MW00834497

THE RHETORIC OF INNOVATION

Self-Conscious Legal Change in Rabbinic Literature

Aaron D. Panken

Studies in Judaism

University Press of America,® Inc.
Lanham · Boulder · New York · Toronto · Oxford

Copyright © 2005 by
Aaron D. Panken

University Press of America,®️ Inc.
4501 Forbes Boulevard
Suite 200
Lanham, Maryland 20706
UPA Acquisitions Department (301) 459-3366

PO Box 317
Oxford
OX2 9RU, UK

Library of Congress Control Number: 2005922591
ISBN 0-7618-3166-5 (paperback : alk. ppr.)

Studies in Judaism

To my wife,

Lisa Messinger

with the greatest love,
admiration and gratitude,
for her boundless insight,
integrity, belief and support
these past thirteen years.

שלי ושלכם שלה הוא
(בבלי נדרים נ' א')

For what is mine,
and what is yours,
are truly hers.
(Babylonian Talmud Nedarim 50a)

Contents

Tables

Preface

The debate over flexibility in Jewish law has become one of the central items of discourse in the contemporary Jewish world. Distinctly different approaches compete for communal attention, some stringently opposed to updating law in any way, others in favor of far more leniency. All, however, attempt to honor their inherited tradition as worthy of study and a valid basis for ongoing decision-making, in whatever way their proponents see fit.

This study is not intended to address directly the broad spectrum of contemporary Jewish opinions on this issue. Rather, it is meant to lay a certain foundation for that discussion: before one can make decisions in the current situation, a more informed view of prior patterns and opinions is a necessary building block. A core principle of this work, then, is that the ideas and tendencies present in rabbinic literature can and must inform present-day scholars and communal decision-makers.

What may be learned from the texts and rhetoric studied herein is that the rabbis had specific ideas and ideals they believed were worthy of prompting legal change, even despite a number of serious limiting factors (the concept of a divinely inherited tradition being the major one). These ideas and ideals varied over time and place, and did not always adhere to concrete, identifiable guidelines. Nonetheless, literary evidence of unquestionably self-conscious legal change has serious implications for current communal questions and challenges.

It is hoped that the reader will emerge from his or her interaction with this study better informed about some of the many specific instances of self-conscious legal change presented explicitly in rabbinic texts. Such information can, hopefully, inform and shape future choices. If this work spurs further discussion in this direction, it will have added a useful voice to an ongoing sacred discourse that attempts, in every age, to balance tradition with innovation, continuity with change.

Aaron D. Panken
New York, New York
November 2004

Acknowledgements

Many wonderful individuals and institutions have given generously of their time and effort in the service of creating this work. First and foremost, I am deeply grateful to my advisor, Lawrence H. Schiffman, for his constant wisdom, patient guidance and many helpful suggestions during my years at New York University, both in the context of this work and on a wide variety of other questions. He has consistently served as a model of a committed professor whose encyclopaedic knowledge, broad intellectual interests and leadership abilities combine to achieve extraordinary ends in both the academy and the community at large. It has been, simply, a true privilege to be his student.

The members of my doctoral committee, Jeffrey Rubenstein and Robert Chazan, also receive my warmest thanks. Jeff was enormously generous in reading multiple drafts of this work and was unfailingly helpful in providing vital correctives on issues that went to the core of its methodology, literary analysis and theoretical concerns. His probing questions and ready assistance were always a welcome part of the process of preparing this thesis. I can safely say that I never once left his office (or his classroom, for that matter) without learning an important new insight into the study of rabbinic literature. That is the mark of an inspired teacher.

Robert Chazan, whom I first came to know well through the Wexner Graduate Fellowship, has served as a steadfast support during my time at New York University. From sage advice on academic matters to questions on career choices, from discussing innovations in curriculum development to pondering university management, his assistance has always been quietly elegant, deep and invaluable. It is no wonder that a generation of graduate students and professors turn to him for ideas and direction. I am proud to be counted among them. I am also deeply indebted to my two readers, Alfred Ivry and Daniel Fleming, for their enthusiasm, time and effort in considering my work, as well as their helpful thoughts and suggestions.

My sincere gratitude is extended to Jacob Neusner, whose renowned intellect has made such groundbreaking contributions to the field of Rabbinics. Many of the major conversations that have arisen in this field were propelled by his initial studies, which often inform this work. I am immensely grateful to him for accepting this book for publication in his series, *Studies in Judaism*.

William Scott Green, a tremendously respected scholar in this field, has been consistently encouraging and helpful with respect to the publication and methodology of this work, and I greatly appreciate his thoughtful guidance, friendship and interest.

Other professors who have been influential upon my thinking include Yakov Elman, David Weiss-Halvni, Richard Kalmin, J.J. Schachter and Elliot Wolfson. A number of graduate students at New York University, Columbia University and the Jewish Theological Seminary have shared in *hevruta*, friendship and discussion that helped shape this work, and I would especially like to thank Beth Berkowitz, Shoshana Gelfand, Jonathan Klawans, Meesh Hammer-Kossoy and Marina Rustow. Shayne Figueroa was also instrumental in managing the process that led to the completion of this work, and I thank her for her support on many occasions.

I could not imagine a more committed and supportive group of colleagues and friends than those I am blessed with at Hebrew Union College-Jewish Institute of Religion in New York, where I serve as dean. I owe David Ellenson, beloved president of the College-Institute, a profound debt for his foresight in allowing me to dedicate the summer of 2002 to the full-time research and writing that led to the completion of this study. David has encouraged me every step of the way: for his confidence, friendship and trust I am extremely grateful. Norman Cohen, esteemed provost of HUC-JIR, likewise supported both concept and execution of my summer of full-time study. Norman's marvelous commitment and companionship, since he was my teacher when I was a student at HUC-JIR, have been among the most precious gifts granted me in my tenure at the College-Institute. Sheldon Zimmerman, former president of the College-Institute, was also highly supportive of the completion of this work, and I thank him for all his care and concern over the years.

A number of colleagues at HUC-JIR have contributed to the completion of this work through their personal support and dedication. I am deeply grateful to Jo Kay and Nancy Wiener, who graciously and professionally shouldered the burdens of the deanship over the summer I was away; to Shirley Idelson, who shares the compelling vision and the hard work of rabbinical education that we are shaping together at HUC-JIR/New York; to my co-deans from the other campuses of HUC-JIR, Lewis Barth, Ken Ehrlich and Michael Marmur, for their constructive partnership; to my colleagues from HUC-JIR from whom I have learned much and with whom I have discussed parts of this work over the years: Carole Balin, Eugene Borowitz, Michael Chernick, Martin Cohen, Ruth Gais, Israel Goldstein, Alfred Gottschalk, Lisa Grant, Lawrence Hoffman, Mark Kligman, Sharon Koren, Leonard Kravitz, Bernard Mehlman, Leon Morris, Stanley Nash, Carol Ochs, Russell Pearce, Benjie Schiller, S. David Sperling, Paul Steinberg, Andrea Weiss, and Wendy Zierler; to my cherished colleagues in the Reform movement who have always helped and, simultaneously, challenged me, among them Glynis Conyer, Lisa Greene, Rick Jacobs, Jan Katzew, Robert Levine, Serge Lippe, Jack Stern, Michael White and Moshe Zemer; to my students at HUC-JIR and elsewhere, who, as the aphorism goes, have taught me more than anyone; to the New York Board of Overseers, and especially the two chairs with whom I have served, Robert Heller and Sam Perelson, for their commitment to excellence; to Trudy Wallace and Anita Rogers, my steadfast and committed assistants, whose energy, grace and deep sense of responsibility never flag; and to those in the HUC-JIR system who have been of great assistance in innumerable ways: Jean Bloch Rosensaft, Eve Starkman, Phil Miller, David Gilner, and Lou Massone.

The Wexner Foundation provided me with generous financial and moral support during my graduate school years, and this was a gift more valuable than words can express. Larry Moses, president of the foundation, provides an unsurpassed model of inspired and visionary leadership that achieves noble goals in unassuming ways. I cherish both his friendship and the experiences he was kind enough to provide for me. Cindy Chazan, director of alumni relations for the foundation, has become an admired friend, co-teacher, confidante and personal advisor. Elka Abrahamson, director of the graduate fellowship program, a treasured friend, has taught me much through her deep intelligence, insight and terrific sense of humor.

During my time as a Wexner Graduate Fellow, I was privileged to be part of a community of graduate students who enriched my learning experience immeasurably. Dear friends, too numerous to list, but especially my classmates Warren Bass, Alyssa Gray, Shaul Kelner, Angela Warnick-Buchdahl and Dov Weiss, share a commitment to both the Jewish community and the rigors of the academic life, and were the true gifts of the Wexner experience. For these and their many other gifts, I am deeply grateful to Leslie and Abigail Wexner for their gracious benefaction.

A number of research libraries have contributed to this work, and it is only proper to express gratitude to them and their fine staffs: the Bobst Library at New York University; the Klau Libraries at HUC-JIR; the library of the Jewish Theological Seminary; the New York Public Library; the libraries of Manhattanville College, SUNY Purchase, Hebrew University, Union Theological Seminary and Columbia University; and the fine local libraries that provided a refuge for a wandering graduate student who needed some peace and quiet, the Larchmont, Mamaroneck and Scarsdale, New York public libraries and the libraries of Great Barrington, Lenox and Lee, Massachusetts.

More than anyone else, I must thank my family for their extraordinary support and forbearance. For these past eight years, my wife, Lisa, and my children, Eli and Samantha, have given up Sundays, early mornings, late evenings and much time during the summers to accommodate courses, papers, comprehensive exams, a proposal and the research and writing of this work. Eli's endless curiosity, love for music, baseball and all things mathematical, biological or mechanical, have strengthened my own curiosity and wonder at the marvels of the world. Samantha's inspired mind, sense of humor, aesthetic sense and adventurous nature have added light and levity to our family. For Lisa, my dedication says what words can say.

My parents, Beverly and Peter Panken, and my sister, Rabbi Melinda Panken, have accepted a reduced number of visits and less attention than should have reasonably been granted them, yet have graciously and enthusiastically provided constant moral support and discussed ideas related to this work over the course of time. My wife's parents, Joan and Martin Messinger, and her extended family, have generously provided places to study and time to do so, when they rightfully could have expected other, more familial things from a son-in-law. It is only with their support and understanding that I have been able to complete this task. The greatest gift I have ever received is their love and care, and they should only know how much I appreciate and love them in return.

Excerpts from **Society and Legal Change, Second edition,** by Alan Watson, are reprinted by permission of Temple University Press. ©2001 by Temple University. All Rights Reserved.

Excerpts from the *JPS Hebrew-English TANAKH,* ©1999, The Jewish Publication Society, have been reprinted with the permission of the publisher, The Jewish Publication Society.

Introduction

> For the historian it is a basic principle that tradition is to be interpreted in a
> sense different than the texts, of themselves, call for. He will always go back
> behind them and the meaning they express to inquire into the reality they ex-
> press involuntarily. Texts must be treated in the same way as other available
> historical material—i.e., as the so-called relics of the past. Like everything else,
> they need explication—i.e., to be understood in terms of not only what they say
> but also what they exemplify.[1]

The German philosopher and literary critic, Hans-Georg Gadamer, argued that
historians studying ancient sources must look behind the texts to probe the distinct reality they involuntarily evoke. Throughout almost two millennia, the corpus of Jewish legal texts from the rabbinic period has been subject to ceaseless
investigation in the pursuit of manifold ends. In some cases, the purpose of such
examination was direct and theological: rabbis and other religious authorities
sought enduring meaning in every jot and tittle of the law, reading with the specific goal of imbuing Jewish observance with clear direction and ultimate meaning. In other cases, historians plumbed the depths of texts intent on building a
richer comprehension of Jewish life and its development throughout the ages
and locales where Jews survived and thrived. Still others were philosophers,
who scanned such sources to delineate the intellectual currents and eddies that
swirled through the times and places of Jewish life.

Many of the rabbis and authorities who brought a modern religious sensibil-
ity to the study of these texts fostered a conservatism they based on what they
saw as ancient religious ideals. For these thinkers, the Sinaitic origins of the
Written Torah, combined with the Oral Torah reportedly delivered alongside it,
provided bedrock for the hermeneutical process that allowed the building of
large and active religious structures, designed to withstand the test of time.
Within the very strict limits of such an approach, any legal evolution found
within these texts had to comport itself appropriately in the face of certain longstanding principles: change had, generally, to come in the form of re-
interpretation of a prior sacred text or the adjustment of legal outcomes to "better reflect" the aims inherent in an already-extant Sinaitic tradition.

Such was the case for post-Enlightenment Orthodox rabbis. In their seeking
of religious guidance in Jewish legal texts, innovation was not generally a desideratum, and, even when permitted, it was rarely admitted. This trend was expressed in the extreme in the well-known aphorism of the Hatam Sofer (the
Hungarian Rabbi Moses Sofer, né Moses Schreiber, 1762-1839): "This is the
general rule: the new is forbidden from the Torah in any place and in any time."[2]
More liberal opinions certainly existed among the early Reformers in Germany

and their inheritors, who opposed this highly restrictive stance. Nonetheless, many writers who concerned themselves with Jewish legal studies continued to cling to a relatively conservative hermeneutic that denied or frowned upon change. The two major schools of approach on this argument, what we might dub "change as appropriate" vs. "change as anathema," still continue a vocal struggle even today.

Academic students of Jewish legal history bring a different lens to the problem. Studies of Jewish legal history take two main approaches: historical-critical scholars use refined literary tools to understand changes in rabbinic law within the broader historical context, comparing and contrasting Jewish legal development with the ongoing march of surrounding cultures, literatures and legal systems, while those in the *Mishpat Ivri* school tend to look at the internal diachronic stream of legal development within Jewish law itself, much as a jurist in any culture would analyze a developing system of jurisprudence. Each method has both its proponents and its advantages, but a useful academic analysis of legal evolution in Jewish law demands the incorporation of lessons from both schools of thought.

Modern Jewish philosophers, by contrast, mine rabbinic legal texts for meta-halakhic ideas and ideals capable of transplant to the modern world, with hopes of addressing the current intellectual situation and informing relevant aspects of the modern Jewish condition. More often than not, these thinkers read sources for concepts contained within the tradition that help define principles that held currency among ancient intellectuals, while at the same time drawing support for viewpoints they themselves find sensible. In the process, they deconstruct the elements of a prior tradition in quest of ancient support for and historical rooting of modern religious concepts.

This study is intended to be an admixture of the academic and philosophic approaches. While it will not, in any way, attempt to deny the religious meaning found in these texts by the proponents of the first school of thought, the focus will be, instead, on the historical development of ideas gleaned from documentary evidence compiled during a well-restricted period. Since the existence of an idea in a text does not prove or disprove its actualization among the populace, this evidence does not permit evaluation of the history of societal activities. Instead, the hope is to trace the development of ideas that the authors/editors of rabbinic legal compilations included in their works. It is thus meant to be a work of intellectual history on a textual tradition, as opposed to a work of social history.

In keeping with the thrust of Gadamer above, our approach will be to view these texts as relics of an age that must be closely examined to provide useful information about both the legal and philosophical development of Jewish thought in the rabbinic period (from 70 CE through approximately the sixth century CE). The approach taken here will focus on understanding the historical circumstances that shaped and influenced the texts at hand and the philosophical biases that these texts bespeak. It will center, heavily, upon the actual language of the texts, including analysis of manuscript differences, linguistic, literary and semantic concerns, stated rationales and implied meanings.

In a postmodern age, it is at least foolhardy, if not downright impossible, to suggest that we can recapture any "original" meanings of texts studied. Authorial intention is, likewise, beyond our grasp. Nonetheless, through a careful tracing of statistical data over large bodies of citations and through close examination of the differences in parallel texts, we aim to come to conclusions about the wide array of ideas about halakhic change in play in the various places, times and texts.

While this study takes a new approach toward understanding the rhetoric of legal change, it is not entirely unprecedented. Prior works have attempted parts of this endeavor. Some have focused on the development of Jewish law as a whole, looking to the rabbinic period as one small temporal slice of their legal historical work.[3] Other more synchronic studies have attempted to collect every occurrence of a term or concept that appears in rabbinic literature, tracing that particular area and its growth. What will make this study distinctive is the fact that it utilizes specific words as semantic markers for change and fully explores every occurrence of these words in the extant body of rabbinic legal literature. This comprehensive approach is relatively new in the study of Jewish legal development in the rabbinic period.[4] Only when legal evolution is admitted through the presence of a semantic indicator does it qualify for inclusion in this study.

Three terms will provide the literary foundation of this study, serving as semantic foci for analysis of the rhetoric of change. They are: *barishonah* ("at first"), *takkanah* ("enactment" or "repair [of the law]") and *gezerah* ("decree"). Each represents a distinct trend in legal evolution. The fact that each and every change in law cited is an instance when the editors *self-consciously* noted the change themselves, prevents falling into eisegetical tendencies that may have crept into prior works searching a bit too hard to promote the idea of legal change.

Our first term, *barishonah*, most often points to a reflective tendency: it claims that prior stages of Jewish law were considered carefully for their efficacy, and, when they did not meet appropriate standards of completeness, suitability for the current situation or fairness to members of the community, they were reshaped, rejected or renewed. Reflection upon prior law and its efficacy is a foundational strategy in most developing legal systems, as we shall see presently when we review theories of legal change.

With the term *takkanah*, we have the embodiment of a markedly different developmental tendency: that of sheer innovation. The largest subcategory of legal changes introduced with this term shows the initiation of new practices that respond to an unmet need poorly served by the present state of the law. Innovation is not easily justified in a system of law that granted almost limitless power to a divinely sanctioned Torah and its revered oral accompaniment. Nonetheless, the rabbis brilliantly opened the "repair" of the law as an avenue for innovation, grafting necessary additions onto the legal canon without doing violence to the idea of its eternal and unchanging core. Thus, *takkanot* generally represent innovations in law that layer entirely new practices, prayers or regulations never considered before onto the already accepted corpus of Jewish custom and law.

While our third term, *gezerah*, shares innovative characteristics with its sibling *takkanah*, it is innovative in an entirely different way. Instead of liberally expanding the purview of law as we so often find with *takkanot*, *gezerot* tend to employ an innovative legal approach to act conservatively—utilizing the radical device of creating new law to prevent the violation of older, accepted law. While the legal outcome is ultimately conservative in nature, it must be said at once that such a rhetorical choice is radically innovative at the same time. Despite their ironically dual nature, *gezerot* show the highest level of consistency of the three marker terms studied, evincing a trend that is quite consistent in its application.

Each of the more than 1,000 reported changes in law examined for this study sheds light on the thought process of the contributors to and editors of individual rabbinic legal texts. We will never obtain substantial historical proof as to whether the editors of these texts or those to whom these changes were attributed held functional leadership positions that influenced the course of human affairs in Palestine, Babylonia or elsewhere. Nonetheless, since these texts represent the best available collection of the intellectual and legal opinions of a subset of scholars who lived during this period, and, since they received subsequent validation and acclamation by the Geonim and later Jewish leaders, analyzing them is our best heuristic window into understanding the intellectual processes of the rabbinic period.

Theories of Legal Evolution

Literary and legal critics, both recently and in the dimmer past, have searched for a general understanding of legal evolution. One of the earliest great modern legal minds turned toward the question was that of the German historical theorist Fredrich Karl von Savigny (1779-1861). Von Savigny defined three phases in the development of law within a society. In the first phase, law is expressed directly through the practices of the people with little technical expression in general rules and no well-defined and logical method of applying them. During the second phase, a separate class of jurists emerges that represents the people in the more technical aspects of law. Their emergence causes a bifurcation in the law, splitting it into a popular part, intelligible to the mass of people, and a technical part, essentially a discipline reserved for jurists alone. In the third phase, during the declining period of the nation, its law loses its popular attraction and becomes merely the property of a few experts. Thus, in general terms, Savigny saw law as developing in a separate realm, far from the interfer-

ence of specific individuals and lawgivers, as an autonomous process that proceeded independently.[5]

Savigny's taxonomy of legal change suggested clear phases of evolution
that never varied in the development of any nation's legal system, and saw law
as a living entity that grew in and of itself. Two British law professors, Jeremy
Bentham (1748-1832) and John Austin (1790-1859), moved away from such
limiting models to a more fluid understanding of legal evolution. Bentham
proved to be a very active influence on British law, while his disciple Austin,
best known as the founder of the school known as legal positivism, was responsible for an extension of legal theory in bold, new directions.

Austin and his followers, the legal positivists,[6] hold that legal evolution has
its own interior *Weltanschauung*: jurists, lawyers and other authorities work
within the tight confines of legal reasoning, pressing law forward as it develops
over time. To adherents of this school of thought, legal change is essentially an
act internal to the legal community (whatever the make-up of that community—
whether lawyers, judges or rabbis). Thus, law is the result of an inexorable process of internal legal consideration, with little input or influence by the surrounding community. The law stands by itself and develops on its own.[7]

Contrast this with the general approach favored by legal realists: they posit
a far greater emphasis on the external community, believing that, to a very great
extent, society and its influences force the ongoing redefinition of law as it faces
new realities. To realists, law responds, directly and inevitably, to actions taking
place in society. No rarified legal clique is responsible for the march of legal
evolution: instead, the everyday actions and situations that occur in the world
propel law forward as it struggles with fresh, new realities.[8]

Somewhere between the classic positivist and realist positions falls the contemporary author Alan Watson, a prominent theorist of legal change, who gen-
eralized from his studies of Roman and English law to suggest the sources,
mechanism and parties involved in legal evolution. In his trenchant analysis,
Watson stakes out a middle ground, indicating that most legal change should be
considered a result of the process of both internal juristic deliberation and pressing societal need, though often in a timeframe that is delayed substantially from
the onset of the root cause. In the final chapter of his *Society and Legal Change*,
he states a series of conclusions about legal change that will inform this study:

> The first conclusion must simply be that there does not exist a close, in-
> herent, necessary relationship between existing rules of law and the society in
> which they operate. Law is not in any mystical sense 'the spirit of the people.'
> Many rules are contrary to the ethos of society, its needs and desires, and do
> not correspond to the interests or wishes of the ruling elite. Moreover, when we
> take into account the longevity of legal rules and the frequency of transplants
> we see that usually legal rules were not created for the society in which they
> now operate...

A second conclusion is that in developed society at least law does not emerge easily from society. As society grows, as institutions are created to cope with changes, then some might think . . . that law would keep in step. . . . This is far from the truth. . . . The force of inertia is very relevant to keeping institutions and rules alive when their unsatisfactory nature has been revealed. The force of inertia, it will be recalled, is often successful because the body or person who has legislative power has other concerns, the interpreters of the law have limited power, and legal scaffolding for a variety of reasons operates to hide the need. Inertia operates both to prevent a legal rule from developing to a satisfactory state and to inhibit change when society changes.

The third conclusion—perhaps the most startling and certainly one that informs all others—is that the great extent of the divergence is not readily apparent. If it had been, much attention would be focused on it, theories would take it more into account . . . the truth seems to be that at any time only a relatively small number of people actually suffer badly from a legal rule being out of step, and are conscious that their misery could be alleviated by a change in law.
. . .

Fourthly, the present shape of a rule of private law has more to do with history than with the present structure of society. 'History' here is used in the widest possible sense: history of the nation, its feuds, intellectual contacts, past social, economic and political conditions and its languages; history of legal life, the activity of the legislature, powers of the interpreters of law, energy and opinions of individual lawyers... All this means, of course, that to have any real understanding of a legal rule, its scope, purpose, utility and suitability, one must know its history.[9]

To sum up his points thus far, Watson describes a separation between law and society, following, at this point, a positivist approach. Law is not set in any direct way by members of society, nor does it respond directly, or in a timely manner, to new societal challenges. While we might have imagined that the momentum of evolution propels law along by some mystical societal spirit eager to make change, Watson argues that it is instead held to a halt by the inertia of historical precedent and practice. To further slow the pace, few individuals are aware enough to recognize both the injury done them and the possibility of law evolving. Even when individuals are aware of the possibility of changing law, busy jurists charged with weighty societal responsibilities rarely have the time to disengage and look beyond the quotidian tasks the law assigns them to re-evaluate prior positions. The law remains, by and large, mostly unchanged for all these reasons.

Watson later continues:

[As] has been emphasized several times before in this volume, there must be some relationship between the needs and desires of society and its legal rules. . . . The forces of inertia are so great that each time a legal change is made society reveals something important about itself. The changes should be examined from the perspective both of the rule or principle or proposition which is created and that which is abrogated. The latter viewpoint, which is easily overlooked, is at times especially significant since it not infrequently happens that the concern is more to abolish an existing rule than to introduce a particular reform.[10]

For Watson, to know the history of a society's legal evolution is to understand what is important to that society. Since legal change has to overcome the inertia of history, the busy state of jurists, the lackluster knowledge of plaintiffs and defendants and various other delaying factors, when we uncover an instance of legal change recorded by a society, we can be certain that it represents a considered priority that arose in the course of that society's life. The obligation, Watson explains, is to examine both the prior law and the later law to understand the change and to learn what motivated the society to overcome its reluctance and engage in a process of change.

Watson suggests a few other ideas with relevance to this study. Here, he describes what he calls "causes of divergence:"

[Legislation] drastically affecting the development of private law may be introduced for reasons, even the most personal reasons, affecting the ruling elite at that time, without any concern being shown for the state of the law in general or for other interests. Thus, the decree of the Roman senate permitting marriage with a brother's daughter was the work of senators who wished to please the Emperor Claudius. They had no concern with the general question of marriage reform, and if Agrippina had been Claudius' sister's daughter, the decree would certainly have permitted marriage with that kind of niece and retained as invalid marriage with a brother's daughter.[11]

Thus, to Watson, the whim or political exigencies of those in power may supply the cause of divergence between law and contemporary societal need. Another source for divergence is to be found in hasty action:

Legislation—even on private law—is very often a 'gut reaction,' an immediate, strong response to some particular event. The danger here is not that the legislation fails to correspond to the immediate wishes of the people, but that the over-reaction can entail harmful consequences as well, and that, legislation being what it is, the situation may never be put right.[12]

Here, Watson observes that hasty reaction to novel or emergent surroundings may cause potential legislative solutions to over-reach, setting up practices and laws that do not ultimately serve the desired purpose.

Finally, Watson describes two strategies that societies use to slow the process of legal change: the first he calls "legal scaffolding." The idea here is that scaffolding is created around law that no longer meets the needs of the society.

Instead of canceling the law entirely, the jurists create a scaffold that holds the divergence to a manageable level, rather than allowing a chasm to grow and force legal change. Scaffolding, Watson suggests, is necessary when a body with legislative abilities fails to act in response to a societal need.[13]

The second strategy is that of legal transplants. Sometimes, when the divergence between societal need and law grows too wide, solutions are imported from neighboring societies that have already confronted the problem. This, too, is a strategy for managing the divergence between older law and societal needs.[14]

Watson's broad insights on legal change help set the stage for research into legal change within rabbinic literature. The same forces and ideas at work within any legal system also apply to rabbinic law, with one major difference: whereas most legal systems rely, ultimately, on humanity as the creator of law, Jewish law in the rabbinic period is predicated upon the divinity of a core text (the Written Torah), often accompanied by a companion set of oral laws (the Oral Torah, claimed to be of some sort of divine origin as well) that modified it, which together supply the initial starting point for rulings. This increases the inertial factor significantly, for changing law becomes tantamount to ignoring or distorting prior divine commands. Nonetheless, despite this increase in resistance to change, change is present on a very regular schedule. Applying Watson's principles only serves to highlight the fact that rabbinic legal alteration had to be based upon strongly held values to overcome significant resistance and empower the manifold changes recorded in our texts.

Rhetorical Concerns

No legal system can exist without the legal change described above. Laws once effective in a prior historical moment cannot realistically be expected to have continued relevance and efficacy indefinitely. So, as Watson suggested, legal systems need means for legal change that respond to societal need. A related matter of some import is the question of how legal systems employ rhetoric to analyze and justify the changes that must occur. This is a significant question for rabbinic law, and one that has not received due attention in prior studies.

Heinrich Lausberg, a well-respected German scholar of rhetoric, drew upon both ancient writers and modern scholarship to describe the rhetorical forms associated with revising law. The ancient rhetoricians, Lausberg wrote, knew general legal rhetoric, as *genus iudiciale* (the type of rhetoric known as "judicial"). This contained two subsets: the *genus rationale* and the *genus legale*. The *genus rationale* was a rhetorical form that dealt with the evaluation of a particular deed based on the law—trials and hearings are two examples of this sort of rhetorical structure. The *genus legale*, of more interest to this study, was a rhetoric of evaluation of the law itself, through the process of interpretation and in comparison with appropriate norms of justice:

The *genus legale* deals with the assessment of a law, generally on the account of a *factum* [deed, act] (deserving of punishment or reward) which has been or is to be performed. Thus the *genus legale* comes into force if an action to be judged in accordance with the *genus rationale* is such that its relationship to the law is difficult from a legal point of view. A cause for the development of the *genus legale* is, therefore, the (real or supposed) imperfection in the wording of the laws: laws cannot unambiguously encompass the variety of possible actions; they need interpretation which sets the content of the laws in relation to the variety of possible (and occurring) actions.[15]

Once a problem arose with a law that required the rhetorical approach outlined here, two factors came into play, which Lausberg calls the "binomial:" 1) the *scriptum* or *vox* (the linguistic formulation of the written or oral statement of the law) which was then analyzed from the perspective of natural linguistic usage and 2) the *voluntas* (the intention of the speaker/author of the legal text) which was analyzed from the perspective of *aequitas* (the natural sense of justice). Lausberg, following ancient rhetoricians, set up a useful dichotomy between the written or oral statement of law in effect and the external sense of equity or justice that law had to meet to remain effective.

Law could require change, in this rhetorical structure, for two reasons: either the *scriptum* or *vox* had become distanced far enough from current linguistic usage that it required linguistic change, or the *voluntas* of the law did not meet current standards of *aequitas*. Combining Watson's ideas with Lausberg's: when either of these two balances between legal texts (written or oral) and society (on the level of linguistic formulation or ensuring just outcomes) moved too far out of balance, eventually, society pressed for legal change.

Our main concern is the rhetoric the rabbis of this period utilized to explain and justify the legal change they promoted. In biblical literature, the authors employed what Bernard Levinson has called a "rhetoric of concealment"[16] with respect to legal change, which tended to conceal changes of law rather than highlight them. Rabbinic literature made a conscious choice to utilize new forms of rhetoric, some extending the trajectory of biblical rhetoric, while others were drawn from surrounding Greek and Roman societies. Rabbinic literature often tended to employ what we will now call a "rhetoric of disclosure." This rhetoric called for both a way of announcing legal change that acknowledged prior law and the revisions it had undergone, and, additionally, a way of justifying it within the philosophical-theological system of Judaism. This study will attempt to understand both the implicit acknowledgements and the explicit ways of explaining the changes in law that are recorded in the rabbinic period, with the hope of estimating the core motivations that flowed from important values closely held by the authors of rabbinic literature.

The Challenge of Ancient "Legal History"

This study focuses on legal history—understanding and tracing the development of law in the rabbinic period—thus it is important to make clear just what legal history means in both the ancient and the modern worlds. In narrative studies, a number of scholars have shown that ancient historians had a far different understanding of writing history than do modern scholars. Writing about Hellenistic historians, for example, one scholar recently explained:

> There is a general consensus of scholarly opinion that with few exceptions Hellenistic historians sought primarily to 'charm, divert and edify' and paid at most 'lip-service to truth'; 'if they deal with events already narrated by others, their overriding aim is not to outdo their predecessors in accuracy or balanced judgment, but to outshine them in splendid and dramatic description. Often the theme is chosen on artistic criteria, being a self-contained whole like a plot for a tragedy', and mere fables or irrelevant digressions are introduced 'to alleviate the tedium of continuous narrative.'[17]

This tendency for privileging artistic embellishment over commitment to truth was not merely a Hellenistic tendency—instead, one may move outward from the specific case of Greek historical narratives to learn about the tendencies of the ancient historian in general. Ancient historians often readily sacrificed truth for a variety of stylistic and audience-related reasons.

The ancient world did not apply the strict separations between genres of writing that we take for granted in a modern context. As another recent scholar wrote about the Roman author Cicero's theory of history:

> Though we today see poetry, oratory and historiography as three separate genres, the ancients saw them as three different species of the same genus— rhetoric. All three types of activity aimed to elaborate certain data in such a way as to affect or persuade an audience or readership.[18]

Such thinking was clearly at work in Jewish narrative in antiquity as well, as Jeffrey Rubenstein has proven in his studies of Talmudic *aggadah*.[19] Ancient historians aimed to persuade or affect an audience or readership, not necessarily to prove historical fact in any modern sense.

What applies in ancient narrative history applies in ancient legal history as well. Rather than assuming that reconstructions of legal history present in rabbinic texts are to be accepted at face value, we will remain cognizant of the great potential for embellishment and fabrication in the ancient world. While narrative authors may have had artistic goals in mind when they "elaborated certain data," legal authors also did so for reasons other than sheer artistry. For the sake of plausibility, rabbis generated explanations that rooted legal change in individuals who had been granted authority, experience and knowledge in applicable areas by biblical texts. Incidents that provoked legal change were embellished to strengthen the acceptance of the resultant adaptation. Many legal changes invoked events and traditions of prior eras, to further shore up the antiquity and authenticity of alterations favored by the rabbis.

In each of these cases, and others, the line between modern and ancient historical approaches is clearly drawn. The task of the modern legal historian is to muster all available evidence to attempt to discern what intellectual development is represented in rabbinic texts, despite what the texts themselves may say.

Methodology

In preparing this work, every example of each term of reference in Mishnah, Tosefta, the Halakhic Midrashim, the Palestinian Talmud and the Babylonian Talmud was consulted. The occurrences of these terms were found through root searches of the comprehensive Bar Ilan University Responsa Project database. These occurrences were then reviewed and categories of various rationales for legal evolution were constructed, based on my analysis of the stated motivation for change present in each example. Among these categories, I then selected for analysis and commentary one or a few examples that best typified that category's rationale for change.

Available manuscripts were examined to determine the best readings for the texts involved. Commentaries and translations, where available, were then consulted to determine the spectrum of potential understandings possible for each passage.[20] Historical and legal secondary works were also utilized to provide general background on the issues inherent in the texts and for their direct analyses of the texts involved. Parallels in all extant rabbinic texts (whether aggadic or halakhic) were then traced, to see if they shed any relevant light on the legal evolution or the rationale itself. Finally, clusters of related passages with further information were then reviewed for any germane contributions they might provide. All translations of primary rabbinic texts and Hebrew secondary material in this study are original, though strongly influenced by the factors and sources mentioned.

Situating this work within the greater currents of contemporary intellectual thought in Jewish Studies, explicit admission of a few assumptions would be prudent. First, this work attempts to follow in the traditions of many accepted principles now *de rigeur* within the academic field of Rabbinics. In a major advance initially propelled by Jacob Neusner but followed by substantial subsequent scholarship, recent authors have shown that firm claims of historicity must remain forever out of reach, both with regard to rabbinic biography and with respect to the proper attribution of rabbinic statements.[21] While such strict limits on uncritical historical conclusions are certainly warranted, Shaye J.D. Cohen has raised an additional concern:

> Neusner has sounded a salutary warning against the facile use of rabbinic texts
> for the writing of the history of pre- and post-70 C.E. Judaism. . . . we still need
> to discover firm criteria by which we can determine how and why the rabbinic
> texts are reliable for some things but not for others.[22]

Thus, the suggested course would be to heed Neusner's warning, while entertaining the elusive possibility of learning history from rabbinic texts. It is clear that ironclad criteria for determining history from these texts do not yet exist, if indeed they ever will.

Second, Jacob Neusner was also the first scholar to forge a new approach to rabbinic texts that treats each particular text as an individual document that can provide information only on the ideas and opinions of its editors.[23] Neusner suggested that scholars should pay primary attention to the documentary context in which discrete passages appear. Source criticism is compatible with this approach, and helps create a more valid and complete analysis.[24]

While minding these two important cautions, however, there must also be some level of acknowledgment that text and history are, indeed, connected. What is to be learned from the study of rabbinic texts is not information about specific people, places or events: instead, the literature itself should be treated as cultural artifact. These artifacts provide entrée into the intellectual streams present in the rabbinic world—currents of thought that were not at all systematic or uniform even in any one particular time or locale, let alone across numerous countries and centuries. A survey of these highly diverse ideas cannot provide us with any neat system of "rabbinic thought"—that must remain unattainable. However, it can give us a window into what ideas were "in play" in the period between 70 CE and the close of BT. This work attempts to forage for the ideas preserved in these texts in order to apprehend the breadth of possible thinking about legal change that existed in this period, without giving in to facile oversimplification or generalization. That, ultimately, is the goal of this study.

Notes

1.   Hans-Georg Gadamer, *Truth and Method* (New York: Continuum Publishing Company, 2003), p. 336.

2.   See the Responsa of the Hatam Sofer, OH 28, 148, 181 and YD 19 and 286, for a few of the instances of this famous statement.

3.   See, for example, Menachem Elon's *magnum opus, Jewish Law: History, Sources, Principles,* Bernard Auerbach and Melvin J. Sykes, translators (Philadelphia: Jewish Publication Society, 1994).

4.   Michael Chernick has completed this sort of study with the Hebrew forms *gezerah shavah, klal u-ferat u'klal,* and *ribui u-miut,* in his publications. See *idem, An Investigation of the Middot "K'lal u-ferat u'klal" and "Ribui u-miut" in the Midrashim and the Talmudim* (Lod: Mekhon Haberman for the Study of Literature, 1984) and *The Middah "Gezerah Shavah:" Its Forms in the Midrashim and Talmudim* (Lod: Mekhon Haberman for the Study of Literature, 1994).

5.   Here, we rely heavily on the summary of Savigny's theories found in Peter Stein's *Legal Evolution* (Cambridge: Cambridge University Press, 1980), pp. 56-65.

6.   For a recent scholar's cogent statement of legal positivism, consult H.L.A. Hart, "Positivism and the Separation of Law and Morals," in R.M. Dworkin, ed., *The Philosophy of Law* (Oxford: Oxford University Press, 1977), pp. 17-37. Dworkin's article rejecting positivism follows immediately thereafter in the volume, providing a good entrée to the debate between the two schools.

7.   Austin extends Savigny's construction of legal evolution. It could be argued that this approach to legal studies coheres with the school of thought called *Mishpat Ivri,* which, in its purest form, focuses on the internal process of legal development, divorced from external communal pressures.

8.   This outlook would seem to be related to the historical-critical method of studying Jewish texts in its interest in both the surrounding world and the historical situation of the Jews in each context.

9.   Alan Watson, *Society and Legal Change* (Philadelphia: Temple University Press, 1977 and 2001), pp. 130-133.

10.   Watson, *op. cit.,* p. 135.

11.   Watson, *op. cit.,* p. 116

12.   Watson, *op. cit.,* p. 117.

13.   See Watson, *op. cit.,* pp. 87-97, for a complete description of his concept of legal scaffolding.

14.   See Watson, *op. cit.,* pp. 98-111, for a complete description of his concept of legal transplants.

15.   Heinrich Lausberg, *Handbuch der literarischen Rhetorik* (Ismaning bei München: Max Hueber Verlag, 1960), § 198.

16.   See the full discussion of this in the introductory section of chapter one.

17.   P.A. Brunt, *Studies in Greek History and Thought* (Oxford: Clarendon Press, 1993), p. 181.

18. A.J. Woodman, *Rhetoric in Classical Historiography* (Portland, OR: Aeropagitica Press, 1988), p. 100. In this vein, see also Christopher Gill and T.P. Wiseman, *Lies and Fiction in the Ancient World* (Austin: University of Texas Press, 1993).

19. Jeffrey L. Rubenstein, *Talmudic Stories: Narrative, Art, Composition and Culture* (Baltimore: Johns Hopkins University Press, 1999).

20. Commentaries and critical editions have been consulted especially in the preparation of the primary rabbinic sources, primarily those of Kehati and Albeck for M; Lieberman and Zuckermandl for T; Rashi, Rabbenu Hananel, Tosafot and Adin Steinsaltz for BT; and the *Penei Moshe* and *Korban HaEdah* for PT. Translations have occasionally been consulted, including Blackman, Danby and Neusner's translations of M, Neusner's translation of T, the Soncino, Steinsaltz and Schottenstein series for BT, and Neusner's translation of PT. Biblical texts follow the translation from the *JPS Hebrew-English Tanakh* (Philadelphia: Jewish Publication Society, 1999).

21. Erwin R. Goodenough's *Jewish Symbols in the Greco-Roman Period* (Kingsport, TN; Kingsport Press, 1965), Volume XII, Summary and Conclusions, was, perhaps, the first major nail in the coffin of the naïve acceptance of rabbinic texts as history. Neusner was the next major scholar to apply the lessons learned directly and firmly to rabbinic literature. For a most vivid example of his application of this idea, one need only turn to the introduction of the third edition of his five-volume *History of the Jews of Babylonia* (Leiden: Brill, 1965-70), where he utterly rejected his earlier approach as inconclusive. Also see Neusner's "The Present State of Rabbinic Biography," in Gerard Nahon and Charles Touati, *Hommage à Georges Vajda: Ètudes d'histoire et de pensée juives* (Louvain: Peeters, 1980), pp. 85-91. Consistently, his later works present a far more skeptical approach to learning history from rabbinic sources. For a concise review of the problems of rabbinic biography and attributions, see H.L. Strack, and G. Stemberger, editors, *Introduction to the Talmud and Midrash* (Minneapolis: Fortress Press, 1992), pp. 62-68.

22. Shaye J.D. Cohen, "The Modern Study of Ancient Judaism," in *idem* and Edward R. Greenstein, *The State of Jewish Studies* (New York: Jewish Theological Seminary of America, 1990), p. 65.

23. See Jacob Neusner, "The Synoptic Problem in Rabbinic Literature," *JBL* 105 (1986), pp. 499-507, for Neusner's statement of the problem and his suggested solution.

24. See Shaye J.D. Cohen, ed., *The Synoptic Problem in Rabbinic Literature* (Providence: Brown Judaic Studies, 2000), especially his introduction, pp. vii-xiii, and the first article by Robert Goldenberg, "Is the Talmud a Document?" pp. 3-10.

Abbreviations

ABD	*Anchor Bible Dictionary*
Arakh.	Arakhin
ARN	Avot deRabbi Natan
AZ	Avodah Zarah
BA1-6	Babylonian Amora from Generation 1-6
BASOR	*Bulletin of the American Schools of Oriental Research*
BB	Bava Batra
BCE	Before the Common Era
BK	Bava Kama
BM	Bava Metzia
BT	Babylonian Talmud
Bekh.	Bekhorot
Ber.	Berakhot
Betz.	Betzah
Chron.	Chronicles
ca.	circa
CE	Common Era
d.	died
Dan.	Daniel
Dem.	Demai
Deut.	Deuteronomy
Ed.	Eduyot
Eccl.	Ecclesiastes
Eruv.	Eruvin
Est.	Esther
Ex.	Exodus
Ez.	Ezekiel
Gen.	Genesis
Git.	Gittin
GR	Genesis Rabbah
Hab.	Habakkuk
Hag.	Hagigah
Hal.	Hallah
Hor.	Horayot
Hos.	Hosea
HUCA	*Hebrew Union College Annual*
Hul.	Hullin
IEJ	*Israel Exploration Journal*
Is.	Isaiah
JBL	*Journal of Biblical Literature*
JHCS	*Journal of Halacha and Contemporary Society*

JJS	*Journal of Jewish Studies*
Josh.	Joshua
JPS	*Jewish Publication Society*
JQR	*Jewish Quarterly Review*
JSJ	*Journal for the Study of Judaism in the Persian, Hellenistic and Roman Period*
JSS	*Journal of Semitic Studies*
Jub.	Jubilees
Kel.	Kelim
Ker.	Keritot
Ket.	Ketubbot
Kgs.	Kings
Kid.	Kiddushin
Kil.	Kilayim
Kor.	Korbanot
Lam.	Lamentations
Lev.	Leviticus
lit.	literally
LR	Lamentations Rabbah
M	Mishnah
Maas.	Maaserot
Macc.	Maccabees
Mak.	Makkot
Makh.	Makhshirin
Mal.	Malachi
Meg.	Megilah
MegTa	Megilat Taanit
Men.	Menahot
Mid.	Middot
Mik.	Mikvaot
MK	Moed Katan
MRSBY	Mekhilta DeRabbi Shimeon bar Yohai
MRY	Mekhilta DeRabbi Yishmael
Ms.	Manuscript
Mss.	Manuscripts
MS	Maaser Sheni
Men.	Menahot
MT	Mishneh Torah
Mtan	Midrash Tannaim
Naz.	Nazir
Ned.	Nedarim
Neg.	Negaim
Neh.	Nehemiah
Nid.	Niddah
Num.	Numbers

Oho.	Oholot
PA1-5	Palestinian Amora from Generation 1-5
PAAJR	*Proceedings of the American Academy for Jewish Research*
Par.	Parah
Pes.	Pesahim
PR	Pesikta Rabbati
PT	Palestinian Talmud
RB	Revue Biblique
RH	Rosh HaShanah
San.	Sanhedrin
SB	Sifre Bemidbar
SD	Sifre Devarim
Sem.	Semahot
Shab.	Shabbat
Shek.	Shekalim
Shev.	Shevuot
Shevi.	Sheviit
Song	Song of Songs
Suk.	Sukkah
SZ	Sifrei Zuta
T	Tosefta
T1-5	Tanna from Generation 1-5
Ta.	Taanit/Taaniyot
Tam.	Tamid
Tem.	Temurah
Ter.	Terumah
Toh.	Tohorot
TY	Tevul Yom
Yad.	Yadayim
Yev.	Yevamot
YK	Yom Kippurim
Zav.	Zavim
Zev.	Zevahim

Chapter One

The Reflective Tendency: *Barishonah*

Introduction

The rhetorical term בראשונה (*barishonah*, "at first") often serves as a marker of self-conscious innovation in rabbinic literature. The word itself appears slightly more than 400 times[25] in the legal corpus[26] of rabbinic literature, where one can discern four basic categories of meaning within these many occurrences. *Barishonah* occurs:

a) referring to objects or people cited in numerical lists, where the first of two or more items listed is specified with the addition of the preposition -ב;[27]

b) as a literary indicator at the start of an excursus into mythic history;[28]

c) as a literary indicator of an historical note;[29] or,

d) as an indicator of self-conscious recognition of change in halakhic or customary positions.

Our focus in this chapter will be on the final category, as it points to a number of intriguing examples where rabbinic sources state significant changes in law as well as their explicit motivations. The use of the word *barishonah* in these texts implies an explicit acknowledgement of legal change on the part of the authors of these rabbinic texts. Though there are a great many instances of legal change in this corpus, these examples and the ones cited in the chapters to follow present clear literary signs of self-conscious innovation, frankly admitted. For this reason, they provide fertile ground for the study of the intellectual history of halakhic change during the rabbinic period (70 CE through the closure of the Talmud in approximately the sixth century CE).

Secondary Literature and Parallels

By way of introduction, we will first examine the limited available secondary literature on the term *barishonah*. A number of prior scholars recognized the value of studying this term and its use in rabbinic literature. Zecharias Frankel was the first to note the function of this term in his study of M:

במאמר ר׳ עקיבא זכרנו דברים אשר נשתנו על ידי ר׳ עקיבא מאשר היו נהוגים לפנים בישראל. . . . יש תועלת בידיעת מנהגים קדמונים לחופשי

מקור ההלכה, לכן נציג גם פה הלכות ומנהגים של ימים הראשונים, אשר
נשתנו בימים הבאים. והמנהגים האלה והשתנותם הובאו במשנה
ותוספתא במאמר "בראשונה."

In the article about Rabbi Akiba [here, Frankel is referring to an earlier
section of his book where he discusses Akiba's role in halakhic
change], we noted matters that were changed by Rabbi Akiba from the
way they were practiced before among Israel. . . . There is a benefit in
knowing earlier customs for those who search for the source of *halakhah*, therefore we will present also, here, *halakhot* and customs of the
early days, which were changed in the days that followed. And these
customs and their changes were brought in the Mishnah and the Tosefta
with the term *barishonah*. [30]

Frankel describes the use of this term as an indicator of halakhic and customary
innovation in the two major Tannaitic legal works, specifically addressing the
benefit to historians (or others who might search for the origins of *halakhot*) in
knowing both the earlier and later phases of legal development. Similarly, Ephraim Urbach points out that these passages grant us useful access into legal issues confronted during the earliest periods of the development of Jewish law:

עובדה היא, שההלכות שהגיעו לידינו מתקופת הזוגות ומזמנם של
התנאים הראשונים נמסרו רק בצורת הגזרה והתקנה, המעשה והעדות,
והמסורת שמקורה במנהג. הגזרה והתקנה מקורן בסמכות הרשויות
המתאימות, אם היו אלה כהנים גדולים, שרים וזקנים, הכנסת הגדולה או
הסנהדרין. מספרן היה גדול בהרבה ממה שנראה לכאורה על יסוד ותן
ההלכות הנקראות במפורש "תקנות" ו"גזרות." די להזכיר את ההלכות
השנויות בנוסח "בראשונה היה. . ., התקין. . .", "בראשונה היו. . .
התקינו. . .", "בראשונה היו. . . משרבו התקינו. . ." ואין בין נוסחאות
אלו לבין "בראשונה היו אומרים. . . חזרו לומר", ולא כלום. בנוסחאות
אלו שנויות למעלה משישים משניות ובריתות. מהן כוללות תקנות
קדומות לתקופת החשמונאים שנדחקו ובוטלו על-ידי תקנות חדשות
בתוקף התנאים האובייקטיביים שנשתנו. כמה וכמה הלכות נשנו במקור
אחד בצורתן האחרונה, אבל מקור אחר שמר על השלבים הקדומים,
ואפשר ללמוד מן המפורש על הסתום ולהסיק שתהליך דומה עבר גם על
הלכות אחרות, שלא נשמרו אלא בנוסח אחד.

The fact is that the *halakhot* that reach our hands from the period of the
zugot[31] and from the first *Tannaim*[32] were passed down only in the form
of the *gezerah* and the *takkanah*, the story and the testimony and the
tradition that has its source in custom. The *gezerah* and the *takkanah*
have their source in the authority of the suitable authorities, whether

these were high priests, ministers and elders, the Great Assembly or the Sanhedrin. Their number is much larger than is apparent from the *halakhot* that are called explicitly "*takkanot*" or "*gezerot*." It is enough to mention the *halakhot* taught in the form "at first . . . he enacted . . .", "at first . . . they enacted . . .", "at first . . . once they increased they enacted . . ." And there is no difference between these forms and "at first they used to say . . . they went back to say . . . ", at all. Over 60 *mishnayot* and *baraitot* are taught in these forms. Among them are ancient *takkanot* from the period of the Hasmoneans that were repealed and canceled by new *takkanot* by force of the objective conditions that changed. A great many *halakhot* were taught in one source in their latest form, but another source preserved the ancient strata, and it is possible to learn from the explicit that which is implicit, and to conclude that a similar process occurred for other *halakhot*, which are only preserved in one form.[33]

Urbach suggests three important points for our study of the term *barishonah*. First, he posits that texts transmitting ancient versions of *halakhot* give us entrée to glimpse earlier forms of Jewish law and their subsequent development. Second, he explains that appropriate authorities in each age made changes to Jewish law in response to objective changes in surrounding conditions, a statement that later authors prove to be an overly positivistic approach to reading the history of this period from its text. Third, Urbach infers that this sort of halakhic development occurred *sub rosa*, even when not explicitly mentioned in the texts, implying that even those laws extant only in one formulation had a prior history of development, which has been lost to later students.

Comparative legal studies have also offered fruitful directions for investigation into the use of this term. As the citations from Alan Watson in the Introduction showed, one should not suppose that this sort of acknowledged development of law is, in any way, a phenomenon unique to Jewish law. Martin Jaffee[34] points to a series of parallels to the term *barishonah* in a variety of ancient legal systems. The earliest is a Hittite formulation mentioned by Bernard Levinson:[35]

> If anyone blinds a free person or knocks his teeth out, formerly (*karū*) they would pay 1 mina of silver, but now (*kinum*) one pays 20 sheqels of silver; he shall pledge his estate as security.[36]

Levinson determines that fully 12% of the 200 laws that comprise the Hittite collection involve cases of an older precedent being replaced by a newer one, all employing this form *karū . . . kinum*.

Levinson then reasons by analogy: "If legal amendment manifests itself so extensively within a century or two of the promulgation of the Hittite laws, we should expect that similar accommodation of older law to newer circumstances would equally become necessary in the literature of ancient Israel, which spans an even longer period."[37] Oddly enough, though, he finds only one example of anything close to the Hittite precedent in the Hebrew Bible, in Ruth 4:7:

וזאת לפנים בישראל על הגאולה ועל התמורה לקים כל דבר שלף איש נעלו
ונתן לרעהו וזאת התעודה בישראל:

Thus formerly it was done in Israel in cases of redemption or exchange: to validate any transaction, one man would take off his sandal and hand it to the other. Such was the practice in Israel.

It is possible that this passage simply represents Ruth's later author describing legal procedure from a prior age. Still, in Levinson's citation of the most explicit example of disclosed legal change in the Bible, all we find is the subtle trace of a law that was once in effect. No new replacement law is specified at all. Levinson notes that even this is an oddity amongst biblical laws—in every other case the authors utilize what he calls a "rhetoric of concealment" that serves to camouflage any dynamism in the actual history of the laws.[38] While there is certainly innovation rooted within the biblical text,[39] the authors did not make it wholly explicit, due to an ideology of constancy and respect for a divinely transmitted core. To explicitly update such laws was to cross a forbidden ideological line. Aside from the text in Ruth 4, then, there are no explicit precedents of what we might call a "rhetoric of disclosure" to be found in the entire Bible.

Gershon Brin, in his study of time in the Bible and Dead Sea Scrolls, points out that the biblical use of the term *barishonah* differs significantly from its use in rabbinic literature.[40] Biblically, it is simply a term that indicates a reference to events of a prior time, generally connected with Israel, lacking any implicit or explicit implication of legal change. It also occurs in the Qumran corpus, where it preserves essentially the same meaning as it has biblically.[41]

We find another set of parallels in one of the best-known Roman legal textbooks, *The Institutes of Gaius*. Gaius (*fl.* 2nd century CE), one of the most renowned Roman jurists, was born under Hadrian and lived in Rome. He was the author of over 100 works dealing with Roman law.[42] Two examples of the many cited by Jaffee will suffice to illustrate the *Institutes'* parallels with halakhic texts. The first concerns safeguarding the rights of a testamentary heir to his inheritance:

224) In ancient times it was permissible to exhaust the whole estate by legacies and gifts of liberty, and to leave nothing but the empty title of heir. And the law of the Twelve Tables[43] seemed to allow this, by pro-

viding that whatever a man had by his will enjoined regarding his property should hold good, the words of the statute being: 'as a man shall have legated of his property, so let law be.' In consequence, testamentary heirs would abstain from the inheritance, and thus many persons used to die intestate.

225) Hence was enacted the *Lex Furia*,[44] whereby no one except certain persons was allowed to take more than 1,000 asses by legacy or gift *mortis causa*. But this statute failed of its purpose. For a man having, for example, an estate worth 5,000 asses could exhaust the whole estate by giving a legacy of 1,000 to each of five persons.

226) Later, therefore, the *Lex Uoconia*[45] was enacted, providing that no one might, by legacy or gift *mortis causa* take more than the heirs . . . but a similar defect came to light. For by distributing his estate among numerous legatees a testator was able to leave his heir so very little that it was not the latter's interest to shoulder the burdens of the whole inheritance for so little gain.

227) Consequently, the *Lex Falcidia*[46] was enacted, providing that a testator may not legate more than three-quarters of his estate. An heir is thus bound to get a quarter of the inheritance. And this is the law observed today.[47]

Here, we may observe a rhetoric of disclosure quite similar to that found in rabbinic literature. The text cites an initial formulation of the law, followed by an elaboration of problems with its application. Subsequent authorities then overturned the initial statement of law and replaced it with a new law that offered superior performance. Multiple distinct phases follow in its legal development, an eventuality also occasionally present in rabbinic literature. The stated purpose of the changes made was to provide a fairer and more just outcome for the parties involved. In the *Institutes,* Gaius shows that innovations in the Roman laws of inheritance worked to ensure that the heir received an appropriate percentage of his/her due inheritance, despite any other intentions of the involved parties.

In an extension of this principle, we find that Gaius reported a decision made during the time of Hadrian, emperor from 117-138 CE:

287) Again, at one time a trust could be left in favour of an uncertain person or an afterborn stranger, though such persons can neither be instituted heirs nor be left legacies. But by a senatusconsult[48] made on the

authority of the late emperor Hadrian the same rule has been established for trusts as for legacies and inheritances.[49]

Precisely during a particularly important period of rabbinic creativity, Roman legal experts were reconsidering earlier positions and formulating new laws to ensure the equity of inheritance (in fairness, this sort of reconsideration appears to have been a constant theme in every period of Roman legal development). It is impossible to say with any certainty whether Jews in Roman Palestine followed the acts of the Roman emperors closely enough to be aware of this form of legal revision. Since their lives and livelihoods were often directly bound up with the vicissitudes of Roman rule, it is entirely likely that Palestinian Jews were aware of the revision of laws occurring in their Roman host culture, as Christine Hayes has argued.[50] Other authors, though, entirely reject this possibility.[51]

One further parallel from Gaius deserves attention:

184) In earlier times, when the *legis actiones*[52] were in use, a tutor used to be appointed if there was a *legis actio* between a tutor and his ward, whether a woman or a male under puberty. For, inasmuch as the tutor could not himself give *auctoritas*[53] in a matter in which he was himself interested, another tutor used to be appointed his *auctoritas*. He was called a *praetorius tutor*, because appointed by the urban praetor.[54] Some hold that since the abolition of the *legis actiones* this case of appointment of a tutor has gone out of use, but another view is that it is still available if the proceedings in view be by *iudicium legitimum*.[55]

A number of striking parallels to Jewish law emerge. In Roman law, responsible adults stood in on behalf of minors or others who required representation in official legal proceedings. A tutor involved in the case at hand (whose relationship with his charge, presumably, denied the possibility of objectivity) was not allowed to participate, for fear of his interfering with a just outcome. As we often see in M and elsewhere, the final formulation of this law is multi-vocal—two views are presented, with no guidance for which is the correct one to follow in future situations. Finally, and most importantly, this individual law changed based upon changes to other laws that rendered it too difficult to uphold. Here, an altered legal context led to revised law.

Two final sources for parallels require discussion. Morton Smith[56] suggests a set of parallels to rabbinic literature's use of *barishonah* in Jesus' Sermon on the Mount, from Matthew 5:21-48, with a focus on 27-30:

27) You have heard it said by the elders:[57] You shall not commit adultery. 28) But I say to you that whoever looks at a woman in lust has committed adultery with her already in his heart. 29) And if your right eye offends you, pluck it out, and cast it away from you; for it is better that one of your members should perish that your whole body should not be cast into hell. 30) And if your right hand offends you, cut it off and cast it away from you; for it is better that one of your members should perish that your whole body should not be cast into hell.

Smith calls this sort of parallel to rabbinic literature a "parallel of idiom." Though the language is not exactly parallel, he argues that the function of the expression is. As Smith explains:

> [T]he words in Mat[thew] are parallel to the expression בראשונה (at first), often found in the Mishnah and Tosefta in the context בראשונה היו אומרים . . . חזרו לומר ('At first they used to say . . . They came round to saying') (and its variants). At any event, there is no doubt that the corresponding words in Mat[thew] are related to the rabbinical tradition . . . the peculiar use which they have in this chapter of Mat[thew] . . . [is] to introduce a legal opinion contradicting that generally accepted.[58]

Whether Smith's idea of parallels of idiom is correct or not[59] and whether this truly introduces legal rather than ethical or theological innovation is debatable. Nonetheless, both the New Testament and Gaius' *Institutes* show that controversial and innovative ideas were often brought forth with certain formulae that differentiated the old from the new. Thus, the formulae we find in rabbinic literature extend a long tradition of disclosed innovation first extant in early Hittite legislation and later shared by Roman and early Christian law.

Finally, one later parallel bears mentioning as well. In a Pahlavi text known as *The Book of a Thousand Judgments*, Sassanian law exhibits a similar form to *barishonah* as well:

> It is said that up to (the reign) of Vahram [a legal commentator], persons became the owners of a slave born of a father . . . but not of such a mother. For Sosyans stated that the child belongs to the father, but now, it is said (that he belongs) to the mother.[60]

Similarly, we find this example:

And Vahram has said: "I too think the same, because if she receives (a judicial document regarding her) misconduct, than any material benefit that she has (received) from her husband shall return to the husband." Now, however, it is said concerning a disobedient wife: that she cannot be left without income.[61]

In both these examples, the texts report earlier law that is supplanted by later opinions stated as new norms. This text is best dated to *ca.* 620 CE, making it somewhat late for our purposes. Nonetheless, while Tannaitic texts had virtually no chance of influence by Sassanian laws, it is possible that later texts, especially BT, were shaped, to some extent, by their surrounding Sassanian context.

The Rationales

With these parallels in mind, we now turn to the study of the rabbinic texts. By thoroughly reviewing carefully selected citations from rabbinic legal literature, we will attempt to create a more nuanced understanding of the term *barishonah* and build a typology of the rationales for legal change utilized in the texts of the Tannaitic and Amoraic periods.

One hundred and sixty-two passages show evidence of the use of this term as a marker for self-conscious legal change in the rabbinic legal corpus. Rationales are explicitly stated that justify the changes reported in 139 of the 162 passages cited (fully 86%).[62] This chapter will categorize the passages according to their stated rationales, examine the frequency of occurrence of each rationale, and attempt to define the spectrum of acceptable justifications for innovation in the rabbinic mind.

Within the citations enumerated above, we find eight explicitly stated rationales for change that appear in conjunction with the word *barishonah* in the entirety of Tannaitic and Amoraic legal literature. We will progress from the most common rationale to the one most rarely offered.

1) An Incident Shows the Problem with a Law

It is not an uncommon experience in any age or place. A leader or communal body, in formulating legal guidelines, makes a thoughtful decision to establish a law that appears to adequately address all foreseeable future possibilities. The trouble is, though, that new, unanticipated possibilities lurk slightly beyond the purview of the legislative parties involved. Frequently, this sort of dissonance between law and reality garners attention via an incident that occurred during the actual application of the law over time. Often, our sources suggest, it

was only after a law had been in effect for some time that its ineffective or in-
complete nature became clear.

In 15 distinct cases within the legal corpus of rabbinic literature, the term
barishonah points to a situation where a relatively negative experience with the
application of a law shows that the early formulation did not fully address the
altered situation at hand.[63] These "learning experiences" varied from the humorous to the tragic, highlighting everything from spirited competition with
neighboring sects of Judaism to the vicious savagery of war with the Romans.
When the application of a law led to clear and present danger or other highly
unacceptable consequences, rabbinic texts suggest that the rabbis felt free to
modify it as they saw fit.

Fighting for Life on Shabbat

Since the earliest recorded moments of Jewish history, weighing two important values against one another has led to multiple potential legal outcomes. Few
examples of this balancing act are more poignant than the interplay between
self-defense and Shabbat.

No mention of self-defense on Shabbat occurs in the Bible at all, though
Moshe D. Herr suggests that it is highly likely that long wars (such as the battle
for Canaan or King David's wars) were waged on Shabbat.[64] Herr cites a number of Second Temple period texts that reflect an outlook wholly opposed to
Sabbath warfare, including Josephus' account of Ptolemy son of Lagos's successful Sabbath attack on Jerusalem[65] and the victorious battle against Nikanor
that had to be terminated before Shabbat began. In both these cases, war on
Shabbat was prohibited, and restraint from fighting and other protective activities led to significant loss of Jewish life and property. Herr also cites the narratives found in I Macc. 2:39-41 and II Macc. 8:12-29, which describe Mattathias
leading a group of citizens in a war of self-defense on Shabbat. From Herr's
reconstruction of history, warfare on Shabbat was entirely forbidden before the
incident with Mattathias, but after Mattathias' decision to fight on Shabbat, the
practice of defensive war on Shabbat was thereafter permitted.[66]

In the Qumran corpus, we find another item of interest to the development of this halakhic concept. Defense of property or other wealth was forbidden on Shabbat, as we see in this text from Qumran, the Damascus Document
11:15:

אל יחל איש את השבת על הון ובצע בשבת.

No one shall violate the Sabbath for the sake of wealth or profit on the
Sabbath.[67]

Here, while no violation of Shabbat is permissible for the sake of preserving wealth, the text does not address the permissibility of personal or communal self-defense on the Sabbath. Lawrence H. Schiffman suggests two possible interpretations of this text: either it shows that the Qumran sect did allow defensive activities when life was at stake or that it is a simple reiteration of the prohibition against commerce on Shabbat.

Jub. 50:12-13 also sheds some light on this complex issue:

12) And (as for) any man who does work on it [i.e., the Sabbath], or who goes on a journey, or who plows a field . . . or who fasts or makes war on the day of the Sabbath,

13) let the man who does any of these on the day of the Sabbath die so that the children of Israel might keep the Sabbath according to the commands of the Sabbaths of the land just as it was written in the tablets which he placed in my hands so that I might write for you the law of each time and according to each division of its days.[68]

In Jubilees, a Palestinian text dated to the second century BCE,[69] a more stringent tendency appears. Here, it is clear that Sabbath violators are to be put to death, and violation *includes* fighting a war on Shabbat. Since the distinction between defensive war and offensive war is not drawn here, the author of Jubilees would classify participants in any sort of warfare on the Sabbath as liable to capital punishment.

Even Roman historians were aware of the Jewish hesitation to fight a war on Shabbat. Menahem Stern cites the following statement from Sextus Julius Frontinus, a Roman historian of the first century CE:[70]

Divus Augustus Vespasianus Iudaeos Saturni die, quo eis nefas est quicquam seriae rei agree, adortus superavit.

The deified August Vespasian attacked the Jews on the day of Saturn, a day on which it is sinful for them to do any business, and defeated them.[71]

Here, notwithstanding Frontinus' error in identification of the general responsible for the downfall of Jerusalem, the evidence suggests that Jewish aversion to war on Shabbat was a factor in Vespasian's choice of Saturday for his attack.

With these prodigious conflicting precedents, we can confidently say that the opinion on defensive war on Shabbat was mixed during the period immediately preceding the destruction of the Second Temple. Turning to the evidence in rabbinic literature, T Eruv. 3:5 provides our first example of the use of *barishonah*, and offers a picture of a chilling incident that the rabbis claim led to changes in law:

גוים שבאו על עיירות ישראל יוצאין עליהן בזיין ומחללין עליהן את השב.
אימתי? בזמן שבאו על עסקי נפשות. לא באו על עסקי נפשות אין יוצאין
עליהן בזיין ואין מחללין עליהן את השבת. באו לעיירות הסמוכות לספר
אפילו ליטול את התבן ואפי׳ ליטול את הקש יוצאין עליהן בזיין ומחללין
עליהן את השבת. בראשונה היו מניחין זיין בבית הסמוך לחומה פעם אחת
חזרו עליהן והיו נדחקין ליטול את זיין והרגו זה את זה. התקינו שיהא כל
אחד ואחד מחזיר לביתו.

Gentiles[72] who came [to wage war] on the towns of Israel—they go out against them with weapons and violate Shabbat [to defend against them]. When? When they have come intent on taking life. If they did not come with the intent to take life, they may not go out against them with weapons nor may they violate Shabbat [to defend against them]. If they come against towns near the border, even to take straw, even to take stubble of straw, we go out against them with weapons and violate Shabbat [to defend against them].

At first, they [the Jews, upon return from battle outside the city walls on Shabbat] would leave their weapons in a house close to the [city] wall.[73] One time they [the enemies] returned against them and they [the Jews] were pressed to take their weapons [quickly], and they killed one another [in the ensuing melee].

They enacted that each individual would return [his weapon] to his home [after the initial battle outside the walls].

In the initial section of T above, the root issue is the balance between Shabbat observance and the use of weapons. Using a weapon in battle certainly involves touching it, which is prohibited—since a weapon falls into the category of *muktzeh*. Carrying weapons is also prohibited, since once one passed a distance greater than four cubits outside one's private dwelling[74] such carrying would constitute a violation of the prohibition against work on Shabbat. Since slaughtering is also forbidden on Shabbat, it is clear that numerous violations would accrue quickly through any Sabbath use of a weapon. The passage notes that when enemies come *with the intent of taking lives*, utilizing a weapon in such direct violation of Shabbat is permitted, since then the principle of

"פיקוח נפש דוחה את השבת"—"saving a life takes precedence over the observance of Shabbat," comes into effect.[75]

The passage indicates both an early way of handling this situation, and a later revision: at first, soldiers would leave their weapons in a house near the city wall upon returning from battle. This would substantially reduce the carrying of weapons from the public areas of the city to the soldiers' private domains, thereby minimizing the violation of Shabbat as much as possible. Given the two values at stake, this initial solution appeared to present a fine compromise, as it allowed maximal protection of life concurrent with minimal violation of Shabbat.

However, once this incident occurred, T explains, the earlier approach had to be overturned. T suggests that, after taking their weapons from their home to fight the initial battle, these Jewish warriors returned their weapons to the storehouse at the edge of the city. In this case, though, the enemies attacked again, whereupon the Jewish soldiers ran to retrieve their weapons from the storehouse near the city wall, but killed one another in the massive confusion of quickly arming themselves for battle in such confined quarters. In the aftermath of such an event, no one could continue to argue that leaving weapons in a cache near the wall upon returning home from battle would advance the paramount value of saving lives, since the confusion led to far more disastrous consequences than the violation of Shabbat. Though aware that Shabbat observance would suffer from the new approach, the editor of T privileged the protection of human life over Shabbat observance, and the people were instructed to return their weapons to their homes for storage until the next time they were needed.

Preventing such injuries in places of storage may, in fact, represent a literary *topos* in rabbinic legal texts. In M Suk. 4:4, we find that similar concerns applied to the *lulav*, originally stored at the Temple to prevent extensive carrying when Shabbat and the first day of Sukkot coincided:

מצות לולב כיצד? יום טוב הראשון של חג שחל להיות בשבת, מוליכין את
לולביהן להר הבית והחזנין מקבלין מהן וסודרין אותן על גב איצטבא,
והזקנים מניחין את שלהן בלשכה. ומלמדים אותם לומר "כל מי שמגיע
לולבי בידו הרי הוא לו במתנה." למחר, משכימין ובאין והחזנין זורקין
אותם לפניהם, והן מחטפין ומכין איש את חבירו. וכשראו בית דין שבאו
לידי סכנה, התקינו שיהא כל אחד ואחד נוטל בביתו:

The commandment of *lulav*, how [is it observed]? When the first day of the festival falls on Shabbat, they bring their *lulavim* to the Temple Mount and the *hazanim*[76] gather [the *lulavim*] from them and arrange them upon the bench, while the elderly place theirs in a chamber. And they teach them to say: "my *lulav* is presented as a gift to whomever it may come."

The next day, they would arise early and come [to the Temple] and the *hazanim* would throw them [the *lulavim*] before them, and they would snatch them up, striking one another. And when the court saw that they were endangered, they enacted that each person would take up [i.e., observe the *mitzvah* of waving the *lulav*] in his home.

From this statement we learn that altering Shabbat storage practices to prevent injury, whether by weapons or by improper use of an important ritual object like a *lulav*, was a consistent position the rabbis utilized to permit minor violations in pursuit of a greater good.

The Toseftan text above has a number of significant later parallels that enhance our discussion. An account from BT Eruv. 45a cites a parallel passage as an anonymous *baraita*. The beginning of this *sugya* deals with those who participate in a rescue mission on Shabbat. Then, the text goes on to respond to M Eruv. 4:3 and portrays the Shabbat war incident in even starker terms:

והא אמרת: כל היוצאין להציל חוזרין למקומן, אפילו טובא. אמר רבי יהודה אמר רב שחוזרין בכלי זיין למקומן. כדתניא: <u>בראשונה</u> היו מניחין כלי זיינן בבית הסמוך לחומה, פעם אחת הכירו בהן אויבים ורדפו אחריהם, ונכנסו ליטול כלי זיינן, ונכנסו אויבים אחריהן. דחקו זה את זה, והרגו זה את זה יותר ממה שהרגו אויבים. באותה שעה התקינו שיהו חוזרן למקומן בכלי זיינן.

And did you [not] say [M Eruv. 4:3], "All who go out to save [lives] may return to their place?" Even [if they travel] quite a distance [i.e., over two thousand cubits and thus beyond the Shabbat limit]? Rav Yehuda said in the name of Rav:[77] that they return to their places with their weapons [i.e., they carry their weapons home for storage].

As it was taught: <u>At first,</u> [upon returning from the initial battle] they would return their weapons to a house close to the [city] wall. Once the enemies noticed them and pursued them, and they [the Jews] came in to take their weapons, and the enemies entered after them. They pushed one another, and they killed each other more than the enemies did. At that time, they enacted that they should return to their places [i.e., their homes] with their weapons.

The BT narrative leaves us with a graver image of the incident at hand.[78] Instead of the rush of grabbing weapons causing the deaths of the Jewish warriors involved, BT's account suggests that the enemies actually followed the Jews inside the storehouse. In this version, it was both the crush itself and the direct attacks of the enemy who pursued and cornered them in the storehouse that led

to the deaths of Jewish soldiers. Thus, BT reframes the issue as more than simple confusion and the press of rushing to fight a daunting battle, labeling it a
tactical concern—consciously avoiding the gathering of any significant number
of Jewish warriors into a small, enclosed space where either mass confusion or
vicious attackers may gain the upper hand. In the end, though, the root principle
at work is the same: maximizing the saving of Jewish life.

One other part of the BT's rendering of this passage sheds some small light
on our analysis of the dating of this passage's events. While both T (above) and
PT (below) provide very little useful evidence for dating this incident because
both passages are entirely anonymous, BT provides us with at least some modicum of information on the chronology of this incident and the subsequent revision of the law. The attributions to Rav, if accurate, provide a *terminus ad quem*
for the incident at hand in the early third century CE. Herr suggests this passage
is based upon an actual event in the Hasmonean period.[79] However, it is clear
that none of the passages studied thus far provides any sort of complete data that
would allow precise determination of the date of this event, if it even happened
at all.

In PT Eruv. 4:3, 28a-b there is still a third account:

תני : גוים שבאו לעיירות הסמוכות לספר ליטול מהן אפילו תבן אפי׳ עצים
יוצאין עליהן בזיין ומחזירין את הזיין למקומן. באו לעיירות המובלעות,
אין יוצאין עליהן בזיין אלא אם כן באו לעיסקי נפשות. <u>בראשונה</u> היו
מוליכין את הזיין לבית שהוא סמוך לחומה. פעם אחת באו עליהן השונאין
היו מדחקין ליטול את הזיין אילו והרגו אילו מאילו יותר ממה שהרגו מהן
השונאים. התקינו שיהא כל אחד ואחד נוטל בביתו.

It was taught: Gentiles who came to the towns near the border to
take from them even straw, even wood, they [the Jews] go out against
them with weapons [on Shabbat] and return the weapons to their places
[after the initial battle]. If they came against cities that were surrounded
[by Jewish populations], they do not go out against them with weapons
[on Shabbat] unless they come for the purpose of taking lives.

At first, they [the Jews] would bring their weapons to a house that
was close to the [city] wall. Once the enemies came against them, and
they were pressed to take the[ir] weapon[s quickly] and they killed each
other more than the enemies killed them. They enacted that each would
take [his weapons] in his home. [80]

PT, following T, rules that once a town has been surrounded by enemy landholdings, the demarcation line for acceptable Shabbat violation changes, a factor

not mentioned in BT's version at all. Interior towns surrounded by friendly neighboring populations, were less crucial to the task of defense, thus a higher level of danger was required to trigger permission for the Shabbat violation associated with the use of weapons. Here, PT did not grant blanket permission to violate Shabbat unless it was clear that life and limb were at stake. PT's formulation of this difference in application of the law is novel, yet sensible.

Notably, the Palestinian versions (T, PT) both suggest an earlier provenance in the Tannaitic period and report the main passage anonymously. They also indicate that the Jews who pressed to reach their weapons quickly were responsible for the loss of life. BT, in contradistinction, is the only text that shows invaders actually entering the storehouse of weapons itself—surely a more dangerous rendering of the incident than any of the other version. It is only in BT, as well, that the attribution of this idea to a later figure appears—Rav, an early Amora who spent most of his adult life in Babylonia.

While all three of these texts agree that this incident precipitated halakhic change, these significant differences point to the hand of editors who wanted to highlight aspects of the law at hand given their own context. BT looked to strengthen the "violent outsider" aspect of the story, for its own polemical purposes and to attribute this Hebrew (and thus probably, originally, Tannaitic) tradition to Rav, a prominent early Babylonian Jewish personage. In contrast, Palestinian traditions may have tended to root this tradition in earlier contexts, to bolster its integrity and enhance the stature and history of the permission to engage in defensive war on Shabbat. Whatever the case may be, here we find stark literary evidence of the rabbinic notion that incidents can and should lead to halakhic change.

The Overzealous Priest

The incident and resultant change above mark only one of a number of instances in rabbinic literature where the danger to life and limb provoked a change in Jewish law. M Yoma 2:1-2 tells of another dangerous incident, when overzealous priests rushed forward to participate in their service at the altar:

א) <u>בראשונה</u> כל מי שרוצה לתרום את המזבח, תורם. ובזמן שהן מרובין, רצין ועולין בכבש, וכל הקודם את חברו בארבע אמות זכה. ואם היו שניהם שוין, הממונה אומר להם הצביעו. ומה הן מוציאין? אחת או שתים, ואין מוציאין אגודל במקדש :

ב) מעשה שהיו שניהם שוין ורצין ועולין בכבש, ודחף אחד מהן את חברו, ונפל ונשברה רגלו. וכיון שראו בית דין שבאין לידי סכנה, התקינו שלא יהו תורמין את המזבח אלא בפיס. ארבעה פיסות היו שם, וזה הפיס הראשון :

1) <u>At first,</u> any [priest] who wanted to remove [ashes] from the altar
would remove them. And when there were many, they ran up the incline and whoever preceded his colleague(s) into the four cubits [of the
altar] won [the right to remove the ashes]. And if two arrived simultaneously, the appointed priest said: "hold out fingers!" And what would
they hold out? One [finger] or two, but they do not hold out the thumb
in the Temple.

2) [There was] a case when there were two who arrived simultaneously, and they were running up the incline, and one pushed the other,
and he fell and his leg was broken. And when the court saw that they
were coming to danger [when using this system], they enacted that they
should only remove the ashes from the altar by lot. There were four lot-
teries there, and this was the first lottery.[81]

As in the prior case, the texts report that the law changed here only after the incident occurred. Once it became clear that the competition in ascending the
ramp up to the altar could lead to injury, the court was quick to remedy the
situation by enacting a new rule to create a fair and safe way to select the priest
designated to clear the altar of its ashes. Note, here, that the court (though precisely which court is omitted) is reported to be the ultimate decisor in this matter.

BT Yoma 23a presents a *baraita* with an even more dramatic version of the
events:

תנו רבנן: מעשה בשני כהנים שהיו שניהן שוין ורצין ועוליןבכבש,
קדם אחד מהן לתוך ארבע אמות של חבירו - נטל סכין ותקע לו
בלבו.

Our rabbis taught: [There was] a case when there were two priests who
arrived simultaneously, and they were running up the incline, and one
of them arrived at the four cubits [of space that defined the domain of
the Altar][82] before his colleague did. [The second one] took a knife and
drove it into his colleague's heart [killing him].

T, PT and BT all show more violent versions of this story, though they all ultimately end the passage with the same discussion and conclusion that we found
in M above. Here is another example in which the editor of later texts, especially
BT, substantially heightens the dramatic tension in the portrayal of the incident
to ensure that the point is driven home: while a broken limb is one level of moti-

vation for change, T, PT and BT raise the stakes to provide an even more compelling justification.

The rest of the discussion in BT considers which incident came first, concluding that the murder actually came first, but that the rabbis at first believed it to be mere anomaly. Later, when the broken leg occurred, the rabbis understood that danger was truly present, and they chose to make an enactment that changed the law to prevent any further harm.

These texts show a keen awareness of the delicate balance between two values, and the way a precipitating incident (or incidents, as BT would suggest) can highlight that tension, eventually evoking legal change. On the one hand, the enthusiasm and competition of the priests represent a sincere willingness to rush to do God's command. On the other hand, the supreme value that limits this enthusiasm is the protection of life and wellbeing. When faced with the essential danger inherent in a practice, the sacrosanct principle that law should not induce physical harm prompted the court to update current law based on the new information the incident brought to light. As in our prior example, the inclusion of this passage highlights the ideology of the editors of rabbinic literature and shows their willingness to consider adapting law when provoked by an incident.

Refusing a Minority Betrothal

Sometimes, as in the two cases above, rabbinic law changed after an earlier incident illustrated the presence of danger to life and limb. In other cases, precipitating events led to less dire consequences. Here we will find that law shifted after an incident showed that confusion would result as opposed to injury. As they discussed revisions to the law, the rabbis appear to take into account both the direct, immediate consequences and the more subtle longer-term ramifications.

In this next example, we find discussion of the legal concept of מיאון (*miun*, "refusal"), a girl's right to refuse a betrothal established by her mother or brothers after her father's death. In this scenario, after the death of her father, the mother or brothers of a minor girl could betroth her to a suitor. The girl's knowledge of the betrothal was a necessary element in validating it. If a betrothal occurred without her awareness, no refusal was necessary at all—it was, by definition, invalid, with no legal action needed to cancel it. However, if a betrothal took place with her knowledge, and she later did not want to accept the betrothal, she retained the right to repudiate it before a *beit din*, without the need for a *get*. Beit Hillel is cited as holding that the refusal was to apply to both betrothal (אירוסין) and marriage (נישואין) and had to take place before a *beit din*. Beit Shammai disagreed, arguing that refusal could only occur before the marriage was completed, during the stage of betrothal alone.[83] In either case, the act of refusal represented a volitional severing of a significant relationship on the part of the young woman involved, contrary to the stated wishes of her mother and/or brothers. While this refusal was similar to the traditional *get* or writ of Jewish divorce, it was considered a lesser sort of divorce, somewhat akin to the modern concept of annulment, because the betrothal was considered as if it had never occurred.

M Yev. 13:1-2 is the earliest rabbinic text to mention this sort of refusal. There, M traces the basic outlines of the process of refusal. The more interesting passage for the study of halakhic change comes in T Yev. 13:1:

בראשונה היו כותבין שטרי מיאונין : לא שפיה ליה ולא רעיה ליה ולית היא צביא לאיתנסבא ליה. ב״ה אומרים בבית דין ושלא בב״ד ובלבד שיהו שלשה. ר׳ יוסי בי ר׳ יהודה ור׳ לעזר בי ר׳ שמעון אומרים אפילו בפני שנים. כיצד מצות מיאון? אמרה : אי אפשי בפלוני בעלי אי אפשי בקדושין שקידשני אמא או אחי, אפילו היא יושבת באפריון והלכה אצל מי שנתקדשה לו, ואמרה בפניו : אי אפשי בפלוני בעלי זה, אין מיאון גדול מזה. ר׳ יהודה אומר אפילו נכנסה ליטול חפץ מחנוני ואמרה בפניו : אי אפשי בפלוני בעלי זה, אין מיאון גדול מזה. יתר על כן א״ר יהודה אפילו אורחין מסובין, ואמרה בפניהם אי אפשי בפלוני בעלי, אין מיאון גדול מזה.

At first, they would write writs of refusals [thus]: "she does not in-cline toward him, she does not desire him, and she does not wish to be married to him." Beit Hillel say: in [the official sitting of] a court or not in [the official sitting of] a court, but it must be [before] three. Rabbi Yossi son of Rabbi Yehuda and Rabbi [E]leazar son of Rabbi Shimon say: even in front of two.[84]

How [does one observe] the *mitzvah* of refusal? She says: "I do not want Ploni[85] my husband. I reject the betrothal that my mother or my brothers betrothed for me." Even if she were sitting on her bridal litter and she went to [the home of] the one to whom she was betrothed and said before him: "I do not want this Ploni as my husband," there is no refusal greater than this.

Rabbi Yehuda says: even if she went in to get an object from a shopkeeper,[86] and she said before him: "I do not want Ploni my hus-band," there is no refusal greater than this.

More than this: Rabbi Yehuda says even if there are guests reclin-ing [around the table][87] and she said before them: "I do not want Ploni my husband," there is no refusal greater than this.

The text begins with a description of the earlier practice. The earliest form of the writ included a three-fold written statement of her desire to be rid of her betrothed:

a) she does not incline toward him
b) she does not desire him
c) she does not want to be married to him

T suggests that this series of statements be written out. After writing out utterly unambiguous statements like these in front of at least two witnesses, if not before an official session of a court, their relationship was firmly put to rest.

The subsequent position articulated in this same text, in contrast, utilized speech in place of writing to effect the adjustment in status. The changeover to oral form as cast in T specifies that the potential bride need merely indicate orally to either the groom, a shopkeeper or guests assembled for dinner that she does not wish to marry him. She is no longer required to create any document, and no hint of public (i.e., court or witness) action is necessary. The reason for the change from written to oral remains unstated in T.

PT San. 1:2, 19a presents a new twist on this issue. Here, a more precise statement of the earlier text of the refusal appears, despite a silence about the contours of the later phase:

תני : <u>בראשונה</u> היו כותבין שטרי מיאונין במעמד פל' ופל' מיאנה
פלנית בת פל' בפל' בר פל' בפנינו : לא רעינא ביה לא שוייהנא ליה
לא צבינא להיתנסבא ליה.

It was taught: <u>At first</u>, they would write writs of refusal: "In the presence of Ploni and Ploni,[88] Plonit[89] daughter of Ploni refused [to marry] Ploni son of Ploni before us, [saying:] "I do not desire him, I do not care for him [and] I do not wish to be married to him."

Since PT is mute on the later evolution of this process, we can only discuss the original clause. Despite the differences in wording, it is clear that PT favors what T calls Rabbi Eleazar bar Rabbi Shimon and Rabbi Yossi son of Rabbi Yehuda's approach over Beit Hillel's, since two witnesses are mentioned in a מעמד (*maamad*, "a moment of testimony") as opposed to holding the proceedings before a *beit din*. Despite this decision, the report of the basic framework of the early process remains intact, and, without a report on a later stratum to examine, there is not much more to be excavated from this text.

The key to understanding the development of this law comes from the version presented in BT. While T indicates the starting and ending positions of Jewish law on this topic of refusal, and PT provides a glimpse at the starting point, neither spells out precisely why this change occurred. BT Yev. 107b-108a goes substantially further in its explicit explanation of the major reason behind this legal change, and that is where we find reported the essential rationale related to the adaptation of this law:

אמר רב יהודה, ואמרי לה במתניתא תנא : בראשונה היו כותבין גט מיאון
לא רעינא ביה ולא צבינא ביה ולית אנא בעיא להתנסבא ליה, כיון דחזו
דנפיש דיבורא, אמרי : אתי לאיחלופי בגיטא, תקינו הכי : ביום פלוני
מיאנה פלונית בת פלוני באנפנא.

> Rav Yehuda said, and they said it about what was taught in the Mish-
> nah: At first, they would write the *get* of refusal: "I do not desire him
> and I do not want him and I do not wish to be married to him." When
> they saw that this was too wordy and expansive, they said: it may come
> to be confused with the *get*. They enacted this: "On day X, Plonit bat
> Ploni refused [to remain married] in our presence."

This later text from BT fills the lacuna, suggesting that the change from oral to written *miun* would prevent confusion between documents of refusal (rejecting a particular type of minority betrothal) and true documents of divorce (rejecting a marriage itself). This highlights the essential difference between *miun* and *get*: once a husband effected a divorce and the wife received her *get*, her legal status changed significantly: she is considered a divorcée forever, with attendant changes in any future *ketubbah* payments and in her ability to marry a priest. Contrary to this, in the process of refusal, the woman who refused to marry a potential husband assigned through betrothal never assumes the status of divor-cée—in any future wedding, she would be treated as a virgin. In legal terms, she is treated as if her wedding or betrothal never took place at all.[90] BT's text thus focuses on one major issue: for the girl involved, avoiding any confusion with a true divorce and its subsequent limitations was of paramount concern. Making a clear separation between *miun* and *get* was critical to her future wellbeing.[91]

With this in mind, the two transformations in this group of texts become clear. In T above, changing the process of refusal to an oral process may have helped differentiate it from the written process of divorce, though T does not supply an explicit reason for the legal change. In BT, by contrast, both processes remain written, but an ironclad distinction was set between the language and style of the two writs. According to the later report of the process as we find it in BT, the writ of refusal had to be short and to the point, whereas the divorce writ was far longer and more complicated. BT, here, provides the most complete explanation and justification of the change in law. This shows the common ten-dency on the part of the editors of BT to embellish, explain and provide context for prior decisions they restated. Whether based upon written statements or oral precedents, BT's editors were comfortable, here, in adding logical statements that explained, justified and rationalized the change in law.

Ultimately, BT's report suggests that confusion was mounting on the difference between the two legal procedures of refusal and divorce, and this uncertainty constituted a grave and gathering danger to the societal fabric. Since divorce created major changes in the status of at least two individuals (not to mention potential longer term damage to offspring) and greater ambiguity between the legal actions of refusal and divorce thus had significant ramifications on personal status, the rabbis chose to create a new form for *miun* that made it perfectly clear that a refusal was not a divorce. Here, a growing lack of clarity coupled with a compelling social interest is portrayed as causing a rewriting of the terms of a legal document and a reconsideration of its essential oral or written nature. Whether this is simply an apologia utilized by BT to justify legal change, or a valid sociological reason for it, is unascertainable from the data available.

In each of these three cases, the texts record a danger that arose through the application of a law that provoked the rabbis to re-examine their legal position. Whether these instances record historical reality or not is almost beside the point. The fact that the editors of rabbinic texts included these examples shows that they viewed legal change as admissible and appropriate in response to difficult incidents that highlighted problems in the current application of law. Certain sacrosanct values, such as the protection of life and personal status, also contributed to the ideology of permitting legal change in these cases.[92]

2) Changes in Business and Agricultural Practices

In 15 occurrences of the term *barishonah*, rabbinic texts report a gradual change in social, agricultural or economic conditions that led the rabbis to review and reconfigure a prior legal decision.[93] These examples range from the simple reporting of a change that occurred in business practices with few ramifications to reported examples of significant halakhic alteration that resulted from contextual changes in the agricultural and economic landscapes. Two specific examples will suffice to illustrate the greater principle at work in this group of sources.

The Buyer Vanishes: The Challenge of Ancient Real Estate Deals

M Arakh. 9:3-4 provides an instance of economic change that led to legal innovation. These *mishnayot* address the question of private landholdings, with a special focus on their sale and subsequent redemption. The discussion revolves around the mechanics of buying back property when an owner chooses to employ his biblically assigned right to reclaim it within a defined period of time after a sale.

According to M Arakh. 9:3,[94] a family that sold its home in a walled city[95] retained the ability to buy it back for the first year following the date of sale. Should the original owners decide to reclaim their home, they could redeem it from the buyer by paying the original purchase price plus the appropriate amount of interest/rent the buyer had lost in the transaction. Further, if the initial owner had died, his son or other heirs retained the right to redeem the property during the course of the twelve months. After the twelve months had elapsed, the property remained permanently in the hands of the buyer and would not revert to its original owner even in the time of the Jubilee when landholdings were remitted. Thus, after twelve months, the buyer achieved complete long-term ownership with no later redemption by the seller possible.

The primary concept at work in this passage derives from Lev. 25:29-31:

(כט) ואיש כי ימכר בית מושב עיר חומה והיתה גאלתו עד תם שנת ממכרו
ימים תהיה גאלתו : (ל) ואם לא יגאל עד מלאת לו שנה תמימה וקם הבית
אשר בעיר אשר לא חמה לצמיתת לקנה אתו לדרתיו לא יצא ביבל : (לא)
ובתי החצרים אשר אין להם חמה סביב על שדה הארץ יחשב גאלה תהיה
לו וביבל יצא :

29) If a man sells a dwelling house in a walled city, it may be redeemed until a year has elapsed since its sale; the redemption period shall be a year. 30) If it is not redeemed before a full year has elapsed, the house in the walled city shall pass to the purchaser beyond reclaim throughout the ages; it shall not be released in the jubilee. 31) But houses in villages that have no encircling walls may be classed as open country: they may be redeemed, and they shall be released through the jubilee.

Property in walled cities, like the valuable agricultural fields that surrounded them, often represented long-term holdings of individual families. A temporary economic downswing might force a family to execute a highly unwelcome sale, releasing their connection to a property that had been "in the family" for years. If the family had no recourse in regaining the lost property, the stability of family landholdings and the value of these dwellings might be adversely affected.

To stabilize this situation, the Torah defined a system that protected family holdings in walled cities for one year after their sale, allowing a family to retain a limited level of claim upon their sold property. The law, as stated in Lev. 25 above, permitted displaced families to take back their ancestral holdings within the year, if financial circumstances allowed.

M Arakh. 9:3-4 highlights a self-conscious change in this understanding based upon behavior the rabbis noticed among the sellers and buyers of homes in their time. An unethical business practice threatened to undermine the essence of this law, and the rabbis shifted their legal practice to compensate for the changed business environment:

ג) המוכר בית בבתי ערי חומה הרי זה גואל מיד וגואל כל שנים עשר חדש. הרי זה כמין ריבית ואינה ריבית. מת המוכר יגאל בנו. מת הלוקח יגאל מיד בנו. אינו מונה לו שנה אלא משעה שמכר לו, שנאמר "עד מלאת לו שנה תמימה." וכשהוא אומר "תמימה" להביא חדש העיבור. רבי אומר יתן לו שנה ועיבורה:

ד) הגיע יום שנים עשר חודש ולא נגאל, היה חלוט לו. אחד הלוקח ואחד שנתן לו מתנה. שנאמר "לצמיתות." בראשונה היה נטמן יום שנים עשר חודש שיהא חלוט לו. התקין הלל הזקן שיהא חולש את מעותיו בלשכה, ויהא שובר את הדלת ונכנס. אימתי שירצה הלה, יבוא ויטול את מעותיו:

3) One who sells a house among the houses in walled cities, he may redeem it immediately and he may redeem it for 12 months. This is a kind of interest, but it is not truly interest.[96] Should the seller die, his son may redeem it. Should the buyer die, he [i.e., the seller] may redeem it from his [i.e., the buyer's] son. He must count a year from the time that he sold it to him, as it is said: "before a full year has elapsed" (Lev. 25:30). And when it says "full," it includes the intercalary month. Rabbi [Yehuda HaNasi] says: He must give him a year and its intercalary [days].[97]

4) [If the final] day of the twelfth month arrived, and it [the property] is still not redeemed, the buyer gains permanent ownership.[98] It is the same in the case of one who buys it and one who gives it as a gift. As it says (Lev. 25:30): "beyond reclaim throughout the ages."

At first, he [the buyer] would hide at the end of the twelve months, so that he would gain permanent ownership. Hillel the Elder enacted that he [the seller] should place his coins in escrow in the Temple treasury,[99] break down the door and enter the property. When he [the buyer] would like, he may come and take his money.[100]

In the initial formulation of the law in 9:3, an unhappy seller was forced to find the buyer to complete the transaction of sale *in person* to regain his landholding before the yearlong protective period expired. Mishnah 9:4, though, indicates that buyers began to make themselves unavailable at the critical time when the seller needed to contact them to redeem the property, thus preventing the seller from timely completion of the transaction before his option expired. A legal alteration in response to this behavior is attributed to Hillel the Elder, but may be of an Ushan origin, if Jacob Neusner's reading of the sources is correct.[101]

Hillel is portrayed as responding to this difficulty in the application of the law by enacting a revision that permitted fuller adherence to the underlying principle of protecting family claims on dwellings in walled cities. Hillel suggests establishing a system of placing the funds in escrow at a neutral, well-regarded place, the Temple,[102] where the seller may concretely establish the legal act of reclamation of his dwelling in a timely manner and then immediately enter the property, by force if necessary, even if the buyer should be enjoying an inconveniently long absence.

Through the application of a new transactional device, the escrow deposit, M reports that Hillel altered the original law to respond to new economic and social conditions. This new enactment permitted the spirit of the law to continue, despite a change in its mode of application. Most importantly, it continued to protect the same group protected by the initial form of the law, despite a change in business climate that threatened to render it obsolete. Whether the attribution to Hillel stands or not, this mishnah shows unequivocal evidence of an ideology of self-conscious legal development in response to sociological change.

New Law for New Wines

Another example of halakhic change in response to new business and agricultural circumstances relates to the manufacture of wine in Judaea. Zeev Safrai has shown that agriculture in Roman Palestine was based primarily upon three major crops: wheat, olives and grapes. While growing any of these staples was a profitable endeavor, grapes were the most lucrative of the three. Grapes were rarely eaten fresh, and in a society without refrigeration and with limited means of preservation, fresh grapes did not last more than a few days past harvest time.[103] The grape's most regular fate was to be pressed and fermented, resulting in wine that could be sold locally, transported long distances or stored for future sale. Vinegar resulted when wine was intentionally fermented for a longer period or when inferior wine production allowed wine to sour. It was most often used for pickling and seasoning or atop certain sorts of olives.

During the Second Temple and early Tannaitic periods, strict prohibitions against the consumption of wine produced or stored by Gentiles kept the production and transportation of wine firmly concentrated in Jewish hands, even as the population of Judaea became more mixed. Wine used in the Temple had to meet even stricter standards for purity, and was of generally higher quality than other wine produced in Judaea.[104]

The methods of producing wine did not remain static throughout the entirety of the Tannaitic and Amoraic periods. Wine was available in a variety of types,[105] and methods used in its production varied both geographically at any given moment in history and diachronically in the same locale. This led, naturally, to changes in the legal treatment of wine and vinegar over space and time as well.

T Dem. 1:2 contains a short statement that reflects developments in wine production in Judaea over time:

בראשונה היה חומץ שביהודה פטור מפני שחזקתו מן התמד. עכשיו
שחזקתו מן היין חייב:

At first, vinegar [made] in Judaea was exempt [from the suspicion that tithes had not been taken from it], because it was under the presumption that it was made from *tamad*[106] [an inferior wine made from husks and stems of pressed grapes steeped in water].

Now that it is under the presumption of [being made from] wine [made from the fruit of grapes], it is liable [to suspicion of being untithed].

The passage requires some unpacking, due to both the agricultural and legal concepts at work within it. On the oenopoetic front, we recognize that this passage presents vinegar that came about in one of two ways: either it came from *tamad*, an inexpensive mash fermented from the husks and stems of grapes already pressed for their juice or via a more costly fermentation process starting with the actual grapes themselves. Since *tamad* was a mixture that came from inedible stems and husks as opposed to the edible fruit itself, the rabbis ruled that it did not fall into the normal category of fruit fit for human consumption. During the earlier phase of this law, no worry about tithing was necessary because the fermenting mash was not itself considered fruit. Thus, any resultant product could not be subject to tithing. Since the vast majority of Judaean vinegar was initially made this way, it was acceptable to presume that there was no risk of Judaean vinegar being *demai*—suspected of coming from untithed fruit.

It is stated in this Toseftan passage, though, that at some moment in the economic and agricultural development of Judaea, methods of wine production changed. After this, the rabbis realized that the majority of Judaean vinegar originated in wine made from grapes themselves, as opposed to wine derived from *tamad*. Given this more direct connection to the actual, edible fruit, any tithe applicable to grapes would now also apply to the resultant vinegar, and, thus, the presumption that existed previously had to be overturned.[107]

A parallel in PT Demai 1:1, 21d sheds further light on the development of this law:

תני : אמ"ר יודה : <u>בראשונה</u> היה חומץ שביהודה פטור מן המעשרות שהיו
עושין יינן בטהרה לנסכים, ולא היה מחמיץ, והיו מביאין מן התמד.
ועכשיו שהיין מחמיץ חייב. מחלפא שיטתיה דר' יודה, דתנינן תמן :
המתמד ונתן מים במידה ומצא כדי מידתו פטור ורבי יהודה מחייב, וכא
הוא א' הכן. אמ' ר' לא : <u>בראשונה</u> היו ענבים מרובות, ולא היו חרצנים
חשובות, ועכשיו שאין ענבים מרובות, חרצנים חשובות.

It was taught: Rabbi Yehuda said: <u>At first</u>, vinegar which was [made] in Judaea was exempt from tithing, for they used to make their wines in purity for their libation offerings, and it did not sour [i.e., turn to vinegar], and they would make [their vinegar] from *tamad*. But now that the wine [itself] sours [and turns to vinegar], one is obligated [to tithe it].

The view of Rabbi Yehuda contradicts what he said elsewhere! As we taught there:[108] "One who mixed *tamad*[109] with a measure of [plain] water and found enough in it to make the measure [that would require it to be tithed], is exempt [from tithing it], but Rabbi Yehuda says he is obligated [to tithe it]." But here he said the opposite!

Rabbi [I]la[i] said: <u>At first</u>, grapes were abundant, so that husks were not considered [edible], but now that grapes are no longer abundant, even husks are considered [edible].[110]

PT offers greater detail than T on both the sequence and rationale of this halakhic change. A *baraita* begins the discussion in PT, stating the essential difference between vinegar and wine production in Judaea. As in T, wine was originally made from grapes, while vinegar was a product of fermenting *tamad*. However, after the practice of making vinegar from wine (and not from *tamad*) became commonplace, the presumption had to be changed to fit a new context.

PT's *baraita* is transmitted in the name of Rabbi Yehuda. The *stam* then counters with an objection against the reported early position of Rabbi Yehuda, questioning whether his opinion in M Maas. 5:6 comports with his stated opinion of the first phase here. The conflict devolves from the opinion attributed to him with respect to plain water mixed with *tamad* in sufficient quantity to qualify for tithing. The difficulty comes when we compare Rabbi Yehuda's two statements: if he considers *tamad* edible in the initial case, he must be consistent and hold that *tamad* is edible in M. Maas 5:6 as well.

Rabbi Ilai's statement resolves this tension and explains the need for legal change in this passage: he notes that when grapes were abundant, their husks and stems were not thought of as edible. After all, who would choose to eat husks and stalks if the actual grapes were also available? Eventually, scarcity and famine in Judaea led to a change in culinary standards and thereafter even husks and stems of grapes were considered food. As a response to economic downturn, then, tithing became applicable to anything made even from *tamad*, since the base material comprising it had now been reclassified as food.

Here, we see that the redactor of PT has reshaped received traditions into a passage sporting a coherent chronological sequence, complete with the prior tradition's earlier and later phases, but adding an explicit reason and an authority figure associated with the change. The alteration of law is fully disclosed, justified and made coherent with other opinions, through an Amoraic overlay that brings a resolution to apparent Tannaitic contradictions. Such greater attention to the issues of justification and coherence are part and parcel of the Talmudic approach to legal change, often absent from M, T and the Halakhic Midrashim. In this instance, it is PT that provides the most complete explanation of the change.

BT Pes. 42b provides one further parallel text on this issue, framed around the slightly different concern of the Babylonian editor:

תניא, אמר רבי יהודה: ביהודה, <u>בראשונה</u> הלוקח חומץ מעם הארץ - אינו צריך לעשר, מפני שחזקה אינו בא אלא מן התמד. ועכשיו, הלוקח חומץ מעם הארץ - צריך לעשר, שחזקתו אינו בא אלא מן היין.

It was taught: Rabbi Yehuda said: In Judaea, <u>at first</u> one who took vinegar from a common person[111] did not need to tithe it, because it was presumed to have come solely from *tamad*. And now, one who takes vinegar from a common person must tithe it, for it is presumed to have come from wine [which came from grapes].

The *baraita* from BT adds only one new element not present in the other texts: the reception of the vinegar from an *am haaretz*—a common person who was not a member of the elite *havurah*. Initially, in Judaea, when one who was strictly observant of tithes (a *haver*) accepted vinegar from one who was less observant (an *am haaretz*), it was presumed to have come from *tamad*, and since *tamad* was not considered edible fruit there was no concern necessary regarding its tithing. This *baraita's* portrayal of the move to the later stage is in harmony with the explanation provided in PT, with one major difference. Where PT suggests that economic distress led to *tamad* being considered comestible, the *baraita* in BT (similar to the text found in T) suggests only that the methods of vinegar production changed.

The inclusion of the question of receiving wine from an *am haaretz*, though, shows one important aspect of the BT redactor's outlook. Here, BT altered the formulation of this *baraita*, shaping it to focus more heavily on its own concerns.[112] Babylonian purity issues and a different fiscal outlook led to a different understanding of the development of the law from that found in PT, where questions related to agriculture and the land still caused greater concern.

These three texts about wine reflect a change in rabbinic law due either to an alteration in the manufacturing process of wine in Judaea or to the definition of certain foodstuffs and their edibility. It is also important to note how each editor took some liberty with the traditions received, inserting local concerns into the material being edited.

From the two examples above, it is clear that rabbinic editors claimed, at times, that changes in business and agricultural standards led to resultant changes in rabbinic law. Again, here, we see that all strata exhibit a rhetoric of disclosure—unabashedly reporting that changes in life led to changes in law. The marked difference we see evolving between the Tannaitic way of expressing these changes and the approach favored by the Amoraim is an important finding that will continue to arise as we review other reasons for legal change.

3) Changes in Municipal and Authority Structures

In 16 cases related to the term *barishonah*, distinct changes in either internal or external authority structures provoked significant adaptations in rabbinic law.[113] Internally, for instance, the rabbis reconsidered the minimum standards for an individual's being classed as a *talmid hakham* (disciple of the wise), thus redefining the authority structure within the Jewish community. They also altered the balance of power in relationships between rabbis of different locales as these communities changed. External challenges also led to the evolution of law: legal alterations are justified on the basis of changes in the relationship between the sages and other communities: e.g., the Samaritans. A review of just a few of these examples will illustrate the process at work here.

The Altered Authority of the Rabbinate(s)

The relationships among competing rabbinical authorities of an age are always a saucy mix of competitive vying for power tempered by mutual admiration and respect. Recent scholarship indicates that the Palestinian Amoraic rabbinate had a relatively weak position of leadership with respect to the surrounding populace. That weakness, coupled with its immersion within a constantly Christianizing Roman Empire, fostered a natural challenge to its power from the swiftly developing Amoraic rabbinate of Babylonia.[114] The Palestinians' eastern compatriots, more comfortably nestled under a friendlier power, eventually overtook them, setting the scene for the later Babylonian centralization of power in the Geonic period.[115] This series of texts does not exhibit the ultimate outcome of this power shift, but it does grant us an early window into the thinking of one of the two broad groups of authorities vying for regional recognition and power.

In an early discussion of the recognition of foreign *gittin*, M Git. 1:1 reports the case of a messenger from a place outside the land of Israel (*medinat ha-yam*)[116] who brought a *get* to a woman in Israel. In discussing this case in PT Git. 1:1, 43b, the rabbis asked what criteria should be employed to determine the validity of a writ of divorce:

אתא עובדא קומי ר׳ יהושע בן לוי : תמן אמר רבי יהושע בן לוי שנייא היא
שאינן בקיאין בדיקדוקי גיטין. והכא אמר אכן. חברייא בשם דר׳ יהושע
בן לוי הדא דאת אמר <u>בראשונה</u> שלא היו חבירים מצויין בחוץ לארץ. אבל
עכשיו שחבירים מצויין בחוץ לארץ בקיאין הן.

A case came before Rabbi Yehoshua ben Levi. There [in PT Git. 1:1, 43a],[117] Rabbi Yehoshua ben Levi said it [i.e., this *get* from outside Israel] is different, since they [the rabbis from outside Israel] are not expert in the precise laws of divorce documents. But here[118] he said the opposite! The *havraya*[119] [said] in the name of Rabbi Yehoshua ben Levi: that which you said is <u>at first</u>, when there were not *haverim* [rabbinical colleagues] outside the land of Israel. But now that there are *haverim* outside the land of Israel, they are [considered] experts [in the writing of *gittin*].

Here, PT provides a striking picture of a Palestinian view of the relationship between the two primary groupings of rabbinic leadership. The text indicates an early Palestinian mistrust of Diasporan divorce proceedings. In this early Amoraic ethos, PT privileged rabbis of Palestinian provenance, suggesting they were the only authorities that could competently complete so serious and detailed a legal transaction.[120] While there were surely *gittin* issued outside of Israel, this did not comport with the expressed desires of the Palestinian rabbinic leadership.

Later, though, as the situation changed, PT reports a new level of acceptance. Rabbi Yehoshua ben Levi, who lived in Lydda, was one of the preeminent Amoraim in Palestine in the first half of the third century.[121] Reporting his two apparently conflicting statements, this text explains that his opinion changed over time. At the time of his earlier opinion, those leaders outside the land did not meet the rigid standards for acceptance into the group known as the *havurah*. Later, however, when there were *haverim* outside Palestine, the necessary level of knowledge and observance was present to be able to complete *gittin* correctly, and it was permitted.

The passage explains that by the time of the *havraya*[122] any prior imbalance in *get*-related knowledge had melted away, thanks to the growth of the Babylonian rabbinate. The editors of PT reported this shift in the authority over *gittin* from an exclusively Palestinian domain to a more balanced and more equitable bipartisan construct that better responded to the new distribution of rabbinic power. One cannot entirely discount the possibility that this section represents a Palestinian polemic against the growing Babylonian community of rabbinic leadership. Nonetheless, the admission of the shift in balance due to changes in the relative level of knowledge implies that PT's editor accepted this kind of reasoning as adequate justification for halakhic change.

The Developing Meaning of *Talmid Hakham*

> [Of tremendous] importance to the academic side of rabbinic education was the practice of *discipleship* with a scholar, the 'service' of a pupil (*talmid hakham*) under a rabbi. Such discipleship lasts for years and is often connected with a closely-knit common life and a shared household. This training is the only way to full-fledged membership in rabbinic society; without it one remains despite all knowledge uneducated, an *am ha'aretz* (Sotah 21b-22a). [123]

The status of *talmid hakham* (literally "disciple of the wise" or "wise disciple")[124] represented a liminal stage in the development of an individual as a Jewish religious leader. The *talmid hakham* was the quintessential apprentice, involved in the daily chore of learning his craft and imbued with some authority, but not yet complete in his own development. Many scholars have discussed the meaning of this ubiquitous term.[125]

In PT MK 83b, 3:7 we find a fascinating discussion of the definition of a *talmid hakham* that reflects significant changes in the meaning of this term over time:

אי זהו תלמיד חכם? חזקיה אמר: כל ששנה הלכות ועוד תורה. א״ל ר׳
יוסי: הדא דאת אמר בראשונה, אבל עכשיו אפילו הלכות. ר׳ אבהו בשם
ר׳ יוחנן: כל שהוא מבטל עסקיו מפני משנתו. תני: כל ששואלין אותו והוא
משיב. א״ר הושעיה: כגון אנן דרבבינן משגחין עלינו ואנן מתיבין לו. אמר

רבי בא בר ממל: כל שהוא יודע לבאר משנתו. ואנן אפילו רבבינן לא
חכמין מבארה מתניתן.

Who is a *talmid hakham*? Hezekiah said: anyone who has studied *halakhot* [the body of practically applicable Jewish law created by the rabbis] and more Torah.[126]

Rabbi Yossi said to him: that which you said is at first, but now, [one who has studied] even *halakhot*.

Rabbi Abbahu [said] in the name of Rabbi Yohanan: anyone who cancels his business for the sake of his study.

It was taught: anyone of whom they ask [questions of law] and he answers.[127] [Rabbi] Hoshaya said: like us, since our rabbis supervise us and we answer to them.

Rabbi [Ab]ba bar Memel said: anyone who knows how to explain his Mishnah.[128] And [with] us, even our rabbis are not wise enough to [fully] explain the Mishnah.[129]

PT begins by quoting an initial statement from Hezekiah,[130] an Amoraic immigrant to Babylonia from Palestine who lived in Tiberias in the early third century. Hezekiah understood the study of *halakhot* and "more Torah" to be the *sine qua non* of discipleship, representing the minimum acceptable level of achievement for this premium status to take hold.

Next, we see Hezekiah's statement overturned, classed as out of date by a statement attributed to Rabbi Yossi, a later emigrant in the opposite direction—from Babylonia to Palestine. Rabbi Yossi, also known as Assi or Issi, was a student of Rabbi Yohanan bar Nappaha in Tiberias, who lived in the mid- to late third century, two generations after Hezekiah. This is the first of three opinions from students of Rabbi Yohanan that we find cited here. Rabbi Yossi's statement dropped the minimum acceptable standard for a *talmid hakham* to a lower level when he defined the requirements as: "now even one who has studied *halakhot*." Removed from Rabbi Yossi's requirements is the crucial clause "and more Torah."

The third view presented in this pericope is attributed to the Palestinian Amora Rabbi Abbahu (d. 309 CE), citing Rabbi Yohanan (*ca.* 200-279 CE),[131] representing the least stringent of the views presented so far. Rabbinic legend described Rabbi Yohanan as the preeminent leader of Jewish life in Tiberias during the mid-third century. Rabbi Abbahu was his student and a contemporary of Rabbi Yossi (the prior opinion), situated in Caesarea in the late third to early fourth century CE. To qualify for discipleship in R. Yohanan's *Weltanschauung*, one needed only to prioritize the study of Torah over one's business obligations. Here, there was no requisite modicum of knowledge at all, simply a show of commitment to study at some personal expense.

A *baraita* forms the next piece of our passage, bringing with it the idea that anyone who participates in dialogic inquiry about Jewish law qualified as a *talmid hakham*. This earlier stratum is inserted to offer a new way to look at the question: being a *talmid hakham* does not imply meeting certain objective standards of Jewish practical and textual knowledge, nor is it required that one downplay the focus upon one's livelihood. Instead, one must have enough ready knowledge to be able to engage in the ongoing shaping of Jewish law through asking and answering questions. In other words, if one asked this *talmid hakham* about any of a number of issues drawn from the broad range of *halakhah*, he had to be ready with an answer. This implies a commitment to the understanding and transmission of appropriate law given the questions being asked at the specific time and place of the disciple's life. Thus, in the *baraita*, the minimum requirement is a steady engagement with the ongoing legal debates of one's day and having ready halakhic answers based on an appropriate level of background knowledge.

One other important implication may be derived from this *baraita*. A distinct element of communal acceptance may also be hidden in its words: community members will only turn to an individual to answer their questions if that individual is considered worthy of providing them with counsel. Thus, this *baraita* also suggests that the community of learners/questioners has a role in defining a person's status as a *talmid hakham*: after all, if no one asks these questions of a scholar, then the initial clause of the definition can never be satisfied.

Hoshaya,[132] an unordained shoemaker and the third student of Rabbi Yohanan in Tiberias encountered in this text,[133] applied this *baraita* to his contemporary situation, indicating that he and his colleagues, who ask and answer questions but are still supervised by their elders, qualified as *talmidei hakhamim* under this definition. Here, the text hints at a delicate communal tension: a *talmid hakham* was neither master nor ordinary person—instead he was a master-in-training. As such, he was able to provide answers to certain halakhic questions, but was still firmly under supervision. Such oversight safeguarded the interests of both the community and the disciple, ensuring that no serious mistake in interpretation or ruling harmed either.

Another implication of this passage is that the *talmid hakham* was responsible for his actions: he *answered*, literally, to his masters. They had the right to question his determinations and to demand a response. Such oversight was not inherent in any of the prior definitions of *talmid hakham* and may have been most visible to one who held the status of *talmid hakham* himself, such as Hoshaya. Here, the true flavor of the apprenticeship was visible.

Rabbi Ba bar Memel, a Palestinian Amora from the same period as Hoshaya known as Abba Bar Memel in BT,[134] concludes this pericope with a statement that rebuts Hoshaya and tells the final truth of this passage all at once: to qualify as a *talmid hakham* no objective level of knowledge can be expected in any absolute terms. Even the greatest of his contemporaries, who constantly supervise disciples, did not achieve total comprehension of what they study.

It is clear, then, that this text reports that the standards for becoming a *talmid hakham* underwent a significant shift over time. Hezekiah's initial definition formed the basis for a useful further discussion. That discussion, if it was indeed historical, most likely took place in Tiberias, as all the voices belong to students of the prominent Tiberian master Rabbi Yohanan. Regardless of whether this is the record of an actual conversation, or a literary construct that a later editor pasted together from transmitted statements, the result is the same: when the redactor finalized this passage, he included a variety of different opinions on the nature of a *talmid hakham* that spanned several generations and clearly evinced a forthright awareness of significant change in its definition over time. While the opinions from Tiberian authorities may well be cotemporaneous, the opinion contained in the *baraita* is clearly portrayed as originating in an earlier period. Rabbi Yossi's claim in this pericope is that an older opinion no longer held currency because conditions that related to authority and leadership had changed.

The Appointment of Judges

Like the changes in the definition of discipleship over time, we also find that rabbinic texts demonstrate that the process of appointing authorities also underwent major modification as time went on. Before we look at the specific texts that show the development of the appointment process, we must first examine precedents that set the stage for this later development.

In Num. 27:15-17, God commanded Moses to place his hand (וסמכת את ידך עליו) on Joshua bin Nun, to appoint him to serve as leader of the entire Israelite community. Alternate versions of this story appear in Deut. 34:9, where the laying on of Moses' hands actually confers leadership capability upon Joshua, and in Deut. 31:1-8, where a different account ignores the involvement of hands entirely, an oral declaration of Joshua's leadership sufficing to mark the transfer of power. Moses' appointment of the 70 elders in Num. 11:16-17 and 24-25 also avoids any mention of the laying on of hands, as does the account in Ex. 18:13-26. The Qumran texts use the term for the laying on of hands quite sparingly, mostly in connection with laying hands on sacrifices or, in one instance, when Abraham heals the Pharaoh called Zoan, the king of Egypt, through touch.[135]

If it were taking place, the practice of *semikhah* (the laying on of hands) as a method of appointment to an office of leadership goes mostly unreported in extant Tannaitic texts. Generally, when an authority is placed into an official position in the community, the verb ישב ("to sit") is used, most often in a transitive form (הושיב) ("to seat"), with no unambiguous indication of the laying on of hands. Lawrence Hoffman argues that in Tannaitic texts the word *semikhah* appears only in connection with laying hands on a communal sacrifice, and not once in the context of appointing leadership.[136]

The *locus classicus* for appointment rites is a pair of short parallel texts in M and T that provide much grist for later interpretive mills. These Tannaitic texts may originally have had little to do with the appointment of religious authorities, before the editors of the Talmuds utilized them as starting points for the discussion of this issue. M San. 1:3 discusses the placing of the elders' hands on a communal sacrifice:

סמיכת זקנים ועריפת עגלה בשלשה, דברי רבי שמעון. ורבי יהודה
אומר בחמשה.

The laying on of hands of the elders and the breaking of the neck of the heifer, [require] three [judges, i.e., a *beit din*]. These are the words of Rabbi Shimeon. And Rabbi Yehuda says: [they require] five.[137]

According to virtually all interpreters of this mishnah, the subject here is a communal sacrifice, which the elders were obliged to lay hands upon before it was offered. This laying on of hands represented the acceptance of the animal as a communal vehicle for redemption from sin and provided a public ritual by which this acceptance could take place. It seems highly unlikely that this mishnah originally had much to say about appointing leadership.

T San. 1:1 provides a parallel that offers further explanation:

דיני ממונות בשלשה. ר' אומר בחמשה, כדי שיגמר הדין בשלשה. הביצוע
בשלשה דברי ר' מאיר, וחכמ' אומ' ביחיד. סמיכה בשלשה, וסמיכות
זקנים בשלשה. ר' יהודה אומ' בחמשה.

Monetary cases [require] three [judges]. Rabbi [Yehuda HaNasi] says: [these require] five, in order that the sentence will be completed by three.[138] A settlement [requires] three. These are the words of Rabbi Meir. And the Sages say: one. Laying hands [on a sacrifice requires] three, and the elders' laying on of hands, three. Rabbi Yehuda says: five.

Again, though we might be tempted to read this text as referring to the appointment of leaders, the commentators caution against it. *Semikhat zekenim*, the laying on of hands *of* elders, does not imply laying hands *on* the elders—rather it means the elders' laying on of *their* hands onto a communal sacrifice offered on *Yom Tov.*[139]

Nevertheless, in the Talmuds we find the connection made between the sacrificial laying on of hands and the sort that appoints a leader to a new role in the community. The word used is not exactly the same, for the Palestinian rabbis substitute *semikhut* for the earlier *semikhah*, to distinguish the two sorts of laying on of hands from one another. The interesting fact, here, is the placement of this discussion by the editors of PT. Clearly, they saw a relation between laying hands on a sacrifice and laying hands on a communal leader, because this discussion, from PT San. 1:2, 19a cites a *baraita* that clearly responds to M San. 1:3:

תני : הסמיכות בשלשה. לא סמיכה היא סמיכות? תמן קריי למנוייה סמיכותא. א״ר בא <u>בראשונה</u> היה כל אחד ואחד ממנה את תלמידיו כגון רבן יוחנן בן זכיי מינה את רבי ליעזר ואת רבי יהושע ורבי יהושע את רבי עקיבה ורבי עקיבה את רבי מאיר ואת רבי שמעון. אמר : ישב ר׳ מאיר תחילה. נתכרכמו פני ר׳ שמעון. אמר לו רבי עקיבה : דייך שאני ובוראך מכירין כוחך. <u>חזרו</u> וחלקו כבוד לבית הזה. אמרו בית דין שמינה שלא לדעת הנשיא אין מינויו מינוי, ונשיא שמינה שלא לדעת בית דין מינויו מינוי. <u>חזרו</u> והתקינו שלא יהו ב״ד ממנין אלא מדעת הנשיא ושלא יהא הנשיא ממנה אלא מדעת ב״ד.

It was taught: appointment [of judges requires] three [judges, i.e., a *beit din*]. Is not *semikhah* [as mentioned in the Mishnah], the same as *semikhut* [as mentioned in the baraita]? There [in Babylonia], they call *minui*[140] [i.e., appointment] *semikhuta.*

Rabbi [Ab]ba [bar Memel] said: At first, each person would appoint his students, just as Rabban Yohanan ben Zakkai appointed Rabbi [E]leazar and Rabbi Yehoshua; and Rabbi Yehoshua appointed Rabbi Akiba; and Rabbi Akiba appointed Rabbi Meir and Rabbi Shimeon.

He said: Rabbi Meir should sit first. Rabbi Shimeon became angry. Rabbi Akiba said to him: it is enough for you that your Creator and I recognize your strength.[141]

They went back[142] and showed honor to this house [i.e., the house of the patriarch]. They said: a *beit din* that appointed without the knowledge of the patriarch, their appointment is no appointment. And a patriarch who appoints without the knowledge of a *beit din*, his appointment is [still] an appointment.

They went back and enacted that a *beit din* may only appoint with the knowledge of the patriarch, and the patriarch may only appoint with the knowledge of the *beit din*.

First, we must recognize (as Hoffman points out)[143] that there are three phases of development present in the rite as depicted here, rather than the usual two in the majority of cases of the term *barishonah* that we have seen. The initial statement appears in a *baraita*, and sets boundaries for the overall process. Following the *baraita*, Rabbi Ba describes the initial step in the process of development, replete with examples of appointed rabbis and one story of conflict over such an appointment. Two later stages are then presented, with very little information as to their provenance. Despite the imbalance in the literary structure, it is clear that this passage suggests a three-phase historical development in the process of ordination.

As recalled by Rabbi Ba, during the first phase local leaders could appoint their students directly, apparently without any need for communal approval in the form of a decision from a *beit din*. This initial phase describes a time when those judges already appointed were able to make additional unilateral appointments. Jacob Neusner, mining this passage for information about Rabban Yohanan ben Zakkai, notes:

> R. Ba's statement stands by itself, with no relationship to what precedes. The tradition dates, at the earliest, from the generation following 'Aqiva, presumably from Meir's school. It is followed by the story of 'Aqiva's arrangements in his own academy, in good Mishnaic Hebrew. We have no clear idea of how R. Ba concluded that ordination began with Yohanan. No earlier evidence pertained to the issue. [144]

Neusner's dating places the events described in phase one during the time of Rabbi Akiba, or, at the latest, during the generation following his (that of Rabbi Meir).

From a literary perspective, it is also vital to note that in Rabbi Ba's statement we find this study's first *attributed* case of the term *barishonah*. Rabbi Ba, known as Rabbi Abba in the BT, or Rabbi Abba II, lived in the third Amoraic generation, during the late third to early fourth century. He began his life in

Babylonia, traveled later to Palestine, and eventually settled in Caesarea.[145] This tells us that Rabbi Ba's statement is likely made approximately 150-200 years after the events depicted in phase one.

Rabbi Ba's statement then proceeds with a review of the development of the process of appointment. In phase two, which begins with a key literary term that indicates a revision, *hazru*, the text states that an appointment made by the court must be approved by the patriarch, while an appointment made by the patriarch does not require any formal approval from a court. Phase two represents a moment in history when the redactors portray the patriarchate as the nexus of power. Without entirely emasculating the *beit din*, their role has been severely curtailed in favor of "showing honor to the patriarch." While we cannot argue, in any way, that this text provides us with ironclad historical truth from the period it purports to define, it does speak to the attitudes of the editor(s) of this text and their view of the balance of power between the patriarchate and *beit din*. At least one recent historian, for example, would argue that both patriarch and *beit din* were entirely marginal to Palestinian society anyway, suggesting that this power struggle had little actual import.[146]

Phase three represents an historical moment during which the patriarch's power has waned. It is a synthesis of both preceding phases, in some sense, because both patriarch and *beit din* are now required for a successful appointment. In this way, both goals of the prior phases are still met: the community is represented through the *beit din*, while honor and power are still wielded by the patriarch. In sum, then, this text provides us with a schema for the development of the process of ordination. The texts imply that this process changed due to the shifting relationship between the communal rabbinic leadership and its centralized authority figure, the patriarch.

Changing Samaritan Attitudes

While internal changes in the authority structures of the Jewish community had a significant impact on law, external groups and their developing relationship with the Jewish community also led to other kinds of changes in law. In the case of the Samaritans, the relationship with the Judaean community grew terribly strained over time and led to a substantial distance between these competing neighboring populations on the Palestinian landscape.

Two theories of the origin of the Samaritan schism permeate the relevant modern scholarly literature. The first, based upon II Kgs. 17, begins with the Assyrian policy of population transfer after the destruction of Northern Israel in 722 BCE. This theory claims that the Cuthites, placed by the Assyrians in Judaea, intermarried and intermingled excessively with local peoples, leading to a strong rejection by the Judaeans who were trying to preserve their own national identity. The second theory rejects the biblical basis of the schism, seeking its origin in John Hyrcanus' attack on Shechem (a holy place for the Samaritans) in 128 BCE.[147] Whatever the true origin, the Tannaitic and Amoraic periods saw a marked decline in the relationship between rabbinic Judaism and its Samaritan competitors.

A passage in PT Pes. 1:1, 27b posits a downward spiral of Samaritan ritual observance:

תני: רבן שמעון בן גמליאל או': כל מצוה שהכותים נוהגין בה הם
מדקדקין בה יתיר מישראל. אמר ר' שמעון: הדא דתימר בראשונה שהיו
משוקעין בכופרניהן, אבל עכשיו שאין להן לא מצוה ולא שירי מצוה
חשודין הן ומקולקלין הן.

It was taught: Rabban Shimeon ben Gamaliel says: any commandment that the Samaritans observe, they are more exacting in their observance than Israel. Rabbi Shimeon said: that which you said is at first, when they were isolated in their villages. But now that they do not have commandment[s], nor the remnant of commandment[s], they are suspected [of improperly observing the commandments] and they are corrupted.[148]

This exchange suggests[149] that at one point in history, it was the case that the Judaeans saw the Samaritans as highly observant of at least certain commandments.[150] R. Shimeon's statement, though, deftly rejects this view as antiquated and depicts the Samaritans quite differently, critiquing a highly negative development in their observance patterns. His statement implies that their initially isolated existence led to a reasonably secure transmission of Torah to their people, since little outside influence was able to interfere with their practices and traditions. After that isolation waned and the Samaritans intermingled with surrounding cultures to a greater extent, the transmission process was disrupted, leading to a situation in which Rabbi Shimeon claimed they "do not have commandments nor the remnants of commandments." His position may also suggest that their traditions became garbled (whether through syncretism or the sheer ignorance of custom facilitated by greater levels of assimilation), leaving them with no solid basis upon which to rely for accurate guidance in their religious practice.

An attempt at dating this shift is best done in light of two articles on the Samaritan schism. Schiffman[151] and Crown[152] both argue that the final split between the Jews and the Samaritans intensified in the mid-second century CE, in response to the loss of the Temple in Jerusalem in 70 CE, the later Hadrianic persecutions and the increased messianic activities during the Bar Kokhba revolt. Other factors included the increased desire of Jews to define themselves as different from other religions and new Samaritan activities that rewrote or added to the written Torah. These combined factors completed the enduring process of the split that had been taking place for many years and led to the subsequent declaration by R. Shimeon in the text above that the Samaritans are polluted entirely and not to be accepted in their observance of any Jewish law.

Thus, due to a variety of external pressures, the rabbis claimed to have shifted their stance on the Samaritans, recognizing first an initial and then a revised formulation of Jewish law with respect to their activities. Such adaptation of law worked to ensure that rabbinic strictures would continue to be observed despite the challenge of those outside authorities who disagreed and behaved differently.

The Romans and the Sabbatical Year

External influence on the halakhic process was not limited to groups that battled over radically different interpretations of Jewish authenticity. Some of the most influential external groups were, in fact, not Jews at all. Our next example shows the influence that Roman authorities had upon the formation of rabbinic law as reported in at least one instance. A text in PT reviews the laws of the Sabbatical Year, during which active farming of Jewish-held land was prohibited. Here, the rabbis discussed the precise definition of active farming and debated whether certain actions (removing thorns, plowing once or twice, etc.) constituted the threshold for violation of the biblical prohibitions listed in Leviticus in relation to the Sabbatical Year.[153]

To understand the Talmudic passage below, one must first be aware of the order of preparing a field for planting after the Sabbatical Year. In general, the process began with clearing the field of all the various detritus that had accumulated naturally over the course of months without human tending. Removing rocks and thorns set the stage for an initial plowing, designed to break up the hard earth into manageable clods that could then be plowed further. In some cases, plowing once would have been enough to prepare a field for planting, while in others, it might have required numerous passes to ensure that the furrows were deep enough for the seeds of a particular crop to take root and survive.

With this background in mind, we turn first to M Shevi. 4:2:

שדה שנתקוצה, תזרע במוצאי שביעית.

A field that has been cleared of thorns, may be planted at the exit of the Sabbatical year.

Here, M implicitly acknowledged that some farmers were clearing their fields during the end of the Sabbatical Year. Immediately after the conclusion of the seventh year, planting such cleared fields was permitted. Thus, some improvement of the field was occurring prior to the completion of the Sabbatical Year, though the actual planting could not take place before year-end.

Looking at our main source, PT Shevi. 4:2, 35a, we find it begins with a quote from the mishnah above:

"שדה שניקוּוצה כוּ'" תמן אמרין בשניטלו קוציה. ורבנין דהכא אמרין משחרש. על דעתיהו דרבנין דהכא, אי זהו הטייוב? כל העם חורשין פעם אחת, והוא חורש שתי פעמים. וכא כן? א"ר יוסי בי רבי בון : תמן אין המלכות אונסת, ברם הכא המלכות אונסת. <u>בראשונה</u> כשהיתה המלכות אונסת, הורי רבי ינאי שיהו חורשין חרישה ראשונה. חד משומד הוה עבר, חמיתון רמיין קובעתה. אמר לון : האסטו! שרא לכון מירדי? שרא לכון רמיין קובעתה?

"A field that has been cleared of thorns," etc. There [in Babylonia],[154] they say: when they have removed its thorns [by hand]. And the rabbis from here [Palestine] say: when [he removed the thorns] by plowing.

According to the opinion of the rabbis from here [in Palestine], what is "improvement" [which constitutes the act forbidden during the seventh year]? All the people plow once, and he [the one who violates the prohibition] plows twice.

But here [in Palestine] is that the rule? Rabbi Yossi son of Rabbi Bun said: there [in Babylonia] the government does not oppress [us with high taxes that force us to violate the Sabbatical year], however, here [in Palestine], the government does oppress [us with high taxes that force us to violate the Sabbatical year].

At first, when the government was forcing [them to grow crops], Rabbi Yannai taught that they should plow the first time. One apostate was passing[155] and he saw them throwing clods of earth up into the air [to break them up]. He said to them: Oh perversion of the law! Are you permitted to rebel? Are you permitted to throw clods into the air [to break them and thus, plow]?

The crux of the matter rests on the interpretation of M Shevi. 4:2. For the Babylonian rabbinic leadership, "cleared" in the mishnah is quite logically understood to mean that a field has had its thorns and other agricultural refuse removed from it, improving its condition and preparing it for plowing. In Palestine, the rabbis go one step beyond this, permitting the owner to prepare the field for planting by breaking up clods, essentially permitting an initial plowing. The Palestinian position suggests an assumption that plowing once does not fully prepare the land for seeding, and thus does not yet encroach upon the prohibition against active farming. To the Palestinians, the first plowing is merely an extension of the clearing.

Rabbi Yossi son of Bun, the last eminent halakhist in late antique Palestine, *fl.* 350-400 CE,[156] is credited with a suggestion for the reason behind the differing viewpoints in Babylonia and Palestine. He suggests that the Babylonians, thanks to a relatively warmer relationship with the government, could afford to hold to a more stringent outlook on this issue. In Palestine, however, the Romans never showed such warmth, and therefore the Palestinian community was forced to remain as flexible and lenient as possible, permitting plowing and preparing the soil in advance to avoid economic ruin under heavy Roman taxation.

Rabbi Yannai, who states this rule, lived in Sepphoris, and was among the first of the Palestinian Amoraim in the late second century.[157] The main point of the story is straightforward: at this point in Palestinian Jewish history, the practice of plowing once during the Sabbatical Year was forbidden. Moreover, this prohibition was such common knowledge that even a guard knew it was forbidden. The question is: why would Rabbi Yannai have ruled that plowing be permitted at all during a sabbatical year? The *Penei Moshe* suggests it is:

> In order to hurry the seeding along, so that they would have something from which to pay the tax to the government.[158]

Since the Romans did not relieve the tax burden of the Jewish community during the Sabbatical Year through the remission of taxes, Rabbi Yannai's ruling permitted preparing for the heavy tax burden by doing whatever could be done to be ready for immediate seeding at the conclusion of the seventh year. In a grave situation, where land and livelihood hung in the balance, this response was a rather pragmatic one.

Note, also, the mocking term of condemnation craftily utilized in the text, "האסטו,"[159] ascribed to a passerby to show that even he regarded their act a serious violation of the laws of the Sabbatical Year. The guard is probably more of a rabbinic projection of guilt over altering this law than anything else.[160] Had the Romans acted similarly to the Persians, this loosening of the Palestinian laws of *shemitah* might never have taken place. The mocking "האסטו," then, came when the passerby realized that committed Jews were bending the laws derived from the Torah in order to conform to the will of a human authority, and a Roman authority at that.

In essence, this example shows that the editors of PT acknowledged the Roman government's decisions, and the concomitant change in Jewish law these decisions caused. While the use of the passerby incident to close the pericope suggests a certain unease with this legal alteration, nonetheless, this passage shows that the editors of this section explicitly admitted that actions of external authorities altered the course of the development of Jewish law in significant ways.

In reviewing the cases above, and the other examples where alterations in Jewish law are justified by the changes in municipal and authority structures, one important conclusion comes immediately to the fore. In all of the other categories of change marked with the term *barishonah* we find what appears to be a mixed distribution of Palestinian and Babylonian sources. That is, both Palestinian and Babylonian textual sources are represented in fairly balanced numbers. This category of reflective legal change, however, is entirely unique in one respect: almost every textual source and tradent cited is Palestinian. There is only one case in which a Babylonian text is involved, BT Ket. 25a, which is parallel to an earlier passage from T Peah 4:6 and probably derivative of it or crafted from the same inherited traditions. Thus, in every example where *barishonah* occurs and Jewish law is altered because of a change in authority structures, the text comes from a Palestinian milieu with Palestinian tradents.

It is quite sensible, given the consistently strained relations between the Palestinian leadership and the Roman government, to think that Palestinian legal change might appear more often in this category than Babylonian. The break with prior trends is a significant finding that highlights a noticeable difference between Babylonia and Palestine in their respective rhetorical approaches to change.

4) Changes in the Behavior of the Populace

Another of the explicitly stated rationales that the rabbis tendered for halakhic change is the sociological fact that the behavior of the populace had changed. There are 10 main texts with 12 parallels[161] where this reason appears attached to the term *barishonah*, and, in each of them the rabbis indicate an unwelcome downturn in the behavior of their contemporaries when compared to communities past. In no case do we see the more optimistic possibility of the improvement of behavior leading to a leniency—in every case it was the lack of proper observance and appropriate behavior that led to more stringent restrictions being enacted. We will explore two examples here and save one interesting text for the latter part of this chapter.

The Shifting Question of Levirate Marriage

Many ancient Near Eastern legal systems offered protection to widows in society who were most vulnerable, though often with an overriding focus on the assurance of continuing a family name.[162] In one of the most interesting manifestations of this legal tendency, the Torah promulgated a law that supported a widow whose husband had died and left her without a male child. In this scenario, a late husband's surviving brother would marry his widow, a process called levirate marriage, with the intent of providing her with safe haven and keeping the family name alive. While the Torah was not unique in advocating this sort of legal remedy, the involved parties and required procedures did differ across cultures.[163]

The commandment in the Torah that forms the basis for the concept of levirate marriage comes from Deut. 25:

(ה) כי ישבו אחים יחדו ומת אחד מהם ובן אין לו לא תהיה אשת המת החוצה לאיש זר יבמה יבא עליה ולקחה לו לאשה ויבמה : (ו) והיה הבכור אשר תלד יקום על שם אחיו המת ולא ימחה שמו מישראל : (ז) ואם לא יחפץ האיש לקחת את יבמתו ועלתה יבמתו השערה אל הזקנים ואמרה מאן יבמי להקים לאחיו שם בישראל לא אבה יבמי : (ח) וקראו לו זקני עירו ודברו אליו ועמד ואמר לא חפצתי לקחתה : (ט) ונגשה יבמתו אליו לעיני הזקנים וחלצה נעלו מעל רגלו וירקה בפניו וענתה ואמרה ככה יעשה לאיש אשר לא יבנה את בית אחיו : (י) ונקרא שמו בישראל בית חלוץ הנעל :

5) When brothers dwell together and one of them dies and leaves no son, the wife of the deceased shall not be married to a stranger outside the family. Her husband's brother shall unite with her: he shall take her as his wife and perform the *levir's* duty. 6) The first son that she bears shall be accounted to the dead brother, that his name may not be blotted out in Israel. 7) But if the man does not want to marry his brother's widow, his brother's widow shall appear before the elders in the gate and declare: "My husband's brother refuses to establish a name in Israel for his brother; he will not perform the duty of a *levir*." 8) The elders of his town shall then summon him and talk to him. If he insists, saying, "I do not want to marry her," 9) his brother's widow shall go up to him in the presence of the elders, pull the sandal off his foot, spit in his face, and make this declaration: Thus shall be done to the man who will not build up his father's house! 10) And he shall go in Israel by the name of "the family of the unsandaled one."

What distinguishes this commandment from the vast majority of other biblical laws is the presence of a choice in its observance, even in its initial formulation. However, even if the biblical text explicitly grants choice, levirate marriage is clearly portrayed as preferable. An insistent brother of the deceased may surely choose *not* to marry his brother's widow, but biblical law disincentives this choice via an embarrassingly public ritual "slap" for any surviving brother who exercises this option.

In rabbinic texts, this idea of choice was preserved, but altered to fit a new social reality. M Bekh. 1:7 presents a passage themed around three commandments for which a choice in observance exists:[164]

לא רצה לפדותו, עורפו בקופיץ מאחריו וקוברו. מצות פדיה קודמת
למצות עריפה, שנאמר (שמות יג) "ואם לא תפדה וערפתו." מצות יעידה
קודמת למצות פדיה, שנאמר (שם כא), אשר לא יעדה והפדה. מצות יבום
קודמת למצות חליצה. <u>בראשונה</u> שהיו מתכונין לשם מצוה, ועכשיו שאין
מתכונין לשם מצוה, אמרו מצות חליצה קודמת למצות יבום.

> If he did not wish to redeem it (i.e., the lamb set apart in place of a first born ass, which then died before being sacrificed), he must break its neck from behind with a hatchet and bury it. The commandment of redemption takes precedence[165] over the commandment of breaking its neck, since it is written (Ex. 13:13): "if you will not redeem it, then break its neck."[166]

> The commandment of betrothing a Hebrew bondwoman takes precedence over redeeming her, since it is written (Ex. 21:8): "if he has not betrothed her, he must let her be redeemed."

> The commandment of levirate marriage (*yibum*) takes precedence over the commandment of release (*halitzah*). [This was] at first, when they had the intention of observing the religious duty, but now that they do not have the intention of observing the religious duty, they said: the commandment of release from levirate marriage takes precedence over the commandment of levirate marriage.

While these three commandments are all rooted in sections of the Torah that give two options for fulfillment of the commandment involved, only in the last case do we find explicit rabbinic reflection on a shift in priorities and the stated cause for that shift. Originally, according to M, those men who lost brothers with no offspring would step in out of a sense of religious duty—they would marry their sisters-in-law for the sake of following through on their perceived obligation to God and Torah. As time went by, however, such religiously admirable motivations became mixed with other more human motives, driven more by emotions and passion than observance of commandments. As Rabbi Obadiah of Bartenura suggests,[167] there are two ulterior motives that might come into play when a *yavam* (a brother required to marry or release his sister-in-law) must choose how he wishes to fulfill this commandment. He may find his late brother's wife attractive, in which case, he may well marry her due to sexual attraction. Or, perhaps he may find her monetary assets irresistible. One can also imagine many variations on this theme—among them: revenge and pressure on his current wife in this not-fully-monogamized society. Whatever the case, the difficulty here arose from the fact that the brother married his sister-in-law not out of a sense of religious duty, but for his own gain. Note, too, that the widow involved may well have her own set of ulterior motives, though it is clear that at this point in history she was not the deciding party.

M claims that the increased likelihood of passion, greed and emotion playing into the decision of the *yavam* brought about by a change in people's behavior led to a resultant alteration of rabbinic law. The preferred outcome shifted from levirate marriage to release, to slow a trend toward observance of a *mitzvah* for the wrong reasons. Unstated here, but surely at the root of this decision, was the fact that this commandment was originally designed to provide protection for the widow and to provide a son to perpetuate the name of the late husband. M's claim, then, is that when other motives interfered with the sacred root principle, release became preferable over levirate marriage.

BT Yev. 39b, quoting this mishnah, provides us with another report of how individuals chose between release and levirate marriage:

תנן התם: מצות יבום קודמת למצות חליצה. בראשונה שהיו מתכוונין
לשם מצוה, עכשיו שאין מתכוונין לשם מצוה, אמרו: מצות חליצה קודמת
למצות יבום. אמר רב: אין כופין. כי אתו לקמיה דרב, אמר להו: אי בעית
חלוץ, אי בעית ייבם, בדידך תלא רחמנא (דברים כ״ה) ״ואם לא יחפוץ
האיש,״ הא ״אם חפץ,״ אי בעי חליץ, אי בעי ייבם.

It was taught there: [in the mishnah cited above]: "the commandment of levirate marriage takes precedence over the commandment of release. [This was] at first, when they had the intention of observing the religious duty, but now that they do not have the intention of observing the religious duty, they said: "release takes precedence over levirate marriage."

Rav said: We do not force [him]. When they came before Rav, he would say to them: If you wish, release [her], if you wish, marry [her], God gave you the choice, (Deut. 25:7) "and if the man does not want [to take his brother's wife]." This implies that, if he wishes, he may release her [by doing *halitzah*], and if he wishes he may marry her [by doing *yibum*].

According to the opinion attributed to Rav, the choice must remain entirely with the living brother. The other citation of this mishnah in the Babylonian Gemara[168] exhibits this opinion as well. Rav's statement, here, clarifies the mishnaic precedent: while the later stage indicated that *yibum* was preferable over *halitzah*, Rav made it clear that forcing him to do one or the other was still an unacceptable option. Rav's words imply that while preference continued, choice was assured.[169]

Later on the same page of Gemara, we find this mishnah repeated, with further commentary. As usual, BT gives us the most fully developed description of the relevant legal change:

בראשונה שהיו מתכוונין לשם מצוה, מצות יבום קודמת למצות חליצה,
ועכשיו שאין מתכוונין לשם מצוה, אמרו: מצות חליצה קודמת למצות
יבום. אמר רמי בר חמא א״ר יצחק, חזרו לומר: מצות יבום קודמת
למצות חליצה. א״ל רב נחמן בר יצחק: אכשור דרי? מעיקרא סברי לה
כאבא שאול, ולבסוף סברי לה כרבנן; דתניא: אבא שאול אומר: הכונס
את יבמתו לשם נוי, ולשום אישות, ולשום דבר אחר כאילו פוגע בערוה,
וקרוב אני בעיני להיות הולד ממזר; וחכמים אומרים: (דברים כ״ה)
"יבמה יבא עליה," מכל מקום.

"At first, when they had the intention of observing the religious duty, [they said:] the commandment of levirate marriage took precedence over release; but now that they do not have the intention of observing the religious duty, they said: release takes precedence over levirate marriage."

Rami bar Hama said in the name of Rabbi Yitzhak: they went back and said that the commandment of levirate marriage takes precedence over the commandment of release.

Rav Nahman bar Yitzhak said to him: Did the generations improve [in their morals]?

At the beginning, they held [that *halakhah* accorded] with Abba Shaul but in the end they held [that *halakhah* accorded] with our Sages, as it was taught: Abba Shaul said: one who marries his late brother's wife for the sake of beauty, for the sake of marriage[170] or for the sake of "something else."[171] It is as if he has violated the laws of incest, and I am close to holding that the child is a *mamzer*.[172] But the Sages say: (Deuteronomy 25:5) "[her husband's brother] he shall go in to her," [thus he shall marry his late brother's wife] in any case.[173]

In this passage, we find report of a third stage in the development of the laws relating to levirate marriage. Rami bar Hamah, a Babylonian Amora who lived in the early fourth century, suggested that the rabbis went back and re-enacted their prior preference for levirate marriage, at some unspecified later moment.

The respondent in this case, Rav Nahman bar Yitzhak, lived at the same time as Rami bar Hama, and served as a leading authority in Pumbedita.[174] Rav Nahman bar Yitzhak expressed surprise at Rami bar Hama's suggestion of a rabbinically-legislated reversal in this law, asking whether it was ever realistic to say that the morals of the generations have improved. Rav Nahman does not dispute Rami bar Hama's idea of altering *halakhah* because of sociological change,[175] but will not accept the idea that generational decline is reversible.[176]

Rav Nahman's statement and the following Aramaic passage (which could either be a continuation of his statement or a Stammaitic gloss) reframes the discussion entirely. Instead of ongoing legal change in response to sociological change, this section presents the change in law as two older opinions from the Tannaitic period in opposition here, that of Abba Shaul and the Sages. Over time, the rabbis vacillate: first following one opinion and then migrating to the other, then returning back. Between the initial formulation of this law in M and its later formulation as we see it in the words of the *stamma deGemara*, this law has shifted twice, creating a total of three stages.

Fascinating, here, is the *stam's* rhetorical choice: instead of simply acknowledging, as both Amoraic rabbis in the prior discussion do, that law changed over time, the *stam* instead sets up two far earlier polar opposite legal precedents, in order to assure the reader that mere sociological change is not the sole motivating factor in deciding law. This suggests a potent late Babylonian Amoraic brew of hesitation connected with changing *halakhah* for sociological reasons, even as it admits of legal change between two polar opposites. This reflects a certain ideological approach in the latter part of the Amoraic period in Babylonia that looked to distance itself from sociologically-driven halakhic change, in favor of rooting ideas into prior opinions already stated by important sages.[177]

Finally, the presence of the rhetorical term *hazru lomar* is also significant in this BT passage. Here, it indicates a return to a prior position already established and discarded once. It is both an admission of the mercurial nature of legal change and an acceptance of the possibility that certain potential solutions may not work.

The Twelve-Letter Name of God

The use of God's sacred name is another area where the rabbis admit of a change in legal outlook due to an altered social context. T preserves a tradition that points to an early leniency in sharing the name of God with the *hoi polloi*. While the new position on this point appears without any stated reason, T Sotah 13:8 gives us a sense of the timeframe, and that is where its import lies:

משמת שמעון הצדיק, נמנעו אחיו מלברך בשם.

[After the death of] Shimeon HaTzaddik, his brothers [the priests] refrained from blessing [the people] with the Name [of God].

Here we have our first reference to the moment when the priests ceased utilizing the full name of God in their worship. We find this statement in the context of an ongoing homage to Shimeon HaTzaddik (*fl. circa* 200 BCE) and others who lived in the Second Temple period. From it, we can set the stage for a later series of texts that discuss precisely how and why the rabbis believed that movement away from using God's name took place.[178]

In BT Kid. 71a and PT Yoma 3:7, 40d we find parallel constructions of this moment of change in Jewish legal history. BT Kid 71a reads:

ת״ר: <u>בראשונה</u> שם בן שתים עשרה אותיות היו מוסרין אותו לכל אדם, משרבו הפריצים היו מוסרים אותו לצנועים שבכהונה, והצנועים שבכהונה מבליעים אותו בנעימת אחיהם הכהנים. תניא: אמר רבי טרפון: פעם אחת עליתי אחר אחי אמי לדוכן, והטיתי אזני אצל כהן גדול, ושמעתי שהבליע שם בנעימת אחיו הכהנים.

> Our rabbis taught: <u>At first</u>, they would give out the twelve-letter name [of God] to everyone. Once the impudent[179] multiplied, they would give it out to the modest ones among the priests, and the modest ones among the priests would swallow[180] it in the chant of their brothers, the priests.

> It was taught: Rabbi Tarfon said: One time, I went up after my mother's brother to the *dukhan*,[181] and inclined my ear to the high priest, and I heard that he swallowed [the] name [of God] among the chant of his brothers, the priests.

While PT Yoma 3:7, 40d has this version:

בראשונה היה אומרו בקול גבוה, משרבו הפרוצין היה אומרו בקול נמוך.
אמ' ר' טרפון: עומד הייתי בין אחיי הכהנים בשורה והטיתי אזני כלפי
כהן גדול ושמעתיו מבליעו בנעימת הכהנים. בראשונה היה נמסר לכל
אדם, משרבו הפרוצים לא היה נמסר אלא לכשירים. שמואל הוה עבר,
שמע פרסייא מקלל לבריה ביה, ומית. אמר אזל גוברא ומאן דשמע שמע.

At first, he would say it [i.e., God's twelve-letter name] in a loud voice. Once the impudent multiplied, he would say it in a low voice.

Rabbi Tarfon said: I would stand in line among my brothers, the priests, and I inclined my ear toward the high priest, and I heard him swallow it [i.e., the name] in the chant of the priests.

At first, it [i.e., God's name] was transmitted to anyone. Once the impudent multiplied, the name was sent only to the suitable.

Shmuel was passing by and he heard a Persian cursing his son with it [the twelve-letter name] and he [the Persian's son] died. He [Shmuel] said: a man went [about his business] and whoever heard it, heard it.[182]

The rabbis, and the priests before them, believed in the significant power of the sacred names of God.[183] Anyone who utilized God's name was thought to have power over other human beings, wielding the ability to create miracles and bestow blessings and also the potential to effectively curse people and places. According to these parallel texts, before the "impudent ones" multiplied, the name was shared freely. However, once impudence spread, the name became a jealously guarded secret. Only the high priest knew the twelve-letter name of God, it was only recited on certain holy days, and then, only when it was carefully guarded from the hearing of the surrounding people who were kept at a distance from the *dukhan*. The high priest's "swallowing" of the name in the chant of his brother priests, here, was a clever compromise—the use of the name in worship could continue, but it was no longer publicly known such that the impudent might use it improperly. Nor did unsuitable priests (apparently, including Rabbi Tarfon) have access to it. However, with respect to the Persian's actions, Shmuel is cited as acknowledging that there was little to be done, *post facto*, if such information were shared inappropriately.

Both Talmudic passages are labeled as *baraitot,* thus they are ostensibly Tannaitic and Palestinian in provenance. This tradition, then, appears to be a rabbinic reminiscence on a halakhic change that took place in the Second Temple period. The reasons that prompted the action, though, imply a Tannaitic and later Amoraic acceptance of the principle of sociological change as a rationale for self-conscious halakhic innovation.

Coupled with the prior passage on levirate marriage and the other cited examples, it is clear that the rabbis utilized the idea of an ongoing decline in the behavior of the people at large as a frequent rhetorical justification for legal change. While earlier generations may have been able to appropriately respect God's ineffable name, these texts report that there came a time when, to eliminate blasphemy, false oaths and other abuses of its inherent power, its use was severely limited. The rabbis claimed that Jewish law changed, here, to slow a perceived downward spiral that signified a growing disrespect for God as expressed through the inappropriate usage of the divine name.[184]

In the two examples reviewed here, as in all the citations related to this rationale, legal change was justified by fear of declining behavioral standards. Such a dim view of certain public behaviors was clearly an accepted part of the worldview of the editors of rabbinic texts. The actual offending behaviors varied: from rising impudence and greed to greater levels of sorcery to students not serving their masters well. What they had in common was that there was no expectation that improvement in future generations was bound to occur. On the whole, this perceived decline produced more halakhic stringency, though in at least one case (the arguable leniency of preferring *halitzah* over *yiboom* mentioned above) it led to the opposite. What remains clear is that the rabbis cited sociological change as an appropriate motivating factor for legal innovation.

5) The Teachings of a Revered Sage

Our legal corpus provides nine instances of self-conscious change in law denoted by the term *barishonah* that were based upon the novel teachings of a revered sage. Remarkable, here, is the fact that the sage simply teaches his viewpoint, and that is enough impetus to revise law—no *derashah* or other scriptural proof is required to modify the regnant halakhic stance.

Rabbi Akiba figures most prominently in these examples, appearing in five of the nine occurrences, all found in M and T.[185] Frankel sees this as evidence that Rabbi Akiba was a prominent promulgator of lenient halakhic change.[186] Epstein, examining these texts from a literary perspective, suggests that these statements are all transmitted in the name of Rabbi Yehuda, Akiba's student, since one of the cases (M MS 5:7) comes to us in his name. He further believes that this material proves that Rabbi Akiba played an important part in the early editing and redacting of M, often changing and finalizing halakhic positions.[187] Albeck sees these particular examples as entirely parallel to the term

משנה ראשונה (*mishnah rishonah*, "the first mishnah"), which he believes also indicates halakhic change from an earlier to a later formulation.[188]

Aside from the statements of Rabbi Akiba, there are four other occurrences where texts report that either an individual sage or a later *beit din* decisively ruled on an issue that altered Jewish law.[189] What unites these cases is that the incisive teaching of the sage overturns an entirely plausible way of understanding a situation in favor of a newly defined approach.

The Complete Vow

Vows held a definite importance in the ancient world that is often hard for modern individuals to fathom. The particular case we will analyze comes from M Ned. 9:6 and concerns the idea of התרת נדרים (*hatarat nedarim*, "releasing of vows"), the process by which a sage released others from vows. In this case, a vow was made that precluded eating for periods of time encompassing a Sabbath or festival day:

פותחין בימים טובים ובשבתות. בראשונה היו אומרים אותן הימים מותרין, ושאר כל הימים אסורין, עד שבא רבי עקיבא ולימד שהנדר שהותר מקצתו הותר כולו :

> One may release [individuals from vows] through the mechanism of holidays and Sabbaths. At first, they would say these same days [i.e., Shabbatot and holidays] they were released [from fulfilling the vow], and the rest of days they were forbidden [to eat]. Until Rabbi Akiba came and taught that the vow of which part has been released, all of it is released.[190]

Fasting was prohibited on Sabbaths and festivals, as we know from a number of pre-Tannaitic and Tannaitic sources.[191] If an individual vowed to fast for a period of time that encompassed a Sabbath, then it was clear that a certain contradiction had crept into the formulation of the vow—at least for the period of Shabbat contained within the vow's limits, since fasting was both enjoined by the vow and absolutely prohibited by other law. This created within the vow a small area that conflicted with standing law. Such a contradiction could allow a sage to release the vower from the required continuation of observing the vow, as it denied the integrity of part of its terms.

There were two possible ways to resolve this contradiction, and that is where we witness the ultimate development cited in this passage. The earlier phase shows that the rabbis understood this vow to remain in effect only during the days that were not Shabbat or holy days, when fasting was prohibited. During חול (*hol*, "regular days"), the vow was in effect, because there was no con-

tradiction to countermand its efficacy. In phase one, it was understood that
Shabbat produced a loophole that allowed release only from that small slice of
time when there was a direct conflict between the vow and the laws against fasting. Outside this small overlap, the integrity of the vow remained, according to
the pre-Akiban way of reading this situation.

The later phase began with the statement attributed to Rabbi Akiba. This
new analysis, a compelling ideological re-reading of this vow, produced surprising results. Through a more stringent reading that demanded total integrity of
the vow in question, ironically, a substantial and innovative leniency emerged.
Rabbi Akiba's position asked that each and every vow exhibit utmost integrity—not only some of the time, but, rather, all of the time. As soon as any piece
of the vow produced a loophole that allowed release from any part of its obligations, Akiba claimed, then a sage could release the entirety of the vow.

Since the sages were often reported as the ones who released individuals
from their vows by finding invalidating contradictions, Akiba's conceptual re-
interpretation of the vow provided a promising way to release people from over-
reaching vows they may have made in error, especially when there was some
conflict between the structure of the vow and other external standing conditions
it would violate. This approach also follows a Hillelite position, articulated in M
Ned. 3:2.[192] A number of other texts also voice opinions that demand this same
complete integrity in the entirety of the vow.[193]

Here, we see our first example of the power of a revered sage to promote a
new way of interpretation that changed the way Jewish law handled an important topic. M appears to replace the earlier understanding of this law with
Akiba's way of interpretation. This may be because Rabbi Akiba or his students
edited this particular mishnah and it was then included in the final version by a
later editor, or it may be that his opinion was transmitted to and accepted by a
final editor. It is also possible that this change was made after Rabbi Akiba and
that his name was simply invoked to lend added *gravitas*. Here, as in the next
example, Rabbi Akiba was portrayed as directly responsible for updating a philosophical stance that had major ramifications on the law.

Approaching the Bench

Another instance in which Rabbi Akiba was reported as promoting halakhic
change through new philosophical reasoning appears in a discussion on the relationship between Jews and non-Jews on Shabbat. T MK 2:14-15 records this
passage:

(יד) יושבין על ספסל של גוים בשבת. <u>בראשונה</u> היו אומרים אין יושבין על
ספסל של גוים בשבת, עד שבא ר' עקיבא ולימד שיושבין על ספסל של גוים
בשבת.

(טז) מעשה ברבן גמליאל שהיה יושב על ספסל של גוים בשבת בעכו. אמרו
לו : לא היו נוהגין להיות יושבין על ספסל של גוים בשבת, ולא רצה לומר
להם מותרין אתם, אלא עמד והלך לו.

(14) One may sit on the bench of non-Jews on Shabbat. <u>At first</u>, they
used to say that one may not sit on the bench of non-Jews on Shabbat,
until Rabbi Akiba came and taught that one [may] sit on the bench of a
non-Jew on Shabbat.[194]

(15) There is a story of Rabban Gamaliel,[195] who was sitting on the
bench of non-Jews on Shabbat in Akko. They said to him: they were
not accustomed to sitting on the bench of a non-Jew on Shabbat, and he
did not want to say "you are permitted." Rather, he stood and walked
off.

This Toseftan passage begins with an anonymous and apodictic prohibition: it is
forbidden to sit on a non-Jew's bench on Shabbat. One might legitimately wonder what possible harm might come from the mere act of sitting? BT Pes. 51a
suggests that Jews who sit on the bench of a non-Jew on Shabbat will look as if
they are engaging in buying and selling.[196] The purpose of prohibiting Jews
from sitting on a non-Jew's bench is thus to prevent מראית עין (*marit ayin,* "the
semblance of sinning"), that is, to ensure that Jews are not even suspected of
said violations.

There is, however, a hint of ambivalence cast into the scene by the tale of
Rabban Gamaliel's behavior. While the local custom in Akko is clearly not to sit
on Gentile-owned benches,[197] Rabban Gamaliel seems to have had a different
understanding of the law than the surrounding townspeople. Rather than upset
their observance, he complies with the more restrictive local custom and moves
on.

There is one challenge inherent in reading this text, and it arises through a
closer look at the purported chronology of the passage. Rabban Gamaliel I, one
of the first of the Tannaim, lived a few decades before the time of Akiba. Even if
we are to say that the personage in the text is Rabban Gamaliel II, he is, at the
latest, cotemporaneous with Rabbi Akiba, and would have been significantly
older. The portrayal of Rabban Gamaliel's acts in the story above tell us that he
already believed it to be permissible to sit on a non-Jew's bench on Shabbat. In
Rabban Gamaliel's actions, we have possible evidence of the existence of this
opinion *before* Akiba's teaching of it, right in this same passage.[198]

It is likely that Akiba was cognizant of Gamaliel's prior action, but that
Akiba was the first to provide a grander philosophic explanation for his deeds

and teach it to others. Perhaps it was Akiba who ultimately promulgated and explained this law in a satisfactory way, applying a more lenient reading that allowed him to open a gate in an old fence around the Torah. Or, perhaps he had sufficient authority or persuasive power to enact legal change based on his personal decisions.

A third way to understand this is to utilize the concept of collections of λόγοι mentioned earlier. Jacob Neusner and other scholars suggest that great rabbis often had collections of sayings attached to their names. It may be that Akiba represented a particularly liberal viewpoint on certain key issues of his day. These two factors may have combined to make him the literary receptacle for a number of liberal opinions that changed Jewish law without clear precedent or proof, which were then reported in his name to give them authority.

Finally, there is one more mundane alternative. It is possible that this is simply a certain kind of scribal error, an *ashgarah*, though one should always show restraint in such suggestions. It is possible that the scribes who copied the Toseftan manuscripts, which are, after all, the only texts that contain any mention of Akiba in connection with this halakhah, copied over the phrase "עד שבא ר' עקיבא ולימד" that is present in a prior halakhah, MK 2:10, and included it in MK 2:14 by mistake. This seems far less likely than the other possibilities, but is not out of the question.

Setting aside the possibility of scribal error, there is much to be learned here in the area of intellectual history. To do so, we need to examine two parallel texts to T, the first one found in PT Pes. 4:1, 30d:

רבי אלעזר בשם רבי אבין : כל דבר שאינו יודע שהוא מותר וטועה בו
באיסור, נשאל והן מתירין לו. וכל דבר שהוא יודע בו שהוא מותר והוא
נוהג בו באיסור נשאל אין מתירין לו. יושבין על ספסלו של גוי בשבת?
מעשה ברבן גמליאל שישב לו על ספסלו של גוי בשבת בעכו. אמרו לו לא
היו נוהגין כן להיות יושבין על ספסלו של גוי בשבת, ולא רצה לומר להן
מותר לעשות כן, אלא עמד והלך לו.

Rabbi Eleazar said in the name of Rabbi Abin: Any matter where one does not know that it is permitted, and one mistakenly acts as if it is prohibited, if one asks [the sages] they may make it permissible to him. But any matter where he knows that it is permitted, and he acts upon it as if it is prohibited, if one asks [the sages] they may not make it permissible to him.

[For example, what about] the case of sitting on the bench of a non-Jew? There is a story about Rabban Gamaliel who sat on the bench of a non-Jew on Shabbat in Akko. They said to him: [here] we are not accustomed to sitting on the bench of a non-Jew on Shabbat. He did not want to say to them: you are permitted to do thus. Rather, he stood and walked off.

PT employs the same Toseftan story to support a legal position stated by Rabbi Eleazar and Rabbi Abin. Rabbi Abin was a Palestinian Amora, either Abin I or Abin II, placing him in the fourth Amoraic generation, which suggests a later provenance for this retelling. Here, PT includes only the traditions that make up the second half of T, and there is, therefore, no mention of Akiba. Unlike T and what we will see in BT, there is no apodictic statement of law beyond the specific case of the bench-sitting in Akko. In short, PT is an extension of T's version, with only a few significant lacunae: no mention of earlier or later phases, no sign of Rabbi Akiba's involvement and no specific statement of final law for the Akko case. PT resembles the next text, BT, in that it used this case as fodder for supporting a broadened final rule.

The final text in this trio is from BT Pes. 51a:

גופא, דברים המותרין ואחרים נהגו בהן איסור—אי אתה רשאי להתירן בפניהן. אמר רב חסדא: בכותאי עסקינן. וכולי עלמא לא? . . . ויושבין על ספסלי נכרים בשבת, ואינן יושבין על ספסלי נכרים בשבת בעכו. ומעשה ברבן [שמעון בן] גמליאל שישב על ספסלי נכרים בשבת בעכו, ולעזה עליו כל המדינה, אמרו: מימינו לא ראינו כך. נשמט על גבי קרקע, ולא רצה לומר להן מותרין אתם.

The text states: In matters that are permitted, but others treat them as forbidden, you are not allowed to permit them in their presence. Rav Hisda said: This refers to the Samaritans. But does it not refer to everyone? . . . [199]

And they may sit on the benches of non-Jews on Shabbat, but they do not sit on the benches of non-Jews in Akko on Shabbat. And there is a story about Rabban [Shimeon ben] Gamaliel who sat on the benches of non-Jews on Shabbat in Akko, and the whole state mocked[200] him. They said: we have never seen anything like this in our lives! He slipped to the ground, and he did not want to say to them: you are permitted.

In BT's reformulation, this text becomes part of a broader discussion of permitting what one knows is permissible, even if the majority of the community holds opinions to the contrary. The text implies that it is better to keep your opinion to yourself. While the same *halakhah* ultimately results, BT contains no compari-

son of earlier and later phases, and no hint whatsoever of Rabbi Akiba. BT re-
fines the stated *halakhah*, in that an explicit reference to Akko is now incorporated into the apodictic statement of the law, thus showing respect for the specific situation of the citizens of Akko.

Finally, there is one charming rhetorical flourish BT adds as well: instead of
Rabban Gamaliel standing and walking away, he slips to the ground, certainly a
more appropriate action for one so humbled by the locals. BT also does not imply that Rabban Gamaliel walked away from the non-Jew's bench—instead he
remained in close proximity.

What we see here is that T is more concerned with connecting the innovation with Rabbi Akiba than the other texts that follow it chronologically. This is
not an anomaly at all, but appears to be but one example of a small pattern of the
usage of *barishonah* in Tannaitic texts. Reviewing the entire group of usages of
barishonah where Akiba is cited as changing Jewish law using the form
עד שבא עקיבא ולימד, we find the following statistical breakdown:

M	2 occurrences
T	3 occurrences
BT	1 occurrence (only a citation from M, not original)
PT	0 occurrences

Carefully assessing this highly limited set of examples, we note that Rabbi
Akiba is cited with this phraseology far more often than other individuals credited with legal change. In fact, if we examine the use of the form עד שבא
רבי (X) ולימד alone, we find that 20 out of the 32 occurrences in our legal corpus
are attached to Rabbi Akiba. Rabban Gamaliel is the closest competitor, with
only five usages connected with him. This points to the recognition of a unique
position for Akiba's teachings within the tradition, especially with respect to
legal change. That recognition appears to be stronger in the Tannaitic period,
where more citations are concentrated.

This either indicates that the Tannaim would accept the power of Akiba's
teaching as a compelling reason to alter Jewish law, or that Akiba, as an editor
or the teacher of another editor, had his own viewpoints placed into initial for-
mulations (whether oral or written) that were ultimately incorporated into the
final redactions of M and T.[201] Also possible, though less likely, is that later
opinions were retroactively attached to Akiba's name to lend *gravitas*. Whatever
the case may be, it is clear that the editors of M and T believed that the name of
one exceptional individual had enough power to change law during the Tannaitic period, but that his name seems to have lost currency as time went by.

6) Catastrophic Historical Events

In the rabbinic legal corpus, there are seven examples of usages of the term *barishonah* that occur in connection with catastrophic historical events. Two events are referenced: the Destruction of the Temple in 70 CE and the Hadrianic persecutions in 132-135 CE.[202] Both these events involved major persecution and extensive damage to the Jewish community at the hands of the Romans. We will examine one example here, as the others follow a very similar formal pattern.

Lost and Found the Ancient Way

This example of Jewish law changing in the wake of a catastrophic event actually provides two separate rationales to explain resultant alterations of law. As the development of this law unfolds, we will see the rationales combined to move in stages toward a final determination of the law. The law at hand confronts the issues of restoring lost property to its owner, based on a biblical commandment found in both Num. 5:6-8 and Deut. 22:1-3. There is another relevant passage in Lev. 5:21-26, where the Torah discusses the case of one who finds a lost object and takes a false oath to retain it. Further evidence exists in the Cairo genizah's version of the Zadokite Fragments (known as the Covenant of Damascus, or Damascus Document in its version at Qumran), for the early legal obligation of returning lost property.[203]

M BM 2:6 sets the earliest Tannaitic scene with a מחלוקת (*mahloket*, "a dispute") between Rabbi Meir and Rabbi Yehudah:

ועד מתי חייב להכריז עד כדי שידעו בו שכניו דברי רבי מאיר. רבי יהודה
אומר : שלש רגלים ואחר הרגל האחרון שבעה ימים כדי שילך לביתו
שלשה ויחזור שלשה ויכריז יום אחד :

And how long is one obligated to announce [a lost article]? Until [he is sure] his neighbors know about it, [and these are] the words of Rabbi Meir. Rabbi Yehuda says: [the finder must announce it until] three festivals [have passed] plus seven days after the last festival, in order that he [the owner] may go toward his home for three days, return for three days and declare [the lost item] for one day.

David Tzvi Hoffmann saw Rabbi Yehuda's opinion as the *mishnah rishonah*, the earlier statement of Jewish law, because it carried with it the assumption of pilgrimage—a Temple-based activity that ceased after 70 CE. Thus, Hoffman concluded that Rabbi Yehuda's opinion had to be a *halakhah* from an earlier period—it cannot be his own.[204] Rabbi Meir's opinion, in contrast, is a later one, set in the context of a destroyed Temple, with no mention of a central public place suitable for declaration or pilgrims to hear it. M, then, shows a simple dispute between two Tannaim, with no explicit reference to legal development.

The sequence of legal development starts to become clear when we look at T BM 2:16-17:

(טז) <u>בראשונה</u> כל הבא ונותן סימניה היה נוטלה. משרבו הרמאין, התקינו שיהא זה נותן סימניה ומביא ראיה שאינו רמיי.

(יז) <u>בראשונה</u> היו מכריזין עליה שלשה רגלים, ואחר הרגל האחרון שבעת ימים. ומשחרב בית המקדש, התקינו שיהו מכריזין עליה שלשים יום. ומן הסכנה ואילך, התקינו שיהא מודיע בה לשכיניו ולקרוביו ולמיודעיו ולאנשי עירו ודיו.

(16) <u>At first</u>, anyone who came [to claim lost property] and gave its specific signs would take it. Once the deceivers multiplied, they enacted that it should be thus: one would give its specific details[205] and bring proof that he is not a deceiver.

(17) <u>At first</u>, they would announce it [the lost property] for three festivals, and after the last festival for seven days. Once the Temple was destroyed, they enacted that they would announce it for thirty days. And from the danger[206] and thereafter, they enacted that they would inform his neighbors, his relatives, his acquaintances and the people of his town and that would suffice.[207]

T reports that the initial shift came due to the increase in the number of deceivers. According to T, in earlier times, before people's behavior patterns grew so deceptive, it was sufficient to provide only the information necessary for identification to release the item from the lost-and-found area.[208] Once the deceivers became so numerous as to have a deleterious effect on the claims process, the leadership required stricter standards. Thereafter, any claimant had to provide not only the specific details of the lost article, but also proof that s/he was not one of the numerous repeat offenders who regularly aimed to deceive others to collect lost items for unwarranted fiscal gain. At some point, these deceivers made enough trouble to cause a revision of the legal rules in effect for lost property within the entire community.[209]

The second halakhah quoted above, T BM 2:17, delineates three stages. These particular changes in the laws of returning lost property related to the timing and distribution of the announcements of the loss. In the initial phase, there was an extended waiting period of one year (the usual amount of time to complete the three pilgrimage festivals), plus seven days beyond the last festival. This allowed any loss suffered by a pilgrim visiting Jerusalem to be recouped during the next visit, even if s/he visited only once per year. In other words, if a specific person came to Jerusalem only for Sukkot (the premiere festival that garnered the highest attendance in this time), this ruling made reclamation of the item possible during the following year's Sukkot festival and seven days past it. The seven days provided time for the pilgrim who may have arrived home, noticed a lost item, and returned to Jerusalem to reclaim it.

The second phase of the reported development came when the Temple was destroyed. Here, the conclusion was quite logical. Once the Temple was destroyed, and pilgrimage to Jerusalem ceased, it became clear that the one-year waiting period, so closely connected to the timing of pilgrimage festivals, no longer made sense. After the destruction, it was highly unlikely that a lost item belonging to an out-of-town visitor would be returned during a subsequent visit at the same time next year.

This report tells us, then, that after a catastrophic event and the resulting devastation of communal patterns and institutions, the rabbis saw it as acceptable to shift the particulars of this legal construct to function better in its new environment. As for the selection of thirty days, this is a common unit of time mentioned frequently in both M and T, probably linked to the lunar month.

During phase two, T is silent as to whether the lost property reclamation system continued in Jerusalem, or if, as it implies about phase three, it was removed to each local community. This may be a reflection of the hopes among the Tannaim that Jerusalem would be rebuilt, which would allow the lost and found system to be re-established. In the time of the Tannaim, post-Hadrianic Jerusalem was known as Aelia Capitolina, and it would have been impossible for Jews to even visit the city, let alone announce their missing items with any degree of comfort. After 135 CE, Jews were not permitted even to enter the city or its environs, except on one day each year: the Ninth of Av, when they were permitted access to mourn the loss of the Temple and their holy city. Even with the more favorable outlook on relations with the Jews under the Antonines, sustained access to Jerusalem was difficult, at best.[210]

If Jews were forbidden to enter Jerusalem, then the prior lost and found system could no longer function. This Roman prohibition against entering Jerusalem may well have given rise to the rabbinic construction of history we see in phase three. Phase three claims to be based on the situation that prevailed after the Hadrianic persecutions. This situation forced the creation of what the rabbis denoted as a new, locally based system. Local announcements shared information about the lost item more efficiently with those most likely to know its whereabouts. Smaller scale announcements also precluded inadvertent notification of the Roman government or other hostile forces, who might have been tempted to confiscate the lost item for their own fiscal gain. E.S. Rosenthal suggests that, with the closing of schools and synagogues, and Hadrian's pronouncement that banned public gatherings, it was no longer possible to establish anything other than a limited system amongst local community members.[211] Living in this hostile climate, the authorities seem to have done their best to reconstruct ways to maintain any linkage to old communal patterns, while still responding to changed realities.

Here, once again, we see a report that the rabbis' understanding of Jewish law responded to external stimuli they could not ignore. BT BM 28b confirms this with its own version of the pericope, extending the development one step further and offering a different rationale:

תנו רבנן: <u>בראשונה</u>, כל מי שמצא אבידה—היה מכריז עליה שלשה רגלים, ואחר רגל אחרון שבעת ימים, כדי שילך לביתו שלשה ויחזור שלשה ויכריז יום אחד. משחרב בית המקדש התקינו שיהו מכריזים בבתי כנסיות ובבתי מדרשות. ומשרבו האנסים התקינו שיודיע לשכניו ולקרוביו, ודיו. מאי משרבו האנסין? דאמרי: אבידתא למלכא. רבי אמי אשכח אודייא דדינרי, חזייה ההוא רומאה דקא מירתת. אמר ליה: זיל שקול לנפשך, דלאו פרסאי אנן דאמרי אבידתא למלכא.

Our rabbis taught: <u>At first</u>, anyone who found a lost article would announce it for three festivals, and for seven days after the last festival, in order that he [i.e., the party who lost the property] would go home for three days, and return for three days and declare [his ownership] for one day.

Once the Temple was destroyed, they enacted that they would announce it in synagogues and in houses of study.

And once the oppressors multiplied, they enacted that he would notify his neighbors and his relatives,[212] and that was enough.

What is [the meaning of] "once the oppressors multiplied?" Those who said: "lost property belongs to the king."

Rabbi Ami found a purse of dinars. One Roman saw that he was afraid [literally, he was trembling]. He said to him: go, and take it for yourself, for, we are not Persians who say "lost property belongs to the king."

While the same general notions are at work here, there are some fascinating divergences. First, note the presence of more highly developed communal organs in the Bavli's rendition: while T's intermediate phase above provides only for a thirty-day announcement period, the *baraita* in BT is more explicit on the mechanics of the announcement procedure, naming synagogues and houses of study as the new vehicles of community that replaced the Temple as the central gathering place. This presents a very different intermediate step that relied upon burgeoning communal institutions as places of gathering, a factor noticeably absent from the account in T. It reflects a growing investment in these institutions by the Amoraim, which the compilers of T, living at an earlier time in their development, did not share. Furthermore, this shows how the editor of this passage in BT retrojected their contemporary communal institutions back into an earlier period. At the same time, it also reflects the greater emphasis on the synagogue in Babylonia than in Palestine.[213]

Next, note the Amoraic overlay that follows the *baraita*. This stratum provides a window into an Amoraic understanding of the concept of "multiplication of deceivers." The rabbinic construction of the Persian viewpoint says that any lost property may immediately be seized for the king. The reported prevailing viewpoint in the Roman Empire at the time differs, as indicated by the story of Rabbi Ammi, a highly respected Palestinian Amora who lived and taught in Tiberias during the reign of Diocletian in the late third century CE.[214] Roman law did, in fact, provide a legal means for dealing with lost property, which entailed granting the finder official recognition of an acquisition after a certain period of time had passed. It clearly did not grant immediate title to the king for lost property, as the Gemara suggests Persian law did. Unfortunately, it is extremely difficult to know which Roman laws were in effect at any given time in the provinces, making the Roman's statement hard to verify.[215]

Ultimately, in these texts[216] we see that the rabbis perceived various events of Roman-Jewish history as depriving the Jews of their fundamental rights, patterns and primary religious institutions, and responded to preserve the core values of the community.[217] This reconstruction shows more stringent standards applied to avoid theft of lost property and ensure that it was returned correctly, whenever possible.

While changes in law that responded to catastrophic historical events have always been among the most frequently taught and cited in the secondary literature, it is surprising to see the meager number of occurrences where this rationale actually is employed by the editors of rabbinic legal literature: a mere seven main textual occurrences with the term *barishonah* and a similarly scant set of references in later chapters. This should serve as a cautionary note to historians: the rabbis who edited Jewish legal works attributed far more changes to other, more mundane reasons than to major historical crises. The devastating nature of these events evidently attracts historians' attention in a skewed way, and makes for interesting storytelling, even though these legal changes surely do not make up the preponderance of the evidence of rabbinic legal change.

7) Preventing Embarrassment

We find four examples in the corpus of rabbinic legal literature using the term *barishonah* in connection with a change in Jewish custom for the sake of preventing the embarrassment of an individual participating in the life of the Jewish community.[218] It is important to note that here we are not dealing with activities strictly defined as *halakhah*, instead, these changes hover at the edge of lawmaking, subtly shifting customs that are reported to be in active use, to replace them with close analogues that are less hurtful to the parties involved. We will examine two of these texts closely.

My Father was an Illiterate Aramean

Deut. 26 commands the ritual of ביכורים (*bikkurim*, "first fruits") for the Israelites upon their initial arrival into the land of Israel. The ceremony was relatively straightforward: it required the farmer to bring a basket of select produce from the first fruits of his land to a priest who placed them before God in the chosen place (i.e., in the Temple in Jerusalem), whereupon the farmer then recited a text that reminded him of his historical link to God and his ancestors. The recitation of the biblical verses from Deut. 26:5-10 served as the key element in the ceremony.

Our particular area of attention is that of the reading of the declaration. Since Deut. 26 prescribed a specific oral statement, generations observing this ritual subsequent to the writing of the Torah were obligated to follow the wording exactly, requiring farmers to recite the selected verses in their entirety. This seems a straightforward requirement, until we remember that the ancient world's level of literacy differed markedly from that in the Western world today. For successful farming, literacy was not a requirement at all, and the rabbis explain that this cast the recitation of the declaration as a daunting task for the illiterate farmer.

William V. Harris[219] has written extensively on the levels of literacy in the Near East in late antiquity. Harris estimated that Roman society in imperial times had a literacy rate of 10-15%, if literacy is defined as the ability to read literary texts in one language and write more than one's signature oneself.[220] Meir Bar-Ilan argued that the Jewish literacy rate in the first century CE was even lower than the Roman rate, somewhere in the vicinity of 3%.[221] Catherine Hezser, in a book-length study dedicated to determining Jewish literacy levels in Roman Palestine, provided a more nuanced reasoning, even as she suggested that the Judaean Jewish community had a similarly low rate of literacy.[222] While Hezser's research indicated a high valuation placed on Torah study, it nevertheless remained clear that the vast majority of Jews in Roman Palestine could not read or write much more than their names. It was only the exceptional students, studying in educational groupings that catered to their growth, who succeeded in developing significant literary skills. Rural students and those with other occupations were far more likely to end up in a permanent state of effective illiteracy. Many Palestinian Jewish farmers, therefore, found the task of learning to read a written declaration in public nearly insurmountable.

Against this background, we now turn to M Bik. 3:7, which discusses the farmer's reading of the declaration:

בראשונה כל מי שיודע לקרות, קורא. וכל מי שאינו יודע לקרות, מקרין
אותו. נמנעו מלהביא. התקינו שיהו מקרין את מי שיודע ואת מי שאינו
יודע:

At first, anyone who knew how to read, would read. And anyone who did not know how to read, they read for him.[223] They refrained from bringing [the *bikkurim*], so they enacted that they would read [both] for those who knew how to read and for those who did not.

M clearly outlines the issues here: for illiterate farmers, the declaration that accompanied the bringing of the *bikkurim* could turn into a belittling ritual. According to Urbach's reading of this text,[224] in the beginning, when literacy was almost non-existent in the Jewish community of the Second Temple period, the ritual of the *bikkurim* continued undisturbed, because low levels of reading were accepted across the community and no farmer felt particularly embarrassed by his low level of literacy. Later, when many members of the community (whether more urbanized Jews or Romans) became more literate, farmers recognized that their skills were insufficient and began to avoid the ritual altogether. Whether Urbach's historical approach is warranted, here, or not, we cannot say with certainty. What is sure is that the authorities of the day accepted the idea of changing customary boundaries for the sake of avoiding embarrassment and promoting observance, and thus reported the altering of the personal requirement in Deuteronomy, allowing surrogate readers to step in for the literate and illiterate alike. Establishing universal surrogate readers was, after all, the best potential way to mitigate embarrassment of the illiterate.

In a parallel text in *SD* 301:5,[225] we find an identical stance, with a very different approach in one respect:

וענית ואמרת: נאמר כאן "עניה" ונאמר להלן "עניה", מה עניה האמורה
להלן בלשון הקדש אף עניה האמורה כאן בלשון הקדש. מיכן אמרו:

בראשונה כל מי שהוא יודע לקרות קורא, ושאינו יודע לקרות מקרים
אותו. נמנעו מלהביא. התקינו שיהו מקרים את היודע, ואת מי שאינו
יודע. סמכו על המקרא "וענית." אין עניה אלא מפי אחרים.

"And you will answer and say." It says here "answer," and it says
later on in the text "answer."[226] Just as later on the word "answer"
means in the sacred tongue, so, too, here it means in the sacred
tongue.[227]

From this, they [the rabbis] said: <u>At first</u>,[228] anyone who knew how
to read, would read. And anyone who did not know how to read, they
read for him. They refrained from bringing [the *bikkurim*. So] they enacted that they would read for those who knew how to read and for
those who did not.

They relied upon this biblical verse: "and you will answer." There
is no answering other than through the mouths of others.

The major difference between these two texts resides not in their outlook on the
custom's outcome, but in the way they support the conclusion that the practice
required changing at all. In M, characteristically, there is no hint of a biblical
source supporting the action of the rabbis in permitting surrogate readers. M
simply understood the situation from a rational perspective: if there is anything
the rabbis could do to reduce the embarrassment connected with this act and
increase the ability of Jews to observe the initial commandment, then they
should do it. This logical reasoning does not appear to be enough for the authors
of *SD*. Instead, they probe the biblical text to root the rabbis' action back into
the written tradition, resorting to a *gezerah shavah* to buttress the position that
rational thought promotes. This is a typical difference between the hermeneutics
utilized in M and the Halakhic Midrashim.

The final sentence of *SD* indicates that its authors used the initial word in
Deut. 26:5, וענית, to prove the biblical text implies that another party is involved.
This is *sui generis*—there are no other occurrences of this reading of the root
לענות in the Halakhic Midrashim.

The final text that influences our understanding of this issue[229] comes from
PT Bik. 3:4, 65d, and is, more than likely, a corruption of the version preserved
in *SD* above:

תני: אין ענייה אלא מפי אחד. ולא עוד אלא שסמכו למקרא "וענית
ואמרת."

It was taught: There is no "answering" except from the mouth of <u>one</u>.
And nothing else, other than that they relied on the text: (Deut. 26:5)
"you shall answer and you shall recite."

PT, here, is quite similar to the end of *SD*, with one important distinction. Instead of "the mouths of others," as we find in *SD*, in PT we have "the mouth of
one." More than likely, this is a simple corruption (replacing אחר with אחד).

In conclusion, the history of this practice in Tannaitic and Amoraic texts
shows that the rabbis instituted a relatively minor change to reduce embarrassment, all for the sake of promoting observance. Though the mechanism of justification differed between the various sources, the resultant change remained
quite consistent.

In Death as in Life

Oddly enough, embarrassment was not limited to cases that only concerned
the living. In one case, we find alterations in a series of customs that deal with
the treatment of the dead in order to prevent embarrassment. Why? Embarrassment of the dead led to concurrent shaming of the living who found themselves
in related situations. Thus, the death of any impoverished individual, for example, and the treatment of his/her corpse in a dishonorable way, might lead to
feelings of shame and inadequacy on the part of the living poor.

Before we turn to rabbinic texts that take on the issue of dignity and modesty in burial, we should make a brief detour to Josephus, where this tendency
appears as well:

Our law has also taken care of the decent burial of the dead, but without
any extravagant expenses for their funerals, and without the erection of
any illustrious monuments for them; but has ordered that their nearest
relations should perform their obsequies; and has shown it to be regular, that all who pass by when anyone is buried, should accompany the
funeral, and join the lamentation.[230]

This general statement honors modesty in burial, and suggests that this attitude
was already a part of some strands of Jewish thought in the Second Temple period. This directive toward modesty becomes more explicit later in the legal development reported in rabbinic legal texts.

The earliest rabbinic stratum of this development is found in T Nid. 9:16-
17:

(טז) <u>בראשונה</u> היו מטבילין על גב הנשים המתות נדות, חזרו להיות
מטבילין על כל אחת ואחת מפני כבוד הנשים. <u>בראשונה</u> היו מוציאין

מוגמר לפני חולי מעיים, וחזרו להיות מוציאין לפני כל אחת ואחת מפני
כבוד המתים. <u>בראשונה</u> היו מוציאין עשירים בדרגש ועניים בכליבא, חזרו
להיות מוציאין בין בדרגש בין בכליבה מפני כבוד העניים :

(יז) <u>בראשונה</u> היו מוליכין לבית האבל עניים בכלי זכוכית צבועה, עשרים
בכלי זכוכית הלבנה, חזרו להיות מוציאין בין בצבועה בין בלבנה מפני
כבוד עניים. <u>בראשונה</u> כל מי שיש לו מת היו היו יציאותיו קשות עליו יותר
ממתו. התחילו הכל מניחין מתיהן ובורחין. הנהיג רבן גמליאל קלות ראש
בעצמו, נהגו הכל כרבן גמליאל :

16) <u>At first</u>, they would immerse those [vessels][231] touched by a menstruant women who had died. They went back [on that ruling] to immerse those [vessels] touched by all women [who had died], because of
the honor of [menstruant] women. <u>At first</u>, they would bring out an incense pan before those who had [died of] intestinal illnesses. They went
back [on that ruling] to bring out the incense pan before everyone [who
had died], for the sake of the honor of the dead. <u>At first</u>, they would
bring out the wealthy [dead] on a *dargesh*[232] and the poor [dead] in a
klibah.[233] They went back [on that ruling] to bring everyone [who had
died] out on either a *dargesh* or a *klibah* for the sake of the honor of the
poor.

17) <u>At first</u>, they would bring [food] to a house of mourning, the poor
in colored glass, and the wealthy in white glass. They went back [on
that ruling] to bring [food] in either colored or white glass, because of
the honor of the poor. <u>At first</u>, anyone who had a death [in the family],
his expenses were harder on him then the death itself. People began to
leave their dead[234] and flee. Rabban Gamaliel treated his own honor
lightly,[235] and everyone became accustomed to act as Rabban Gamaliel
did.[236]

Three aspects unite these five rulings: first, they all indicate that there was an
earlier and later phase of the funerary practices mentioned. Second, the embarrassment of a group of disadvantaged people was considered reason enough for
revising custom, and the rabbis are portrayed as taking action by going back and
changing their rulings to ensure that the weaker parties in their society were not
hurt by the customs and practices they instituted. Finally, the action taken to
equalize the groups at odds within society was either asking everyone to assume
the custom of the weaker group or mixing the customs in use, in either case ob-
fuscating the difference between the groups involved. In doing so, the rabbis

removed the negative valence from the act to ensure that all parties were treated fairly and honorably.

BT MK 27a presents this text in a very similar condition, but there are a few small differences:[237]

תנו רבנן : <u>בראשונה</u> היו מוליכין בבית האבל, עשירים בקלתות של כסף ושל זהב, ועניים בסלי נצרים של ערבה קלופה, והיו עניים מתבייישים. התקינו שיהו הכל מוליכין בסלי נצרים של ערבה קלופה, מפני כבודן של עניים. תנו רבנן : <u>בראשונה</u> היו משקין בבית האבל, עשירים בזכוכית לבנה, ועניים בזכוכית צבועה, והיו עניים מתבייישין. התקינו שיהו הכל משקין בזכוכית צבועה, מפני כבודן של עניים. תנו רבנן : <u>בראשונה</u> היו מגלין פני עשירים ומכסין פני עניים, מפני שהיו פניהן מושחרין בשני בצורת, והיו עניים מתבייישין. התקינו שיהו מכסין פני הכל, מפני כבודן של עניים. תנו רבנן : <u>בראשונה</u> היו מוציאין עשירים בדרגש, ועניים בכליכה, וכן בסמוך, והיו עניים מתבייישין. התקינו שיהו הכל מוציאין בכליבה, מפני כבודן של עניים. תנו רבנן : <u>בראשונה</u> היו מניחין את המוגמר תחת מתי חולי מעים, והיו חולי מעים חיים מתבייישין. התקינו שיהו מניחין תחת הכל, מפני כבודן של חולי מעים חיים. <u>בראשונה</u> היו מטבילין הכלים על גבי נדות מתות, והיו נדות חיות מתבייישות. התקינו שיהו מטבילין על גבי כל הנשים, מפני כבודן של נדות חיות. <u>בראשונה</u> היו מטבילין על גבי זבין מתים, והיו זבין חיים מתבייישין. התקינו שיהו מטבילין על גבי כל האנשים, מפני כבודן של זבין חיים. <u>בראשונה</u> היתה יציאתו של מת קשה לקרוביו יותר ממיתתו, [עד שהיו קרוביו עד שבא רבן גמליאל ונהג קלות ראש בעצמו ויצא בכלי פשתן, ונהגו העם אחריו לצאת בכלי פשתן. אמר רב פפא : והאידנא נהוג עלמא אפילו בצרדא בר זוזא.

Our rabbis taught: <u>At first</u>, they would bring [food] to the house of mourning, the wealthy, in silver and gold baskets, and the poor in wicker baskets woven from peeled willow twigs, and the poor were ashamed. They enacted that all would bring[238] [food] in wicker baskets woven from peeled willow twigs, for the sake of the honor of the poor.

Our rabbis taught: <u>At first</u>, they would bring drinks to the house of mourning, the wealthy in white glass, and the poor in colored glass, and the poor were ashamed. They enacted that all would bring drinks in colored glass, for the sake of the honor of the poor.

Our rabbis taught: <u>At first</u>, they would uncover the face of the wealthy, and cover the face of the poor,[239] because their faces were blackened in years of scarcity, and the poor were ashamed. They enacted that they would cover the face of everyone [who died], for the sake of the honor of the poor.

Our rabbis taught: At first, they would bring out the wealthy on a *dargesh*, and the poor on a *klibah*, and similarly on pillows,[240] and the poor were ashamed. They enacted that everyone would bring out [their dead] on a *klibah* for the sake of the honor of the poor.[241]

Our rabbis taught: At first, they would lay the incense pan beneath those who died of intestinal illness, and those living with intestinal illness were ashamed. They enacted that they would lay it beneath everyone, for the sake of the honor of those living with intestinal illness. At first, they would immerse the vessels touched by menstruant women who had died, and living menstruant women were ashamed. They enacted that they would immerse vessels touched by all women for the sake of the honor of living menstruant women. At first, they would immerse the vessels touched by men with emissions who had died, and living men with emissions were ashamed. They enacted that they would immerse instruments touched by all men [who had died], for the sake of the honor of living men with emissions.

At first, the costs of [burying] the dead were more difficult for his relatives than his death itself [until relatives were leaving him (i.e., the dead body) and fleeing],[242] until Rabban Gamaliel came and behaved lightly toward his own honor, and came out [to his burial] dressed in plain linen garments, and the people after him became accustomed to[243] being brought out in plain linen garments.

Rav Papa said: But nowadays, the world is accustomed to being brought out in a coarse canvas garment worth one *zuz*.[244]

In BT, this thematic collection of customs is highly similar to the version in T, and the few differences are mostly the result of a creative editor. The editor of BT has intensified the section on bringing food to the house of mourning to accentuate the differences between wealthy and poor by having the wealthy serve their victuals in gold and silver, while the poor person's food is relegated to wicker baskets. The colored or white glass issue, which appeared in T, is then rehearsed, but is clearly reshaped to discuss drinks brought to a house of mourning, where T leaves some ambiguity as to the nature of edibles brought in these vessels. BT also adds the stark depiction of starvation entailed in the debate over covering the face of the dead. BT paints the lines between rich and poor with a far sharper brush than in T.

With respect to the issues related to the menstruant women, BT takes an interesting tack. In adding an parallel situation for men, that of the *zab* (a man suffering with emissions from his genitals), the editor of this passage in BT supplied an analogous idea that was a short logical jump from what existed in prior recensions (oral or written) of the text. Including this analogous situation brings a greater sense of fairness and equality to the practice involved, though it may be anachronistic to suggest that this was the author's intent. Once again, BT steps beyond the boundaries established in the T tradition.

A similar phenomenon appears in BT's reference to the garment in which Rabban Gamaliel was buried being made of plain linen.[245] While plain linen may have been replaced with another, cheaper fabric, the idea of burying both the poor and wealthy in lesser garments is one that has certainly carried on, even into the contemporary Jewish community. Replacing this fabric with another indicates, as well, that the editors of BT were not afraid to replace older details with newer ones. Oral transmission of traditions may also have played a part in this updating.

Finally, we find one other interesting difference in comparing BT and T. In T, the terminology employed is "חזרו להיות" or "they went back to being," as opposed to the terminology utilized in the BT, "התקינו שיהו" or "they enacted that." While T shows a community that revised its customary stance, this is very different than the usual meaning of a legal enactment. The editor of this segment of BT, then, saw these decisions as having more legal weight, and used a more significant term (*hitkinu*) accordingly, implying that the rabbis actually enacted legal change on these issues. Here, the rhetoric of change employed in T and BT differs significantly.

One other parallel text warrants mention: Boaz Cohen[246] points out that there are significant parallels to these pericopae in T and BT in the fifth century BCE Roman legal text known as the Twelve Tables. In Table X, we find:

IV) No greater expenses or mourning than is proper shall be permitted in funeral expenses.

V) No one shall, hereafter, exceed the limit established by these laws for the celebration of funeral rites.

VI) Wood employed for the purpose of constructing a funeral pyre shall not be hewn, but shall be rough and unpolished.

VII) When a corpse is prepared for burial at home, not more than three women with their heads covered with mourning veils shall be permitted to perform this service. The body may be enveloped in purple robes, and when borne outside, ten flute players, at the most, shall accompany the funeral procession. . . .

XI) No wine flavored with myrrh, or with any other precious beverage, shall be poured upon a corpse while it is burning; nor shall the funeral pile be sprinkled with wine.

XII) Large wreaths shall not be borne at a funeral; nor shall perfumes be burned on the altars. . . .

XV) Gold, no matter in what form it may be present, shall, by all means, be removed from the corpse at the time of the funeral; but if anyone's teeth should be fastened with gold, it shall be lawful either to burn, or to bury it with the body.[247]

As we can see, Jewish law may be responding to prior adaptations in Roman law. While the laws of the Twelve Tablets predate these texts by nearly six centuries, such evidence shows that the intellectual conception of downplaying personal differences between individuals at funerals was present in the Roman world. While Cohen is reticent to reach the conclusion that Roman law directly influenced Jewish decision-making at this particular point,[248] given the fact that the Twelve Tables were promulgated in *circa* 450 BCE, Roman intellectual currents could have played some part in provoking this leveling of privilege within the Jewish community.

What emerges from this section is the fact that the authors and redactors of these texts were keenly sensitive to the shame of others and were willing to justify changes in custom as a result of these factors. No prooftexts appear to support this idea; it is simply assumed to be a valid motivating rationale for the change of Jewish custom during the Tannaitic and Amoraic periods.

8) For the Sake of Communal Welfare

Four examples of changes in Jewish law using the term *barishonah* occur that revolve around the principle of תיקון העולם (*tikkun haolam* - "the repair of the world").[249] The original appearances of this term are to be found in M. In the numerous uses that appear there, the meaning of the term is somewhat akin to "for the sake of preserving/improving social welfare."[250] In the two examples we will review here, Jewish law changed for just this reason: in response to situations that arose where harm to social welfare could result if *halakhah* were not altered.

One point of immediate interest is that all the citations arise in the legal area of divorce law and, moreover, in the specific tractate of Gittin. Two factors probably led to this concentration of appearances. First, with the corpus of Written Torah that deals with marriage law severely limited (it encompasses no more than a few relevant verses),[251] there was simply more leeway to make changes for the sake of social welfare in rabbinic divorce law than in most other areas of law. Second, the rabbis had pressing social needs with which to contend, and, on the whole, the development of Jewish divorce law during the rabbinic period tended toward expanding rights for women, without entirely dismantling the decidedly patriarchal construction of divorce, as Judith Hauptman has shown.[252] This being the case, it is no surprise that this area provided a fertile ground for the creative and sustained alteration of rabbinic law over time.

Rethinking Divorce

M Git. 4:2 provides an example of rethinking the laws of divorce for the sake of protecting social welfare. The writ of divorce had a very specific form and content, well documented in both M and later rabbinic texts. It was given from the husband directly to the wife, or via each party's agents, and was not considered valid until the wife accepted it into her hand. The *get* provided both the husband and the wife with clear documentation of the act of divorce, thus protecting their future ability to marry others. It also provided an official date of divorce, which helped certify the legal status of any future children the divorced woman might have.[253] Finally, it included the resolution of the *ketubbah*, a sum of money the husband gave to his wife in the event of divorce, usually assumed to give her some margin of protection if she were not financially stable. In all its aspects, the *get* was an important mechanism to ensure that marriages had an official termination procedure that protected both parties involved, with a special emphasis on the protection of the woman.

During the Tannaitic period, only the husband could initiate divorce. There is some evidence of early examples of ancient Semitic law where bi-lateral requests for divorce were accepted: i.e., either the husband or the wife could request a divorce.[254] By the Tannaitic period, though, there was no acceptable way for a woman to file for divorce, a possibility provided for by most modern legal systems in the Western world. Hints of women asking the court to compel her husband to grant her a divorce did begin to appear in the Amoraic period, but compulsion to divorce may well have been a rare occurrence. It was somewhere between difficult and impossible for a woman to initiate divorce proceedings in the rabbinic period, outside of a few very specific situations where women were explicitly granted the right to request a court's assistance.[255]

In the first section of M Git. 4:2, we find the case of an unsettled husband in the process of sending a *get* to his wife. Once he had the scribe write the *get*, he entrusted it to an agent charged with the task of bringing it to his wife for acceptance, as the procedure demanded. However, after the *get* left the husband's hands, he had a change of heart, and wanted to rescind the *get* before it effected the official divorce. Normally, one would intercept the agent, if possible, thus preventing the reception of the *get* by the wife. If he could not stop the agent, the divorce would be finalized when the wife accepted the document. However, M Git. 4:2 tells us that in an early stage of Jewish legal development, there was another way to handle this situation:

בראשונה היה עושה בית דין במקום אחר, ומבטלו. התקין רבן גמליאל
הזקן שלא יהו עושין כן מפני תקון העולם. בראשונה היה משנה שמו
ושמה שם עירו ושם עירה, והתקין רבן גמליאל הזקן שיהא כותב איש
פלוני וכל שם שיש לו, אשה פלונית וכל שום שיש לה מפני תקון העולם :

At first, he would convene a court in another place, and cancel it [i.e., the *get*]. Rabban Gamaliel the Elder enacted that they would not do this for the sake of *tikkun haolam*.

At first, he would change his name and her name, the name of his city, and the name of her city. Rabban Gamaliel the Elder enacted that he [the scribe writing the *get*] would write "Ploni" and any name that he had, "Plonit" and any name that she had, for the sake of *tikkun haolam*.[256]

The first of the two problems addressed here was, as explained above, the divorcer who changed his mind. If he could not intercept the *get* and still wanted to prevent his divorce, during the earlier phase of development of this law he could instead convene a different court and invalidate the *get*. On one level, this makes sense: rabbinic law generally accepted the idea that an appropriately configured court could intervene and cancel actions that took place before two witnesses, such as the completion of a *get*.

There were some extraordinarily challenging difficulties with utilizing this procedure. The rabbis had a serious problem with leaving the (ex-?) wife with a vaguely determined marital status. Imagine the worst possible outcome of this: what if the wife had already received and accepted her *get* by the time the new court had cancelled it, or, if she never learned of the cancellation? In the ancient world where communication was slow, before word reached her of the second court's action, she may well have married another, and already consummated her next marriage. Any offspring that arose from this second union would be of highly dubious social status—liable to receive the title of *mamzer*.[257] Since this problem arose not from her own adulterous misdeed, but from the confusion of her (possibly) ex-husband, it was a heavy and unjust price to pay for her and her new family. With such a possibility looming, it is no wonder that the rabbis altered law to prevent it.

The significant social problems present in the earlier ruling are avoided with Rabban Gamaliel's enactment, which states that one may not void a *get* in another court, for the sake of *tikkun haolam*, or the social welfare of the human beings involved. This prevented any of the wife's new offspring from acquiring a lowered birth status, gave her a definite marital status, and forced the husband to be more careful about his decision to divorce. This went far in ensuring that the process of divorce had integrity to it.

The second case outlined in M Git. 4:2 relates a situation fraught with similar ambiguity. In the ancient world, as today, there were those who traveled often in pursuit of their livelihood. While they were known by one name at home, their names may have been different in Greek or the language of any other place where they did business.[258] This became a problematic aspect of writing a *get*, because it was critical that any official divorce be valid and binding everywhere in the world, under whatever name the husband or wife might choose to employ in any given community.

In the earlier phase of this law's development, M indicates that either party might change names, utilizing any desired name when writing a *get* in a given locale. Furthermore, even the town involved might be known by different appellations as well, opening the possibility of changing the name of the place as well.[259] With mercurial town names and personal names, the precise identity of the parties divorcing could not be defined to an acceptable level of certainty. In light of this problem, Rabban Gamaliel acted to ensure that all the possible names involved would be included in the *get*, to ensure that the disadvantaged party (in this instance, usually the woman) would not be left holding a *get* of dubious value. Again, this statement indicates that the social welfare of disadvantaged parties to a divorce was of primary concern for the rabbis.

The Toseftan parallel to this passage, T Git. 3:3,[260] follows the same general lines of argument, but includes a few slight differences that make a brief discussion worthwhile:

קדם אצל אשתו או ששלח אצלה שליח, אמ' לה "גט ששלחתי ליך אי
אפשי שתתגרשי בו" ה"ז בטל. בראשונה היה עושה ב"ד במקום אחר
ומבטלו. אם בטלו מבוטל, דברי ר'. רבן שמעון בן גמליאל אומר: אין יכול
לבטלו, ולהוסיף על תנאו.

If he reached his wife before the *get*, or he sent a messenger to her, and said to her "regarding the *get* that I sent you—it is not my desire that you be divorced with it," then it is cancelled.

At first, he would convene a court in another place and cancel it. If he cancelled it, it is cancelled, [and these are] the words of Rabbi [Yehuda HaNasi]. Rabban Shimeon ben Gamaliel says: He is not able to cancel it or add to its provisions.

The initial piece of T parallels M closely. At the end, however, we see two opinions not present in M's version. Rabbi Yehuda HaNasi held that if a *get* were cancelled by another court, it indeed remained cancelled. Rabban Shimeon ben Gamaliel, an earlier authority, took the stricter position, and denied the other court the ability to make any changes to the terms of the *get* at all.

Comparing M with T, we find that the same two possibilities are presented in an entirely different way. While the term *barishonah* at the start of the Toseftan passage does show the recognition of legal development, the two outcomes in T appear as conflicting opinions of prominent rabbis. The later opinion (i.e., that of Rabbi Yehuda HaNasi) is the one that coheres with the earlier stage represented in the process indicated in the first part of both M and T. Rabban Gamaliel, the enactor in M, has disappeared from the scene entirely. The closest we find in T to any mention of his role is that of his son: Rabban Shimeon ben Gamaliel, who held essentially the same viewpoint represented by his father's enactment in M.

Rabbi Yehuda HaNasi's position is best understood this way: he believed that *post facto*, the canceling of the divorce was to be accepted, because a legal act (even if undesirable and with ill effects) had been completed and was valid and binding. *Ab initio*, though, it appears that he would not have advised them to behave this way. Despite the societal difficulties inherent in the action, this serious act taken by a *beit din* was still to be considered efficacious.

In BT Git. 32b-33a, two later glosses add to the information present in M and T. The first question raised is that of the composition of the *beit din*. Rav Nahman considered two witnesses to be sufficient, while Rav Sheshet required a full *beit din*. The second point made in BT relates to the very essence of this change in law. BT points out that the rabbis are uprooting a law from the Torah for the sake of the welfare of this woman.[261] BT makes its claim unabashedly, asserting that the power of defining the parameters of marriage rests entirely with the rabbis. This is in keeping with the prevalent rhetoric of disclosure active in BT.

In sum, then, we see that the rabbis have re-created their stance on this law to uphold social welfare, especially the welfare of the disadvantaged party. Sometime in the late first century, this difficulty became serious enough to prompt a rethinking of *halakhah*, and a restrictive solution to a thorny problem that had ramifications for both present and future generations.

Full Names and Fuller Names

A second example in the category of *tikkun haolam* involved the writing of the names of the required witnesses to a *get*. Witnesses were required to sign a *get*, to ensure that there were at least two men who could testify before a *beit din* as to the validity of the document should the need arise. Their signatures effected the *get*, in essence, because it was not valid without them. This was vitally important for all official documents, but especially so in the case of a *get*, because if one of the parties required proof of status, witnesses could certify the correct marital status (married or divorced) for the parties involved.

BT Git. 36a revolves around the written documentation of witnesses, and quotes the following *baraita*:

כדתניא : <u>בראשונה</u> היה כותב אני פלוני חתמתי עד. אם כתב ידו יוצא
ממקום אחר—כשר, ואם לאו—פסול. אמר רבן גמליאל : תקנה גדולה
התקינו, שיהיו מפרשין שמותיהן בגיטין, מפני תיקון העולם.

As it was taught: <u>At first</u>, he [i.e., a witness] would write "I, Ploni, signed this as witness." If his handwriting could be found on other documents, it was acceptable, and if not, it was not acceptable. Rabban Gamaliel[262] said: they [i.e., the rabbis] enacted an important enactment, that they [i.e., the witnesses] would write their full names in *gittin*, for the sake of *tikkun haolam*.

At issue here is the difference between signing and sealing a critical document with "I, John, seal this as witness," and "I, John Quincy Smith, also known as Johnny, of New York City, New York, seal this as witness." The more information provided, and the larger the handwriting specimen, the better the likelihood of the authorities recognizing the signature, and, if necessary, finding the witness after he had left the proceedings, whether he was nearby or halfway around the world. With fuller names and more information, the ability to find witnesses was greatly increased, and the woman's (and her offspring's) level of protection was, likewise, significantly increased.

A parallel text in T Git. 7:13 without *barishonah* prompts Lieberman to comment on the necessity for this change in law:

And in ancient times many were not found who knew how to write, except in cities and towns, and signing (*hatimah*) served as the sealing (*hotemet*) [of a document] in our period, and according to the majority they knew who the witness was, or the witnesses were, and it was possible to uphold the signature based on another place. And for this reason, afterwards as well, they found it suitable to use the signature of famous *hakhamim*, even if they did not write out their name at all, and even if they did not write suitably.[263]

Thus the major issue was the requirement of identifying and tracking the witnesses. With the general familiarity that existed in smaller communities, and with supporting evidence from other documents where this witness utilized a similar signing pattern (whether in suitable print or not), the *get* was valid because there was enough information present to make tracking possible. Again, we see that either Rabban Gamaliel or Rabban Shimeon ben Gamaliel showed concern in providing for the welfare of the disadvantaged within the social network of their time.

This category of changes in law, then, aimed at enhancing the specificity of law that dealt with social relations, and, in particular, avoiding the harm of leaving a person in dubious status within the social web. It also attempted to avoid long-term harm that might come to children or other relatives, especially when the act that created this harm was not directly under the control of the harmed party.

Chapter One - Conclusions

After close study of the examples detailed above and the other texts related to the term *barishonah*, a number of patterns emerge. First, there are a number of precedents for this type of legal change: Hittite, Roman and Sassanian law as well as the New Testament all exhibit the same formal pattern of disclosing legal development. Biblical law, with the exception of one passage that comes close, does not ever freely admit of this kind of legal change.[264] This establishes a core evolution that took place between the time of the Bible and the era of rabbinic legal literature: the move from a biblical rhetoric of concealment to a rabbinic rhetoric of disclosure: biblical texts tending to hide legal change, rabbinic editors making a conscious decision to disclose the development of law. This choice clearly reflects an underlying change in philosophic outlook.

The examples chosen from the eight different rationales in this chapter provide a select overview of the various rationales the rabbis employed for justifying legal change. The employment of a rationale does not imply, of course, any activation of new law in general practice. Studies by Goodenough, Schwartz and others[265] have shown it is foolhardy to assume that laws found in rabbinic texts actually imply any level of communal observance in their time period. Instead, praxis in a given age is more a combination of the various influences on the people involved: rabbinic ideas, cultural norms absorbed from the Greco-Roman world, concepts from art and literature the people encountered, etc. So, from reading these texts, we cannot determine with any specificity if or how these laws were actually brought to life in the community. Nonetheless, what we can glean from these texts are the various philosophical viewpoints on legal change the editors of rabbinic legal works accepted, and how that philosophy shifted over time and space.

As discussed in the introduction, the term *barishonah* is used 162 times throughout the legal corpus of rabbinic legal literature in reference to self-conscious alterations of Jewish law. In 139 of these occurrences, rationales appear that explain the halakhic change in the example. Chart 1 shows a breakdown of the various rationales offered for halakhic change, and their frequency of occurrence in rabbinic legal sources.

From the data in Chart 1, we note that the editors of certain works had distinct propensities for certain rationales. M does not contain the use of the term *barishonah* with reference to significant rethinking of law due to changes in leadership structures. Factoring in the recent study of Seth Schwartz, which attempts to discern the historical picture of the patriarchate and its influence open the general Palestinian Jewish community, we arrive at a potential reason for this lacuna. Schwartz suggests:

> that the core ideology of Judaism . . . ceased, after the two revolts, to function as an integrating force in Palestinian Jewish society. The intermediaries of the Torah lost not only their legal authority, but also their status as cultural ideals. . . . Both rabbis and patriarchs were probably convinced they had a right to exercise legal authority over the Jews by virtue of belonging to the class empowered by the Torah itself. Yet in the wake of the Destruction and the Bar Kokhba revolt, and the imposition of direct Roman rule in Palestine, the Torah and its representatives lost their institutional position and much of their prestige, and they and their successors spent the rest of antiquity struggling to restore them. For the rabbis, the struggle did not finally succeed until the rise of Islam, at the earliest.[266]

Schwartz's position takes into account archeological data and literature that transcends the more limited rabbinic account. If Schwartz is correct, then M's silence could be indicative of the lack of access to effective leadership opportunities for rabbis in the Tannaitic Palestinian milieu. With the possibility of actual leadership quashed at the hands of an overbearing Roman government, any legal change that devolved from changes in authority structure may well have been essentially irrelevant to the rabbis of M.

In contrast with M are the records of T and PT, both of which contain some examples of change in authority structure that lead to alteration of law. T, probably edited after M during the late 3rd century in Palestine,[267] was created during a period that rabbinic historiography suggests was confronting a divergence of its extant centralized authority in a post-Rabbi Yehuda HaNasi world. In PT, we find a slightly more extensive picture of legal change in response to shifts in authority structures. While T confronts issues that looked back into history, such as the ancient definitions of tribal borders, changes in municipal limits to the town of Tiberias and problems that might invalidate *gittin*; PT discusses legal issues that go to the very painful heart of the matters relating to the Jewish community at the time of its writing: relations with the Roman government, the shifting definition of religious leadership and changes in ordaining and appointing judges.

BT's examples of law that changed as a result of shifting authority structures are all paralleled by earlier texts, and therefore probably redacted into BT from earlier traditions. This indicates a preserving trend, rather than an editor addressing compelling novel issues. From this array of texts, we can see that the use of *barishonah* in different ways in each work reflects the influences at work on the editors, in their particular context.

Another striking fact is that PT does not refer at all to catastrophic historical events (such as the destruction of the Temple and the Hadrianic persecutions) to justify halakhic change with *barishonah*. BT used this rationale only gingerly: in one case it speaks of a change in a long-abolished practice—the dispatching of runners to notify the Diaspora of the new moon. In another, BT repeats a text also preserved in T about lost items, which relies upon both the destruction of the Temple and the Hadrianic persecutions for dating successive stages of development that alter law to fit a new Diasporan, post-Temple context. Thus, both PT and BT downplay the destruction as a rationale for change, and BT only includes prior statements that happen to include this rationale if they are germane to its Diasporan setting.

Under the rationale we call "Akiba or others teach," we find that Akiba appears only in literary settings traceable to the Tannaitic period. This indicates that the power of his name held currency only in the period during and immediately following his life. Other scholars' names seem to have had enough clout to accomplish similar justification of halakhic change in later works, and yet, Akiba was cited in reference to five distinct cases, while no other teacher warrants more than one citation apiece. We find, then, that M and T gave Rabbi Akiba a special role in halakhic change connected with the term *barishonah*, and no other authority shared precisely that same spotlight.

Table 1
Rationales for Halakhic Change Utilizing
the Term בראשונה in Textual Sources

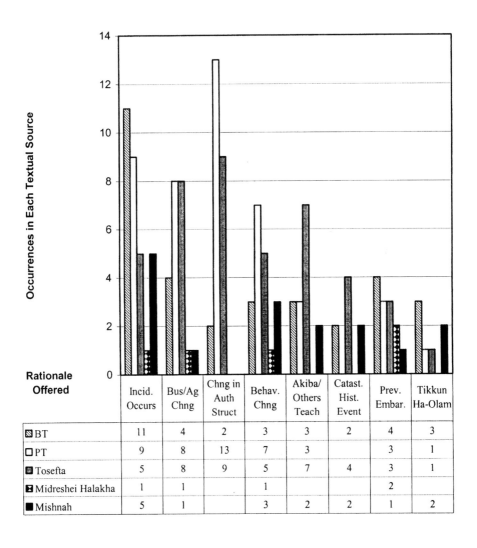

Rationale Offered	Incid. Occurs	Bus/Ag Chng	Chng in Auth Struct	Behav. Chng	Akiba/ Others Teach	Catast. Hist. Event	Prev. Embar.	Tikkun Ha-Olam
BT	11	4	2	3	3	2	4	3
PT	9	8	13	7	3		3	1
Tosefta	5	8	9	5	7	4	3	1
Midreshei Halakha	1	1		1			2	
Mishnah	5	1		3	2	2	1	2

BT also adds details to the traditions that make the texts more appropriate for their later audience. One example stands out: in the texts on reclaiming lost articles, BT is the only source to mention synagogues and study houses as places where one may make an announcement of a lost item. While PT was edited in a context in which these communal institutions surely existed, for some reason, BT's editors felt more at liberty to incorporate new material.

One other interesting issue is the distribution of sources. In every source, there is very little indication of legal change in the orders Tohorot and Kodashim. In fact, the passages that utilize *barishonah* in these orders are almost entirely parallels that are better suited to their original tractates. The two passages that do fit well into their tractate (in Niddah) refer to menstrual purity laws that were more likely to have been in active use in this period than other material dealing with other obsolete purity or sacrifice issues in the remainder of these tractates. This bespeaks a particular focus in the changing of law using the rhetorical term *barishonah*: in the post-destruction context, laws that were abrogated due to historical circumstances alone were generally not changed with the term *barishonah*. Thus, changes discussed with this term do not appear to include a large theoretical or utopian subset, but were, most likely, limited to laws of contemporary concern.

One final point on the distribution of rationales: it is surprising to note that the rationale that appears in the smallest quantity of all is that of *tikkun haolam*—for the sake of social welfare. Furthermore, it is limited to occurrences of *barishonah* related to marriage law. It would appear that the use of the combination of *barishonah* and *tikkun haolam* is very limited—meaning that it applied to changing law for the sake of preserving the status of the woman, the disadvantaged party in this case. Thus, the "repair of the world" implies attentiveness to the ramifications of legal action on the party in the currently weaker position.

Attributed and Non-attributed Occurrences

Citations of the Term ראשונה with Halakhic Change[268]

Source	Attributed Usages	Enactor[269]	Unattributed
Mishnah	3 (17%)	3 (17%)	11(65%)
Tosefta	12 (29%)	4 (9%)	26 (62%)
Midreshei Halakhah	0 (0%)	1 (25%)	3 (75%)
Palestinian Talmud	20 (44%)	1 (2%)	24 (53%)
Babylonian Talmud	4 (13%)	4 (13%)	23 (74%)

If we look at the 139 occurrences (including parallels) from a literary-critical perspective, we begin to find some interesting results. The table above shows the number of attributed vs. unattributed uses of the term. Notice that throughout the entire corpus of texts studied, the number of unattributed uses of this term far exceeds the number of attributed uses. In all the sources except the PT, there are more than twice as many unattributed uses as attributed ones. Only in PT are the numbers anywhere close to even, with the attributed usage (46%) nearing half of all occurrences. This is a significant finding, and suggests one of three possibilities.

First, it may reflect choices in the editing of PT. It is possible that the editors of PT preserved these statements with the names of their tradents attached, while BT and other sources chose to preserve them anonymously. This may have been an effort to neutralize these texts by providing them with a clean history and a stronger, "*stam*" format which led to greater acceptance.

A second possibility is that the editor of PT was closer (geographically or temporally) to the sources of these statements, and thus we see a better preservation of more "local" material. If the editors were closer to the sources of the statements, it is reasonable to assume that they would have had better access to the information needed to cite each statement בשם אומרו (*b'shem omro*—"in the name of the one who said it").[270]

Third, this may provide a window into a significant difference between the Palestinian and Babylonian communities and the way they used this term. More on this third option, which is the most likely one, follows in the next section.

Geographic and Chronological Distribution of Attributed Uses of *Barishonah*

First, a methodological note: dating a literary trend by observing individual authorities who utilize a certain term is always a dicey business, especially when one relies upon one or a few citations. However, as Jacob Neusner suggests, using the dating of citations of rabbis can indicate broad generational patterns, especially in earlier texts.[271] Looking statistically over all of the occurrences of this term can thus give a promising idea of its usage, and the quantity of citations reviewed helps to correct errors that may crop up in specific texts.

When we look more closely at attributed uses of this term, splitting them according to the generation and location of the tradents involved, the results are profound. In the Tannaitic sources, we find that *all* attributed uses come from the period before the fourth Tannaitic generation, implying that use of this term began in the start of the Tannaitic period and continued through the end of that period, much as we would expect since the documents involved are edited after the end of the fourth Tannaitic generation.

What is remarkable is what we find in the later generations when we compare BT and PT's use of this term. Chart 2[272] shows the distribution of attributed occurrences of the term throughout our textual sources, along with the generation and provenance of the attached tradent. While one might expect that this term would appear equally attributed to Babylonian and Palestinian tradents, this is not the case at all. Indeed, amongst all attributed uses, we find a far larger number of citations of Palestinian Amoraim represented (35 instances in all), with *only four citations of Babylonian Amoraim* in connection with this term at all.

The four citations of Babylonian Amoraim include: the father of Rabbi Abin (BA1 cited in BT Git.), Rav Huna (BA2 cited in PT Sotah.), Rav Sheshet (BA3 cited in three parallel texts in BT BB, BT Men. and BT Hul.), Rav Hisda (BA3 cited in PT Sotah) and Rav Huna (BA2 quoted by Rav Hisda in the same part of PT Sot.). In the four BT citations, though, there is evidence of simple carry-over from earlier materials: in BT Gittin, the quoted statement of the father of Rabbi Abin is introduced with *detani*, even though the father of Rabbi Abin is identified as one of the earliest of Amoraim. It is justifiable to dismiss this as an entirely Amoraic citation. As for Rav Sheshet, who appears in the three parallels in BT BB, Men. and Hul., his only role is to quote the words of a Tanna, Rabbi Shimeon Shezuri, who is also introduced with *detanya*. So, essentially, the entirety of the attributed material associated with this word in BT is Tannaitic in origin.[273]

Table 2 must be viewed in light of the distribution of *memrot* in each generation. Based on a highly approximate survey done on the Bar-Ilan University Responsa Project software, coupled with David Kraemer's count of *memrot* of different authorities found in BT,[274] we may utilize the following very rough estimates of the relative number of statements present in rabbinic literature from each generation of authorities, based also on the listing of rabbis in Strack and Stemberger's chronology. The methodology (admittedly far from perfect) was to select the two best known authorities with unique names from each generation, and search for appearances of their names in PT and BT. At best, it can give an approximate representative sense of the relative number of occurrences connected with each generation. (K) indicates Kraemer's counting, otherwise the numbers are results derived from searching the Bar-Ilan system.

Table 2
Attributed Occurrences of בראשונה in Textual Sources

	T1	T2	T3	T4	T5		PA 1	PA 2	PA 3	PA 4	PA 5		BA 1	BA 2	BA 3
▨ BT			2	1									1		3
☐ PT			5				6	5	23	1				1	1
▥ Tosefta		2	6	3											
■ Mishnah			3												

Authority/Generation	*Appearances* in PT	*Appearances* in BT
PA1 – R. Yehoshua ben Levi	482	517
R. Hoshaya	490	100
PA2 – R. Yohanan	1249	2781
Resh Lakish	483	858
PA3 – R. Abbahu	594	270
R. Ammi	154	287
PA4 – R. Yermiyah	734	446
R. Huna	282	1573

Authority/Generation	*Memrot* in BT[275]
BA1 – Rav	2250 (K)
Shmuel	1076 (K)
BA2 – Rav Yehuda/ Rav Huna	137 (K)
BA3 (whole generation)	2015 (K)
BA4 – Abbaye/Rava	2125 (K)

Looking again at Table 2, we see that in PT, on the other hand, we find ample usage of the term *barishonah* throughout the Amoraic period. Notice, though, that the peak of usage occurs in PA3, the generation of Rabbi Abbahu, Rabbi Eleazar ben Pedat and Rabbi Assi, all students of Rabbi Yohanan bar Nappaha, a leader in Tiberias. From the distribution of the occurrences of this term, and the tradents cited in connection with it, we arrive at the conclusion that the students of Rabbi Yohanan bar Nappaha in Tiberias were major proponents of this sort of halakhic change, and utilized this term more intensely than other groupings in either the Amoraic or the Tannaitic periods. When we review the chart above that shows frequency of citation of the names of those in the generation of PA3, we see that the aggregate number of appearances connected with the PA3 generation is actually smaller than most other generations. This is a very significant finding, which tells us that the editors of PT located the time of greatest activity for the use of this term in the PA3 generation, perhaps because they had more traditions involving the term that came down to them from that generation. After that generation, though, there is a marked drop-off in the attributed use of the term.

Table 3
Number of Occurrences of the Term בראשונה
in Tannaitic and Amoraic Material from PT and BT

	Incid Occ	Bus/ Ag Chng	Chng Auth Struct	Behv Chng	Akva/ Oth. teach	Cat. Hist. Event	Prev Embr	Tkn Ha-Olam		Strict er (NR)	More Len. (NR)
▨ BT - Amoraic											
☐ PT - Amoraic	1	1	6	3	3					3	2
▨ BT - Tannaitic	10	4	2	3	3	2	4	3			6
■ PT - Tannaitic	8	7	7	4	.	2	3	1		2	1

Y-axis label: Number of Occurrences. X-axis label: Rationale Offered (NR = No Rationale)

One other method of analysis confirms this point. If we examine Chart 3, and look at the uses of *barishonah* in BT, we see that the marker terms we associate with Tannaitic material (such as תנן, תנו רבנן and the like) indicate that all uses of this term in BT stem from either citations of *mishnayot* or *baraitot*. No occurrence of *barishonah* is Amoraic in origin, when viewed through the criterion of language (all the statements connected to *barishonah* in BT are in Hebrew). Furthermore, none are embedded in an Aramaic stratum, for they do not use Aramaic introductions, nor do they include Aramaic terminology in the statements themselves. Clearly, then, the use of this term is strictly limited to the Tannaitic material in BT.

In reconstructing the intellectual development associated with this term, then, we find that it was in use throughout the Tannaitic period in Palestine. With the conclusion of the Tannaitic period, the Palestinian Amoraim continued using this term to indicate prior and later stages of development in Jewish law. The Babylonian Amoraim, unlike their Palestinian counterparts, shifted away from use of this term. Thus, there is continuity in usage found throughout the Palestinian texts we have studied and a disjunction between the Palestinian and Babylonian textual traditions.

Chronologically, we find that the occurrences of this term began in the earliest days of the Tannaitic period, and extended through the fifth Amoraic generation in Palestine, giving us an historical range for the use of this term in Palestine of 70 CE – *circa* 380 CE. If the later attributions of the use of this term are accurate, then the appearance of Rabbi Halakhah, Rabbi Yossi bar Abin and Rabbi Mana, give us proof that this term was in use in Palestine through the late fourth century CE in Palestine. BT only includes material with this term already placed in it—there is no evidence that any Amora or the stammaitic editors create new material with this term in it in BT at all.

Enactors of Change

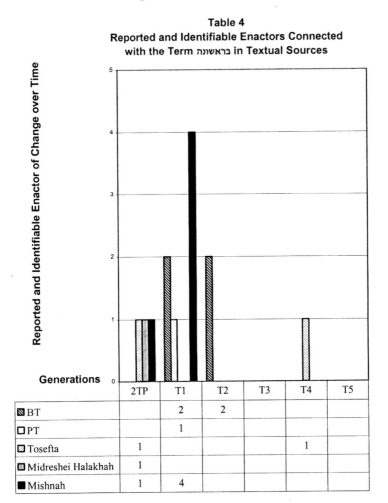

Table 4
Reported and Identifiable Enactors Connected
with the Term בראשונה in Textual Sources

Generations	2TP	T1	T2	T3	T4	T5
⧄ BT		2	2			
☐ PT		1				
⊡ Tosefta	1				1	
⊞ Midreshei Halakhah	1					
■ Mishnah	1	4				

Looking at Table 4, there is one more insight to be gained, and it is a bit of a foreshadowing of the work to come. When we examine the texts that end in a *takkanah* being enacted, we find that all of the named enactors come from either the very late Second Temple Period (Shimeon ben Shetah and Hillel HaZaken) or from the Tannaitic period (Rabban Yohanan ben Zakkai, Rabban Gamaliel HaZaken, Rabban Gamaliel and Rabbi Yehuda HaNasi and his court). There are two statements in which temporally indeterminate parties enact law: an unspecified *beit din* and *hakhamim*. No statements appear that indicate any individual later than Rabbi Yehuda HaNasi enacting a *takkanah* connected with the term *barishonah*. Finally, we should also note that all the enactors mentioned served as patriarch at some point in their careers. This indicates either that the term *barishonah* is often connected with Tannaitic legal change by authorities at the highest level, or that later editors only felt comfortable attributing reflective legal change to leaders of a certain status.

Barishonah, then, denoted reflective legal change over the period from the first to the fourth centuries CE, predominantly in Palestine, with its apex during the third generation of Palestinian Amoraim. The editors of rabbinic legal works utilized this term when reflection upon prior legal decisions showed them to be insufficient. This reflection could be on a philosophical level, or, in other cases, forced by events or incidents. Finally, the editors of rabbinic legal works utilized a rhetoric of disclosure, which represented a major change from the rhetoric present in the Hebrew Bible and other precursors. This indicates a greater comfort with the idea of legal change and development.

Thus, the outlines of the use of this term become clear. More examples and conclusions await us at the end of the next two chapters, where we will consider this term's close siblings *takkanot* and *gezerot*.

Notes

25. The precise count in the printed editions is as follows: Mishnah-31, Tosefta-64, Halakhic Midrashim-27, Yerushalmi-147 and Bavli-148, for an exact total of 417 documented occurrences. Differences in the use of this term in various manuscripts may, however, bring the total up or down by several occurrences.

26. For this study, we will define the legal corpus of rabbinic literature to include the following: Mishnah, Tosefta, the Palestinian Talmud, the Babylonian Talmud and the Halakhic Midrashim (including *MRSBY, MRY, Sifra, SB, SD, SZ*, and the reconstruction known as *Mtan*). Translations of these texts are the author's, unless otherwise noted.

27. Items in these lists include the first of the two Temples (cf. M Ta. 4:6, PT Yoma 4b, BT Ta. 26b and 29a, RH 18b, etc.); the notes blown on a shofar (cf. BT RH 27a, 28a and 33b, PT RH 15a, 3:4; first, as opposed to second, wives (BT Yev. 9b, 18b and 27b); halakhic statements (cf. BT BM 37a); and a variety of other items.

28. Cf. T Sot. 15:1-6 (with its parallel in PT Sot. 44b, 9:14) and PT Kil. 28a, 8:2 for two prime examples of this literary *tendenz*. It is, of course, likely that the rabbis considered this actual history, thus making possible a folding of categories b) and c) into one.

29. Examples include PT MK 4b, 1:5, PT Yoma 4a, 1:1, T Ber. 7:29, T Shev. 8:1, T Ket. 1:4 (and parallels: BT Ket. 12a and PT 3a, 1:1) and BT BB 100b.

30. Zecharias Frankel, *Darkhei HaMishnah* (Tel Aviv: Sinai, 1959), p. 146.

31. That is, from the period of the five great pairs of Jewish leaders (it is an anachronism to call them "rabbis") as they are reported in rabbinic literature. Listed in chronological order, they were: Yose ben Yoezer and Yose ben Yohanan; Yehoshua ben Perahya and Mattai; Yehuda ben Tabbai and Shimeon ben Shetah; Shemayah and Avtalyon; and Hillel and Shammai. The last of these leaders were Hillel and Shammai, according to available traditions of rabbinic history. Cf. Strack and Stemberger, *Introduction*, pp. 69-72.

32. *Tannaim* ("teachers" or "repeaters") is the name for rabbis active during the Tannaitic period, from 70 CE to approximately 225 CE. This period begins with the destruction of the Second Temple and concludes with the closing of the Mishnah.

33. Ephraim E. Urbach, ‏"הדרשה כיסוד ההלכה ובעית הסופרים"‏ *Tarbiz* 27 (1956-7), p. 168.

34. Martin Jaffee, "The *Taqqanah* in Tannaitic Literature: Jurisprudence and the Construction of Rabbinic Memory," *JJS* 41.2 (1990), pp. 204-225.

35. Bernard Levinson, "The Human Voice in Divine Revelation" in *Innovation in Religious Traditions* (eds. Michael A. Williams, Collett Cox and Martin S. Jaffee; New York: Mouton De Gruyter, 1992), pp. 41-44.

36. Levinson, "Human Voice," p. 42, translated from Hittite Laws § 7.

37. Levinson, "Human Voice," p. 43.

38. Levinson, "Human Voice," p. 45.

39. Cf. Bernard Levinson, *Deuteronomy and the Hermeneutics of Legal Innovation* (Oxford: Oxford University Press, 1997) and the other instances cited in Levinson, "Human Voice."

40. Gershon Brin, *The Concept of Time in the Bible and the Dead Sea Scrolls* (Leiden: Brill, 2001), pp. 73-74.

41. 4QFlorilegium 1.1 and 1.5; 11QTemple[a] 21.5 and 11QTemple[b] 54.6 show clear evidence of the use of this term in a historical mode. Another possible source is 11QTemple[a] 15.18, where the word is reconstructed, probably appropriately.

42. M. Cary et al., *The Oxford Classical Dictionary* (Oxford: Clarendon Press, 1950), pp. 375-6.

43. The Twelve Tables is the earliest codification of Roman law, promulgated in 451-450 BCE, and published on bronze (or wood) tablets in the Forum in Rome.

44. *Lex Furia* probably refers to *Lex Cincia* of 204 BCE, but is certainly before 169 BCE, the date of the *Lex Uoconia.*

45. *Lex Uoconia* is dated to 169 BCE.

46. *Lex Falcidia* is dated to 40 BCE.

47. Francis De Zulueta, tr., *The Institutes of Gaius* (Oxford: Clarendon Press, 1946), pp. 130-3.

48. This was the formal advice of the Senate to the magistrates. While in Republican times it had no legal force, it was *de facto* binding. In Imperial times, especially with Hadrian and thereafter, it immediately had the force of law. Cf. M. Cary et al., *Dictionary*, s.v. *Senatus Consultum.*

49. De Zulueta, *Institutes*, pp. 148-9.

50. See Christine Hayes, "The Abrogation of Torah Law: Rabbinic *Taqqanah* and the Praetorian Edict," in Peter Schäfer, *The Talmud Yerushalmi and Graeco-Roman Culture* (Tübingen: Mohr Sieback, 1997), pp. 643-674, especially the section on the Praetorian Edict, where Hayes argues that Palestinian Jews were indeed aware of at least some Roman legal developments.

51. See Bernard S. Jackson, "Evolution and Foreign Influence in Ancient Law," *American Journal of Comparative Law* 16 (1968): 372-390.

52. These are strict, specific rituals that require the oral statement of a legal action. Cf. W.W. Buckland, *A Text-Book of Roman Law from Augustus to Justinian* (repr. Cambridge: Cambridge University Press, 1966), pp. 609-616.

53. *Auctoritas* is the assigned legal authority over any individual not recognized as independent by the Roman court, who requires representation in legal proceedings. As in Jewish law, one who is involved in the case at hand in some way (נוגע בדבר) may not represent the party with whom they are involved.

54. An urban praetor was the Roman official charged with governing a city.

55. A trial—that is, if the proceedings progress to the point where a full trial becomes necessary, then a tutor may be appointed, according to this opinion. De Zulueta, *Institutes*, p. 58-59.

56. Morton Smith, *Tannaitic Parallels to the Gospels* (Philadelphia: Society of Biblical Literature, 1951), pp. 28-9.

57. The Greek formulae "'ηκούσατε 'ότι 'ερρέθη τοῖς 'αρχαίοις" ("You have heard it said by the elders") and "'εγὼ δὲ λέγω" ("I say to you") are the formulaic elements that tie this pericope together, as noted by Smith, *Parallels*, pp. 28-9.

58. Smith, *Parallels*, p. 28.

59. Cf. Jacob Neusner's scathing indictment of the entire concept of these parallels in his *Are There Really Tannaitic Parallels to the Gospels* (Atlanta: Scholars Press, 1993).

60. Chapter XVI, 1:2-4, in Anahit Perikhanian's text and translation of *The Book of a Thousand Judgments* (Costa Mesa, CA: Mazda Publishers, 1997), p. 27. Thanks are extended to Dr. Yakov Elman of Yeshiva University for his suggestion of examining this legal text as a source for later legal parallels.

61. *Op. cit.*, Chapter XLVII, A3:13-4,4, p. 253.

62. Two additional categories may be discerned from the occurrences of *barishonah* that do not have an attached rationale: there are cases when the *halakhah* shifts to be more lenient, and there are cases in which the *halakhah* becomes stricter. The law is changed to be stricter in: M Ned. 11:12; M Nid. 10:6; T Kel. BM 8:5; PT Shek. 7:3, 50d; PT Shab. 3:3, 6a; and PT Ket. 5:4, 29d. The law is changed to be more lenient in: M RH 2:6 (parallel to BT Eruv. 25a); M Git. 6:5 (parallel to M TY 4:5, BT BB 146b, BT Menahot 30b and BT Hul. 75b); T Dem. 3:4 (parallel to PT Dem. 2:3, 23a and BT Bekh. 31a); T Shev. 4:16; T Shab. 15:14 (parallel to PT Shab. 17:1, 16a and BT Shab. 123a); and PT Betz. 1:1, 60a (parallel to PT AZ 2:7, 41c). Since these cases do not have stated rationales, we will not include them in the main discussion in this chapter.

63. These 15 citations and their 21 parallels are: M Shek. 7:5; M Yoma 2:1; M RH 2:1; M RH 2:2 (parallel to T RH 1:15-2:2, BT Betz. 4b-5a); M RH 4:4 (parallel to BT Betz. 4b-5a); T Eruv. 3:5 (parallel to BT Eruv. 45a, PT Eruv. 4:3, 21d and BT RH 23b); T Suk. 4:1 (parallel to BT Suk. 51a (where there are two parallel texts within the page); T Yev.13:1 (parallel to BT Yev. 107b-108a and PT San. 1:2, 19a); T Ket. 12:1 (parallel to PT Ket. 8:11, 32b and BT Ket 82b); T Kor. 11:7 (parallel to T Men. 13:18 and BT Pes. 56b-57a); BT Ber. 23a-b (parallel to PT Ber. 2:3, 4c); BT RH 31b (parallel to BT Yoma 67a (two parallels), PT Yoma 6:5, 43d and PT Shab. 9:3, 12a); PT MS 1:2, 39c; PT MS 4:3, 55a; and PT MS 5:2, 55a (parallel to PT Sot. 9:11, 24a and PT Pes. 3:1, 29d).

64. M. D. Herr, "לבעיית הלכות מלחמה בשבת בימי בית שני ובתקופת משנה והתלמוד," *Tarbiz* 30 (1961), pp. 242-56, 341-56. Cf., especially, p. 242, n.1, on his view of war on Shabbat in the Bible.

65. Josephus' *Antiquities* 12.1.1.

66. Herr, "הלכות מלחמה," pp. 242-247.

67. Lawrence H. Schiffman, *The Halakhah at Qumran* (Leiden: E.J. Brill, 1975), pp. 124-5. Cf. his commentary and notes on this issue.

68. James H. Charlesworth, *The Old Testament Pseudepigrapha* (New York: Doubleday, 1985), p. 2:142.

69. O.S. Wintermute makes this claim in Charlesworth, *Pseudepigrapha*, p. 2:44.

70. M. Cary *et al.*, *Dictionary*, pp. 371-2.

71. Menaham Stern, *Greek and Latin Authors on Jews and Judaism* (Jerusalem: The Israel Academy of Sciences and Humanities, 1974), pp. 1:510-11.

72. Various censored versions of this word exist in both the printed version and some manuscripts of T. The Vienna edition, the *editio princeps* for Lieberman's edition, is followed here and throughout this study, unless otherwise noted.

73. Rashi to BT Eruv. 45a reads this as implying that they would store their weapons in the first house outside the wall that they reached while returning to the city from battle. This would minimize any further carrying of weapons on Shabbat not in the service of self-defense.

74. The traditional limit for Shabbat carrying, cf. M Shab. chapter 11.

75. Cf. B. Shab. 132a for the *locus classicus* of this debate. Cf. also BT Yoma 84b-85a.

76. The *hazan* served in an administrative role in the Temple and in the synagogue afterwards. See M Yoma 7:1, M Sot. 7:7-8 and M Mak. 3:12 for examples of the involvement of the *hazan* in ritual activities. Note that the term *hazan* is not used in anything like our modern sense, where it now means something akin to "Cantor."

77. The attribution in this passage is particularly difficult. The Munich manuscript has the following attribution: "Rav Pappa said in the name of Rabbi Yehuda in the name of Rav." *Dikduke Sofrim ad loc.* reports another manuscript that has only "Rav said," but rejects this as a scribal error.

78. Note, however, that manuscript differences do play a serious role in our reading of this particular text. In some manuscripts the text leaves out the element of the enemies entering the storehouse—in the Munich manuscript and in the version recorded in the Rif, we find that the mention of the enemies pursuing the Jews into their storehouse is handled quite differently. *Dikduke Sofrim* suggests that these witnesses to the BT imply a reading of the story in this way: that the enemies first entered the storehouse with intent to ambush the Jews, and were then followed by the Jews, whereupon the ensuing melee occurred. Cf. *Dikduke Sofrim ad loc.*

79. Herr, "הלכות מלחמה," pp. 242-249.

80. This text comes from the Leiden Manuscript of PT, the best available text, from Saul Lieberman, *Palestinian Talmud Leiden Ms., Codex Scaliger 3* (Jerusalem: Kedem Publishing, 1970). All future citations of PT will utilize this edition, unless otherwise noted.

81. The parallel text in BT Tam. 28a basically replicates this version.

82. Equally violent versions of this story appear in T Shev. 1:4 and PT Yoma 2:1, 39d. The reading suggested by these two passages, that "the priest arrived at the four cubits of the altar" is followed in interpreting BT's more difficult phrasing.

83. See Boaz Cohen, *Jewish Law and Roman Law: A Comparative Study* (New York: Jewish Theological Seminary of America, 1966; repr. Holmes Beach, Florida: Gaunt, Inc., 2001), p. 1:320. In note 224, Cohen also points out that BT Yev. 107b-108a suggests that a second betrothal also effects the renunciation of her first marriage.

84. The argument between Rabbi Yossi and Rabbi Elazar is over whether this proceeding requires two witnesses or a full court. This points, further, to the ambiguity inherent in this action: if it is a legal divorce, then a court should be required; if it is something short of a legal divorce, then two witnesses should suffice.

85. Ploni is the generic Hebrew name, a rough equivalent of "John Smith" in American parlance.

86. BT Yev. 108a has her entering a store at the command of her husband, perhaps to collect something that belonged to her.

87. Perhaps gathered for the wedding?

88. These are the two male witnesses.

89. Plonit, the feminine Hebrew form of Ploni, roughly equates to "Jane Smith."

90. Saul Lieberman, *TK* 6:147, suggested a different possibility, rooting this text into a specific moment in time. He believed that this changeover occurred because of the confusion that resulted from the Hadrianic persecutions:

> Without the writing of the *get* and its [proper] handing over to the woman, she would not be divorced, but with respect to *halitzah* and *miun* where the writ is only for evidence alone, here logic tells us that the Sages enacted [this] in a time of persecution—that they would no longer write the documents of *halitzah* and *miun* at all, so that they would not place themselves in any unnecessary danger, for when she desired to get married she could bring witnesses about [her] *halitzah* and *miun*.

Here, Lieberman explained that witnesses to her *halitzah* and *miun* were enough to prove that she did it, with no written record required. He also suggested a potential specific anchor in history to the process of updating the halakhic procedure of refusal. There is little concrete proof to support his claim that the persecutions of the 130s were causal of this legal change.

91. Cf. M Yev. 13:4 for some aspects of the significant status differences between a ממאנת and a גרושה.

92. Cf. Moshe Halbertal, *Interpretive Revolutions in the Making* (Jerusalem: Magness Press, 1997), for a detailed study of how core values affect the interpretive process.

93. There are 15 occurrences of main texts, and 6 parallels. The texts are M. Arakh. 9:4 (parallel to *Sifra Behar* 4:8); T Dem. 1:2 (parallel to BT Pes. 42b and PT Dem. 1:1, 21d); T Dem. 1:11; T MS 4:5; T Ket. 6:4; T AZ 8:1 (parallel to BT AZ 48b and PT AZ 4:9, 44b); T AZ 8:1 (another occurrence in this same *halakhah*); T Makh. 3:5-6; BT Pes. 56b-57a; BT AZ 31a (parallel to PT AZ 5:4, 44d); PT Peah 7:1, 20a; PT Kil. 9:4, 32d; PT Shev. 6:4, 37a; PT Sot. 1:8, 15d; and PT Kid. 1:5, 60c.

94. Cf. Jacob Neusner, *The Economics of the Mishnah* (Chicago: University of Chicago Press, 1990), pp. 101-2.

95. According to Neusner, *op. cit.*, walled towns were predominantly Jewish in population, whereas cities were home to a mixed Jewish and Gentile populace. There were only 11 walled cities in Roman Palestine: Caesarea, Beit Shean, Jerusalem, Gaza, Ashkelon, Akko, Neopolis, Tiberias, Emmaus, Beit Guvrin and Ashdod. Cf. Jacob Neusner, "The Experience of the City in Antique Judaism," in *Approaches to Ancient Judaism Volume V: Studies in Judaism and its Greco-Roman Context* (ed. William Scott Green; Chico, CA: Scholars Press, 1985), pp. 37-52, especially pp. 42-22; Daniel Sperber, *The City in Roman Palestine* (New York: Oxford University Press, 1998), pp. 117-127; and Yaron Dan, חיי העיר בארץ ישראל בשלהי העט העתיקה (Jerusalem: Yad Yitzhak ben Tsvi, 1984), p. 59. Hayim Lapin offers another approach to determining the pattern of cities and settlements in his *Economy, Geography and Provincial History in Later Roman Palestine* (Tübingen: Mohr Siebeck, 2001), pp. 78-100, though his map and listing reflect later evidence from the Amoraic period. There are also texts that eliminate Jerusalem from the list of towns included in the group of walled cities. See *ARN* 1:35, where a list

of rules that pertain to Jerusalem exempts it from the 12-month rule, allowing that houses may be redeemed by the original owner at any time, even after the 12-month period has passed. Parallels to this text include T Neg. 6:2, where even renting homes in the city is forbidden, and BT BK 82b. Daniel Sperber "Social Legislation in Jerusalem during the Latter Part of the Second Temple Period," *JSJ* VI:1 (June, 1975): 86-95, suggests that the regulations changed over time as living conditions were drastically altered.

96. This is like interest, since the value of the home may rise or fall, and the difference might be considered interest upon the house's redemption. However, since we are dealing with a sale that may ultimately be permanent, we cannot truly consider this in the category of interest.

97. The difference between the majority opinion and that of Rabbi Yehuda HaNasi, here, is significant. The majority opinion, which ultimately becomes Jewish law, calls for the entire intercalary month to be included in the waiting period, thus creating a thirteen-month waiting period in years when a second Adar is added. Rabbi Yehuda HaNasi calls for the 354-day lunar year plus the 11-day correction that harmonizes the lunar and solar calendars. The difference between the two opinions can amount to up to 19 days.

98. This means he would not have to return the property to the previous owners, even in the time of the Jubilee. Cf. the comments of Hanokh Albeck, ששה סדרי משנה (Tel Aviv: Devir Publishers, 1952-8) in his commentary on this mishnah.

99. חולש, here, is synonymous with מפקיד or מטיל, and literally means "to cast in," according to Saul Lieberman. He suggests that the money was put in a vessel together with a note containing the name of the man to whose credit the money was deposited, much as it was done at pagan temples throughout the Greco-Roman world. Cf. Saul Lieberman, *Hellenism in Jewish Palestine* (New York: Jewish Theological Seminary, 1950), p. 169.

100. Parallels to this text do not exist in our corpus, aside from a quotation of this mishnah in BT Git. 74b-75a.

101. Hillel the Elder lived at the time of Herod, late first century BCE to early first century CE. Cf. Strack and Stemberger *Introduction*, pp. 71-2. However, Neusner and other scholars believe that many of the attributions to Hillel in rabbinic literature are inaccurate or undeserved reassignments of statements made by others to Hillel's name, as in the Greek practice of collecting λόγοι. Cf. Jacob Neusner, *Formative Judaism* (Chico, CA: Scholars Press, 1982), pp. 45-63. Cf. also his *The Rabbinic Traditions About the Pharisees Before 70* (Leiden: Brill, 1971), 3:209-10, where he suggests that this particular tradition is probably Ushan in its formulation, since the texts that verify it are all Ushan in origin.

102. Cf. Lieberman, *Hellenism*, pp. 164-179, for a discussion of the treasury functions of the Temple and how such activity compared to practice throughout the Greco-Roman world.

103. Drying was, of course, possible, turning the grapes into raisins.

104. Zeev Safrai, *The Economy of Roman Palestine* (New York: Routledge, 1994), pp. 104-136, especially pp. 126-136. See also Jack Pastor, *Land and Economy in Ancient Palestine* (London: Routledge, 1997).

105. Cf. Safrai, *Economy*, p. 134, where he suggests that there were at least three distinct kinds of wine in Roman Palestine: wine made from fresh pressed grapes, wine made from raisins, and wine from the husks and stems of already pressed grapes.

106. For a description of *tamad*, consult M Dem. 1:1, and especially the commentaries of Rabbi Obadiah of Bartenura and Hanokh Albeck. Lieberman, relying on Sukenik, points out that *tamad* is a term that has been in use since the Second Temple period. Cf. *TK* 1:194, and E. L. Sukenik's original article, "משמעותן של הכתובות "למלך"," *Kedem* 1 (1942): 32-36.

107. Daniel Sperber, *Roman Palestine*, p. 41, suggests that we read this text another way: "descriptions of what went on in Judea often may indicate some miraculous happenings due to the extraordinary powers of the Temple." With this comment, he files this passage away in a list of exaggerated descriptions of larger-than-life Judean products. While we cannot dismiss the possibility that this text promotes such a hyperbolic outlook, it seems unlikely that the rabbis would present a change of Jewish law with significant potential fiscal ramifications if it were only predicated on a mere exaggeration.

108. M Maas. 5:6.

109. Cf. Rashbam to BT BB 97a, s.v. *hametammed*.

110. This explains Rabbi Yehuda's apparent contradiction: according to Rabbi Ilai's explanation of his view, the opinion he expresses in M Maas. is to be understood as after a famine in Palestine, when even the husks were considered food. Once this extra explanation is factored in, we see that the Mishnah represents an earlier stratum, and the *baraita* a later one.

111. The term *am haaretz* means, essentially, a person who is not strict with their tithes and ritual purity concerns. S/he would not have been included in the exclusive society of the rabbis, known as the *havurah*, and would have been subject to numerous restrictions when interacting with its membership. There is an enormous literature on this term, including the following early studies: Adolf Büchler, *Der Galiläsche 'Am-Ha'rets Des Zeiten Jahrhunderts* (Vienna: N.P., 1906); Solomon Zeitlin, "The Am Haarez," *JQR* (N.S.) 23 (1932): 45-61 and Aharon Oppenheimer, *The 'Am Ha-aretz* (Leiden: E.J. Brill, 1977), who refutes the prior two authors to provide the start of the understanding generally followed by more recent scholars. Recent studies germane to this topic include Stephen G. Wald, *Perek Elu Ovrin: Bavli Pesahim, Perek Shlishi* (New York and Jerusalem: Beit HaMidrash LaRabbanim Ba-Amerikah, 2000), where Wald dissects the various layers of the views contained within a long *sugya* from BT Pes. 49a-b; and a chapter from a forthcoming work graciously shared by Jeffrey L. Rubenstein in which he concludes that BT, unlike the other works in the corpus, expresses "a degree of contempt and disgust for non-rabbis that is completely unprecedented in other rabbinic works." He locates the source for this negative attitude in the Stammaitic layer, and attributes it to necessary acts that foster self-definition and self-justification—a hyperbolic expression of the core rabbinic ideology that places ultimate worth on Torah study.

112. Literary reshaping of *baraitot*, even to the point of creating entirely fictitious *baraitot*, appears to have been a tendency not uncommon for the editors of BT. The original proponent of this position was Isaac Hirsch Weiss in his דור דור ודרשיו (Jerusalem: Ziv, 1964), 2:242-244. Abraham Weiss disagreed in his לחקר התלמוד (New York: Feldheim, 1954), but Louis Jacobs maintains a position some-

where between the two Weisses in "Are There Fictitious Baraitot in the Babylonian Talmud?" *HUCA* 42 (1971), pp. 185-196. His conclusion, there, is that the "redactors did use fictitious baraitot for the purpose of literary device and as a pedagogical means" (p. 196). An important recent work that provides explicit examples of this tendency is Jeffrey L. Rubenstein's *Talmudic Stories*, especially pp. 261-264, where he shows that some purportedly Tannaitic sections written in Hebrew actually originate in Amoraic, Aramaic sections that predate them. The most recent study of Babylonian reworkings of prior material is Shamma Friedman's "Uncovering Literary Dependencies in the Talmudic Corpus" in Shaye J.D. Cohen's *The Synoptic Problem in Rabbinic Literature* (Providence: Brown Judaic Studies, 2000), pp. 35-57, where Friedman argues for the acceptance of the idea of edited parallels, rather than independent parallels. His theory would suggest that this particular *baraita* was reshaped from its earlier version close to its T manifestation to the later version we see in BT.

113. The 16 cases and 9 parallels are: T Peah 4:6 (parallel to BT Ket. 25a and T Ket. 3:1); T Eruv. 5:2 (parallel to PT Eruv. 5:6, 22d); T Sot. 15:7 (parallel to PT Sotah 9:12, 24b); T Git. 1:1; T BK 8:16-17 (parallel to BT BK 81b); T San. 7:1 (parallel to PT San. 1:4, 19c); T Oho. 18:15; PT Dem. 2:1, 22d; PT Shev. 4:2, 35a (parallel to PT San. 3:5, 21b); PT MS 5:5, 56d (PT Sotah 9:11, 24a); PT Pes. 1:1, 27b; PT Yoma 1:1, 38c; PT MK 3:7, 83b; PT Ket. 1:5, 25c (parallel to PT Git. 5:7, 47b); PT Git. 1:1, 43b; and PT San. 1:2, 19a.

114. For a provocative recent view on the weakness of rabbinic leadership and the effects of the Christianization of the Roman Empire on Palestine in the second through fifth centuries, see Seth Schwartz's book, *Imperialism and Jewish Society: 200 B.C.E. - 640 C.E.* (Princeton: Princeton University Press, 2001). His work relies on both documentary and archaeological evidence to show that rabbis and patriarchs were far less powerful than rabbinic texts tend to suggest, especially in light of the way that recent scholars have read them. His most stunning conclusion is that factors including the centralization of Roman rule and its subsequent Christianization actually propelled an explosion of Jewish life, contrary to the generally accepted viewpoint that these processes led to decline.

115. Contrary to Seth Schwartz above, see Joshua Schwartz, "Tension Between Palestinian Scholars and Babylonian Olim in Amoraic Palestine," *JSJ* 11 (1980), pp. 78-94. Joshua Schwartz argues that growing Babylonian prosperity, the perceived abandonment of Palestinian families by those emigrating westward and new, distinctive Babylonian customs all led to enmity between the two communities during the Amoraic period. All of these are signs of the waning influence of the Palestinian rabbis and the ascent of the Babylonians.

116. Any area outside the land of Israel is generally referred to as *medinat hayam* ("a state of the sea") in this tractate. According to Albeck's interpretation of M Git. 1:1, *medinat hayam* includes land beyond the western border of the land of Israel (thus the reference to the sea), but comes to mean any land beyond Israel. Cf. Albeck, *Mishnah, Nashim*, pp. 268, 273. See also *Korban HaEdah* and *Penei Moshe* to PT Git. 1:1, 43b, which agree that *medinat hayam* included all areas outside Israel, thus, most importantly, Babylonia.

117. This refers to the very first words of this *halakhah* in PT. In this initial *sugya*, the opinion is stated that *gittin* are different from other writs, in that they require a messenger bringing them from foreign lands to say the formula, "it was written before me and sealed before me." This is not required with other types of writs, and Rabbi Yehoshua ben Levi explains in the text that this is because the people of foreign lands were not experts in the exact regulations of divorce documents.

118. In the case that Rabbi Yehoshua ben Levi was then adjudicating.

119. The *havraya* are best defined by Lee Levine: "a group centered in Tiberias and known as 'the Sages.' Flourishing during the same period as the 'Rabbis of Caesarea,' from the mid-third to the mid-fourth centuries, these rabbis quoted R. Johanan and R. Shimeon ben Lakish, and discussed legal questions...They apparently functioned as a group . . . several members of this rabbinical association are mentioned by name: R. Hanania, R. Abimi and Oshaia the younger. Such guild-like associations were, however, a passing phenomenon in the history of rabbinism, partly a reflection of contemporary society, partly a residue of Second Temple sectarian roots." Lee I. Levine, *Caesarea Under Roman Rule* (Leiden: E.J. Brill, 1975), p. 97. Cf., also, Reuven Kimelman, *Rabbi Yohanan of Tiberias: Aspects of the Social and Religious History of Third Century Palestine* (New Haven: Dissertation, Yale, 1977), pp. 137-9. Kimelman adds that the students of Rabbi Yohanan formed the major part of this fellowship. He explains that the name *havraya* is based on the expression *havirei Torah*, or "fellowship of Torah." In contrast with Levine who called this grouping a rabbinical association, Kimelman concludes that this association was a collection of rabbinic apprentices—unordained and still in training.

120. It is interesting to note an opinion of Rava presented in BT Git. 2a that also implied concern over the abilities of those rabbinic authorities outside the land of Israel with respect to the precise terms of divorce law. The difference is, however, that BT's concern is a far more limited one: whether the authority that presided over the writing of the *get* understood that *gittin* were written for a specific woman alone. No wholesale discarding of authorities outside Palestine takes place in the same way we see in PT's version. Nor does the text deploy the term *barishonah* to indicate legal change in the same way.

121. Strack and Stemberger, *Introduction*, pp. 92-3.

122. Levine, *Caesarea*, p. 89, dates the *havraya* to no earlier than 250 CE, the date of the death of Rabbi Hoshaya I, when the seat of rabbinic power transferred from Caesarea to Tiberias. The precipitating event for this exodus was, most likely, Decius' persecution of the Caesarean Christian Church and the subsequent pagan revival, which probably led to a significant evacuation of sages from the beleaguered city of Caesarea. Tiberias provided somewhat of a respite, far from the Caesarean seat of Roman rule in Palestine. The *terminus ad quem* for this passage, however, is most likely during the lifetime of Rabbi Yehoshua ben Levi, since his statement is the initial gambit in the discussion. If Levine and the dating in the passage are both correct (which is hard to say with any certainty), this suggests a tentative dating of events in this passage no later than the early 4th century, *circa* 300 CE.

123. Strack and Stemberger, *Introduction*, pp. 14-15.

124. This second definition is less likely, since the plural form, *talmidei hakhamim*, suggests that this term is *smikhut* (a construct form), as opposed to a noun with a following adjective.

125. Cf. Aharon Oppenheimer, *The 'Am Ha-aretz*, pp. 170-199; Catherine Hezser, *The Social Structure of the Rabbinic Movement in Roman Palestine* (Tübingen: Mohr Siebeck, 1997), pp. 78-93 and 332-352; Louis Ginzberg, *Students, Scholars, and Saints* (Lanham, MD: University Press of America, 1985), pp. 35-58; Robert Kirschner, "*Imitatio Rabbini*" *JJS* 17 (1986), pp. 70-9; Jacob Neusner, *Talmudic Judaism in Sassanian Babylonia* (Leiden: E.J. Brill, 1976), pp. 46-135; and *idem, Contemporary Judaic Fellowship in Theory and in Practice* (New York: Ktav, 1972), pp. 13-30; Gedaliah Alon, *The Jews in Their Land in the Talmudic Age* (Jerusalem: Magnes Press, 1984), pp. 479-514; Ephraim E. Urbach, *The Sages* (Jerusalem: Magnes Press, 1975), pp. 620-30; and Richard Kalmin, *The Sage in Jewish Society of Late Antiquity* (New York: Routledge, 1999) among numerous others.

126. Two major commentators to PT dispute the meaning of this odd phrase: the *Penei Moshe* suggests that this implies one who has studied enough *halakhot* that he understands how they are derived from the Torah. The *Korban HaEdah* suggests we follow its variant reading of the text, which states: הלכות בכל יום ועוד תורה כל ששונה "all who study *halakhot* each day, and more Torah." The *Korban HaEdah* goes on to interpret that, in addition to being expert in *halakhot* through regular study, he must also be an expert in Torah. David Weiss Halivni, in his *Midrash, Mishnah and Gemara* (Cambridge: Harvard University Press, 1986), pp. 19-21 and nn. 17-20, strongly countermands the claim of Lauterbach that this passage represents early evidence for the development of the midrashic form, chiding Lauterbach for his neglect of Ms. Leiden's reading of ועוד תורה and the profusion of *rishonim* who prefer this reading. Taking this as a possibility, it may be that the text here implies that a *talmid hakham* must serve as a living witness to Torah. Given the rest of the literary structure of the passage, though, this seems less likely than the reading selected above, even if it is a more poetic choice.

127. There are two ways to read this *baraita*: alone, it seems to suggest that a *talmid hakham* is anyone who is questioned by another about Jewish law, who has some ability to answer questions. When read in conjunction with the statement of Rabbi Hoshaya that follows it, though, it appears that a *talmid hakham* is an authority in that he is questioned by others, but not the final authority, in that he has another authority who supervises him. The latter reading is more in keeping with the rest of the material in PT here, as well as with the explanation of the *Penei Moshe* (*ad loc.*).

128. Literally, this could mean "explain his Mishnah," or "explain his study." Lee Levine suggests the latter translation in his *The Rabbinic Class of Roman Palestine in Late Antiquity*, (New York: Jewish Theological Seminary, 1989), p. 43, n. 1. The *Penei Moshe* suggests that this is the "way of modesty," saying that by the time this text was written, the generation involved did not have the ability to fully explain what it was studying to an ignorant person. This may reflect either a lack of teaching prowess or an underwhelming knowledge when compared to prior generations.

129. This difficult clause can either suggest that the rabbis themselves were not sufficiently knowledgeable to explain the Mishnah, or, potentially, that the students were not up to the task. Here, it is translated according to the former interpretation.

130. Hezekiah and Yehuda were the two sons of Rabbi Hiyya, who came with their father from Babylonia to Palestine, living in Tiberias and working in the silk trade at the very end of the Tannaitic period, in the early third century.

131. Strack and Stemberger, *Introduction*, p. 98 on Rabbi Abbahu and p. 95 on Rabbi Yohanan. For more detailed studies of the lives of these two prominent rabbis, see Lee Levine, "Rabbi Abbahu of Caesarea," in *Christianity, Judaism and Other Greco-Roman Cults: Studies for Morton Smith at Sixty* 4 (Leiden: E.J. Brill, 1975), pp. 56-76 and Kimelman, *Yohanan*.

132. Here it is prudent to suggest a slight emendation of the text: though Hoshaya is not ordained, in our text he is referred to as Rabbi Hoshaya. Since the majority of the statements in this pericope are from students of Rabbi Yohanan, it is logical to assume that this gloss comes from Hoshaya II, who was not ordained a rabbi, according to the information we have about him. It is not, however, entirely possible to rule out the prospect that the gloss on this *baraita* came from the earlier (and far more prominent) Rabbi Hoshaya I Rabba, a key figure in Caesarean Jewry, *fl.* 230-250 CE. The content of the gloss and the other rabbis cited all point to its author as Hoshaya II, who may well have experienced supervision by other authorities that Hoshaya I would not have warranted.

133. Strack and Stemberger, *Introduction*, p. 100. Hoshaya II was usually known as Oshaya in BT.

134. Strack and Stemberger, *Introduction*, p. 100.

135. Cf., for example, 1QWords of Moses 4.9 and 11QTemplea 15.18, where hands are laid upon sacrifices. The healing incident occurs in 1QGenesis Apocryphon 20.22-29.

136. Lawrence A. Hoffman, "The Origins of Ordination," *CCAR Yearbook* 90 (1982), 71-94, especially pp. 73-75, shows that Tannaitic sources do not utilize the word *semikhah* in their appointment of religious leadership. Hezser, *Social Structure*, pp. 78-93, provides a good summary of the relevant sources and concepts associated with the appointment of rabbinic leadership. Cf. Hanokh Albeck, "סמיכה ומינוי ובית דין" *Zion* 8 (1943), 85-93 for a more detailed treatment of some relevant citations.

137. BT San. 3b suggests that Rabbi Yehuda's reasoning is based on his understanding of Lev. 4:15, where the elders lay their hands on the sacrifice. Rabbi Yehuda reasons that since "elders" is plural, that implies two judges, and since "shall lay their hands" is also plural, that implies another two judges. Since one may not have an even *beit din* (since it could become deadlocked) one more judge joins in, leaving a total of five.

138. Note here that Rabbi Yehuda HaNasi provides a logical explanation (as opposed to the biblical justification mentioned in BT San. 3b) for the reasoning behind having five initial judges: if five start out, and the *beit din* is split, there will be at least three judges responsible for any decision that arises.

139. See Lieberman, *TK* 5:1300, lines 68-9, for a discussion of the use of the word *semikhah* in the Tosefta. Cf. the notes of Hanokh Albeck, *Mishnah Moed*, p. 511. Both disagree on the exact meaning of this term, but neither ventures to tie it to the appointment of leadership.

140. This reflects a certain outlook: among Palestinian Amoraim, generally, the verb employed for appointments to communal office was the root מנה. Corroborative evidence is available in Hezser, *Social Structure*, p. 87. *Minnui* does not, in any way, imply the laying on of hands, as the verb *samakh* may.

141. The *Penei Moshe* explained this interaction in the following way: Rabbi Meir was older than Rabbi Shimeon, but Shimeon was more talented in his understanding of Jewish law. When Meir sat as a judge first, Shimeon grew angry that Meir had been recognized first, despite Shimeon's greater abilities. Akiba chastised Shimeon, saying

that Akiba and God both knew that he surpassed Meir in wisdom, and that should have been enough for him. Due to Meir's age, he was installed as a judge prior to Shimeon to avoid embarrassing him. The twin priorities of talent and honor are thus reconciled here.

142. חזרו, "they went back," is terminology that implies that the rabbis involved re-examined their prior position and revised it.

143. Hoffman, "Origins," pp. 76-77. Hoffman calls the three periods Personal (before some date in the range of 135-200 CE), Centralization (from that date to sometime in the third century) and Compromise (commencing after that latter date in the third century), based on the definitions supplied in the text at hand.

144. Jacob Neusner, *Development of a Legend: Studies on the Traditions Concerning Yohanan ben Zakkai* (Leiden: E.J. Brill, 1970), p. 138. Cf. Hoffman, "Origins," pp. 76-77 as well.

145. Strack and Stemberger, *Introduction*, p. 100.

146. Schwartz, *Imperialism*, pp. 103-128.

147. Cf. Lawrence H. Schiffman, "Samaritans in Tannaitic Halakhah," *JQR* 75 (April, 1985), pp. 323-50, especially 323-5 and 349-50, for a review of the Tannaitic material on the origin of the Samaritan schism. A complementary study that corroborates Schiffman's findings through study of non-rabbinic evidence is Alan D. Crown's "Redating the Schism between the Judaeans and the Samaritans," *JQR* 82 (July-October , 1991), pp. 17-50. Other major studies on this topic include R.J. Coggins, *Samaritans and Jews* (John Knox Press: Atlanta, 1975); James D. Purvis, "The Samaritans," in W.D. Davies and Louis Finkelstein, eds., *Cambridge History of Judaism Volume II* (Cambridge: Cambridge University Press, 1989), pp. 591-613; *idem,* "The Samaritans and Judaism" in Robert Kraft and George W.E. Nickselburg, eds., *Early Judaism and its Modern Interpreters* (Atlanta: Scholars Press, 1986), pp. 81-98; and Alan D. Crown, *The Samaritans* (Tübingen: JCB Mohr, 1989).

148. Many parallels exist for this text, though, interestingly, none of them uses the *barishonah* construct. Cf. T Pes. 2:1-3; BT Kid. 76a; BT Hul. 4a and BT Git. 10a. Toseftan manuscripts have one difference worth noting: in place of מדקדקין, "more exacting," two manuscripts (Ms. London and Genizah fragments) have בקיאין, "more expert," implying that the Samaritans had more knowledge about certain commandments.

149. According to the interpretation of the *Korban HaEdah, ad loc.*

150. The parallel text in BT Hul. 10a suggests that the commandments that were best observed by the Samaritans were those that were fully explained in the written Torah, a very sensible position given the ideology of the Samaritans.

151. Schiffman, "Samaritans," pp. 348-50.

152. Crown, "Redating the Schism," pp. 38-50.

153. The biblical *locus classicus* may be found in Leviticus 25:1-8.

154. Most opinions hold that there was no observance of the agricultural aspect of the Sabbatical Year in Babylonia. This text, then, represents the rabbis of Babylonia helping to understand this practice in Palestine. On the other hand, the more unlikely idea that the Babylonians actually practiced the Sabbatical Year is suggested by the reading of Shlomo Sirillo, *ad loc.*, as printed in Kalman Kahana, ed., *Masekhet Sheviit* I (Benei Brak: Lipa Freedman Press, 1972), p. 93.

155. Here, the printed edition has: חד משמד הוה אני עבר חמייתון דמיין קובעתה, which makes little sense. A parallel from PT San. 3:5, 21b has: חד משומד הוה איעבר חמתון רמיין קובעתיה, which is helpful in resolving the puzzling word אני in the printed edition. This is a very difficult phrase, with three possible meanings based on different textual witnesses: it can mean either "a guard passed" (according to Ms. Leiden), "an apostate passed" (according to the printed edition) or "an evil one passed" (as suggested by the *Penei Moshe*). What unites these readings is that all indicate someone outside the accepted Jewish community passed by and made this comment. Yehuda Feliks, in his critical edition, תלמוד ירושלמי מסכת שביעית (1979, ירושלים: אות-צור-הוצאת), p. 1:288, suggests that we must read this text as "one apostate was passing," which seems to be the best of the possibilities. Beyond that, certainty is difficult.

156. Cf. Strack and Stemberger, *Introduction*, p. 106.

157. Strack and Stemberger, *Introduction*, p. 91-2, and cf. Oppenheimer, *The 'Am Ha'aretz* (Leiden: E.J.Brill, 1977), pp. 190-191.

158. *Penei Moshe* to PT Shevi. 4:2, 35a, s.v. חד משומד.

159. Jastrow, *Dictionary*, p. 328, notes the Samaritan origin of this term, similar to the Aramaic root סטי, "to go astray" or "leave the right path." Sokoloff, *Dictionary*, p. 158, suggests that it arose from the Aramaic הא, "this," combined with the Greek "'έστω," meaning "be it!"—a sort of bilingual exclamation meaning "so be it!"

160. See Christine E. Hayes, "Displaced Self-Perceptions: The Deployment of *Minim* and Romans in B. Sanhedrin 90b-91a," pp. 249-289 in Hayim Lapin, *Religious and Ethnic Communities in Later Roman Palestine* (Bethesda: University Press of Maryland, 1998). In this article, Hayes explored the role of the non-Jew as a projection of certain Jewish exegetical and ambivalent philosophic tendencies. A similar pattern may well be at work here.

161. The citations are: M Shevi. 4:1 (parallel to T Shevi. 3:8 and PT Shevi. 4:1, 35a); M. Shek. 1:2 (parallel to BT MK 6a-b and PT Shek. 1:2, 46a); M Bekh. 1:3 (parallel to BT Yev. 39b); T Shevi. 3:9; T MS 4:3; T BM 2:16-17 (parallel to BT BM 28b, PT BM 2:6, 8c and *Mtan Devarim* 22:2); T San. 7:1 (parallel to PT Hag. 2:2, 77d and PT San. 1:4, 19c); BT Kid. 71a (parallel to PT Yoma 3:7, 40d); PT Dem. 3:3, 23c (parallel to PT AZ 1:8, 40a); and PT Ter. 2:2, 41c.

162. Levirate marriage has been shown to exist in Ugarit, and is also present in the Middle Assyrian and Hittite law codes, and possibly in the Nuzi texts. The primary concern, in all these texts, is with producing a male child to carry on the name of the deceased husband. See "Marriage (OT and ANE)," *ABD* 4:567, and the bibliography there for the sources that support this statement.

163. Jeffrey H. Tigay, *Deuteronomy: The Traditional Hebrew Text with the New JPS Translation/Commentary* (Philadelphia: Jewish Publication Society, 1996), pp. 482-3, points out examples in Hittite and Middle Assyrian laws that are parallel to Deut. 25, with some differences. For example, in the Hittite legal system, the presence of children is immaterial to the obligation to the widow. In Middle Assyrian laws, the father of the deceased may marry the widow instead of his brother.

164. Frankel, *Darkhei HaMishnah*, p. 314, points out that the editor of this mishnah grouped these three laws together here because of similarities in style, and not content. Since each of these laws provides choice in its observance, it is sensible to group them in

one mishnah. Note that there is no thematic linkage among the laws at all: sacrifice, levirate marriage and betrothing a handmaid are all otherwise unrelated, and the latter two would not belong in this tractate of M at all. See Yaakov Nahum Epstein, *Mevo'ot LeSifrut HaTannaim* (Jerusalem: Magnes Press, 1957), p. 453.

165. Cf. Lieberman, *TK* 5:1203, where he justifies this reading of the text.

166. Note that the biblical order is the determinant here: since the redemption is mentioned first, the Rabbis assume that it is the preferable *mitzvah*.

167. Cf. Rabbi Obadiah of Bartenura on this mishnah, *s.v.* בראשונה.

168. BT Ket. 64a.

169. Many *rishonim* and *aharonim* note that Sura preferred *yiboom*, while Pumbedita and Nehardea both inclined toward *halitzah*. Cf. Shmuel Kalman Mirsky, ed., שאילתות דרב אחאי גען (Jerusalem: Slomin, 1977), Deut., pp. 37-40 (*sheilta* 172 in the clarifications and notes section) for a full list of citations on this issue in the *rishonim* and *aharonim*. For the later history of the development of this issue, see Jacob Katz, *Divine Law in Human Hands* (Jerusalem: Magnes Press, 1998), pp. 45-49.

170. This can mean either that he marries her for the sake of being married itself, for the sake of some change in his status in society or for the very fact of wanting a wife and loving her. Normally, marrying the widow of your deceased brother would be considered forbidden, except when accomplished in the process of a valid *yiboom*. Once done for any other reason, it is a violation of the laws of consanguinity.

171. Here it was probably sexual attraction, or another similar sort of ulterior motive, that might urge him on to levirate marriage for less than sacred reasons.

172. A *mamzer* is the offspring of an adulterous or consanguineous relationship who would not be allowed to marry within the Jewish community, except to another of the same diminished status.

173. Even if an ulterior motive is the motivating factor—here the Sages appear to favor the following of the commandment with the preferences expressed in the biblical text.

174. Strack and Stemberger, *Introduction*, p. 105.

175. Sociological change is the term used by Joel Roth in reference to this passage. Cf. Joel Roth, *The Halakhic Process* (New York: Jewish Theological Seminary of America, 1986), pp. 249-51.

176. For a complete study of this concept in rabbinic literature, consult Menachem Kellner, *Maimonides on the "Decline of the Generations" and the Nature of Rabbinic Authority,* (Albany: SUNY Press, 1996), especially pp. 1-26.

177. Hayes, "Abrogation," p. 663, where Hayes confirms this tendency in the *takkanot* she studied. Further, cf. Abraham Goldberg, "התפתחות הסוגיא בתלמוד הבבלי" in *Memorial Volume for Rabbi Hanokh Albeck* (Jerusalem: Mossad HaRav Kook, 1963), pp. 101-113, where Goldberg shows that this is also present among *gezerot*.

178. Cf. Lieberman, *TK* 8:746, where he cites a manuscript of Rashi to BT Men. 109b explaining that the practice of the priests' using God's name stopped so that the common people would not hear it and misuse it. This interpretation is, doubtless, based upon Rashi's knowledge of the two pericopae cited from BT and PT.

179. Literally: "wild ones" or "ones who break out"

180. Here, the meaning of this word is that the high priest spoke the name in such a way as to prevent others from hearing it amongst the chant of the other priests.

181. The *dukhan* was the platform upon which the priests stood when they blessed the people, using the sacred name of God.

182. The story relating to Shmuel recited here comes in an Aramaic stratum, and thus is most likely later than the preceding Hebrew material.

183. Cf. Urbach, *The Sages*, pp. 124-134 for a discussion of the power of divine names.

184. This is certainly in keeping with the rabbinic concept of *yeridat hadorot* ("the diminution of the generations"), which suggests that each successive generation experiences lower levels of knowledge, insight and wisdom. Cf. Kellner, *op. cit.*

185. M MS 5:7; M Ned. 9:6; T Pes. 1:7; T MK 2:10; and T MK 2:13-16.

186. To my knowledge, Zecharias Frankel was the first to have noticed this tendency in citations about Rabbi Akiba, cf. Frankel, *Darkhei HaMishnah*, p. 125: "Rabbi Akiva relied upon his breadth of knowledge to instruct leniently against what the earlier authorities instructed or the accepted strict customary behavior that existed until his day."

187. Epstein, *Sifrut HaTannaim*, pp. 71-76.

188. Cf. Hanokh Albeck, *Mavo LaMishnah* (Jerusalem: Bialik, 1943), p. 75, n. 15.

189. T Naz. 5:1 (paralleled by T Oho. 4:13 and PT Naz. 7:2, 56c); T San. 2:10-13 (parallel to T Ed. 3:1, PT Peah 5:1, 18d and PT Shek. 1:2, 46a); BT Ket. 82b; and BT Nid. 31a.

190. The only parallel to this text, BT Ned. 18a, merely cites this mishnah, providing no additional information.

191. Cf. M Ta. 2:10, 4:3, 4:7, and also *MegTa*, on p. 333 in Hans Lichtenstein, "Die Fastenrolle: Eine Untersuchung Zur Jüdisch-Hellenistischen Geschichte," *HUCA* 8-9 (1931-2), pp. 257-351.

192. In M Ned. 3:2, Beit Hillel and Beit Shammai argue over a vow made mistakenly by the owner of a fig tree who approached his property from a distance to find unknown persons eating his figs. He vows that the figs are forbidden to them, and only upon reaching the tree does he realize that his father and brothers are among the party consuming his property. Since he never intended that his father and brothers be prohibited from eating the figs, a part of the vow is invalid. Beit Shammai decide that the vow on the rest of the party at the tree stands, while Beit Hillel affirms that any vow in which a part has been invalidated is entirely void.

193. Cf. T Ned. 5:1, the *baraita* attributed to Rabbi Natan in PT Ned. 9:6, 41c and BT Ned. 26b for parallels.

194. The Zuckermandl printed edition, and its primary text, Ms. Erfurt, both lack the mention of Rabbi Akiba in this *halakhah*. Lieberman includes it in his text because of its presence in Ms. Vienna. Cf. Lieberman, *TK* 5:1261.

195. The printed version of the BT parallel (BT Pes. 51a) has Rabban Shimeon ben Gamaliel as the protagonist in this story. All other versions of the text (all manuscripts of T and PT, and every manuscript of BT) show Rabban Gamaliel himself. This odd misattribution in the printed edition of BT entirely puzzles the editor of *Dikduke Sofrim*, see his words *ad loc.*

196. בשלמא ספסלי נכרים - משום דמחזי כמקח וממכר

197. Aharon Oppenheimer, *HaGalil BeTekufat HaMishnah* (Jerusalem: The Zalman Shazar Center, 1991), p. 121, points out that this is one of a number of occasions when the Galileans correct members of the patriarch's house as to proper Galilean observance. In all cases, the patriarch or his representative acceded to the local custom.

198. Unless we accept BT's printed edition as the correct text, in which case the protagonist was Rabban Shimeon ben Gamaliel, there is a chronological problem here. Unfortunately, BT's printed edition is the sole witness to this version, and it does not even appear in BT's manuscripts. Furthermore, all parallel texts refer to Rabban Gamaliel, ultimately proving this to be a very unlikely reading. Thus, we are stuck with a certain level of anachronism in this passage.

199. The text as cited here removes two other examples that intervene in the discussion. They are not relevant to ours.

200. The verb used here, לעז, means "to cast suspicion upon," or "to discredit." It is possible that people were spreading tales that emphasized this action as discrediting Rabban Gamaliel. It is also possible that this word is mistaken for another Hebrew verb, לעג, "to mock." Though there are no manuscripts to support this emendation, it does appear to be a strong possibility for a probable alternate reading, and it is followed in the translation above.

201. For a discussion of Akiba's significant role as "father" of M, see Shmuel Safari, *The Literature of the Sages* (Philadelphia: Fortress Press, 1987), pp. 215-222. See, also, Albert I. Baumgarten's article on the Akiban School as challenger to the Hillelite patriarchs—this may have been a factor in the publication of these opinions in Akiba's name. Cf. A.I. Baumgarten, "The Akiban Opposition," *HUCA* 50 (1979), pp. 179-197.

202. The sources are: M Suk. 3:12 (paralleled by M RH 4:3); M RH 4:3 (a second example); M RH 4:4; T Ket. 9:5-6; T Ned. 4:7; BT RH 21b and the example to be covered here: T BM 2:16-17 (paralleled by BT BM 28b, PT BM 2:6, 8c and *Mtan* to Deut. 22:2).

203. See Lawrence H. Schiffman, *Sectarian Law in the Dead Sea Scrolls* (Chico, CA: Scholars Press, 1983), pp. 111-123 for the relevant texts and his interpretation.

204. Hoffmann, *Mishnah Rishonah*, p. 43.

205. סימנים (*simanim*, "signs") are the specifics of a lost item—details so particular as to be useful in distinguishing the object at hand from others like it. Examples might include the particular markings on an animal, patterns, rips or other identifying marks on a garment, or any other irreproducible marks that create a unique identity for a material object.

206. This term often refers to Hadrian's persecutions connected to the Bar Kokhba revolt.

207. Cf. Urbach, *The Halakhah*, p. 13, for his analysis of this text.

208. Cf. BT BM 28b, where there is a *baraita* describing a stone where lost and found items were kept. While there is no specific reference to it in T BM 2:16-17, this passage illuminates both the process and the potential place considered in a contemporary rabbinic text:

> Our rabbis taught: There was stone of claims in Jerusalem. Anyone who lost something would turn there, and anyone who found something would turn there. This one would stand and announce [what had been found], and this

one would stand and give its specific details and take it. And this is in accordance with what we taught: "go and see if the stone of claims is covered."
The concluding quotation of this section is from BT Ta. 19a, the story of Honi the Cir-
clemaker, where Honi gauges the amount of rain that has fallen by whether it has covered
the stone of claims. From this story we can learn two characteristics of this stone: it was a
well-known geographic marker, and it must have been on relatively high ground for the
story to make sense. M itself, however, has: אבן הטועים.

209. This also accords with our conclusions in the previous section of this chapter
on Changes in the Behavior of the People, above.

210. E. Mary Smallwood, *The Jews Under Roman Rule* (Boston: Brill Academic
Publishers, repr. 2001), pp. 457-469.

211. E.S. Rosenthal, ירושלמי נזיקין (Jerusalem: Israel Academy of Sciences and Humanities, 1983), pp. 136-7.

212. A number of manuscripts and the printed version add "and his acquaintances"
to the list of those notified. Cf. Rabbinovicz, *Dikduke Sofrim, ad loc.* Following Ms. Munich and the majority of others, the text and translation above leave this out.

213. Cf. Lee Levine, *Ancient Synagogues Revealed* (Detroit: Wayne State University Press, 1982), especially the section on synagogues of the Diaspora, for comparisons
between Palestinian and Babylonian synagogues and their relative importance to each
community during this period. Isaiah Gafni, in his "Synagogues in Babylonia in the Talmudic Period," in Dan Urman and Paul V.M. Flesher, eds., *Ancient Synagogues* (Leiden:
E.J. Brill, 1995), pp. 220-231, suggests that Babylonian synagogues had a far more limited practical role, and were seen mostly as places of prayer, linked to the Temple. Steven
Fine disagrees in his book, *This Holy Place* (Notre Dame: University of Notre Dame
Press, 1997), especially pp. 95-158, where he asserts that Palestinian and Babylonian
synagogues had similar levels of sanctity in their respective communities.

214. Strack and Stemberger, Introduction, p. 98.

215. Cf. Buckland *Text-Book of Roman Law*, especially pp. 206-7 on *Occupatio* and
pp. 218-9 on *Thesauri Inventio*, two Roman legal concepts that apply to lost property. In
neither case is the property transferred to the realm in the way the Gemara suggests is
typical of Persian legal procedures, so the Gemara may well have a correct understanding
of the Roman law in this case. However, Sohrab Jamshedjee Bulsara's *The Laws of the
Ancient Persians As Found in the* "Mâtîkân Ê Hazâr Dâtastân" (Bombay: Hoshang T.
Anklesaria, 1937), pp. 430-2, does not support the Gemara's understanding of Persian
law. In this Persian legal text from the Sassanian period, we find: "it has been written in a
place that when a property that is not such as has been purchased (by the man) for a value
or has been given to him as a gift, happens to belong to him under any circumstance,
then, notwithstanding that, it can be sold by him (or) pass (to another) as gift (from
him)." Such a statement flies in the face of Persian royalty exerting ownership rights over
all lost property. It is difficult to say whether this later law code represents Persian law as
it was actually practiced in an earlier period, so the ultimate answer remains unattainable
from the sources we have.

216. There are two other parallel texts to be found in PT BM 2:6, 8c and *Mtan* 22:2,
though they add little to the discussion. The only interesting factor in PT BM 2:6, 8c, is
that it presents a three day waiting period, most likely a scribal error. See also Lieberman,
TK 9:161-2.

217. This is not a singularity in rabbinic literature. See also the series of negative events listed in M Sot. 9:9-15 that led to major changes.

218. The citations are: M Bik. 3:7 (paralleled by *SD* 301 and *Mtan* to Deut. 26:5); T Yev. 12:15 (paralleled by PT San. 1:2, 19a); T Nid. 9:16-8 (paralleled by BT MK 27a-b, BT Ket. 8b-9a and BT Nid. 71a); and BT San. 19a (paralleled by PT Ber. 3:2, 6b and PT San. 2:2, 20a).

219. William V. Harris, *Ancient Literacy* (Cambridge: Harvard University Press, 1989), p. 13.

220. Harris, *op. cit.*, p. 328.

221. Meir Bar-Ilan, "Illiteracy in the Land of Israel in the First Centuries C.E.," in Simcha Fishbane and Jack Lightstone, eds. *Essays in the Social Scientific Study of Judaism and Jewish Society II* (Hoboken: Ktav, 1992), p. 55.

222. Catherine Hezser, *Jewish Literacy in Roman Palestine* (Tübingen: Mohr Siebeck, 2001), pp. 496-503.

223. Most commentaries interpret this to mean that a literate individual (probably the priest involved) recited the statement, which the illiterate individual thereupon repeated word for word. See, for example, Albeck, *Mishnah, Zeraim*, p. 320.

224. Urbach, *The Halakhah*, p. 11.

225. Text from Louis Finkelstein, *Siphre ad Deuteronomium H.S. Horovitzii schedis usis cum variis lectionibus et ad notationibus* (New York: Jewish Theological Seminary Press, 1969), pp. 318-319.

226. The later text refers to the Levites, who speak on behalf of the people in Deut. 27:14, where the text says: וענו הלוים ואמרו אל כל איש ישראל קול רם. The use of the same root, לענות, is taken to imply that the agency of the Levites on behalf of the people in this verse authorizes the use of a similar agent as surrogate reader in the case of *bikkurim*.

227. The interpretation, here, is that this declaration must be in Hebrew, as opposed to the vernacular.

228. At least one manuscript omits the word בראשונה here. Cf. the critical apparatus in Finkelstein, *Siphre, ad loc.*

229. There is one other parallel: the reconstructed *Mtan* to Deut. 26:5, but the components present in this parallel are well represented in the texts we have already reviewed.

230. Josephus, *Against Appion*, 2:205. See David Kraemer's treatment of this and other Second Temple texts in his *The Meanings of Death in Rabbinic Judaism* (London: Routledge, 2000), pp. 14-23.

231. Rashi, discussing a parallel text quoted below from BT MK 27a, explains that this implies that immersion is required for those vessels touched by menstruating women before their death. Another possible reading is that the clothing they wore required immersion.

232. A fancy couch used to carry the body of a wealthy deceased person. This is furniture of a far higher caliber than the one used by the poor. Cf. BT San. 20a for the Gemara's definition.

233. A common wooden box, or coffin. While *dargesh* is relatively well attested, this text and its parallels represent the only attested usages of the word *klibah* as a coffin. In other citations it means simply "box."

234. In the street, so that the community would become responsible for the burial of their dead, thus saving the relatives the tremendous sums of money involved in burial during this early phase.

235. By being brought out to burial in modest dress, see the discussion below.

236. Rabban Gamaliel's actions help the rest of the community begin to utilize a new custom. This is not, in any sense of the word, *halakhah*, but it is a significant change in communal behavior attributed to the valiant actions of a patriarch.

237. Parallels to parts of this text exist in BT Ket. 8b and BT Nid. 71a.

238. No mention of pillows appears in the printed text, but it does appear in an early manuscript and Geonic witnesses such as the *Rif,* the *Sheiltot* and others. Cf. Rabbinovicz, *Dikduke Sofrim, ad loc.*

239. Wealthier families could afford to ensure that the signs of illness or starvation could be avoided either by better nutrition during their lives, or by covering up or removing them from the face by makeup applied after death. The poor had neither the resources nor the leisure time to ensure proper food in life, and certainly could not procure cosmetic help after death.

240. No mention of pillows appears in the printed text, but it does appear in an early manuscript and Geonic witnesses such as the *Rif,* the *Sheiltot* and others. Cf. Rabbinovicz, *Dikduke Sofrim, ad loc.*

241. Note the complete capitulation to the custom of the poor in this case.

242. In the brackets is an explanatory insertion found in the printed text, but not present in the manuscripts.

243. Here, too, is an explanatory insertion found in the printed text.

244. BT uses the word צרדא, a popular pronunciation of the Latin *sordida*, from which we derive the English word "sordid." Cf. Jastrow, *Dictionary*, s.v. צרדא.

245. Frankel, *Darkhei HaMishnah*, p. 60, identifies him as Rabban Gamaliel (I) the Elder. This would give us a likely provenance for this incident in the late first century CE in Yavneh.

246. Cohen, *Jewish and Roman Law*, p. 22.

247. S.P. Scott, *The Civil Law* (New York: AMS Press, 1973), pp. 74-6.

248. Cohen, *Jewish and Roman Law*, p. 22.

249. The four examples are: M Git. 4:2 (paralleled by T Git. 4:1, PT BB 10:4, 17c and BT Git. 32b); M Git. 4:2 (another example in this same mishnah); T Git. 4:4 (paralleled by BT Git. 53a and BT BK 117a); and BT Git. 36a.

250. Cf. Roth, *Halakhic Process*, pp. 273-279 for a review of the scope of this term.

251. Cf. Rachel Biale, *Women and Jewish Law* (New York: Schocken Books, 1984), chapter 2, for a summary of the relevant textual background.

252. Judith Hauptman, *Rereading the Rabbis* (Boulder, CO: Westview Press, 1998), pp. 102-127. See also Judith Romney Wegner, *Chattel or Person?* (Oxford: Oxford University Press, 1988), pp. 45-50.

253. Without a *get*, any future children she would have might be considered the offspring of adulterous sexual relations, known in Jewish tradition as *mamzerim*, who have reduced social status and limited marriage options for themselves and their offspring.

254. See Michael L. Satlow, *Jewish Marriage in Antiquity* (Princeton: Princeton University Press, 2001), p. 214, and the works he cites there.

255. Hauptman, *Rereading the Rabbis*, pp. 114-120.

256. Epstein, *Mavo LeNusah HaMishnah,* pp. 867 and 995, comments that this mishnah is found in a chain of mishnayot that revolve around actions taken for the sake of certain privileged values, including the support of those who have repented (*mipnei takkanat hashavim),* the ways of peace (*mipnei darkhei shalom*) and for the sake of repair/upkeep of the altar (*mipnei tikkun hamizbeah*). The editorial choice demonstrates the link these value-driven halakhic choices have in the mind of the editor of M. Alternatively, they may be collected together as a mnemonic device.

257. Two potential opinions of Resh Lakish appear in PT Git. 4:2, 45c, which bring up these two very real possibilities of *agunah* and *mamzerut.* In BT Git. 32b-33a, these appear in a discussion between Rabbi Yohanan and Resh Lakish.

258. For a modern-day analogue, consider the businessman (or worse, professor!) who travels often between the United States and Israel. In the U.S., he may be known by his American name of Isaac. When in Israel, for the sake of better relations with the local business community, he may be known by his Hebrew name of Yitzhak. This is certainly not an unimaginable scenario.

259. This was especially true in the rabbinic period, when the Romans constantly changed the names of cities and towns, naming them after the latest Emperor, and upgrading or lowering their status due to political concerns.

260. T Git. 4:1, in Ms. Erfurt.

261. Cf. Yitzhak Gilat, "בית דין מתנין לעקור דבר מן התורה" in *Annual of Bar-Ilan University* VII-VIII (1970): 117-132, especially pp. 119-20.

262. Ms. Munich and Mss. Vatican 139 and 140 have Rabban Shimeon ben Gamaliel as the enactor of this *takkanah.* Cf. Meyer S. Feldblum, *Dikduke Sofrim Masekhet Gittin* (New York: Horeb, 1966), *ad loc.*

263. Lieberman, *TK* 8:913.

264. See Ruth 4:7, as mentioned in the introduction to this chapter.

265. Cf. Goodenough, *Jewish Symbols,* where he argued that the laws against icons that are so pervasive in rabbinic literature are not upheld in actuality when one looks at the art present in the remains of synagogues in the region. One can be virtually certain that this concept would apply in all other areas of life in this period as well. For a more recent and comprehensively argued case, see Schwartz, *Imperialism,* who argues that rabbinic texts are not very worthwhile as a source of community history. Neusner, in his introduction to the third edition of his *History of the Jews of Babylonia* also puts to rest the notion of reading history from texts.

266. Schwartz, *Imperialism,* pp. 103-4.

267. Cf. Abraham Goldberg, "The Tosefta" in Safrai, *Literature of the Sages,* pp. 283-302. Some authorities, including Albeck, consider the Tosefta to be a much later work. However, scholarly consensus dates its origin to the mid- to late third century CE, as a closely associated add-on (thus the name *Tosefta*) and expansion of M.

268. This chart does not include those instances where *halakhah* becomes more lenient or stricter, where no rationales are stated.

269. In cases we are calling "enactor," the text reports that one individual scholar changed the law. Note that in cases where Rabbi Akiba teaches a new philosophical outlook, he is not counted as the "enactor."

270. The ideal of quoting statements in the name of their originator is cited in M Avot 6:6. There, it is said to be one of the practices that brings redemption to the world.

271. See Jacob Neusner, "The History of Earlier Rabbinic Judaism," *History of Religions* 16 (1977), pp. 216-36.

272. Note that Table 2 contains data for all occurrences of the use of the term *barishonah*, both with rationales and without.

273. It is possible that some Tannaitic texts are translated into Aramaic and inserted with Aramaic terms into BT, though this study did not find parallels that utilized that approach. A comprehensive study of Aramaic terms of legal change would be a valuable future endeavor.

274. David Kraemer, *Stylistic Characteristics of Amoraic Literature* (Ph.D. Dissertation: Jewish Theological Seminary, 1984).

275. Kraemer did not study occurrences in PT, thus the information here is limited to BT. Another useful measure of the relative size of the generations of scholars may be found in the estimates given in Lee I. Levine, *The Rabbinic Class of Roman Palestine in Late Antiquity* (New York: Jewish Theological Seminary of America, 1989), pp. 66-69. Since this does not provide accurate account of the number of occurrences in literature, but attempts to estimate the size of the population of scholars in general, it is only useful as collateral information, and will not be relied upon in this study.

Chapter Two

The Innovative Tendency: *Takkanot*

Introduction

The term *barishonah* points to a trend of reflection upon prior law that inspired reports of numerous significant legal changes throughout the rabbinic period. In chapters two and three, we will examine two other terms, more significant both in their frequency of occurrence and in their implications, which often serve as similar harbingers of change to that highlighted by the term *barishonah*.

In this chapter, we will explore the uses of the root תקן (*tikken* – "enacted"), and in the next, the root גזר (*gazar*, "decreed"). Each of these terms occurs hundreds of times in the corpus of rabbinic literature, encompassing a multiplicity of meanings that must be sorted carefully before one can fully understand the various nuances of halakhic change they signify. Both chapters will begin with a discussion of the semantic range of the pertinent root, followed by a review of the scholarly and traditional opinions on the meaning of the terms, then by a detailed discussion of a series of examples of usages related to various modes of legal change. The objective is to provide a complete examination of the halakhic change denoted by each root in the legal literature of the rabbinic period.

The Meanings of the Root תקן

The root תקן carries a tremendous semantic range. In the Bible, the root occurs only four times, three times in the Hebrew of Ecclesiastes and once in an Aramaic cognate in Daniel. In Ecclesiastes, we find two usages that reflect the meaning "to make straight," while the third shows a meaning more akin to "setting a literary form:"

Eccl. 1:15

מעות לא יוכל <u>לתקן</u>, וחסרון לא יוכל להמנות :

A twisted thing that cannot <u>be made straight</u>, a lack that cannot be made good...

<u>Eccl. 7:13</u>

ראה את מעשה האלהים! כי מי יוכל <u>לתקן</u> את אשר עותו!

Consider the work of God! For who can <u>set straight</u> what God has made crooked?

<u>Eccl. 12:9</u>

ויתר שהיה קהלת חכם עוד למד את דעת את העם ואזן וחקר <u>תקן</u> משלים
הרבה :

A further word: Because Kohelet was a sage, he continued to teach wisdom to the people. He listened to, investigated and <u>fixed</u>[276] [the literary form of] many maxims.

The earliest stratum of Hebrew usage appears to convey the sense of "to make straight," as we see in the first two occurrences in Ecclesiastes. This is the simplest of the meanings, and is found in direct apposition to a root with more frequent biblical appearances: עות, "to be bent, crooked." This antonym appears 11 times in the Bible, with occurrences in texts ranging from Amos and Psalms to Lamentations and Job.[277]

In the text from Daniel 4:33, we find the earliest Aramaic usage of the term:

ועל מלכותי <u>התקנת</u> ורבו יתירה הוסף לי.

And I was restored to my rule, and added greatness was given me.

In the Aramaic, as well, the root meaning appears to be connected to reestablishing the straightness of something that has gone crooked, in both a literal and figurative sense.

Brown *et al.* suggest that the meaning "to make straight" arises from the Assyrian root, *takânu*, which means "to be well ordered."[278] They also suggest that we look to the Wisdom of Ben Sira 47:9-10 for another early occurrence of this root:

(ט) נגינות שיר ל[פני מזבח ו[ק]ו]ל [מזמור בנבל]ים <u>תיקן</u> : (י) [נתן]
ל[חגים הדר <u>ויתקן</u> מועדים שנה בש]נה :

(9) Music of song [before the altar] and the voice of song <u>he set</u> with lutes; (10) He gave the festivals beauty, and <u>fixed</u> the seasons each year.[279]

Again, we find a usage similar to that of our last Ecclesiastes text: *tikken* here means to fix the form of a composition – in this case, an art song utilized in worship. Since verse 10 is so heavily restored, it is not wise to argue for "fixing seasons" as a possible early meaning, especially as it is not attributed elsewhere during this period. Ben Sira, then, provides an additional witness to the use of this verb in the first quarter of the second century BCE.[280]

This term, therefore, is a rather late starter when it comes to biblical literature: no occurrences appear in the Torah or the Prophets at all, and in Writings its appearances are limited to two of the very latest books. Ecclesiastes, with its late estimated date of composition during the third century BCE, shows the first attestation of this term in Jewish literature. The Book of Daniel, which reached its present form somewhere in the second century BCE, is an even later source.[281] Ben Sira, with its composition approximately cotemporaneous with Daniel, provides another source of proof for the emergence of this term. Thus, we can say with some confidence that this term has a late provenance, first arriving in our literary sources during the late third to early second century BCE.

Both Jastrow[282] and Sokoloff[283] suggest many possible meanings for the root and its derivatives within rabbinic literature and its antecedents. Combining their lists with our further research in rabbinic texts, we may delineate the following group of meanings for this family of words:

Meanings of the root תקן Appearing in Rabbinic Literature
a)   to make straight, firm, right; to mend, repair[284]
b)   to set in order, make ready, prepare[285]
c)   to make things legally fit for use by giving priestly dues[286]
d)   to make an arrangement or agreement[287]
e)   to place, arrange[288]
f)   to set, in a literary or morphological sense[289]
g)   to set the size of measures[290]
h)   to establish, institute, introduce a legal measure, ordain, decree, reform

A few of the many examples of each of these meanings are cited in the notes below, excluding the final meaning listed, for it will constitute the main focus of this chapter.

One interesting fact to note at the start of our discussion is the total number of occurrences of this term compared to the number of usages related to the final meaning (meaning "h") listed above:

Text	Occurrences of root תקן[291]	Usages related to "h" above [292]
Mishnah	148	35 (23%)
Tosefta	191	27 (14%)
Halakhic Midrashim	111	20 (18%)
Babylonian Talmud[293]	1317	526 (40%)
Palestinian Talmud	504	117 (23%)

One can see immediately from these figures that the usage of this term in the meaning of "enacting legal measures" is numerically more pronounced in the Babylonian Gemara (40%) than in any of the Palestinian sources (14-23%). Already, in this initial, superficial analysis, we see a pronounced preference in the Babylonian text favoring the use of this root as an indicator of halakhic change over other potential uses.

Secondary Literature and Parallels Related to תקן

Before moving to an exploration of the various sorts of halakhic change denoted by the root תקן, it will serve us well to take a brief excursion into the prior scholarship on this question. The scholarship is relatively limited, despite the important nature of the question, though a number of authors have made significant individual contributions to the study of the nature of *takkanot*.

The first attempt at work in this field in the late pre-modern period was by Rabbi Elijah Mevorakh Galipapa, a Turkish rabbi of the late seventeenth to early eighteenth century. His major work, ידי אליהו (*Yedei Eliyahu, The Hands of Elijah*)[294] was published in Constantinople in 1728. It was republished in 1989 or 1990.[295] Galipapa's work is fairly comprehensive and includes many of the *takkanot* from the rabbinic period, but it is not framed around the corpus of law from the rabbinic period. Instead, Galipapa chose to key his work to the codification of the commandments found in Maimonides' *Mishneh Torah*. He cited the appearance of each particular *halakhah*, and then followed it with commentary and analysis. While he did refer to prior Jewish legal sources, his work is limited in that he only included those *takkanot* mentioned by Maimonides. Though excellent in its scope, it does not provide a perfect base for our study of the earlier rabbinic period, as it does not offer a complete grouping of the enactments from our period of interest.

One early modern scholar who deserves mention is Rabbi Tzvi Hirsch Chajes, born in 1805 in Brody, in Northeast Galicia.[296] His well-known work מבוא התלמוד (*Mevo HaTalmud, Introduction to the Talmud*), first published in 1845, was translated into English as *The Student's Guide Through the Talmud*.[297] Chajes made an important contribution to the study of *takkanot* and *gezerot* by serving as the first collector of *takkanot* and *gezerot* from the rabbinic sources themselves, as opposed to relying upon Maimonides' later codification. He ordered his collection according to the approximate chronology of the cited authorities responsible for enacting each *takkanah* and *gezerah*, allowing his reader a more progressive understanding of the development of law. Though his work was decidedly uncritical, and not completely comprehensive in that it did not include every occurrence of each word, it proved helpful in grounding future attempts at a more comprehensive and ordered collection.

The next important contribution to the study of *takkanot* was made by Rabbi Moshe Aryeh Bloch (1815-1909), the author of the best-known work in the field to date.[298] His massive work of seven volumes, composed between 1879 and 1902, reprinted in 1971, known as שערי תורת התקנות (*Shaarei Torat HaTakkanot, Gates of the Instruction of the Enactments*), provides an enormous compilation of every *takkanah* and *gezerah*, along with a very useful commentary.

While Bloch was comprehensive in his approach, he is not to be counted amongst even the early critical students of these texts. He railed against Graetz, Hertzfeld and Isaac Hirsch Weiss, his contemporaries, who brought a critical approach to the material. In his introduction, for instance, Bloch singled out Weiss' work, *Dor Dor VeDorshav*, in particular, as an example of the undesirable critical approach he specifically tried to avoid. Bloch rails against the following example of Weiss' problematic approach:

ומריבי הקבלה עוד יתעצמו בהראותם כי כן היתה תכונת החכמים
הקדמונים שלפעמים היו מיחסים דברים לקדמוני קדמונים, לא מהיות
קבלה בידם אמנם מהשערה או לסבה אחרת . . . וביחוד נמצא כמה חקים
ותקנות אשר יחסו לדגולי אנשי שם בזמן קדום. ואם נתבונן בהם נראה כי
לא סמכו בזה על קבלת איש אחר איש אלא על השערות, ולרוב דקות
ורחוקות. והסבות אשר הורגלו בזה היו מונחות לרוב בשכחת מקורי
הדברים. כי דברים רבים היו נמצאים וחיים בעם ובמשך הזמן שכחו
מקורם והתחלתם. והנה בא האחד וחשב, לפי דרכם, למצוא להם רמז
וסמוכים בדברי אחד מהקדמונים אשר לפי השערתו נרמז בהם תקנה או
חקה כך וכך, ולמי שבא אחריו כבר היתה ההשערה לדבר ברור, ובמשך
הזמן לדבר מקובל . . . הן לשלמה המלך יחסו גזרות ותקנות. ואם נשאלו
מאין היה להם כן? אין התשובה שכן קבלו איש מפי איש, אלא שיצא להם
כן ממובן הכתובים, לפי דרכי מדרשם, שנאמר אזן וחקר ותקן משלים
הרבה (עירובין כ״א: יבמות כ״א.) ודרשו מלת תקן על התקנות ויצא להם
מזה ששלמה תקן תקנות, ויחסו לו תקנות אשר מקורם והתחלתם כבר
נעלם מהם.

And the adversaries of the tradition will again argue when they see these (*takkanot*) that such was the disposition of the early sages that they sometimes would attribute words to the earliest sages, not because they had a tradition in their hands, but from a conjecture or for some other reason. . . .

And especially there are some statutes and *takkanot* that are connected to people of great reputation in a prior time. And if we look at these, we will see that they did not rely, in this, on a tradition [transmitted directly] from one mouth to another, but instead on conjectures, in most cases weak and distant ones. And the reason that they became accustomed to this lay mostly in the forgetting of the sources of the matters. For there were many matters present and living among the people, and over time they forgot their source and their beginning. And one came and thought—according to their way—to find for them a hint and supports in the words of their predecessors that through conjecture was hinted that they made a *takkanah* or such and such a statute, and for the one who came after him already the conjecture became a clear thing, and over time an accepted thing. . . .

So, to Solomon the King they attached *gezerot* and *takkanot*. And if we ask where did they derive this? The answer is not that they received a tradition mouth to mouth, but rather that they derived it from the meaning of the text – according to their *midrash* – as it is said: "he listened to, investigated and fixed many parables," (Ecclesiastes 12:9 – Eruvin 20a; Yevamot 20a). And they interpreted the word *tikken* into *takkanot*, and they derived it from this that Solomon enacted *takkanot*, and they attached [to him] *takkanot* whose source and beginning had already escaped them.[299]

Weiss' critical eye on Solomon's purported *takkanot* was more than Bloch could bear. To Weiss, the *takkanot* of Solomon were the antithesis of true history – they were the dreamy exegetical outcome of one short verse in a book merely attributed to Solomon, which created an idea entirely lacking in any direct path of transmitted tradition. In essence these *takkanot* were baseless conjectures that time sealed as tradition, balanced on the head of a midrashic pin, intended to explain and strengthen laws and regulations whose genesis had been forgotten.

This sort of analysis was not an acceptable option for Bloch. In his introduction, Bloch went on to explicitly state his approach to the study of *takkanot*, showing both his awareness and his conscious rejection of a modern critical outlook:

ולא נעלמה ממני דרכי המבקרים החדשים אשר אינם משגיחים על עדות
חז״ל בעניין זמן התקנה ושם המתקן. ואומריי כי מפאת שלא היה להם
ז״ל ידיעה ברורה בדבר הרחיקו את זמן התקנה עד הזמן היותר קדום
ויחסוה לאחד מגדולי הקדמונים לתלותה באילן גדול. . . . . אבל אנוכי
אחזתי רק דרך הקבלה ומינה לא אזוע ודברי רז״ל יהיי לי למאירת עינים.

And the ways of the new critics who do not abide by the testimony of
the sages in the matter of the time of the *takkanah* or the name of the
enactor have not escaped me. And they say that because the sages did
not have clear knowledge in a certain matter, they pushed back the date
of the *takkanah* to an earlier period, and tied it to one of the great ones
among their predecessors to "hang it on a big tree. . . ." But I hold only
to the way of the tradition, and from it I will not waver, and the words
of our rabbis will be for me a light for the eyes.[300]

From this passage, we see that Bloch's method stood in sharp contrast with that
of Weiss and the others who employed nascent critical methodology. Bloch
categorized the *takkanot* and *gezerot* he studied according to their stated authorship, and left it at that. He did not confront the thorny question of the reliability
of attributions, nor did he attempt to provide a critical comparison of the textual
sources or manuscript differences that underlay the instances he cited. Bloch
provided an estimated date for each *takkanah* he cited, based, it appears, solely
on the attributions found in the texts. While his work certainly provides a useful
starting point in assessing these enactments, his investigations could have bene-
fited greatly from the many years of critical scholarship that antedated his death.
In light of some of the concerns about attributed sayings and their historical implications that recent scholars have noted,[301] his material on authorship, manuscripts and dating must be approached carefully, to say the least.

 Ephraim Urbach also delved into the world of *takkanot* and *gezerot*, in a
short study within his work *The Halakhah*. In this book, Urbach collected *takkanot* according to their authors and period of creation. He sifted through them
critically and responsibly, unafraid to point out the unlikely nature of some of
the attributions. Conceptually, his work sets a baseline for this study, though his
work was less comprehensive in scope.[302]

 Another major study exists that is not as well known as Bloch's, but is as
comprehensive and detailed in its approach. In 1991, Rabbi Israel Schepanksy
published his התקנות בישראל (*HaTakkanot BeYisrael, The Enactments in Israel*),[303] a four-volume work that traces *takkanot* from the earliest recorded instances attributed to Moses through enactments associated with the Jewish
community in the modern period. In the first two volumes of *HaTakkanot BeYi-
israel*, Schepansky covers all the *takkanot* assigned to rabbinic authorities, carefully counting the number of *takkanot* assigned to each authority, bringing ap-

propriate parallels and supporting evidence from sources in the rabbinic period
and interpreters thereafter, and analyzing the reason for each *takkanah* and *gezerah* he discusses. Like Bloch, though, he is unwilling to examine the *takkanot*
critically, accepting attributions and statements at face value. Nor does he enter
into historical-critical assessment of manuscripts, philology or the identity of
authorities involved. So, while the work is extremely valuable from the perspective of collecting data, finding parallels, explaining the operative halakhic parameters and the later interpretative history of each enactment, his analysis could
also benefit greatly from a more modern scholarly approach.

Menachem Elon, a noted legal scholar and former associate Chief Justice of
the Israeli Supreme Court, is the other major scholar who has written a work
defining the parameters of *takkanot* and *gezerot*. An authority on both Jewish
Law and general legal theory, his approach allows us to benefit from the vast
insights provided by both these bodies of knowledge.[304]

Elon's *magnum opus*, called המשפט העברי (*HaMishpat HaIvri, Jewish Law:
History, Sources, Principles*),[305] is where he presents a most informative study
on the effect of legislation on the development of Jewish law. While Elon does
not attempt or claim to provide comprehensive coverage of all the *takkanot* and
gezerot in rabbinic legal texts, his work offers some distinct advantages over the
work of Bloch, Galipapa and Schepansky. First and foremost, his methodology
is entirely academic. While there are certainly pronounced differences between
the approach of the *mishpat ivry* and the historical-critical schools in their unpacking of halakhic history from rabbinic texts, there is no doubt that Elon's
investigation represents the best modern attempt yet to shed light on the history
of *takkanot* and *gezerot*.

Second, beyond simply collecting, categorizing and commenting on the
texts, Elon extends the theoretical background of his predecessors on the foundational issues relating to *takkanot* and *gezerot*. He explores the authorizing
directives for legislative innovation in Jewish law, which he claims come from
the Torah itself. He also honestly examines the problems that inhere in shaping
any process of change that some see as revising divinely ordained commands
within an eternal, unchanging core of Jewish law. Finally, Elon provides a series
of examples of *takkanot* and *gezerot*, to clarify the parameters of this process of
growth in Jewish law. He orders these examples according to modern legal
categories, giving us a diverse array selected from many different areas of law.
For our study, it is important to note that he is not attempting to create an intellectual history of the rabbinic period, nor does he dwell at length on the reasons
offered for these *takkanot*. Instead he sees these as particular stopping points in
the broad continuum of Jewish legal development throughout the ages.

One other note is in order here. Neither Bloch nor Elon (nor, by the way,
any other prior student of *takkanot* and *gezerot*) consistently relies on the linguistic markers of the texts to determine what constitutes a *takkanah* or *gezerah*.

In some instances, they will declare changes in law to be *takkanot* or "legislation," when the texts involved do not explicitly use the specific term. While these texts do indicate halakhic changes that reportedly occurred, our present study will employ more restrictive controls: we will discuss only those texts that include uses of these specific marker terms, avoiding making any undue assumptions about equality between *takkanot*, *gezerot* and other sorts of halakhic change reported in the texts.

Two other authors have written important individual articles on the topic of *takkanot* and *gezerot*.[306] Martin Jaffee's article provides an overview of a form-critical literary approach to the *takkanah* in the literature of the Tannaitic period (*circa* 70-225 CE), determining that the *takkanah* is a new hermeneutical development that comes about during the Tannaitic period as a way of dealing with the limitations of interpretation of older traditions. Jaffee notes that the *takkanot* attributed to the most ancient authorities are all found in the latest stratum of PT and BT. He then suggests that *takkanot* attributed to Tannaim in Amoraic strata may also be retrojections. Next he points out that many *takkanot* that appear in PT and BT have their sources in passages in M and T that do not indicate a *takkanah* at all. Instead of reading the later texts as more historically accurate (as some do), he suggests that we consider these as rabbinic re-interpretations of history. Jaffee sees the development of "*takkanah*-literature" as later than M, resulting from rabbinic reflection upon the few reports of *takkanot* in M. Ultimately, he concludes that we cannot learn actual legislative history from the record of *takkanot*, but we can learn about the thinking of the late Tannaitic and Amoraic editors and redactors who utilized this hermeneutic on prior material.[307]

Christine Hayes' article compares Amoraic *takkanot* to Roman *edicta*, providing a useful set of reference points to the external legal processes that surrounded the development of Jewish law in Palestine during the Amoraic period. Hayes demonstrates the presence of stronger revisionist tendencies in PT than in BT, and attributes these to the influence of the Roman legal system upon the Palestinian Jewish community.[308]

This study will differ from previous ones in a few significant ways in both purpose and method. The hope is to preserve the best of the previous major works, yet add to the discourse by creating a complementary work. Galipapa, Bloch and Schepansky in essence, were comprehensive, but not thoroughly critical. Elon was critical, but not comprehensive. None attempted to fully place these instances of Jewish legal development within the greater historical context of the rabbinic period, nor did they focus on manuscript variations, attribution issues or other concerns of historical-critical scholars.

What will distinguish this work from the studies of Bloch or Elon is an adherence to the historical-critical method. This involves a clear differentiation between stated and hypothetical rationales for halakhic change; examination of available manuscripts to produce the best available witness for each text; where possible, dating of texts and tradents with whatever precision historical-critical scholarship will allow; assessment of differences between Palestinian and Babylonian, Tannaitic and Amoraic and other contexts; review of parallel texts and institutions in surrounding cultures and legal systems and the application of critical techniques to statements within the text itself. This process will result in a reconstruction of the intellectual history of the development of the legal concept of *takkanah* in the rabbinic period, which will help define the contours of halakhic change and innovation during an important period of legal creativity.

The Characteristics of *Takkanot*

Definitions of *Takkanah* and *Gezerah*

Rabbinic literature is devoid of any descriptive material that directly defines the theoretical boundaries or limitations of *takkanot* and *gezerot*. It is only after the Tannaitic and Amoraic periods that later authorities began to take a retrospective look at the terms and their usage to attempt to formulate a definition *post facto*. The available literature[309] points to Maimonides as the initial authority to endeavor to invent a categorical definition of these terms in the introduction to his *Commentary on the Mishnah*. In his categorization of types of law one finds in M, sections four and five, he explains his understanding of *gezerot* and *takkanot*:

והחלק הרביעי: הם הדינים שתקנו הנביאים והחכמים בכל-דור ודור, כדי לעשות סיג וגדר לתורה. ועליהם צוה הקב״ה לעשותם, והוא מה שאמר במאמר כללי: ושמרתם את משמרתי (ויקרא יח ל), ובאה בו הקבלה: ״עשו משמרת למשמרתי.״ והחכמים יקראו אותם: ״גזרות. . . .״

והחלק החמישי: הם הדינים העשויים על-דרך החקירה וההסכמה בדברים הנוהגים בין בני-אדם, שאין בם תוספת במצוה ולא גרעון; או בדברים שהם תועלת לבני אדם בדברי תורה, וקראו אותם: ״תקנות ומנהגים,״ ואסור לעבור עליהם. וכבר אמר שלמה, עה״ש, על-העובר עליהם: ופרץ גדר ישכנו נחש (קהלת י, ח). ואלו התקנות רבות מאד ונזכרות בתלמוד ובמשנה: מהן בענין איסור והתר; ומהן בענין הממונות; ומהן תקנות שתקנו נביאים, כמו תקנות משה ויהושע ועזרא, כמו שאמרו: ״משה תקן להם לישראל שיהיו שואלים ודורשים בהלכות פסח בפסח.״ ואמרו: ״משה תקן הזן, בשעה שירד שמן לישראל.״ אבל תקנות יהושע ועזרא הן רבות. ומהן תקנות מיוחסות ליחידים מן החכמים, כמו שאמרו: ״התקין הלל פרוזבול;״ ״התקין רבן גמליאל הזקן;״ ״התקין רבן יוחנן בן זכאי.״ והרבה בתלמוד: ״התקין רבי פלוני,״ ״התקין רבי פלוני.״ ויש מהן תקנות מיוחסות להמון החכמים כמו שאמרו: ״באושא התקינו״ או כמו שאמרו ״תקנו חכמים״ וכדומה לזה הרבה.[310]

And the fourth category—these are the laws that the prophets and the sages in each generation enacted in order to make a fence and a boundary for the Torah. And God commanded [us] to do them, and this is as God said in the general statement "You shall keep My charge" (Leviticus 18:30). And the tradition comes [to explain] that this means "Make a guard for My charge," and the sages would call these "*gezerot*." . . .

And the fifth category—these are the laws that are promulgated through investigation and agreement in the matters that occur between human beings, that do not involve any addition to nor subtraction from a commandment; or laws that effect matters between human beings in matters of Torah, and they called them "*takkanot*" and "*minhagim*," and it is forbidden to violate them. And Solomon, may he rest in peace, already said about one who violates them: "one who breaches a fence, a snake will bite him"[311] (Ecclesiastes 10:8). And there are very many *takkanot* mentioned in the Talmud and the Mishnah: among them— matters of ritual practice; and among them—matters of civil law; and among them—takkanot that the prophets enacted, such as the *takkanot* of Moses, Joshua and Ezra, as they said: "Moses enacted for Israel that they should be asking and interpreting the laws of Passover during Passover." And they said: "Moses enacted [the first blessing in *Birkat HaMazon*, known as] *HaZan*, at the time when *mannah* came down for Israel." But the *takkanot* of Joshua and Ezra are many. And among them—*takkanot* attributed to individuals from the sages, as they said: "Hillel enacted the *prosbul*;" "Rabban Gamaliel the Elder enacted;" "Rabban Yohanan ben Zakkai enacted." And often in the Talmud: "Rabbi Ploni enacted;" "Rabbi Ploni enacted." And there are *takkanot* tied to a large group of sages, as they said: "In Usha they enacted" or as they said: "the sages enacted" or "*takkanot* of the sages" and many similar cases.

Rambam's explanation still stands as the most cogent early definition of the difference between *takkanot* and *gezerot*, and forms the basis for most future attempts at understanding these terms. As we will see throughout this chapter and the next, though, there are some fundamental problems with it. At times, the words *takkanah* and *gezerah* are used almost interchangeably in rabbinic literature, so that it is clear that the redactors of these texts did not always adhere to a well-defined difference between them. Furthermore, *gezerot* appear in our sources that do not, by any means, place a fence around the Torah. With regard to *takkanot*, there are a number of examples where an unbiased reader would have difficulty supporting the claim that they do not add to nor subtract from the commandments. Finally, and perhaps of greatest import, it remains entirely unlikely that these terms were used in any well-conceptualized systematic way throughout the vast expanse of rabbinic literature. Thus, no systematic categorization can do justice to the myriad utilizations of these terms. With all those caveats in mind, though, Maimonides' claim best captures the essence of what lies behind the majority of *takkanot* and *gezerot*.

A late medieval commentator supplies us with another possible definition of the difference between *takkanot* and *gezerot*. In Rabbi Moses ben Joseph Trani's[312] introduction to *Kiryat Sefer*, chapter 4, Trani suggests that *takkanot* and *gezerot* each have four aspects. For *gezerot*, all four revolve around the uniform ideal of creating a fence around the Torah to avoid violation of its commandments. Trani's four aspects of *takkanot* are more instructive – they include: a) commandments of the rabbis; b) commandments of the rabbis that have some limited basis in the Torah (*asmakhta*); c) *Takkanot* that the rabbis enacted because of an incident that occurred; and d) practices that were the custom of the prophets.[313]

In the early modern period, Chajes, in his *Mevo HaTalmud*, provided us with a thoughtful categorization of the six different sorts of law that arise from the rabbis, describing *takkanot* and *gezerot* carefully:

> There is still another category of observances, cited in the Mishnah and Gemara and in several *beraitoth*, that are of different character, and bear no relationship to those before-mentioned. They come under the category of '*takkanoth*' (enactments) and '*gezeroth*' (decrees) which were found necessary by the Rabbis as precautionary measures to safeguard the Torah.

> Every Talmudic teacher in his own period, understanding the conditions of his own days, felt the need of promulgating various enactments and decrees for the purpose of protecting the walls of the law against breaches. These *takkanoth* and *gezeroth* belong to the category of Rabbinic laws, and they carry no authority even for the infliction of the ordinary punishment of flogging upon the disobedient, let alone that of capital punishment. Transgressors of such rabbinic decrees, however, were liable to *makkath marduth* (beating for rebellion).[314]

Here, Chajes stakes out an interesting position. First, he notes that the entire purpose of both *takkanot* and *gezerot* is "protecting the walls of the law against breeches." This followed Maimonides' understanding of *gezerot* above, but veered far from his definition of *takkanot*. Contrary to Maimonides, Chajes saw *takkanot* and *gezerot* as entirely rabbinic, and he did not consider violators of them liable to penalties associated with violations of Torah laws. Maimonides, on the other hand, held that violators of *takkanot* and *gezerot* suffered penalties for violating rules from the Torah, since the Torah provides for their observance.[315] Finally, Chajes' apt characterization of *takkanot* and *gezerot* as responses to their time sets the stage for an understanding of the dynamic development of Jewish law as it responds to objective changes in surrounding conditions.

Bloch essentially follows Maimonides, directly citing his introduction to the *Commentary on the Mishnah* at the very beginning of his own introduction:

> [According to the Rambam] the definition of *gezerot* is a warning and a negation that the sages decreed and prohibited this from that. But the definition of a *takkanah*, according to the majority, is a positive obligation and command to do that which the sages enacted to do such and such.[316]

Elon follows Maimonides' view as well, but enhances his definitions with this critical caveat:

> It may therefore be said that, in the main, the term *gezerah* denotes legislation prohibiting the performance of a particular act that the Torah does not prohibit; the objective of a *gezerah* is to extend a prohibition established in the Torah, in order to decrease the likelihood that the Torah's prohibition will be violated. *Takkanah*, on the other hand, generally denotes an enactment that imposes a duty to perform a particular act for the benefit and welfare of the community or any of its members. These general rules, however, do not always apply.[317]

Elon and Bloch suggest a series of sources that show the difficulties of applying their shared viewpoint, thus the stated reservations.[318] We are left with a heuristic definition, at best, for understanding these two terms as they are utilized in rabbinic legal literature, which all authors, including the current one, acknowledge as imperfect, but generally accurate.

The Authority to Make *Takkanot* and *Gezerot*

Menachem Elon, in his section on legislated change in Jewish law, suggests a useful typology of Jewish jurisprudence that flows from general legal theory. He begins by making a distinction between supreme and subordinate legislation:

> Legislation is defined as the promulgation of principles and rules by a competent, authoritative body for the purpose of giving those principles and rules binding legal effect. There are two basic categories of

legislation: supreme legislation and subordinate legislation. Supreme legislation includes those legal principles and rules (whether "constitutional," "basic," or "ordinary") promulgated by the highest legislative authority of the legal system. Subordinate legislation consists of those legal principles and rules enacted by an agency of inferior rank that is subject to the system's highest legislative authority . . .

The Written Law (*Torah she-bi-khe-tav*—Scripture) is the supreme legislation of the Jewish legal system. It is the written "constitution" of Jewish law, having its ultimate source in divine revelation. Every other legislated rule is subordinate legislation because legislators derive their legislative power not from inherent authority but pursuant to formal delegation of that power—an express authorization conferred by the supreme legislation, namely the Written Law.[319]

Whether one sees the Written Law—the supreme legislation—of the Jewish people as divinely revealed, divinely inspired or the result of hundreds of years of literary development, the point remains the same: *takkanot* and *gezerot*, as well as any other forms of change within the Jewish legal system, require some source rooted in the Written Law that permits their promulgation. Without some authorization in the *Torah shebikhtav*, the creation of new laws would violate a number of directives contained within the Written Law, including Deut. 13:1, which Maimonides cited in his Mishneh Torah in explaining that changes to the eternal law contained in the Torah are essentially forbidden:[320]

את כל הדבר אשר אנכי מצוה אתכם אתו תשמרו לעשות לא תסף עליו
ולא תגרע ממנו.

Be careful to observe everything which I enjoin upon you; neither add to it, nor take away from it.

Without some other verse to countermand this limitation, it would seem that inferior courts and religious authorities would have little room to alter Jewish law. Many texts, both ancient and modern, are utilized to provide a variety of sources that supply the necessary authorization for halakhic change.

Rabbinic sources suggest that the *locus classicus* for the authority to make alterations in Jewish law may be found in a few specific textual locations. Elon cites BT Shabbat 23a and its discussion of the Hanukkah blessing as one noteworthy example. At issue is the fact that the blessing over the Hanukkah candles includes the word "וצינו," "and God commanded us," a formulation usually reserved for activities commanded in the Written Torah. The problem, here, is that

the historical events that initiated the celebration of Hanukkah did not occur
until 164-5 BCE, long after the completion of the Torah. The *stam* of the BT
then sensibly inquires: how it is that God's command to the Jewish people to
light Hanukkah candles exists in the Torah, when the very events they com-
memorate have certainly not yet occurred at the time of the Torah's completion?
Since one is not authorized to deviate to the right or the left, as we saw above,
how can one affirm this commandment as actually commanded, and not as a
violation of the limitation in Deut. 13:1? This question is asked and answered in
BT Shab. 23a:

מאי מברך? מברך "אשר קדשנו במצותיו וצונו להדליק נר של חנוכה."
והיכן צונו? רב אויא אמר: (דברים יז) מ-"לא תסור." רב נחמיה אמר:
(דברים לב) "שאל אביך ויגדך זקניך ויאמרו לך."

What blessing does one say [over the Hanukkah candles]? One says:
"who has sanctified us with commandments and commanded us to kin-
dle the light of Hanukkah." But where did God command us? Rav Avia
said: From the verse "You must not deviate" (Deut. 17:11). R. Nehemiah[321] said: "Ask your father, he will inform you, your elders, they
will tell you" (Deut. 32:7).[322]

Rav Avia's suggested verse also appears as the basis for the authority to alter
Jewish law in another rabbinic source, *Mtan* to Deut. 17:11, from Hoffman's
reconstruction of a lost midrashic work:

ד"א: "על פי התורה אשר יורוך" על דברי תורה חייבין מיתה ואין חייבין
מיתה על דברי סופרים: "ועל המשפט אשר יאמרו לך תעשה" זו מצות
עשה בכל מצוה לשמוע להן, אפילו <u>בגזרות ותקנות</u> שהרי הוא אומר "על פי
התורה אשר יורוך" אלו <u>גזירות ותקנות ומנהגות</u> שיורו בהן לרבים כדי
לחזק הדת ולתקן העולם:

Another matter [regarding] "in accordance with the Torah that they will
teach you" (Deut. 17:11): according to words of Torah, one may be put
to death, and not according to words of the scribes. "And you shall do
according to the ruling handed down to you;" this is a positive commandment to obey every commandment, even *gezerot* and *takkanot*, for
the text says, "according to the Torah that they will teach you," this
means *gezerot*, *takkanot* and *minhagot* that they will teach to the many
in order to strengthen religion and ensure the orderly functioning of society.

Since this is a reconstruction, we can never be entirely certain that this understanding is not a later addition. However, it does cohere nicely with the ideas
expressed in the section from BT Shabbat above. This gives us some slim evidence that the operative hermeneutic that authorized *takkanot* and *gezerot* came
to be during the Tannaitic period, if not before.

Nonetheless, one must question this hermeneutic. At first glance, Deut.
17:11 and 32:7 both serve well as potential sources for authorizing subordinate
legislation, but when one examines their original context, their usage in this
manner is not at all a foregone conclusion. Deut. 17:11 comes in the midst of the
discussion of procedures for adjudicating a legal case that is too baffling to decide:

(ח) כי יפלא ממך דבר למשפט בין דם לדם בין דין לדין ובין נגע לנגע דברי
ריבת בשעריך וקמת ועלית אל המקום אשר יבחר יהוה אלהיך בו : (ט)
ובאת אל הכהנים הלוים ואל השפט אשר יהיה בימים ההם ודרשת והגידו
לך את דבר המשפט : (י) ועשית על פי הדבר אשר יגידו לך מן המקום ההוא
אשר יבחר יהוה ושמרת לעשות ככל אשר יורוך : (יא) על פי התורה אשר
יורוך ועל המשפט אשר יאמרו לך תעשה לא תסור מן הדבר אשר יגידו לך
ימין ושמאל : (יב) והאיש אשר יעשה בזדון לבלתי שמע אל הכהן העמד
לשרת שם את יהוה אלהיך או אל השפט ומת האיש ההוא ובערת הרע
מישראל : (יג) וכל העם ישמעו ויראו ולא יזידון עוד :

8) If a case is too baffling for you to decide, be it a controversy over
homicide, civil law or assault—matters of dispute in your courts—you
shall promptly repair to the place that the Lord your God will have chosen, 9) and appear before the levitical priests, or the magistrate in
charge at the time, and present your problem. When they have announced to you the verdict in the case, 10) you shall carry out the verdict that is announced to you from that place that the Lord chose, observing scrupulously all their instructions to you. 11) You shall act in
accordance with the instructions given you and the ruling handed down
to you; you must not deviate from the verdict that they announce either
to the right or to the left. 12) Should a man act presumptuously and disregard the priest charged with servicing there the Lord your God, or the
magistrate, that man shall die. Thus you will sweep out evil from Israel:
13) all the people will hear and be afraid and will not act presumptuously again.

A few items stand out in reading this passage: first, this text is clearly focused
on a specific case (criminal, capital or civil) that is too difficult for a local court
to decide. Second, this challenging case is to be brought to a higher authority,

the court in Jerusalem,[323] for ultimate judgment. Third, the verdict of the high court must be followed scrupulously, on penalty of death.

Despite the clarity of the instruction above, we must recognize that using Deut. 17:11 as the authorizing basis for *takkanot* and other rabbinic innovations represents a significant hermeneutical jump away from the *peshat* ("direct or simple meaning") of these biblical texts, and points to an interpretive stance that endorsed legal change. The original biblical authorization given here was tightly limited to individual cases too baffling for a local court to decide. Furthermore, this authority was granted only to the single "place where the Lord your God will have chosen," and not explicitly to successor courts such as the ones in Yavneh, Usha and so on, nor was it distributed to individuals in any way. Lastly, no blanket authorization was given to make sweeping provisions that exceeded the boundaries of handling the presenting case. It was only when the redactors of works such as *Mtan* to Deut. 17:11 and BT Shab. 23a lifted this text from its context and reinterpreted it in a radical new way that circumvented the *peshat*, that it became an authorization for greater legal change.

The second potential text said to authorize rabbinic legislation comes from Deut. 32:7:

(ז) זכר ימות עולם בינו שנות דור ודור שאל אביך ויגדך זקניך
ויאמרו לך : (ח) בהנחל עליון גוים בהפרידו בני אדם יצב גבלת
עמים למספר בני ישראל : (ט) כי חלק יהוה עמו יעקב חבל
נחלתו :

7) Remember the days of old,
Consider the years of ages past;
Ask your father, he will inform you,
Your elders they will tell you:

8) When the Most High gave nations their homes
And set the divisions of humanity,
God fixed the boundaries of peoples
In relation to Israel's numbers.

9) For the Lord's portion is God's people,
Jacob, God's own allotment.

While the first Deuteronomic text we reviewed was tied, at least, directly to legal adjudication, Rabbi Nehemiah's choice of prooftexts is even more difficult. This text is pure poetry, taken from Moses' final statement before he climbs Mount Nebo to die. It is simply a text that asks Moses' charges to pay heed to their history, and to respect their elders as conduits of information. There is not

even a hint of any endorsement of legal change in this verse, let alone any of the
wide power ascribed to it by Rabbi Nehemiah. Rabbi Nehemiah, like his coun-
terpart Rav Avia, suggested utilizing this biblical prooftext to uphold a philosophy of legal change that far exceeded its *peshat*.

From these verses we may learn that the Torah requires regard for one's
elders, respect for their knowledge of history and tradition, and, in a limited
number of baffling cases, turning to a Jerusalem-based central authority, when
possible, for decisive innovative action. Nowhere in these authorizing texts do
we see the sort of legal *carte blanche* assumed by rabbinic lawmakers in the
texts studied in the rest of this chapter. A further irony is the fact that both these
texts come from Deuteronomy, long considered the latest part of the Torah by
critical scholars, and a major source of legal change itself.[324]

Following Nahmanides, Elon suggests another interpretation of a verse that
he claims specifically authorized *gezerot*. In Lev. 18:29-30, after a long list of
abhorrent prohibited practices that run the gamut from incest to idol worship, the
chapter ends with these two verses:

(כט) כי כל אשר יעשה מכל התועבות האלה ונכרתו הנפשות העשת מקרב
עמם : (ל) ושמרתם את משמרתי לבלתי עשות מחקות התועבת אשר נעשו
לפניכם ולא תטמאו בהם אני יהוה אלהיכם :

29) All who do any of these abhorrent things – such persons shall be
cut off from their people. 30) You shall keep My charge not to engage
in any of the abhorrent practices that were carried on before you, and
you shall not defile yourselves through them: I am the Lord your God.

Elon then cites *Sifra Aharei Mot* 9:22, which interprets Lev. 18:30 in the following manner:

"ושמרתם את משמרתי" שמרו לי משמרת, ושמרתם משמרתי להזהיר
בית דין על כך, "לבלתי עשות מחוקות התועבות אשר נעשה לפניכם," ולא
תטמאו בהם.

"You shall keep My charge" – preserve a safeguard for Me, and guard
My charge [i.e., My laws]; this is an instruction to the court to avoid
following the abominable laws that had been followed before them, and
that they will not defile themselves through them.[325]

Similar to what we found above, the biblical passage deals only with abhorrent
sexual and worship practices. *Sifra* does offer permission to create boundaries
that serve as "fences around the Torah" within these specific, limited areas.

Again, however, there is little cause to understand the statement of the *Sifra* as fully authorizing the manifold and expansive changes in law arising through *gezerot*.

The strategies Maimonides and Nahmanides utilized in supporting the authorization of legislation (following Rabbis Avia and Nehemiah, respectively)[326] attempt to provide adequate validation of the rabbis' accepted power to change Jewish law. The texts cited, though, seem to have been lifted from their original contexts and vested with far wider power than one would imagine them to imply, had one simply read them *in situ*. This points to one conclusion: the rabbinic editors interpreted these verses from Scripture with a hermeneutic determined to justify the rabbinic power to legislate and to alter law when necessary.

Takkanot and Torah Law

Takkanot are classed as דרבנן (*derabbanan*, "of our rabbis," i.e. rabbinic in origin).[327] No definition or text in any source clashes with this basic principle. Some texts imbue *takkanot* with a certain status that hovers somewhere above the other rabbinic precepts of our tradition, close but not exactly equivalent to Torah law itself. In other texts, quite the opposite is the case. To understand this difference, we will look at two short texts that form a rather striking counterpoint.

Our first example deals with the question of מרור (*maror*, "bitter herbs") during the eve of Passover in Jerusalem. At issue in BT Pes. 39b is the question of whether an item already dedicated to one religious purpose may be used to fulfill another religious purpose—namely that of eating bitter herbs in fulfillment of the Torah's command.[328] An Amora, Rami bar Hamah, begins the discussion by asking whether one may discharge his obligation to eat *maror* during Pesah with *maror* that has been brought to Jerusalem in fulfillment of the requirement for second tithes, since this *maror* was already dedicated to a prior sacred purpose:

בעי רמי בר חמא: מהו שיצא אדם ידי חובתו במרור של מעשר שני
בירושלים? אליבא דרבי עקיבא לא תיבעי לך, השתא במצה דאורייתא
נפיק, במרור דרבנן מיבעיא? כי תיבעי לך, אליבא דרבי יוסי הגלילי. מאי?
במצה דאורייתא הוא דלא נפיק, אבל מרור דרבנן נפיק או דילמא כֹּל
דתקינו רבנן - כעין דאורייתא תקון. אמר רבא: מסתברא, מצה ומרור.

Rami bar Hama asked: What is the law as to whether a person fulfills his obligation with *maror* [if it were made] from second tithe produce in Jerusalem? According to the opinion of Rabbi Akiba, there is no need to ask: since [if one can fulfill the obligation of *matzah* from second tithe produce, and] *matzah* is an obligation from the Torah [and *matzah* dedicated to the tithe may still be employed to fulfill the obligation to eat *matzah* at Passover], surely [in the case of the] *maror* from second tithe produce, which is only a rabbinical obligation [in our time, because there is no paschal sacrifice anymore], one can fulfill the obligation [from *maror* already dedicated to the second tithe].

It is a question for you, then, according to the view of Rabbi Yossi HaGalili [who ruled that *matzah* from the second tithe is not acceptable for fulfillment of the *mitzvah*]. What is the law [regarding *maror*]? With *matzah*, which is an obligation from the Torah, he may not fulfill his obligation [if he eats it from second tithe *matzah*], but with *maror*, which is only an obligation from our rabbis, he may [fulfill his obligation with food already dedicated to the tithe]? Or, perhaps, <u>all that our rabbis enacted, they enacted as if it is similar to biblical law</u> [and therefore he may not use second tithe produce for either *matzah* or *maror*]? Rava said: it is logical, then, to say [that both] *matzah* and *maror* [follow the same laws—and thus neither may be eaten from the second tithe produce to fulfill their respective obligations at Pesah].

Germane to our discussion is the underlined phrase: "all that our rabbis enacted, they enacted as if it is similar to biblical law." Not a unique occurrence, this phrase appears nine times throughout BT, always in the Stammaitic layer. It does not occur even once in any Palestinian legal texts from the period.[329]

The phrase, as it is utilized above and elsewhere, indicates a tendency within BT to grant enhanced authority to the *takkanot* of the rabbis. Generally, the term is used where a biblical commandment is no longer in effect, and a rabbinical commandment has replaced it. While it clearly does not say that *takkanot* are truly equal in authority to Torah law, the very fact that they are "like" laws in the Torah classes them as closer to Torah laws than other rabbinic decisions. This phrase also demands that *takkanot* follow the general tendencies and outlines indicated in the laws from the Torah that they resemble. In the passage in BT Pes., above, כל דתקינו רבנן כעין דאורייתא תקון is invoked to resolve the difficulty posed by Rabbi Yossi HaGalili (T2, *fl.* early 2nd century CE), and it must be accepted as a valid statement for the *sugya* to be resolved appropriately. Rava (BA4, d. 352 CE) is quoted as approving of the premise.

In contradistinction to the tendency in BT, we find a different approach in PT. In PT, there are a number of pericopae that differentiate very carefully between *takkanot* and laws from the Torah,[330] and we never find a statement that grants *takkanot* the sort of broad power that BT hands over. Instead, it appears that PT takes a more circumspect view of the power of rabbinic enactment.

One of the more interesting examples of PT's tendency to delineate precisely what arises from Torah and what from rabbinic enactment, is a text that questions the validity of a גט (*get*, writ of divorce) brought from abroad. PT Git. 2:1, 44a gives a final determination that its validity derives half from Torah and half from a *takkanah*:

ר׳ יוסי בעי : אמר בפני נכתב ובפני נחתם אלא נתייחד ברשות הבעלים בין
כתיבה לחתימה. נישמעינה מן הדא : אחד אומר בפני נכתב ואחד אומר
בפני נחתם, פסול מפני שאחד אומר בפני נכתב ואחד אומר בפני נחתם.
אבל אם אמר בפני נכתב ובפני נחתם אלא שנתייחד ברשות הבעלים בין
כתיבה לחתימה, כשר. רב חסדא בעי : חציו מתקנה וחציו מדבר תורה.

> Rabbi Yossi asked: [what is the law if the agent carrying the *get* said] "before me it was written and before me it was signed," but it was left alone in the domain of the owner between the [time of its] writing and the [time of its] signing?[331]

> Let us learn the answer from this [other case in M Git. 2:1]: if one says "before me it was written" and another says "before me it was signed," it is invalid, because one said "before me it was written" and another said "before me it was signed," but if one said "before me it was written and before me it was signed, but it was left alone in the domain of the owner between the writing and the signing," it is valid.

> Rav Hisda remarked:[332] half of it is from a *takkanah* and half of it is from a command of the Torah.

The logic behind this section of the *sugya* is that one witness from a distant locale who watched the creation of a *get* was considered trustworthy to validate it, so long as he observed the entire process. This required one single witness to have seen both the writing and signing of the *get*. The problem, here, is that it remained in the possession of the husband alone, which may have allowed him time and opportunity to alter it in his favor. If it were left in the husband's possession unwatched by a witness, the *get* was considered suspect and thus invalid.

Rav Hisda's closing remark is the central piece of this text for our purposes. The *Penei Moshe* understands him to say that the invalid *get* mentioned in the earlier part of this paragraph is considered cancelled partly because of a *takkanah* and partly because of a matter of Torah. On the one hand, because it was brought together (and left for some time, apparently) in the private domain of a property owner (whether the husband or another person remains unclear), it is invalid according to the enactment of the rabbis, since any suspicion that a *get* may have been switched with another *get* invalidates it. Rav Hisda terms this opinion of the rabbis a *takkanah*. On the other hand, the *Penei Moshe* continues, the Torah grants a court the right to make decisions based on their investigation of the evidence. With this in mind, the Torah actually allows the court to decide that this *get* is invalid on its own discretion. Therefore, this decision is based half on a *takkanah* and half on the Torah.

Such attention to the sources of rulings, whether from a *takkanah* or the Torah, is not uncommon in PT. In BT, there are only two places where this sort of analysis takes place where the word *takkanah* is used explicitly.[333] Since the term *takkanah* itself occurs almost twice as often in BT as in PT, and in light of the solely Babylonian use of the phrase "כל דתקינו רבנן כעין דאורייתא תקון" it seems appropriate to conclude that the Babylonian redactors were far less squeamish about the power inherent in *takkanot*, ranking their legislation at nearly the level of the supreme laws found in the Torah.

A *Takkanah* upon another *Takkanah*

Another issue that arises in our texts is the question of whether rabbinical law permits one enactment to be modified by another. This question is addressed seven times in Talmudic settings: four times in PT[334] and three in BT.[335] Such second order change is regularly forbidden in both BT and PT.

One example where a second order change is discussed, yet ultimately rejected, concerns the nature of the festival of Sukkot as it is observed after the destruction of the Temple. PT RH 4:3, 59b explores which parts of the festival observance have their basis in the Torah, and which come from *takkanot*. The passage ends with a statement that rejects the idea that one *takkanah* may be layered upon another:

כתיב "ושמחתם לפני יי' אלהיכם שבעת ימים." אית תניי תני בשמחת שלמים הכתוב מדבר, אית תניי תני בשמחת הלולב הכתוב מדבר. מאן דאמר בשמחת הלולב הכתוב מדבר, ביום הראשון דבר תורה ושאר כל הימים דבר תורה, ורבן יוחנן בן זכיי מתקין על דבר תורה. מאן דאמר בשמחת השלמים הכתוב מדבר, ביום הראשון דבר תורה ושאר כל הימים מדבריהן, ורבן יוחנן בן זכיי מתקין על דבריהן <u>ויש תקנה אחר תקנה?</u>

It is written: "and you shall rejoice before the Lord your God seven days."[336] There are Tannaim who taught that the text is speaking of the joy associated with the *shelamim* offerings.[337] There are [also other] Tannaim who taught that the text is speaking of the joy associated with the *lulav*.

For the one who says this verse is speaking about the joy of the *lulav*,[338] the offerings of the first day are from the Torah,[339] and the rest of the days are [also] from the Torah, and Rabban Yohanan ben Zakkai is making a *takkanah* on a matter of Torah.

For the one who says this verse is speaking about the joy of the *shelamim* offerings, the [waving of the *lulav* on the] first day is from the Torah,[340] and the rest of the days are from their words [i.e., the words of the rabbis], and Rabban Yohanan ben Zakkai is making a *takkanah* upon their [the sages'] words. And is it permitted to make a *takkanah* upon a *takkanah*? [No, of course not!]

In this section of PT Rosh Hashanah, we find the *stam* of PT rejected the possibility that a *takkanah* may ever be utilized to alter prior rabbinic enactments (i.e., a *takkanah* may not be made on another *takkanah*), but only to alter laws that arose from the Torah itself.

In the BT passages, we see examples of the same stance. The discussion in this next passage concerns the question of two oaths. The first is an oath imposed by the Torah, when there is a partial claim made regarding ownership of money or property. The second sort of oath, technically known as a consuetudinary oath, is an oath taken to validate (or invalidate) a complete claim: where one involved party denies the claim of another party in its entirety. A *sugya* in BT Shev. 41a focuses on the difference between these oaths:

מאי איכא בין שבועה דאורייתא לשבועה דרבנן? איכא בינייהו: מיפך שבועה, בדאורייתא לא מפכינן שבועה, בדרבנן מפכינן. ולמר בר רב אשי דאמר: בדאורייתא נמי מפכינן שבועה, מאי איכא בין דאורייתא לדרבנן? איכא בינייהו: מיחת לנכסיה, בדאורייתא נחתינן לנכסיה, בדרבנן לא נחתינן לנכסיה. ולרבי יוסי דאמר: בדרבנן נמי נחתינן לנכסיה, דתנן: מציאת חש"ו, יש בהם גזל מפני דרכי שלום, ר' יוסי אומר: גזל גמור; ואמר רב חסדא: גזל גמור מדבריהם, למאי נפקא מינה? להוציאו בדיינין, מאי איכא בין דאורייתא לדרבנן? איכא בינייהו: שכנגדו חשוד על השבועה, בדאורייתא, שכנגדו חשוד על השבועה אפכינן ליה שבועה ושמו אאידך; בדרבנן, <u>תקנתא היא, ותקנתא לתקנתא לא עבדינן.</u>

What is the difference between an oath imposed by the Torah, and an oath imposed by the rabbis? This is [the difference] between them: transference of the oath.[341] In the case of an oath imposed by the Torah, we may not transfer the oath, but in the case of the oath imposed by the rabbis, we may transfer it.

And according to Mar bar Rav Ashi, who said: "we also may transfer the Torah-imposed oath," what is the difference between the Torah-imposed oath and an oath imposed by the rabbis? This is [the difference] between them: the seizure of his property. With the Torah-imposed oath, we may seize his property, but with the rabbinically imposed oath we may not seize his property.

And according to Rabbi Yossi, who said that with a rabbinically imposed oath we may seize his property, as we learned: the found property of a deaf-mute, an imbecile or a minor comes under the law of theft for the sake of peace. Rabbi Yossi said: it is true theft. Rav Hisda said: this [i.e., Rabbi Yossi's statement] implies true theft according to the words of the rabbis. What is the difference between them [i.e., the positions that the oath is *derabbanan* or *deoraita*]? The seizing [of assets/property] by the court.[342]

[According to Rabbi Yossi, then,] what is the difference between a Torah-imposed oath and a rabbinically imposed oath? There is a difference when one party is suspected of swearing falsely: in the case of a Torah-imposed oath, where the party is suspected of swearing falsely, we transfer the oath to the other one,[343] but in the case of a rabbinically-imposed oath, it is a *takkanah*, and we do not impose one *takkanah* onto another *takkanah*.[344]

In this case, we see again that no *takkanah* may be applied to a prior one. Here, the consuetudinary oath is non-transferable, because its origin is in a *takkanah*. The biblically derived oath, on the other hand, may be transferred. Most important for our purposes, the analytical overlay of this *sugya* does not permit the imposition of one *takkanah* upon another. This limits the extent of the changes to Jewish law that *takkanot* may bring. In all three cases in which this statement appears in BT, it is accepted immediately as probative, ending the line of discussion that led to it. Thus we see conclusive evidence that the editors of both PT and BT state similar views on the idea of a *takkanah* upon another *takkanah*: it was definitively not to be permitted.

Refraining from a Beneficial *Takkanah*

According to the legal sources from the rabbinic period, when the rabbis imposed a *takkanah* that led to the benefit of an individual, that individual could refuse to take advantage of the *takkanah*, and reject it. This statement is universally attributed to Rava,[345] and appears four times, in BT alone.[346] Turning down the benefit does not invalidate the *takkanah* in any way; it simply allows an involved party to disavow his/her access to an unwanted perk that may have other undesirable ramifications.

One example of the application of this principle occurs in BT Git. 77a. This *sugya* flows from M Git. 8:1, where M asks about the validity of a *get* thrown into the hand of a woman by her divorcing husband. The Gemara begins by showing the Torah-based aspects of the divorce process, basing its discussion on Deut. 24:1:

כי יקח איש אשה ובעלה, והיה אם לא תמצא חן בעיניו כי מצא בה ערות
דבר, וכתב לה ספר כריתת ונתן בידה ושלחה מביתו :

A man takes a wife and possesses her. She fails to please him because he finds something obnoxious about her, and he writes her a bill of divorcement, hands it to her, and sends her away from his house.

BT Git. 77a bases its understanding of the *get* on this verse, paying special attention to the mention of placing the *get* into her hand:

מנא הני מילי? דתנו רבנן : (דברים כ"ד) ונתן בידה, אין לי אלא ידה ; גגה,
חצרה וקרפיפה מנין? ת"ל : ונתן, מכל מקום. . . . חצרה, מה שקנתה אשה
קנה בעלה! א"ר אלעזר : בכותב לה דין ודברים אין לי בנכסיך. וכי כתב לה
הכי מאי הוי?! והתניא : האומר לחבירו דין ודברים אין לי על שדה זו, ואין
לי עסק בה, וידי מסולקת הימנה, לא אמר כלום! אמרי דבי ר׳ ינאי :
בכותב לה ועודה ארוסה ; וכדרב כהנא, דאמר רב כהנא : נחלה הבאה לו
לאדם ממקום אחר, אדם מתנה עליה שלא ירשנה ; וכדרבא, דאמר רבא :
<u>האומר אי אפשי בתקנת חכמים כגון זו, שומעין לו.</u>

What is the source that supports these words [in the Mishnah]? As our rabbis taught: "And he shall give it into her hand" (Deut. 24:1). This can mean nothing other than her hand. [How do I know that it may be placed on] her roof, [or in] her courtyard or her enclosure? The text says: "give," which implies putting it in any place [that is hers]. . . .

"Her courtyard," but since everything a wife owns is owned by her husband, how can this be? Rabbi Eleazar said: we presume that he gave her a statement in writing that said "I have no right nor claim on your property." But even if he did so, what effect does it have? As we have learned: If a man says to his partner "I have no claim on this field, I have no interest in it, I dissociate myself from it," his words are of no [legal] effect.

The School of Rabbi Yannai said: the case is one where he wrote her a document [disavowing any claim to her property] while they were still betrothed; and we follow Rav Kahana, as Rav Kahana said: an inheritance that comes to a man, he may make a stipulation upon it [that he will not take it]; and this is based upon Rava, as Rava said: one who says I do not wish to take advantage of the *takkanah* of the sages [made for my benefit] such as this, we listen to him.

Here, when a husband attempted to give a *get* to his wife by placing it on her property (in her courtyard, on her roof, etc.), there was a significant problem. Since all the property owned by his wife was, technically, considered his property, the School of Rabbi Yannai had to posit the presence of a prenuptial document that deprived the husband of his marital right to his wife's property. Rava is cited as holding the opinion that the sages made a *takkanah* that assigned these rights to the husband in the first place. With this in mind, Rava declared that the husband could revoke his rights to the benefit granted him in the *takkanah* of the sages. Rava's statement granting the right of refusal to those benefiting from a *takkanah* was accepted as law wherever it appeared, leading us to conclude that this opinion was acceptable in the worldview of the editors of BT.

Takkanot Do Not Inflict Unnecessary Loss

A related statement, found three times also only in BT, provides a corollary to the idea that one may refuse a benefit offered by a *takkanah*. In BT BB 35b,[347] we find the assumption that the rabbis would not have made a *takkanah* that would have led to personal loss. This *sugya* speaks of a case where the prior landholder is disputing ownership with the current resident, claiming that the current resident is merely a tenant farmer, and not the new owner of the property:

חזקתן שלש שנים מיום ליום וכו'. א״ר אבא: אי דלי ליה איהו גופיה צנא
דפירי, לאלתר הוי חזקה. אמר רב זביד: ואם טען ואמר לפירות הורדתיו,
נאמן. וה״מ בתוך שלש, אבל לאחר שלש לא. א״ל רב אשי לרב כהנא: אי
לפירא אחתיה, מאי הוה ליה למעבד? א״ל: איבעי ליה למחויי. דאי לא
תימא הכי, הני משכנתא דסורא דכתב בהו: במשלם שניא אלין תיפוק
ארעא דא בלא כסף, אי כביש ליה לשטר משכנתא גביה ואמר לקוחה היא
בידי, הכי נמי דמהימן? מתקני רבנן מידי דאתי ביה לידי פסידא? אלא
איבעי ליה למחויי, הכא נמי איבעי ליה למחויי.

"Their *hazakah*[348] [the *hazakah* of the current landholder] is in effect for three years from the day, etc." Rabbi Abba said: If the one who claims ownership helps the current landholder to lift a basket of fruit, this creates an immediate [new] presumption [that the land belongs to the current landholder].[349] Rav Zevid said: If he [the claimant] claims that he placed him on the land as a tenant farmer [and thus the basket of

fruit was simply helping him with his share], then he is to be believed.
And these words apply only when it is within three years, but not later.

> Said Rav Ashi to Rav Kahana: If he had made him a tenant farmer
> [for longer], what should the landholder do [to protect himself from the
> tenant farmer's possible claim that the land was now his after a three-
> year uncontested use of the property]? He said to him: he [the claimant]
> should have lodged a protest [within three years]. For if you did not ac-
> cept this premise, then what of the "mortgage of Sura,"[350] which has
> written in it: "at the end of these years the land shall go out [and return
> to the prior owner] without any monetary exchange." But if the lender
> hides the security document and claims that he bought the land, should
> we also believe him? Would the rabbis make a *takkanah* that would
> lead to [the owner's] financial loss? Rather, since [there] the borrower
> should have lodged a claim within three years [to protect his interest in
> the land], here, also, he [the current landholder] may protect himself by
> lodging his claim within three years.

Here, due to the statement by the rabbis in M BB 3:1 recognizing the *hazakah* of
the landholder, it is possible that the true owner of the land might experience
serious financial losses. The rule of the sages is assumed to allow a three-year
window for the current landowner to make an official claim before witnesses. In
the final analysis, as long as the three-year statute of limitations is observed, and
the current landholder or lender had the reasonable opportunity to stake their
claims, even if they did not take advantage of it, then they were sufficiently protected. Here, then, we see that a basic principle of *takkanot* was assumed to be
that they not inflict unnecessary financial loss on those whom they affected.

A Few Singularities

Through the many examples reviewed in the latter part of this chapter, we
will mark out the general contours of the use of the term *takkanah* in rabbinic
literature. However, there are a few other statements worth mentioning because
they highlight important moments in the process of making *takkanot*, the attitude
toward making *takkanot* and the thinking of the rabbis responsible for the acceptance of the very idea of enacting new legal standards.

In T Yev. 1:9, we capture a glimpse into what we might label *takkanah in-
terrupta*. The context is the setting of ייבום (*yiboom*, "levirate marriage.") This
Toseftan passage hints at the ramifications of these marriages upon their offspring:

נתיבמו, בית שמיי אומרים הן כשירות והולד כשר; בית הלל אומרים הן
פסולות והולד ממזר. אמר ר' יוחנן בן נורי: בא וראה היאך הלכה זו
רווחת בישראל! לקיים כדברי בית שמיי הולד ממזר כדברי ב"ה, אם
לקיים כדברי בית הלל הוולד פגום כדברי בית שמאי. אלא <u>בוא ונתקין</u>
שיהו הצרות חולצות ולא מתיבמות. ולא הספיקו לגמור את הדבר עד
שנטרפה שעה.

If they [the surviving co-wives] entered into levirate marriage
[with any of the surviving brothers of their late husband], the school of
Shammai says: they [the remarried co-wives] are fit, and the children
are fit;[351] the school of Hillel says: they are unfit and the children are
mamzerim.[352]

Rabbi Yohanan ben Nuri said:[353] come and see how this law will
affect Israel – if you follow the school of Shammai, the child is a
mamzer according to the school of Hillel; if you follow the school of
Hillel, the child is a *pagum*[354] according to the school of Shammai.[355]
Rather, let us come and enact a *takkanah* that co-wives release [their
surviving brothers-in-law from the obligation of marrying them] and do
not marry [one of their surviving brothers-in-law]. And they did not
succeed in completing the matter before the situation deteriorated.[356]

Our report here states that under the guidance of Rabbi Yohanan ben Nuri, the
rabbis began the process of instituting a *takkanah*. According to this source,
unwelcome events prevented Rabbi Yohanan ben Nuri and his colleagues from
completing the task of revising the law to ease the effect these two divergent
understandings of levirate marriage had upon the community of Israel.

In BT BK 96a, we have an interesting window on the question of the applicability of *takkanot* to those outside the Jewish community. In a discussion
about a non-Jew who unknowingly purchased from a thief a stolen item that
originally belonged to a Jew, we find:

בעי רבא: השביח עובד כוכבים, מהו? א"ל רב אחא מדפתי לרבינא:
<u>תקנתא</u> לעובד כוכבים ניקו ונעבוד? אמר ליה: לא צריכא, כגון דזבניה
לישראל. סוף סוף הבא מחמת עובד כוכבים הרי הוא כעובד כוכבים! לא
צריכא, כגון דגזל ישראל וזבנה ניהליה והשביחה עובד כוכבים, והדר עובד
כוכבים וזבנה לישראל, מאי? מי אמרינן: כיון דמעיקרא ישראל והדר
ישראל, עבדי רבנן <u>תקנתא</u>, או דלמא כיון דאיכא עובד כוכבים באמצע, לא
עבדו ליה רבנן <u>תקנתא</u>? תיקו.

Rava inquired: if a non-Jew [bought a stolen item and] improved it, what then? Rav Aha from Difti said to Ravina: should we get up and make a *takkanah* for [regulating the behavior of] non-Jews? He said to him: no, we need this [statement of law] for the case in which he sold it [the stolen item] to a Jew. [He replied:] in the end, one who claims [a stolen object] through [the intermediary of] a non-Jew is [treated] like the non-Jew! [He said to him:] No, we need this [statement of law] for the case in which a Jew stole an object and sold it to a non-Jew who improved it, and then sold it back to another Jew—what then? Should we say, since at the beginning it was a Jew and then it was again a Jew, the rabbis make a *takkanah*—or, perhaps, since there was a non-Jew in the middle, our rabbis did not make a *takkanah*? Let it stand.

In this theoretical discussion, thanks to the interplay between Jew and non-Jew, and the rabbinic reluctance to make an enactment regulating the activities of non-Jews, the issue is ultimately abandoned with the rabbinic phrase *teyku*, indicative of the fact that the rabbis had no final answer for this problem.[357] Here, though no new *takkanah* is made, a *takkanah* in progress is considered, and it is clear that the application of *takkanot* to non-Jews is not fully accepted (nor fully rejected).

In another fascinating singularity, we find the term *takkanah* used in a way that is more often typical of the term פסק (*pesak*, "determined law") in later Jewish law.[358] In PT Eruv. 4:1, 21d, there exists a long debate between two chains of authorities that disagree on the *halakhah* in the case of establishing a Sabbath dwelling. The difference of opinion relates to the use of a shed, stable or a ship as a place for dwelling on Shabbat: some opinions suggest that one may traverse the entire area of the dwelling, while others argue that the traditional limit of four cubits should apply even within these three defined areas. These opinions are carried by Rabban Gamaliel and Rabbi Eleazar ben Azariah on the one hand, and Rabbi Yehoshua and Rabbi Akiba on the other, and already appear in M's initial presentation in 4:1. The applicable moment for our study comes at a point in the discussion in PT where a decision is ultimately reached:

חנניה בן אחי רבי יהושע אומר: כל היום היו דנין אילו כנגד אילו, עד שבא אחי אבא והכריע ביניהן והתקין שתהא הלכה כרבן גמליאל וכרבי אלעזר בן עזריה בספינה, וכרבי יהושע וכרבי עקיבה בדיר וסהר.

Hananya the son of the brother of Rabbi Yehoshua said: All day they were debating, these against those, until my uncle came and decided between them, and enacted that *halakhah* would follow Rabban Gamaliel and Rabbi Eleazar ben Azariah with regards to the ship, and following Rabbi Yehoshua and Rabbi Akiba with regards to the shed and the stable.

Without wandering into a longer discussion of the details in this complicated *sugya*, it is important to note that the term *takkanah* is used in describing a decision made between two positions. This enactment is not an innovation by any means, instead, it is the selection of an appropriate halakhic decision from two viable options, intended to set Jewish law for the future. This is quite different from the majority of usages of the term that we encounter in the rest of the literature, and suggests that some *takkanot* in other passages could simply have been the ultimate decision reached in a process of halakhic debate, rather than being the result of innovation or legislation made up by the rabbis reporting it.

Another interesting singularity appears in BT BM 112b, where the discussion revolves around an enactment that a hired laborer may swear he did not receive his due pay in order to receive the wages owed him:

שכיר בזמנו נשבע ונוטל וכו'. שכיר אמאי תַקִינוּ ליה רבנן למשתבע ושקיל?
אמר רב יהודה אמר שמואל : הלכות גדולות שנו כאן. הני הלכתא נינהו?
הני תקנות נינהו! אלא, אמר רב יהודה אמר שמואל : תַקְנוֹת גדולות שנו
כאן. גדולות מכלל דאיכא קטנות? אלא אמר רב נחמן אמר שמואל:
תַקְנוֹת קבועות שנו כאן.

"A laborer who claims wages when they are due, may swear and receive his wages." [The Gemara now assumes this to be a rabbinic enactment without discussing it.][359] Why did the rabbis enact that a laborer may swear and take [his wages from an employer]? Rav Yehuda said in the name of Shmuel: they taught major *halakhot* here. Are these *halakhot*? These are enactments! Rather, Rav Yehuda said in the name of Shmuel: Major enactments they taught here. Major [enactments]? Does this imply that there are minor [enactments as well]? Rather, Rav Nahman said in the name of Shmuel: Fixed enactments they taught here.

שכיר (*sakhir*, "day laborer") implies that this laborer had been hired for a specified short period of time, usually one day's work. According to Lev. 19:13, the employer is obligated to pay the employee immediately at the end of the workday—wages may not be held by an employer overnight. However, the Torah did not provide a specific legal remedy should an employer choose to withhold wages. Thus, the rabbis instituted a *takkanah* that a day laborer could swear regarding money owed him, and he must be paid. This procedure protected the weaker party from the whim or wickedness of the stronger party.

The text raises an interesting question: can a distinction be made between ephemeral and more long-lasting *takkanot*? Can there be a distinction between major and minor *takkanot*? The *stam* rejects both of these potential distinctions, while accepting a third: the differentiation between fixed *takkanot* and some other, unnamed category. This suggests that there were some *takkanot* promulgated that were worthy of being fixed for all time, thus they were not meant to be temporary measures, but permanent. Others, one may learn from this text, were meant as ephemeral solutions to momentary problems, and were not ever intended to be in effect for the long term. Unfortunately, it also provides us with very little further information on this conceptual categorization, and provides little evidence of a systematized distinction. Since this is the only occurrence of this sort of statement, we are left without much concrete information, but simply a glimpse of one potential typology of various *takkanot*.

A final singularity provides a fascinating look into one rabbinic view of the biblical text. In BT Ket. 10b, the subject matter is the word אלמנה (*almanah* – "widow") and the amount of money provided in the *ketubbah* of a widow who remarries:

מאי אלמנה? אמר רב חנא בגדתאה: אלמנה, על שם מנה. אלמנה מן
האירוסין מאי איכא למימר? איידי דהא קרי לה אלמנה, הא נמי קרי לה
אלמנה. אלמנה דכתיבא באורייתא מאי איכא למימר? דעתידין רבנן
דמתקני לה מנה. ומי כתב קרא לעתיד? אין, דכתיב: (בראשית ב') "ושם
הנהר השלישי חדקל הוא ההולך קדמת אשור," ותנא רב יוסף: אשור, זו
סליקא, ומי הואי? אלא דעתידה, הכא נמי דעתידה.

What is an *almanah*? Rav Hana of Baghdad said: "*almanah*"—
"because of *maneh* [100 *zuz*]."[360]

A widow from betrothal [and not from marriage itself], what is there to say [since the value of her *ketubbah* is still 200 *zuz*, though she is still called an *almanah*]? Since this one is called *almanah*, so, this one is also called *almanah*.

[The word] "*almanah*" written in the Torah—what is there to say [about this, since the *ketubbah* was not instituted in biblical times]?[361] That its future was that the rabbis would enact for her [a *ketubbah* worth] 100 *zuz*. Does the Torah write about the future? As it is written: (Genesis 2:14) "and the name of the third river is Hiddekel, and it is the one that goes to the east of Assyria." And Rav Yosef taught, Assyria, this is [the city of] Seleucia.[362] And did Seleucia already exist? Rather, it was to exist in the future, and so, too, for her [i.e., for the 100 *zuz* of the widow].[363]

Here, the Torah text is granted the ability to peer into the future, and to respond to contingencies not yet extant at the time of its composition. This passage implies that the rabbis, in making this *takkanah*, were simply following the intentions present *sub rosa* in the biblical text. This passage relies upon a folk etymology to show that the fixing of the value of a widow's *ketubbah* was not simply made up, but rather had a firm base in a Torah so prescient that it could actually predict future situations and provide adequate responses to them in advance.

These passages represent very limited portals into an understanding of the intellectual history of the rabbis' approach to legal change, but they do help to create a more detailed picture of rabbinic legal development amongst the Tannaim, Amoraim and Stammaim. There is no evidence, here, of any systematized ideology. Nonetheless, we do see the *ad hoc* use of ideas connected to *takkanot* to analyze and solve various problems. This is helpful in sketching a broad and complete (though asystematic) idea of the use of the term in rabbinic literature.

We now turn to the main task of this chapter, where we will look carefully at the wide variety of *takkanot* that exist in rabbinic literature so as to apprehend the viewpoints of the rabbis who promulgated them, the stated rationales connected with them and the various categories of enactments that we find scattered about our texts. As before, we hope to open a window of understanding onto the editors and redactors of the various texts we study, to help reconstruct the intellectual development that took place during this period.

The Rationales—Initiation *Takkanot*

In 726 distinct occurrences of the root *tkn* related to enacting revisions or amendments to rabbinic law or custom, we find a total of 12 distinct rationales employed to justify their innovations in Jewish law. We will examine closely a few examples of each of these rationales, except for those rationales already covered in the first chapter, which will simply be listed for the sake of brevity. We will conclude the chapter with an analysis of the distribution of these rationales over time and space, as we did in chapter one.

Initiation of New Practices

The largest category, by far, of *takkanot* found in our texts is the group of *takkanot* that initiate new practices, laws and customs. In 60 discrete cases, our corpus credits authorities, ranging from Adam to the late Amoraic rabbis, with the creation of *takkanot* that start new practices. Included among the initiators are: the prophets, Moses, the Men of the Great Assembly, Ezra, David, Solomon, the *tzofim* ("prophets"), numerous individual authorities and the rabbinical assemblies of both Yavneh and Usha.

Ultimately, it is highly unlikely that *all* of these attributions are accurate, as Martin Jaffee has argued,[364] though we cannot entirely rule out the possibility that some are. It is clear that these texts do not necessarily provide us with completely reliable and discernable historical background on the true initiators of these changes in practice or ideology, nor do they point precisely to the era of said developments. Nonetheless, there is definite information to be gleaned pertaining to intellectual development within rabbinic thought by the very fact of the inclusion of these passages in Jewish legal works. The initiation of new practices cited in these texts and the attributions given them can help us delineate active trends in the intellectual history of the rabbis, as well as the major differences in thought patterns among divergent communities. To effectively utilize this material, rather than simply accepting the suggested attribution and rationale, we must consider why the rabbis attributed legal changes to each party, and what that says about the rabbinic worldview during the editor's time.

We will begin by looking at accounts of the initiation of new practices that are attributed to pre-rabbinic figures such as Adam, Moses, Ezra and others. Thanks to large chronological gaps and the influential position in rabbinic historiography held by these early leaders, these are the most suspect of attributions, and need to be viewed with much skepticism.

Accounts of Pre-Rabbinic Initiation of New Practices

Our rabbinic legal corpus includes 39 references to initiation attributed to important pre-rabbinic figures.[365] The earliest of these figures, according to biblical chronology, is Adam, the first human being created. The latest is the group of leaders rabbinic tradition names אנשי כנסת הגדולה (*anshei kenesset hagedolah,* "the Men of the Great Assembly"). The attributed origins, thus, span thousands of years and reflect many different situations within the spectrum of development of the Jewish people. The most numerous citations center on Ezra, Moses and the prophets, a reflection of the rabbis' consideration of their important leadership roles at pivotal moments in Jewish history, and the relatively rich possibilities inherent in the descriptions of their actions in biblical texts. Most provocatively, all of these reported innovations exhibit a thematic tie between the initiated practice and a verse or situation associated with the initiator. The verses are often used midrashically to support the initiation account. This tends to reinforce the critical questioning of these traditions, implying that a later editor may have searched the past for a firm anchor for a developing practice, designed to hold it safely to a strong historical seabed in the person of these respected leaders.

Adam, the First Human Initiator?

PT AZ 1:2, 39c provides us with the only example of Adam as initiator of religious practices. The rabbis did not portray Adam as changing law—after all, not much law was in place at his moment in history. Instead, they attribute to Adam the initiation of a basic calendrical rubric. The fascinating piece is that he is shown as initiating part of the *Roman* calendar:

רב אמר: קלנדס אדם הראשון התקינו כיון דחמא לילייא אריך. אמר אי
לי שמא שכתוב בו ״הוא ישופך ראש ואתה תשופנו עקבי״ שמא יבוא
לנשכיני. ואומר ״אך חושך ישופיני.״ כיון דחמא איממא ארך, אמר
״קלנדס,״ ״קלון דיאו.״

> Rav said: *Calends*—Adam the first [human being] instituted it. When he saw the nights lengthening [as the fall season turned to winter], he said: "Woe is me, perhaps [the snake,] the one about whom it is written 'he will strike at you with his head and you will strike at him with your heel' (Genesis 3:15) will come to bite me." And he said: "surely darkness will cover me."[366] (Psalm 139:11) When he saw that the days were lengthening [again when spring began], he said: *"Calends," "Calon Dio."*

קלנדס is from the Greek word καλάνδαι, which gives rise to the Latin *calandae*, and to the later English *calendar*, but in the Greek accusative form instead of the nominative form.[367] The word means, simply, the first day of the Roman month. *Calends* was a piece of the coordinating calendrical scheme already present in the earliest Roman calendar, which divided each of the ten months into three parts centered around *calends* (the first day), *nones* (the seventh day) and *ides* (the middle of the month, the fifteenth day).[368] The two final words of the passage provide Rav's folk etymology for the Greek term *calends* in καλόν δύε, a Greek term that Lieberman identifies as meaning "set well," a fond farewell spoken to the sun by a reassured Adam who then knew it would continue to rise each day. Rav's point, here, was that the Roman *calends* festival was a creation occasioned by Adam's first joyful notice of the sun when the days began to lengthen during earth's first springtime.[369]

A closer analysis of the situation reveals more. If we search the prehistory of the Roman calendar, we find that legend attributes the development of the earliest Roman calendar (with the tripartite monthly *calends, nones, ides* system mentioned above) to Romulus, the founder of Rome, who started his calendar with year 1 at Rome's founding in the year 735 BCE. Romulus' original 304-day calendar was far from perfect: with its 61.25 day discrepancy with the solar year, the seasons it enumerated wandered quite a bit. Nonetheless, it did eventually lead to the more sophisticated descendant calendars of 355 days, and finally 365.25 days. *Calends* was still observed during late antiquity as a regular monthly celebration in Roman life.[370]

If we look to the only extant text that is somewhat parallel, we find something entirely different. *PR* 23:6,[371] a later midrashic compilation, begins with this same trope of Adam and his fear of darkness as the sun wanes in winter, absent any reference to the Roman counting of time. In contrast, the *PR* passage concludes with an explanation of the blessing over the candle during *havdallah*, the service recognizing the end of Shabbat at sunset, also a time when light was diminishing but would return again. *PR* is a Palestinian text, composed sometime in the ninth century.[372] Thus, we have two witnesses to a story about Adam and diminishing light that circulated in the Palestinian context, but these two different authors chose to adapt the Adam motif to their chosen message in varying ways.

With this information before us, we can now understand better what the PT passage is actually doing. Instead of simply attributing the beginning of a custom to Adam, it is drawing on Adam's universality as primogenitor of all humanity to undermine the very Roman-ness of an important aspect of the Roman calendar. Instead of crediting the first-man of Rome, Romulus, with this element of the world's most advanced calendrical system, the universal first-man created by the God of the Jews, Adam, is given responsibility for the creation of even a Roman calendrical celebration. Adam is chosen as initiator because he represented the earliest universal human being who could be vested with this act, and he arises from a Jewish source of history—the Torah. This rejection of the Roman nature of the calendar is coherent with other rabbinic decisions to distance the Jewish community from Roman celebrations.[373]

This passage, then, is a thinly veiled slap against the more advanced calendar system of the Romans, reassigning credit to Adam for one of the Romans' most successful ideas.[374] Its internal etiology for a calendrical custom is an ideological statement of either Rav's generation in Babylonia and his attitude toward the Romans, or that of the redactors of PT. Both its Aramaic skeleton and attribution to Rav remind us that it is Amoraic in origin. Forms such as איממא (daytime), which appear only in PT, prove its Palestinian origin or substantial refashioning by Palestinian redactors to fit their language and style.

Finally, the passage does utilize the exact form of other initiation *takkanot*, which gives us a good first hint that we must carefully evaluate each of these occurrences and not accept them at face value. This text shows that the editors of PT desired to send a certain message about Jews and Romans, and the relative antiquity of their contributions to humankind, and they utilized Adam's unique position in humanity to do so. This also shows that the root *tkn* did not always strictly indicate legal change, but can be employed as a rhetorical form that served other functions—especially that of assigning an origin to a practice or idea.

The Patriarchs as Initiators

Following biblical chronology, the next initiating *takkanah* mentioned in our legal sources is said to arise from the *avot*, the three patriarchs Abraham, Isaac and Jacob.[375] One opinion in BT Ber. 26b credits them with initiating the three daily prayer services, though an opposing opinion declares the *tefillot* a later rabbinic innovation based on the sacrifices. Despite this dispute, BT Ber. does make clear through the use of the verb *tkn* that it seriously considered the possibility that the patriarchs were the initial instigators of the three daily services. The end of this *sugya* resolves the disagreement with a compromise: the patriarchs enacted these services, while the rabbis supported them from the daily sacrifices. Thus, the credit for this innovation is shared between two groups that were widely divergent. For BT, the real issue here is the balance between admitting the novelty of the practice and an attempt to root it back into the earliest corridors of the people's history, to provide a strong anchor for a new practice.

Moses as Initiator

The next group of initiatory *takkanot* is attributed to Moses, whom many commentators view as an initiator in a truly unique situation. Schepansky, for example, spends a number of pages discussing the *takkanot* of Moses to determine if they are to be classed as biblically ordained (*deoraita*) or rabbinically-ordained (*derabbanan*). His pre-critical argument proceeds this way: traditionally, since Moses himself was responsible for transmitting the Torah from Mount Sinai, any law originating with him could, perhaps, qualify as biblically ordained. The rabbinic and medieval sources, however, do not uphold this position. Schepansky rehearses a variety of opinions by Maimonides, Nahmanides and the *rishonim* and *aharonim*, and his pages conclude with a clear sense that Moses' *takkanot* were to be considered exclusively *derabbanan*, to distinguish the Written Torah from his personal innovations taught after Sinai. This distinction also clarifies Moses' dual roles as lawgiver and as later initiator of change in law.[376]

Though Bloch and Schepanksy accept *takkanot* attributed to Moses in our sources as *bona fide* history, among the seven examples of Moses' initiating of new customs and practices, all are quite problematic from a critical perspective. In BT Shab. 30a, we find a statement that expounds on the general theme of the initiating activities of Moses:

דבר אחר : מנהגו של עולם, שר בשר ודם גוזר גזרה ספק מקיימין אותה
ספק אין מקיימין אותה, ואם תמצי לומר מקיימין אותה, בחייו מקיימין

אותה, במותו, אין מקיימין אותה. <u>ואילו משה רבינו, גזר כמה גזירות</u>
<u>ותיקן כמה תקנות, וקיימות הם לעולם ולעולמי עולמים</u>. ולא יפה אמר
שלמה ושבח אני את המתים וגו׳!

Another matter: the custom of the world is that when a ruler of
flesh and blood makes a decree, there is a question as to whether they
observe it and or whether they do not observe it. And if you want to
say that they observe it—in his life they observe it, but after his death
they do not observe it.

But what about Moses our teacher? <u>He decreed many decrees, and</u>
<u>enacted many enactments, and they stand [after his death] for all eter-</u>
<u>nity</u>. And did not Solomon speak well [when he said]: "I accounted
those who died [more fortunate than those who are still living]" (Eccl.
4:2).[377]

Here, without any mention of Moses' specific innovations, we see a statement of
general attitude with regard to Moses' innovations in lawgiving. Note that the
statement is in Hebrew—a linguistic indicator of an earlier statement within BT,
usually from the Tannaitic period. The statement suggests his *takkanot* are
clearly *derabbanan*, but that there is a qualitative difference between Moses and
other lawmakers in the eyes of the rabbis. Moses' work lived on long after his
death, while in their opinion others' work lacked the same exalted longevity.

We find an early specific instance of innovation attributed to Moses in *SB*
66:[378]

וידבר משה אל בני ישראל ״לעשות הפסח.״ למה נאמר? לפי שהוא אומר
״וידבר משה את מועדי ה׳ אל בני ישראל,״ (ויקרא כג מד) ומה ת״ל
״וידבר משה אל בני ישראל לעשות הפסח?״ אמר להם שמרו את הפסח
בזמנו, נמצאו מועדות בזמנם. ד״א: מלמד ששמע פרשת מועדות מסיני,
ואמרה לישראל וחזר ושנאה להם בשעת מעשה. ד״א: אמר להם הלכות
פסח בפסח, הלכות עצרת בעצרת, הלכות החג בחג. מיכן אמרו: משה <u>תקן</u>
להם לישראל להיות שואלים בענין ודורשים בענין.

And Moses told the children of Israel to "observe the Pesah."
(Num. 9:4) Why is this said? Since it says: "And Moses declared to the
Israelites the set times of the Lord," (Lev. 23:44) why does the text
[also have to] say "Moses spoke to the children of Israel and told them
to observe the Pesah?" (Num. 9:4) He said to them: observe Pesah at its
proper time—that festivals must be observed at their proper time.

Another matter: this teaches that he heard *parashat moadot* [the biblical text about the festivals] from Sinai, and spoke it to Israel, and went back and taught them again at the time of its observance.

Another matter: he said to them: [study] the laws of Pesah during Pesah, the laws of Shavuot during Shavuot, the laws of Sukkot during Sukkot. From this they said: Moses <u>enacted</u> for Israel that they ask questions on the subject [at hand] and interpret [biblical texts] on the subject [at the appropriate time].

Here, in a passage that speaks of the observance of Passover, there is a *takkanah* that sets a further requirement upon Israel not explicitly present in the Written Torah. Playing on the apparent redundancy of the two verses that prescribe observance of Pesah, the midrash inferred that Moses initiated the requirement of timely study of laws pertaining to each festival. This should include, according to this midrash and its Talmudic parallels,[379] asking questions about the festival and interpreting the biblical texts related to it.

SB supplies three divergent interpretations to resolve the redundancy between these two verses: a) that the additional verse shows that Moses directly instructed the Israelites to observe the festivals in a timely manner; b) that Moses heard the explanation of the biblical passages relating to the festivals at Sinai, and then went back and taught them at the time of their observance each year; or c) that Moses gave them an entirely separate oral command to study the laws of each holiday during that holiday, and they *inferred* from his statement that Moses initiated this practice for them. The use of the phrase מיכן אמרו (*mi-kan amru*, "from this they said") is an important clue to understanding the history of this passage: this phrase explicitly admits that the assignment of the *takkanah* to Moses is derived as opposed to inherited.

This is the critical point: in *SB* above, the editors utilized a redundancy in biblical texts to infer that this initiation of practice came from Moses. In contrast, in every other rabbinic discussion of this matter, we find a *baraita* that states a two-fold obligation: a thirty-day time period before Pesah for study in the assembly (with a minority opinion of Rabban Shimeon ben Gamaliel of two weeks), and study during the duration of the holiday for the general community. Interestingly, these *baraitot* show no hint of any connection with Moses. The earliest of the many occurrences is in T Meg. 3:5:

שואלין הלכות הפסח בפסח והלכות עצרת בעצרת והלכות החג בחג. בבית
הועד שואלין בהלכות הפסח קודם לפסח שלשים יום. רבן שמעון בן
גמליאל אומר שתי שבתות.

They ask [questions and study] about the laws of Pesah during Pesah,
the laws of Shavuot during Shavuot and the laws of Sukkot during
Sukkot. In the assembly, they ask [questions and study] about the laws
of Pesah for thirty days before Pesah. Rabban Shimeon ben Gamaliel
said: for two weeks.

In this section, as in its many parallels,[380] we find Tannaitic traditions concerning the origins of this practice, with no mention of Moses' role in initiating it at
all. The most logical reconstruction of the tradition's history, then, would point
to the Tannaitic or pre-Tannaitic existence of a tradition of timely study of the
laws associated with festivals. Most editors incorporated these traditions wholesale as anonymous *baraitot*, without attempting a reconstruction of attribution
for the initiation of the practice. The editors of *SB*, however, decided to anchor
this practice more firmly into the written tradition, and chose a handy biblical
repetition to forge a link with Moses, designed to bolster the authority of the
practice. By the time of the Amoraim, however, the practice was accepted
enough that it no longer required explicit pre-rabbinic justification.

One other initiation of Moses requires our attention. In PT Meg. 4:1, 75a,
Moses is assigned responsibility for enacting the regular Torah readings on
Shabbat morning, festivals, intermediate days of festivals and on ראש חודש (*Rosh
Hodesh*, "the start of the month"), while Ezra is given responsibility for initiat-
ing the Torah readings during the week and at Shabbat Minhah:

משה <u>התקין</u> את ישראל שיהו קורין בתורה בשבתות ובימים טובים
ובראשי חדשים ובחולו של מועד, שנאמר "וידבר משה את מועדי יי׳ אל
בני ישראל." עזרה <u>התקין</u> לישראל שיהו קורין בתורה בשני ובחמישי
ובשבת במנחה.

Moses <u>enacted</u> that Israel would read in the Torah on Sabbaths, holidays, the beginning of the month and the intermediate days of festivals,
as it is said: "And Moses declared the festivals of God to the people of
Israel" (Lev. 23:44). Ezra <u>enacted</u> that Israel would read in the Torah
on Monday, Thursday and Shabbat at Minhah.

Here, too, Moses was portrayed as the institutor of a vital practice with serious
communal ramifications. However, there are contradictory texts that attribute
this practice to "the Prophets,"[381] or "the Prophets and the Elders."[382] Furthermore, there is firm scholarly evidence that indicates that this practice did not
begin until later times. Albeck's assessment of Moses' involvement is succinct
and on target: this *takkanah* is assigned to Moses solely through the means of
later biblical interpretation.[383] As in the other case above, the editors turned a
slim hint in a well-worn verse into a radical statement of origin.

From these texts, and the remainder like them, it is clear the rabbis were hanging vital practices that they wanted to bolster for communal reasons on their greatest, most ancient authority, the initial transmitter of law himself. Torah reading times, *Birkat HaMazon*, study during festivals, seven days of mourning or feasting and parts of the form of the *amidah* are all attributed to Moses' initiation. A few facets unite these various cases where the rabbis fashion a Mosaic initiation: all represent important customs that created activities that gathered individuals together for communal study or prayer. All lacked clear lines of biblical authority, but were in keeping with (and, at least in *SB*, were explicitly justified by) strong connection with extant biblical laws. Finally, the character of Moses as teacher and leader is accentuated by the rabbis' choice of these practices: for the rabbis, Moses represented the apex of learned and religious leadership, and the initiations attached to him reflect this outlook. This assigning of innovations to suitable individuals, based upon their specific traits as tradition defined them, will repeat often with respect to a number of other pre-rabbinic leaders, as we shall presently see.

The Ten *Tenaim* of Joshua

Joshua received credit in rabbinic legal sources for initiating a number of practices sustained by later Jewish law. While in Joshua's case, his innovations are called תנאים (*tenaim,* "stipulations") as opposed to *takkanot*; there are two extant instances where the Amoraim directly refer to them as *takkanot*, rendering them eligible for inclusion in this study.

Joshua is quoted as instituting a *takkanah* in BT Ber. 48b, during a discussion of the origin of *Birkat HaMazon* (the grace after the meal). He also appears in BT Eruv. 17a, where we find a discussion of legal limits on the actions of an army:

תנו רבנן: מחנה היוצאת למלחמת הרשות—מותרין בגזל עצים יבשים. רבי יהודה בן תימא אומר: אף חונין בכל מקום, ובמקום שנהרגו שם נקברין. מותרין בגזל עצים יבשים. האי תַקנתא דיהושע הוה, דאמר מר, עשרה תנאים התנה יהושע: שיהו מרעין בחורשין ומלקטין עצים משדותיהן.

Our rabbis taught: a camp [of soldiers] that goes out to fight a discretionary war[384] is permitted to commandeer dry wood. Rabbi Yehuda ben Teimah said: They may even camp[385] anywhere, and in the place where they are killed, there they are buried.

They are permitted to commandeer dry wood. This was an <u>enactment</u> of Joshua, as the Master said: Joshua stipulated ten stipulations:

that they are allowed to pasture their cattle on uncultivated land and
that they may collect wood from their [i.e., others'] fields.

In the *baraita* above, an advancing army is granted license to fulfill its basic
needs wherever it happens to march: soldiers may camp anywhere, seize wood
for fires or siegeworks and take burial places for fallen soldiers from the surrounding community. The Amoraic commentary that follows says that the
source for permission to take firewood resides in a *takkanah* promulgated by
Joshua, from amongst his ten *tenaim*, though only two are quoted in this particular text. When we look at the parallel text in T Eruv. 2:6, though, we find that it
does not give credit to Joshua at all; it only repeats the essence of the *baraita*
with the same opinion of Rabbi Yehuda ben Teimah:

מחנה היוצאת למלחמת הרשות מותרין לגזול עצים יבשין. ר׳ יהודה בן
תימא אומר: שורין בכל מקום, ומקום שנהרגין שם נקברין.

A camp that goes out to a discretionary war is permitted to commandeer dry wood. Rabbi Yehuda ben Teimah said: they may camp [with-
out permission of the owners] in any place,[386] and where they are
killed, there they are buried.

We see immediately that this nearly equivalent text, stated in the name of the
same authority, lacks the connection we saw above to Joshua. Another parallel,
this one in M, which discusses the collecting of dry wood by an army, is devoid
of any relationship to Joshua as well.[387] It is only in BT's Aramaic layer of
commentary that we see these traditions portrayed as a *takkanah* of Joshua, a
sign that BT was willing to re-envision the nature of prior legal opinions, reassigning both their authorship and their legal status.

These traditions in BT tended to collect around Joshua when they related to
an advancing army. This is no literary lark; since Joshua was the first military
commander of the Israelites when they began their most important battles, it is
perfectly logical that enactments related to war would accrete around him. As a
literary stratagem, then, either the rabbis or the editor of BT Eruv. attributed this
law to Joshua, without reliance upon an inherited tradition or specific prooftexts.
It simply made sense.

Furthermore, it was only in the Tannaitic period, long after Joshua's time,
that a dualistic concept of war began to emerge with even the beginnings of a
sense of clarity.[388] The combination of these data show that the editors of BT felt
comfortable claiming alteration of earlier law, even as they created a retrojection
of this change onto Joshua to bolster it. This represents a common strategy employed often in the justification of initiatory *takkanot*.

In perhaps the most important rabbinic source relating to Joshua, BT BK 80b-81a, we find a *baraita* with a full listing of all ten *tenaim*, though here they are not called *takkanot* at all. Interestingly, there are not just ten in the printed version, but actually eleven:

תנו רבנן : עשרה תנאין התנה יהושע : שיהו מרעין בחורשין, ומלקטין עצים
בשדותיהם, ומלקטים עשבים בכל מקום חוץ מתלתן, וקוטמים נטיעות
בכל מקום חוץ מגרופיות של זית, ומעין היוצא בתחילה בני העיר
מסתפקין ממנו, ומחכין בימה של טבריא ובלבד שלא יפרוס קלע ויעמיד
את הספינה, ונפנין לאחורי הגדר ואפילו בשדה מליאה כרכום, ומהלכים
בשבילי הרשות עד שתרד רביעה שניה, ומסתלקין לצידי הדרכים מפני
יתידות הדרכים, והתועה בין הכרמים מפסיג ועולה מפסיג ויורד, ומת
מצוה קונה מקומו.

Our rabbis taught: Joshua made ten stipulations:
1) they may graze [cattle] on uncultivated land;[389]
2) they may collect wood in their [private] fields;[390]
3) they may collect grasses anywhere except a place where there is fenugreek;[391]
4) they may cut shoots [from a plant] except from the shoots of olive trees;[392]
5) [when] a spring emerges for the first time, the people of the town may drink from it;
6) they may fish with hooks and line in the Sea of Tiberias as long as they do not spread a sail and interfere with the boat[s];[393]
7) they may relieve themselves behind a fence even if the field is full of saffron;[394]
8) they may walk via paths on private land until the coming of the second rain;[395]
9) they may turn aside and walk on the sides of roads [and thus cross private property] to avoid the road-pegs;[396]
10) anyone who is lost in a vineyard may cut his way up and cut his way down [in order to get out]; and
11) that a dead body acquires the spot where it is found.[397]

Dikdukei Sofrim on this passage suggests no substantial manuscript differences, and certainly none substantial enough to account for the differential between the formulaic counting of "ten" and the actual count of eleven. Traditions of ten abound in Jewish lore (cf. Ezra's ten *takkanot* (discussed below), the ten *puncta extraordinaria* of the Torah,[398] Abraham's ten trials, the Ten Commandments and so on), providing a fine grouping for oral memorization naturally suited to the digits of the human hand. There is also a very strong thematic tie between all these laws: they all relate to communal life in settled towns, something that Joshua would have first established.

The most likely explanation of this text's development is that these legal stipulations, easements that formed the basis of Judaean property laws, formed externally and individually, and were then brought together thematically by an editor, based around the formulaic notion of a group of ten assigned to Joshua. The first four laws relate to farming, defining the parameters of grazing, collecting wood and grass and the protection of future agricultural sources. Laws five and six relate to water rights. Laws seven through eleven provide easements on the use of private land by individuals who do not own it. What unites these ten (actually, eleven) laws is their relevance to a people living on their own land.

What emerges from this *baraita*, then, is a picture that is created in the Tannaitic period, designed to attach laws to Joshua because of his strong position in Jewish memory as a superior warrior and an allocator of tribal lands. The language, place names and activities referenced do not cohere with the time of Joshua, indicating a definite later origin for these *takkanot* amongst the Jews living under Roman influence. The most responsible reconstruction understands this passage as the result of the rabbinic desire to root customs in the earliest possible generation of leadership, connecting them to the most appropriate predecessor for their theme. Since Joshua was portrayed as the first major Israelite leader responsible for the initial capture and fortification of the land of Israel, it made great literary sense to promulgate these laws in his authoritative name. Doing so lent *gravitas* to these laws, and created an appropriate literary structure to support innovation in areas related to a shifting balance between communal and individual rights in a settled society. As we are beginning to see, this is a common occurrence amongst the *takkanot* attributed by the rabbis to leaders before and during the Second Temple Period. Other examples will be found in our next section, where the rabbis summon forth a variety of distinguished personages to reinforce a series of *takkanot* that relate to their particular moments in history.

Takkanot Ascribed to Prophets, Kings and Other Leadership

A few examples exist that show other individuals initiating practices during the period following Joshua. These include David,[399] Solomon,[400] the *tzofim* (prophets),[401] the *neviim* (also prophets)[402] and the *anshei hakenesset hagedolah* or "the Men of the Great Assembly."[403] Like the examples involving Joshua above, these too are the results of rabbinic retrojection of practices onto earlier strata of history for the purpose of strengthening the mandate of observance. Often these texts provide a pseudo-history of the practice, rooting major developments in the fertile soil of earlier revered leadership. These re-creations do not represent history, but are the later creative work of rabbis looking to anchor their practices to the authoritative texts and personalities of past generations. In this respect, they are significant, for they provide us with insight into how the rabbis viewed and employed the great characters of the past who held weight in their eyes.

One compound example of the rabbinic exposition of such retrojection appears in texts that describe the development of the system of watches in the Temple in Jerusalem. We begin by looking at M Ta. 4:2, a text that does not use the term *takkanah* at all, but is the earliest rabbinic reference to the system of watches in the Temple:

אלו הן מעמדות לפי שנאמר (במדבר כ״ח) "צו את בני ישראל ואמרת
אליהם את קרבני לחמי." וכי היאך קרבנו של אדם קרב והוא אינו עומד
על גביו? התקינו נביאים הראשונים עשרים וארבע משמרות, על כל משמר
ומשמר היה מעמד בירושלם של כהנים, של לוים ושל ישראלים. הגיע זמן
המשמר לעלות, כהנים ולוים עולים לירושלם, וישראל שבאותו משמר
מתכנסין לעריהן וקוראין במעשה בראשית :

These are the *maamadot*, as it is said: "Command the Israelite people and say to them: [be punctilious in presenting to Me at stated times] the offerings of food due Me" (Num. 28:2). And since when is the offering of a man brought near [to God] and he does not stand next to it? The early prophets[404] <u>enacted</u> 24 watches, and for each of these watches there was a *maamad* in Jerusalem [made up] of priests, Levites and Israelites. When the time came for them to come up to stand watch, the priests and Levites would go up to Jerusalem and the Israelites in that same watch gathered in their cities and read the story of creation.

A *maamad* is, literally, a "standing" at a post—completing a necessary watch in the rotation of sacrificial duties in the Temple. Here, M exhibits a one-phase pattern of initiation. T, on the other hand, offers us three stages in the original creation of the system of twenty-four *maamadot* in the Temple. T Ta. 3:2 suggests that the development of the system of watches began with Moses, continued with David and Samuel, and then concluded with the "prophets who were in Jerusalem:"

שמנה משמרות תיקן משה לכהונה, ושמנה ללוייה. משעמד דוד ושמואל
הרואה, עשאום עשרים וארבע משמרות כהונה, ועשרים וארבע משמרות
לויה, שני "המה יסד דוד ושמואל הרואה באמונתם," אילו משמרות
כהונה ולויה. עמדו נביאים שבירושלם וקבעו שם עשרים וארבעה עמודים
כנגד עשרים וארבע משמרות כהונה ולויה, שני "צו את בני ישראל ואמרת
אליהם את קרבני לחמי." אי איפשר לומר כל ישראל, אלא מלמד ששלוחו
של אדם כמותו.

Moses <u>enacted</u> eight watches for the priesthood and eight watches for the Levites. When David and Samuel the seer, arose, they set 24 watches for the priests and 24 watches for the Levites, as it is said: "David and Samuel the seer, established them in their office of trust" (I Chron. 9:22). These are the watches of the priesthood and the Levites.

The prophets who were in Jerusalem arose and fixed there 24 groups [for the *maamadot*] corresponding to these 24 watches for the priests and the Levites, as it is said: "Command the Israelite people and say to them: [be punctilious in presenting to Me at stated times] the offerings of food due Me" (Num. 28:2). It is impossible to say all Israel [will handle these offerings themselves]. Rather, this teaches that the agent of a person is [considered] equivalent to the person himself/herself.

The Toseftan version gives a very detailed account, identifying steps from no fewer than three moments in history that contribute to the final form, and defending its understanding through the use of evidence gleaned from biblical verses. In contrast, note the utter lack of involvement of Moses, David and Samuel in the mishnaic version. The entire practice of the *maamadot*, according to M, sprang fully-grown from the heads of some undefined early prophets. Note, as well, the difference in terminology: in T, the verb used to describe the action of the early prophets was קבעו, "fixed," while M used התקינו, "initiated," or "made a *takkanah*." This seems reflective of a desire on the editors' (or, potentially, earlier tradents') part to root this practice in the earliest tradition possible. M, on the other hand, seems quite content to rely upon the early prophets alone.

Finkelstein suggested a different origin: he stated that 24 was the correct number for the task, not because of three groupings that cumulatively moved from eight to 16 to 24, but because the yearly cycle was exactly 50 weeks long. Removing two full weeks of pilgrimage holidays (Sukkot and Pesah) when no coverage was needed because everyone was in Jerusalem anyway, this left exactly 48 weeks—a perfect fit for the 24 groups in a duty cycle who would each be required to serve two weeks per year.[405]

Albeck[406] looks to I Chron. 24:7-19 to support the origin of the 24 watches:

(ז) ויצא הגורל הראשון ליהויריב לידעיה השני. . . . (יח) לדליהו שלשה
ועשרים למעזיהו ארבעה ועשרים: (יט) אלה פקדתם לעבדתם לבוא לבית
יהוה כמשפטם ביד אהרן אביהם כאשר צוהו יהוה אלהי ישראל:

7) The first lot fell on Jehoiarib; the second on Jedaiah. . . .
18) The twenty-third on Delaiah; the twenty-fourth on Maaziah.

19) According to this allocation of offices by tasks, they were to enter
the House of the Lord as was laid down for them by Aaron their father,
as the Lord God of Israel had commanded him.

This text is the earliest enumeration of twenty-four divisions among the sons of
Aaron, and, as such, is the most logical prooftext there could be for the position
found in M and T. It is mildly surprising, to say the least, that it does not appear
in either text as a justification for the 24 watches. This text also does not make
any mention of the role of Moses, David or Samuel.

A parallel text from Qumran, *The War of the Sons of Light Against the Sons
of Darkness* (1QM II:1-4) describes the priestly *mishmarot* as 26 in number,
with 12 Levites serving one for each tribe. This Qumran source also lacks any
mention of Moses, David or Samuel as instigators of the practices described.[407]

A later parallel text, PT Pes. 4:1, 30c, provides an Amoraic suggestion that
the reason for the *maamadot* is to prevent every Israelite from taking too much
time away from critical agricultural duties, namely, the harvesting of crops at the
appropriate times:

אמר ר' יונה: אילין תמידין, קרבנותיהן של כל ישראל אינון. אם יהיו כל
ישראל עולין לירושלם לית כתיב אלא "שלש פעמים בשנה יראה כל
זכורך." אם יהיו כל ישראל יושבין ובטילין, והכתיב "ואספת דגנך?" מי
אוסף להן את הדגן! אלא שהתקינו הנביאים הראשונים עשרים וארבע
משמרות, על כל משמר ומשמר היה עומד בירושלם של כהנים ושל לוים
ושל ישראלים.[408]

Rabbi Yonah said: these daily sacrifices, they are the offerings of all Israel. If all Israel would go up to Jerusalem—but it is only written [in
this verse]: "three times each year your males will be seen . . . " (Ex.
23:17) If all Israel would sit and avoid working—but is it not written,
"you shall gather in your new grain" (Deut. 11:14)? Who would gather
the new grain for them? Rather, that the early prophets <u>enacted</u> 24
watches. For each watch, there would stand in Jerusalem a group of
priests, of Levites and of Israelites.[409]

Here, the same 24 watches are cited as instituted by the early prophets, but the
textual justifications for the reasons given to justify these watches differ substantially. All Israel is not required to go to Jerusalem on a constant basis, instead the commandment only applies three times each year, during the pilgrimage festivals. In addition, the text invokes the value of preserving a vital part of
the work force for the important agricultural goal of harvesting crops. PT's text
then suggests that all three groupings (priests, Levites and Israelites) spent their

watch working in Jerusalem, in contradistinction to the claims of M and T. Again, no mention of Moses, David or Samuel appears.

The final text in this quartet is BT Ta. 27a:

אמר רב חסדא: משה תיקן להם לישראל שמונה משמרות. ארבעה
מאלעזר וארבעה מאיתמר. בא שמואל והעמידן על שש עשרה, בא דוד
והעמידן על עשרים וארבעה, שנאמר: (דברי הימים א' כ״ו) ״בשנת
הארבעים למלכות דויד נדרשו וימצא בהם גבורי חיל ביעזיר גלעד.״
מיתיבי: משה תיקן להם לישראל שמונה משמרות, ארבעה מאלעזר
וארבעה מאיתמר. בא דוד ושמואל והעמידן על עשרים וארבע, שנאמר:
(דברי הימים א' ט׳) ״המה יסד דויד ושמואל הראה באמונתם!״ הכי
קאמר: מיסודו של דוד ושמואל הרמתי, העמידום על עשרים וארבע. תניא
אידך: משה תיקן להם לישראל שש עשרה משמרות, שמונה מאלעזר
ושמונה מאיתמר, וכשרבו בני אלעזר על בני איתמר חלקום והעמידום על
עשרים וארבע, שנאמר: (דברי הימים א' כ״ד) וימצאו בני אלעזר רבים
לראשי הגברים מן בני איתמר, ויחלקום לבני אלעזר ראשים לבית אבות
ששה עשר, ולבני איתמר לבית אבותם שמונה, ואומר: (דברי הימים א'
כ״ד) ״בית אב אחד אחז לאלעזר ואחז אחז לאיתמר.״ מאי ואומר? וכי
תימא: כי היכי דנפישי בני אלעזר, הכא נמי דנפישי בני איתמר, שמונה
מעיקרא ארבעה הוו. תא שמע: ״בית אב אחד אחז לאלעזר ואחז אחז
לאיתמר.״ תיובתא דרב חסדא! אמר לך רב חסדא: תנאי היא, ואנא
דאמרי כי האי תנא דאמר שמונה.

Rav Hisda said:[410] Moses <u>enacted</u> eight watches for Israel—four from [the family of] Eleazar and four from [the family of] Itamar. Shmuel came and increased it to 16 [watches], David came and increased it to 24 [watches], as it is said: "In the fortieth year of the reign of David, they searched and they found among them men of substance in Jazer-Gilead" (I Chronicles 26:31).

An objection was raised against this [by citing this conflicting version of the tradition from another *baraita*]: Moses <u>enacted</u> eight watches for Israel, four from Eleazar and four from Itamar. David and Shmuel came and increased it to 24 [watches], as it is said: "David and Shmuel, the seer, established them in their office of trust" (I Chronicles 9:22). This is what it [the *baraita*] is saying: from the foundation of [both] David and Shmuel the Ramathite [together], it was raised to 24.[411]

Another [dissenting *baraita*] taught: Moses <u>enacted</u> sixteen watches for Israel, eight from Eleazar and eight from Itamar, but when the descendants of Eleazar grew more numerous than the descendants of Itamar, they [i.e., the watches] were split again and increased to 24, as it is said: "The sons of Eleazar turned out to be more numerous by male heads than the sons of Itamar, so they divided the sons of Eleazar into 16 chiefs of clans and the sons of Itamar into eight clans" (I Chronicles 24:4). And it says: "one clan more taken for Eleazar for each one taken of Itamar"[412] (I Chronicles 24:6). What is the meaning of this additional verse? If you would say that just as the children of Eleazar increased in number, so did the children of Itamar increase from an original four to eight.

Come and hear: "one clan more is taken for Eleazar for each one taken from Itamar" (I Chronicles 24:6). This *baraita* refutes the opinion of Rav Hisda. But Rav Hisda would answer: Tannaim disagree on this question, and I accept the opinion of the Tanna who says [that Moses enacted] eight [watches].

By the end of this *sugya*, there are two possibilities: either Moses instituted eight watches, and later authorities came to add the next 16, for a total of 24 watches; or Moses enacted 16, and then eight more were added when the watches were split in the time of the sons of Eleazar and Itamar. The final opinion is cited in Rav Hisda's name: that this is a *mahloket Tannaim*—a dispute between Tannaim, showing that in the eyes of BT, the earlier traditions had still not been resolved to a comprehensive solution.

At the end of this examination, we realize that the traditions are conflicting and we are left with no verifiable final explanation of the historic pattern of development of the watches in Jerusalem. Here we have dueling traditions attached to earlier giants, which clash which one another, and are each supported by prooftexts selected to retroject the origin of practices onto Moses, the prophets, Samuel and David. Each of these potential initiators provides a meritorious possible choice due to their special place in the history of the Israelites and Jerusalem.

Ezra as Initiator

With the destruction of the First Temple in 586 BCE, those who lived in Judaea faced new challenges never before encountered by the nascent Jewish people. After the Babylonian exile, and an approximately seventy-year hiatus away from the dual pillars of land and Temple that provided pre-exilic Judaism's central foci, the Jews returned to Judaea to resettle their homeland and confront a new political, religious and social landscape. It was during this return that a new sort of leadership arose, in the persons of Ezra and Nehemiah. The books of the Bible that bear Ezra and Nehemiah's names tell the story of their new approaches to the problems of their time: resettlement, the re-sanctification of the Temple, the need for new rituals that suited their time and the untangling of the web of intermarriage and assimilation created in Babylonia.

Among scholars, a few wax eloquent in granting Ezra an enormous role in the origins of post-exilic Judaism. Two examples come from Koch and Halivni. Koch's view is the most expansive with respect to Ezra's role:

> The role of Ezra in post-exilic history can hardly be overestimated. He was one of the greatest men within a people which was truly not deficient in great men! He had succeeded in moving the apparatus of a huge empire for the sake of a people, a small one in number and an unimportant one in political and economic regards. Even if his final intention did not last and the united people of twelve new tribes was not realized, his work was probably as far-reaching as that of Moses.[413]

Halivni, while providing a more muted approach, still veers into an overextended homage:

> No other steward of God's word could be so aptly likened to Moses in Jewish tradition as Ezra, and yet the difference between these two figures is crucial as well. . . . Ezra was not only the final biblical prophet, he also was the prophet in whose time the people of Israel, at long last, embraced the Torah. Moses, by tradition, was the prophet of original revelation, the medium through which God's will came to the people. But the people of Moses' time, also, according to tradition, were unfit and unprepared to hear the word of God. The people "stood at a distance" as the Torah was revealed. Only in Ezra's day did the nation gather around, willing and eager to receive the written word. In this sense, the work of Ezra completes the work of Moses.[414]

Along these lines, much has been made of Ezra's role in initiating new practices and reviving old ones.[415] For our limited purposes, there are 13 occurrences where rabbinic legal texts mention initiations of new practices by Ezra using the term *takkanah*,[416] and, interestingly enough, the majority of these (ten of the thirteen) are first found in PT. This is in contradistinction to the overall trend in *takkanot*, which tend to be more heavily concentrated in BT. Since Ezra was, ultimately, one of the founders of renewed Jewish settlement in Palestine, and thus a heroic precursor of the Palestinian Jewish community of the rabbinic period, it is not at all surprising to find an enhanced emphasis on his role in PT.

PT and BT both include versions of Ezra's ten *takkanot*. Chronologically, PT was redacted first, so we begin by reviewing that text. The formulaic concept of ten *takkanot* is never mentioned explicitly in PT, although exactly ten *takkanot* attributed to Ezra do appear in PT's version. Our superimposed numbering, added to the list in PT Meg. 4:1, 75a, shows the innovations attributed to Ezra:

עזרה התקין לישראל שיהו קורין בתורה בשני ובחמישי ובשבת במנחה,
הוא התקין טבילה לבעלי קריין, הוא התקין שיהו בתי דינין יושבין
בעיירות בשיני ובחמישי, הוא התקין שיהו הרוכלין מחזרין בעיירות מפני
כבודן של בנות ישראל, הוא התקין שיהו מכבסין בחמישי מפני כבוד
השבת, הוא התקין שיהו אופין פת בערבי שבתות שתהא פרוסה מצויה
לעני, הוא התקין שיהו אוכלין שום בלילי שבתות שהוא מכניס אהבה
ומוציא תאוה, הוא התקין שיהו הנשים מדברות זו עם זו בבית הכסא,
הוא התקין שתהא אשה חוגרת בסינר בין מלפניה בין מלאחריה. א"ר
תנחום בר חייה : מפני מעשה שאירע. מעשה באשה שבעלה קוף מכדרכה
ושלא כדרכה. הוא התקין שתהא אשה חופפת וסורקת קודם לטהרתה
שלשה ימים.

1) Ezra <u>enacted</u> for Israel that they would read Torah on Monday and Thursday and during the afternoon service on Shabbat;
2) He <u>enacted</u> immersion for men who had seminal emissions;[417]
3) He <u>enacted</u> that [Jewish] courts would sit [in formal session] in towns on Monday and Thursday;
4) He <u>enacted</u> that spice peddlers may circulate in the towns for the sake of the honor of the women of Israel;[418]
5) He <u>enacted</u> that they would do laundry on Thursday, in honor of Shabbat;
6) He <u>enacted</u> that bread should be baked on Friday, so that there might be a bit of bread for the poor [for Shabbat];[419]
7) He <u>enacted</u> that they eat garlic on Friday, for it brings in love and brings out sexual desire;[420]
8) He <u>enacted</u> that women speak to one another in the restroom;[421]
9) He <u>enacted</u> that a woman must wear a *sinnar*[422] both in front and behind her. Rabbi Tanhum bar Hiyya said: this is because of the case that occurred. A case when an ape raped a woman [having both] vaginal sex and anal sex [with her];[423]
10) He <u>enacted</u> that a woman must wash and comb her hair three days before her purification [by immersion].

Ezra is a highly rational choice for an editor to make in looking for an innovator of many of these *takkanot*. *Takkanot* attributed to Moses tended to represent religious and educational practices. Those connected with Joshua coalesced around themes related to war and initial community easements. In contrast, the *takkanot* that became associated with Ezra in rabbinic literature tended to cluster around two main areas: 1) regular community events that, though they had no easily discernible commandment in the written Torah that compelled their observance, took place on a weekly basis; and 2) those rules revolving around broadly defined purity concerns—including both sexual and ritual purity.

In tying these innovations to Ezra, the message the editor(s) sent was: these practices, though they lacked ultimate, direct basis in the words of the Written Torah, had their origins as far back as the beginning of the Judaean community's first post-exilic leadership. This granted these practices an extra modicum of authority, and set their observance on as high a plane of obligation as possible outside that of the written canon. At the same time, the selection of Ezra also served to highlight the Judaean nature of these practices. Since many (Torah reading, correct preparation for and observance of Shabbat, purity concerns, etc.) were vital elements in maintaining communal cohesion in Judaean society, the rabbis attempted to shore up continued Judaean practice by bolstering their observance through an ersatz, but highly plausible, history.

Choosing Ezra as the initiator of these practices also comports well with his portrayal in the Book of Ezra, where he is shown to be a leading figure in re-establishing ritual in the life of the returning exilic community. A thematic connection between these select *takkanot* and Ezra's areas of interest as he is portrayed in the biblical text is a vital link to understanding the editors' choices in this passage. Half of these ten *takkanot* relate, in large part, to establishing a regular rhythm for Jewish life. *Takkanot* 1, 3, 4, 5 and 7 portray Ezra as concerned with scheduling various weekly events that helped define Judaean communal life. The most interesting, from a textual perspective, is *Takkanah* 1, the establishment of a cycle of reading for the weekly Torah portion, a responsibility related to education and affirmation established once on each of the two market days (Monday and Thursday) and twice on Shabbat (at *Shaharit* and *Minhah*) to take advantage of the times when the populace of Judaea would be in town or at leisure. These time selections allowed the largest number of listeners to be present whenever Torah was read, best assuring a *minyan*, and also made optimal use of the free time allotted on the day of rest.

Takkanah 1's attribution to Ezra, in particular, is fraught with difficulty. First, within rabbinic literature itself, there are at least two opposing opinions as to the origin of this custom. The first comes from PT Meg. 1:1, 70b:

רבי יוסטא בי רבי שונם בעא קומי רבי מנא: ולא עזרא תַיקַן שיהו קורין
בתורה בשני ובחמישי ובשבת במנחה? ומרדכי ואסתר מַתקינים על מה
שעזרה עתיד לְהַתקין? אמר ליה: מי שסידר את המשנה סמכה למקרא
"משפחה ומשפחה ומדינה ומדינה ועיר ועיר."

Rabbi Yosta son of Rabbi Shunam asked before Rabbi Minna: Did not Ezra [later] <u>enact</u> that they would read Torah on Monday, Thursday and

on Shabbat afternoon? And [does this truly mean that] Mordecai and
Esther enacted [this enactment based] on what Ezra was to enact in the
future? He said to him: the one who ordered the Mishnah relied on this
text: "family by family, province by province, and city by city" (Esther
9:27).[424]

Here, PT actually admits that the suggestion of Mordecai and Esther's involvement in the enactment of weekly Torah reading is based solely on the reading of
a verse in Esther, explaining that the editor of the Mishnah ascribed the initiation
of weekly Torah reading to them based on his reading of Esther 9:27.

Another more intriguing possibility is that found in *MRY*,[425] where it states
that the *neviim rishonim* (early prophets) and the *zekenim* (elders) were responsible for the innovation of the reading cycle in an effort to stem the rebellion that
resulted from separation from the Torah for three days or more:

דורשי רשומות אמרו : "ולא מצאו מים." דברי תורה שנמשלו למים. ומנין
שנמשלו למים? שנאמר "הוי כל צמא לכו למים." (ישעיה נה'א) לפי שפרשו
מדברי תורה שלשת ימים, לכך מרדו. ולכך התקינו להם הנביאים
והזקנים שיהיו קורין בתורה בשבת בשני ובחמישי. הא כיצד? קורין
בשבת, ומפסיקין באחד בשבת. וקורין בשני, ומפסיקין בשלישי וברביעי.
וקורין בחמישי, ומפסיקין בערב שבת.

Those who interpret marks[426] said: "and they did not find water" (Exodus 16:22). [This refers to] words of Torah that are compared to water.
And how do we know that they are compared to water? As it is said:
"Ho, let every thirsty person go to the water" (Isaiah 55:1). Once they
separated from the words of Torah for three days, then they rebelled.
And so the early prophets and the elders enacted for them that they
would read the Torah on Shabbat, on Monday and on Thursday. How
[is this done]? [They] read on Shabbat, and pause on Sunday. Read on
Monday, and pause on Tuesday and Wednesday. Read on Thursday
and pause on Friday.

Here, the instigators of the decision to regularize the Torah reading are "the
early prophets and the elders."[427] Recall, as well, that we saw above a text that
suggested Moses had a hand in this development as well. Earlier references in
M,[428] Josephus,[429] and the New Testament all suggest other possibilities,[430] so it
is established that the cycle of Torah reading came from an ancient era. However, we can also see that there is nothing close to complete agreement on crediting Ezra with this innovation.

Scholarly opinion varies with respect to the dating of regularized Torah reading. Charles Perrot wrote:

> [I]t became customary to read the Tora on the afternoon of the Sabbath as well as on the *market days* [emphasis added] Monday and Thursday. Thus people too far from the synagogue on Sabbath mornings could have the benefit of Tora readings, though they lacked the accompanying haftara. Later this institution was attributed to Ezra, or the Elders who preceded the Great Synagogue. In fact there is scarcely any trace of this custom before the Destruction of the Second Temple; at least, earlier documentation never mentions it. [431]

Perrot's conclusion is bolstered by two more recent studies by Lawrence H. Schiffman and Lee Levine.[432] Schiffman analyzed the Qumran corpus, Philo, Josephus and other Second Temple period sources, in addition to extant Tannaitic traditions, to find that public Torah reading was certainly a prominent part of the synagogue ritual by the first century CE, and that public reading of the Torah most likely took place in Qumran, though he freely admits that few details are available. He then concludes:

> It would seem that these widespread and organized reading rituals in Pharasaic-rabbinic circles so soon after 70 CE lead to the conclusion that the reading of the Torah and most of its procedures . . . would have been practiced in synagogues in the early first century, even before the destruction.[433]

Schiffman thus provides a *terminus a quo* in the early first century CE for widespread public acceptance of the rituals of Torah reading.

Levine places the general acceptance of the practice at a similar point in time, bringing evidence for public Torah reading from 1 and 2 Macc., Josephus and Philo. While each of these sources indicates the public reading of Torah on a specific occasion, Levine, like Perrot, is unwilling to conclude that these early mentions implied a weekly Torah reading. In fact, Levine explains:

> Whatever the early stages of the Torah-reading ceremony, the question arises as to when it became fully institutionalized as the central component in the non-sacrificial liturgy. The chronological parameters are probably to be fixed between the fifth and third centuries B.C.E. On the one hand, the terminus post quem is undoubtedly the period of Ezra and Nehemiah, when the first public Torah-reading ceremony appears to have been held. By the third century, on the other hand, the existence of

a regular communal Torah-reading framework was probably a prime factor in the creation of the Septuagint. . . . This liturgical practice was probably brought to Egypt from Judaea and was not the creation of the fledgling Diasporan community; there is no evidence of such a custom in the earlier Elephantine community, which flourished in Upper Egypt in the fifth century B.C.E. The brief account of the high priest Ezekias reading to his friends from the Torah (lit., scroll) upon his arrival in Egypt may well point to such a practice. . . . By the first century, a weekly ceremony featuring the communal reading and study of holy texts had become a universal Jewish practice. It was a unique liturgical feature in the ancient world: no such form of worship was known in paganism.[434]

Thus, though earlier traces of the practice do appear, regularized public Torah reading was not a generally accepted practice until well into the first century CE. It was acceptable, in the eyes of editors of parts of PT and BT, to assign this innovation to Ezra in order to help bolster it. However, other editors (*MRY*'s in particular) chose to attribute this practice to Moses, the early prophets or other more ancient leadership. One could argue that this represents a nuanced difference of opinion on the actual meaning of public Torah reading: linking public Torah reading to Ezra, the innovator *par excellence* of regularized communal activities, suggests an understanding of public Torah reading as regularly scheduled weekly activity designed to enhance communal cohesion. Assigning it to Moses, on the other hand, may represent a more educational focus, or, perhaps, a sense of replaying the ancient drama of Sinai. Thus, various editors, depending on their outlook on the role of the Torah service, designed pedigrees that fit their beliefs. Ezra, as the lone biblical character shown actually reading Torah in public, and as a leader portrayed by the rabbis as innovating weekly practices that established important communal rhythms, was an ideal choice for this initiation. He was not, however, the only possible choice, as we see in the selections made by other editors.

Before we leave Ezra, it is instructive to note the subtle differences between BT and PT in the texts that tell of the ten *takkanot*. BT BK 82a reads:

עשרה תקנות תיקן עזרא: שקורין במנחה בשבת, וקורין בשני ובחמישי, ודנין בשני ובחמישי, ומכבסים בחמישי בשבת, ואוכלין שום בערב שבת, ושתהא אשה משכמת ואופה, ושתהא אשה חוגרת בסינר, ושתהא אשה חופפת וטובלת, ושיהו רוכלין מחזירין בעיירות, ותיקן טבילה לבעלי קריין.

Ezra enacted ten *takkanot*:
1) that they read [publicly from the Torah] at Minhah on Shabbat;

2) that they read [publicly from the Torah] on Monday and Thursday;
3) that they sit in judgment on Monday and Thursday;
4) that they do laundry on Thursday;
5) that they eat garlic on Friday;
6) that a woman must rise early to bake;
7) that a woman must wear a *sinnar*;
8) that a woman must comb and immerse;
9) that spice peddlers may circulate through towns; and
10) he enacted immersion for men who had seminal discharges.

There are a number of differences worth noting. First, notice the change in order between BT and PT. PT's order provides little in the way of recognizable structure to the *takkanot*. In PT, *takkanot* 2 and 4 interrupt the list of events during the week, and the issues related to women are not grouped together. In BT, the order is substantially more logical. BT begins with time-based events (1-5), and uses that as a transition to a woman's time-based responsibilities. The next section (6-8) covers women's responsibilities, ending with beautification/purification, which is a thematic connector to the spice peddler (9), the supplier of cosmetics to women beautifying themselves. Finally, in keeping with the idea of beautification/purification, the male analogue is mentioned (10) as a conclusion to this piece. BT's version is, not surprisingly, far better edited than PT, and its thematic progression is quite well crafted here.

Other differences occur in the enumeration of the *takkanot*: BT's *takkanot* 1 and 2 are combined in PT. PT's *takkanah* 8 does not appear in any form in BT. Also, a modicum of explanatory material is present in PT, which is whittled away by the editors of BT to keep the list succinct.

Finally, there is one concrete difference in the practices at hand between PT and BT, which appears in *takkanah* 6 in both sources. In PT, women may arise at any time, as long as they bake bread for Shabbat on Friday with the express purpose of providing for the poor. In BT, on the other hand, women must wake early in the morning with no single day specified, for no particular charitable reason.

Since there are more than ten *takkanot* attributed to Ezra in the rabbinic corpus, it is clear that we have here an early tradition of Ezra's ten *takkanot* that was revised and reinterpreted in two specific contexts, to reinforce certain community-based customs in ways coherent with their place and time. With the variations between these lists, and with the extra *takkanot* listed in references above, we learn that the rabbis editing legal texts felt free to retroject innovations to promote and support values and practices they wished to promote, based loosely, where possible, on information present in biblical texts.

The Men of the Great Assembly

Rabbinic legal sources present four *takkanot* preserved in the name of the אנשי כנסת הגדולה (*anshei kenesset hagedolah*, "Men of the Great Assembly" (or "Men of the Great Synagogue," as some authors call them). The Men of the Great Assembly occupy a rather challenging place for students of Jewish history—the sources about them are scarce, and the accretion of legendary material often obscures any potential for an accurate historical view of their activities, if they even existed as more than a construct at all. Louis Finkelstein and Hugo Mantel are the two scholars who wrote most extensively on the question of their identity and the time of their activity, though their approach has come under significant recent scrutiny, most notably in the work of I.J. Schiffer.[435]

Finkelstein saw the group as a legislative and judiciary body, empowered to formulate, interpret or apply Jewish law, called into being by Ezra and Nehemiah sometime in the sixth century BCE as their foil against an overbearing priestly and aristocratic leadership. Finkelstein credited the group with the creation of the *amidah* and *Birkat HaMazon*, two innovations that the Talmud assigns to them, though not utilizing *takkanah* terminology. He set a completion date of the *anshei kenesset hegedolah's* activities in the temporal vicinity of 175 BCE. Most important, though, is Finkelstein's explicit caveat: this is all to be seen as only "highly probable," because the evidence is indeed scant.

Hugo Mantel concludes that the word *kenesset* is based on a literal translation of the Greek word σύνοδος (*sunodos*, "assembly," "guild" or "national gathering"),[436] and that the *kenesset hagedolah* was the overall controlling body of a social-religious society. The institution arose, argued Mantel, during a time when the prevalence of this sort of governing group was growing widely throughout the Hellenistic world, and such influence was surely felt among the Judaeans as well. Its purpose was to extend the work of Ezra—to enlarge and expand the Oral Torah among the people, and to educate them about the laws of purity that were at the ritual heart of the society. Mantel also tied this group to precedents in Ugaritic society and elsewhere in the ancient Near East. He saw it as a natural outgrowth of Hellenistic social influence combined with Ezra's fierce adherence to the Torah. Mantel claimed that the work of the *anshei kenesset hagedolah* began at the start of the Second Temple period (at the time of Ezra and Nehemiah in the sixth century BCE) and concluded around the time of 200 BCE.[437]

While these two scholars represent an attempt of a certain age at historicizing the *anshei kenesset hagedolah*, one earlier and almost all recent scholars agree that any attempt to make history out of the literary traces that pertain to this group is highly suspect.[438] Notable among them is Ira Jeffrey Schiffer, who is to be credited with the most methodologically complete approach to the topic thus far:

This analysis of the traditions concerning the Men of the Great Assembly suggests that the name was created by the mishnaic masters interested in establishing a continuous chain of authority from Moses to the Pharisees. The early Amoraic masters then identified this name with the assembly described in Neh. 8-9. They ascribed to it liturgical and exegetical concerns based on the activity of the group in Neh. Once this had become established, related activities not specified in Neh. could be credited to them. This included the writing of books which the rabbis believed were from the period of the Men of the Great Assembly. We thus have an active and formative period of development probably at the end of mishnaic times and during the early Amoraic generations.[439]

Schiffer defines an accretive process by which activities were first assigned to the *anshei kenesset hagedolah* because the activities resembled those listed in Neh. 8-9. Later, activities not specified in Neh. also were ascribed to them, when the rabbis believed they originated in their period. Schiffer makes clear that this occurred far later, at the end of the Tannaitic period into the early Amoraic period. He does not accept, at any point, that this group actually existed or functioned as a legislative body, as Finkelstein and Mantel believed.

To gain a clear understanding of the rabbis' report of the role of the *anshei kenesset hegedolah* we will examine two[440] *takkanot* ascribed to the *anshei kenesset hagedolah*, beginning with BT Ber. 33a, which analyzes the blessings associated with *havdallah*:

רבי עקיבא אומר אומרה ברכה רביעית כו'. אמר ליה רב שמן בר אבא
לרבי יוחנן מכדי אנשי כנסת הגדולה <u>תקנו</u> להם לישראל ברכות ותפלות
קדושות והבדלות, נחזי היכן <u>תקנון</u>? אמר ליה: בתחילה קבעוה בתפלה,
העשירו, קבעוה על הכוס; העני, חזרו וקבעוה בתפלה. והם אמרו:
המבדיל בתפלה צריך שיבדיל על הכוס. איתמר נמי, אמר רבי חייא בר
אבא אמר רבי יוחנן: אנשי כנסת הגדולה <u>תקנו</u> להם לישראל ברכות
ותפלות קדושות והבדלות. בתחלה קבעוה בתפלה, העשירו, קבעוה על
הכוס; חזרו והענו, קבעוה בתפלה. והם אמרו: המבדיל בתפילה צריך
שיבדיל על הכוס. איתמר נמי, רבה ורב יוסף דאמרי תרוייהו: המבדיל
בתפלה צריך שיבדיל על הכוס.

Rabbi Akiba said: he says it as the fourth blessing, etc. Rav Shemen bar Abba said to Rabbi Yohanan: let us see where the *anshei kenesset hagedolah* <u>enacted</u> for Israel blessings, prayers, sanctifications and *havdallot* [separations]. Let us see where they <u>enacted</u> them? He said to him: at the beginning they fixed it in the *tefillah* [the *amidah*, since the people of this time were poor and could not afford wine], when they became wealthy, they fixed it over the cup [of wine], and when they became impoverished [again], they went back and fixed it in the *tefillah* once again. And they said: one who says *hamavdil* [the prayer of separation in the *havdallah* service] during the *tefillah* must go back and say it again over the cup [of wine, if this is financially possible].

It was also said: Rabbi Hiyya bar Abba said in the name of Rabbi Yohanan: The *anshei kenesset hagedolah* enacted blessings, prayers, sanctifications and *havdallot* (separations) for Israel. At the beginning they fixed it in the *tefillah*, when they became wealthy, they fixed it over the cup [of wine], and when they went back and became poor, they fixed it in the *tefillah*. And they said: one who says *hamavdil* during the *tefillah*, must go back and say it again over the cup.

It was also said: [it was] Rabbah and Rav Yosef [who] both said: one who said *hamavdil* in the *tefillah* must say it again over the cup.[441]

This discussion centers on the place of the *havdallah* blessing, recited on Saturday night during the *amidah* to mark the conclusion of Shabbat. Three *memrot* form the body of the argument, and the first two carry the message that the *anshei kenesset hagedolah* enacted the blessing of *havdallah*, among other blessings. The first two *memrot* involve Rabbi Yohanan, one of the earliest Amoraim, which is in keeping with Schiffer's suggestion as to the origin of these traditions.

The economic situation of the people is the key determinant of the placement of this blessing. In a good fiscal climate, they would highlight the *havdallah* blessing by saying it over a separate cup of wine, instead of reciting it during the fourth blessing of the *amidah*. In poorer times, the entire ritual would occur during the *amidah*, so as to minimize the added expense of more wine. The ultimate outcome at the end of this *sugya* was that the later authorities came and decided that saying *hamavdil* during the *amidah* alone was not sufficient. Each of the three Amoraic positions stated in this *sugya* repeats that essential idea, and it became the resultant legal position upheld in the outcome of this argument. Here, we find an example of a constructed narrative that justified and explained contemporary practice.[442]

Joel Roth, based on the Maharik (Rabbi Joseph ben Solomon Colon, ca. 1420-1480) views the upholding of this ancient custom as a prime example of new law shaped by older custom. Despite the fact that an extraneous recitation of this blessing would certainly violate the accepted law that one should not take God's name in vain and utter a *berakhah levatalah* (an extraneous blessing), in this *sugya* Rav accepts the redundancy because of its origin in inherited custom assigned to a powerful source.[443]

An alternate tradition of a Tannaitic dispute on the placement of the *havdallah* blessing exists in M Ber. 5:2:

מזכירין גבורות גשמים בתחיית המתים. ושואלין הגשמים בברכת השנים.
והבדלה בחונן הדעת. ר׳ עקיבא אומר: אומרה ברכה רביעית בפני עצמה.
רבי אליעזר אומר בהודאה.

We recite "the Might of the Rain"[444] in the [section of the second blessing on] resurrection of the dead; and we ask for rain in the [section of the ninth] blessing for the year; and *havdallah* [is said] during the [fourth] blessing on "who bestows understanding."

Rabbi Akiba says: say it as the fourth blessing in and of itself.
Rabbi Eliezer says: [say it] in the [18th blessing on] thanksgiving.

This text bears witness to a problem with ascribing creation of the *havdallah* blessing to the *anshei kenesset hagedolah*, and its placement in the fourth blessing of the *amidah*. Scholars do agree that proto-*amidot* existed before the *amidah* itself was formulated. However, the fixing of the *amidah* in any sort of complete form occurred substantially later than even the very latest activity that could possibly be recognized as connected with the *anshei kenesset hagedolah*. Joseph Heinemann, the pre-eminent scholar of liturgical development, recognized that the text from M Ber. 5:2 above proves that it is only at the *end* of the Tannaitic period that the placement of *havdallah* in the fourth blessing was set.[445]

Combining Schiffer's, Roth's and Heinemann's claims, we see that the rabbis constructed this tradition of the *anshei kenesset hegedolah* fixing the *havdallah* blessing to provide firm footing for a still-developing custom, and to link that claim into a continuous chain of tradition. Since the *havdallah* ceremony lacks clear precedent in the Bible, the rabbis ascribe its origins to their "catchall" group from the Second Temple period, the *anshei kenesset hagedolah*.

The other text we will examine is from BT Meg. 2a, which suggests that the *anshei kenesset hagedolah* were responsible for the practice of reading *Megillat Esther* on the holiday of Purim:

מגילה נקראת באחד עשר. מנלן? מנלן? כדבעינן למימר לקמן: חכמים
הקילו על הכפרים להיות מקדימין ליום הכניסה כדי שיספקו מים ומזון
לאחיהם שבכרכים! אנן הכי קאמרינן: מכדי, כולהו אנשי כנסת הגדולה
תקנינהו, דאי סלקא דעתך אנשי כנסת הגדולה ארבעה עשר וחמשה עשר
תקון אתו רבנן ועקרי תקנתא דתקינו אנשי כנסת הגדולה? והתנן: אין

בית דין יכול לבטל דברי בית דין חבירו אלא אם כן גדול ממנו בחכמה
ובמנין, אלא פשיטא, כולהו אנשי כנסת הגדולה <u>תקינו</u>, היכא רמיזא? אמר
רב שמן בר אבא אמר רבי יוחנן : אמר קרא (אסתר ט') "לקים את ימי
הפרים האלה בזמניהם. " זמנים הרבה תקנו להם.

The *Megillah* is read on the 11th [of Adar]. What is the source for
this? [How can you ask] what the source is for this [for it is clearly not
a scriptural decree]? As we are going to say below [i.e., later on in this
Gemara], the sages conceded to the villages that they might advance
their day of reading to the previous day of assembly in order that they
could supply water and food for their brothers in the towns.[446] This is
what we meant to ask: let us see, the *anshei kenesset hagedolah* <u>enacted</u>
all these dates, for would you think to say that the *anshei kenesset
hagedolah* <u>enacted</u> [reading on] the 14th and 15th, and our rabbis came
and uprooted an <u>enactment</u> that the *anshei kenesset hagedolah* <u>enacted</u>?
Was it not taught: No court may uproot the ruling of another court
unless it is greater in number and wisdom?[447]

Rather, it is simple—the *anshei kenesset hagedolah* <u>enacted</u> it.
Where is the hint [in our biblical text that this took place]? Rav Shemen
bar Abba said in the name of Rabbi Yohanan: the text says (Esther
9:31) "to observe these days of Purim at their times"—[from the plural
form of the word "times," we realize] they <u>enacted</u> more than one specific time for them.

Here, the tradition that attributed the innovation of the reading of the *Megillah* is
supported by an interpretation of a verse in Esther. The verse used for proof
cites Esther alone, or Mordecai and Esther together, as the individuals credited
with the innovation of reading the story each year at the same time.[448] No mention of the *anshei kenesset hagedolah*, or any assembly of persons, appears in
the base text, which makes it suspect, at best, as a proof for their connection
with the custom of the reading of *Megillat Esther*. One could postulate that the
anshei kenesset hagedolah reaffirmed the earlier statement of Mordecai and/or
Esther, but to do so is to argue from silence.

Finally, it is also important to note that here, too, we see a tradition from
Rabbi Yohanan connecting a practice to the *anshei kenesset hagedolah*. It appears that he is the overwhelming propagator of this set of traditions related to
initiation and this group.

Shimeon ben Shetah or Rabbanan? The Origin of the Ketubbah

In the latest of the attributed pre-rabbinic initiations reported, we find Shimeon ben Shetah credited with the creation of the Jewish marriage contract, the *ketubbah*. The biblical record provides us with a plentitude of narrative information on individual marriages, but little in the way of material that defines the legal limits of the marital bond. The best information available from the Second Temple and Tannaitic periods comes from the few *ketubbot* found in the documents from Elephantine, in the Babatha archives and in the Cave of Letters.[449] An Edomite marriage contract from 176 BCE shows that formulae from Jewish documents were substantively parallel to extant traditions among other peoples.[450] This evidence suggests that the custom of writing marriage contracts existed before the advent of the Tannaitic period, and that the practice continued throughout the time of the Tannaim. While *ketubbot* were clearly in use, this material lacks any explicit reference to the origin of the written *ketubbah*, or its specific initiators.

The authority cited as responsible for the creation of the *ketubbah* was Shimeon ben Shetah, who lived in the late second to early first century BCE. He and Yehuda ben Tabbai were considered the third of the five pairs who served as religious leaders in the period preceding the destruction of the Temple.[451] From the data we have here, a picture emerges of a first century BCE sage who was constructed as wielding significant power, and was often directly involved in the workings of governance in the latter part of the Hasmonean period.

In a pair of texts from BT, we find an explicit mention of the origin of the *ketubbah*. A *baraita* from BT Shab. 14b notes:

דתניא : יוסי בן יועזר איש צרידה ויוסי בן יוחנן איש ירושלים גזרו טומאה
על ארץ העמים ועל כלי זכוכית. שמעון בן שטח תֵּיקַן כתובה לאשה, וגזר
טומאה על כלי מתכות.

As it was taught: Yossi ben Yoezer of Zeridah and Yossi ben Yohanan of Jerusalem decreed impurity on the land of non-Jews and upon glassware. Shimeon ben Shetah <u>enacted</u> the *ketubbah* for a woman, and decreed impurity upon metal implements.

This short list of *takkanot* and *gezerot* depicts the institution of the legal mechanism of the *ketubbah* by Shimeon ben Shetah. All of the authorities mentioned in this particular listing lived during the Second Temple period. Yossi ben Yoezer and Yossi ben Yohanan were the first of the *zugot* (pairs) of great leaders, and may be classed as proto-rabbis.[452]

A second BT text provides us with slightly different information on Shimeon ben Shetah's role in the origin of the *ketubbah*. BT Yev. 89a states:

אין לה כתובה. מאי טעמא <u>תקינו</u> לה רבנן כתובה? כדי שלא תהא קלה
בעיניו להוציאה, הא, תהא קלה בעיניו להוציאה!

> "[The case: a woman whose husband went to a country beyond the sea, who remarried after being told that her husband had died. If her husband subsequently returned, she must leave both husbands, and] she has no claim to her *ketubbah* [payment from either husband]." What is the reason that our rabbis <u>enacted</u> a *ketubbah*? In order that it would not be easy in his [i.e., the husband's] eyes to divorce her, however, in this case, [when she is in such a difficult legal position being married to two men simultaneously], let it be easy [for him] to divorce her [and thus sever a prohibited, adulterous marriage]!

Here, Shimeon ben Shetah is not mentioned explicitly at all, nor does he appear in two other citations that speak of the genesis of the *ketubbah* in BT and PT.[453] Instead, credit for the institution of the *ketubbah* is given here to the general רבנן (*rabbanan*, "our rabbis"), a term that usually indicates the opinion of a group as opposed to a single authority.

The BT Shab. text is a *baraita*, and thus from a Tannaitic stratum. The BT Yev. text has a later provenance, most likely Amoraic, because it is explanatory in nature and uses Aramaic connective material between its statements. Further, all the authorities cited in the BT Shab. text are earlier authorities, making it far more likely that this piece survived as a whole unit from an earlier period. It seems safe to conclude that the BT Shab. *baraita* predates the text from BT Yev.

One other *baraita* from BT Ket. 82b provides some support for the representation in BT Shab. by indicating Shimeon ben Shetah's involvement in setting the terms and limitations of the *ketubbah*. This section is preceded by Shimeon ben Shetah's enactment that all the husband's property could be mortgaged to guarantee his wife's *ketubbah* settlement:

תניא נמי הכי: בראשונה היו כותבין לבתולה מאתים ולאלמנה מנה, והיו
מזקינין ולא היו נושאין נשים, <u>התקינו</u> שיהיו מניחין אותה בבית אביה;
ועדיין כשהוא כועס עליה, אומר לה לכי אצל כתובתיך, <u>התקינו</u> שיהיו
מניחין אותה בבית חמיה, עשירות עושות אותה קלתות של כסף ושל זהב,
עניות היו עושות אותה עביט של מימי רגלים. ועדיין כשכועס עליה, אומר
לה טלי כתובתיך וצאי, עד שבא שמעון בן שטח <u>ותיקן</u>, שיהא כותב לה כל
נכסי אחראין לכתובתה.

It was also taught in a *baraita*: At first, they would write *ketubbot* for virgins at 200 [*zuzim*] and for widows at 100 [*zuzim*], and they would grow old and never marry women [because the amount at stake was too high, and all the men's property could be seized to fulfill this debt, potentially bankrupting the men. Since the men would not mortgage so much property, the women had trouble finding husbands]. They en-acted that they would place it [the amount of the *ketubbah*] in the house of her father. But still, when he [i.e., the husband] was angry, he would say: "go to your *ketubbah*." So they enacted that the [amount of the] *ketubbah* would be deposited in the house of her father-in-law. Wealthy women converted it into silver or gold baskets, and poor women into vessels for the collection of urine.[454] And still, when he [the husband] was angry with her, he would say to her "take your *ketubbah* and go!" until Shimeon ben Shetah came and enacted that he would write to her "all of my property is mortgaged to your *ketubbah*."[455]

This pseudo-history of the *ketubbah* is constructed to explain why the *ketubbah* works as it does, and why other options are not tenable. Here, Shimeon ben Shetah is depicted as an involved party in the re-structuring and limiting of the effect of the *ketubbah*, with this text's editors utilizing both the term *barishonah* to indicate review of prior law, and the term *tikken* for innovative activity. If no ketubbah existed before his time, it is highly unlikely that the sort of language we see above ("until Shimeon ben Shetah came and enacted") would be used to describe his contribution to the later development of the document.

Michael Satlow argued that the Tannaim radically reworked the very idea of a *ketubbah*: originally, both husband and wife had the ability to call for a divorce. The Tannaim shifted this at some point, restraining the wife's ability to divorce the husband, and concentrating the power to dissolve a marriage in the husband's hands, while at the same time originating a fine for the husband who divorced his wife. The reason for the fine was to maintain some balance—with this shift, there had to be some concomitant replacement of protection for the wife—thus the idea of a *ketubbah* payment was created. Satlow's proof for this development is the fact that most *ketubbot* found in the ancient Near East either have equal fines for men and women, or lack fines entirely. Other evidence also exists for a shift between pre-Tannaitic and Tannaitic permissions to call for divorce.[456]

From the three texts above, we see that during the Tannaitic period, some knowledge that Shimeon ben Shetah was involved in the design of the *ketubbah* document circulated in rabbinic circles. However, as time went by, the Amoraim may not have generally known who was responsible for the innovation of the individual sections of the *ketubbah*. Nonetheless, as we see here, the connection with Shimeon ben Shetah remained, with some authorities claiming the *ketub-*

bah originated with him, while others granted him limited responsibility for the redesign of parts of the document.

As for the reasons behind this particular innovation: it was clearly designed to protect the marital bond of its time, with the intent (as implied in BT Ket. 82b) to encourage marriage and procreation, and generally to discourage divorce. From this perspective, we could categorize this *takkanah* as a "social welfare" initiation that created a new legal process to encourage the proper functioning of society. So, while it was certainly a rabbinic initiation, it was also a change in Jewish law to benefit Jewish society at large.

Rabbinically Initiated Practices

Twenty-one of the 60 occurrences of initiation utilizing *tkn* that occur in our corpus cite rabbis, as individuals or collectively, who initiated a law or practice.[457] A few notable properties appear at once in the distribution of citations. First, we immediately see that no citation appears in any purely Tannaitic collection amongst these many occurrences (i.e., not one is found in M, T or any of the Halakhic Midrashim). Second, note that the weighting strongly favors BT, which has 13 occurrences, whereas PT has merely three—all of which appear in relation to the same mishnah and topic, and all of which actually indicate literary fixing as opposed to initiation of new practice. It would appear from this data that the redactors of BT are more likely than those who edited PT to use this term to admit diverse instances of innovation by rabbis.

It would also appear that this formulaic usage is predominately an Amoraic one. Though there are two instances of this sort of assignment falling within the confines of a *baraita*, the majority (14 of the 16 total occurrences (13 BT, 3 PT) = 87.5%) occur in strictly Amoraic contexts, when judged by the tradents cited and language utilized in the statements,[458] and the general characteristics of the discussion that surrounds the statements. So, we are left with a set of predominately Amoraic, Babylonian statements, with just two exceptions.[459] It is also possible that these two exceptions are not truly Tannaitic *baraitot*, but the evidence does not allow any concrete proof one way or the other.

One other factor stands out in this usage: the rabbis' initiation of new practices is limited to two rather small areas of Jewish life: what moderns would class as "religious ritual" and marital relations. In religious ritual, the rabbis are portrayed as innovating in the following areas: the blessings of the prayer service; the number of required cups of wine at a Passover Seder and a house of mourning; the exact standards for sounding the shofar on Rosh Hashanah; the saying of *Birkat HaMazon* in Hebrew; and allowing the incoming and outgoing watches of priests to come together and eat when their course of duty coincided with Shabbat. In marital law, the rabbis (and Shimeon ben Shetah, as we saw just above) were said to have instituted the *ketubbah*, set the amounts of payment upon divorce required for brides of various social status, and set certain other terms of the marital relationship.

This distribution suggests an attitude among the Babylonian Amoraim (or later editors) that initiation of new practices could only be attributed to the rabbis when there was sufficient legal room for novelty within a particular area of Jewish law. Both the shaping of certain ritual acts (prayer, sounding the shofar, etc.) and the outlines of marital responsibility had a very limited set of biblical references governing their development. This allowed the editors of BT (mostly) and PT (somewhat) more freedom to re-shape these practices through the use of *takkanot*. Here, unlike the many other examples already seen in this chapter, the editors did not feel the need to resort to retrojections to far earlier religious leadership (the prophets, Moses, etc.) to bolster their authority to innovate, because these areas still allowed for some flexibility, even at a later date. Even if these attributions are retrojections to Yavneh, Usha, and other great moments of rabbinic power, it is still important to note that the retrojections point to individuals far closer to the contemporary scene of the authors, and not in the more highly mythic past.

Finally, even more interesting is the fact that all of PT's three occurrences appear in PT Ber., implying an even more limited (and perhaps, more reticent) view on rabbinic initiation of new practices by the editors of PT. Furthermore, these initiations are entirely limited to the shaping of blessings within the *amidah*. In fact, it is quite possible to read these as occurrences of the use of the root *tkn* to indicate the literary fixing of a prayer-text into its finalized form. If this is the case, the point may be made even more strongly: PT shows a pronounced difference from BT in its attitude toward explicit acceptance of rabbinic initiation. Though many of the issues discussed appear in both Talmuds, PT's reluctance to use the term *takkanah* as a marker of rabbinic initiation is remarkable.

Rabbinic Initiation 1: Prayer

> Prayer was, of course, customary among the Israelites from earliest times. Prayer at fixed times is already alluded to in the Bible as the practice of individuals. . . . But neither the spontaneous prayers of individuals (nor, for that matter, of the community as a whole when the occasion demanded), nor the cultic prayer-hymns of the Levites are the equivalents of the institution of fixed, communal prayer, which constituted a radical innovation of the Second Temple Period, and which made an indelible impress on the entire religious life of the people by providing them with a completely novel form of religious expression.[460]

Joseph Heinemann's thoughtful insight sets the scene for our glimpse into an instance of the rabbinic initiation of prayer. Moshe Greenberg, in a similar vein, showed that during the biblical period, spontaneous, extemporized prayer, unmediated by priests or other ritual experts, enabled individuals to have "[c]onstant, familiar intercourse with God" that "strengthened the egalitarian tendency . . . that was rooted in Israel's self-perception."[461] Prayer, as it appeared throughout the Bible, was essentially creative, spontaneous and individualized, even if it did utilize certain patterns modeled after inter-human hierarchical communication. This mode of prayer formed a counterpoint to the main worship event of the day: the sacrifice, managed and controlled by Israel's priesthood.

Fragmentary texts found at Qumran indicate the presence of a daily liturgy, with special texts recited for each day of the month and supplicatory prayers on various days of the week.[462] Lee Levine suggests that prayer was an integral part of Diaspora worship, though a lesser part of Judaean worship during the time of the Second Temple. He admits, however, that we have no way of "determining the exact nature, composition, and extent of Jewish prayer in the Diaspora during the Second Temple period."[463] In Judaea there is no evidence of communal prayer during the Second Temple period at all. It appears that fixed, communal prayer was an innovation that arose, at the earliest, in the Diaspora during the Second Temple period, but by and large remained outside the Judaean community until the Tannaitic period. The exceptions to this general rule were the various sects (Qumran, Essenes, Therapeutae, etc.), who may well have sought to actualize a variant set of worship practices to differentiate themselves from the cult in Jerusalem they abhorred. It was only after 70 CE, with the Temple's destruction, that prayer widely replaced sacrifice as Judaism's authentic, accepted mode of communal worship, valid in both Diaspora and Judaea.

Heinemann points out that the wording and structure of the prayer service was not rigidly set until after the rabbinic period:

> Only gradually, over a period of time, were all the details of the statutory prayers standardized; and last of all was the precise wording fixed. In fact, this process did not end until the period of the *Geonim* (c. 600-1100 C.E.); and even when the exact wording of the prayers was finally determined, different versions became authoritative in Babylonia and Palestine.[464]

One can see, immediately, that Heinemann viewed the statutory liturgy as a developing, growing entity within the body of Jewish prayer, one that was not fully fixed until long after the close of the two Talmuds. This piece of Heinemann's view has become the accepted schema amongst scholars of liturgy, and other authors suggest a similar pattern of development, though they may differ on the specific timetable and locale of certain changes. All agree that the rabbinic period was a time of enormous flexibility in the statutory prayers, probably because of the very limited biblical basis for the practices involved.[465]

BT Ber. 33b provides a fine example of an innovation attributed to two Amoraim through the use of the root *tkn*. In the midst of a discussion between Rabbi Eliezer and Rabbi Akiba about precisely when one says the blessings of *havdallah* at the end of a festival day, the Gemara presents a statement of Rav Yosef's that supplies us with an instance of liturgical innovation reportedly made by Rav and Shmuel:

אמר רב יוסף: אנא לא האי ידענא ולא האי ידענא, אלא מדרב ושמואל
ידענא דתקינו לן מרגניתא בבבל: ותודיענו ה' אלהינו את משפטי צדקך
ותלמדנו לעשות חקי רצונך, ותנחילנו זמני ששון וחגי נדבה ותורישנו
קדושת שבת וכבוד מועד וחגיגת הרגל, בין קדושת שבת לקדושת יום טוב
הבדלת ואת יום השביעי משׁשת ימי המעשה קדשת, הבדלת וקדשת את
עמך ישראל בקדושתך, ותתן לנו וכו'.

Rav Yosef said: I do not know this, nor do I know that, but of Rav and Shmuel I do know that they have <u>enacted</u> for us a pearl in Babylonia [when they coined this text that incorporates *havdallah* into the Yom Tov blessing]:[466] "You have made known to us, Adonai our God, Your righteous judgments and taught us to do the statutes of Your will,[467] and bequeathed us times of joy and festivals of freewill offerings, and sent us the holiness of Shabbat, the honor of the season, and the celebration of the festival. You separated between the [greater] holiness of Shabbat and the [lesser] holiness of Yom Tov, and sanctified the seventh day from the six days of work. You separated and sanctified the people Israel with your holiness and gave them, etc."

Though a relatively minor point in a lengthier *sugya*, the simple attribution to Rav and Shmuel of the initiation of saying the *havdallah* blessing during the fourth blessing of the *amidah* stands as a reported example of rabbinic innovation in prayer. Whether they were the first to recite this prayer, or simply the first to fix its literary form, the text does not clarify. Elbogen cites a number of textual witnesses that trace the development of this blessing in the periods following the closure of the Talmuds, but the text quoted is already remarkably close to the current form of the *havdallah* blessing in use today.[468]

When the Tannaim can reach no agreement, we see the Amoraim resolving the earlier question of precisely when the blessing of *havdallah* should be said during the *amidah*. Next, the Amoraim supply a final text of the liturgy for their time, setting the exact wording that should be said within the blessing that surrounds it. In the first Babylonian Amoraic generation, Rav and Shmuel set this new prayer in response to an unanswered Tannaitic question. Nearly 100 years later in the early fourth century C.E., Rav Yosef felt it appropriate to restate their opinion as a satisfying answer to the question that arose before him. And, far later, the redactors of BT themselves tacitly indicated their acceptance of this change by including this statement in the final text. This suggests openness to the idea of self-conscious initiation in liturgy that continued well into the Amoraic period and beyond it, at least until the redaction of BT.

One caveat, as mentioned above, is that it is possible to read this pericope as something other than the wholesale initiation of the *havdallah* ceremony. It could be the report simply presents the designation of this text's fixed, permanent wording, selecting one option to certify as proper in the observance of a long established practice. Even if this were the case, the idea of selecting one text as the established procedure is, in and of itself, innovative, and certainly qualifies as a change in law that reduced the diversity of practice and privileged one liturgical mode over others. As we shall see in the next sections, liturgy was just one of the many areas in which this sort of initiation occurred.

Rabbinic Initiation 2: Yavnean Innovation and Fixing Liturgy—A Pseudo-History of the *Birkat HaMazon*

In terms of collective rabbinic initiation, two specific groupings situated in towns where groups of rabbis met to discuss law appear in the corpus of texts: Yavneh and Usha. Citations of rabbinic innovation in Yavneh are less frequent than those of Usha; only two extant citations of *takkanot* exist in rabbinic literature from Yavneh as opposed to five examples from Usha.[469]

The two *takkanot* connected with Yavneh both confront issues of emergent liturgy. In this respect, they deal with the fixing of liturgical texts and practices, and provide pseudo-histories that explain the creation of the prayers at hand. Since the prayers are required ones, it is logical to include these two examples among the legal *takkanot*. In this multi-layered example in BT Ber. 48b, Yavnean leadership was shown as responsible for connecting the text of the fourth blessing of the *Birkat HaMazon* with painful historical events:

אמר רב נחמן : משה תַקַן לישראל ברכת הזן בשעה שירד להם מן, יהושע
תַקַן להם ברכת הארץ כיון שנכנסו לארץ, דוד ושלמה תַקְנוּ בונה ירושלים.
דוד תַקַן על ישראל עמך ועל ירושלים עירך, ושלמה תַקַן על הבית הגדול
והקדוש, הטוב והמטיב ביבנה תַקְנוּהַ כנגד הרוגי ביתר. דאמר רב מתנא :
אותו היום שניתנו הרוגי ביתר לקבורה תַקְנוּ ביבנה הטוב והמטיב, הטוב,
שלא הסריחו ; והמטיב, שניתנו לקבורה.

Rav Nahman said: Moses enacted for Israel *Birkat HaZan*[470] at the time
when *mannah* came down for them; Joshua enacted *Birkat HaAretz*[471]
when they entered the land [of Israel]; David and Solomon enacted
boneh yerushalayim.[472] David enacted the words "for Israel Your people and for Jerusalem Your city,"[473] and Solomon enacted "upon this
great and holy house."[474] "Who is good and does good:" in Yavneh
they enacted it for the sake of those who were martyred in Betar.[475] As
Rav Matena said: On the same day that the dead of Betar were taken to
be buried, they enacted in Yavneh "who is good and does good." "Is
good," that they did not decay; and "does good," that they were permitted to be buried.

The passage is stated in the name of Rav Nahman. The two cited authorities,
Rav Nahman (bar Yaakov) and Rav Matena, were both students of Shmuel, and
thus second or third generation Babylonian Amoraim, active in the late third to
early fourth centuries CE.

This passage, moving as it does from the earliest times to the latest, supplies
a purported origin for all four blessings within *Birkat HaMazon* linked thematically to critical moments in the history of the Jewish people. Even leaving aside
the reliance on the miracles of the manna and the non-decaying bodies to justify
certain blessings, the chronology of this passage is somewhat suspect. It is not
that *Birkat HaMazon* could not have developed as early as the biblical period.
Indeed, many prominent scholars argue for an early origin to *Birkat HaMazon*,
including Heinemann[476] and Finkelstein.[477] Deut. 8:10 is the biblical basis generally cited to justify the commandment for this blessing in the first place.[478]
Despite this possibility, the earliest text Finkelstein cited as a potential proto-
Birkat HaMazon comes from Jub. 22:6-9 (a section of Jubilees not found at
Qumran), where we find a prayer supposedly recited by Abraham after he ate, in
celebration of the feast of the first fruits:

6) [A]nd he ate and drank and blessed God Most High who created
heaven and earth and who made all the fat of the earth and gave it to
the sons of man [and woman], so that they might eat and drink and
bless their Creator. 7) "And now I thank you, my God, because you
have let me see this day. Behold, I am one hundred and seventy-five
years old, and fulfilled in days. 8) And all of my days were peaceful for
me." [479]

The most reliable dating of this retelling of Genesis we know as the Book of
Jubilees is to the time of the Hellenistic reform, around 168 BCE.[480]
Another early reference to *Birkat HaMazon* cited by Heinemann comes
from the fictitious Letter of Aristeas, and shows slight promise of being serious

evidence of an early blessing after the meal—in fact, in the epistle itself, it is even uttered *before* the meal.[481] Moshe Weinfeld notes an early *Birkat HaMazon* in a Qumran text (4Q434), though he admits that the order and form of the blessings differ markedly from those we find in rabbinic sources.[482] While one cannot deny that these texts contain themes parallel to the blessings of *Birkat HaMazon*, it hardly seems likely that these were early versions of the grace after meals. A final pre-Tannaitic trace of the presence of *Birkat HaMazon* may be found in the *Didache*, an early Christian Palestinian text from the first century CE, which preserves a text that follows a very similar pattern to *Birkat HaMazon*.[483] This final text, though, appears to be only slightly pre-Tannaitic, if it predates 70 CE at all.

M, T and a number of *baraitot* use the term *Birkat HaMazon* without explanation, indicating that it must have been a solid part of tradition during the Tannaitic period. But such usage does not indicate any particular form for this blessing—it merely indicates that the concept of blessing after a meal was present. In fact, there are even cases of Amoraim arguing over whether *Birkat HaMazon* was made up of three or four blessings, indicating that the final form had still not been completed well into the Amoraic period.[484] Ultimately, not one of the early sources provides any firm evidence that *Birkat HaMazon* was a four-part prayer, or that its sections developed in the order suggested by Rav Nahman's statement.

The basic concept of the blessing after the meal has existed since biblical times, but the familiar four-blessing structure of *Birkat HaMazon* remained fluid at least into the Tannaitic, and probably the Amoraic period. The passage in BT Ber. provides a late reconstruction of the origins of this practice, based on prominent biblical personalities and the literary motifs attached to them by their portrayal in the Bible.

Even the assignment of *hatov vehametiv* to Yavneh, the closest chronological stage to the Amoraim, has been proven false, as Finkelstein first explained:

> We have noticed that this benediction is mentioned by R. Eliezer b. Hyrkanos. . . . But we know that R. Eliezer b. Hyrkanos died before the outbreak of the rebellion of Bar Kokhba. How then could he mention a benediction that was composed in celebration of the relenting of the government toward those who had taken part in it? It is clear that the Amoraic tradition regarding this benediction cannot be accepted, although the benediction was doubtless added to the Grace within a half century after the destruction of the Temple.[485]

Ahistorical as it is, this construct in BT created a distinguished and longstanding history for the *Birkat HaMazon*. Here, again the rabbis felt comfortable hanging their creations onto the great authorities of the past, to lend them added relevance and *gravitas*. Furthermore, this text admits of a certain acceptance of the very idea of liturgical development, for it sees the very creation of the *Birkat HaMazon* as a long-term process of accretion. The prayer itself, when viewed through the frame established in BT, becomes a reminder that tradition is fluid in the long-term, and is affected and shaped by the various forces and moments of Jewish history. This fluidity is freely admitted, and recognized as appropriate.

The editors of this passage selected appropriate personages from history, who represented various biblical moments that cohered with the rabbis' perception of the meaning of each blessing in *Birkat HaMazon*, and linked them to the prayer as initiators, or, possibly, as those who fixed the final literary form of the prayer. Moses, whom the Bible showed was present for the miracle of the *mannah,* became representative of the ongoing divine sustenance acknowledged in *Birkat HaZan*. Joshua, first military conqueror of the land, symbolized the value of the land of Israel connected to *Birkat HaAretz*. David and Solomon, biblically responsible for the founding of Jerusalem and the Temple, respectively, became the exemplars of *boneh yerusahalayim*. Betar, scene of Bar Kokhba's last stand, represented a chronologically closer miracle that the rabbis at Yavneh were said to have honored with the formation of the final blessing—*hatov vehametiv*.

It appears that the rabbis scanned biblical texts and recent history to find referents who sensibly promoted the values the rabbis desired to promote. It is hard to say whether that process took place in Yavneh, in the time of Rav Nahman and his peers, or four hundred years later among the editors of BT. Whenever it did occur, this constructed pseudo-history expressed the values of its editors via a strong connection with prior biblical tradition.

As for the other initiation in Yavneh, it pertains to the development of another element of worship in Jewish life: the *amidah*. Here, too, the tone is one of liturgical formulation, rather than strict legal enactment, though it is sensible to include this example because stating this blessing ultimately became a legal obligation. There is an ongoing discussion in Amoraic literature, mirrored in modern scholarship, about the development of the 18 or 19 benedictions of the *amidah*. The following text from BT Ber. 28b attributes the creation of the 12th blessing in the *amidah*, the blessing that asks that heretics have no hope, to the rabbis at Yavneh:

הני תמני סרי, תשסרי הוויין! אמר רבי לוי : ברכת המינים ביבנה
<u>תקנוה</u>. כנגד מי <u>תקנוה</u>? אמר רבי לוי : לרבי הלל בריה דרבי
שמואל בר נחמני : כנגד (תהלים כ״ט) ״אל הכבוד הרעים,״ לרב
יוסף : כנגד אחד שבקריאת שמע; לרבי תנחום אמר רבי יהושע
בן לוי : כנגד חוליא קטנה שבשדרה. תנו רבנן : שמעון הפקולי
הסדיר שמונה עשרה ברכות לפני רבן גמליאל על הסדר ביבנה.
אמר להם רבן גמליאל לחכמים : כלום יש אדם שיודע <u>לתקן</u>

ברכת המינים? עמד שמואל הקטן ותקנה, לשנה אחרת שכחה.
והשקיף בה שתים ושלש שעות ולא העלוהו.

These 18 [benedictions of the *amidah*], they are [actually] 19!

Rabbi Levi said: *Birkat HaMinim*, they <u>formulated</u> it at Yavneh.
And to what does it correspond? Rabbi Levi said: According to Hillel
the son of Rabbi Shmuel bar Nahmani, to the verse: "the God of Glory
thunders" (Psalm 29:3); according to Rav Yosef, to the "One" in the
Shema; according to Rabbi Tanhum in the name of Rabbi Yehoshua
ben Levi, to the small vertebrae in the spinal column.

Our rabbis taught: Shimeon Hapakuli ordered the eighteen benedictions before Rabban Gamaliel in Yavneh. Rabban Gamaliel said to
the Sages: Is there no one who knows how to <u>fix</u> *Birkat HaMinim*?
Shmuel the Small stood and <u>fixed</u> it, but another year he forgot it, and
he tried to remember it for two or three hours, and they did not remove
him [from leading the prayer].

Much ink has been spilled on this passage and its parallels.[486] The *baraita* in BT
reflects the fluid nature of the *amidah* during the Tannaitic period. While 18
blessings were fixed, it was still possible to add a new one and set its definite
form, bringing the total up to 19. The text justifies the additional blessing by any
of three reasons, which vary considerably in their theological outlook. From the
second half of the passage, it is also clear that the exact formulation of this particular blessing was not yet fixed in the Tannaitic period, either.

Note again the usage of the root *tkn* in its meaning of literary formulation. It
remains impossible, given the available evidence, to rule out the possibility that
the rabbis considered the literary formulation of a blessing a form of legal enactment. Formulation of a blessing certainly had legal ramifications in its effect
upon later worshippers, yet it still remained primarily an act of literary formulation—technically different than that of legal enactment. Nonetheless, this particular usage of the term blurs the line between the two categories.

Rabban Gamaliel's question indicates that, according to rabbinic historiography, only one of the numerous sages gathered in Yavneh knew how to recite
this blessing in its finalized form, sure proof of the novelty of this final edition.
Conversely, Shmuel the Small's lengthy attempt at remembering the correct
version in this source does indicate that there was already a nascent sense of a
"fixed" liturgy for this prayer that had priority over other forms.[487]

After this analysis, it is clear that Yavneh, while potentially a seat of innovation, was portrayed as highly conservative and limited when it came to inno-

vating law using the term *takkanah*, with only one reliable tradition indicating the use of a *takkanah* in the entirety of our extant sources from the rabbinic period. Both instances when Yavnean *takkanot* are reported represent cases when the rabbis set the final form of liturgical pieces. In this respect, the collective group of rabbis at Yavneh was not considered responsible for an innovation using the term *takkanah*, beyond the setting of two very small parts of greater liturgical pieces. Rabban Yohanan ben Zakkai, however, is portrayed as responsible for a number of innovations, which we will discuss below. The collective, here, shown as responsible for only very limited legal change (if any), was overshadowed by a dominant leader credited with more significant alteration of law.

Rabbinic Initiation 3: Usha and Marital Relations

Usha, a town in the Galilee near Sepphoris and Shefaram, served as the seat of Jewish leadership in the period following the Bar Kokhba revolt (roughly 135-170 CE). According to our texts, Usha was the reported site of five examples of rabbinic initiation. These appear tightly grouped in one literary unit in BT Ketubbot 49b-50a. They also form one grouping in a legal sense, as well: all five enactments focus on familial responsibilities. Further, another linkage resides in the fact that three of the five *takkanot* were stated in the name of Rabbi Elai, a third generation Palestinian Amora, a scholar in third century Tiberias.[488] Two other *takkanot* were stated in the names of Rabbi Yitzhak, another third generation Palestinian Amora, and Rabbi Yossi ben Hanina, a second generation Palestinian Amora. This places all the tradents associated with these traditions firmly in early third century Palestine.

The *takkanah* that is arguably the most interesting in this quintet is one that sets a new limit upon the spending of one's assets for *tzedakah*, found in BT Ket. 50a:[489]

א״ר אילעא: באושא התקינו, המבזבז, אל יבזבז יותר מחומש. תניא נמי
הכי: המבזבז, אל יבזבז יותר מחומש, שמא יצטרך לבריות; ומעשה באחד
שבקש לבזבז יותר מחומש ולא הניח לו חבירו, ומנו? רבי ישבב, ואמרי לה
רבי ישבב, ולא הניחו חבירו, ומנו? רבי עקיבא. אמר רב נחמן, ואיתימא רב
אחא בר יעקב: מאי קרא? (בראשית כ״ח) וכל אשר תתן לי עשר אעשרנו
לך. והא לא דמי עישורא בתרא לעישורא קמא! אמר רב אשי: אעשרנו
לבתרא כי קמא, אמר רב שימי בר אשי: ושמועות הללו מתמעטות
והולכות, וסימניך: קטנים כתבו ובזבזו.

Rabbi Elai said: In Usha they enacted that one who spends liberally [on *tzedakah*] may not spend more than one fifth [= 20% of his/her assets].

It was taught in another *baraita*:[490] One who spends liberally may not spend more than one fifth, lest he become dependent on other people.

There is a story of one who wanted to spend liberally [more than a fifth] and his colleague did not allow it. Who was it [who did not allow it]? Rabbi Yeshebab.[491] Others say that [the one who wanted to spend] it was Rabbi Yeshebab. Who did not permit him [i.e., Rabbi Yeshebab, to spend it]? Rabbi Akiba.

Rav Nahman said, but some say Rav Aha bar Yaakov said: What is the prooftext? "And all that You will give to me, I will surely set aside a tenth." (Genesis 28:22).[492]

But the second tenth is not like the first tenth? Rav Ashi replied: "I will give a tenth of it," implies that the second is like the first.[493]

Rav Shimi bar Ashi said: These reports are decreasing,[494] and the mnemonic is: minors wrote and spent liberally.[495]

The last words of this section are our strongest indicator that this material on Ushan innovation traveled as a unit, even orally before the writing of the Gemara. The reference to "minors" serves as a trigger to the memory of the first *takkanah* on this page, which speaks of fathers supporting their minor children through the provision of food. The second *takkanah* directs that even if a man writes that his full estate should be turned over to his sons, he and his wife still have the right to support themselves from the estate's assets. The third in this trail of mnemonic aids refers to the one who spends liberally, spending 20% instead of 10% on *tzedakah*, as cited on the prior page.

The parallel in PT Peah 1:1, 15a-b has much to teach about the history of this *takkanah*:

דמר רבי שמעון בן לקיש בשם רבי יהודה בן חנינא נמנו באושא שיהא
אדם מפריש חומש מנכסיו למצות. . . . מעשה בר' ישבב שעמד והחליק את
כל נכסיו לעניים. שלח לו רבן גמליאל: והלא אמרו חומש מנכסיו למצות?
ורבן גמליאל לא קודם לאושא היה?!? רבי יוסי בי ר' בון בשם רבי לוי: כך
היתה הלכה בידם ושכחוה, ועמדו השניים והסכימו על דעת הראשונים,
ללמדך שכל דבר שבית דין נותנין נפשן עליו, סוף הוא מתקיים כמה
שנאמר למשה מסיני.

As Rabbi Shimeon ben Lakish said in the name of Rabbi Yehuda ben Hanina: they voted and decided in Usha that a person may distribute one fifth of his/her property to charity. . . .[496]

A story of Rabbi Yeshebab, who stood up and distributed all his property to the poor. Rabban Gamaliel sent to him: Did they not say 'one fifth of his/her property [may go] to charity?

But did not Rabban Gamaliel precede Usha? Rabbi Yossi son of Rabbi Bun said in the name of Rabbi Levi: this was the law in their hands, and they forgot it. And the later ones [lit. "second ones"] stood up and agreed upon the opinion of the earlier ones [lit. "first ones"]. This is to teach you that anything that a court decides upon, in the end it will be upheld like that which was said to Moses at Sinai.

There are a few fascinating divergences between the versions in PT and BT. First, where BT utilizes the verb *tkn*, in PT we find the very different *nimnu ve-gamru*, indicating that PT saw this as a vote taken within the Ushan context. The final statement in the pericope from PT leaves no doubt as to the power its editors placed in the hands of a court—to compare the court's decision favorably with something said to Moses at Sinai is, without question, a strong statement of the permanence of its ruling.

The most interesting divergence is PT's understanding of the role of Rabban Gamaliel, an authority who predated Usha, whom PT reported as citing an Ushan tradition. Combining the tradition of Ushan origin with this statement from Rabban Gamaliel results in a mettlesome anachronism, which inspires further questioning in the *sugya*. PT's resolution is to harmonize the two sources by explaining that the law was forgotten and then re-created accurately in the image of the prior law at Usha. This concept, of a law that the rabbis knew but then forgot is utilized five times in PT only, never appearing in another source in these precise terms.[497] It appears to be a rhetorical device that answers possible objections by showing the approved answer to be a prior *halakhah*.

If we consider the historical situation in which the Ushans found themselves, the sorts of concerns we find addressed in the Ushan *takkanot* make perfect sense. Hadrian (117-138 CE), the Roman Emperor who reigned at the very beginning of the rise of Usha, ended a long line of Roman Emperors who had extremely hostile relations with the Jews. Subsequently, with the advent of more benevolent Emperors such as Antoninus Pius (138-161 CE) and Marcus Aurelius (161-180 CE), the Ushan School thrived in a period of relative calm with respect to the Roman government. Nonetheless, the persecutions and attacks that took place during Hadrian's time, and the upheavals associated with the Bar Kokhba rebellion, would certainly have left many families torn apart. Thus, it is not at all surprising to find *takkanot* that confront the pressing issues of family responsibilities and limitations on *tzedakah*, to help limit the number of indigent people as the Ushan leadership attempted to stabilize a badly hurt community on a better path. This either indicates true Ushan origin, or that later editors shared a certain picture of the Ushan context and retrojected accordingly.

Reviewing Ushan and Yavnean *takkanot*, the critical finding is that *takkanot* created when the rabbis worked singly or in groups centered at the seat of power are tightly limited to two areas: worship and marital/family relationships. In worship, especially, much of their reported activity centered on the literary fixing of prayer texts. As mentioned before, these were areas where there was more flexibility in Jewish law due to the paucity of Torah texts that dictated the specifics of *halakhah*. Certainly the distribution of these *takkanot* reflects a tacit acknowledgement that there was either more latitude for initiation and innovation in these areas, especially in the minds of the redactors of BT where the majority of citations appear, or, alternatively, greater pressing need to make changes.

Enactments of The Sages

While groups of rabbis in specific, identifiable locales are cited as making significant changes to Jewish law, the more general "sages" are also credited with initiating new practices as well. In 11 occurrences in BT and three in PT,[498] individual rabbis or the general terms for distinguished collectives of rabbis, denoted by the terms רבנן (*rabbanan*, "our rabbis") or חכמים (*hakhamim*, "sages") are presented as making novel enactments included in our legal texts. We will analyze one *takkanah* promulgated in the name of the sages, and a series promulgated in the name of one individual—Rabban Yohanan ben Zakkai.

One interesting attempt at initiation by the sages comes in BT Ket. 8b, a passage that sets the parameters of what David Kraemer called "a ritual of comfort" that took place in a house of mourning.[499] The specific part of this text that captures our interest is its reference to an abortive *takkanah* requiring that ten cups of wine must be consumed in a house of mourning:

אמר עולא, ואמרי לה במתניתא תנא : עשרה כוסות תַּקָנוּ חכמים בבית האבל, שלשה קודם אכילה, כדי לפתוח את בני מעיו, שלשה בתוך אכילה, כדי לשרות אכילה שבמעיו, וארבעה לאחר אכילה, אחד כנגד הזן, ואחד כנגד ברכת הארץ, ואחד כנגד בונה ירושלים, ואחד כנגד הטוב והמטיב ; הוסיפו עליהם ארבעה : אחד כנגד חזני העיר, ואחד כנגד פרנסי העיר, ואחד כנגד בית המקדש, ואחד כנגד רבן גמליאל, התחילו היו שותין ומשתכרין, החזירו הדבר ליושנה.

Ulla said, and some say it was taught in a *baraita*: The sages en-acted ten cups in the house of mourning: three before the meal, in order to open his intestines; three during the meal, in order to help digest the food that is in his stomach; and four after the meal—one for the [first prayer in the *Birkat HaMazon* called] *Birkat HaZan*, one for the [second] blessing [of *Birkat HaMazon* called] *Birkat HaAretz*, one for the [third] blessing [called] *boneh yerushalayim*, and one for the [fourth] blessing [called] *hatov vehametiv*.

They added four to these: one for the community workers [who at-tended to burying the dead and other communal needs], one for the keepers of the communal funds [who released funds to pay for burials that the poor could not afford],[500] one for the Temple and one for Rab-ban Gamaliel.[501] They began [to observe this], and they were drinking and becoming intoxicated. They returned the matter to its prior state [that of requiring only ten cups at a house of mourning].

This *takkanah* promulgated by the sages clearly led to adverse effects that did not cohere with the original intent of the enactment. The original enactment at-tempted to achieve three purposes: first, to prepare the intestines of the mourner for the food he or she needed to eat to remain well during the intensity of the mourning period; second, to serve as a *digestif* during the meal; and third, to set off the *Birkat HaMazon* in a house of mourning from other occasions, as was also done during the seven days following a wedding.

With the latter four cups, though, the sages aimed to recognize relevant par-ties to the funeral with individual toasts, honoring them for their assistance to the mourning family. Community workers and keepers of communal funds each played a part in the actual labor and financing of the burial, so they deserved recognition. The destruction of the Temple, the prototypical mourning moment for the entire Jewish people, was then recalled with its own cup. A final cup remembered Rabban Gamaliel, who by his actions as a communal leader set a modest course for all funerals that followed. There may also be a link to Greek and Roman funeral customs.[502]

By the end of this pericope, though, the sages have realized the error of their ways: requiring fourteen cups of wine, even well-diluted with water and accompanied by food, would leave most mourners inebriated. Since inebriation was not the desired outcome, the sages reversed direction to ensure the dignity of the funerary observance. We find a parallel text with the same sentiment, but a different enumeration of cups in Sem. 14:14, and with an interesting inter-change of the term *gezerah* for *takkanah*:

עשרה כוסות שותין בבית האבל, שנים לפני המזון, וחמשה בתוך המזון,
ושלשה לאחר המזון, אחד לברכת אבלים, ואחד לתנחומי אבלים, ואחד
לגמילות חסדים. חזרו והוסיפו עוד שלשה, אחד לראש הכנסת, ואחד לחזן
הכנסת, ואחד לרבן גמליאל. וכשראו חכמים ובית דין שמשתכרין ויוצאין,
גזרו עליהם והחזירום למקומן.

They drink ten cups at the house of mourning: two before the meal, and
five during the meal, and three after the meal, one for the blessing of
the mourners, and one for the comforting of the mourners, and one for
acts of lovingkindness. They went back and added another three, one
for the head of the *kenesset*, and one for the *hazan haKenesset*,[503] and
one for Rabban Gamaliel. And when the sages and the court saw that
they would become inebriated and leave [the house of the mourners],
they <u>decreed</u> upon them [i.e., the extra cups], and returned them to their
place.[504]

While the numbers of cups and the reasons supporting them changed, the basic
principle remained the same. The one added piece of information in this text
brings the entire passage into focus: the concern here was beyond the simple
dignity of the custom—if those comforting the mourners became drunk, they
would depart, leaving the mourners alone and defeating the purpose of the meal
of consolation entirely.

A second parallel text, very similar to the above, from PT Ber. 3:1, 6a, bol-
sters this argument, but provides a few other conflicting details:

תני: עשרה כוסות שותין בבית האבל: שנים לפני המזון, וחמשה בתוך
המזון, ושלשה לאחר המזון: אילו שלשה שלאחר המזון: אחד לברכת
המזון, ואחד לגמילות חסדים, ואחד לתנחומי אבילים. וכשמת רבן שמעון
בן גמליאל, הוסיפו עליהן עוד שלשה: אחד לחזן הכנסת, ואחד לראש
הכנסת, ואחד לרבן גמליאל. וכיון שראו בית דין שהיו משתכרין והולכין,
גזרו עליהן והחזירום למקומן.

It was taught: They drink ten cups in the house of mourning: two before
the meal, and five during the meal, and three after the meal. These are
the three after the meal: one for the *Birkat HaMazon*, and one for acts
of loving-kindness and one for comforting the mourners. And once
Rabban Shimeon ben Gamaliel died, they added another three: one for
the *Hazan HaKenesset*, one for the head of the *kenesset* and one for
Rabban Gamaliel. But when the court saw that they were becoming
inebriated and going [out from the house of mourning], they <u>decreed</u>
and returned them to their place [i.e., reinstated the prior observance].

While the texts from Sem. and PT agree on the original enumeration and the later additions the sages made to this custom, their versions of the story vary considerably from the BT text. Both PT and Sem. utilize the word *gezerah* instead of *takkanah*, though it is clear that BT defines an enactment as the mechanism employed for halakhic change. This example reinforces our prior conclusion that BT is more inclined to utilize the language of *takkanah* than any of the Palestinian sources. This suggests that BT is more inclined to present rabbis as empowered than PT, at least when it came to rabbinic legislation.

The very interesting fact that arises in PT that we have not seen elsewhere is the element of timing: PT places the initiation of this custom at the time of the death of Rabban Shimeon ben Gamaliel I, the father of Rabban Gamaliel II, who served as *nasi* in the late first century CE.[505] Also of note is the fact that Sem. and BT both explicitly attribute this change to the sages, while PT does not, giving credit for any changes to either an unnamed "they," or to the generic court.

In these three texts we find an adaptation of older laws that initiated new honors for those involved in funerary rites in Palestinian Jewish society. Though the number of cups and reasons for the change differed, the three parallel reports suggest that additional cups were added to the practice of drinking at a mourners' home at some point during the Tannaitic period, probably late in the first century, but were then rapidly removed in order to maintain dignity and sustain the emotional support required by the mourners. The sages or the court were involved in the process, with credit allotted differently in the relevant sources.

Enactments of the *Nasi*: Rabban Yohanan ben Zakkai

In another passage, we find a collection of innovations brought forward in the name of one individual: Rabban Yohanan ben Zakkai. As Urbach sees it:

> Rabban Johanan b. Zakkai's greatest achievement was the creation of a legal-religious institution in Yavneh and the solution of problems which arose because of the destruction of the Temple. His main aim was to re-establish the religious life on the assumption that the Temple would not be speedily rebuilt but in the firm belief that ultimately it would. Not all of Rabban Johanan's *takkanot* were immediately accepted.[506]

M RH 4:1-4 and the Gemara commenting on it in BT RH 31b point out exactly nine *takkanot* attributed to Rabban Yohanan ben Zakkai.[507] In BT, we find:

תנו רבנן: אין כהנים רשאין לעלות בסנדליהן לדוכן, וזו אחד מתשע
תקנות שהתקין רבן יוחנן בן זכאי. שית דהאי פירקא, וחדא דפירקא
קמא. ואידך? דתניא: גר שנתגייר בזמן הזה צריך שיפריש רובע לקינו.

אמר רבי שמעון בן אלעזר: כבר נמנה עליה רבן יוחנן וביטלה מפני
התקלה. ואידך: פלוגתא דרב פפא ורב נחמן בר יצחק. רב פפא אמר: כרם
רבעי, רב נחמן בר יצחק אמר: לשון של זהורית.

Our rabbis taught: priests are not permitted to ascend the *dukhan* in
their sandals.[508] And this is one of the nine *takkanot* that Rabban Yohanan ben Zakkai enacted. Six in this chapter, and one in the first chapter,[509] and the other one? As it is taught: a convert who converts at this
time[510] needs to set aside a quarter [of a shekel] for his nest [i.e., a pair
of birds].[511]

Rabbi Shimeon ben Eleazar said: Rabban Yohanan [and his court]
already voted on this, and cancelled it because of stumbling.[512]

And the other one? There is a disagreement between Rav Papa and
Rav Nahman bar Yitzhak. Rav Papa said: the fourth year vine; and Rav
Nahman bar Yitzhak said: the scarlet thread.[513]

Rashi conveniently lists the various *takkanot* involved as follows:[514]

1) priests are not permitted to ascend the *dukhan* in sandals (here, a
   baraita in BT RH 31b);
2) the Shofar should be blown when Rosh Hashanah falls on Shabbat
   wherever a *Beit Din* is present (M RH 4:1);
3) the Lulav should be taken up for seven days outside Jerusalem (M
   RH 4:3);
4) on the day of the waving of the Omer (16 *Nissan*) eating new produce is forbidden entirely (M RH 4:3);
5) the court in Jerusalem would accept testimony on the new month
   throughout the whole day (M RH 4:4);
6) witnesses (traveling to testify about the new month at the court in
   Jerusalem on Shabbat) may only go to the place where the court is
   sitting, but may not travel farther (M RH 4:4);
7) messengers may violate Shabbat to inform the populace of the new
   month only for *Nissan* and *Tishrei* (BT RH 21b);[515]
8) a convert must set aside a quarter of a shekel for a pigeon's nest (a
   baraita in RH 31b);[516] and
9) either: the *takkanah* suggested by Rav Papa (the fourth year vine)
   or the one suggested by Rav Nahman bar Yitzhak (the scarlet
   thread) (both here, BT RH 31b).

Each of these initiations (except the potential *takkanah* of the scarlet thread, which comes under much chronological scrutiny later in this page of Talmud) reflected a focus on aspects of religious life that had to be sustained despite massive changes in the objective conditions that surrounded the Jews. They tended to extend earlier religious practices into a new context—where rites were purely Temple-based, retainable elements of Temple practice were incorporated to evince a connection to prior practice. In some cases, new elements of ritual and new justificatory patterns were also created that stretched historic precedents into functional new rites.

From a source critical perspective, eight of the *takkanot* recorded in Rabban Yohanan ben Zakkai's name are clearly of Tannaitic origin. *Takkanot* two through six come directly from M, while *takkanot* numbered one, seven and eight are contained in *baraitot* in BT. It is only number nine that has a distinctly Amoraic origin, and that is the one that is disputed. A tradition of nine *takkanot* must have existed, and at least one of the *takkanot* was forgotten. Both Rav Papa and Rav Nahman bar Yitzhak attempted to recreate the tradition correctly, and disagreement resulted. Here, despite the Amoraic gloss of the final *takkanah*, we are confronting a predominantly Tannaitic record of Rabban Yohanan ben Zakkai's activity.

It is also worth remarking upon the fact that we find nine substantial *takkanot* that have significant ritual ramifications in the name of Rabban Yohanan ben Zakkai, while the *takkanot* associated with the collective at Yavneh are limited to two that deal only with liturgical finalization. This indicates a specific editorial choice: it was more effective to connect legal change to powerful leaders at critical points of time, than to groups of lawmakers. A lone, powerful leader, acting at a critical moment, made for a better story, and led, often, to the accretion of legal and legendary material around his actions. A similar pattern occurred with Rabbi Akiba's role in philosophical change in chapter one.

In these nine *takkanot*, we find record of a leader whose work was reported to have reshaped many important aspects of Jewish religious practice at a critical moment in Jewish history. These reports focus, as does *aggadah* connected to Rabban Yohanan ben Zakkai, on his daring innovations at a time of extreme need—through these changes in law, Rabban Yohanan ben Zakkai was portrayed as finding ways to preserve and sustain (often through enormous alteration) practices that would otherwise have been utterly decimated after the Destruction.

These *takkanot* of initiation are reported to have created a sizable, new landscape of innovative rites and practices for the Jewish people, and responded to many novel and challenging situations that required great ingenuity. The process of initiating practices through *takkanot* was a vital tool in the hand of a rabbinic leadership confronting many significant challenges in the Tannaitic and

Amoraic period, and the documents we have indicate that they used it, when necessary, to alter the face of Jewish tradition.

Other Categories

Outside of the most popular category, initiation, *takkanot* are introduced with many other rationales attached to them. Some of these rationales have already received treatment in chapter one, but some are entirely different.

For the Sake Of Communal Welfare

Thirty-six occurrences state that *takkanot* were enacted for the sake of communal welfare.[517] Each of these enactments exhibits rationales similar or identical to those we saw in chapter one above, in the section on changes in law for the sake of communal welfare. Since this sort of rationale was discussed extensively above, we will list the *takkanot*, but will not stop to analyze them. The basic trends demarcated in chapter one apply here as well.

Encouraging Proper Behavior

Rabbinic legal sources report that the rabbis often made *takkanot* to encourage the community to act properly. In 30 cases throughout our texts, we find examples of *takkanot* that were intended to lead members of the community to act appropriately in selected situations where misbehavior was a distinct possibility.[518] We will review only two of these cases.

Remitting the Remitting: The *Prosbul*

Perhaps the most famous of all *takkanot* was the *prosbul* attributed to Hillel the Elder. This enactment was designed to help the poorest members of society survive times of great duress, while at the same time encouraging the wealthy to continue making loans to poor comrades to fulfill their obligations to engage in *tzedakah*. By excusing the wealthy from having to observe the scheduled remission of debts in the Sabbatical Year, this legal maneuver provided both a righteous observance for the wealthy and access to seed, food and other necessities for the poor, further sustaining the economy despite the severe limitations placed upon it by the Torah's construct of the Sabbatical Year.

M Shevi. 10:3-4 bears the first Tannaitic notice of this revolutionary change in Jewish law:

ג) פרוזבול אינו משמט. זה אחד מן הדברים <u>שהתקין</u> הלל הזקן, כשראה
שנמנעו העם מלהלוות זה את זה, ועוברין על מה שכתוב בתורה (דברים
טו) "השמר לך פן יהיה דבר עם לבבך בליעל" וגו'. <u>התקין</u> הלל לפרוזבול:

ד) זהו גופו של פרוזבול: "מוסר אני לכם איש פלוני ופלוני, הדיינים
שבמקום פלוני, שכל חוב שיש לי, שאגבנו כל זמן שארצה." והדיינים
חותמין למטה או העדים:

3) A [loan secured by a] *prosbul* is not cancelled [by the Sabbatical Year]. This is one of the matters that Hillel the Elder <u>enacted</u>, when he saw that the people refrained from lending [money] to one another [in the Sabbatical Year because they were concerned that the debt would be cancelled and they would lose the principal of their loan], and were violating what is written in the Torah (Deut. 15:9): "Be careful lest there be a base thought in your heart," etc. Hillel <u>enacted</u> the *prosbul*.

4) This is the substance of the *prosbul*: "I transmit to you, Ploni and Ploni, the judges in place Ploni, that any debt due me I may collect whenever I wish." And the judges sign below, or the witnesses.

The *prosbul* ascribed to Hillel was the rabbis' answer to the restrictive prohibitions in the Torah that prevented loans from being upheld over the period of the Sabbatical Year. Deut. 15:1-3, as mentioned in the mishnah above, provides the root text for the earliest level of Jewish law in this matter. The Torah's account of the seventh year provides no escape clause whatsoever from the remission of debts between Israelites. Every creditor was included, and the commandment was written in a classic command form, making its observance incumbent upon everyone in the community. M reports that Hillel was able to adjust it in a significant way, thanks to a strict constructionist reading: the text in Deut. 15:2 states that every *individual creditor* must remit all claims due from other individuals. It does not, however, specifically require that a *court* remit claims due it, or claims that have been turned over to it for payment. Utilizing a close reading to open a loophole, Hillel created a legal fiction: the act of turning personal loans over to a court, so that the court may, in effect, permit the continuance of the obligation between individuals, despite the commanded remission of individual obligations during the Sabbatical Year.

Not surprisingly, the editor of this section of M felt the need to further bolster this explanation with a *derashah* to support it: Deut. 15:9 commands "Be careful lest there be a base thought in your heart," and M interprets this as proof positive that creditors are commanded to continue making loans, despite the looming remission scheduled for the seventh year. The verse utilized is an *asmakhta* (a weak textually-based support), even if somewhat enhanced by the proximity of the verse in the same chapter of Deuteronomy. Oddly enough, a parallel source, M Git. 4:3, ignores any form of *derashah* as support for this *takkanah*, relying solely on the logical apprehension of the positive impact on general social welfare: *mipnei tikkun haolam*.

Quite a number of scholars have discussed this *takkanah*, and the text in M has many parallels and commentaries that devolve from it, so there is no end to the possibilities for analysis.[519] First, scholars point out the word *prosbul* itself, which is clearly not of Hebrew origin. It arose, some suggest, from the abbreviation of a Greek phrase: $\pi\rho\grave{o}\varsigma\ \beta o \upsilon \lambda \tilde{\eta}\ \beta o \upsilon \lambda \epsilon \upsilon \tau \tilde{\omega} \nu$, "before the assembly of counselors,"[520] indicating that the loan had been transferred from the individual realm to an assembly of distinguished representatives of the community. Emil Schürer, on the other hand, found its origin in a different word: $\pi\rho o\sigma\beta o\lambda\acute{\eta}$, a multiply-defined word which he explicitly admitted had never been attested with this particular meaning in extant Greek sources, but which he nonetheless believed to be the correct origin.[521] There is some promise to his conjecture. Liddell and Scott[522] present two meanings that cohere with the rabbinic sense: one arises from the idea of marking down the ownership of a lot during an auction, a legal function that records the transfer of funds between two parties; the other describes firmly placing a stake in the ground to give it a strong hold, which might be connected on a metaphoric level to the process of a loan "holding" despite communal remission. BT suggests that the word comes from פורסא דמילתא—the setting in order of a matter—and combined this further with בולי, a Hebrew transliteration of the Greek $\beta o\upsilon\lambda\acute{\eta}$, the ruling council of a city.[523] Any of these meanings could potentially give rise to the rabbinic *prosbul*, though the majority of scholars do favor the "assembly of counselors" tack above.

Several scholars have attempted to date this innovation to various specific moments in Jewish history during the Second Temple Period. Silberg, following Salo Baron's assessment, gives the most cogent attempt: he suggests that with the advent of the Herodian period, a semi-capitalistic system was introduced into the country, which led to the obvious need for a credit system. Such a credit system would have been greatly hindered by the periodic remission of debts commanded by the Torah. So, in an effort to ensure the ongoing economic prosperity of the people in this new economic context, Hillel responded with this innovation.[524] This is certainly a fair argument, but we should remember that no dating of this sort can be considered entirely verifiable, nor can we confirm that this commandment was widely observed in the Second Temple period.

The first parallel text we find to M Shevi. above attempts to explain a supposed basis in Torah for the transfer of the debt to the court. Playing upon the fact that Deuteronomy 15:3 says *yadkha*, "your hand," *SD* Piska 113 reads the text as implying that this excludes notes held by a court:

"את אחיך תשמט ידך." ולא המוסר שטרותיו לבית דין. מיכן אמרו
<u>התקין</u> הלל פרוסבול מפני תיקון העולם, שראה את העם שנמנעו מלהלוות
זה את זה ועברו על מה שכתוב בתורה, עמד <u>והתקין</u> פרוסבול. וזהו גופו
של פרוסבול: מוסרני אני לכם פלוני ופלוני הדיינים שבמקום פלוני, כל
חוב שיש לי שאגבנו כל זמן שארצה. והדיינים חותמים למטה או העדים.

"You must remit whatever is due you (literally "your hand") from your
kinsmen"—and not the one who hands over his notes to the court.
From here, they said: Hillel <u>enacted</u> *prosbul* for the sake of repairing
the world, for when he saw the people were avoiding lending to one
another, and they were transgressing what was written in the Torah, he
stood up and <u>enacted</u> *prosbul*. And this is the body of *prosbul*: "I declare before you, Ploni and Ploni, the judges in the place Ploni, each
debt that I have I may collect whenever I wish." And the judges sign
below, or the witnesses.[525]

SD reads the word *yadkha* as implying permission to transfer the debts to the
court to avoid remission during a Sabbatical Year. It implies that Hillel based his
enactment upon the biblical interpretive process, and not upon logical apprehension. As David Kraemer reads this midrash, its message is clear: "Whatever the
language of the Mishnah, *prosbul* gains strength from the Torah. Indeed, the
midrash claims, Hillel did nothing beyond what the Torah itself would permit."[526]
Another source that tends to downplay the revolutionary nature of Hillel's
enactment is PT Shevi. 10:2, 39c. Referring to M's prooftext from Deut. 15:9,
PT is not as certain of *prosbul's* Torah origin:

מיכן סמכו לפרוזבול שהוא מן התורה. ופרוזבול דבר תורה?! <u>כשהתקין</u>
הלל, סמכוהו לדבר תורה. אמר ר' חונה קשייתה קומי רבי יעקב בר אחא
כמאן דאמר מעשרות מדבר תורה, והלל <u>מתקין</u> על דבר תורה. אמר רבי
יוסי וכי משעה שגלו ישראל לבבל, לא נפטרו מן המצות התלויות בארץ.
והשמט כספים נוהג בין בארץ בין בחוצה לארץ דבר תורה. חזר רבי יוסי
ואמר: וזה דבר השמיטה שמוט: בשעה שהשמיטה נוהגת דבר תורה,
השמט כספים נוהג בין בארץ בין בחוצה לארץ דבר תורה. ובשעה
שהשמיטה נוהגת מדבריהן, השמט כספים נוהגת בין בארץ בין בחוצה
לארץ מדבריהם. תמן אמרין אפילו כמאן דאמר מעשרות דבר תורה, מודה
בשמיטה שהיא מדבריהן, דתני: וזה דבר השמיטה שמוט.

From here, they supported the *prosbul*, asserting that it is from the
Torah. And is the *prosbul* from the Torah? When Hillel <u>enacted</u> it, they
supported it from the Torah.

Said Rav Huna: I asked before Rabbi Yaakov bar Aha: for one who says that tithes are from the Torah [and not just a rabbinical enactment], then Hillel is making an <u>enactment</u> upon a matter from the Torah. Rabbi Yossi said: And since the time when Israel was exiled to Babylonia, were they not exempted from the *mitzvot* that depend upon the land? But the remission of debts is observed both in the land and outside the land, as it is a matter from the Torah. Rabbi Yossi changed his mind and said: this is the meaning of "you shall surely remit:" when the Sabbatical Year is being observed as a matter of Torah, remission of debts is observed whether in the land or outside of the land as a matter of Torah. And when the Sabbatical Year is being observed as a matter from the rabbis, the remission of debts is observed whether in the land or outside of the land as a matter from the rabbis.

There [in Babylonia] they said: even one who said that tithes are a matter from the Torah would admit that the Sabbatical Year [observed at this time] is due to the rabbis, as it was taught: "this is the meaning of you shall surely remit."

PT suggests that the development of the enactment occurred this way: Hillel made the enactment, and in response there was some concern that he had uprooted a matter from the Torah. The *sugya* in PT then goes out of its way to show that this was not a problem, for in fact after the Babylonian exile the Sabbatical Year itself was considered entirely *derabbanan* (rabbinically ordained), and not a matter based in the Torah. Thus, PT resolved the difficulty by showing that Hillel did not alter a matter of Torah, but merely a rabbinic law, which is permitted in the ideological system of the editors of PT. Thus, instead of entering the rhetorical task of supplying a support from verses in the Torah, which might have compared unfavorably to the direct statements that commanded the remission of debts, PT sidestepped the problem entirely, reworking the axiological basis of the observance to place it firmly in the work of the rabbis, to ensure the added legal maneuvering room necessary to effect such a change. If the observance of the Sabbatical Year was *derabbanan*, then Hillel (or another rabbi) was within his rights to cancel or adjust its observance.

BT Git. 36a-b, in contrast, sees Hillel's enactment as far more radical:

ומי איכא מידי, דמדאורייתא משמטא שביעית, <u>והתקין</u> הלל דלא
משמטא? אמר אביי: בשביעית בזמן הזה, ורבי היא; דתניא, רבי אומר:
(דברים ט״ו) "וזה דבר השמיטה שמוט." בשתי שמיטות הכתוב מדבר,
אחת שמיטת קרקע ואחת שמיטת כספים, בזמן שאתה משמט קרקע,
אתה משמט כספים, בזמן שאי אתה משמט קרקע, אי אתה משמט

כספים ; <u>ותקינו</u> רבנן דתשמט זכר לשביעית. ראה הלל שנמנעו העם
מלהלוות זה את זה, עמד <u>והתקין</u> פרוסבול. ומי איכא מידי, דמדאורייתא
לא משמטא שביעית, <u>ותקינו</u> רבנן דתשמט? אמר אביי : שב ואל תעשה
הוא. רבא אמר : הפקר בית דין היה הפקר.

Is there such a thing [i.e., is it possible], that the Torah commands to remit loans in the seventh year, and Hillel <u>enacted</u> that we do not remit loans?[527] [No, this does not entirely make sense, as Hillel was not granted the power to uproot a commandment of the Torah.]

Abaye said: [this statement refers to the situation] nowadays, in the seventh year, and it is [the opinion of] Rabbi, as it was taught: Rabbi said: (Deuteronomy 15:2) "This shall be the nature of the remission," the text speaks about two remissions, the remission of landholdings and the remission of monies [or debts]. When you remit landholdings, you remit debts; when you do not remit landholdings, you do not remit debts,[528] but our rabbis <u>enacted</u> that you remit debts as a reminder of the seventh year.[529] [When] Hillel saw that the people were avoiding granting loans to one another, he arose and enacted *prosbul*.

And is there such a thing [i.e., is it possible], that the Torah did not command that we remit loans in the seventh year, and our rabbis <u>enacted</u> that we do indeed remit loans? [No, this does not entirely make sense.]

Abaye said: [this is a] sit and do nothing [situation].[530] [This is a situation in which the rabbis enacted that people should sit and do nothing, which the rabbis were, in fact, empowered to do, as we see in this *memra*:] Rava said: property declared ownerless by a *beit din* was ownerless.[531]

Here, Abbaye's opinions grant legitimacy to Hillel's *takkanah* by taking a different course from that found in PT: reclassifying the debt remission as *deoraita*, and then showing that a court can ask community members to ignore a positive commandment by "sitting and doing nothing." At the same moment, it goes farther than PT in providing two justifications, attributed to Abaye and Rava, for Hillel's right to make such a change. As David Kraemer, reviewing this part of the BT and the following pericope, explains:

> In contrast with the earlier sources, the intent of the Bavli here has been to emphasize the innovative boldness behind the *prozbul* and to assert,

in a broader way, rabbinic prerogative vis-à-vis Torah. . . . Why would
the Bavli want to state its support of rabbinic power so forthrightly?
Why would it not wish, as do its predecessors (excluding the Mishnah),
to hide the assertion of rabbinic power behind the veil of scriptural justification? The answer lies in the Bavli's broad theory of rabbinic "Torah" and its relation to Written Torah. . . . [T]he application of their
own reason was deemed in no way inferior to the explication of Written
Torah. To make this point, the Rabbis of the Bavli did not hesitate to
emphasize the distance of some of their laws from the Written Torah.[532]

Kraemer articulates what we have now seen consistently throughout this study
of *takkanot*: BT is far more willing to utilize what Kraemer called "the assertion
of Rabbinic power," and shows less need to cloak its changes in scriptural clothing. What becomes clear, even from only this small group of passages related to
the remission of debts, is that we have a remarkable instance of rabbinic leadership changing a Torah matter for the sake of encouraging proper behavior
amongst the people Israel. Without this *takkanah*, the economic situation of the
poor would continue to degrade. It was only with the encouragement that this
takkanah provided to the wealthy, and the positive reassurance that their precious loaned assets would not vanish during the seventh year, that the community could continue this important economic activity. The further bolstering of
the practice by rooting it into proofs based on verses from the Torah, plus the
coupling of this *takkanah* with a revered leader in the person of Hillel, all work
to highlight the import of this major change in law.

Takkanat Hashavim: Benefits for those who Repent

Similar to the category above is another one that encourages proper behavior, though in a slightly different way. In three cases, our legal texts determine
that individuals should receive beneficial treatment because of completing a
repentant act—in their correcting of their prior inappropriate behavior, they have
shown good faith, and should be rewarded for it.[533] The earliest occurrence is in
the Tannaitic text of M Git. 5:5:

העיד רבי יוחנן בן גודגדה : על החרשת שהשיאה אביה שהיא יוצאה בגט.
ועל קטנה בת ישראל שנשאת לכהן שאוכלת בתרומה, ואם מתה בעלה
יורשה. ועל המריש הגזול שבנאו בבירה, שיטול את דמיו מפני תקנת
השבים. ועל חטאת הגזולה שלא נודעה לרבים, שהיא מכפרת מפני תקון
המזבח :

Rabbi Yohanan ben Gudgedah testified that [in the case of] a deaf-mute
girl whose father married her off [before the age of majority and thus

still under his legal jurisdiction], she may go out [i.e., be divorced] with a *get*;[534] and that a minor female Israelite who was married to a priest may eat *terumah*,[535] and that if she dies, her husband inherits her [belongings]; and about one who built a stolen beam into a residence, that he [the owner of the beam] should take the money [instead of requiring destruction of the residence to retrieve the beam], because of *takkanat hashavim*;[536] and that a stolen sin-offering [whose stolen status was] not known to the public, still made atonement.[537]

There are two possible ways to read the meaning of *takkanat hashavim*: first, one might infer that there was actually a *takkanah* at some point in history that granted recognition and privileges to those who were repenting. More likely, though, is the idea that we simply call the concept "repair for the penitent," and decide that there was no specific time in history when there was such a decision *qua* enactment. Thus, the idea is included in this study since it still represents the altering of law in accord with a basic, underlying value: in order to encourage positive behavioral change among the populace.

There is enough evidence, though, to delineate the concept in clear terms. Looking at the mishnah above, we note that the original owner of stolen building materials that were incorporated into a building could legitimately require any individual who built a home using them to wreck it, in order to return the specific stolen boards or beams involved. After all, since the stolen property still rightfully belonged to the original owner, it would be within his/her rights to require its return, and, by extension, the destruction of the house built from it. However, when the builder admits that he stole the materials, and shows interest in making amends for his prior inappropriate behavior, M responds with some compassion for his situation, because he is repenting his prior misdeed. In this sense, above and beyond the actual letter of the law, M recognized and rewarded repentant behavior. This is the essence of the term *takkanat hashavim*—encouraging proper later behavior by rewarding it in ways that lessen the ill consequences of prior illegal acts.

This discussion also appears as a disagreement between Beit Hillel and Beit Shammai preserved in T BK 10:5:

הגוזל את המריש ובנאו בבירה, בית שמאי אומרים יקעקע את הבירה
ויטול את המריש, ובית הלל אומרים מחשב כל מה שהיה שוה ונותן
לבעלים מפני תַקְנַת שבין.

One who steals a beam and built it into a residence, Beit Shammai say that he must tear down the residence so that he [the owner of the beam] may take the beam; and Beit Hillel say, calculate its value, and give it to the owners because of *takkanat shavim*.

When M simply supplies an answer with the necessary actions to be taken, it is clearly holding to the position that T connected to Beit Hillel. This response was a bit more lenient than Roman law, which demanded double payment in this situation, as Boaz Cohen pointed out:

> Of particular interest is the rule concerning stolen materials from buildings and vineyards, which reads as follows in the XII Tablets: "A man is not permitted to dislodge a stolen beam when fixed in buildings or vineyards or to lay claim to it." This the Law affected with an eye to prevent buildings from being disturbed under this pretext. Nevertheless, it grants action for double the amount of damages against such a person who has been found guilty of fixing such beams. . . .
>
> Jewish legal opinion on this point underwent some development in the course of time. It seems that in an early period, the law required that an object obtained by robbery be returned to its owner, no matter what shape or form it had assumed. This view was retained by Beth Shammai who obliged the person that used stolen timber in building a house, to demolish the structure and to restore the beam. The later and more liberal opinion advocated by Beth Hillel that the robber should defray only the cost of the beam, became the established norm, and is the only one recorded in the Mishna. The reason given for this reform of legislation is that it would encourage repentant sinners to make reparation for stolen objects.[538]

Cohen, therefore, saw the two opinions in M and T above as representing two discrete phases in the development of Jewish law—an earlier phase where the *mahloket* preserved in T between Beit Hillel and Beit Shammai existed, and a later phase in which the appropriate reaction was already chosen and justified, resulting in what we see in M.

The essence of the ideal of *takkanat hashavim*, then, was to provide a way for those who had committed a transgression to restore the earlier state without overwhelming disruption of the outcomes achieved through their other good works. This would, in turn, encourage others to repent for their misdeeds, leading to both an overall increase in repentance and a downturn in sin in the entire society. The suggested penalty for stealing in this passage was not nearly as harsh as the maximum standards possible in the Bible[539] or M.[540] This lenient choice emphasizes that the overriding desire to strengthen the will to repentance was deemed more important to the broad fabric of the community then one individual's repayment of a single specific theft.

In this section, then, we see that the editors of our legal texts were not afraid to invoke *takkanot* to spur the community toward better practice. Whether it involved practice that led to positive economic outcomes, or the leaving behind of illegal or immoral behaviors, *takkanot* were employed to help guide the community toward a better way of life.

Changes in Business and Agricultural Practices

As we saw in chapter one, there were a number of halakhic changes that resulted from changes in business and agricultural practices. Fourteen of these cases utilize the root *tkn*. These follow the patterns described in chapter one very closely, and do not require further discussion here.[541]

An Incident Shows the Problem with the Law

In ten cases, the root *tkn* appears in our sources in connection with an incident that shows a specific and irresolvable problem with a current law. These cases are also very similar to the formulation we saw above with the term *barishonah*, and therefore do not require further consideration here.[542]

Catastrophic Historical Events

In nine cases, the root *tkn* occurs indicating changes in law in response to catastrophic historical events. Similar to the changes noted in chapter one under this heading, these events range from the destruction of the Temple to the Hadrianic persecutions to the end of the Bar Kokhba revolt. The changes in law following the destruction of the Temple tend to center around personalities such as Rabban Yohanan ben Zakkai, as we saw above.[543] Again, these resemble the examples in chapter one closely enough to allow us to forego further discussion.

Changes in the Behavior of the Populace

As in chapter one, the root *tkn* is utilized to indicate halakhic change that resulted from change in the behavior of the populace. There are nine occurrences of this rationale for halakhic change in our sources.[544] It is important to note that no new occurrences of this rationale occur in PT (they are all preceded by appearances in M or T).

Preventing Embarrassment

The editors of rabbinic legal texts report five instances when the rabbis changed halakhic positions to avoid the embarrassment of individuals involved in various practices. These *takkanot* function identically to the examples of legal change shown in chapter one under this heading.[545]

Changes in Municipal and Authority Structures

As in chapter one, we see a variety of changes in Jewish law that result from differences in authority structures. Five cases involve the use of the root *tkn*.[546] While some of these are internal changes, others result from external authorities and the pressure they exerted upon the Jewish community. Though we did analyze a number of these cases in chapter one, we will pause to look at one case where texts report that the Roman authorities and their power structure had an immense and extremely unwelcome impact on the marriage regulations of the Judaean Jewish community.

Roman Cruelty Prompts Judaean Permissiveness

PT Ket. 1:5, 6a reports that the laws of marriage underwent a considerable loosening in response to savage behavior allowed by the Roman leadership. The story begins in M Ket. 1:5, where we find a surprising statement that if an unmarried Judaean couple dined in the bride's father's home without chaperones, the potential husband involved may no longer make a claim about his wife's virginity thereafter:

האוכל אצל חמיו ביהודה שלא בעדים אינו יכול לטעון טענת בתולים מפני
שמתייחד עמה.

> One who eats in the home of his father-in-law in Judaea without witnesses is not [thereafter] permitted to lodge a claim about [his wife's] virginity because he was secluded with her.

M provides us with a basic first look at the situation in Judaea. Once a betrothed man ate unaccompanied in the home of his father-in-law in the presence of his bride-to-be, he could not, thereafter, claim that someone else had sexual relations with her before their marriage, as would have been his right had he not been sequestered with her. M explains that this situation did not apply in every corner of the world, though: it was geographically limited to Judaea. Outside this province, a bride in this situation would still qualify as a virgin, and the resultant claim of *betulim* (virginity) could still be addressed in court. Why this looseness in Judaean sexual mores? Another mishnah, M Yev. 4:10, adds a bit more color to the picture:

היבמה לא תחלץ ולא תתיבם עד שיש לה שלשה חדשים. וכן כל שאר
הנשים לא יתארסו ולא ינשאו עד שיהיו להן שלשה חדשים, אחד בתולות
ואחד בעולות, אחד גרושות ואחד אלמנות, אחד נשואות ואחד ארוסות.
רבי יהודה אומר הנשואות יתארסו והארוסות ינשאו חוץ מן הארוסות
שביהודה מפני שלבו גס בה. רבי יוסי אומר כל הנשים יתארסו חוץ מן
האלמנה מפני האיבול:

A widow may not perform *halitzah* or enter into a levirate marriage until she has [waited] three months [after becoming a widow].[547]
And similarly, all the rest of the [categories of marriageable] women
may not become betrothed and may not marry until they have [waited]
three months: it is the same for virgins and non-virgins, divorcees and
widows, married women and betrothed women.

Rabbi Yehuda says: married women [who divorced or were wid-
owed] may become betrothed [immediately, without waiting three
months to see if they are pregnant], and betrothed women may marry
[immediately, without waiting three months to see if they are preg-
nant],[548] except a betrothed woman of Judaea, because he [i.e., her fi-
ancé] is familiar with her [i.e., they may already be engaging in sexual
relations]. Rabbi Yossi says that all women may be betrothed [immedi-
ately] except for widows, because of their intense grieving.

Here, too, is an implication that premarital relations in Judaea differed from
what was found elsewhere. The core concept at work is that the Galileans were
more careful in avoiding premarital seclusion and sexual relations, whether due
to a different tradition or a simple difference in behavior.[549] Thus far, both of
these Tannaitic pericopae reinforce this consistent difference in behavior between Judaea and Galilee: Judaean men, sequestered with their fiancées, were
possibly having sexual relations with them, while Galilean men were not.

In M, this decision is not yet portrayed as a *takkanah*. It is only when we
arrive at the portrayal in PT that the language of *takkanah* becomes apparent.
PT, in fact, provides a far more detailed and potentially fabricated justification
for this presumption, relying upon the application of an ancient idea, the *jus
primae noctis*, a law that entitled a male of superior status to the first intercourse
with a female virgin. The roots of this legal idea go back as far as the Gilgamesh
Epic, and its aftereffects appear as late as the late Middle Ages.[550] To be sure,
most scholars dismiss it as nothing more than a literary motif,[551] but Tal Ilan, for
one, acknowledges its power as a polemical explanation and justification for
behavior, while entirely rejecting it as historical fact. Ilan also brings supporting
evidence from the Babatha archive that shows at least one other example of
premarital cohabitation in Judaea in the aftermath of the Bar Kokhba revolt,

indicating that Judaean premarital cohabitation may have been a regular occurrence, though it is clearly impossible to make any large scale societal determination based on one piece of evidence.[552]

When we examine the text of PT Ket. 1:5, 6a, we immediately see the substantial change the picture has undergone in its reworking since the Tannaitic
period:

בראשונה גזרו שמד ביהודה, שכן מסורת להם מאבותם שיהודה הרג את
עשו דכתיב (בראשית מט) "ידך בעורף אויביך." והיו הולכין ומשעבדין
בהן, ואונסין את בנותיהן, וגזרו שיהא איסטרטיוס בועל תחילה. התקינו
שיהא בעלה בא עליה עודה בבית אביה, שמתוך שהיא יודעת שאימת
בעלה עליה, עוד היא נגדרת. מכל מקום אין סופה להיבעל מאיסטרטיוס.
אנוסה היא, ואנוסה מותרת לביתה. כהנות מה היו עושות? מטמינות היו.
ויטמינו אף בנות ישראל! קול יוצא, ומלכותא שמעה, ואילין ואילין
מתערבבין. מה סימן היה להן? קול מגרוס בעיר: משתה שם, משתה שם,
אור הנר בברור חיל, שבוע בן, שבוע בן. אף על פי שבטל השמד, המנהג לא
בטל. כלתו של רבי הושעיה נכנסה מעוברת.

At first, they [the Romans] decreed religious persecution upon
Judah [the Judeans], for there was a tradition they had from their ancestors that Judah had killed Esau[553] as it is written: "Your hand is upon
the neck of your enemy." (Gen. 49:8)[554]

So they [the Romans] would go and subjugate them [the Jews], and
rape their daughters. And they decreed that a [Roman] soldier would
have the first intercourse [with a virgin Jewish woman before marriage
to her husband].[555]

They [the rabbis] enacted that her husband would come to [have
intercourse with] her while she was still in her father's house, since if
she knew that the fear of her husband was upon her, she would guard
herself and] remain chaste, [preventing herself from being raped by the
Roman soldier].[556] In any case, if it were her end to be raped by a soldier,[557] she is [considered] an *anusah* [a woman who has been raped]
and an *anusah* is permitted to her husband [if he is an Israelite].

What did they do with the wives of priests [who, if they were
raped, were no longer permitted to return to their husbands]? They hid
them away. But they could hide the Israelite women away, too! The
word would get out, and the [Roman] government would hear, and
these and these would be mixed up with one another.[558] What sign did

they [the Roman authorities] have? The sound of the wheel grinding flour in the city told them, "A feast is there, a feast is there!"[559] the light of the candle in Berur Hayil, "the week of a son, the week of a son."[560]

> Even though the persecution ended, the custom did not end. The daughter-in-law of Rabbi Hoshaya entered [under the *huppah*] pregnant.

First of all, here we see the appearance of a *takkanah* where none existed at all in Tannaitic texts. PT sets this change of law in an emergent historical moment, as a response to persecution not directly indicated in either M or T. Had this been the motivation for the change in law, one must wonder why it is that M and T both avoid mention of it, especially since such perpetration of such a heinous crime against Jewish women would serve as a strong justification of legal change.

That is, in effect, what PT does with its earlier tradition: the editors of this passage reshaped their inherited tradition, called it a *takkanah*, and applied reasoning that motivated it, all in an effort to reframe the passage as a response to an emergent condition. It is telling that they felt that such a leniency as permitting premarital sex required such an enormously compelling reasoning.

We must not ignore the overwhelming possibility that this Amoraic explanation is either polemical or apologetic. As polemic, this construction of the text would allow the Amoraim both to attack the Romans for their brutality and to dwell upon the pervasive sense of Jewish powerlessness under their rule. As apologetic, it provided a defense for a generally unacceptable leniency on Judaean premarital cohabitation by situating it in a constructed social reality that validated it as a legal decision. Given Ilan's interpretation of the text from the Babatha archive mentioned above, which provides evidence of at least one other known case of Judaean premarital cohabitation, and the complete lack of Tannaitic depiction of this Roman behavior, the editors of PT created a text depicting an understandably negative view of the Romans that allowed a necessary leniency.

Avoiding the Profanation of God's Name

In four cases that do not resemble anything we saw in chapter one, we find *takkanot* reported to have been made to prevent the profanation of God's name.[561] We will examine one of these cases to understand the general parameters at work.

The Sinful *Av Beit Din*

The אב בית דין (*av beit din*, "father of the court") was a position of leadership that was second only to the *nasi* (the patriarch) in the described authority structure of the Sanhedrin.[562] The title's earliest citation appears in M, referring to the junior members of the *zugot* (pairs) during the late Second Temple Period.[563] PT and BT both utilize the title, and in later times, it was used in reference to the officers of the post-Amoraic Babylonian academies as well.[564]

The question arose in BT MK 17a as to the correct course of action should an *av beit din* commit a sin that would make him liable to נידוי (*niddui*, "being banned from the community"):[565]

אמר רב הונא : <u>באושא התקינו</u> : אב בית דין שסרח, אין מנדין אותו, אלא
אומר לו : (מלכים ב' י"ד) "הכבד ושב בביתך." חזר וסרח, מנדין אותו,
מפני חילול השם. ופליגא דריש לקיש. דאמר ריש לקיש : תלמיד חכם
שסרח, אין מנדין אותו בפרהסיא, שנאמר (הושע ד') "וכשלת היום וכשל
גם נביא עמך לילה." כסהו כלילה.

Rav Huna said: <u>In Usha they enacted</u>: An *av beit din* who sinned,[566] they do not ban him, instead one says to him: "save your dignity and remain at home" (II Kgs. 14:10).[567] If he sinned again, they ban him, because of the profanation of God's name.[568]

But this is in opposition to the statement of Resh Lakish! For Resh Lakish said: a *talmid hakham* who sinned, they do not ban him publicly, as it is said: "so you shall stumble by day, and by night a prophet shall stumble as well" (Hos. 4:5)—cover it up, like the night.

Immediately, we note that this passage does not portray reflective legal change, but *ab initio* legal decision-making. In this respect, it resembles an initiation *takkanah* since the passage does not indicate the presence or the details of any initial legal stance.

Rav Huna's statement attempts to balance a number of values inherent in the situation. First, it endeavored to give the *av beit din* another chance, allowing him to repent and save his dignity despite his initial sin. In fact, this text states that he was even permitted to continue serving in his role, without being banned. Only after he sinned a second time, could he be banned from the community, because his continuing actions disgraced God's name on earth, since he could be perceived as a representative of God within the community.

Resh Lakish's statement staked out a more difficult position, with one significant difference in its application. Whereas Rav Huna's statement is only concerned with the *av beit din*, Resh Lakish's position is applicable to all *talmidei hakhamim*. Any *talmid hakham* who sins, according to Resh Lakish, was never to be banned publicly. Instead, whatever punishment was meted out to him must be done so quietly, avoiding any unnecessary sharing of information, in order to preserve the dignity of God's name, the reputation of the *talmid hakham* involved, and the authority of the sages as a collective.

PT MK 3:1, 81d provides the only parallel text to this section:

רבי יעקב בר אביי בשם רב ששת: נמנו באושא שלא לנדות זקן, ואתייא
כיי, דאמר רבי שמואל בשם רבי אבהו: זקן שאירע בו דבר, אין מורידין
אותו מגדולתו, אלא אומרין לו "היכבד ושב בביתך".

Rabbi Yaakov bar Abaye in the name of Rav Sheshet: They voted in Usha that they would not ban an elder, and it is in accordance with that said by Rabbi Shmuel in the name of Rabbi Abbahu: if something [untoward] happens to an elder, we do not lower him from his [position of] greatness, but say to him: "save your dignity and stay home" (II Kgs. 14:10).

Thus there are two reports of this decision placed in an Ushan context, pointing to a Palestinian decision in the late Tannaitic period. While the *av beit din* is not named explicitly in PT, the treatment of the elder (clearly one with some respected position in the community, though not specifically the *av beit din*) is precisely the same as we saw in BT.[569] Here, too, we see that PT's report signified the decision with the terminology of voting, while BT chose to utilize the idea of a *takkanah*. This again points to a greater perception of rabbinic power in BT than PT, as we have now seen a number of times.

It should be noted that the authorities citing this Ushan *takkanah* made to avoid the profanation of God's name are all Babylonian Amoraim. Rav Huna, who brought this *takkanah* in BT was a second generation Babylonian Amora, while Rav Sheset, the authority who cited it in PT, was a third generation Babylonian Amora, both of whom lived in the third century.

This *takkanah* provided an impetus and justification for the cover-up of inappropriate activity on the part of a communal leader for the sake of preserving the dignity of God's name. While this did not represent a change of law *per se*, it does formulate rabbinic policy on handling deviance within communal leadership. The quiet sacrifice of a person's position did greater good for the community than the public shaming of one perceived as a representative of God.

Takkanot Made Because of Danger

Rabbinic legal sources include two *takkanot* made to preempt danger.[570] We will examine one of these sources.

Recalling *Yom Tov* in the Shabbat Evening Service

In BT Shab. 24a-b we find a discussion of the recitation of blessings related to Hanukkah during the afternoon service of Shabbat or *Rosh Hodesh*. Since Hanukkah falls on the 25th of Kislev and lasts for eight days, each celebration of this festival of lights stretched across both a Sabbath and the beginning of the next Hebrew month, Tevet. The central issue in this *sugya* is whether the *shaliah tzibbur* (service leader) at an afternoon service on Shabbat or Rosh Hodesh should recite the additional prayer (the *al hanissim*) for Hanukkah. The *takkanah*, though, relates to mentioning other holy days during the evening service on Shabbat:

איבעיא להו: מהו להזכיר של חנוכה במוספין? כיון דלית ביה מוסף
בדידיה, לא מדכרינן, או דילמא: יום הוא שחייב בארבע תפלות? . . .
דאמר רבי יהושע בן לוי: יום הכפורים שחל להיות בשבת המתפלל נעילה
צריך להזכיר של שבת, יום הוא שנתחייב בארבע תפלות. קשיא הילכתא
אהילכתא! אמרת: הילכתא כרבי יהושע בן לוי, וקיימא לן: הילכתא
כרבא. דאמר רבא: יום טוב שחל להיות בשבת, שליח ציבור היורד לפני
התיבה ערבית אינו צריך להזכיר של יום טוב, שאילמלא שבת אין שליח
צבור יורד ערבית ביום טוב. הכי השתא! התם, בדין הוא דאפילו בשבת
נמי לא צריך, ורבנן הוא <u>דתקוני משום סכנה</u>, אבל הכא, יום הוא שנתחייב
בארבע תפלות.

It was asked of them [the sages]: What is the ruling on mentioning Hanukkah [i.e., reading *al hanissim*, a Hanukkah addition] during *musaf* [the additional service on Shabbat or Rosh Hodesh that falls during Hanukkah]? Since Hanukkah does not have a *musaf* of its own, we do not recall it [during the *musaf* of Shabbat or Rosh Hodesh that falls during Hanukkah].[571] Or, perhaps: it is a day that requires four *tefillot* [anyway, and therefore we do mention it in every *tefillah*]?[572] [An argument on this topic ensues.] . . .

As Rabbi Yehoshua ben Levi said: Yom Kippur that fell on Shabbat, one who prays the *neilah*[573] service must mention Shabbat, for it is the day [of Yom Kippur] that requires four services.[574] There is a difficulty between this and another *halakhah*! You said: the law follows Rabbi Yehoshua ben Levi, and we hold: the law follows Rava, as Rava said: A *Yom Tov* that fell on Shabbat, the *shaliah tsibbur* who goes down in front of the ark for the [Friday] evening service [to repeat the abridged repetition of the Shabbat *maariv* prayer known as the *me-ein sheva/magen avot*] is not required to mention *Yom Tov*, since if it were not Shabbat, the *shaliah tsibbur* would not go down in front of the ark on *Yom Tov* [at all, because there would be no repetition required].

So, now! [How can you compare these two cases?] There [in the case of recalling a *Yom Tov* that fell on Shabbat], it is right that even on Shabbat we do not need [to recall *Yom Tov*], and it is our rabbis who <u>enacted</u> it because of danger, but here [in the case of Hanukkah] it is the day [itself] that requires four services.

Regarding this danger, Rashi explains:

משום סכנה: מזיקין, שלא היו בתי כנסיות שלהן בישוב, וכל שאר לילי החול היו עסוקין במלאכתן, ובגמרו מלאכתן מתפללין ערבית בביתן, ולא היו באין בבית הכנסת. אבל לילי שבת באין בבית הכנסת, וחשו שיש שאין ממהרין לבא ושוהין לאחר תפלה, לכך האריכו תפלת הצבור.

Because of danger—[from] demons, for their synagogues were not in the settlement [areas], and all the rest of the nights of regular days they were busy with their work, and when they finished their work, they prayed the evening service in their homes, and did not come to synagogue. But on the eve of Shabbat they came to the synagogue, and they were afraid that there were those who would not hurry to come, and would tarry after the prayer, [remaining alone and, thus, exposed to demons] so they lengthened the communal prayer.

Here, in responding to a dangerous situation, the rabbis are cited as proactively reducing danger by elongating the prayer on Friday evenings: through mandating the addition of a repetition of the *me-ein sheva/magen avot* that mentions *Yom Tov* in the Shabbat evening service, they increased the length of the service and better protected their community. Rashi explains that synagogues were located well outside the busiest population centers, and thus leaving individuals alone in the synagogue completing prayer, or allowing them to return home from the Shabbat evening service by walking the streets alone at night, left people unprotected, potentially exposing them to injury at the hands of both supernatural and more mundane creatures: demons, brigands or other undesirables. Worshippers who lingered after the service might find themselves isolated and vulnerable to attack. By extending the worship service, the rabbis gave those who came late the possibility of completing their worship and leaving with the others, ensuring they would not walk home alone. Here, the Stam justified liturgical change on the grounds of security concerns, formulating a prayer to serve an external purpose quite apart from the standard goals of liturgical creation.

To Preserve Social Status

In two cases, the rabbis are reported as acting to preserve the privilege enjoyed by protected social classes.[575] We will examine one of these two cases.

The Enhanced *Ketubbah* of the Priestly Class

In M and T we find two texts that sharply differentiate between the Israelite class and the priestly class in matters of the payment of the *ketubbah*. Though the Temple had been destroyed for some time before this *halakhah* was fixed in the written texts of M and T, and the priestly class had suffered some substantial setbacks in their social status, there is indication that the vestigial remnants of priestly power were still protected by the rabbis. Our first text appears in M Ket. 1:5:

בית דין של כהנים היו גובין לבתולה ארבע מאות זוז, ולא מיחו בידם
חכמים :

A court of priests would collect 400 *zuz* for [the *ketubbah*] of a virgin [daughter of a priest, whether she married a priest or non-priest], and the sages did not object.

M states that the *ketubbah* for a virgin daughter would be 400 *zuz*. Though not stated overtly, this was presumably a virgin of priestly descent; otherwise this court of *kohanim* makes little sense. Due to her enhanced social status, the value of her *ketubbah* was double that of a regular virgin Israelite woman.[576] Here the law is simply stated without any indication that it is a formal *takkanah*, but control of the practice is still vested in a court of priests.

In T Ket. 1:2, this same law was stated differently, this time with the utilization of a *takkanah*:

הנושא ונותן בכהונה, והנותן בה, תקנה שהתקינו בבית דין : בת ישראל
לכהן, ובת כהן לישראל נותן ארבע מאות זוז.

One who negotiates [a *ketubbah*] with [a potential spouse from] the priesthood, and one who gives her, [his daughter, in marriage to a priest, should abide by] the *takkanah* that they enacted in court: [marrying] a daughter of an Israelite to a priest, and [marrying] a daughter of a priest to an Israelite, one pays 400 *zuz* [for the *ketubbah* payment].

There is one very surprising fact to be noted in T's text. One could certainly anticipate that the Israelite male who married a woman from a priestly family

would have to pay an enhanced *ketubbah*, since the social status of the priestly
widow is higher than that of her prospective husband. The surprise is in the balance put forward by T. One would not expect that an Israelite woman marrying
a male priest should deserve an enhanced *ketubbah* of 400 *zuz*. Commentators
suggest that either the priesthood did not want to be liable to suspicion of haugh-
tiness, or that this was a penalty for a male *kohen* who married below his class.
BT explains this as representing "an aristocratic marriage," as aristocracy was
then defined.[577] Most important for our purposes is that T states the change in
law as a *takkanah*, quite the opposite of its precursor's (M's) apodictic portrayal
above. This is further evidence of the elasticity of the claims that certain laws
were *takkanot* while others were not.

The final text in this group comes from BT Ket. 12a-b, commenting on M
Ket 1:5 above, and it bears witness to three stages of development:

תנא: ואלמנת כהנים, כתובתה מאתים. והאנן תנן: אחת אלמנת ישראל
ואחת אלמנת כהנים, כתובתן מנה! אמר רב אשי: שתי תקנות הוו,
מעיקרא תקינו לבתולה ארבע מאות זוז ולאלמנה מנה, כיון דחזו דמזלזלי
בהו, תקינו לה מאתן. כיון דחזו דקא פרשין מינייהו, דאמרי: עד דנסבינן
אלמנת כהנים ניזיל ניסיב בתולה בת ישראל, אהדרינהו למלתייהו.

> It was taught: And the widow [who was the daughter] of priests—
> her *ketubbah* is two hundred [*zuz*]. And did we not also learn [in M
> Ket. 1:5]: both [the *ketubbah* of] the widow of an Israelite and [the
> *ketubbah* of] the widow of priests are the same—their *ketubbah* is 100
> [*zuz*]!

> Rav Ashi said: there were two enactments [concerning a widow
> who was the daughter of a priest]. At the beginning, they enacted for a
> virgin 400 *zuz* and for a widow 100 *zuz*. When they saw that they were
> dishonoring them [the widows of priests], they enacted [a *ketubbah* of]
> 200 *zuz* [for the widows of priests, as we saw in the *baraita*]. When
> they saw that they were avoiding [marrying] them [i.e., the widows of
> priests], as they say: "before we would marry the widow of priests, let
> us go and marry a virgin daughter of an Israelite," they returned them
> to their [original] state [of having *ketubbot* of 100 *zuz* like every other
> widow].

Rav Ashi's statement above harmonized the two sources he had before him by
creating a diachronic review of the development of this law. Rav Ashi saw two
takkanot that delineated three phases of historical development with respect to
the amount of a priestly widow's *ketubbah*:

Phase I: (original state) (represented in M Ket. 1:5)
                      Ketubbah of widow (Israelite or priest) = 100 *zuz*

Phase II: (after seeing that widows of priests are disgraced)
                      (represented in the *baraita* in BT Ket. 12a-b)
                      Ketubbah of Priestly widow = 200 *zuz*

Phase III: (after seeing men hesitate to marry widows of priests)
                      (represented, again, in M Ket 1:5)
                      Ketubbah of priestly widow = 100 *zuz*

This reconstruction of history promoted in the name of Rav Ashi harmonized the two Tannaitic sources he had before him. PT, similarly, goes through an equivalent exercise of harmonization.[578]

Michael Satlow argued that a shift occurred in marriage priorities during the rabbinic period: at its start, marriage to a priest was preferable. By the time the period had ended, however, the texts tend to privilege marriage into a family of scholars over a family of priests.[579] BT's approach in this particular instance may reflect a greater shift in attitude than that prevalent in other texts from this period.

These texts, then, show an early Tannaitic consideration for the priests and their social status, even though their power diminished in the long term. The report of Rav Ashi's retrospective leaves us with two possibilities: read as history, it suggests that both respect for the priesthood and practical realties played a role in the decisions made regarding *ketubbot*. Due to the rabbinic derivation of the *ketubbah*, the amount involved remained alterable for a significant period of time. Read as apology, Rav Ashi's reconstruction works to obviate a problem between two sources that demands resolution.

Unclassifiable *Takkanot*

As in chapter one, eleven examples of changes in law are recorded without any clear statement of their justification.[580]

Chapter Two—Conclusions

After this in-depth review of select uses of the term *tkn* in revising rabbinic law, we can now describe the evolution of the use of this term. First, we note that the earliest usage of the root *tkn* in biblical literature comes from the third century BCE, in the book of Ecclesiastes. During this period, the term showed a bifurcated usage: it could indicate either the making straight of something that

was crooked, or the literary fixing of a text or parable. During the rabbinic period, the meaning of "literary fixing" was utilized on a continuing basis, while
the new meaning, that of "initiating new law," gained greater prominence as
well.

After a review of previous scholarly work on this topic, we then turned to a
number of statements that directly addressed issues related to *takkanot*, including: attempts at a definition for *takkanot* created by later authors; discussion of
their status as *derabbanan* or *deoraita*; the biblical texts various later authorities
used to grant permission to make *takkanot*; permission for an individual to refrain from a beneficial *takkanah*; the idea that *takkanot* are assumed not to inflict
unnecessary loss; the permissibility of making a *takkanah* upon another *takkanah*; and a few other singularities that reflected certain attitudes that may or
may not have been widely held. No well-conceived system was at work here—
there are simply the various *ad hoc* pieces of evidence found in our texts that
help to sketch the contours of the use of this term.

Takkanot were generally considered to be *derabbanan*, though BT tended to
privilege them slightly more than other rabbinic legal statements, classifying
them as very close to biblical law in their authority. Both PT and BT prohibited
takkanot upon other *takkanot*. BT cited Rava as saying that one may entirely
refrain from taking advantage of any beneficial *takkanah* that the rabbis made,
should it be undesirable to the one affected by it.

Takkanot could not be made instantaneously—in fact, we saw at least one
example of a *takkanah* that was interrupted and never completed. *Takkanot* were
only applicable to members of the Jewish community. In one case in BT, the
involvement of a Gentile stumped the rabbis, who left off their discussion with
"*teyku.*" In another case, the root *tkn* was utilized in the sense of *pasak*, setting a
final halakhic stance in place for a difficult question. We also found at least one
takkanah justified by a "prescient" Torah, which utilized a word meant to be
interpreted later in a specific way that became known as a *takkanah.*

We will now turn our attention to a summary of the distribution of stated
rationales that impelled halakhic change, the balance between attributed and
unattributed material, and the periods and places these attributions indicate. As
before, our study will be informed by the fact that the textual citation of legal
development tells little about its ultimate implementation—rather it gives us a
window into the editors' philosophical outlook on Jewish law at the time of the
creation of the work. We will continue to be highly skeptical about single attributions, but more positivistic in assessing the date and locale of groups of attributions.

Among the 726 appearances of the root *tkn*, there are 185 basic texts (single
texts or texts with groups of parallels)[581] that show discernible instances of halakhic change with their accompanying rationales. As noted above, there are
also 11 instances where halakhic change is indicated, but without explicitly

stated reasons. The distribution of the most frequently stated rationales in these texts is shown in Table 5.

In examining Table 5, we immediately notice several aspects of the usage of the terminology of *takkanah* in rabbinic legal literature. First, in looking at the most popular usage of the term, that of initiation of new practices, we see a tremendous discrepancy between Tannaitic sources and Amoraic sources. In the predominately Tannaitic sources (M, T and the Halakhic Midrashim), a total of six new practices are explicitly introduced by the term *tikken*, while PT and BT contain a total of 90 specific references. The implication here is that Amoraic editors were far less squeamish about including explicit statements that indicated the initiation of new practices with the term *takkanah*. Even in the limited number of examples covered in this chapter, we saw a number of instances in which Amoraic editors revised the presentation of a prior law and called it a *takkanah*, where Tannaitic sources showed no indication of explicit legal change.[582] Even factoring in the sheer difference in size of the collective Talmuds versus M, T and the Halakhic Midrashim, the number of Amoraic usages of this term is far greater than what we find in its Tannaitic complement.

It is a well-known fact that the very nature of the texts edited in or after the Amoraic period differs from those edited in the Tannaitic period: after all, Amoraic texts include substantial debate, theoretical questioning and justifications and explanations, while Tannaitic texts more often resemble later codes in their apodictic and straightforward rendering of the law.[583] This points to conscious literary choices made by the editors of various works and shows further evidence of the trend illuminated in chapter one: in the balance between a rhetoric of disclosure and a rhetoric of concealment, the editors of Amoraic legal texts tended toward disclosure more than their predecessors who edited earlier Tannaitic texts. This indicates a continuation of the trajectory away from the biblical rhetoric of concealment in altering law, toward a more open approach to legal development that admitted of alteration of law at the hands of rabbinic authorities.

Attributed innovations marked as *takkanot* are connected far more often to *earlier* authorities than to later ones. This displays a certain outlook on initiation that may best be summed up this way: new practices could be instituted as long as the justification was strong, or (to borrow Weiss's words mentioned earlier) they were hung on the branches of a big tree from an earlier time. Further evidence to support this notion may be found by examining the various assignments of responsibility for the initiation of new practices. Of 60 base texts that deal with the creation of new practices, 39 provide pre-rabbinic rootings in individuals recognized as important leaders by either biblical or rabbinic texts. Twenty-one initiations of new practice are assigned to rabbis, fourteen to a variety of individuals and seven to collective groups: five to the academy in Usha, and two to Yavneh.

Table 5
Most Frequent Rationales for Halakhic Change Utilizing
the Root TKN in Rabbinic Legal Sources

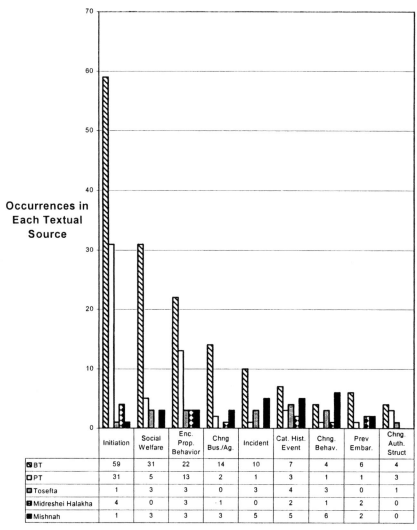

	Initiation	Social Welfare	Enc. Prop. Behavior	Chng Bus./Ag.	Incident	Cat. Hist. Event	Chng. Behav.	Prev Embar.	Chng. Auth. Struct
BT	59	31	22	14	10	7	4	6	4
PT	31	5	13	2	1	3	1	1	3
Tosefta	1	3	3	0	3	4	3	0	1
Midreshei Halakha	4	0	3	·1	0	2	1	2	0
Mishnah	1	3	3	3	5	5	6	2	0

Occurrences in Each Textual Source

Rationale Offered

Remarkable in this collection of occurrences is the following fact: PT never once assigned an initiation to *any* figure in the Tannaitic or Amoraic periods. Out of 31 *takkanot* assigned by PT to various individuals, we find absolutely none that give credit for innovation to any rabbis at all. The closest PT came to representing the rabbis as initiators is in PT Ber. 2:4, 4d-5a, where we find three examples of rabbis finalizing prayer texts in the *amidah*. Furthermore, not even one Palestinian text in our study (from all the occurrences of this root in M, T, Halakhic Midrash and PT) ever utilizes the term *takkanah* in connection with an initiation attributed to rabbinic innovation. In stark contrast, BT more willingly admits the idea of rabbinic innovation, with fully 32 texts (including base texts and parallels) that mention creation of new practices at the hands of the rabbis, whether individually or collectively. This represents a profound difference in outlook on innovation of new practices between the Palestinian texts in our study and the Babylonian texts.

In this distribution, there exists evidence of a significant difference in the relative idea of rabbinic power between Palestinian and Babylonian editors. Palestinian editors were willing to retroject the creation of new practices on to prior authorities, from the biblical and Second Temple periods, but were not confident enough in their own rabbinic leaders to utilize their reputations to bolster *takkanot* that initiated new practices. Babylonian editors, in contrast, certainly felt comfortable enough using rabbinic exemplars to bolster the initiation of new practices, thus exhibiting much greater levels of confidence in their own leadership.

The choices made in retrojecting each *takkanah* of initiation to particular pre-rabbinic parties were also telling: in general, biblical characters were selected because they fit the needs of the initiation at hand, either through a biblical reference that lent some connection to the practice (as in, for example, Moses or Ezra with the initiation of public Torah reading—Moses made sense because he initially transmitted the Torah; Ezra made sense because he was the first to read it publicly); because the individual cited was known to stand for a related value (such as David and Solomon's stipulation of the *boneh yerushalayim* prayer in *Birkat HaMazon*) or because the individual cited was the earliest authority who might have related to the practice (such is the case with Joshua and the easements on settled land). In every case, pre-rabbinic authorities are selected because they served the rhetorical purpose of the rabbis in bolstering new practices, and provided added plausibility.

Geographic and Chronological Distribution of Attributed Uses of the root *Tkn*

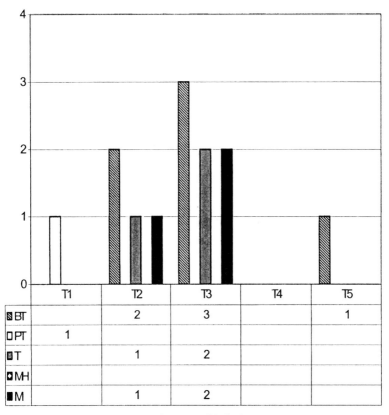

Tannaitic Attributions of Takkanot
Table 6

	T1	T2	T3	T4	T5
▨ BT		2	3		1
◻ PT	1				
▨ T		1	2		
◪ MH					
■ M		1	2		

Generation of Attribution

Tables 6 and 7 show data on the generations (and, thus, a heuristic dating) of the various authorities cited in the extant attributed statements utilizing the root *tkn*. It is important to remember that these are attributions, not assignments: these individuals are cited as making statements about *takkanot*, but are not assigned credit for the activity of making the initial legal change itself. As we did in chapter one, we will utilize this data over numerous occurrences, in order that

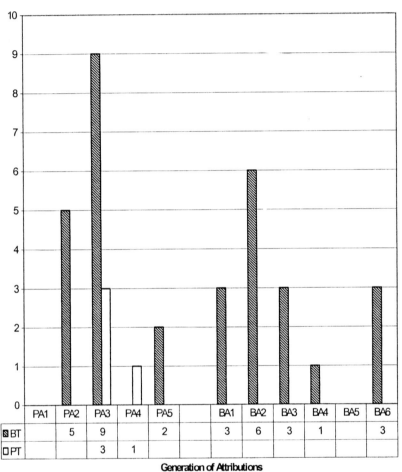

Amoraic Attributions of Takkanot
Table 7

Generation of Attributions

	PA1	PA2	PA3	PA4	PA5		BA1	BA2	BA3	BA4	BA5	BA6
BT		5	9		2		3	6	3	1		3
PT			3	1								

we may overcome the difficulties of employing individual attributions. In the aggregate, such data should reliably point to the broad outlines of which communities and generations were constantly discussing halakhic change, and which communities and generations did so to a lesser extent.

Throughout the Tannaitic period, we find a scant collection of attributed *takkanot* connected to each generation, except for T4. In the Amoraic period there is more data, and this allows for some useful findings. PT shows only four attributed uses of the root *tkn*, and those only appear connected to tradents from PA3 and PA4. BT, likewise, shows its largest spike in the number of attributed discussions of usage in PA3, with a good number of attributions based in PA2 as well. Based on this data, we can posit that the editors of PT and BT either collected material conceived during these generations, or simply believed that there was a significant increase in the discussion of *takkanot* in the Palestinian context during the period roughly defined as PA2-PA3.[584] This result coheres well with the results found in our study of the term *barishonah*. As noted there, the Palestinian authorities centered around Rabbi Yohanan bar Nappaha in Tiberias formed a central kernel that shows up consistently bearing *takkanot* in our sources. Here, too, we find representatives from that same group figuring prominently in making statements on *takkanot*: Rabbi Abbahu, Rabbi Hiyya bar Abba and his student Rav Shmuel bar Yitzhak, Rabbi Eleazar ben Pedat and Rabbi Yitzhak, to name just a few, are all cited as originating traditions that utilize the rhetoric of *tkn*. Once again, the Tiberian school is portrayed as having a sustained interest in the alteration of *halakhah* based on new circumstances.

In BT, we find a further datum that helps us pinpoint the temporal outlines of activity related to *takkanot*. While BT shows its largest spike of attributed *takkanot* in PA2 and PA3, it also shows a concordant significant rise in BA1-BA3. There is a slowing of this activity in BA4-5, and a slight rise once again when we arrive at BA6. Finding this pattern suggests that BA1-3 were the height of activity in Babylonia, with a subsequent tapering off of attributed statements relating to *takkanot*. Thus, the major period of growth in the use of the root *tkn* and discussion of *takkanot* was during the first through third Amoraic generations, with a slight dominance amongst Palestinian Rabbis, and a smaller but healthy number of Babylonian Rabbis as well.

These findings accord with what we saw in chapter one—the early Amoraic period showed a blossoming of the use of the term *barishonah* as well. The reflection upon prior legal decisions occasioned by the use of the term *barishonah* was matched by an innovative trend in the employment of *takkanot*. These two trajectories are matched by a more conservative tendency that we will explore in chapter three, where we discuss the use of the term *gezerah*. All three, however, represent the growth of a novel and self-conscious sense of Jewish legal development in the early Amoraic period—based, surely upon prior tendencies—but with a new life and a new philosophic stance of disclosure and retrojection all its own.

Notes

276. Here, we make use of the JPS translation, with some modifications. The term *tikken* in Eccl. 12:9 is translated in the JPS version as "tested the soundness of many maxims," which seems to be missing the point. Ibn Ezra (the 12th century Italian commentator) and the *Metsudat David* (the 18th century Galician commentary by David Altshuler), *ad loc.*, suggest that the term indicates that Solomon (the reputed author of Ecclesiastes) created and composed 3000 aphorisms, following I Kings 5:12. While the vastness of his composition is not our concern here, the fact that this verb implies literary composition to both Ibn Ezra and the *Metsudat David* provides additional (yet admittedly slim) supporting evidence for the fact that this meaning did exist as early as the time of composition of Ecclesiastes. Cf. James L. Crenshaw, "Ecclesiastes, Book of," *ABD* 2:271-280.

277. Cf. Avraham Even-Shoshan, קרית ספר ירושלים:(קונקורדנציה חדשה, 1987), p. 846.

278. F. Brown, S.R. Driver and C.A. Briggs, *A Hebrew and English Lexicon of the Old Testament* (Oxford: Clarendon, 1966), p. 1075.

279. Hebrew text from Moshe Tzvi Segal, מוסד ביאליק ירושלים: ספר בן סירא השלם, 1958), p. 324.

280. For the dating of Ben Sira, see Alexander A. Di Lella, *The Wisdom of Ben Sira* (New York: Doubleday, 1970), pp. 8-16.

281. John J. Collins, "Daniel, Book of," *ABD* 2:29-37.

282. Cf. Jastrow, *Dictionary*, pp. 1691-1693 for a long list of potential meanings of this root and its derivatives.

283. Michael Sokoloff, *A Dictionary of Jewish Palestinian Aramaic of the Byzantine Period* (Ramat-Gan, Israel: Bar Ilan University Press, 1992), pp. 589-90.

284. See, e.g., M Shek. 1:1, where the word suggests *repair* to the roads and *SD* 308, ד"ה דור עקש, where a crooked staff is *made straight* by burnishing it in a flame.

285. See, e.g., M Dem. 4:7 or 7:7, where the word means the preparing of food; or M Suk. 5:2, where the word suggests a massive making-ready in anticipation of the coming festival.

286. See, e.g., PT Dem. 5:8, 24d, where the term indicates the setting aside of gifts for the priests.

287. See, e.g., PT AZ 1:2, 39c, where the Roman and Egyptian governments reach an agreement with one another.

288. See, e.g., PT Ber. 9:2, 13d, where eggs are placed/arranged on a plate with this verb.

289. This meaning seems entirely absent from the listings of both Sokoloff and Jastrow. For a few examples, see the following: BT Eruv. 21a, where תיקן משלים is used to describe Kohelet's literary fixing of parables; BT Yev. 64b, where the Gemara asks מאן תיקן with reference to a particular mishnah; PT Shek. 5:1, 48g, where Rabbi Akiba is said to have set (whether orally or in writing, we cannot be sure) *midrash, haggadot* and *halakhot*. The most interesting example is the one where the symbolic forms of the final

letters are set by a group of individuals referred to as צופים (*tzofim*, "seers" or "prophets"), in BT Meg. 3a. Lieberman was the first to comment on this meaning in *Hellenism*, pp. 90-91. He drew a parallel between the Aramaic root תקן and the Hebrew root סדר ("to order"), explaining that they both mean " to edit." He also aligned these verbs with the Greek διορθοῦν, which has the technical meaning "to edit."

290. See, e.g., BT Ber. 22a-b, where various rabbis set the values of a series of measures.

291. This accounting is based on the results of a careful search of the Bar Ilan University Responsa Project database to find all occurrences of the root in the Jewish legal corpus of the rabbinic period. Since some manuscripts utilize the root at certain points, and drop the root at other points, this exact total has some malleability based on manuscript selection. Nonetheless, on a statistical basis, the results of these comparisons are still quite valid and suggest certain tendencies on the part of the authors of the texts involved.

292. This number is based on the Bar Ilan University Responsa Project search indicated above, filtered through personal reading of every result, and a determination of the meaning of the root involved. While we may be relatively confident that the determinations are accurate, still, there is always the possibility that one might read these sections differently, and results might well differ by a few occurrences in one direction or another depending on the reader. Nonetheless, as stated above, the results would remain statistically valid due to the large number of citations reviewed.

293. Note that the number of occurrences in both BT and PT are based, of course, only on the respective Gemaras of these works, excluding the occurrences reproduced in the included mishnayot.

294. Rabbi Elijah Galipapa, ידי אליהו (Repr. Brooklyn, New York: Beigeleisen Brothers, 1989/90).

295. Simon Marcus, "Elijah Mevorakh Galipapa," *Encyclopaedia Judaica* 7:271. Galipapa was born in Sofia (in present-day Bulgaria) in the latter part of the 17th century, and immigrated to Jerusalem in 1702. Fleeing a significant tax burden imposed upon him by the Ottoman authorities, he arrived in Rhodes in 1704, where he became deputy to the chief rabbi. He died in Rhodes in 1740, where his tombstone still stands today.

296. A descendant of a celebrated intellectual family, Chajes became *Kreis-rabbiner* (district rabbi) in Zolkiev, Galicia, by 1827 at the young age of 22. He completed a doctoral degree in Philosophy at Lemberg University, and had a close relationship with both Nahman Krochmal and Samson Bloch. In 1852 he was appointed to the rabbinate in Kalish, Poland, but died shortly afterwards in Lemberg in 1855.

297. Tzvi Hirsch Chajes, *The Student's Guide Through the Talmud*, translated and with an introduction by Jacob Shachter (London: East and East Library, 1952), pp. xi-xiv. An 1845 edition of the Hebrew original of this work was consulted at the Jewish Theological Seminary Library.

298. Bloch was born in Ronsperg, Bohemia, and served as a congregational rabbi, Talmud and Codes Professor and Rector of the rabbinical seminary in Budapest. See Moshe Nahum Zobel, "Moses Bloch," *Encyclopaedia Judaica* 4:1107-8.

299. I.H. Weiss, *Dor*, 1:3.

300. Bloch, *Takkanot*, Author's Introduction, n.p.

301. Cf., for example, William Scott Green, "What's in a Name?—The Problematic of Rabbinic 'Biography,'" in *idem, Approaches to Ancient Judaism I* (Missoula: Scholars Press, 1978), pp. 77-96; Jacob Neusner, "The History of Earlier Rabbinic Judaism," *History of Religions* 16 (1977), pp. 216-36 and David Halivni, "Doubtful Attributions in the Talmud," *PAAJR* 46-7 (1979-80), pp. 67-83.

302. Urbach, *The Halakhah*, pp. 7-29 and 71-75.

303. Israel Schepansky, *התקנות בישראל* (ירושלים: קוק הרב מוסד, 1991).

304. Justice Elon was born in Dusseldorf in 1923, and immigrated to Palestine in 1935. He served as Adviser on Jewish Law to the Ministry of Justice, and as a Professor of Jewish Law at the Hebrew University. See "Menachem Elon," *Encyclopaedia Judaica*, 1:29.

305. See Elon, *Jewish Law* 2:477-880 for Elon's discussion of legislation in Jewish law. While "Jewish Law" is a fair translation of the title, the implication of the Hebrew term is something akin to "Jewish Law investigated from a jurisprudential perspective," in that this work views the Jewish legal "system" as a whole, and seeks to determine its basic values, concepts and modes of thought. See the introduction to this work, pp. lii-liii, and the translator's introduction, pp. lvii-lix, for a summary of this approach.

306. Another excellent though somewhat dated article is by S. Ochser, "Takkanah," *Jewish Encyclopedia* 11:669-676.

307. Martin S. Jaffee, "The Taqqanah in Tannaitic Literature: Jurisprudence and the Construction of Rabbinic Memory," *JJS* 41.2 (1990), pp. 204-225.

308. Christine Hayes, "The Abrogation of Torah Law: Rabbinic Taqqanah and Praetorian Edict," in Peter Schäfer, *The Talmud Yerushalmi and Graeco-Roman Culture* (Tübingen: Mohr Siebeck, 1997), pp. 643-674. Bernard Jackson takes the opposite position on Roman influence, finding no evidence of it at all. See Jackson, "Evolution."

309. Cf. Bloch, *Takkanot*, Introduction, p. I, and Elon, *Jewish Law*, pp. 490-493.

310. Rabinowitz הקדמות לפירוש המשנה (של רבינו משה בן מימון) (Jerusalem: Mossad HaRav Kook, 1961), pp. 40-41.

311. This verse is typically understood in rabbinic literature as a severe warning against breaching any fences around the Torah, with the implied result being personal harm. See, for example, BT AZ 27b and T Hul. 2:23.

312. Rabbi Moses ben Joseph Trani (the מבי"ט, 1500-1580) was born in Salonika and immigrated to Safed via Adrianopol at a young age. He was one of the four students Jacob Berab ordained in his effort to restart ordination, and later became spiritual head of the entire community of Safed upon the death of Joseph Karo. Cf. "Trani, Moses ben Joseph," *Encyclopaedia Judaica*, 15:1315.

313. The original text of this description was unavailable, thus this synopsis relies upon the summary in Schepansky, *HaTakkanot*, p. 4.

314. Zvi Hirsch Chajes, *Mevo HaTalmud* (Lvov: Margulies, 1845) p. 13. Here we have followed the translation found in Chajes, *Student's Guide*, p. 35.

315. Cf. *MT Hilkhot Mamrin*, 1:1, where Rambam tied obedience of *takkanot* and *gezerot* to Deut. 17:11.

316. Bloch, *Takkanot*, Introduction, p. 1.

317. Elon, *Jewish Law*, p. 492.
318. Elon, *Jewish Law*, p. 490-2 and Bloch, *Takkanot*, Introduction, pp. I-IV.
319. Elon, *Jewish Law*, p. 478.
320. Cf. *MT Yesodei HaTorah* 9:1.
321. Ms. Munich cites this tradition in the name of Rav Nahman bar Yitzhak instead.
322. Deut. 32:7. The passage from BT comes from BT Shab. 23a.
323. Though the text does not explicitly use the proper name "Jerusalem," it is clear that this is the meaning of "the place the Lord has chosen." Tigay comments upon this in his introduction to Deut., p. xvii: "Unique in Deuteronomy's laws is the rule that sacrificial worship may take place only in a single sanctuary. This law transfers virtually all important activities that were previously performed at sanctuaries throughout the country—sacrifice, festivals, rites of purification, and certain judicial activities—to the central sanctuary in the religious capital." Consult the rest of the introduction, pp. xiii-xxviii for his discussion of the Josianic reform, the "finding" of the scroll of Deuteronomy in 622 BCE, and the political forces that led to the singling out of Jerusalem as capital during this period.
324. See Levinson, *Deuteronomy and the Hermeneutics of Legal Innovation* (Oxford: Oxford University Press, 1997), pp. 3-22, for full coverage of the history of this claim.
325. I.H. Weiss, *Sifra* (Vienna: 1852, Repr. New York: Um Publishers, 1947), p. 86b. Elon, *Jewish Law*, p. 482-3, also cites BT Yev. 21a and BT MK 5a, where Rav Kahana and Rav Ashi, respectively, interpret this verse as authorization to make "fences" around Torah law. The passage in BT Yev. concerns prohibited sexual unions, securing a direct connection with the Torah text's original context in Leviticus. As for BT MK, the text discusses the marking of graves so as to prevent unsuspecting passersby from becoming impure by straying over them. In both cases, it is clear that ritual purity is the root issue, an issue that arises directly from the biblical text. Why this authorization would extend beyond these concerns remains an open question.
326. Cf. *MT Mamrin* 1:1-2, Nahmanides' Glosses to Maimonides' *Sefer Hamitzvot*, *Shoresh* 1, and the discussion in Elon, *Jewish Law*, pp. 483-5.
327. See, for example, Maimonides' Introduction to his *Commentary on the Mishnah*, where he includes the *takkanot* among the sections of rabbinic legal categories.
328. In Ex. 12:8, the command reads: "And they shall eat the meat this night, roasted in fire, with *matzah* on *maror*."
329. BT Pes. 30b, 39b (as cited above) and 116b; BT Yoma 31a; BT Yev. 11a; BT Git. 64b and 65a (with discussion); BT AZ 34a and BT Bekh. 54a.
330. Cf. PT Shevi. 10:2, 39c, parallel to PT Git. 4:3, 45c; PT Eruv. 1:10, 19d; PT Shek. 7:3, 40d; PT Git. 5:1, 46c; PT RH 4:2, 59b and PT Shev. 7:1, 37d.
331. The issue, here, is whether the *get* is valid if it were not completed in one step and constantly observed thereafter by appropriate witnesses. Since the writing and the signing constituted separate steps on the way to the final completion of the *get*, doing them in different places complicated the matter by requiring appropriate testimony both to validate each piece, and to ensure that the document had not been tampered with in the

meantime. The *Korban HaEdah* suggests another possibility here: that the *get* may have been switched for an entirely different document, making it, of course, completely invalid. Securing it in the private domain of a property owner was the best way to ensure that nothing interfered with its validity during this intermediate period.

332. Here, the *Korban HaEdah* suggests a version that substitutes "אמר" for "בעל," though there are occurrences of the latter that may be understood as "remarked" as well. Cf., *e.g.*, PT Ber. 1:1, 2b.

333. BT Ket. 10a and BT Suk. 41b.

334. PT Suk. 3:11, 54b; PT RH 4:2, 59b; PT RH 4:3, 59b and PT Hal. 1:1, 57c.

335. BT Shev. 41a; BT Shev. 46a and BT BM 5a-b.

336. The complete verse of Lev. 23:40 reads: "On the first day you shall take the product of *hadar* trees, branches of palm, boughs of leafy trees and willows of the brook, and you shall rejoice before the Lord your God seven days."

The initial problem, here, is that the commandment to wave the *lulav*, based on this verse, is limited to the first day, since the commanding verb ולקחתם is immediately followed by the limiting phrase ביום הראשון. Thus, the crux of this *sugya* is how we know that the *mitzvah* of *lulav* continues beyond the first day of the festival due to rabbinical enactments, and not due to a statement in the Torah itself.

337. These are offerings of well-being, which are burnt whole on the altar during the festival of Sukkot in compliance with the command in Num. 29:12-38.

338. This reading comports with both the *Korban HaEdah* and the *Penei Moshe*, though it is the opposite of what is contained in the manuscripts and printed edition. Logically, it is the best reading.

339. Lev. 23:40.

340. See, again, Lev. 23:40.

341. Generally, in cases where one party owed money (or the value of property) to another party, the debtor swore an oath claiming that s/he already paid the amount in question. In such cases, the Torah imposed an oath that cited monetary amounts less than those at stake in the case (ensuring that the divine name was not taken in vain if the total referenced amount exceeded the money involved in the case). The rabbis, on the other hand, imposed a consuetudinary oath over the entire amount. The idea of transferring the oath implies having the creditor say the oath in place of the debtor, in case there is any reason to believe that the debtor might swear falsely. Cf. BT Shev. 40b.

342. This means that if a person without adult status (e.g., a deaf-mute, imbecile or minor) loses something, the court may not, according to Rabbi Yossi, seize the assets of the finder in order to compensate the victim. According to Rabbi Hisda, who sees finding items belonging to any of these parties as actual theft according to the understanding of גזל in the Torah, the court may take action and seize assets.

343. This suggests that the court require the other party swear to his/her claim, instead of the one we believe is swearing falsely.

344. For more discussion of this rule in BT and this particular *sugya*, see Schepansky, *HaTakkanot*, pp. 1:93-99. Schepanksy does not, however, discuss the PT's texts on this topic at all.

345. Rava bar Yosef bar Hama, d. 352 (BA4), was a student of Rav Nahman who taught in Mehoza. Strack and Stemberger, *Introduction*, pp. 104-5.

346. BT Git. 77b; BT Ket. 83a; BT BK 8b and BT BB 49b.

347. The two other examples are BT BM 100a and BT BB 38a.

348. A *hazakah* is a presumption—not fully proven according to law, but strongly suspected to be true. The case here is that a person who currently holds the land claims that it was given to him as a gift, or purchased by him, though the deed was subsequently lost. Thus, since he currently holds the land, he has a presumption of ownership, but not full proof. According to the statute of limitations expressed in the Mishnah, this presumption is only effective for three years. After the completion of three years, the landholder gains a real claim to ownership that cannot be uprooted by other claims.

349. The logic here is that by helping the current landholder, the claimant is making a *de facto* admission that the landholder owns it. Otherwise, why would he help?

350. The "mortgage of Sura" is a mortgage deed that developed in the Amoraic period. Control over the land granted by this deed generally lasted for three years, unless trouble intervened, whereupon the ownership of the land returned to the prior owner. See Asher Gulak, החיוב ושעבודיו (Jerusalem: Hebrew University Press, 1939), p. 76.

351. "Fit," (*kasher*) here, simply means that they would be permitted to marry any Israelite, with no degradation of their status due to their *yiboom*.

352. The term *mamzer* is a technical legal term for any child born as a result of adulterous or consanguineous relations. If the children are declared *mamzerim*, they suffer from significant and detrimental long-term ramifications: with this status they and their offspring are forbidden to marry Jews of normal status.

353. Based on this attributed statement, Adolf Büchler, *Das Synedrion in Jerusalem* (Vienna: Verlag der Israel-Theol. Lehranstalt, 1902), p. 81, n. 6, places the creation of the enactment in Yavneh.

354. *Pagum* represents another defective legal status in a family's history, caused by a marriage that took place where a difference in status would make the union forbidden. It held far fewer negative legal ramifications than the status of *mamzer*. A *pagum* is generally assigned the lower status of his/her parents. For example, if a high priest married a widow, the status of the offspring would follow the widow's status as opposed to the high priest's.

355. Louis Finkelstein, *Siphra*, 1:130, reads this pericope as proof of the extreme concern of the rabbis with the gravity of the disagreements between the houses of Hillel and Shammai.

356. Lieberman, *TK* 6:5, points out that BT and PT disagree on the ultimate disposition of this *takkanah*: BT Yev. 27a brings a statement in the name of Rav Nahman bar Yitzhak that they went back and completed the *takkanah* at a later date. PT Yev. 3:1, 4c, on the other hand, claims that the *takkanah* was never completed. M Yev. 1:4 also holds a relevant report: it indicates that the two schools respected one another's opinions, choosing not to disqualify from marriage those with defective status under the stance of the opposing school. This may represent a pre-*takkanah* compromise position that held sway until the situation deteriorated sufficiently to require other legal remedy.

357. See Louis Jacobs, *Teyku: The Unsolved Problem in the Babylonian Talmud: A Study in Literary Analysis and Form of the Talmudic Argument* (London: Cornwall Books, 1981), for a review of the use of this term in Talmudic sources, though Jacobs' stress is entirely on BT rather than PT. Some commentators, reading *teyku* as an acronym, suggest this statement is an indication that this debate will be left until the time of the Prophet Elijah for an answer.

358. *Pasak* (פסק) is the general term for the deciding of law by an authority or authorities. Once an authority rules between two possible alternatives, the law is considered finalized.

359. See the parallel in BT Shev. 45a, where the text acknowledges *ab initio* that this is an enactment of the rabbis.

360. *Maneh* is equivalent to 100 *zuz* (a monetary value), the amount of the *ketubbah* payment specified in a widow's marriage contract as noted in the relevant mishnah. Rav Huna's statement is playing on the linguistic similarity between *maneh* and *almanah* to make a connection between these two words. The next two paragraphs in the Gemara attempt to refute this suggested etymology.

361. This statement questions the idea that *almanah* ("widow") implies *maneh* ("100 *zuz*"). Since the word *almanah* is already present in the Torah, and there is no indication of any value of money (let alone *zuz*, which was surely not the currency in effect in the days of the Torah's writing), the idea of connecting *almanah* and *maneh* is not granted automatic acceptance. The anachronism is simply too difficult to allow it to stand without further discussion.

362. Seleucia was a town on the west bank of the Tigris, about 25 kilometers southeast of Baghdad. For extensive citations on the area, see Aharon Oppenheimer, *Babylonian Judaica in the Talmudic Period* (Wiesbaden: Dr. Ludwig Reichert, 1983), pp. 207-223.

363. "Her" being the widow who would receive the 100 *zuz*, who also was to exist in the future, but did not at the time of the writing of the Torah.

364. Jaffee, "Taqqanah," p. 205, notes that the *takkanot* attributed to the most ancient authorities are generally found in the latest strata of the Talmudic texts. He suggests, here, that these attributions, as well as those citations of purportedly Tannaitic origin, are all suspect.

365. In approximate chronological order, they are:

Adam: 1 case in PT AZ 1:2, 39c;

The *Avot* (Patriarchs, i.e., Abraham, Isaac and Jacob): 1 case in BT Ber. 26b;

Moses: 7 cases in *SB* 66 (cf. Horovitz, p. 62) (paralleled by BT Meg. 4a and 32a), BT Ber. 48b, BT Shab. 30a, BT Men. 65a (a mocking statement made by a sectarian trying to invoke Moses' authority to support his unacceptable views on the dating of Shavuot), PT Ber. 7:3,11c (paralleled by PT Meg. 3:7, 74c), PT Meg. 4:1, 75a and PT Ket. 1:1, 25a;

The *tzofim* (whom most commentators connect with the prophets): 1 case in BT Meg. 3a involving the finalizing of the forms of the final letters in the Hebrew language;

The prophets: 6 cases in M Ta. 4:2 (paralleled by T Ta. 3:2, BT Ta. 27a, PT Ta.

4:2, 67d), *MRY Beshallah Masekhet DeVayissa Beshallah, Parashah* 1 *s.v.* ויסע משה (cf. Horovitz, p. 154) (paralleled by *MRSBY* 15:22, PT Meg. 1:1, 70b and PT Meg. 4:1, 75a), *SD* 343:2 (cf. Finkelstein, p. 395) (paralleled by BT Ber. 4b and 9b, BT Meg. 17b and PT Ber. 2:4, 4d), BT Pes. 117a, BT Arakh. 13a, and PT Eruv. 3:9, 21c;

Joshua: 3 cases in BT Ber. 48b, BT Eruv. 13a and BT BK 81a-b;

David: 1 case in BT Ber. 48b;

Solomon: 2 cases in BT Ber. 48b and BT Shab. 14b;

Ezra: 13 cases in BT Ket. 3a-b (paralleled by PT Meg. 4:1, 75a), BT BK 82a-b, BT BK 82b, BT BB 21b (paralleled by PT Meg. 4:1, 75a), PT Yoma 8:1, 44d (paralleled by PT Ta. 1:6, 64c and PT Meg. 4:1, 75a), PT Meg. 1:1, 70b (paralleled by PT Meg. 4:1, 75a), and six other occurrences in PT Meg. 4:1, 75a and

The Men of the Great Assembly: 4 cases in BT Ber. 33a, BT Ber. 33b., BT Meg. 2a and PT Shek. 5:1, 5c.

366. The use of this text plays on the dual meaning of the root שׁיף, meaning "to cover over" or "to poison," to tie the impending darkness in the Psalms verse with the attack of the venomous snake in the Genesis verse.

367. See Saul Lieberman, *Hellenism*, pp. 10-11. Also, cf. Walter Bauer, *A Greek-English Lexicon of the New Testament* (Chicago: University of Chicago Press, 1979), *s.v.* καλάνδαι, p. 398.

368. Cf. David Ewing Duncan, *The Calendar* (New York: Avon Books, 1998), pp. 29-35 for a helpful briefing on the development of the Roman Calendar. For an example of a primary source that indicates Romulus' role in calendar initiation, see the fourth century Roman historian Macrobius' account in *The Saturnalia*, book 1, chapter 12, in Macrobius, *The Saturnalia* (trans. Percival Vaughan Davies; New York: Columbia University Press, 1969), pp. 83-90.

369. Lieberman, *op. cit.*

370. Duncan, *op. cit.*, pp. 30-31.

371. Meir Friedmann, *Pesikta Rabbati* (Vienna: Selbstverlag des Herausgebers, 1880; Repr. Tel Aviv: Esther, 1963), p. 118b.

372. William Braude, *Pesikta Rabbati* (New Haven: Yale, 1968), pp. 2-3. This date arises from an addition in the text indicating that it was composed 777 years after the destruction of the Second Temple. The frequent occurrence of numerous Palestinian authorities suggests a Palestinian provenance.

373. See, for example, Seth Schwartz's article "Gamaliel in Aphrodite's Bath," in Schäfer, *Talmud Yerushalmi in Graeco-Roman Culture*, pp. 203-17. In Schwartz's conclusion on p. 217: "[The rabbis'] modified rigorism, with its uncompromising rejection of anything remotely connected to pagan cult, but acceptance of most non-cultic manifestations of Greco-Roman pagan culture, permitted them to live and function. . . ." Calendar, a vital communal function that ordered the activities and lives of Jews and Romans alike, could better be accepted if it became less "Roman/pagan," and more "Jewish."

374. There are numerous instances of Jewish-Roman cultural competition that exist among Tannaitic and Amoraic texts. See, for example, Louis H. Feldman, *Jew & Gentile*

in the Ancient World (Princeton: Princeton University Press, 1993), who catalogs topics and interactions preserved in literary sources that point to regularly uneasy feelings of competition and antipathy between Jew and Gentile.

375. Schepansky, however, dismisses this *takkanah* (as he also ignored the above reference to Adam's), because until Moses gave the Torah to Israel, the power to make *takkanot* did not officially exist. Schepanksy, *HaTakkanot*, pp. 1:119-120.

376. Schepansky, *op. cit.*, pp. 131-134.

377. In its original context, this text from Ecclesiastes implies that the dead are better off than then living, because they do not have to witness the oppression and miseries of contemporary life. In this passage, it is reapplied to imply that Moses, now dead, is better off than the contemporary rabbis, for his decrees are still followed and will continue to be followed forever, while theirs may or may not be. This proves to be an interesting admission of the shakiness of rabbinic authority.

378. H. S. Horovitz, *Siphre D'be Rab* (Lipsiae: Gustav Fock, 1942; Repr. Jerusalem: Wahrman Books, 1966), p. 62.

379. Parallels to this text, utilizing the root תקן, exist in BT Meg. 4a and 32a. There is little more to be gleaned from the comparative study of these parallel texts.

380. Parallel *baraitot* occur in PT Pes. 1:1, 27b (the Hebrew indicates it is the same *baraita*, though PT omits a marker term such as *tanya* or the like) and in BT in Pes. 6a, RH 7a, Meg. 29b, San, 12b, AZ 5b and Bekh. 58a.

381. BT BK 92a.

382. *MRY* Beshallah, Vayissa 1, p.154 in H.S. Horovitz, *Mekhilta DeRabbi Yishmael* (Jerusalem: Bamberger and Wahrmann, 1931).

383. Albeck, *Mavo LaMishnah*, p. 31.

384. A *milhemet reshut* (discretionary war) requires the king to consult with certain parties before marching out to war: in The Temple Scroll, consultation is with the high priest, who must consult the *Urim* and *Thummim* to discern the will of God with respect to this war (cf. Lawrence H. Schiffman, "The Laws of War in XIQTemple" *Revue de Qumran* 13:1-4 (1988), pp. 306-8, where he reviews 11QT LVIII 11-15 where this consultation is required). In rabbinic literature, the king may lead the people into a discretionary war only after the decision of a representative court of 71 judges (see M San. 1:5). Jewish tradition distinguishes between a "discretionary war," which is made to conquer territory and expand the reach of the people Israel, and an "obligatory war," where the war is focused on settling the land of Israel itself, fighting longtime enemies and former settlers in the land of Israel or defending the Jewish people from aggressive offensive attacks. Cf. M Sot., Ch. 8, and MT *Melakhim*, Chs. 5-6.

385. Rabbinovicz, *Dikduke Sofrim, ad loc.,* shows that several manuscripts have קונין here, that they may "take possession" anywhere, as opposed to "camping" anywhere, but rejects this reading as incorrect, following the printed edition.

386. Lieberman, *Tosefta Moed*, p. 93 suggests this reading in his note to line 22.

387. See M Eruv. 1:10 for a parallel to the words on commandeering dry wood.

388. There is no concept of *milhemet reshut* present in the Torah at all, nor in any of the biblical books. Deuteronomy 20, the *locus classicus* for rules regarding war in the Torah, contains no definitive mention of this term, nor is war clearly divided into two

opposing categories with different rules. The earliest attestations of the term *milhemet reshut* appear in M Sotah 1:7, San. 1:5 and 2:4, and in *SD Piskaot* 190:21, 198:9, 199:10, 203:19, 211:21/10, where the term is used but not completely defined. Furthermore, when the term is finally better defined, in later texts such as PT, BT and, finally, in its most highly evolved incarnation in MT, the definition *specifically excludes* battles for the land of Israel. Joshua's battles would have been categorized as *milhemot mitzvah*, obligatory wars, as opposed to discretionary wars.

Yigael Yadin, in reviewing the regulations on war in the Qumran community's *War Scroll*, notes: "The Pentateuch does not specifically distinguish between the two kinds of war and demands exemption for all the types mentioned in Deuteronomy; Judas Maccabeus acts in agreement with this [cf. I Macc. 3:55-6, where Judah Maccabee exempts all those categories called for in Deut. 20, despite the fact that his war would certainly qualify as *milhemet mitzvah* according to the rabbis' later definition]. The Rabbis distinguish between two kinds of war, exempting all the types in a War of Choice [a *milhemet reshut*] and conscripting them in a War of Duty [a *milhemet mitzvah*]. The [War] scroll apparently conscripts the builders of houses, etc., and exempts the faint hearted."

Here, we see evidence that even as late as the end of the Second Temple period these two categories had not fully solidified. See Yigael Yadin, *The Scroll of the War of the Sons of Light Against the Sons of Darkness* (Oxford: Oxford University Press, 1962), pp. 67-9. See also the War Scroll itself, 1QM, column X, p. 129 in Florentino García Martínez and Eibert J.C. Tigchelaar, *The Dead Sea Scrolls Study Edition* (Leiden: Brill, 1997).

389. Without the permission of the owner. The Gemara suggests that this is only for sheep and goats pastured in large woods, where the owner's land could sustain the animals without being stripped completely bare. The grazing of sheep and goats in small woods, or bovines in big woods, or, worst of all, bovines in small woods, was not permitted without permission of the owner, according to this text.

390. Again, without the owner's permission. Here, too, the Gemara makes a distinction between the different sorts of wood that may be collected, and permits it only as long as the wood was still attached to the ground and wet. This was to prevent a visitor from taking piles of wood set out to dry by the owner.

391. A curly plant that the Gemara says requires grass to thrive, especially when it is being grown to produce seeds.

392. Cf. the parallels to this law at M BB 5:3 and the Gemara at BT BB 80a-b, where the situation of this law is made clear. In this case, one person is purchasing a tree from another, and must cut it down to make use of the wood. The question is: how close to the base may the purchaser cut? The answer given is that enough room must be left to allow the olive tree to sprout again, and thus ensure the continued growth of the seller's tree.

393. This law and the preceding law grant rights to all people to make use of two different sorts of bodies of water, a natural resource considered public property, provided that its utilization respected the rights of others.

394. Even in a field of saffron, the most expensive of spices, one in need of relieving him/herself in dignity behind a fence may remove a pebble from the fence without con-

cern for the severe violation of dislodging the fence, and without worrying about the possibility of loose rocks damaging the expensive plants. Rashi and other commentators suggest that the rock is used to cleanse oneself after defecating. Cf. Fred Rosner, *Encylcopedia of Medicine in the Bible and the Talmud* (Northvale, New Jersey: Jason Aronson, 2000), p. 95, who suggests that this passage implies that small stones were used to clean the anus after defecating. Also cf. BT Ber. 55a and BT Shab. 81a, where re-using pebbles was said to lead to hemorrhoids.

395. The seventeenth of Marheshvan, according to Rashi and his reading of BT Ta. 16a. Once the fields were muddy, though, this practice was forbidden as it caused damage to plants.

396. Jastrow, *Dictionary*, p. 263, explains that these are related to the Hebrew גץ or the Arabic *gypsum*—white pegs that stand by a road made of baked or packed earth, used to mark a cross-path.

397. Literally, "the dead body acquires its place" for its burial.

398. These ten additional dots that are added to words in the Torah are first mentioned in *SB* ch. 69. Cf. Horovitz, *Siphre*, pp. 64-66. The dots are attributed to Ezra's handiwork as a scribe in *Avot DeRabbi Natan*, Version A, ch. 34, see Solomon Schechter, *Avot DeRabbi Natan* (Repr. New York: Jewish Theological Seminary, 1997), pp. 100-101. For a scholarly overview on this issue, see Emanuel Tov, *Textual Criticism of the Hebrew Bible* (Minneapolis: Augsberg Fortress, 1992), pp. 55-57. Lieberman, *Hellenism*, pp. 43-46, explains that this was a common Hellenistic editing tendency that showed emphasis on a certain passage, and did not, as *ARN* suggests, indicate a doubtful section of the text. This chapter of *ARN* also contains mention of a number of other "ten" traditions.

399. Cf. BT Ber. 48b.

400. Cf. BT Ber. 48b and BT Shab. 14b.

401. Cf. BT Meg. 3a.

402. The prophets appear in six examples: M Ta. 4:2 (paralleled by T Ta. 3:2, PT Pes. 4:1, 30c, PT Ta. 4:2, 67d and BT Ta. 27a); *MRY Beshallah Vayissa Beshallah* 1, *s.v. Vayissa Moshe* (paralleled by *MRSBY* 15:22, PT Meg. 1:1, 70b (though here the action is taken by Ezra, not the prophets) and PT Meg. 4:1, 75a); *SD* 343:2, (paralleled by BT Ber. 4b, BT Ber. 9b, BT Meg. 17b-18a and PT Ber. 2:4, 4d); BT Pes. 117a; BT Arakh. 13a and PT Arakh. 3:9, 21c.

403. Cf. BT Ber. 33a and 33b.

404. *Tosafot Yom Tov* follows Rashi in the harmonizing suggestion that the term "early prophets" should be understood as David and Samuel, and also points out the verse in I Chron. 9:22 as it is quoted in T. This shows, simply, that the commentators knew the Toseftan text as well, and were looking for ways to harmonize the two sources.

Louis Finkelstein, *New Light From the Prophets* (London: Valentine, Mitchell & Co., 1969), pp. 49-76, makes much of this mishnaic passage, dating its composition quite early—to the fourth or fifth century BCE and suggesting that the term "early prophets" found here should be read as "the prophets of Jerusalem," as it appears in T below. Y. N. Epstein, *Sifrut HaTannaim*, p. 46, agrees with Finkelstein's assessment of the early dating of this mishnaic.

405. Finkelstein, *New Light,* pp. 72-3.

406. Albeck, *Mishnah, Moed,* p. 341.

407. See Martínez and Tiglchelaar, *Dead Sea Scrolls Study Edition,* 1:114-5.

408. The last six words of this text are a handwritten gloss in Ms. Leiden, Cf. Lieberman, *Leiden Ms.,* p. 447.

409. This text is repeated *verbatim* in PT Ta. 4:2, 67d.

410. The majority of earlier manuscripts bring this statement in the name of Rav Hisda, according to Rabbinovicz, *Dikduke Sofrim, ad loc.* The other possibility, which appears in the printed edition of BT, is that this was transmitted by Rav Hama bar Gorya in the name of Rav.

411. In other words, through the joint effect of David and Shmuel's increases, the ultimate number was 24. This harmonizes the two *baraitot,* resolving the problem.

412. This implies that there were twice as many leaders (16) in Eleazar's family as in Itamar's (eight).

413. K. Koch, "Ezra and the Origins of Judaism," *JSS* 19 (1974): 173-197, p. 195-6.

414. David Weiss Halivni, *Revelation Revealed* (Boulder, CO: Westview Press, 1997), pp. 3-4.

415. For a more balanced view of what we can know about "the historical Ezra," see Robert North's opinion in Freedman, ed., "Ezra," *ABD II*, pp. 726-729, and his helpful bibliography.

416. These thirteen occurrences are: BT Ket. 3a-b (paralleled by PT Meg. 4:1, 75a); BT BK 82a-b (the ten *takkanot* pericope, which also includes one other example of Ezra's *takkanot,* relating to the number of verses one must read in the Torah); BT BB 21b; BT BB 22a (paralleled by PT Meg. 4:1,75a); PT Yoma 8:1, 44d (paralleled by PT Ta. 1:6, 64c and PT Meg.4:1, 75a); PT Meg. 1:1, 70b (paralleled by PT Meg. 4:1, 75a) and another instance in PT Meg. 4:1, 75a (which has six more examples listed within it, in addition to the parallels just listed).

417. This probably arose as a response to use of the root נדה, "polluted," in Ezra 9:11, when the text refers to the polluted land and its inhabitants. It is a slim thread upon which to hang such a serious halakhic innovation. Note, as well, that there was also an important egalitarian tendency in this decision, as it required men to observe purity laws in a way that paralleled women's requirements.

418. Spice peddlers were the primary distributors of cosmetics, and, thus, they were permitted to sell door-to-door in any town, for the sake of beautifying the women of Israel. There is some unease associated with them, though, as we see in BT Yev. 24b, where a *baraita* states: "when the spice peddler goes out, the woman is bound in a petticoat." Spice peddlers may have peddled something a bit spicier, too.

419. Food for the poor on Shabbat is a constant value in rabbinic texts, see M Peah 1:7, and *MRSBY* 20:8. It is also notable that the initial discussion of carrying on Shabbat in M Shab. 1:1 is based on the poor person who comes to ask for support at the door of a home during Shabbat. Such highlighting of the value of *tzedakah* on Shabbat is another way the editors of M put forward this value.

420. Marital relations are encouraged on Shabbat in rabbinic tradition, so the consumption of garlic would lead to better fulfillment of this duty. Garlic was reputed to

have many medicinal and other uses in the ancient world. The genus *allium* includes garlic and onions, and any number of medicinal potions have been concocted from members of this genus. Pliny the Elder in John Bostock and H.T. Riley, translators, *The Natural History of Pliny* (London: Bohn, 1857), pp. 4:225-228, lists 61 remedies from garlic alone, including this delightful description: "Garlic acts as an aphrodisiac, beaten up with fresh coriander, and taken in pure wine. The inconveniences which result from the use of it are dimness of sight and flatulency; and if taken in too large quantities, it does injury to the stomach and creates thirst." Thus the lust-enhancing qualities of garlic were well recognized in the Greco-Roman context. Hans Licht, *Sexual Life in Ancient Greece* (New York: Barnes & Noble, 1963), pp. 513-4, also notes that members of the genus *allium* were recognized aphrodisiacs amongst the ancient Greeks. Cf. also the list of rabbinic sources on garlic contained in Rosner, *Medicine*, pp. 144-5. Parallels to this source also mention the eating of garlic on Friday, including BT Ned. 31a and 63b. For a history of the use of garlic, see Gruffydd Roger Fenwick and Anthony Bryan Hanley, "The Genus *Allium*—Part I," *CRC Critical Reviews in Food and Nutrition* 22:3 (1985):199-271, with emphasis on pp. 199-203.

421. There is a parallel in BT San. 19a, attributing this enactment to Rabbi Yossi of Sepphoris, where a reason is offered for this *takkanah*: it prevents accidental *yihud* (a woman sequestered with a man to whom she is not married)—grounds for suspicion of extramarital relations. For other activities of women in this setting, see BT Yoma 11a.

422. A סינר was a sort of petticoat that engendered modesty and chastity, covering both the front and back of a woman's body. It tended to slide around from front to back, as noted in M Shab. 10:4. Removing it implied engaging in sexually provocative behavior, as we see in BT Shab. 13b and PT Sot. 1:2, 17c.

423. This bizarre reading follows the *Korban HaEdah*. Covering both her front and her back with a closed garment would protect her in either case. The euphemistic Hebrew expression "not according to her way" is the Talmud's preferred way of speaking of anal intercourse.

424. The verse from Esther, in its original context, refers strictly to observance of the holiday of Purim, and has no connection whatsoever to Torah reading on Monday, Thursday or Shabbat. This is probably why the idea that Mordecai and Esther had any role in effecting the institution of these Torah readings is entirely rejected by the *Korban HaEdah*, the *Penei Moshe* and other commentators. Nonetheless, PT here provides us with an alternate source for the *takkanah*.

425. Horovitz, *MRY, Beshallah, Masekhta deVayissa* 1, p. 154.

426. Horovitz, *op. cit.*, note to line 13, suggests that this simply means that the interpretation at hand comes from *midrash aggadah*. Jacob Z. Lauterbach, "The Ancient Jewish Allegorists in Talmud and Midrash," *JQR* (N.S.) 1 (1910-11), pp. 291-333, in the only available scholarly literature on this term, shows that *dorshei reshumot* means those who interpret Torah in allegorical ways. Since Isaiah's "water" is "evidently used as a figure of speech to designate the Divine word, the *Dorshe Reshumot* interpreted it, in a figurative sense, to designate symbolically the Divine law . . ." Lauterbach, on pp. 310-11, also ties this specific passage's allegorical interpretation of water with precedents in

Philo, citing both his *On the Allegories of the Sacred Laws* 2:21 and *On Dreams* 2:31 and 2:38, all of which utilize this same allegorical interpretation of water as Torah.

427. Later *varienta* attribute these changes to "early fathers" (*Pesikta Zutrati*) or "the prophets among them" (*Midrash Sekhel Tov*).

428 M Meg. 4:1.

429. Cf. Josephus *Against Appion* 2:175

430. Acts 15:21.

431. For more on the days of the lectionary cycle, cf. Martin Jan Mulder, ed., *Mikra* (Philadelphia: Fortress Press, 1990), pp. 137-159. This quote is from p. 148.

432. Lawrence H. Schiffman, "The Early History of Public Reading of the Torah," in Steven Fine, ed., *Jews, Christians, and Polytheists in the Ancient Synagogue* (London: Routledge, 1999), pp. 44-56 and Lee I. Levine, *The Ancient Synagogue* (New Haven: Yale University Press, 2000), pp. 135-142.

433. Schiffman, *op. cit.*, p. 54.

434. Levine, *op. cit.*, p. 139.

435. See Louis Finkelstein, הפרושים ואנשי כנסת הגדולה (New York: Jewish Theological Seminary, 1950), chapter 4 and *idem*, "The Men of the Great Synagogue (*circa* 400-170 B.C.E.)," in *The Cambridge History of Judaism II* (Cambridge: Cambridge University Press, 1989), pp. 229-244; Hugo Mantel, אנשי כנסת הגדולה (Israel: Devir, 1983) and I.J. Schiffer, "The Men of the Great Assembly" in William Scott Green, *Persons and Institutions in Early Rabbinic Judaism* (Missoula, MT: Scholars Press, 1977), pp. 237-283.

436. Cf. Henry George Liddell and Robert Scott, *A Greek-English Lexicon* (Oxford: Clarendon Press, 1968), p. 1720 for the various possible meanings of this Greek term, including "meeting," "junction," and "assembly-place," among many others.

437. Mantel, *op. cit.*, pp. 96-7.

438. See Abraham Kuenen, *Gesammelte Abhandlungen zur biblischen Wissenschaft* (Freiburg: Mohr Siebeck, 1894) and Schiffer, "The Men of the Great Assembly."

439. Schiffer, "Men of the Great Assembly," p. 270.

440. Note that other authors give responsibility for many other enactments to the *anshei kenesset hagedolah*, cf., for example, Frankel, *Darkhei HaMishnah*, p. 3, and Albeck, *Mavo LaMishnah*, pp. 37-8. Since we are very carefully limiting the purview of this study to occurrences that use the term *takkanah*, only four fit our criteria for inclusion.

441. See T Ber. 3:9, where this law is brought with absolutely no reference to any individuals, and where the blessing is said only over a cup, with no mention of any recitation in the *amidah*.

442. Cf. the top of BT Ber. 33b, where Ravina asks Rava for the final ruling, and Rava replies: "Like the *kiddush*, which even though it is said in prayer, it is still said over the cup, so, too do we say the *havdallah* blessing over the cup even if it is said during the *amidah*."

443. Roth, *Halakhic Process*, pp. 226-8.

444. An addition to the second blessing of the *amidah* added during the rainy season.

445. Heinemann, *Prayer*, pp. 28-9.

446. This initial explanation suggests that the sages made a concession to the needs of the participants in Megillah reading in the smaller towns, in order to prevent overwhelming numbers of people assembling in underprepared population centers on the same day, thus ensuring sufficient availability of services (water, food, etc.) to meet the demands of those gathering to hear the reading of *Megillat Esther*. Significant, here, is that the sages are credited with permitting the change of date to the 11th (from the 14th), implying that they allowed the shift of their own accord. This idea is subsequently rejected.

447. This explanation suggests that all the dates upon which the *megillah* could be read were enacted by the *anshei kenesset hagedolah*, and that the sages do not innovate here at all, instead they simply explain and implement an enactment that was bequeathed to them by a prior leadership that exceeded their authority, and which they therefore could not alter.

448. See Adele Berlin, *The JPS Bible Commentary: Esther* (Philadelphia: Jewish Publication Society, 2001), pp. 90-3.

449. For specific examples and explanations of the contours of Second Temple period use of *ketubbot*, see Michael Satlow, *Jewish Marriage in Antiquity* (Princeton: Princeton University Press, 2001), especially pp. 93-100, where Satlow helpfully summarizes the characteristics of *ketubbot* from the Elephantine and Babatha archives. The original texts of the Elephantine papyri are available in Betzalel Porten and Ada Yardeni, eds., *Textbook of Aramaic Documents from Ancient Egypt* (Jerusalem: Hebrew University, 1986), B2-3. For the Babatha *ketubbah*, see Yigael Yadin et al., *The Documents from the Bar Kokhba Period in the Cave of Letters: Hebrew, Aramaic and Nabatean-Aramaic Papyri* (Jerusalem: Israel Exploration Society, 2002), pp. 118-141. Two interesting Greek marriage contracts were also found in this cave, and may be found in Naphtali Lewis, *The Documents from the Bar Kokhba Period in the Cave of Letters: Greek Papyri* (Jerusalem: Israel Exploration Society, 1989), pp. 79-83 and 130-133.

450. See the Edomite marriage contract, dated to 176 BCE, which utilizes similar formulary to Jewish *ketubbot*, in Esther Eshel and Amos Kloner, "An Aramaic Ostracon of an Edomite Marriage Contract from Maresha, Dated 176 BCE," *IEJ* 46 (1996), pp. 1-22.

451. See M Avot 1:9 and BT Hag. 16b, for literary records of their connection. Cf., also, Frankel, *Darkhei HaMishnah*, pp. 37-8.

452. Cf. Judah Goldin, "The First Pair (Yose ben Yoezer and Yose ben Yohanan) or the Home of a Pharisee," *Association for Jewish Studies Review* 5 (1980), pp. 41-61.

453. Cf. BT Ket. 39b and PT Ket. 8:11, 42b.

454. Tosafot, *s.v.* עביט של נחושת גרסינן, has a different reading here which suggests "brass baskets" instead of vessels for collecting urine. The deliberate use of urine in this passage, however, works to highlight the plight of the impoverished woman left barely supported by her meager *ketubbah* settlement.

455. This, in effect, allowed the invasion of any portion of the husband's property for the payment of her *ketubbah*, and made him far more liable, thus raising the level of protection for the woman, and, ultimately, further sustaining existing marriages through economic means.

456. Satlow, *Marriage*, pp. 213-6.

457. Rabbis, either as a group or individuals, are cited as innovating in BT Ber. 33b; 40b; BT Shab. 14b (paralleled by BT Shab. 16b (cf. also BT Yev. 89a) and BT Ket. 54a); BT Pes. 109b-110a (paralleled by BT Pes. 117b); BT RH 34a; BT Suk. 56a; BT Ket. 8b; 10a; 12a; 47b (paralleled by BT Arakh. 22a); BT Hul. 26b; PT Ber. 2:4, 4d and 2:4, 5a (two occurrences). There are five innovations that are set in Usha: BT Ber. 49b (two *takkanot*) and BT Ket. 50a (three *takkanot*, one of which has parallels on BT Ket. 67b and BT Arakh. 28a; another has parallels at BT Ket. 78b, BT BK 89a-90a, BT BM 35a and 96b, and BT BB 50a and 139b). Yavneh is the site of two *takkanot*: BT Ber. 28a and BT Ber. 48b.

458. For instance, note the substitution of the Aramaic אתקין in place of the Hebrew התקין.

459. The exceptions are BT Shab. 14b, where Shimeon ben Shetah is cited in a *baraita* as instituting the use of a *ketubbah* in Jewish marriage, and BT Ket. 47b, where the rabbis set down obligations between husbands and wives.

460. Heinemann, *Prayer*, p. 14.

461. Moshe Greenberg, *Biblical Prose Prayer* (Berkeley: University of California Press, 1983), p. 52.

462. Lawrence H. Schiffman, "The Scrolls and Early Jewish Liturgy," in Lee I. Levine, ed., *The Synagogue in Late Antiquity*, pp. 44-45.

463. Lee I. Levine, *The Ancient Synagogue* (New Haven: Yale University Press, 2000), p. 154.

464. Heinemann, *op. cit.*, p. 29.

465. Cf. Ismar Elbogen, *Jewish Liturgy: A Comprehensive History,* Raymond P. Scheindlin, tr. (Philadelphia: Jewish Publication Society, 1993); Zahavy, Tzvee, *Studies in Jewish Prayer* (Lanham, MD: University Press of America, 1990); and Lawrence A. Hoffman, *The Canonization of the Synagogue Service* (Notre Dame: University of Notre Dame Press, 1979) for further understanding of this process of liturgical growth through the Tannaitic, Amoraic and Geonic periods.

466. This "pearl" is the prayer to be added as the fourth benediction on a festival day.

467. Many mss. skip the initial two statements of this prayer ("and You made known to us . . ." and "and You taught us . . ." and begin the prayer from "and bequeathed . . ." Cf. Rabbinovicz, *Didkdukei Sofrim, ad. loc.*

468. For a concise history of the development of the Havdallah blessing in the fourth blessing of the Amidah, see Elbogen, *Liturgy*, pp. 41-2. For one version of the blessing in current usage, see Phillip Birnbaum, *Daily Prayer Book* (New York: Hebrew Publishing Company, 1977), p. 201 or other contemporary prayerbooks.

469. Yavneh is mentioned explicitly in only the *takkanot* that appear in BT Ber. 28a and 48b.

470. This was the first blessing in *Birkat HaMazon*, the grace after meals, thanking God for providing sustenance. The connection with Moses came about through a linkage with the *mannah* that God provided to the hungry people in the desert as they traveled under Moses' leadership to the land of Israel.

471. This is the second blessing in *Birkat HaMazon* and deals with the blessing of the land of Israel. Since Joshua brought the people Israel across the Jordan into Israel, he is an appropriate literary personage to initiate this benediction.

472. *Boneh Yerushalayim*, "builder of Jerusalem," is the third blessing in *Birkat HaMazon*, and asks for the continued well-being and building of Jerusalem. Since David and Solomon built Jerusalem and the Temple respectively, it is only appropriate to give them credit for their completed tasks.

473. Since David was the first to strengthen the position of leadership of the Israelites in the Ancient Near East, and the founder of Jerusalem, it is also appropriate to assign him this prayer.

474. I.e., the Temple in Jerusalem, which Solomon first built.

475. Betar was one of the strongholds of the Bar Kokhba revolt, a fortress southwest of Jerusalem that was the last to fall in the revolt. Many Jews died at the hands of Roman troops when it fell in 135 CE.

476. Heinemann, *Prayer*, pp. 115-122.

477. Louis Finkelstein, "The Birkat Ha-Mazon," *JQR N.S.* XIX (1928-9), pp. 211-262.

478. Cf. BT Ber. 44a for the debate between Rabban Gamaliel and the sages on the contours of this commandment.

479. Translation from James H. Charlesworth, *The Old Testament Pseudepigrapha* (Garden City: Doubleday & Co., 1985), volume 2, p. 97.

480. Michael Stone, ed., *Jewish Writings of the Second Temple Period* (Philadelphia: Fortress Press, 1984), p. 103.

481. Cf. Heinemann, *op. cit.*, p. 115 and Moses Hadas, *Aristeas to Philocrates* (New York: Harper Brothers, 1951), p. 172-3.

482. Moshe Weinfeld, "Grace after Meals in Qumran," *JBL* 111 (1992), pp. 427-440.

483. Huub van de Sandt and David Flusser, *The Didache: Its Jewish Sources and its Place in Early Judaism and Christianity* (Assen: Royal Van Gorcum, 2002), pp. 309-325.

484. Cf. BT Ber. 46a.

485. Finkelstein, "Birkat Ha-Mazon," pp. 221-2. Weiss suggests just the opposite: that a Yavnean dating is too early, and that the *takkanah* must have been made in Usha. Cf. Weiss, *Dor*, Volume 2, pp. 130-1.

486. Cf. Elbogen, *Liturgy*, pp. 24-37 and Heinemann, *Prayer*, pp. 218-250. Lawrence H. Schiffman, writing on this subject in his *Who Was a Jew* (Hoboken: Ktav, 1985), pp. 53-61, argues that the blessing is entirely responsive to the schism that developed between Jews and Christians in the first century CE. Schiffman holds that while the benediction sought to exclude Jewish Christians from active participation in the synagogue service, it did not imply expulsion from the Jewish people. Reuven Kimmelman, on the other hand, in his "Birkat Ha-Minim and the Lack of Evidence for an Anti-Christian Jewish Prayer in Late Antiquity," in E.P. Sanders *et al.*, *Jewish and Christian Self-Definition* (Philadelphia: Fortress Press, 1981), pp. 226-244, suggests that the blessing was actually directed against Jewish sectarians, and that Christians were still welcome in synagogue services throughout this period. In short, there is little scholarly

agreement on any part of the debate connected with this blessing. Lieberman, *TK* 1, pp. 53-54, suggests that a blessing existed prior to Shimeon Hapakuli, but that he adapted it to apply specifically to the *minim* during a time when their separatism was endangering the community.

487. Cf. Heinemann, *Prayer*, pp. 225-6.

488. Strack and Stemberger, *Introduction*, p. 101, calls him either Hela or Ela.

489. Two parallels exist to this text, though without the discussion appended here after the initial *takkanah*: BT Ket. 67b and BT Arakh. 28a. Neither adds any new material to the discussion.

490. This Tannaitic source does not occur in any of our other extant rabbinic texts.

491. Rabbi Yeshabab was one of the ten martyrs reported killed at the hands of the Romans, and lived in early second century Palestine, at the same time as Rabbi Akiba.

492. The verse is interpreted in a creative way, which is hard to follow in translation. The original Hebrew of Gen. 28:22 uses an infinitive construct form that utilizes a repetition of the verb עשר, to tithe at the rate of 10%, based on the word for "ten," עשר, in Hebrew. The double usage of this verb in the biblical text is usually directly interpreted to the semantic end of emphasis—"I will surely tithe"—but the Gemara reinterprets it as doubling the permitted percentage of the tithe, from 10% to 20%.

493. The question at hand, here, is whether the second tithe will be equal in value to the first. The mathematics: begin with $100 in assets. The first tithe is 10% of the total, which is $10. The second tithe can either be 10% of the remaining total of $90, which is $9, or 10% of the original total, which would be $10. Thus, the difference is whether we have a top aggregate *tzedakah* rate of 19% or 20%. Rav Ashi advocates a second tithe equal to the first one, thus a top rate of 20%.

494. If you compare the various *takkanot*, and the tradents listed as reporting them on this page of Gemara, you find that the first *takkanah* is spoken in the name of Rabbi Elai in the name of Resh Lakish who received it from Rabbi Yehudah ben Hanina (though some manuscripts report Rabbi Yossi ben Hanina). The second *takkanah* is reported by Rabbi Elai in the name of Resh Lakish. By the time we reach this third *takkanah*, we find that it is brought only in the name of Rabbi Elai. Thus, the reports are decreasing in number and, perhaps, reliability. This is, clearly, a very late editorial comment, though Rav Shimi bar Ashi was a Babylonian student of Abbaye and Rava, according to Hyman, תולדות תנאים ואמוראים (ירושלים: פרי הארץ, 1987), vol. 3, p. 1114.

495. "Minors wrote and spent liberally" is a mnemonic device that indicates both the order of the enactments, and the relative reliability of them in terms of their attributions. In an oral transmission mode, this order and the reliability of the tradents in each case would matter greatly. This is doubtless a remnant of prior oral transmission that survived the writing of this passage.

496. *Mitzvot* here, as it often occurs in PT, means property that will be donated to charity.

497. PT Peah 2:4, 17a; PT Shevi. 1:5, 33b; PT Suk. 4:1, 54b; PT Ket. 8:8, 32c and the current source.

498. In BT: Ber. 33b and 40b; Pes. 109b-110a; RH 31b and 34a; Suk. 56a; Ket. 8b, 10a, 12a and 47b; and Hul. 26b. In PT: Ber. 2:4, 4d (three occurrences). The fact that the

three occurrences in PT are localized to the same page of Gemara is significant. Further, since all three occurrences deal strictly with the formulation of blessings in the *amidah*, this is stark evidence that PT contained a very limited range of initiation of practices explicitly attributed to the rabbis using the term *takkanah*.

499. David Kraemer, *Meanings of Death*, pp. 127-132.

500. For those who were involved in the process of burial and other community tasks, a drink in their honor at a house of mourning would certainly have been appropriate. This explanation is found in Mirsky, *Sheiltot Bereshit* 15, p. 101, and in certain manuscripts of BT. Cf. Moses Hirshler, *Talmud Bavli* (Jerusalem: *Makhon HaTalmud HaYisraeli HaShalem*, 1972), pp. 53-54.

501. Rabban Gamaliel was portrayed as the first to downplay his honor by being buried in sub par garments, in a valiant effort to teach the greater community to avoid embarrassing the poor through overly elaborate burial practices. See the continuation of this Gemara for a full description of this incident.

502. These customs may well have been modeled after Roman customs, where a special rite was held at the home of the deceased, followed by a funerary feast (called *silicernium*) that was eaten either at the grave or in the home of the deceased on the day of the burial. See J.M.C. Toynbee, *Death and Burial in the Roman World* (Ithaca: Cornell University Press, 1971), pp. 50-51. Greek precedents to these Roman customs included the *perideipnon*, a meal of consolation mentioned in the works of Hegesippos and Menander, who imply that it was eaten at the home of the dead and served as an occasion for relatives to gather, wreathe themselves and speak of the deceased's life and achievements. Frequent mentions of drink offerings also appear in a variety of Greek sources that mention burial. See Donna C. Kurtz and John Boardman, *Greek Burial Customs* (London: Camelot Press, 1971), pp. 145-7.

503. An official of the assembly, the role is rather unclear.

504. Michael Higger, *Treatise Semahot* (Jerusalem: Mekor, repr. 1970), p. 209.

505. It is possible, though very unlikely, that this was the earlier Rabban Gamaliel I. Shamai Kanter, *Rabban Gamaliel II: The Legal Traditions* (Providence: Brown University, 1980), pp. 207-8, agrees that Rabban Gamaliel II is the much more likely referent.

506. Urbach, *The Halakhah*, pp. 271-4.

507. Frankel, *Darkhei HaMishnah*, p. 66, counts ten *takkanot* when he includes another so-called *takkanah* in M Sotah 9:9. We, however, must exclude it because it fails to utilize the term *takkanah*.

508. The *dukhan* was the platform upon which the priests stood when blessing the people. Priests were required to serve in the Temple barefoot, and since the *Birkat Kohanim* was now their only remaining service, it was appropriate for them to do it barefoot as well. Cf. Urbach, pp. 271-4.

509. Cf. BT RH 21b, where the Gemara attributes a *takkanah* to Rabban Yohanan ben Zakkai permitting messengers to travel on Shabbat to notify communities about the new moons of Tishrei and Nissan.

510. I.e., after the destruction of the Temple.

511. While the Temple still stood, a convert to Judaism was required to offer a sacrifice upon joining the Jewish people, the smallest acceptable offering being two pigeons.

After the Temple was destroyed, the convert was still required (as we see in this *takkanah*) to set aside the appropriate sum, for s/he would be obligated to bring the sacrifice once the Temple was rebuilt. See BT Ker. 9a for the source of this obligation. The word "nest," here serves as a euphemism for these two pigeons.

512. This means that a convert might set aside this money as dedicated to Temple use, but then improperly use it for his/her own personal use, thus committing the rather serious offense of using sacred property for a profane purpose. To avoid this, the practice was cancelled.

513. "The fourth year vine" refers to the practice of bringing all produce from grape vines and trees up to Jerusalem from anywhere within a day's walk, in keeping with the rabbinic interpretation of Lev. 19:24. This ensured that the markets of Jerusalem were well stocked with produce during pilgrimage festivals, both because pilgrims would sell their produce outside the city, creating greater availaibility of produce for incoming pilgrims and thereby slowing the purchasing within the walls, and because some would actually bring their produce into the city itself, thus "decorating the streets of Jerusalem with fruit," as suggested later in this Gemara.

The "thread of scarlet" was originally fastened to the door of the Temple court, and if it turned white, the people knew that their sins had been forgiven at Yom Kippur. People would become saddened if it did not change color, so Rabban Yohanan ben Zakkai (or an undefined group, as we find in parallel texts, cf. for example, BT Yoma 67a) enacted that it be moved inside the door of the Temple, out of the sight of the community. People continued to peek in and become sad, so he was then credited with enacting that half be tied to the horns of the goat sent into the wilderness, while the other half remained fastened to a rock at the Temple Mount.

This debate between Rav Papa and Rav Nahman bar Yitzhak goes unresolved in the Gemara, so we do not have a firm final selection of the ninth *takkanah* attributed to Rabban Yohanan ben Zakkai. The fourth year vine *takkanah* makes more sense, since it, at least, could have been observed in a post-Temple milieu.

514. Rashi lists these throughout his commentary on the passage cited above, BT RH 31b.

515. The issue here was that since these months contained important holidays (Pesah and Rosh Hashanah/Yom Kippur, respectively), it was more important that the community be informed of their precise starting dates, to facilitate timely communal observance.

516. It does appear, ultimately, that this *takkanah* was not accepted into practice, despite the concern about misuse of sacred property. Cf. BT Ker. 9a.

517. The occurrences are: M Git. 3:2 (parallels in BT Git. 26a and PT Git. 3:2, 44d); M Git. 4:2 (parallel in PT Git. 4:2, 45c); M Git. 4:3; T Yev. 1:9 (two occurrences); T Ket.1:1 (two occurrences); T Git. 7:13; BT Meg. 2a and 4b; BT Yev. 99a, 108a and 112b; BT Ket. 50b, 57a, 57b and 80a (paralleled by BT BM 39a); BT Git. 15a-b, 34b (parallel to PT Git. 4:2, 45a), 36a, 49b, 50b, (two occurrences), 67b, 75b, 85b, and 86a; BT BK 8b and 62a; BT BM 3a-4b, 17b-18a and 49b; BT BB 21a, 131b (two occurrences), 140b and 160b and PT Git. 5:3, 46d.

518. The sources are: M Shev. 10:3 (paralleled by M Git. 4:3, *SD* 113, *Mtan Devarim* 15:3, BT Git. 36a and PT Shev. 10:2, 39c); M RH 2:8; T RH 1:14; T Ket. 5:7

(paralleled by BT Ket. 82b and PT Ket 8:11, 32b) and 12:1; *SZ* 35:22; BT Eruv. 45a (parallel to PT RH 2:3, 51a); BT Suk. 51b; BT Betz. 30a; BT Meg. 21b; BT MK 6b; BT Sotah 48a; BT Git. 17a (parallel to PT 4:2, 45c) and 47b; BT BK 94b and 103b; BT BM 8a, 10a-b and 51a; BT San. 19a (paralleled by PT San. 8:2, 20a), and two other occurrences on BT San. 19a; BT Men. 51b-52a; BT Bekh. 29a; BT Nid. 4b and 67b; PT Ber. 4:3, 6c; PT MS 4:5, 55a; PT Betz. 1:8, 60d and PT Git. 5:1, 46c.

519. Cf. the symposium in *Sevara* 2:2 (1991), pp. 61-73 for the opinions of Pinchas Shiffman, David Kraemer and David M. Gordis; for coverage of the traditional sources and modern practice, see Alfred S. Cohen, "Pruzbul," in *JHCS* 28 (1994): 17-29; for a literary-critical exposition on the sources, see Neusner, *Pharisees* I, pp. 217-225; for an historical approach, see Emil Schürer, *The History of the Jewish People in the Age of Jesus Christ* (Edinburgh: T & T Clark, 1979), 2:366-7; see also, Albeck, *Mishnah Zeraim*, in the *hashlamot* on pp. 382-3; Elon, *Jewish Law*, pp. 511-12; Bloch, *Takkanot*, 3:92-113 and Schepansky 1:301-313; Moshe Silberg, *Talmudic Law and the Modern State* (New York: Burning Bush Press, 1973), pp. 38-40.

520. Jastrow, *Dictionary*, p. 1218.

521. Schürer, *op. cit.*

522. Lidell and Scott, *Lexicon*, pp. 1504-5.

523. See BT Git. 37a and the *Penei Moshe* to PT Shevi. 10:2, 39c.

524. Silberg, *Talmudic Law*, p. 39.

525. Finkelstein, *SD*, p. 173. The text in brackets is only present in a few of the lesser manuscripts, and doubtless represents an addition lifted wholesale from the text of M Shevi. 10:4.

526. David Kraemer, "*Prozbul* and Rabbinic Power" in *Sevara* 2:2 (1991), p. 67.

527. This statement goes right to the heart of the matter: how can a lone rabbinic leader invalidate a positive commandment in the Torah? If this is the case, then the 248 positive commandments are all vulnerable to revision or rejection at the hands of the rabbis! This is an entirely untenable prospect in a system that deems the Torah its supreme legislation.

528. The idea being that since the Sabbatical Year was no longer observed, the Torah's command was now invalid. It is restored, in some sense, only as a lesser rabbinically ordained commandment.

529. Since, after the Babylonian exile, one could still remit debts even if the remission of landholdings had become impossible, the rabbis enacted that the practice of the remission of debts should continue as a reminder of the prior practice of the Sabbatical Year. This is similar to other cases of remembrances of prior practice in the Temple. This has the important effect of making the practice entirely *derabbanan*, as we saw in PT above.

530. Abaye's understanding is that a "sit and do nothing" situation implies that one should simply not act to observe this commandment, i.e., that debtors should not be required to repay their loans, thus sitting and doing nothing in the face of an obligation. As David Kraemer puts it: this is a "passive transgression (one which involves the failure to perform a particular act), which is not assumed to be a problem . . . The Rabbis here are thus arrogating to themselves the right to annul a significant minority of the Torah's

commands. This supposed resolution, which arguably renders Hillel's *prozbul* less 'radical,' turns out to be quite radical indeed." Kraemer, "Prozbul," p. 68.

531. Rava's understanding is based on the accepted idea that a court has the power to declare property ownerless (the Gemara continues from here to find scriptural support for this idea), which is probative in this case because the court is effectively dissolving the link a property owner has to property. If the court can do this, it can certainly dissolve the link between a lender and his/her owed debt, simply another form of property. À la Kraemer, *op. cit.*: "[T]he court assertedly has the power to declare property ownerless, allowing another party to take rightful possession. In this case, if the obligation to forgive debts derives from the Torah, then the *prozbul*, in effect, declares the borrower's property [= the worth of the loan after the Sabbatical cancellation] to be *hefqer* and thus enables the lender to recover the loan."

532. Kraemer, *op. cit.*, pp. 69-70.

533. The cases are: M Git. 5:5; (paralleled by T BK 10:5, BT Git 55a, PT Git. 5:5, 47a and PT BK 9:1, 6d); BT BK 66a-b and BT BK 84a-85a.

534. Albeck, *Mishnah Zeraim*, pp. 286-7 explains that she may accept the *get* on her own authority, even though, as a minor and a deaf-mute, she was considered to lack the functional mental capacity to marry on her own authority. Even lacking *daat*—the formal legal capacity to carry out her own affairs—she was still considered able to recognize conditions that were so inappropriate for her that she required a *get*, and to act against her father's will to dissolve the marriage.

535. *Terumah* is the food reserved only for those who are priests or priestly dependents. Since she began her life as a *bat-Yisrael,* a non-priest, by allowing her to eat this food, M is including her as a part of the family of priests. This stance is further strengthened by the inheritance rule that follows.

536. In the only parallel text, M Ed. 7:9, and in some versions of M, this explanation is left out. Cf. Epstein, *Mavo LeNusah HaMishnah*, p. 954.

537. BT Git. 55a explains that this is to prevent the priests from worrying that their sacrifices may be stolen, and might not be efficacious. So, to eliminate their concerns, the sacrifice is considered effective even if stolen, thus avoiding the thorny problem of invalid sacrifices upon the sacred altar.

538. Cohen, *Jewish and Roman Law* 1:19-20.

539. See Prov. 6:30-1, where the penalty for theft is seven-fold repayment of the item taken. Ex. 22:6 requires a two-fold repayment for stolen chattels.

540. M San. 1:1, following Ex. 22, would suggest at least a double repayment for thieves who stole chattel, with higher possibilities (four- and five-fold) for stolen livestock.

541. M MS 5:2; M Shek. 7:6; M Arakh. 9:4 (paralleled by *Sifra Behar Parasha*h 4 and BT Git. 74b); BT Kid. 26a (parallel to BT BM 49b); BT Kid. 43b (parallel to BT BM 5a); BT BK 97b; BT BM 27a (parallel to PT Shev. 7a, 37c); BT BM 83a; BT BM 100a; BT BM 112b (parallel to BT Shev. 45a-46a); BT BB 35b (parallel to BT BB 38a); BT BB 172a; BT Men. 107b; and PT MS 5:2, 56a.

542. M. Shek. 7:5-6; M Yoma 2:2 (parallel to BT Yoma 27a and BT Tam. 28a); M Suk. 4:4; M RH 4:4 (two occurrences, one parallel to BT Betz. 5a); T Eruv. 3:6 (parallel

to BT Eruv. 45a and PT Eruv. 4:1, 21d); T Zev. 11:16 (parallel to T Men. 13:18 and BT Pes. 57a); BT Ber. 23a (parallel to PT Ber 2:3, 4c); BT RH 22b; and BT RH 31b (parallel to BT Yoma 67a).

543. The cases are: M. Suk. 3:12 (parallel to M RH 4:3, *Sifra Emor* 12:19 and PT Suk. 3:11, 54a); M RH 4:1 (parallel to BT RH 29b and PT RH 4:2, 59b); M RH 4:4; M Men. 10:5 (parallel to T Men. 10:26, *Sifra Emor* 10:1, BT RH 30b, BT Suk. 41b, BT Men. 68b and PT Hal. 1:1, 54c); T RH 2:9; T Ket. 9:6; T BM 2:17 (parallel to PT BM 2:6, 8c); BT RH 31b; and BT Ta. 31a (parallel to BT BB 121b).

544. The cases are: M Ber. 4:1; M Ber. 9:5 (parallel to T Ber. 6:21 and BT Ber. 54a); M Shevi. 4:1 (parallel to T Shevi. 3:8 and PT Shevi. 4:1, 35a); M Shek. 1:2; M RH 2:1; M RH 2:2 (parallel to BT Betz. 4b); T BM 2:16 (parallel to *Mtan Devarim* 22:2 and BT BM 28b); BT Ber. 54a; and BT Pes. 56a.

545. The cases are: M Bik. 3:7 (parallel to *SD* 301:5 and *Mtan Devarim* 26:5); M Shek. 7:6 (parallel to BT Men. 51b, BT Men. 73b and PT Shek. 7:6, 50d); BT MK 27a (parallel to BT Nid. 71a); BT Sot. 32b; and BT Nid. 61b.

546. The cases are found in: T Yoma 1:7; BT Git. 80a; PT Ket. 1:5, 28c; PT Git. 5:7, 47b; and PT San. 1:2, 19a.

547. Albeck suggests that the reason for this waiting period was that it takes approximately three months for a woman's early pregnancy to show, thus, she was restricted from marrying a new husband until it became clear she was not pregnant with her deceased husband's offspring. This mechanism protected offspring by ensuring that their paternity was clearly known—a desideratum for the purposes of child support and the appropriate setting of custodial responsibilities.

548. The issue at hand here is the lineage of any children born in the first three months. Those women who were fully married (i.e., were both betrothed and married thereafter) before their divorce or widowhood occurred, could potentially be pregnant. Nonetheless, Rabbi Yehuda does not prohibit their immediate betrothal, because betrothal alone did not permit intimacy, and thus the child would clearly belong to the first husband, because the betrothed couple was presumed not to be having sexual relations. The converse is also true: those who were divorced or widowed from betrothal (and not from marriage itself) could marry immediately, since they were presumed not to be having sexual relations during betrothal, and thus any resultant child would belong to the second husband. This presumption did not hold true in Judaea.

549. M Ed. 4:7, M Git. 8:9 and other sources point to the difference between Galilean and Judaean customs in this respect. See Louis M. Epstein, *Sex Laws and Customs in Judaism* (New York: Bloch, 1948), pp. 126-127 and Cohen, *Jewish and Roman Law*, p. 322. Lawrence H. Schiffman, "Was There a Galilean Halakhah?" in Lee I. Levine, ed., *The Galilee In Late Antiquity* (New York: Jewish Theological Seminary Press, 1992), pp. 143-156, denies the idea of specific differences in Galilean laws, arguing that the same body of laws applied to both Judaea and Galilee, but that the Galileans generally exhibited stricter observance and more upright actions than the Judaeans. Thus, to Schiffman, the difference was not in the laws themselves as much as the local behavior in obedience to them.

550. See Jörg Wettlaufer, "The *jus primae noctis* as Male Power Display: A Review of Historic Sources with Evolutionary Interpretation," *Evolution and Human Behavior* 21:2 (2000), pp. 111-123 for a review of the historical sources related to this law.

551. See for, example, Tal Ilan, "Premarital Cohabitation in Ancient Judea: The Evidence of the Babatha Archive and the Mishnah (*Ketubbot* 1.4)," *HTR* 86:3 (1993), pp. 247-64 and William D. Howarth, "'Droit du Seigneur:' Fact or Fantasy," *Journal of European Studies* 1 (1971), pp. 291-312.

552. Ilan, "Premarital Cohabitation," pp. 248-256.

553. Esau is often seen as precursor and symbol for the Romans, especially in Palestinian Jewish sources. Cf., for example, PT Ta. 4:8, 68d; *GR* 65:21 and 67:7; and *SD* 41, ed. Finkelstein, p. 85.

554. When Jacob blessed his sons immediately prior to his death in Gen. 49, he used this phrase in his blessing of Judah. Here, the phrase is put into the mouth of the Romans to justify the particular violence of the Judaean-Roman relationship.

555. Roman soldiers were forbidden to marry provincial women, and even relationships with them were discouraged, as a soldier's first allegiance was always meant to remain with the state and the army. There are, however, many accounts of Roman soldiers involved in both rape and ongoing relationships with women from the provinces in which they were stationed, some of which eventuated in marriage. For a complete study of Roman soldiers and their marriage and sexual habits, see Sara Elise Phang, *The Marriage of Roman Soldiers (13 B.C. – A.D. 235)* (Leiden: Brill, 2001), with special focus on chapter eight where Phang concentrates on the soldiers' relationships with women from the provinces they patrolled. See also Biale, *Women and Jewish Law*, chapter 10, for a review of the basic Jewish legal tenets relating to rape.

556. Accepting the emendation of Lieberman, *TK* 6:187, n. 6, who suggests that we read this as נגדרת, that she would be "chaste," instead of the printed edition's נגררת, that she was "dragged away." *Penei Moshe* also accepted this as a likely alternate reading.

557. There are two possible reasons that this premarital intercourse might help her avoid rape at the hands of a Roman soldier: first, she might be less desirable in the eyes of the Roman soldier as she was no longer a virgin; or, the Roman soldier might understand that her fiancé might attempt to protect her, which might deter him for fear of vengeance. It is also possible that once a husband had intercourse himself with his wife to be, he did not harbor expectations that she be a virgin on their wedding date. Thus, by advancing the moment of first intercourse, it became less likely that intervening intercourse with another would lead to the dissolution of the engagement.

558. I.e., women from both social status categories (Israelites and priests) would be raped.

559. Thus, the preparations for the wedding feast (grinding flour for the baked goods, and other such activity) let the secret be known to the Roman soldiers.

560. The feast of a *brit milah* took place on the eighth day, at the end of the son's first week of life. Similar to the wedding feast, the Roman soldiers knew from the preparations that a celebration was in the offing.

561. The cases are: T Ter. 10:17; BT Yoma 69b; BT MK 17a and BT Ned. 10a.

562. Cf. PT Pes. 6:1, 33a.

563. See M Hag. 2:2 and M Ed. 5:6.

564. For a full treatment of the sources mentioning this term, see Hugo Mantel, *Studies in the History of the Sanhedrin* (Cambridge: Harvard University Press, 1961), pp. 102-129.

565. *Niddui* was the lighter form of ban available to the rabbis—it was imposed for 24 possible reasons (cf. BT Ber. 19a and PT MK 3:1, 81c) including contempt of court, insulting a scholar and causing the public to profane God's name. The *menuddeh* (banned individual) was not allowed to have social relations with the community, but could study in it, teach within it and engage in business dealings with its members.

566. The root סרח also carries with it the nuance of "smelled," "stank" or "decomposed."

567. This prooftext comes from the biblical story of Yehoash, king of Israel, when he replied to a threat from the king of Judah, Amaziah. Yehoash suggested that Amaziah and his forces would be better off to stay at home and avoid war. The selected verse is an apt one, as its continuation shows: "save your dignity and stay home, rather than provoke disaster and fall, dragging Judah down with you." Rashi plays on the root כבד in this text, which he saw as implying that the offending *av beit din* was to sit at home and hang his "heavy" head low. It can also imply having enough respect for one's "honor" (and the honor of the position of *av beit* din) to stay at home and avoid public embarrassment.

568. This implies that when a communal leader sins repeatedly, God's name is profaned. Once he has established a pattern of repeated violations, he can no longer be tolerated as a representative of the community.

569. See Adolf Bèuchler, הסנהדרין (ירושלים :מוסד הרב קוק, 1974), pp. 149-50.

570. The sources are: BT Shab. 24b, discussed here, and PT Ned. 6:1, 40a, where the rules on intercalation of the year are made more lenient due to a time of emergency.

571. This school of thought, associated later in this *sugya* with Rav Huna and Rav Yehuda, explains that since Hanukkah is not a festival that adds an additional service (the *musaf*) to the day (as other holidays, such as Sukkot, Pesah, Shavuot, Rosh Hashanah and Yom Kippur do), one does not make a change to the *musaf* service of Shabbat or Rosh Hodesh because of it.

572. This viewpoint becomes associated with Rav Nahman and Rabbi Yohanan in this *sugya*, and implies that Shabbat Hanukkah and Rosh Hodesh Tevet are, indeed, days when one adds a special prayer to the *musaf* service, because of the confluence of Hanukkah with each of these two other observances.

573. This is the closing service of the day, called *neilah* ("locking") because it symbolized the locking of the gates of the Temple at the end of the Day of Atonement. Cf. PT Ber. 4:1, 7c.

574. Only Yom Kippur requires *neilah*. Since Shabbat does not require this service but is still mentioned in it, the analogy with mentioning Hanukkah on Shabbat and Rosh Hodesh is appropriate, suggesting that mentioning it on these days is the correct course of action.

575. The cases: T Ket. 1:2 and BT Yoma 10b.

576. See M Ket. 1:2, where it says that the applicable *ketubbah* payment for an Israelite virgin is 200 *zuz*.

577. These opinions come from *Shitah Mekubetset* to BT Ket. 24a-b, PT Ket. 1:5, 25c and BT Ket. 24b, respectively. See also Louis M. Epstein, *The Jewish Marriage Contract* (New York: JTSA, 1927), p. 74, n. 60.

578. See PT Ket. 1:5, 25c.

579. See Satlow, *Marriage*, pp. 147-158.

580. Those that make law more lenient with no stated reason are: T Shevi. 1:1; T Shevi. 3:8; T Shevi. 6:27; BT Pes. 73a; BT Suk. 55a; BT BM 27b; PT Shevi. 6:4, 37a and PT Shab. 1:7, 4a. Those cases where law is made stricter with no stated reason are: T Kil. 4:1; BT Shab. 15b; and BT Hag. 24a.

581. From a total of 726 usages in the rabbinic legal corpus, 185 of these occurrences represent unique records of legal development, while the other 541 are parallel occurrences that supplement our knowledge, but do not represent separate cases of legal change. Basic texts, for the remainder of this discussion, are defined as those texts that represent unique discussions of a topic related to change in Jewish law during the rabbinic period. They may be single texts alone, or may also include parallels as well.

582. This coheres, as indicated in the introduction to this chapter, with the results of Jaffee, "*Taqqanah.*"

583. See, on this, David Weiss Halivni, *Midrash, Mishnah and Gemara.*

584. Remembering the listing of statements from each Amoraic generation in the conclusion to chapter one only heightens the effect of this data, and proves further that such a distribution points to actual trends.

Chapter Three

The Conservative Tendency: *Gezerot*

Introduction

In this third chapter, we turn our attention to the root גזר (*gazar*), which represents a conservative tendency in the rabbis' rhetoric of innovation. The word "conservative" does not represent stasis in law, but, rather, signifies a promulgation of new law designed to defend law already in place. It is legal innovation to be sure, but the sort harnessed to the service of protecting and enhancing observance of prior law. This distinguishes it from the reflective trend we saw in chapter one and the predominantly innovative tendencies evinced in chapter two.

More than the terms in other chapters, this family of roots exhibits remarkable consistency throughout rabbinic legal texts. In the vast majority of cases, גזרות (*gezerot*, "decrees") reflect an intriguing combination of the conservative desire to limit potential legal deviation by establishing a "fence around the Torah," combined with the innovative creation of new law. The ultimate goal was to create an overlay of preventive prohibitions that ensured that the essential core of the Written Torah was not violated. Though there are some exceptions to this rule, they are few and far between.

The Meanings of the Root גזר

Like the other terms studied, the root *gzr* reflects a wide semantic range, showing evidence of linguistic development between its earliest biblical occurrences and its usage during the rabbinic period. In the Bible, forms of this root occur 24 times, 16 times in the Hebrew sections, and eight times in the Aramaic of the book of Daniel. Within these occurrences, three basic strands of meaning emerge, arising in this chronological order:

a)   cut (in both noun and verbal forms)[585]
b)   decree/sentence (in both noun and verbal forms)[586]
c)   one who makes decrees, a diviner or exorcist[587]

From close examination of the chronology of these sources, some linguistic development becomes clear. In the earliest texts, we find the purely physical meaning of "cut," along with the direct physical applications of such a definition: "to

cut wood," "an area that is cut off from other space" and the like. The most in-
famous occurrence of this term, I Kgs. 3:25-26, reports King Solomon utilizing
this root to suggest that two competing prostitutes claiming maternal rights to
two babies, one alive and one dead, "cut" the live baby in half. King Solomon's
stratagem works, of course, and the living baby is returned to the proper mother.
In the process, we have two examples of the direct, physical meaning of this
verb in its early biblical phase.

It is only later, in the texts of Job, Esther and Daniel, that the more developed meaning of "decree" or "sentence" appeared. Job, the earliest of these three
texts, dates from the sixth century BCE, and was probably written in a context of
Persian domination.[588] Scholars argue that Esther, an ahistorical book, reached
written completion in two stages: an early version was probably completed in
the fourth century BCE, while the latter edition was likely completed slightly
before or during the Maccabean period, between 167 and 135 BCE.[589] Daniel,
likewise probably carrying on an older oral tradition, reached completion during
the period before 164 BCE.[590] This broad range of historical evidence, then,
shows that a shift in the meaning of *gzr* came about during the early part of the
Second Temple Period, sometime between the late sixth and the mid-second
centuries BCE.

Illustrative of this change is an occurrence of the term in Job 22:27-28,
where three "friends" offer Job their advice in the face of the calamities that
have befallen his family. Eliphaz the Temanite, in his attempted consolation of
Job, suggests that Job should try to forge a closer relationship with God, banish-
ing iniquity from his heart and seeking God's favor. If Job does so, then he may
expect God to accede to any decrees he may enact:

(כז) תעתיר אליו וישמעך ונדריך תשלם :

(כח) ותגזר אומר ויקם לך ועל דרכיך נגה אור :

27) You will pray to God, and God will listen to you, and you will pay
your vows. 28) You will <u>decree</u> and it will be fulfilled, and light will
shine upon your affairs.

Here, the meaning of *gzr* is "to decree"—to make a statement that has efficacy
to change the real state of the world. Thus, by the time of Job, Esther and
Daniel, we find that a new meaning has appeared next to the older one.

How *gzr* came to migrate semantically from "cut" to "decree" warrants attention. Biblically, the synonym כרת (*karat*, also "to cut" but more importantly
"to make a covenant") is used extensively as a legal term for making an enduring covenant.[591] Theorists of covenant ceremonies in the Ancient Near East note
the important function of a ritual act in validating and affirming the agreement

being made between the two parties involved. In the most common ritual, the ratifying of a new covenant culminated in the sacrifice of a live animal, as described by Delbert R. Hillers:

> The most widely attested form of swearing to a covenant, however, involved cutting up an animal. The man taking the oath is identified with the slaughtered animal. "Just as this calf is cut up, so may Matiel be cut up," is the way it is put in the text of an Aramaic treaty from the eight century B.C., and an earlier document describes a similar ceremony: "Abba-AN swore to Yarim-Lim the oath of the gods, and cut the neck of a lamb, (saying): 'If I take back what I gave you. . . . '" The consequence is not expressed and does not need to be. Abba-AN may have drawn his finger across his throat, or it may have been sufficient to point to the slain lamb. Among the Israelites, it seems that a common way of identifying the parties to a covenant with the victim was to cut up the animal and pass between the parts.[592]

Hillers' assessment of this ritual provides some assistance in tracking the developing meaning of the term *gzr*. The literal, physical meaning of *gzr* is synonymous with *krt*, the verb of choice for "cutting" a covenant. The use of this verb to indicate the affirming of a covenant no doubt emerged from the act of "cutting" the animal involved in the ritual completion of the agreement. Over time, *krt* came to acquire a figurative meaning as well: the ratification of a covenant between a more powerful party (usually a king or ruler of some sort) and his/her vassals. Completing a covenant implied a written text, often with curses or penalties for its violation, lists of involved deities and defined obligations incumbent upon each involved party. The shorthand for this process came to be represented by the Hebrew verb *krt*.

The most probable reconstruction of the development of *gzr* is based on the similarity between the functioning of a decree and a covenant. In both cases, the more powerful party would impose an agreement on the less powerful party, sanctioned by the deities involved, naming both the obligations and the substantial penalties and curses inherent in its violation. Thus, the jump from the physical "cutting" of a covenant to the authoritative passing of a "decree" follows closely the development of the root *krt*. Between the sixth and second centuries BCE, then, the root *gzr* moved from a simple verb for "cutting" to a term signifying the ratification of a decree by a powerful ruler that imposed responsibilities and penalties upon relatively less powerful individuals.

Further evidence for this semantic trajectory lies in the parallel development of the Greek verb κρίνω. Early instances of this verb's usage tend to indicate a meaning akin to "separation" or being "cut off." Over time, the meaning changed to include legal decisions made at trial, expression of the determination to do a certain act, and legal decrees relating to major communal issues, all directly parallel to the Hebrew *gzr*.[593]

Decisive evidence for this path of development comes from Joseph Fitzmyer, who notes the original sense of this verb as "to cut in two, divide," and shows a later figurative meaning of "to conclude a pact or treaty." In the Aramaic inscriptions of Sefire, Fitzmyer finds the origin for this usage in a ritual in which a calf is cut in two to conclude a treaty. Citing Dupont-Sommer's treatment of כרת ברית,[594] and Albright's suggestion of an Akkadian parallel,[595] Fitzmyer points to numerous parallel constructions in the ancient world: from *The Iliad* in Homeric Greek (ὅρκια τέμνειν) and the *Aeneid* in Virgil's Latin (*foedus ferire*) to the Akkadian expression *TAR be-ri-ti*. This surfeit of evidence points to the fact that the transformation of terminology from physical cutting to legalistic covenanting was a regular semantic occurrence in the ancient world.[596]

Unlike our prior two terms from earlier chapters, *gzr* also exhibits two occurrences in extant Second Temple literature. In the Qumran text known as 11Q10 or 11QtgJob, the root *gzr* appears in the *targum* to Job 21:21:

צבו לאלהא בביתה,
[ומני]ן ירחוהי גזירין.

Desire for God in God's house,
[and the num]ber of his months are [*sic*] set. [597]

Here, in this verb's passive form, we find further evidence of the shift from its original, physical meaning to a new, more abstract idea in which an all-powerful ruler set the parameters of a person's life. The fact that this verb is not used here in the original Hebrew of Job, but is selected in writing the *targum*, suggests an increasingly frequent and accepted usage of this meaning of the root during the later part of the Second Temple Period.

Another Qumran text from a fragment first published by J.T. Milik in 1956,[598] now known as the Prayer of Nabonidus, shows evidence of the deployment of this term in a different fashion, more exactly parallel to the evidence we found in some sections of Daniel noted above. Frank Moore Cross published a text, translation and commentary on the first few verses of this prayer,[599] in which we find the following:

וחטאי שבק לה. גזר והוא יהודי מ[ן] בני גלות על לי ואמר]
החוי וכתב למעבד יקר ור[ב]ו לשם א[להא עליא].

And God forgave my sin. A diviner—who was a Jew from o[f the Exiles—came to me and said:] "Recount and record (these things) in order to give honour and great[ness] to the name of G[od Most High]."[600]

Cross suggests that this text's lettering is a "characteristic Jewish semicursive," dating from 75-50 BCE. Here we see that the third and latest meaning from the biblical record is alive and well until at least the turn of the era. It is not difficult to imagine how this meaning came to be, either. In the ancient mind, decrees imposed by kings or other powerful figures were extensions of the will of the deities involved. There are cases, in fact, where we find ancient literature that describes kings, wise men and magicians imposing their will on gods who, in turn, do their bidding.[601] A diviner or exorcist (as some translators propose) is also one who imposes the will of a human upon a divine being. Thus, this meaning represents an extension of the verse in Job where he will decree and God will respond. It is, in a sense, an inversion of the usual usage, momentarily empowering the weaker party over the stronger.

Josephus utilized a standard Greek terminology when referring to decrees. Κρίνω, mentioned above for its similar development to *gzr*, became his verb of choice for the promulgation of decrees. He referred to the decrees themselves with the dually defined term that Christian writers also adopted for use when referring to their religious beliefs: δόγμα (*dogma*). Various Roman δόγματα appear in *Antiquities'* description of the relations between the Jews and their Roman rulers.[602]

By the time we arrive at the rabbinic period, we find that many different meanings have evolved, all attached to the basic idea of "cutting," and the subsequent development of "decreeing." Jastrow,[603] Sokoloff[604] and the review of primary texts in this research found the following usages of the root *gzr* (Hebrew and Aramaic) in rabbinic literature:

Meanings of the Root גזר in Rabbinic Literature

A) to cut, shear, split open, go to pieces, harvest[605]
B) to make a covenant or agreement[606]
C) to circumcise (arising directly from the physical meaning "to cut")[607]
D) a legal decision, court sentence, verdict (*gezar din*)[608]
E) a cut off, inaccessible region[609]
F) a hermeneutical principle that utilizes similar language between two texts to prove a legal point (*gezerah shavah*)[610]
G) to decree a communal or individual fast[611]
H) to decree a ban (*niddui*) upon a person[612]
I) a decree resident in the biblical text (*gezerat hakatuv*)[613]
J) balcony, architectural element projecting out of a wall[614]
K) wood, sticks[615]
L) to decree, enact a prohibition as a precautionary measure, prohibit, guard

The last category, (L), is where we will focus our attention throughout this chapter. Note, however, that even within (L) we may discern a variety of different sorts of decrees:

a.   God's decrees[616]
b.   non-Jewish kings' decrees[617]
c.   decrees of the government[618]
d.   decrees made by or upon outside parties[619]
e.   decrees or fences made by individual rabbis or groups of rabbis

Our study will concentrate on the final category, the extant records of decrees and precautionary measures established by the rabbis and other Jewish leadership.

As we did with the root *tkn*, we note at the start of our discussion the total number of occurrences of this term compared to the number of usages related to the final meaning (meaning "L") listed above:

Text	Occurrences of root גזר[620]	Usages related to "L" above[621]
Mishnah	28	13 (46%)
Tosefta	64	27 (42%)
Halakhic Midrashim	344	13 (3.8%)
Palestinian Talmud	308	142 (46%)
Babylonian Talmud[622]	1584	1052 (66%)

We can see from these figures that the usage of this term in the meaning of "enacting legal measures" is far more frequent in the Babylonian Gemara (66%) than in any of the Palestinian sources (3.8%-46%).

Some Characteristics of *Gezerot*

In light of the discussion of *takkanot* and *gezerot* in the introduction of chapter two, it is unnecessary to rehearse the definition, the sources of justification and other basic information about *gezerot*. Nonetheless, there are a number of characteristics present in the rabbinic legal corpus that help define the general characteristics of the *gezerah* in rabbinic usage in ways that transcend prior studies and definitions.

The prior terms, *barishonah* and *takkanah*, both exhibit substantial variations in usage throughout their data sets. For *barishonah*, the rationales employed varied quite a bit, as they did for *takkanot*. As we saw in chapters one and two, no single reason compels the majority of usages of either *barishonah* or *takkanah*. Instead, many different rationales each play major roles in powering the legal change described by these terms. In sharp contrast, the collection of *gezerot* found in our corpus exhibits substantially less variation in rationale: more than 90% of the occurrences are "fences around the Torah:" precautionary measures that extend the limits of negative commandments in order to prevent their violation. None of our other terms exhibit such high stability and consistency as we find in the subject of this chapter's research.

Before moving on to examine various examples of the rather limited scope of rationales that led our editors to include these fences in their texts, we must first examine the general characteristics of *gezerot* as defined by our texts, for the asystematic traces of a rabbinic ideology of legal change they indicate.

Rejecting the Fence

One unique property that divides *gezerot* from our other terms of study is that many *gezerot* mentioned in rabbinic texts do not gain ultimate acceptance in the discussion that follows. Surprisingly, a very large number of hypothetical and/or rejected *gezerot* appear in our texts, well over 100.[623] Besides the rejected ones, we also have a large number of disputed *gezerot*,[624] where two parties discussed both the possibility of accepting and rejecting the same *gezerah* without any final conclusion being reached in the rabbinic textual tradition. Such ambivalence is not the case at all with *takkanot* or with *barishonah*. With just a few exceptions, the prior terms generally indicated changes in law that were accepted by the editors (or at least never explicitly rejected). This was not at all the case with *gezerot*.

The reasons for rejecting *gezerot* turn out to be at least as interesting as the reasons for accepting them. In some instances, the editors of rabbinic legal texts chose to reject *gezerot* because they were not fully accepted by the majority of the surrounding community of Jews. In other cases, these texts rejected *gezerot* that were protective of a rabbinical enactment as opposed to a fence around the Torah itself. In still other cases, *gezerot* were rejected because the authorities discussing them did not believe that the highly skilled individuals involved needed the extra security of a fence around the Torah. We will examine each of these sorts of rejection, reviewing a few examples to make clear the boundaries of each ideological stance.

Communal Acceptance of *Gezerot*

One prominent principle that rabbinic texts suggest motivated the rejection of numerous *gezerot* was the idea that authorities may not make any decree that the majority of the community involved will not be able to bear. The most radical case of this sort appeared in a *baraita* in BT BB 60b, where the authorities involved declared it better to allow Israel to sin without knowledge than to impose a decree that would cause them to sin intentionally, if they were unable to bear the effects of a specific *gezerah*:

תניא: אמר ר' ישמעאל בן אלישע: מיום שחרב בית המקדש, דין הוא
שנגזור על עצמנו שלא לאכול בשר ולא לשתות יין, אלא אין גוזרין גזרה על
הצבור אא"כ רוב צבור יכולין לעמוד בה; ומיום שפשטה מלכות הרשעה,
שגוזרת עלינו גזירות רעות וקשות, ומבטלת ממנו תורה ומצות, ואין מנחת
אותנו ליכנס לשבוע הבן, ואמרי לה: לישוע הבן, דין הוא שנגזור על עצמנו
שלא לישא אשה ולהוליד בנים, ונמצא זרעו של אברהם אבינו כלה מאליו,
אלא הנח להם לישראל, מוטב שיהיו שוגגין ואל יהיו מזידין.

It was taught: Rabbi Yishmael son of Elisha said: From the day that the Temple was destroyed, it would be proper that we <u>decreed</u> upon ourselves not to eat meat and not to drink wine, but <u>we do not make a decree upon the community unless the majority of the community is able to comply with it</u>; and from the day that the evil [Roman] reign spread [over us], who make harsh and evil <u>decrees</u> upon us, and prohibit our observance of Torah and *mitzvot*, and do not permit us to observe the week of the son—and according to another version: "to save the son"[625]—it would be proper that we <u>decree</u> upon ourselves not to marry a woman and bear children, but we would find the seed of Abraham, our father, coming to an end itself, so, rather, <u>let Israel alone, as it is preferable that they sin unintentionally and not intentionally.</u>[626]

The text abandons the two suggested decrees in the *baraita* because they are too onerous for the majority of the Jewish community to uphold. The first decree, an act the text says is reflective of deep mourning in the wake of the destruction of the Second Temple, prohibited eating meat and drinking wine, two symbols of joy that were intimately connected with the Temple and its religious ceremonies. By outlawing these comestibles, the decree would have turned the simple act of daily food consumption into a constant reminder of the intense sadness affiliated with a communal tragedy. However, the text states that the decree was rejected, it being too difficult for the majority of the community to forego meat and wine, major staples in the ancient diet. Without communal acceptance of this law, it would become meaningless violation of a rabbinically imposed stringency instead of profound observance. It was therefore renounced.

In this passage's second *gezerah*, it is the permission to bear children that is at stake, an almost unthinkable restriction with enormous ramifications upon the future of the community. When the Roman government outlawed *brit milah* during the reign of Hadrian,[627] they called into question the community's ability to uphold a central pillar of religious observance. Without initiation rites to affirm a son's entry into the covenant, the identity definitions prevalent for centuries became untenably shaky. The considered *gezerah*, that of prohibiting bearing children, would certainly have solved the problem of uncircumcised sons within the community, but at too high a cost. The *gezerah* ultimately faced rejection because of a deeper, more important value: that of continuing the stock of Abraham into future generations, even if boys had to remain uncircumcised under the pressure of Roman persecution. The procreative drive being what it is, it was clear to the author of this text that human beings would not be able to withhold themselves from the procreation both commanded by the Torah[628] and encouraged by human instinctual drives. Thus, this text suggested it was better to avoid this *gezerah*, and prevent another sin (that of ignoring a rabbinic decree) from being heaped upon the already suffering Jews of the land of Israel, than to promulgate it and have them disregard it anyway. Clearly, this *tanna* saw the role of communal acceptance as significant in determining the ultimate efficacy of decrees.

There are a number of instances when this calculus of communal acceptance comes into play in our legal sources.[629] One fascinating example occurs in BT Hor. 3b in the midst of a discussion of the rules of liability in a case when courts ruled incorrectly. This passage even goes so far as to supply a prooftext to support the community's role in accepting or rejecting decrees:

מתיב רב משרשיא: סמכו רבותינו על דברי רשב״ג ועל דברי ר״א בר׳
צדוק, שהיו אומרים: אין גוזרין גזירה על הצבור אלא א״כ רוב הצבור
יכולין לעמוד בה. ואמר רב אדא בר אבא: מאי קרא? (מלאכי ג׳) ״במארה
אתם נארים ואותי אתם קובעים הגוי כולו,״ והא הכא דכתיב ״הגוי
כולו?״ ורובא ככולא דמי.

Rav Mesharshya objected [with this *baraita*]: our rabbis relied upon the words of Rabban Shimeon ben Gamaliel and upon the words of Rabbi Eleazar bar Rabbi Tzadok, who used to say: [we] may not impose a decree upon the community unless the majority of the community is able to comply with it. And Rav Ada bar Abba said: What is the prooftext [that supports this statement]? "You are suffering under a curse, yet you go on defrauding Me, the whole nation of you," (Mal. 3:9). But surely it is written here "the whole nation of you." [implying that the entirety of the nation must be unable to bear it before a law may be rejected. Even so,] the majority is considered [as though it were] the whole.[630]

The choice of prooftext is fascinating. In Mal. 3:9, God chastised the people roundly for ignoring the tithes. In the BT passage above, Malachi's utilization of the term "whole nation" in speaking on God's behalf is reworked with a common rabbinic concept, that the majority represented the whole, to imply that rejecting *gezerot* is permissible when they prove too difficult for the majority (as opposed to the entirety) of the people to bear.[631]

PT also has its own version of this statement requiring communal acceptance to validate *gezerot*. In PT AZ 2:8, 41d we will read, momentarily, of a decree prohibiting the use of oil that originated in the hands of a non-Jew. This precaution's earliest mention in our corpus comes in M AZ 2:6-7, where it is stated apodictically, followed by an opposing minority opinion:

אלו דברים שלגוים אסורין, ואין איסורן איסור הנאה . . . והפת והשמן
שלהן. רבי ובית דינו התירו בשמן.

> These items of Gentiles are prohibited, but their prohibition is not a prohibition against benefit . . . their bread and their oil. Rabbi [Yehuda HaNasi] and his court permitted the oil.

Probably, the basic idea was that preventing the sharing of oil acted as a fence against the sharing of wine. Preventing the sharing of wine was meant to prevent social intercourse and resultant intermarriage. The Palestinian Gemara, in explaining this fence, retrojected the origin of the prohibition against eating Gentile oil to Daniel's rejection of the food and wine of King Nebuchadnezzar of Babylon, based on a verse that speaks of Daniel's abstention from the food of a non-Jewish king in Daniel 1:8:

וישם דניאל על לבו אשר לא יתגאל בפתבג המלך וביין משתיו ויבקש משר
הסריסים אשר לא יתגאל.

> Daniel resolved not to defile himself with the king's food or the wine he drank, so he sought permission of the chief officer not to defile himself.

Though the Daniel verse does not explicitly mention oil itself, PT assumed it to be included in the food of the king.

Admittedly, there is good evidence for an early origin to this law prohibiting the use of oil made by non-Jews, though not necessarily from the book of Daniel. Joseph M. Baumgarten has shown that this restriction is already present in the apocryphal book of Judith (in 10:5), where oil is listed among the food supplies that the heroine took with her into the enemy camp. Baumgarten also notes the presence of this restriction in both Josephus' writings and in the Damascus Document from Qumran.[632] Thus, the antiquity of this prohibition is well established. The most likely scenario is that an older law was passed on through the generations, and when the editors of PT searched for its origin, they scoured the biblical text for evidence, and landed upon this statement in Daniel. This led them to make a connection between Daniel and what they later termed a *gezerah*.

In response to Daniel's purported rejection of wine from non-Jews, the next phrase of the mishnah notes that Rabbi [Yehuda HaNasi][633] and his later court decided to change the law and permit it. This led to a serious problem in the *sugya*, as PT wondered how it is that Rabbi and his court could have so facilely discarded Daniel's decree, since later authorities were never permitted to reverse prior decisions until they constituted a court greater in both number and wisdom than the earlier authority. In response to this challenge, the passage in PT AZ 2:8, 41d rejected the decision attributed to Rabbi and his court, and looked for another reason to accept the leniency that allowed use of Gentile oil. It finally finds just such a reason in the idea that the community did not accept Daniel's decree, thus invalidating it:

ר׳ יוחנן בעי: ולא כן תנינן שאין בית דין יכול לבטל דברי בית דין חבירו עד
שיהא גדול ממנו בחכמה ובמניין? ורבי ובית דינו מתירין מה שאסר דניאל
וחביריו!!? רבי יוחנן כדעתיה: אמר ר׳ יוחנן מקובל אני מרבי לעזר בי רבי
צדוק שכל <u>גזירה</u> שבית דין <u>גוזרין</u> ואין רוב ציבור מקבלין עליהן אינה
<u>גזירה</u>. בדקו ומצאו <u>בגזירתו</u> של שמן ולא מצאו שקיבלו רוב הציבור
עליהן.

Rabbi Yohanan asked: Did we not learn (M Ed. 1:5) that a court is not permitted to nullify the decisions of another court until it is greater than it in wisdom and in number? And [can it really be true that] Rabbi [Yehuda HaNasi or Nesiah] and his court permitted what Daniel and his colleagues prohibited? Rabbi Yohanan [speaks] according to his view [as it appears in other statements of his]: Rabbi Yohanan said "I have received a tradition from Rabbi Eleazar son of Rabbi Tzadok that any decree that a court decrees and the majority of the community does not accept upon itself, it is no [longer considered an effective] decree. They checked and found regarding the decree against [heathen] oil, and they did not find that the majority of the community accepted it [thus nullifying it].

PT attributes this statement on communal acceptance to Rabbi Eleazar bar R. Tzadok, but, oddly, does not mention Rabban Shimeon ben Gamaliel. Thus the BT's attribution is only half-confirmed. The ultimate outcome of this passage in PT is also rather fascinating. The text shows a claim of what can be considered the essence of rabbinic legal pragmatism: an authoritative body looking to the actual observance within a living community before a final ruling takes full effect. Without communal acceptance of its decrees, even the most well-argued and thoughtful intellectual legal position is doomed to failure in this ideology.

If the attributions in BT and PT are correct, then we have some potential Tannaitic evidence for the idea that a *gezerah* requires communal acceptance. Rabbi Eleazar bar Rabbi Tzadok (T2), cited by both texts, and Rabban Shimeon ben Gamaliel (T1), cited by BT alone, represented the leadership of the period following 70 CE, in the immediate aftermath of the War when Yavneh served as the great seat of Jewish learning. The array of authorities who discussed these opinions also tells us something important: in PT, Rabbi Yohanan bar Nappaha (PA2, d. 279), a leading teacher in Sepphoris, bore the tradition of Rabbi Eleazar bar Rabbi Tzadok. In BT, two contemporaries of Rava (BA4), Rav Mesharshya (BA4) and Rav Ada bar Abba (BA4),[634] brought the tradition in the name of Rabban Shimeon ben Gamaliel and Rabbi Eleazar bar R. Tzadok. Those cited as carrying these ideas forward prove that the concept that a community must show acceptance for a decree to be valid appears to have been in active discussion from first century CE Judaea to mid-fourth century Babylonia, and, ultimately, to the time of the editing of both PT and BT. It remains a longstanding and accepted principle in the ages that follow as well.[635] It also reflects a serious understanding of the interplay between the ideals of law and communal realities.

Finding the Right Frequency

Another major reason for rejecting *gezerot* came from the idea that the rabbis only made decrees on issues that arose frequently. The rabbis often discarded decrees that dealt with rare behaviors, probably because a fence around such actions was unlikely to prevent much of anything, if no one were actually performing the problematic behavior anyway. PT and BT use different language to express this ideal, but the core message is the same. In PT Yoma 1:1, 38d we read about the advance preparation of substitute high priests and substitute wives of high priests, lest some untoward impurity should make the original high priest unclean and thus unable to officiate at the Yom Kippur ritual:

מניין כשם שמתקינין לו כהן אחר תחתיו שמא יארע בו פסול, כך מקדשין
לו אשה אחרת על תנאי שמא יארע דבר באשתו? שנאמר "וכפר בעדו ובעד
ביתו." ביתו: זו אשתו, דברי רבי יהודה. אמר לו רבי יוסה: אם כן, אין
לדבר סוף. מהו אין לדבר סוף? שמא תמות אשה זו, ותמות אשה אחרת.
אמר רבי מנא עד דאת מקשי לה על דרבי יהודה, קשייתה על דרבנן, שמא
יארע קרי לכהן זה, ויארע קרי לכהן אחר. קרי מצוי, מיתה אינה מצויה.
<u>גזרו</u> על דבר שהוא מצוי, ולא <u>גזרו</u> על דבר שאינו מצוי.

What is the textual support for [M Yoma 1:1 when it says] "just as they prepare for him another *kohen* in his place, lest he become unfit, so, too, do we betroth another wife to him on the stipulation that something will make his wife unfit?" As it is said: "he shall make atonement for himself and his house." (Lev. 16:6) "His house," this means his wife, [according to] the words of Rabbi Yehuda. Rabbi Yossi said to him: If so, then there is no end to the matter. What is "there is no end to the matter?" Perhaps this woman will die, and the other woman will die! [Since no one is immune to dying, they could never appoint enough substitutes to totally fend off this liability.]

Rabbi Mana said: Why do you bring up difficulties against Rabbi Yehuda's position, when you should bring up difficulties against the rabbis' position? Perhaps this [first] *kohen* will have a seminal emission, and the other *kohen* will have a seminal emission. Seminal emissions are frequent, while [sudden] death is not frequent. [Thus, the rabbis] <u>decreed</u> upon a matter that is frequent, and did not <u>decree</u> upon a matter that is not frequent.

Rather than accepting that the rabbis made a decree concerning an infrequent occurrence, the editor of this passage has Rabbi Minna's statement initiate a reworking of the justification for the decree in M Yoma 1:1, to ensure that it derived from a frequent matter, that of seminal emissions, rather than the much rarer issue of the death of the high priest's wife during the seven days before Yom Kippur. Since such rare cases of mortality were very unlikely to occur during the precise period of preparing for Yom Kippur, it did not prove a suitable justification for a *gezerah*, and was discarded. Decrees were meant to provide answers to regular situations, not to the occasional oddity that might arise.

In BT, the same concept holds sway, albeit with different wording. BT BM 47a confronts the question of exactly what actions constitute the assumption of ownership during a purchase or barter transaction. In this section of the *sugya*, an Amora asks about a transaction of purchase made verbally with an uncounted bag of coins:

אמר מר: מכור לי באלו: קנה, ויש לו עליו אונאה. לימא סבר רב הונא
מטבע נעשה חליפין? לא. רב הונא סבר לה כרבי יוחנן, דאמר: דבר תורה
מעות קונות. ומפני מה אמרו משיכה קונה? <u>גזירה</u> שמא יאמר לו: נשרפו
חטיך בעלייה. מלתא דשכיחא, <u>גזרו</u> בה רבנן; ומלתא דלא שכיחא, לא
<u>גזרו</u> בה רבנן.

The Master said: [If a purchaser said:] "Sell me [that item for sale in exchange] for these [uncounted coins]" he acquired [the item], and [if the value is over one-sixth below the amount he exchanged for it] he [the buyer] may tender a claim of fraud [against the seller].

Shall we say that Rav Huna holds that coins can effect a barter exchange? No. Rav Huna holds with Rabbi Yohanan, who said: It is a matter of Torah [law] that [transactions made with] coins do effect the purchase.

And why did they say that pulling [an object near (called *meshikha*)][636] acquires [purchases, but the act of the buyer paying the appropriate amount of money to the seller does not]? It was a [precautionary] decree, lest he [the seller] say to him [the buyer]: "your wheat burned in the upper chamber."[637] [But] a matter that is frequent, the rabbis decreed upon it, while a matter that was infrequent, the rabbis did not decree upon it [thus this decree is not accepted as law].

Here, BT discards the decree that only pulling may effect transactions, since the case of a fire destroying the purchaser's property while it remained in the hands of the seller was too rare to justify legal change. Later in this text, this whole approach is ultimately rejected, and a decision made based upon a different principle. In the meantime, though, this tradition rejected a precautionary measure because it did not focus on the regularly occurring situation, but instead concerned itself with the rare act. This sort of reasoning recurs occasionally in both PT and BT.[638]

No Fence Necessary

We now turn to *gezerot* rejected as unnecessary due to the sufficient knowledge of the actors involved. This principle was applied to priests in two cases,[639] as well as to other leaders appointed within the community, as we see in this case where select appointees of the court took action while participating in the willow branch ceremony during Sukkot in BT Suk. 43b:[640]

"ערבה שבעה." כיצד? ערבה בשביעי מאי טעמא דחיא שבת? אמר רבי יוחנן : כדי לפרסמה שהיא מן התורה. אי הכי, לולב נמי לידחי כדי לפרסמו שהוא מן התורה! לולב <u>גזרה</u> משום דרבה. אי הכי, ערבה נמי <u>נגזור</u>! ערבה שלוחי בית דין מייתי לה, לולב לכל מסור.

"The willow branch ceremony [is observed in the Temple] for seven days." How? What is the reason that the willow branch ceremony overrides the Sabbath on the seventh day (of Sukkot [=*Hoshanah Rabbah* that coincided with Shabbat])?[641] Rabbi Yohanan said: in order to publicize that this [commandment] is from the Torah. If so, let the [seven-day obligation to lift the] *lulav*[642] also override the Sabbath, to publicize that it [too] is from the Torah! Regarding the *lulav*, there is a de-

cree in the name of Rabbah [prohibiting it on Shabbat, lest one inadver-
tently carry it four cubits in the public domain, and violate the Sab-
bath]. If so, for the willow branch, let us also make a decree! The appointees of the court bring the willow branch, while the *lulav* is [a
commandment] given for the entire people.

This extensive *sugya* continues far beyond this point, but for our immediate purpose we have read far enough. The stam of BT rejects this *gezerah* because of
the higher standard that is assumed to apply to appointees of the court. As Rashi
points out, possible Shabbat violation in the case of the willow branches was
limited to the priests and those invited to participate by court appointments.
While we might fear that regular members of the community would make mis-
takes in their observance of the willow branch ceremony, the priests and those
whom the court chose for this particular purpose can be assumed to be knowledgeable enough to avoid carrying, fixing or otherwise violating the rules of
Shabbat. Here, a potential *gezerah* was rejected as unnecessary by virtue of the
higher level of education of those involved in carrying out the action.

In a similar case, we find that the rabbis rejected the imposition of a *gezerah*
because it did not consider the physical needs of human beings during a festival.
In discussing permission to place two stones side by side to form a privy on a
festival (potentially prohibited because it might be considered building on Shabbat, a prohibited action), BT Betz. 32b says:

אבנים של בית הכסא, מותר לצדדן ביום טוב. איתיביה רבה לרב נחמן :
אין מקיפין שתי חביות לשפות עליהן את הקדרה! אמר ליה : שאני התם,
משום דקא עביד אהלא. אמר ליה רבה זוטא לרב אשי : אלא מעתה, בנה
אצטבא ביום טוב דלא עביד אהלא, הכי נמי דשרי? אמר ליה : התם, בנין
קבע אסרה תורה, בנין עראי לא אסרה תורה, וגזרו רבנן על בנין עראי
משום בנין קבע. והכא, משום כבודו, לא גזרו ביה רבנן.

Stones of the privy, it is permitted to put them next to one another on
the day of a festival.[643] Rabbah objected to Rav Nahman: We may not
stand two jars side by side in order to put a frying pan upon them.[644] He
said to him: there it is different, since he is making a tent.[645] Rabbah
Zuta said to Rav Ashi: From this [may we learn that] one is also permitted to build a solid seat on the ground during a festival, for one did
not make a tent?[646] He said to him: there, while the Torah prohibited a
permanent building, it did not prohibit a temporary building, but our
rabbis decreed against a temporary building because of a permanent
building. Here, because of his dignity, the rabbis did not make a decree
about it.

Here, while an accepted decree against the building of a temporary structure on a festival is reported, a second potential decree is averted for the sake of the dignity of the human beings involved.

With regard to the second *gezerah*, one might suggest that it made perfect sense to prohibit the creation of a privy on a festival. The building of the privy could surely have been done beforehand, or other alternate means of achieving the same function could have been found. However, here the concerns of dignity played more strongly than the rabbis' wont to prohibit temporary building. Since the seat of a privy has open space below it, it certainly fit the definition of a "tent," the rabbis' prototypical building.[647] Anyone watching could then derive from this permitted building project that it was permissible to build a tent (or more!) on a festival. Since human needs do not stop and start according to the ritual calendar, the rabbis saw that prohibiting such actions was an unreasonable legal stricture, and rejected this *gezerah*.

A *Gezerah* upon another *Gezerah*

In BT Yev. 22a, we find record of a *gezerah* made for reasons related to the image of Judaism in the eyes of those who chose to become Jewish. In this *sugya*, the discussion centers on the question of the applicability of the laws of incest to converts. At issue is the question of the convert's status: since Rabbi Yossi's dictum says that a convert is considered "as a newborn child," and is thus devoid of his or her prior familial connections, the question arises as to whether the laws of incest could still apply in the case of a convert:

אמר ליה רבא לרב נחמן: חזי מר האי מרבנן דאתא ממערבא ואמר, בעו
במערבא: <u>גזרו</u> שניות בגרים, או לא <u>גזרו</u> שניות בגרים? אמר ליה: השתא
ומה ערוה גופה, אי לאו שלא יאמרו באין מקדושה חמורה לקדושה קלה,
לא <u>גזרו</u> בהו רבנן, שניות מיבעיא?

Rava said to Rav Nahman: Did the Master see this [statement] from one of our rabbis who came from the West [from Palestine] and said: they asked in the West, did the rabbis <u>decree</u> second [degree incest regulations][648] upon converts to Judaism, or did they not <u>decree</u> second [degree incest regulations] upon converts to Judaism? He [Rav Nahman] said to him [Rava]: now since with [first degree] incest itself, our rabbis only <u>decreed</u> it [for converts] lest they say that they went from a more severe state of sanctity to a more lenient state of sanctity,[649] can we [even think to] say [that they imposed] second [degree incest regulations upon converts]?

Relying on Rabbi Yossi's dictum of a convert's symbolic rebirth as noted above, the rabbis recognized that converts were not prevented by the Torah from engaging in even the first degrees of incest. However, considering how this might reflect upon the Jewish community in the eyes of others (and probably because of a general recoiling from the very idea of permitting any type of incest in any case), the rabbis are shown to have instituted this prohibition upon the convert preventing him from marrying his closest relatives. Rav Nahman, thereafter, rejects the premise that second degree limitations should be decreed, especially since the first level limitations were instituted only to prevent the perception of Judaism as a more lenient faith that permitted incest. Hence, while assuring the positive perception of Judaism in the eyes of others proved a valid argument for the first level of restrictions, it only went so far. Second level restrictions were not applied to converts in the end, for that would be tantamount to imposing a *gezerah* upon another *gezerah*. The position against this practice of making one decree upon another is strongly represented in both BT and PT, as we shall presently see.

Both Talmuds explicitly reject a number of restrictive laws because they attempted to impose a more stringent preventive measure upon an extant preventive measure.[650] In another occurrence of this rule, in BT Hul. 104a-b, the rabbis struggle over the derivation of the idea itself, even as they rule on the *gezerah* at hand:

ואסור להעלות. אמר רב יוסף: שמע מינה בשר עוף בחלב דאורייתא, דאי
סלקא דעתך דרבנן, אכילה גופה גזירה, ואנן נגזר העלאה אטו אכילה!
ומנא תימרא דלא גזרינן גזירה לגזירה? דתנן: חלת חוצה לארץ נאכלת עם
הזר על השלחן, וניתנת לכל כהן שירצה. אמר ליה אביי: בשלמא אי
אשמועינן חלת חוצה לארץ בארץ, דאיכא למיגזר משום חלת הארץ
דאורייתא ולא גזרינן. איכא למשמע מינה אלא חו"ל, משום דליכא
למיגזר הוא, אבל הכא, אי שרית ליה לאסוקי עוף וגבינה, אתי לאסוקי
בשר וגבינה, ומיכל בשר בחלב דאורייתא. מתקיף לה רב ששת: סוף סוף,
צונן בצונן הוא! אמר אביי: גזירה שמא יעלה באילפס רותח, סוף סוף כלי
שני הוא, וכלי שני אינו מבשל! אלא: גזירה שמא יעלה באילפס ראשון:

"It is forbidden to serve [meat with cheese on the same table]."[651] We learn from this that the meat of fowl [cooked] in milk is [forbidden] by the law of the Torah, for if you might think that it was [a prohibition] from our rabbis that eating [the meat of fowl with milk products] itself is a <u>decree</u>, would we <u>decree</u> against serving it because it leads to eating [it]?

And whence can you say that we do not make one <u>decree</u> upon another <u>decree</u>? As it was taught [in M Hal. 4:8]: the *hallah* [dough offering] of produce grown outside the land of Israel may be eaten with the stranger [i.e., the non-priest] at the table, and may be given to any priest one desires.[652]

Abaye said to him: this [logic] makes sense only if we were told that *hallah* grown outside the land of Israel may be eaten [at the table with a non-priest] inside the land of Israel, for then it would be appropriate to make a decree regarding *hallah* of the land of Israel, which is prohibited by the Torah, but they did not make it. From this [the decision not to make a decree in this case] we may learn [that you do not make a decree upon another decree]. [There is a problem, though:] outside the land, there is no reason to make a decree [thus, there is no way one would make a decree on another decree in this case].

But here [the case is different, for] if you permit him to serve fowl and cheese, he will come to serve meat and cheese, and [eventually] eat meat and cheese [that is forbidden] from the Torah.

Rav Sheshet objected: in the end, it is only cold [food] with cold [food]![653] Abaye said: it is a decree lest it be served in a still boiling stew pot. But in the end it is only [serving it in] a second pot[654] [which was not directly heated on the stove], and a second pot does not cook [and is therefore unable to violate the biblical restriction]! Rather, it is a decree lest it come upon the table in a stew pot [that was heated directly on the stove, with the resultant possibility that it would lead to the cooking of milk and meat together and thus violate the root principle from the Torah].

Here, the very idea of making a decree upon another decree is rejected outright, and this opinion is the accepted position in each and every occurrence of this debate in both BT and PT. While it is clear that the rabbis wanted to make fences around the Torah to ensure that violations were kept to a minimum, it is also clear that they did not desire to extend that process to secondary or tertiary levels. Both Talmuds conclusively reject the making of secondary decrees (in fact, any level beyond the first precautionary measure).

In this case, the final decision prohibited the placing of fowl and cheese together on the table, but not, however, as a *gezerah* upon another *gezerah*. Instead, supplying another reason, this passage reframes the issue in new terms: now, serving fowl and milk products was prohibited to avoid the possibility that, in the end, meat and cheese might be cooked together accidentally when placing these two items on the table in close proximity to a vessel that can cook. Thus, while a *gezerah* does result, it may not be balanced atop another *gezerah*—it must stand on its own in preventing the violation of a law from the Torah.

In PT, though expressed in different language, a similar viewpoint held against the layering of one *gezerah* onto another. PT Shevi. 2:6, 33d provides us with a glimpse of the editor's view on this question:

אין נוטעין ואין מבריכין ואין מרכיבין ערב שביעית פחות משלשים יום
לפני ראש השנה. ואם נטע או הבריך או הרכיב יעקור. . . . לא עקר
פירותיו, מה הן? רבי בא רבי לא הוון יתבין בצור. אתא עובדא קומיהון:
הורי רבי לא ישפכו פירותיו. אמר רבי בא: אני לא נמניתי עמהן בעלייה.
אמרין: נצא לחוץ, נלמד. נפקון ושמעון רבי יונה רבי יצחק בר טבליי בשם
רבי לעזר: אין מחדשין על <u>הגזירה</u>. ר' יוסה רבי יצחק בר טבליי בשם רבי
לעזר אין מוסיפין על <u>הגזירה</u>.

> They do not plant [a tree], and they do not sink [vines into the ground], and they do not graft [plants onto other plants] fewer than thirty days before Rosh Hashanah in the year preceding a Sabbatical Year. But if one planted, or rooted or grafted, one must uproot it. (M Shevi. 2:6). . . .

> If one did not uproot the resultant produce, what then [is its status]? Rabbi Ba [and] Rabbi La[655] were sitting [in a court session] in Tyre. A case came before them [relating to this matter]: Rabbi La taught that one must destroy all the resultant produce. Rabbi Ba said: I was not counted among those in the upper chamber [when a decision was made on this issue. Since I did not help decide it, I cannot rule upon it now].

> They said: let us go outside and learn [what to do in this case]. They went out and heard Rabbi Yonah [and] Rabbi Yitzhak bar Tablai in the name of Rabbi Eleazar [say]: We do not make new [law] based upon a <u>decree</u>.[656] Rabbi Yosah [and] Rabbi Yitzhak bar Tablai in the name of Rabbi Eleazar [said]: we do not add to a <u>decree</u>.

In PT as in BT, we find that the clear and undeniable outcome of this discussion and all others like it is that authorities may not pile one *gezerah* upon another. Though the tree planted during the lead-in to the Sabbatical Year in this case is itself forbidden through a *gezerah*, its fruits are not. The essential problem, here, is that of too many consequences. If prohibiting the fruit were an acceptable halakhic decision, there would be no end to *gezerot*. Ultimately, *gezerot* are limited to those areas where a fence is placed around the Torah. One fence is the maximum allowable.

The Disputed Fence

In a number of cases, fences suggested by the rabbis are disputed, with no final decision stated as to their disposition. There were two main sorts of disputes that fit this category: the first involved *gezerot* accepted by one party but rejected by another. These ultimately remained in their disputed status, with no final decision stated in rabbinic texts. The second set of disputed *gezerot* is actually accepted, but the reasoning behind the *gezerah* allows significant room for multi-vocal argument. Often, in these cases, we see a variety of reasons being offered for the same *gezerah*, with no final agreement on the selected rationale by discussion's end. We will examine a few such examples of both sorts of disputed *gezerot*, to help form an understanding of this phenomenon.

Disputed Decrees I—Indeterminate Decrees

Disputed decrees are those where two or more parties disagree as to whether the decree was acceptable or not. The parties to these discussions range from Palestinian pre-Tannaim (such as Yose ben Yohanan) to fifth generation Babylonian Amoraim such as Rav Papa and Rav Zabed, and their dating spans the first through fifth centuries CE. Discussions of disputed *gezerot* are extant in both Palestinian and Babylonian sources, though BT includes far more instances (50) than PT (only 1), which implies a far greater Babylonian editorial focus on the intellectual underpinnings of this conservative aspect of the process of legal change.[657]

In BT Suk. 14a, the Gemara discusses a dispute between Rabbi Yehuda and Rabbi Meir first mentioned in M Suk. 1:6, about the suitability of planed boards for use as *sekhakh*[658] on the top of a *sukkah*. The mishnah reads:

מסככין בנסרים דברי רבי יהודה, ורבי מאיר אוסר. נתן עליה נסר שהוא
רחב ארבעה טפחים : כשרה, ובלבד שלא יישן תחתיו.

One may use planed boards for *sekhakh*, [these are] the words of Rabbi Yehuda; but Rabbi Meir prohibits it. If one placed upon it [the *sukkah*] a planed board that is four handbreadths wide, it is valid, as long as one does not sleep underneath it.

BT Suk. 14a adds an Amoraic overlay to this Tannaitic dispute, which calls Rabbi Meir's position a *gezerah*:

אמר רב : מחלוקת בנסרין שיש בהן ארבעה, דרבי מאיר אית ליה גזרת
תקרה, ורבי יהודה לית ליה גזרת תקרה. אבל בנסרין שאין בהן ארבעה
דברי הכל כשרה. ושמואל אמר : בשאין בהן ארבעה מחלוקת, אבל יש בהן

ארבעה : דברי הכל פסולה. אין בהן ארבעה, ואפילו פחות משלשה : הא
קנים בעלמא נינהו! אמר רב פפא, הכי קאמר : יש בהן ארבעה, דברי הכל
פסולה ; פחות משלשה, דברי הכל כשרה. מאי טעמא? קנים בעלמא נינהו.
כי פליגי : משלשה עד ארבעה. מר סבר : כיון דליתנהו שעור מקום, לא
<u>גזרינן</u> ; ומר סבר : כיון דנפקי להו מתורת לבוד, <u>גזרינן</u>.

Rav said: the disagreement was about planed boards that were at
least four handbreadths wide, for Rabbi Meir held that a *gezerah* had
been made that prohibited boards that resembled those of the roof of a
house,[659] while Rabbi Yehuda did not hold that a *gezerah* had been
made that prohibited their use as a roofing material [in a *sukkah*]. But
for planed boards that were less than four handbreadths wide, all agreed
they are permitted.[660]

But Shmuel said: the disagreement was over [planed boards] less
than four handbreadths wide, but for [boards] four or more handbreadths wide, all agree that they are invalid.

[But this is a problem: boards whose width is] less than four
[handbreadths], and certainly less than three, these are merely sticks.

Rav Papa said: this is what he [Shmuel] meant: All agree that
[planed boards] four handbreadths or wider are invalid; all agree that
[planed boards] narrower than three handbreadths are valid. What is the
reason? Because they are merely sticks. When they disagreed, it was
about [planed boards] between three and four [handbreadths wide]. One
master [=Rabbi Yehuda] thought: since they have not reached the
measure of "place,"[661] we do not make a <u>decree</u> [that they are invalid];
the other master [=Rabbi Meir] thought: since they do not fit the category of *lavud*,[662] we do make a <u>decree</u>.

Rabbi Meir and Rabbi Yehuda's disagreement is understood in no less than
three different ways, all reinterpreted by opinions attributed to Babylonian Amoraim from the mid-third century.

We may learn from this disagreement of *Tannaim* and its Amoraic overlay
that not every *gezerah* left a clear trail of history in its wake. There are two possible ways to read the legal history suggested within this passage. First, it is possible that this *gezerah* did exist, and while Rabbi Meir knew it, Rabbi Yehuda
never caught wind of its existence. If this were the case, then the preserved discussion of the Amoraim provides an accurate portrayal of the underlying
thought processes that led to the disagreement.

On the other hand, the interplay between M and BT forces us to consider the possibility that no such *gezerah* ever existed at all, or that it did not exist before the Amoraic period. Since we find no explicit mention of a decree in the initial reading of the text in M, but simply two conflicting opinions on the use of planed boards in a *sukkah*, there is no significant Tannaitic evidence of a decree at all. Instead, one may read this decree as wholly part of the Amoraic overlay, where Rav, Shmuel and Rav Papa all *understand* the opinions expressed as indicative of a valid decree accepted by Tannaim. In this case, unfortunately, there is no further information available as to when or where the actual decree was made (if, indeed, it was). The best we can say is that we have evidence of a disputed decree, possibly discussed in the end of the first century CE, upon which Rabbi Meir appears to have based an opinion. It is more likely, however, that here BT assumes (or invents?) a decree based on a Tannaitic hint from M, without out concrete evidence.

In contrast to this possibly Tannaitic and possibly Amoraic record of a *gezerah*, we find another source that provides us with an example of a disputed decree in a purely Amoraic record. BT Shab. 146b begins with a debate based on M Shab. 22:3, where the use of a barrel on Shabbat is the topic of the moment. The particular piece of M that spurs this disagreement, a text centered on the permissibility of sealing a barrel's opening with wax on Shabbat, leads us to this discussion in the Gemara:

ואם היתה נקובה וכו'. מישחא; רב אסר, ושמואל שרי. מאן דאסר : <u>גזרינן</u>
משום שעוה, ומאן דשרי : לא <u>גזרינן</u>. אמר ליה רב שמואל בר בר חנה לרב
יוסף : בפירוש אמרת לן משמיה דרב מישחא שרי.

> "And if it [the barrel] were [already] open, etc." Oil [used for closing the hole of a barrel on Shabbat], Rav prohibited it, but Shmuel permitted it. The one who prohibited it [=Rav] did so as a <u>decree</u> because of wax;[663] and the one who permitted it [=Shmuel, held] that we did not make a <u>decree</u>. Rav Shmuel bar Bar Hannah said to Rav Yosef: explicitly you said to us in the name of Rav that [using] oil [in this way] is permitted.

Here, too, we see a debate on whether a decree occurred or not, but this time it is limited to the opinions of two Amoraim, Rav and Shmuel. Again, here, we see that the degree of uncertainty is high, especially when we take into account the last statement from Rav Shmuel bar Bar Hanah, entirely discounting the stated opinion of Rav. Here, it is clearly the *stam* that calls Rav's opinion a decree, the named Amoraim themselves do not use this terminology.

We are left with a tangled morass of conflicting information, with no clear outcome on the results of this discussion during the Amoraic period. What we can learn, however, is that it was common practice for subsequent generations (whether they are Amoraim or Stammaim) to call earlier decisions *gezerot* when the earlier authorities did not use this terminology. This indicates, once again, the Amoraic and Stammaitic willingness to recast prior information in more legally authoritative terms.

In a short text from BT Git. 21b-22a, we find two fourth generation Amoraim, Abaye and Rava, arguing about the existence of a *gezerah* in much the same manner:

כתבו . . . על עלה של עציץ נקוב, אביי אמר: כשר; ורבא אמר: פסול.
אביי אמר כשר, דשקיל ליה ויהיב ליה ניהלה; רבא אמר פסול, <u>גזרה</u> שמא
יקטום.

> If one wrote [a *get*] . . . on a leaf that grew in a perforated earthenware flowerpot [embedded in the soil, yet removable], Abaye said it is valid; and Rava said it is invalid. Abaye said it is valid, because he may take it [the entire pot] and give it to her; Rava said it is invalid, because it is a <u>decree</u> lest he pluck off the leaf [and give that to her].[664]

Here, similarly, we have the early hint of a decree, but it is only called a decree in the latest layer of text from the *stam*. The *stam* portrayed Rava's opinion as a decree to protect *gittin* written on leaves from being invalidated when a part of the leaf was plucked from the plant. The act of detaching the leaf invalidated it as a legal document. Abaye had no such worries, and saw this as a valid *get*, because one could remove the whole pot (and thus the entire plant) from the earth, which caused no danger to the validity of the *get*. Abaye did not see the detaching of a perforated pot as an intermediary step, since it was already semi-detached by the pot itself. Again, within the rabbinic legal sources, there is no ultimate resolution on the validity of the *gezerah* in this case either.

One last example of a disputed *gezerah* comes from PT Hal. 4:12, 60b, and is the only one like it to be found in the entire PT. In citing a *baraita* that follows from the discussion in M Hal. 4:10, PT portrays Rabbi Hiyya and Rabbi Abba bar Zabda as determining what should be done with *hallah* (dough offering) that is brought into Israel from outside the land:

תני רבי חייה: <u>גזרו</u> עליהן והחזירום למקומן. אמר רבי בא בר זבדא:
איפשר לאוכלה? אין את יכול שלא יאמרו ראינו תרומה טמאה שנאכלת.
לשורפה? אין את יכול שלא יהו אומרים ראינו תרומה טהורה נשרפת.
להחזירה למקומה? אין את יכול שלא יהו אומרין ראינו תרומה יוצא מן
הארץ לחוץ לארץ. הא כיצד? מניחה עד הפסח ושורפה.

Rabbi Hiyya taught: they <u>decreed</u> upon them [i.e., those who brought dough offerings from abroad] and they returned it [the dough offering] to its [original] place. Rabbi [Ab]ba bar Zabda said: [Instead,] is it possible to eat it? You may not eat it, so that the people do not say "we saw unclean *terumah* that was eaten." [Is it possible] to burn it? You may not burn it, so that people do not say "we saw pure *terumah* being burned." [Is it possible] to return it to its [original] place? You may not, so that people do not say "we saw *terumah* leave the land [of Israel] to outside of the land." What then? Leave it until Pesah and burn it [then, with the other leaven acquired over the course of the year as is required in preparation for Pesah anyway].

Once again, we see the suggestion of a decree, but no complete confirmation of its existence, since the following opinions indicate substantial unease with its thrust. Rabbi Abba bar Zabda raises four possibilities (one of which validates the decree, potentially) as alternatives. Rabbi Hiyya (PA3) and Rabbi Abba bar Zabda (PA2) lived in the third century CE, and were students of the school of Rabbi Yohanan in Tiberias.

Examining all *gezerot* that are disputed in BT (50 occurrences) and PT (only one occurrence), we find that the significant variation between BT and PT points to the fact that this does not present an accurate historical record that is to be relied upon. Rather, it appears that BT is more willing to posit theoretical explanations of potential *gezerot* that are later rejected. PT, in contrast, is far less prone to doing so. Here, editorial tendencies had a direct and vital effect on the portrayal of legal change that is not readily to be dismissed.

Disputed Decrees II—Multiple Rationales for the Same Decree

In 14 cases in BT (and none in PT) we find *gezerot* with multiple potential rationales. As opposed to the majority of *gezerot* in our literature, these decrees stand out as ambiguous in reason. Despite such stark lack of unanimity on the reasoning, these *gezerot* are regularly presented as binding law.

One interesting example actually provides the reader with no less than five different possible reasons for the same *gezerah*. BT includes a glimpse of a discussion of the reason for the *gezerah* that prohibited immersion of vessels on Shabbat and Yom Tov. This disagreement is based upon M Betz. 2:2, which treats the premise of immersion on Shabbat of vessels required for use on a subsequent festival:

חל להיות אחר השבת, בית שמאי אומרים מטבילין את הכל מלפני
השבת; ובית הלל אומרים כלים מלפני השבת ואדם בשבת:

When it [=the Festival] fell after Shabbat (on Sunday), Beit Shammai say: one must immerse everything before Shabbat; and Beit Hillel say: vessels must be immersed before Shabbat, but a person [may immerse him/herself] on Shabbat [in order to prepare for the Festival].

BT Betz. 17b-18a builds upon M's foundation, inquiring as to the origin and the rationale for the accepted law:

דכולי עלמא מיהת כלי בשבת לא, מאי טעמא? אמר רבה : <u>גזרה</u> שמא
יטלנו בידו ויעבירנו ארבע אמות ברשות הרבים. אמר ליה אביי : יש לו בור
בחצירו, מאי איכא למימר? אמר ליה : <u>גזירה</u> בור בחצרו אטו בור ברשות
הרבים. התינח שבת, ביום טוב מאי איכא למימר? <u>גזרו</u> יום טוב אטו שבת
. . . רב יוסף אמר : <u>גזרה</u> משום סחיטה. אמר ליה אביי : תינח כלים דבני
סחיטה נינהו, כלים דלאו בני סחיטה נינהו מאי איכא למימר? אמר ליה :
<u>גזרה</u> הני אטו הני. איתיביה כל הני תיובתא, ושני ליה כדשנינן. רב ביבי
אמר : <u>גזרה</u> שמא ישהא. תניא כוותיה דרב ביבי : כלי שנטמא מערב יום
טוב אין מטבילין אותו ביום טוב, <u>גזרה</u> שמא ישהא. רבא אמר : מפני
שנראה כמתקן כלי.

    Everyone agrees that vessels may not be immersed on Shabbat, [but] what is the reason? Rabbah said: It is a <u>decree</u> lest he take it in his hand and bring it four cubits into the public domain [thus violating the prohibition of carrying on Shabbat].

    Abaye said to him: [what if] he has a pit [with water in it] in his courtyard, what is there to say then? He said to him: it is a <u>decree</u> lest [he derive] from the pit in his courtyard [that he may also immerse vessels by going] to a pit in the public domain. This is sensible for Shabbat, but for a festival what is there to say?[665] They <u>decreed</u> [that the prohibition applies] on a festival [as well] lest one [learn from it that one may] violate Shabbat . . . (this line of reasoning is ultimately rejected, so another begins).

    Rav Yosef said: it is a <u>decree</u> to prevent wringing out [wet] clothes [which is forbidden on Shabbat and Festivals]. Abaye said to him: This is sensible for clothing which may be wrung out, but what is there to say about vessels that one is not able to wring out? He said to him: this is a <u>decree</u> [that prevents immersing vessels in order] to prevent that. He objected with all these objections, and we answered him as we answered.

Rav Bibi said: it is a <u>decree</u> lest he delay [immersing until after the Festival began, and use unclean vessels for sacred causes on Yom Tov]. There is a Tannaitic teaching to support Rav Bibi: a vessel that becomes unclean on the day before a Festival, they do not immerse it on the Festival. It is a <u>decree</u> lest he delay.[666]

Rava said: because he would appear to be fixing a vessel [on the Festival, which is forbidden].

This *sugya* is indicative of an important element of the interaction between the Tannaitic opinions set forth in M and T and the Amoraic overlay of discussion these opinions received in BT and PT. Given the apodictic style of M, the Amoraim often had to discern the reasons behind the legal decisions before them. As with any analyst who attempts to discern the original intent of a terse prior author, there arose a few problems. First, as literary critics have shown,[667] to know the original intention of an author with any certainty is impossible. Second, in any legal system, where different jurists may choose the same law for differing reasons, each individual or community of interpreters brings their own set of concerns and ideas to the analysis of law. Here we have a shining example of the challenge faced by the Amoraim in dealing with Tannaitic prohibitions they accepted, but still had to explain.[668]

Another example of a *gezerah* with multiple possible reasons brings us two potential rationales for the *gezerah*, but again shows the fluidity of the Amoraic understanding of Tannaitic decrees. In M AZ 1:1, we read of the limitations placed upon Jewish cooperation with non-Jews in the days leading up to pagan festivals. These limitations are designed to ensure that no Jewish support (monetary or other sorts) is lent to idolatrous practices. M reads:

לפני אידיהן של עובדי כוכבים ומזלות שלשה ימים אסור לשאת ולתת
עמהן להשאילן ולשאול מהן להלוותן וללוות מהן.

Prior to the festivals of idolaters, [for] three days it is forbidden to transact business with them, to lend articles to them or to borrow articles from them, to lend them money or to borrow money from them.

The strict restrictions of this mishnah attempt to break the links between Jew and non-Jew in advance of idolatrous festivities, to be sure that no benefit is derived from Jewish property or equity that will later be employed in the service of idolatry. In a very short Amoraic commentary in BT AZ 6b, though, we find Abaye and Rava discussing the reasoning behind the prohibition against lending and borrowing money:

להלוותם וללוות מהן. בשלמא להלוותם משום דקא מרווח להו, אלא
ללוות מהן, אמאי? אמר אביי: <u>גזרה</u> ללוות מהן אטו להלוותם. רבא אמר:
כולה משום דאזיל ומודה הוא.

"to lend them money or to borrow money from them." It is understand-
able [to prohibit] lending them money, because it supports them [in
their idolatrous activities, which is forbidden for Jews to do], but why
[is it forbidden] to borrow from them? Abaye said: it is a <u>decree</u> that we
prohibit borrowing from them lest we end up lending to them. Rava
said: it is all because he [the non-Jew] will go and give thanks.[669]

Here we see the two most famous fourth generation Babylonian Amoraim discussing their understanding of a prohibition handed down to them from a Tannaitic milieu. Weiss was the first to notice Abbaye's prominent role in this activity.[670] In fourteen distinct instances, we find that Abaye explained the rationale
behind a prohibition passed down to him from Tannaitic sources. This sort of
text reflects a tendency toward ongoing evaluation and analysis of Tannaitic
prohibitions, in an attempt to clarify their reasoning.

Of note in all the occurrences of *gezerot* with disputed reasons is the time
frame of the authorities cited. The distribution of the authorities cited, apart from
two Toseftan exceptions, show that all the disputative activity portrayed in texts
that mention authorities from the latter part of the Amoraic period in a most decidedly Babylonian context. This points to one of two possibilities: either these
later Babylonian Amoraim actually created more disputative material (the oft-
discussed *shakla vetarya*[671] as they attempted to understand the positions of the
earlier authorities who had imposed these *gezerot*; or, alternatively, that these
later Amoraim were more diligent in recording their divergent opinions than
prior generations. A process of re-sifting and re-validating of prior opinions took
place, to create a tighter intellectual framework for decision-making. Thus, even
some earlier prohibitions that were previously accepted faced reevaluation, and
the result is the literary synthesis we find before us in these disputes. Either of
these potential explanations could lead us to the literary product we find in BT's
collection of disputed *gezerot*.

The Authority to Make *Gezerot*

In the prior chapter's introduction, we discussed the variety of scriptural
support that is suggested for both *takkanot* and *gezerot*, though none of the citations proved particularly satisfying. As explained there, one source in *Sifra* and
two sources in BT suggested that the textual authorization for *gezerot* derived
from Lev. 18:30. Aside from these statements, which have their own problems,

the standard legal collections in M, T, PT and BT do not explicitly address the origin of the authority to make *gezerot*. The Halakhic Midrashim alone provide us with a few potential insights into the source for the rabbis' authority to create fences around the Torah.

In *MRY*, we find an interpretation that points to the power to make *gezerot* based on Ex. 15:26. The Torah reports that God showed Moses a method for sweetening the bitter waters of Marah to make them palatable for drinking. In the midst of this divine teaching moment, the Torah records this statement from God to Moses:

ויאמר אם שמוע תשמע לקול יהוה אלהיך, והישר בעיניו תעשה, והאזנת
למצותיו, ושמרת כל חקיו כל המחלה אשר שמתי במצרים לא אשים עליך
כי אני יהוה רפאך.

God said: If you will heed the Lord your God diligently, doing what is upright in God's eyes, giving ear to God's commandments and keeping all God's laws, then I will not bring upon you any of the diseases that I brought upon the Egyptians, for I the Lord am your healer.

MRY on this passage parcels out each part of this verse in typical exegetical style to uphold the power of a different branch of Jewish law:

"לקול יהוה אלהיך," מלמד שכל השומע בקול גבורה מעלה עליו הכתוב
כאלו שימש לפני חי העולמים ברוך הוא. "והישר בעיניו תעשה," זה משא
ומתן, שכל הנושא ונותן באמונה, ורוח הבריות נוחה הימנו, מעלה עליו
הכתוב כאילו קיים כל התורה כולה. "והאזנת למצותיו," אלו הלכות.
"ושמרת כל חקיו," אלו <u>גזירות.</u>

"if you will heed the Lord your God diligently," this teaches that anyone who obeys the voice of the Mighty One, the text considers it as if s/he has served in the presence of the Eternal God, who is blessed.

"doing what is upright in God's eyes," this is in business, for anyone who does business honestly, and people have respect for him, the text considers it as if s/he upheld all the commandments of the Torah.

"and giving ear to God's commandments," these are the *halakhot*.

"and guarding all God's laws," these are <u>decrees</u>.

Thus, through a close exegesis of this biblical verse, *MRY* has attempted to root the practice of making fences around the Torah back into what Elon would call the "supreme legislation" of the Jewish people. A few problems must be considered, though. First of all, if we look at parallel texts, the use of the prooftext varies significantly. In the very same page of this work, we find this version:

"והאזנת למצותיו." אלו <u>גזירות</u>, "ושמרת כל חקיו," אלו עריות.

"and giving ear to God's commandments," these are the <u>decrees</u>. "and guarding all God's laws," these are the sexual prohibitions.

This verse is interpreted, here, in a reversed and altered way, assigning different parts of the verse to quite opposite legal areas. In fact, two other verses, Ex. 18:16 and 18:20, are both also held up as proof for the validity of *gezerot*. In light of this confusion of sources, and their inconsistent usage, it appears that a Tannaitic rabbinic leadership looking for a way to influence the growth of rabbinic law conceived of the authority for *gezerot*. Only after they had conceptualized such an approach, did they set about looking for justificatory prooftexts, upon which they did not universally agree. The collectors of the Halakhic Midrashim included more than one account in serving the ideal of completeness, and did not look for consistency, as we might in the modern world. Thus, we see that more than one attempt was made to justify the power of *gezerot*, and that this inconsistency points to a perceived need to explain and fortify the practice, and to "hang it on a big tree"—the biggest and most firmly rooted tree of all— that of scriptural support.

Breaking Through the Fence – Violations and Penalties

In indicating the penalties for violations of *gezerot*, the rabbis utilized one prooftext in a consistent way. T Hul. 2:22-23 shows the earliest version of this concept:

(כב) מעשה בר' אלעזר בן דמה שנשכו נחש, ובא יעקב איש כפר סמא לרפאותו משום ישוע בן פנטרא. ולא הניחו ר' ישמעאל. אמרו לו : אי אתה רשאי בן דמה. אמר לו : אני אביא לך ראיה שירפאני. ולא הספיק להביא ראיה עד שמת :

(כג) אמר ר' ישמעאל : אשריך בן דמה שיצאת בשלום, ולא פירצת <u>גזירן</u> של חכמים, שכל הפורץ גדירן של חכמים לסוף פורענות בא עליו, שנאמר "ופורץ גדר ישכנו נחש" :

(22) The story of Rabbi Eleazar ben Damah who was bitten by a snake, and Jacob of Kfar Sama came to heal him in the name of Yeshua ben Pantra, but Rabbi Yishmael did not allow it. They said to him: "You are not permitted, ben Damah." He said to him: "I will bring proof that he may heal me," but he did not have enough time to bring proof before he died.

(23) Rabbi Yishmael said: "Happy are you, ben Damah, that you have left this world in peace, and did not break any of the decrees of the sages, for anyone who breaks the fence of the sages, in the end evil will come to him, as it is written 'one who breaches a stone fence, a snake will bite him.'" (Eccl. 10:8)[672]

The message inherent in the Ecclesiastes text is that individuals will bear responsibility for their actions. When one breaks through a stone fence, one creates an entryway for oneself. At the same time, one also creates an egress for a snake enjoying the perfect hiding place either in the next yard or in the stones of the fence itself. Since a *gezerah* is a fence that contains the Torah, and prevents breaches of it, this metaphor is well constructed and quite suitable to the message that danger lurks just outside.

When one considers the context in which the Eleazar ben Damah story occurs, the plot thickens substantially. Herford[673] and Urbach[674] read this story as a strong polemic against healing in an ancient Christian mode. Schiffman utilizes this text to establish a *terminus ante quem* for the halakhic ruling that one may not be healed by a *min*, and to draw conclusions about the close contact between Jewish Christians and Jews in a Palestinian context.[675] In the text, Jacob of Kfar Sama attempted to heal Eleazar ben Damah through the power of the name of Jeshua ben Pantera, but Rabbi Yishmael did not permit it. The use of a name was a standard Christian healing methodology, for which much evidence exists in the New Testament. In Acts 3:6-7, for example, we find Peter and John involved in healing in the name of Jesus near the Temple in Jerusalem:

6) Peter said: "I have no silver and gold, but I give you what I have: in the name of Jesus Christ of Nazareth, walk!" 7) And he took him up by the right hand and raised him up; and immediately his feet and his ankles were made strong.

In light of early Christianity's ringing endorsement of such "medicine," Rabbi Yishmael could hardly allow it, seeing it as a violation of Jewish law to engage other unacceptable spirits in performing miraculous healing. Rabbi Yishmael's prooftext in T is an extremely apt one, for not only does it rail against the violation of Jewish law, but it also serves as a larger metaphor for breaking through the barrier between Judaism and early Christianity.

One could also ask: why would Rabbi Yishmael imagine that Eleazar ben Damah would be happy about his death? One direct answer comes from the parallel text in PT AZ 2:2, 40d-41a. There, PT remarks that if the snake had not bitten him, he would have faced a far worse fate. By transgressing the ordinances of the rabbis, he would have ended up a heretic, and faced far sterner punishment in the world to come. Thus, PT understands his death by snakebite to be a form of mercy for his near-transgression.

A later Amoraic version of this lethal snake trope appears in BT Shab. 110a in a story of divine retribution for violation of rabbinic legal strictures, though without the explicit mention of the term *gezerot*. It appears that by the time the editors of BT did their work, this idea had been applied not only to Christians, but, more broadly, to anyone who violated rabbinic law. In this section, the text describes a cure for a snakebite created from the embryos of a certain kind of pale ass. The only problem: for the cure to work, the ass from which it was taken could not be *trefah*, that is, its lungs had to have been intact and the animal itself had to be pure, and it must have been considered suitable for eating according to rabbinic law:

ההוא בר קשא דפומבדיתא דטרקיה חיויא. הוה תליסר חמרי חיורתא בפומבדיתא, קרעינהו לכולהו ואישתכחו טריפה. הואי חדא בההוא גיסא דפומבדיתא, עד דאזלי מייתי לה, אכלה אריה. אמר להו אביי : דילמא חיויא דרבנן טרקיה, דלית ליה אסותא, דכתיב (קהלת י) "ופרץ גדר ישכנו נחש." אמרו ליה : אין, רבי. דכי נח נפשיה דרב, גזר רב יצחק בר ביסנא דליכא דלימטייה אסא וגידמי לבי הילולא בטבלא, ואזל איהו אמטי אסא וגידמי לבי הילולא בטבלא, טרקיה חיויא ומית.

A snake bit a certain official from Pumbedita. There were 13 white donkeys in Pumbedita, and they tore open all of them, but they found them to be *trefah*. There was one on the other end of Pumbedita, but before they got there to bring it, a lion ate it. Abaye said to them: Perhaps a snake of the rabbis bit him, for which there is no cure, as it is written: "one who breaches a fence will be bitten by a snake." (Eccl. 10:8) They said to him: yes, my teacher. For when Rav died, Rav Yitzhak bar Bisna <u>decreed</u> that no one may bring myrtle and palm branches to wedding feasts with a *tabala*,[676] but he [the official] came bringing myrtle and palm branches to a wedding feast with a *tabala*, and a snake bit him and he died.

Here, Rav Yitzhak bar Bisna is cited as instituting a decree that recognized Rav's death by reducing the joy of weddings through diminished musical and vegetative decoration. The official from Pumbedita did not follow this decree, and, therefore, perished, despite the presence of a quorum of potentially appropriate looking asses. In the end, the story serves its purpose, creating a cautionary tale for anyone considering violating the decrees of the rabbis. Note, however, that it stops well short of mandating death or other penalties at the hands of human beings,[677] but expects only a divinely imposed death penalty.

This story, coupled with the exegesis of Eccl. 10:8 found in T, form a suggestive web that shows the rabbis compelling observance by literary and rhetorical means as opposed to direct punitive measures at the hands of human beings.

A Few Characteristics of *Gezerot*

Tannaitic sources indicate that rabbinic decrees were preserved in written form,[678] and that such decrees remained the property of the court decreeing them.[679] BT Betz. 3b sets forth the principle that decrees were considered entirely rabbinical in origin, and thus any uncertainty in a *gezerah* was to be resolved in a lenient manner, as opposed to commandments that had their direct source in the Torah, where uncertainty had to be resolved in the strictest possible manner.[680]

Another issue that arose was the question of the longevity of a decree responding to the temporary actions of outside authorities. If, for example, the Romans took an action that led to a rabbinic decree in response, if the Roman action were subsequently rescinded, the ongoing validity of the rabbinic decree could be called into question. PT San. 3:5, 21b covers this situation in a discussion of planting during the end of the Sabbatical Year, in anticipation of growing crops early in the next year:

טייב בזמן זה מהו? רבי ירמיה סבר מימר בטל הדין בטלה גזירתא, רבי
יוסי סבר מימר לעולם הגזירה במקומה עד שיעמוד בית דין אחר ויבטלה.

Tilling [the soil early in preparation for planting at the onset of the Sabbatical year] in this time, what [is the ruling]? Rabbi Jeremiah thought to say: when the [Roman] law [imposing a heavy tax burden] was cancelled, the <u>decree</u> was cancelled; Rabbi Yossi thought to say: the <u>decree</u> stands in its place until another court will cancel it.

The reference here is to the fact that Roman law levied taxes on Jewish fields even during the time of the Sabbatical Year.[681] In dire economic circumstances, Jews would plant their fields toward the end of the Sabbatical Year, violating the margins of the Sabbatical laws in order to attempt to meet their heavy tax obligations to the Roman government. The rabbis, in watching this transgression of Torah law, imposed harsh fines upon those who planted their fields at this time.

PT, however, raised the following question here: what should happen when the Romans changed their law, and allowed more leniency in tax requirements to accommodate Jewish observance of the Sabbatical year? Should the decreed rabbinic fine that was imposed be abolished, or was the correct course of action to retain the decree until an appropriate court rescinded it? No definitive answer appears here, just a disagreement between two Palestinian Amoraim of the third generation.

In a similar case, BT considered the eating of cheese made by non-Jews. Here we find a fascinating statement that sheds light on the initial promulgation of *gezerot*. BT notes that the reasons for *gezerot* made in the West (*viz.*, in Palestine) were not shared publicly for the first year. The particulars of the case involved rennet, a curdling agent taken from the intestines of a cow used to make cheese. If the rennet came from animals that had died of illness, had not been ritually slaughtered or had been utilized for sacrifices to idols, the resulting cheese was not kosher.[682] In discussing a potential further stringency in M AZ 2:5, Rabbi Joshua is cited as rejecting limitations on the derivation of benefits from this sort of cheese: Jews were still permitted to derive benefit from it (which they might by selling it, warehousing it, transporting it, etc.), even though they were forbidden to eat it. When Rabbi Yishmael asked Rabbi Joshua about this, the mishnah indicates that he changed the subject. In BT AZ 35a, the Gemara takes the discussion one step further, filling in an interesting picture of BT's view of how certain rabbis dealt with recent *gezerot*:

"השיאו לדבר אחר וכו'." מאי (שיר השירים א) "כי טובים דודיך מיין?!"
כי אתא רב דימי אמר, אמרה כנסת ישראל לפני הקב"ה: רבש"ע, עריבים
עלי דברי דודיך יותר מיינה של תורה. מ"ש האי קרא דשייליה? אמר רבי
שמעון בן פזי, ואיתימא רבי שמעון בר אמי, מרישיה דקרא קא"ל: (שיר
השירים א) "ישקני מנשיקות פיהו," אמר ליה: ישמעאל אחי, חשוק
שפתותיך זו בזו ואל תבהל להשיב. מ"ט? אמר עולא, ואיתימא רב שמואל
בר אבא: <u>גזרה</u> חדשה היא ואין מפקפקין בה. מאי <u>גזירתא</u>? אמר רבי
שמעון בן פזי אמר רבי יהושע בן לוי: משום ניקור. ולימא ליה: משום
ניקור! כדעולא, דאמר עולא: כי <u>גזרי גזירתא</u> במערבא, לא מגלו טעמא עד
תריסר ירחי שתא, דלמא איכא איניש דלא ס"ל ואתי לזלזולי בה ...

"He changed the subject, etc."[683] What is [the meaning of] "for your beloved one is better than wine?" (Song 1:2b) When Rav Dimi came [from Palestine] he said: the assembly of Israel said before God: Master of the universe, the words of your beloved ones are sweeter to me than the wine of the Torah.[684]

Why did he [Rabbi Yishmael] ask him [Rabbi Yohanan] about this particular verse? Rabbi Shimeon ben Pazi, and others say it was Rabbi Shimeon ben Ammi, said: he spoke [i.e., referred to] the first part of the verse: "let him kiss me with the kisses of his mouth" (Song 1:2a). He said to him: Yishmael my brother, press your lips together and do not be anxious for an answer.

What is the reason [he should not be anxious for an answer]? Ulla said, and some say it was Rav Shmuel bar Abba: it was a new <u>decree</u>, and they should not explain it.

What, then, is the reason for this <u>decree</u>? Rabbi Shimeon ben Pazi said in the name of Rabbi Yehoshua ben Levi: because of [the possibility of] a snakebite [since idolaters were not particular about covering their liquids, the milk used to make the cheese may have had snake venom in it]. Then, let him say to him: because a snake may have bitten it [in other words, why not tell him the reason, instead of asking him to keep silent]? It is according to Ulla, as Ulla said: when they <u>decree</u> a <u>decree</u> in the West [in Palestine], they do not reveal its reason for a year of twelve months [i.e., until twelve lunar months later], lest there be a person who does not agree with the reason, and will come to disregard it.

Rashi's explanation for this decision to tightly guard the rationale behind a *gezerah* for the first year helps clarify the idea:

דלמא איכא דלית ליה ההוא טעמא, ולא בדיל מיניה, ומזלזל בה. אבל
השתא דלא מגלו טעמא דמלתא, בדלי מיניה כו״ע דסברי קמו רבנן במלתא
דאתי מיניה חורבא, ואנן הוא דלא בקיאינן בטעמא.

"Lest there be a person" who does not accept this same reason [for the decree], and does not avoid violating it and ignores it. But now that they do not reveal the reason for the matter, the whole world avoids [violating] it, believing that our rabbis ruled on a matter [the violation of] which brings destruction, and it is we who are not expert in the reason [i.e., the rabbis knew that it would bring some harm, and thus decreed against it].

Sometimes, a bit of knowledge is a dangerous thing. To share the rationale for a decree too quickly risked others in the community impugning its motives, to the ultimate detriment of the fence created by the rabbis.[685] Thus, though we have only a single, somewhat *ad hoc* instance of this sort of concealment of the reason behind a *gezerah*, there is a certain impeccable logic to it. With such little evidence, we can merely accept it as an interesting idea, not presume that it was a widespread practice. There is no evidence, here, for a systemic principle, but merely a kernel of an idea that may or may not have been in use.

Only one other rabbinic legal text suggests any sort of waiting period associated with *gezerot*, and that is a source in PT Shevi. 6:1, 36c. After a discussion of whether the town of Ashkelon was considered part of the land of Israel or not, PT records that the rabbis present took a vote and decided that Ashkelon was to be considered outside the land of Israel.[686] In light of this, it was thought to harbor the "uncleanness of other lands," which had ramifications upon the status of produce grown there with respect to the heave offering. The rabbis then proceeded to ask when exactly this *gezerah* went into effect:

אימתי היא טמיאה משום ארץ העמים? א"ר סימון: משתשהא הגזירה
ארבעים יום. אמר רבי ירמיה: ולא בטעות אנו מחזיקים? אלא מיד.

> When is [Ashkelon considered] unclean because of the uncleanness of foreign lands? Rabbi Simon said: after the <u>decree</u> will wait for 40 days. Rabbi Jeremiah said: Did we not make an error [that we are now correcting]? Rather, [it takes effect] immediately.

The implication of the statement attributed to Rabbi Simon is that the original issuance of a *gezerah* required 40 days notice before taking effect. This might allow word to spread to the entire community, though the text is silent as to this practice's ultimate rationale. According to Rabbi Jeremiah, though, in the case of an erroneous prior ruling that the rabbis were correcting, the corrective took effect immediately, probably to reduce accumulation of further error. While there is no other evidence of a 40-day waiting period, this raises the possibility of restrictions on the dissemination and activation of *gezerot*. Note, though, the difference between this source and the one immediately preceding it from BT: there, Palestinian rabbis put a decree into effect immediately, though they held off on telling others the reason publicly. Here, the activation of the entire *gezerah* must wait forty days, with no mention of any regard for the reason involved. Thus, while these two texts share some similarities, they cannot ultimately serve as independent confirmation for one another.

Major Groupings of Decrees

Fences Around the Torah

As we saw earlier in a similar section on *takkanot*, groups of *gezerot* appear in a series of six different collections: three preserved around events or individuals and another three constructed around topics.[687] These small collections of decrees have been brought together through the constructive literary activity of the redactors of rabbinic legal texts. The largest of these groupings is the most interesting, both for the content of the *gezerot* themselves, and because of the descriptive material found within. As an ancillary benefit, these *gezerot* provide excellent examples of the category called "a fence around the Torah," which enables us to cover this category, by far the largest category of *gezerot* made up of 270 basic texts (plus, additionally, their associated parallels), at the same time.[688]

Decrees Based Around Events and People

Showdown in the Attic of Hananya ben Hezekiah ben Gurion

The earliest source for this string of decrees confronts questions of permissible work on Friday afternoon in anticipation of the start of the Sabbath. This text and its three major parallels each bring a basic enumeration of 18 *gezerot*. Most interesting is the interplay between the various sources: while all claim to present 18 decrees, the actual number varies from 13 to 18, and the array of included laws shows major shifts from text to text. In M Shab. 1:4-9, for example, we find the number 18 mentioned, while only 13 laws were included:

(ד) ואלו מן ההלכות שאמרו בעליית חנניה בן חזקיה בן גוריון כשעלו לבקרו נמנו ורבו ב״ש על ב״ה . וי״ח דברים <u>גזרו</u> בו ביום : (ה) בית שמאי אומרים : אין שורין דיו, וסממנים, וכרשינים אלא כדי שישורו מבעוד יום, ובית הלל מתירין : (ו) בית שמאי אומרים : אין נותנין אונין של פשתן לתוך התנור אלא כדי שיהבילו מבעוד יום. ולא את הצמר ליורה אלא כדי שיקלוט העין. ובית הלל מתירין. בית שמאי אומרים : אין פורשין מצודות חיה, ועופות ודגים אלא כדי שיצודו מבעוד יום, ובית הלל מתירין : (ז) בית שמאי אומרים : אין מוכרין לעובד כוכבים, ואין טוענין עמו, ואין מגביהין עליו אלא כדי שיגיע למקום קרוב, ובית הלל מתירין : (ח) בית שמאי אומרים : אין נותנין עורות לעבדן, ולא כלים לכובס עובד כוכבים אלא כדי שיעשו מבעוד יום, ובכולן בית הלל מתירין עם השמש : (ט) אמר רבן שמעון בן גמליאל : נוהגין היו בית אבא שהיו נותנין כלי לבן לכובס עובד כוכבים שלשה ימים קודם לשבת. ושוין אלו ואלו שטוענין קורות בית הבד ועגולי הגת :

4) And these are among the *halakhot* that they stated in the attic of Hananyah ben Hezekiah ben Gurion. When they went up to visit him, they voted, and Beit Shammai outnumbered Beit Hillel. And they de-creed 18 decrees on that same day.[689]

5) Beit Shammai says: one may not soak ink, material for dye or vetches[690] unless there is enough time for the soaking to be complete while it is still day [that is, before Shabbat has begun], but Beit Hillel permits [it].[691]

6) Beit Shammai says: one may not put bundles of flax into the oven unless there is enough time for them to be heated while it is still day. And one may not put wool in to [a vat to] dye unless there is enough time for it to absorb [the dye while it is still day], but Beit Hillel per-mits [it]. Beit Shammai says: one may not set traps for wild animals, birds or fish unless there is sufficient time to trap [them] while it is still day, but Beit Hillel permits [it].[692]

7) Beit Shammai says: one may not sell to a non-Jew, and one may not help load [a beast with cargo] with him, and one may not lift up a pack-age onto him unless he will reach a nearby place [before sunset], but Beit Hillel permits [it].

8) Beit Shammai says: One may not give hides to a non-Jewish tanner or clothes to be washed to a non-Jewish launderer, unless there is suffi-cient time that they be done while it is still day. For all these cases, Beit Hillel permits [it] as long as the sun is shining.[693]

9) Rabban Shimeon ben Gamaliel said: In my father's house, we were accustomed to giving the white clothing to a non-Jewish launderer three days before Shabbat.[694]

Both [schools, Beit Hillel and Beit Shammai] agree that one may load the beams of an olive press or the rollers of a wine press [at dusk, even though they continue to apply pressure throughout the Sabbath].[695]

First, we note the vagaries of language that appear in this mishnah. The two words that are employed to describe the legal activity in progress are the noun *halakhot* and the verb *gazar*. The implication is an important one: laws that are decreed by the rabbis in an official setting such as this one may be assumed to be legally binding *halakhot*. No source argues this question in any of the primary or secondary texts.

Second, we recognize the use of the terminology of voting. These decisions were presented as if endorsed by a limited democratic process, not an inclusive one that involved all citizens to be sure, but a democratic process among the jurists making law. This is the only occurrence of *gezerot* explicitly subject to votes found in this study. It is certainly not a regular facet of decrees.

The number of decrees is stated as 18, but, counting, we find that there are, at most, 13 laws stated in this pericope.[696] The text in M reports that Beit Shammai prohibited the following close to the onset of Shabbat: 1) making ink; 2) using material for dye; 3) soaking vetches; 4) working with bundles of flax; 5) dyeing wool; 6) setting traps; 7) selling to a non-Jew; 8) loading a non-Jew's animal; 9) loading a non-Jew's burden onto his/her shoulders; 10) working hides and 11) the washing of clothes by non-Jews. M grants permission to 12) load the beams of the olive press and 13) load the rollers of the wine press.

The general ideology at work is what we have seen before: a fence around the Torah. In *gezerot* 1-11, activities that might encroach, eventually, on the observance of Shabbat are forbidden. In *gezerot* 12 and 13, however, we notice something different: instead of creating a fence around the Torah, these two laws actually permit activity that one might have prohibited based on the same logic. Since the process of pressing grapes and olives for their wine or oil is one that involves the work of a tool (the beam or roller), there is a halakhic issue with using these tools on Shabbat. Kehati points out a useful distinction between the wine and oil presses and the other cases here: he interprets this action as placing the beam or roller onto the produce only *after* the initial squeezing of the grapes or olives has occurred, to let the residual wine or oil continue to seep out over the course of the Sabbath, and therefore it is not to be considered the original work of the first pressing.[697] Regardless of the exact explanation here, we have two examples of laws termed *gezerot* that do not form fences around the Torah, but do the opposite: create a leniency where there was not one in prior times.

This mishnaic literary unit suffers from some difficulty in following through on its initial premise of 18 *halakhot*, having, as noted above, only 13 laws contained within it. Happily, there is an extensive series of parallels through which we may fill in the blanks and observe its ongoing legal development, the next layer of which occurs in T Shab. 1:16-23:

(טז) אלו מן ההלכות שאמרו בעליית חנניה בן חזקיהו בן גרון. כשעלו לבקרו, נמנו ורבו בית שמיי על בית הלל. שמונה עשרה דבר גזרו בו ביום, והיה אותו היום קשה להם לישראל כיום שנעשה בו העגל. . . . (יח) בו ביום אמרו : כל המטלטלין מביאין את הטומאה בעובי המרדע. ונמנו ורבו בית שמיי על בית הלל. (יט) בו ביום אמרו : השוכח כלים בערב שבת עם

חשיכה תחת הצנור. ונמנו ורבו בית שמיי על בית הלל. (כ) אמרו בית שמיי
לבית הלל: אין אתם מודין שאין צולין בשר בצל וביצה בערב שבת עם
חשיכה, אלא כדי שיצולו? אף דיו, סמנין, וכרשנין כיוצא בהן? (כא) אמרו
להן בית הלל: אי אתם מודין שטוענין קורות בית הבד ותולין עגולי הגת
ערב שבת עם חשיכה? אף דיו, סמנין, וכרשנין כיוצא בהן? אילו עמדו
בתשובתן, ואילו עמדו בתשובתן. אלא שבית שמיי אומרים "ששת ימים
תעבוד ועשית כל מלאכתך," שתהא כל מלאכתך גמורה מערב שבת, ובית
הלל אומרים "ששת ימים תעבד מלאכה," עושה אתה כל ששה. (כב) בית
שמיי אומרים: אין מוכרין לנכרי, ולא טוענין עמו, ולא מגביהין עליו אלא
כדי שיגיע למקום קרוב. ואי זהו מקום קרוב? עד שיגיע לבית הסמוך
לחומה. ר' עקיבא אומר: כדי שיצא מן הפתח ויקדש עליו היום. אמר ר'
לעזר בי ר' צדוק: של בית רבן גמליאל היו מוליכין כלי לבן שלהן לכובס
נכרי שלשה ימים קודם לשבת, וצבועים בערב שבת. לפי דרכנו למדנו
שהלבנים קשין להעשות יתר מן הצבועין. (כג) פותקין מים לגנה בערב
שבת עם חשיכה, והיא שותה והולכת בשבת. נותנין קילור לעין, ואספלנית
למכה בערב שבת עם חשיכה, והן מתרפין והולכין כל השבת כולה. נותנין
גפרית תחת הכלים בערב שבת עם חשיכה, והן מתגפרין והולכין בשבת.
נותנין מגמר על גבי גחלים בערב שבת עם חשכה, ואין נותנין חטים לרחים
של מים אלא כדי שייטחנו.

16) These are among the *halakhot* that they stated in the attic of
Hananya ben Hezekiah ben Gurion. When they went up to visit him,
they voted, and Beit Shammai outnumbered Beit Hillel. They <u>decreed</u>
18 matter[s] on that very day, and that same day was as difficult for Israel as the day when the [Golden] Calf was made. . . .

18) On that day they said: "All carried movable property conveys overshadowing uncleanness if it is as thick as an ox-goad." (M Oho. 16:1).
They voted and Beit Shammai outnumbered Beit Hillel.

19) On that same day they said: "One who leaves vessels under a spout
on the eve of Shabbat at dusk." (M Mik. 4:1).[698] And they voted and
Beit Shammai outnumbered Beit Hillel.

20) Beit Shammai said to Beit Hillel: Do you not admit that one may
not roast meat, onions or eggs on the eve of Shabbat at dusk, unless
there is time for them to be fully roasted (M Shab. 1:10)? So [should
not this limitation also apply to] ink, dye and vetches (M Shab. 1:5)?

21) Beit Hillel said to them: Do you not admit that one may load the
beams of the olive presses and the rollers of the wine presses on the eve
of Shabbat at dusk (M Shab. 1:9)? So [should not this leniency also ap-

ply to] ink, dye and vetches? These stood by their answer, and these stood by their answer.[699] Rather, Beit Shammai says: "six days shall you labor, and do all your work" (Ex. 20:8/Deut. 5:12) [This means] that all your work shall be complete by the eve of Shabbat; and Beit Hillel says: "six days shall you labor, and do all your work" [This means] that you work *all* six days [including Friday until dusk].

22) Beit Shammai say: one may not sell to a non-Jew, and one may not load [a beast with cargo] with him, and one may not lift up a package onto him unless he will arrive in a nearby place [before the Sabbath begins]. And what is [the definition of] a nearby place? [A house] that is near the wall [of the city]. Rabbi Akiba says: Sufficient time for him to go out the door before the day is sanctified. Rabbi Eleazar son of Rabbi Tzadok said: members of the house of Rabban Gamaliel would bring their white clothing to a non-Jewish launderer three days before the Sabbath (M Shab. 1:9), and the colored clothing on the eve of the Sabbath. By the way, we learned [from this] that white clothing is harder to clean than colored clothing.

23) They may open water channels for a garden on the eve of Shabbat at dusk, and it may continue to draw water during Shabbat. They put medicine on the eye,[700] and a compress on a wound on the eve of Shabbat at dusk, and they may continue healing the entire Shabbat. They put sulfur under vessels on the eve of Shabbat at dusk, and they continue sulfuring during Shabbat. They place the incense burner amongst the coals on the eve of Shabbat at dusk, but they do not put wheat into the water-powered mills unless there is enough time for it to be ground [before Shabbat begins].

There are two overall ways of approaching this Toseftan passage. First, one could see this as an independent counting, where each of the halakhic positions enumerated above would count toward the completion of the 18 total decrees. Counting generously, one can actually arrive at 18 *gezerot* in T's version, unlike what we found in M:

1) movable property bigger than an ox-goad may convey uncleanness;
2) leaving vessels under a spout makes them unclean;
3) no roasting meats;
4) no roasting onions;
5) no roasting eggs;

6) one may load the beams of the olive press;
7) one may load the rollers of the wine press;
8) no selling to a non-Jew on the eve of Shabbat;
9) no loading a non-Jew's animal on the eve of Shabbat;
10) no helping load a burden onto a non-Jew's back on the eve of Shabbat;
11) no washing white clothing at a non-Jewish laundry on the eve of Shabbat;
12) washing colored clothing is permitted;
13) one may open irrigation channels before Shabbat and let them run;
14) one may apply medicine for the eye that will continue to heal;
15) one may place a bandage on a wound before Shabbat that will continue to heal;
16) one may place sulfur under vessels that will continue to burn throughout Shabbat;
17) one may place an incense burner in the fire that will continue to burn throughout Shabbat and
18) one may not grind wheat in water-powered mills that continue to operate during Shabbat.

Reading it this way, we see that this creates a combination of stringencies and leniencies, but that all the component pieces center on a discussion of avoiding the continuation of work on the Sabbath.

On the other hand, one could view T's work as supplementary to M, commenting on and adding to the total collection, to explain it and ensure that the 18 are reached in a combination of the two works. If this is the case, we have 13 *halakhot* already mentioned in M, plus the following five add-ons:

14) movable property bigger than an ox-goad may convey uncleanness;
15) leaving vessels under a spout makes them unclean;
16) no roasting meats;
17) no roasting onions; and
18) no roasting eggs.

According to the first reading, T shows more leniencies than M. Of the 18 *halakhot* presented in T as enumerated above, fully seven grant permission to commit an act that continues into the Sabbath, while 11 are prohibitions that create a fence around the Torah, the more traditional meaning of a *gezerah*. In M, the balance is tilted in the other direction: out of 13 rules, 11 are stringencies that protect Shabbat observance, while only two provide for permission to engage in activity that abides past the start of Shabbat. Thus, T presents a more lenient picture of the results of this day of decrees.

T also shows more emotion than M with respect to the significance of this day for the history of the Jewish people. Linking this day to the moment when the Israelites made the golden calf makes a serious statement. The two episodes share some distinct similarities.[701] Comparing this day to the time of the golden calf is a fitting analogue, but one that clearly displays the real ambivalence T's editor felt toward Beit Shammai's strictures. The leniencies that T layers onto M's version further serve to heighten the impression of discomfort.

The two Talmuds reject the basic idea that M (or, potentially, T) contained a complete record of the 18 *gezerot*, and craft their own, quite distinctive lists. PT Shab. 1:4, 3c, in forming its own pericope, takes the standoff to an even more violent level:

תנא רבי יהושע אונייא: תלמידי ב״ש עמדו להן מלמטה והיו הורגין
בתלמידי בית הלל. תני: ששה מהן עלו, והשאר עמדו עליהן בחרבות
וברמחים. תני: שמונה עשר דבר גזרו, ובשמונה עשרה רבו, ובשמונה
עשרה נחלקו, ואילו הן שגזרו: על פיתן של גוים, ועל גבינתן, ועל שמנן, ועל
בנותיהן, ועל שכבת זרען, ועל מימי רגליהן, ועל הילכות בעל קרי, ועל
הילכות ארץ העמים. תמן תנינן: אילו פוסלין את התרומה: האוכל אוכל
ראשון, והאוכל אוכל שני, והשותה משקין טמאין, והבא ראשו ורובו
במים שאובין, וטהור שנפלו על ראשו ורובו שלשה לוגין מים שאובין,
והספר, והידים, והטבול יום, והאוכלים והכלים שניטמאו במשקין. רבנן
דקיסרין אמרו: אלו שגזרו, ממה שרבו, שבעה אינון. ואילין איניין
חורנייתא: מי שהחשיך בדרך נותן כיסו לנכרי, כיוצא בו לא יאכל הזב עם
הזבה מפני הרגל עבירה, כל המיטלטלין מביאין טומאה כעובי המרדע,
כיצד בוצרין בית הפרס, המניח כלים תחת הצינור, על ששה ספיקות
שורפין את התרומה. א״ר יוסי בי ר' בון: אף גידולי תרומה. אלו הן שגזרו
אילין עשרתי קדמייתא. והשאר מן מה דתני ר״ש בן יוחי: בו ביום גזרו
על פיתן, ועל גבינתן, ועל יינן, ועל חומצן, ועל צירן, ועל מורייסן, על
כבושיהן, ועל שלוקיהן, ועל מלוחיהן, ועל החילקה, ועל השחיקה, ועל
הטיסני, ועל לשונן, ועל עדותן, ועל מתנותיהן, על בניהן, ועל בנותיהן, ועל
בכוריהן.

Rabbi Yehoshua of Onaya taught: Beit Shammai stood downstairs and were killing the students of Beit Hillel. It was taught: six of them went upstairs, and the remainder stood against them with swords and shields.

It has been taught: 18 matter[s] they <u>decreed</u>, and on 18 matter[s] they were the majority, and on 18 [matters] they disputed. And these are those they <u>decreed</u>: on the bread of non-Jews, their cheese, their oil, their daughters, their seminal emissions, their urine, on the laws governing one who had a seminal emission, and on the laws governing the uncleanness of their lands.

There we learned: These make *terumah* unsuitable: One who eats first degree unclean food; one who eats second degree unclean food; one who drinks unclean liquids; the one whose head and greater part of the body enter drawn water; the clean one who had more than three *logs* of drawn water fall onto the head and the majority of the body; the [sacred] book; the [unwashed] hands; the one who immersed today and the food and vessels that were made unclean by liquids.

Our rabbis of Caesarea said: Those they <u>decreed</u>, from among those about which they argued, are seven. And these are the others [that they decreed] afterwards: one [traveling] on a road [after Shabbat has begun] must give one's purse to a non-Jew [to hold] (M Shab. 24:1); and, similarly, a *zav* may not eat with a *zavah* because it leads to sin (M Shab. 1:3); all movable property conveys overshadowing uncleanness if it is wider than an ox-goad (M Oho. 16:1); how do they gather grapes in the area of graves (M Oho. 18:1); one who leaves vessels under a spout (M Mik. 4:1); concerning six matters of doubt they burn *terumah* (M Toh. 4:1). Rabbi Yossi son of Bun said: Also that produce that grows from *terumah* is *terumah* (M Ter. 9:18).

These are the ten that they <u>decreed</u> before. And the remainder are those [which derive] from what Rabbi Shimeon bar Yohai taught: on that same day they <u>decreed</u> about their bread, cheese, wine, vinegar, brine, fish brine, preserves, boiled foods, salted food, spelt, ground food [probably grain], peeled barley,[702] language, testimony, gifts, sons, daughters, and firstlings.

First of all, we notice in PT's *sugya* that the confrontation between Beit Hillel and Beit Shammai has turned quite violent. The commentators are divided on this issue, with some doing their best to read around the violence.[703] Lieberman's analysis, though, suggests that this violence does have a legitimately historical basis, in light of other evidence from *MegTa* and elsewhere.[704] This reading helps flesh out T's connection with the golden calf incident, and highlights the awful nature of the events reported.

The *sugya* in PT grapples with many of the same potential decrees we found in T and will soon find when we look at BT. PT first brings a *baraita* that describes eight prohibitions limiting interactions with non-Jews. Following this *baraita* are ten prohibitions cited from M Zav. 5:12, which, when added to the eight in the *baraita*, make up the correct total of 18 decrees. However, the rabbis of Caesarea dismissed the application of the restrictions from M Zav. Instead, these rabbis suggested a different set: the seven prohibitions they then list themselves. However, this does not create a full complement of 18. So, after all is said and done, PT turns to a statement of Rabbi Shimeon bar Yohai, whose ten prohibitions, when combined with the initial *baraita*, make up the perfect number of 18.

Comparing PT's version to those found in M and T, the table on the opposite page shows the various *gezerot* contained in the different Palestinian sources we have examined thus far. Remarkable in this table is the jump that took place between the lists in each stratum. In M, the text is clearly entirely concerned with the observance of Shabbat. T continues that same tight focus. The quantum leap occurred between the early and late Amoraic phases of these texts, when the editors responsible for PT shifted the focus to center upon the issues of purity and separation from idolaters. The turn toward purity concerns represents a trend that we will see continued in BT.

The final layer of rabbinic commentary on our mishnah is found in BT Shab. 13b-17b,[705] which begins with a *baraita* that essentially refutes M and T's counting of these decrees, and then two other *baraitot* that provide a total of eleven different decrees:

אמר ליה אביי לרב יוסף. אלו תנן, או ואלו תנן? ואלו תנן. הני דאמרן, או
אלו תנן, דבעינן למימר קמן? תא שמע: אין פולין לאור הנר, ואין קורין
לאור הנר, ואלו מן ההלכות שאמרו בעליית חנניה בן חזקיה בן גרון. שמע
מינה: ואלו תנן, שמע מינה. ושמנה עשר דבר גזרו. מאי נינהו שמנה עשר
דבר? דתנן, אלו פוסלין את התרומה: האוכל אוכל ראשון, והאוכל אוכל
שני, והשותה משקין טמאין, והבא ראשו ורובו במים שאובין, וטהור
שנפלו על ראשו ורובו שלשה לוגין מים שאובין, והספר, והידים והטבול
יום, והאוכלים והכלים שנטמאו במשקי.

Abaye said to Rav Yosef: Did we learn "these," or "and these?"[706] [If we learned] "and these," [that includes] those we stated [in the previous mishnah], or, if "these," that includes those we are soon to state? Come and hear:[707] We do not delouse [ourselves or our clothing] by the light of the [Shabbat] candle, and we do not read by the light of the [Shabbat] candle, and these are of the *halakhot* that they said in the upper story of Hananya ben Hezekiah ben Gurion. We learn from this that "and these," is the correct answer.

Decree Number	Mishnah	Tosefta	Palestinian Talmud[708]
1	Ink	Movable property wider than ox-goad carries uncleanness	Cheese of the non-Jews prohibited
2	Material for dye	Forgotten vessels under a pipe are unclean	Wine, vinegar, brine and fish-brine of non-Jews prohibited
3	Vetches	Roasting meat prohibited	Preserves and salted food of non-Jews prohibited
4	Bundles of flax	Roasting onions prohibited	Spelt, ground grain and peeled barley of non-Jews prohibited
5	Wool	Roasting eggs prohibited	Language (Greek) and testimony of non-Jews prohibited
6	Setting traps	May load beams of an olive press	Gifts of non-Jews prohibited
7	No selling to a non-Jew before Shabbat	May load rollers of a wine press	Sons and daughters of non-Jews prohibited
8	No loading beast of a non-Jew pre-Shabbat	No selling to a non-Jew before Shabbat	Firstlings of non-Jews prohibited[709]
9	No helping non-Jew load burden before Shabbat	No loading beast of a non-Jew before Shabbat	1st degree of unclean food makes one unclean
10	No giving hides to be worked pre-Shabbat	No helping non-Jew load burden before Shabbat	2nd degree of unclean food makes one unclean
11	No washing clothes at non-Jewish laundry pre-Shabbat	No washing **white** clothes at non-Jewish laundry before Shabbat	Drinking unclean liquids makes one unclean
12	May load rollers of a wine press before Shabbat	No washing **colored** clothes at non-Jewish laundry before Shabbat	Bathing head & majority of body in drawn water makes one unclean
13	May load beams of an olive press before Shabbat	May open irrigation channels before Shabbat	Bathing head and majority of body in >3 *logs* drawn water makes one unclean
14	-	May put medicine in eye before Shabbat	Holy Books make the hands unclean
15	-	May put a bandage on a wound before Shabbat	Unwashed hands are unclean
16	-	May burn sulfur under a vessel on Shabbat	One who immersed today (*tevul yom*) unclean
17	-	May use incense burner on Shabbat	Food touched by unclean liquids is unclean
18	-	May not put wheat into water-powered mills pre-Shabbat	Vessel touched by unclean liquids is unclean

And they <u>decreed</u> 18 matter[s]. What are these 18 matter[s]? As we
learned, (M Zav. 5:12) these make *terumah* unfit: one who eats unclean
food of the first degree; and one who eats unclean food of the second
degree; one who drinks unclean liquids; one whose head and the majority of the body enter drawn water; a clean person who had three *logs* of
drawn water fall on the head and the majority of the body; the book; the
hands; one who immersed that day; and foods and utensils that con-
tracted uncleanness from unclean liquids.

These twelve *gezerot* (Rabbi Meir counts, only eleven) show that the *baraitot*
contained in BT did not simply accept the rulings included in M as part of the
package of 18 *gezerot*, as T did. Instead, these *baraitot* in BT read the last clause
of M Shab. 1:15 ("and they decreed 18 decrees on that same day") as an opening
for a whole new set of laws retrojected to the incident when Beit Shammai prevailed over the votes of Beit Hillel that day. BT goes on to tell us that this collection of eleven is not the end of the decrees, but that there were many more.
BT Shab. 16b-17b lists the rest, pursuing a full count of 18 decrees:

ואידך מאי היא? דתנן: המניח כלים תחת הצינור לקבל בהן מי
גשמים אחד כלים גדולים ואחד כלים קטנים, ואפילו כלי אבנים
וכלי אדמה וכלי גללים, פוסלין את המקוה. אחד המניח ואחד
השוכח, דברי בית שמאי. ובית הלל מטהרין בשוכח . . . ואידך
מאי היא? דתנן: כל המטלטלין מביאין את הטומאה בעובי
המרדע . . . ואידך? הבוצר לגת, שמאי אומר: הוכשר, הלל אומר:
לא הוכשר. אמר לו הלל לשמאי: מפני מה בוצרין בטהרה, ואין
מוסקין בטהרה? אמר לו: אם תקניטני: גוזרני טומאה אף על
המסיקה. נעצו חרב בבית המדרש, אמרו: הנכנס יכנס והיוצא
אל יצא. ואותו היום היה הלל כפוף ויושב לפני שמאי כאחד מן
התלמידים, והיה קשה לישראל כיום שנעשה בו העגל. וגזור
שמאי והלל, ולא קבלו מינייהו, ואתו תלמידייהו גזור וקבלו
מינייהו . . . ואידך? אמר טבי רישבא אמר שמואל: אף גידולי
תרומה תרומה. בו ביום גזרו. מ"ט? א"ר חנינא: גזירה משום
תרומה טהורה ביד ישראל. ואידך? אמר רבי חייא בר אמי
משמיה דעולא: אף מי שהחשיך לו בדרך נותן כיסו לנכרי, בו
ביום גזרו. ואידך? אמר באלי אמר אבימי סנוותאה: פתן ושמן
ויין ובנותיהן, כולן משמונה עשר דבר הן.

And another one? As we learned (M Mik. 4:1): one who leaves
vessels under a spout to collect rainwater, it is the same if they are large
vessels or small vessels, and even a vessel of stone and a vessel of earth
and a vessel of dung, they make the *mikveh* unfit. It is the same if they

leave them there [on purpose] or if they forget them, according to Beit Shammai; but Beit Hillel declares the *mikveh* clean if they forgot. . . .

And another one? As we learned (M Oho. 16:1): Any movable property wider than an ox-goad conveys overshadowing uncleanness. .
. .

And another one? One who cuts grapes to make wine in a vat, Shammai says: it is susceptible [i.e., it may acquire ritual uncleanness]. Hillel says: it is not susceptible. Hillel said to Shammai: Why must we crush grapes in ritual purity, when we need not harvest olives in ritual purity? He said to him: If you provoke me, I will <u>decree</u> that olives must, likewise, be harvested in conditions of ritual purity. A sword was planted in the Beit HaMidrash, and they said: whoever comes in may come in, but no one may leave.[710] And on that day, Hillel sat bent in submission before Shammai like one of the students, and it was as hard for Israel as the day when the [Golden] Calf was made. And Shammai and Hillel <u>decreed</u> it, but they [their students] did not accept it from them. But their students came and <u>decreed</u> it and they [=the community and following generations] accepted it from them [=their students].[711]

And another? Tabbi the fowl trapper[712] said in the name of Shmuel: Even the produce that grows from *terumah* is considered *terumah*. They <u>decreed</u> it on that same day. What is the reason? Rabbi Hanina said it was a <u>decree</u> to prevent pure *terumah* [being retained] in the hands of an Israelite.

And another? Rabbi Hiyya bar Ammi said in the name of Ulla: Even one [traveling] on the road [after Shabbat began] must give one's purse to a non-Jew. They <u>decreed</u> it on that same day.

And another? Bali said in the name of Abimi Sanvatah:[713] Their bread and their wine and their daughters [of non-Jews, all are forbidden to us as a preventative measure] – all are [decrees that are] from the 18 matter[s].

BT's three sets of 18 decrees (according to Rabbi Yossi, Rabbi Meir or Rabbi Tarfon), are substantially different from M, T or PT, as shown in the table on the opposite page. It is evident from the table that the editors of BT significantly expanded a very small phrase in M ("and they decreed 18 decrees"), and created an extended list of *gezerot* imbued with all the Tannaitic authority they could muster, filling this empty construct with additional restrictions on observance they wished to root firmly in a prior historical moment. Retrojection with such a strong hand was a favored tactic of the editors of BT, as we have seen in other parts of this study. Here, however, we see it in its finest hour.

The overriding concern of the editors who created the Amoraic overlays in PT and BT was with rather utopian questions of purity and separation from idolaters, laws that were most likely not observed during the Amoraic period at all. While the original mishnah and even its later interpretation in T were solely based around the analysis of Shabbat observance, and had absolutely nothing to do with purity, in BT's final version, a mere three of the decrees (1, 2 and 16) maintain any connection with Shabbat at all! Thus, the editors of BT have utilized two *baraitot* to pack as many purity restrictions as they possibly could into a gaping hole of history they forced open by creatively rereading the Mishnah. While PT began this process, it is in BT that its ultimate evolution concluded. Thus, we see that the concerns of the late Amoraic editors of these texts came out through their reworking of an earlier historical stratum, by retrojecting their priorities onto a more powerful set of earlier authorizing rabbis.

One final note on these decrees comes from BT AZ 36a, during a discussion covered earlier in this chapter about a decree against the use of an idolater's oil. This leads to the oft-repeated question of whether a court may overturn a prior court's decree, where our 18 decrees are mentioned:

> והתנן : אין בית דין יכול לבטל דברי בית דין חבירו, אלא אם כן גדול
> הימנו בחכמה ובמנין. ועוד : הא אמר רבה בר בר חנה אמר ר׳ יוחנן : בכל
> יכול לבטל בית דין דברי בית דין חבירו, חוץ משמונה עשר דבר, שאפילו
> יבא אליהו ובית דינו אין שומעין לו! אמר רב משרשיא : מה טעם? הואיל
> ופשט איסורו ברוב ישראל.

> And was it not taught: A court is unable to invalidate the decisions of another court, unless it is greater in number and in wisdom. And further: Rabbah bar Bar Hannah said in the name of Rabbi Yohanan: One court may invalidate every matter of another court except for the 18 matter[s], for even if the Prophet Elijah were to come with his court, we do not obey him [if he tries to cancel these 18 decrees]! Rav Mesharshya said: What is the reason? Since the prohibition had spread to the majority of Israel.

BT thus imbued these 18 decrees with an especially privileged status, granted them by the acceptance of the people Israel. Even as worthy a character as Elijah the Prophet, usually endowed with great power, would be unable to invalidate these decrees, even if his court exceeded the number and wisdom of the disciples of Hillel and Shammai on that day. Widespread communal acceptance of *gezerot* lent added *gravitas* to this set of decrees, sealing the validity of these laws forever. The listing below shows the various opinions contained within BT:

Decree	Rabbi Yossi	Rabbi Meir	Rabbi Tarfon
1	No delousing on Shabbat by candle light	No delousing on Shabbat by candle light	No delousing on Shabbat by candle light
2	No reading on Shabbat by candle light	No reading on Shabbat by candle light	No reading on Shabbat by candle light
3	First degree unclean food makes one unclean	First degree unclean food makes one unclean	First degree unclean food makes one unclean
4	Second degree unclean food makes one unclean	Second degree unclean food makes one unclean	Second degree unclean food makes one unclean
5	Drinking unclean liquids makes one unclean	Drinking unclean liquids makes one unclean	Drinking unclean liquids makes one unclean
6	Bathing head & majority of body in drawn water makes one unclean	Bathing head & majority of body in drawn water makes one unclean	Bathing head & majority of body in drawn water makes one unclean
7	Showering head and majority of body in >3 *logs* drawn water makes one unclean	Showering head and majority of body in >3 *logs* drawn water makes one unclean	Showering head and majority of body in >3 *logs* drawn water makes one unclean
8	Holy Books make the hands unclean	Holy Books make the hands unclean	Holy Books make the hands unclean
9	Unwashed hands are unclean	Unwashed hands are unclean	Unwashed hands are unclean
10	One who immersed today (*tevul yom*) is unclean	One who immersed today (*tevul yom*) is unclean	One who immersed today (*tevul yom*) is unclean
11	Food touched by unclean liquids unclean	Food **and vessels** touched by unclean liquids unclean[714]	Food touched by unclean liquids unclean
12	Vessel touched by unclean liquids is unclean	**Forgotten vessels under a pipe are unclean**[715]	Vessel touched by unclean liquids is unclean
13	Movable property larger than an ox-goad can form a tent and transmit uncleanness	Movable property larger than an ox-goad can form a tent and transmit uncleanness	**Forgotten vessels under a pipe are unclean**[716]
14	Vintage grapes in ritually pure conditions	Vintage grapes in ritually pure conditions	Vintage grapes in ritually pure conditions
15	Produce of *terumah* is *terumah*	Produce of *terumah* is *terumah*	Produce of *terumah* is *terumah*
16	Give purse to a non-Jew if on a road after Shabbat starts	Give purse to a non-Jew if on a road after Shabbat starts	Give purse to a non-Jew if on a road after Shabbat starts
17	Bread, wine, oil and daughters of non-Jews forbidden	Bread, wine, oil and daughters of non-Jews forbidden	Bread, wine, oil and daughters of non-Jews forbidden
18	Non-Jewish child is considered a *zav*	Non-Jewish child is considered a *zav*	Non-Jewish child is considered a *zav*

In the development of our most extensive grouping of *gezerot*, we see reflected the concerns of each of the authors in their time, utilizing an earlier textual precedent to create law that altered and expanded received legal formulae. By and large, the reported change here began by employing a conservative hermeneutic, initially broadening the purview of Shabbat limitations to outlaw certain boundary activities that could potentially lead to Shabbat violation. Later, especially in BT, a more flexible ideology was at work, which justified enlarging the circle of purity laws to include new practices. Both legal actions retrojected the existence of these decrees back to a Tannaitic leadership that appeared never even to have explicitly discussed them as *gezerot*.

Muting Joy: In the Wake of the Temple

M Sot. 9:14 brings our next set of grouped *gezerot*, centered this time on a moment in history that required legal response to the vicissitudes of war:

בפולמוס של אספסיינוס גזרו על עטרות חתנים ועל האירוס. בפולמוס של
קיטוס גזרו על עטרות כלות, ושלא ילמד אדם את בנו יונית. בפולמוס
האחרון גזרו שלא תצא הכלה באפריון בתוך העיר. ורבותינו התירו שתצא
הכלה באפריון בתוך העיר:

During the war[717] of Vespasian, they <u>decreed</u> against the crowns of grooms and the [use of the] drum [at wedding celebrations]. During the war of Quietus,[718] they <u>decreed</u> against the crowns of brides, and that a person may not teach his/her son Greek.[719] During the final war,[720] they <u>decreed</u> that the bride would not come out on a palanquin inside the city. And our rabbis[721] allowed the bride to come out on a palanquin inside the city.[722]

This mishnah shows the reported results of a disastrous series of lost battles upon both Jewish morale and the ritual celebration of weddings in Judaea. In the face of the trials of war, prior customs that emphasized the joy of impending nuptials are cancelled, as a reminder to the entire community to recalibrate its sense of stability and happiness. As usual, M presents these texts apodictically, with no discussion of reasoning attached to them.

In T Sot. 15:8-10, we find the only parallel to this grouping of war-related *gezerot*. The parallel text has a number of additions, expansions and explanations:

(ח) בפולמוס של אספסינוס, גזרו על עטרות חתנים. ואילו הן עטרות
חתנים : של מלח, ושל גפרית. אבל של ורד, ושל הדס התירו. בפולמוס של
קיטוס גזרו על עטרות כלות. אילו הן עטרות כלות : אילו זהוריות

מזוהבות. אבל יוצאה היא בכיפה של מלח בבית. ושלא ילמד אדם את בנו
יונית. התירו להם לבית רבן גמליאל ללמד את בניהם יונית, מפני שהן
קרובין למלכות.

(8) During the war of Vespasian, they <u>decreed</u> against crowns of
grooms (M Sot. 9:14). Which are the crowns of grooms [that were for-
bidden]? [Those] of salt and of sulfur. But [crowns made] of roses and
of myrtles they permitted.

During the war of Quietus[723] they <u>decreed</u> against crowns of
brides. Which are crowns of brides [that were forbidden]? [Those] of
silk woven with gold. But she may go out in a cap of salt in the
house.[724] And [they also <u>decreed</u>] that one may not teach one's child
Greek (M Sotah 9:14).[725] They permitted the house of Rabban Shimeon
ben Gamaliel to teach their children Greek, since they were close to the
[Roman] government.[726]

As we can see in this text, the War of Vespasian provided a dire enough circumstance to lead to modification of the legal permissions afforded those involved in
marriage ceremonies. The Roman general Vespasian began his assault on Jerusalem in 67 CE, about three years before his son and successor, Titus, accomplished the ultimate destruction of the Temple and the capture of the entire city
after Vespasian was called away to Rome to assume the position of Emperor.
The tremendous Jewish suffering of this time may be seen mainly in the work of
Josephus, though rabbinic literature is also replete with horror stories.[727]
    Subduing the level of joy inherent in wedding festivities during a difficult
time is symbolized by change in the ritual garb associated with the celebration.
The particulars of the crowns themselves are interesting. The prior grooms'
crowns, made from rock salt and decorated with sulfur drawings on them, were
translucent, attractive and durable. In contrast, the use of vegetative crowns replaced this traditional observance with a more ethereal crown fashioned more by
nature than by humanity. These less extravagant crowns served as a reminder
that the community was still facing war, even in a moment when a couple was
uniting in joy. On the bride's side, there is a concomitant downgrading of
crowns from silk woven with gold to those made of rock salt and sulfur. In both
cases, the casting off of extravagant headgear is meant as a symbol of the pain
felt throughout society, during and after the siege on, and eventual downfall of,
Jerusalem.
    The prohibition on teaching one's child Greek has a prior history to it that
warrants further examination. Lieberman argued[728] that the restriction was not
against either the adult study of Greek language or Greek wisdom, or the teaching of it to adults. Instead, he believed that the concern here was the teaching of

Greek language to children, for until a child has shown enough maturity to be a faithful and community-minded Jewish adult, it was unwise to teach the child a language that could be used to inform on the Jewish community to the Romans. Thus, the concern here was not a broad elimination of Greek language and Greek wisdom from the Judaean community, rather it was to ensure that those who knew Greek used it solely for the benefit of the Jewish community, rather than to its detriment. In this respect, this *gezerah* was more one that shaped the use of political power than one that was driven by any philosophical stand toward Greek language and philosophy.[729]

One could argue that this is a protective fence around the Torah because it prevents the neglect of the study of Torah, since any time spent on the study (or teaching) of Greek language or wisdom would, by definition, be time away from Torah study. In fact, there is at least one source that takes this tack.[730] However, the reasons explicitly tendered here for the creation of this prohibition avoid utilizing this rationale, one that easily could have been stated and justified based on the *mitzvah* of Torah study.

In the continuation of these decrees in T, we find the following:

(ט) ושלא לסוד את ביתו בסיד. בביצת הסיד. אם עירב בו תבן או חול, מותר. ר' יהודה אומר: עירב בו חול, הרי זה טרכי סיד ואסור. אם עירב בו תבן מותר. פולמוס האחרון גזרו על חופת חתנים. אילו הן חופת התנים: אלו של זהב, אבל עושה הוא אפיפירות ותולה בה כל מה שירצה. ושלא תצא כלה באפיריון בתוך העיר. ורבותינו התירו שתצא כלה באפריון בתוך העיר. אף על פלטון גזר ר' יהודה בן בבא, ולא הודו לו חכמים.

(9) And [they also <u>decreed</u>] that one may not plaster one's house with plaster. This is: with the plaster of egg.[731] If one mixed it with straw or sand, it is permitted. Rabbi Yehuda says: if he mixed it with sand, this is a binding plaster, and is forbidden. [During] the last war,[732] they <u>decreed</u> against the *huppah* [wedding canopy] of grooms. These are the [forbidden] wedding canopies of grooms: those that are of gold. But one may make frames and hang from them whatever is desired. And a bride may not go out on a palanquin inside the city. But our rabbis permitted the bride to go out on a palanquin inside the city (M Sotah 9:14). Rabbi Yehuda ben Bava <u>decreed</u> against the use of spikenard oil,[733] but the Sages did not agree with him.

In T Sotah 15:9, we find more customary limitations said to decrease the joy of the memory of Jerusalem after the destruction of the Temple in 70 CE. Plastering one's home in a color and texture reminiscent of Jerusalem is forbidden, extravagant golden wedding canopies are eliminated, and palanquins, bridal

litters that were paraded around town with the bride ensconced within during
Temple times, were now a thing of the past, considered too ornate for the poor
surroundings in post-Temple Judaea. Even spikenard oil, a precious luxury fra-
grance, was not to be used at all according to one minority opinion, though the
sages ultimately permitted it.

This section presents, then, a grouping of *gezerot* that expressed the rabbinic outlook on the destruction, balancing the joy felt at happy occasions with
the intense sadness of communal disenfranchisement, punishment and defeat.
Only one small note of hope rings through: these activities, though altered, never
ceased.

The *Gezerot* of Admon and Hanan ben Avishalom

Similar to the two examples covered above, there is another example of
nine *gezerot* grouped together by the parties who decreed them, two of which
are assigned to Hanan, and seven to Admon. The earliest version of this tradition
comes from M Ket. 13:1-9:

(א) שני דייני גזירות היו בירושלם: אדמון וחנן בן אבישלום. חנן אומר שני
דברים, אדמון אומר שבעה. מי שהלך למדינת הים ואשתו תובעת מזונות,
חנן אומר: תשבע בסוף ולא תשבע בתחלה. נחלקו עליו בני כהנים גדולים,
ואמרו תשבע בתחלה ובסוף. אמר רבי דוסא בן הרכינס כדבריהם. אמר
רבן יוחנן בן זכאי: יפה אמר חנן לא תשבע אלא בסוף: (ב) מי שהלך
למדינת הים ועמד אחד ופרנס את אשתו, חנן אומר: איבד את מעותיו.
נחלקו עליו בני כהנים גדולים, ואמרו ישבע כמה הוציא ויטול. אמר רבי
דוסא בן הרכינס כדבריהם. אמר רבן יוחנן בן זכאי: יפה אמר חנן, הניח
מעותיו על קרן הצבי: (ג) אדמון אומר שבעה. מי שמת והניח בנים ובנות,
בזמן שהנכסים מרובין, הבנים יורשים והבנות ניזונות, ובנכסים מועטים
הבנות יזונו והבנים יחזרו על הפתחים. אדמון אומר: בשביל שאני זכר
הפסדתי! אמר רבן גמליאל: רואה אני את דברי אדמון: (ד) הטוען את
חברו כדי שמן והודה בקנקנים, אדמון אומר: הואיל והודה במקצת
הטענה, ישבע. וחכמים אומרים: אין זו הודאה ממין הטענה. אמר רבן
גמליאל: רואה אני את דברי אדמון: (ה) הפוסק מעות לחתנו, ופשט לו
את הרגל, תשב עד שילבין ראשה. אדמון אומר: יכולה היא שתאמר אילו
אני פסקתי לעצמי אשב עד שילבין ראשי, עכשיו שאבא פסק עלי, מה אני
יכולה לעשו, או כנוס או פטור! אמר רבן גמליאל: רואה אני את דברי
אדמון: (ו) העורר על השדה, והוא חתום עליה בעד. אדמון אומר: יכול
הוא שיאמר השני נוח לי, והראשון קשה הימנו. וחכמים אומרים: איבד
את זכותו. עשאה סימן לאחר איבד את זכותו: (ז) מי שהלך למדינת הים
ואבדה דרך שדהו, אדמון אומר: ילך בקצרה. וחכמים אומרים: יקנה לו
דרך במאה מנה או יפרח באויר: (ח) המוציא שטר חוב על חברו והלה
הוציא שמכר לו את השדה, אדמון אומר: יכול הוא שיאמר אילו הייתי
חייב לך היה לך להפרע את שלך כשמכרת לי את השדה. וחכמים אומרים:
זה היה פקח שמכר לו את הקרקע מפני שהוא יכול למשכנו: (ט) שנים

שהוציאו שטר חוב זה על זה, אדמון אומר: אילו הייתי חייב לך כיצד
אתה לוה ממני? וחכמים אומרים: זה גובה שטר חובו, וזה גובה שטר
חובו:

1) There were two judges of *gezerot*[734] in Jerusalem:[735] Admon and
Hanan ben Avishalom. Hanan says two things, Admon says seven. One
who went abroad, and his wife makes a claim for sustenance, Hanan
says: she must swear at the end, but she must not swear at the beginning.[736] The children of the high priests[737] disagreed with him, and they
said: She may swear at the beginning [as well]! Rabbi Dosa ben
Hyrkanos agreed with their view. Rabban Yohanan ben Zakkai said:
Hanan spoke well, she must swear only at the end.[738]

2) One who went abroad, and [some]one [else] arose who sustained his
wife, Hanan said: he [i.e., the other supporter] lost his money [that he
spent on supporting the other's wife]. The children of the high priests
disagreed with him, and said: he shall swear as to how much he laid
out, and take it [from the husband who went abroad]. Rabbi Dosa ben
Hyrkanos agreed with them. Rabban Yohanan ben Zakkai said: Hanan
spoke well; [the one who supported the other's wife] he left his coins
on the horns of a deer.[739]

3) Admon says seven [things]: one who died and left sons and daughters, in the case where the property was great, the sons inherit and the
daughters are sustained [by the estate until they marry].[740] [In a case]
where the property was small, the daughters are sustained [by the es-
tate] and the sons will go from door to door.[741] Admon says: Because I
am male I have lost out [on benefiting from the estate]? Rabban Gamaliel[742] said: I see the point of Admon's words.[743]

4) [In the case of] one who claims that his colleague owes him jugs of
oil, and his colleague admits to owing him empty jugs, Admon says:
since he admitted to part of the claim, he will swear; and the sages say:
this is not an admission of part of the claim. Rabban Gamaliel said: I
see the point of Admon's words.[744]

5) One who stipulated [to give] money to his son-in-law,[745] but then re-
neged, she will sit until her head turns white.[746] Admon says: She is
able to say: If I had stipulated myself, I would sit until my head turned
white, however since my father stipulated for me, what can I do?[747] Ei-

ther [my betrothed] must marry me or divorce me! Rabban Gamaliel said: I see the point of Admon's words.

6) One who contests the ownership of a field who is also a signatory [as a witness on the deed],[748] Admon says he may claim: the second [person involved] is easier for me, the first is harder than him;[749] but the sages say: he has lost his right [to any claim on the field]. If he made a boundary mark [for a nearby field that indicated his acknowledgment of the other's ownership of the field he is challenging], he has lost his right [to the field.][750]

7) One who went abroad and the path to his field was lost,[751] Admon says: he may walk via the shortest path; while the sages say: He must buy a path even for 100 *maneh*, or fly through the air.[752]

8) One who brings a bond of debt against his debtor [to enforce payment in court], and the debtor provides a bill of sale[753] that proves he [recently] sold the lender the field, Admon says: He can say "if I were [truly] obligated to pay you, you should have taken what was yours when you sold me the field;" but the sages say "This one was prudent when he sold him the field, since he can [now] take it as security."[754]

9) Two [people] who brought forth bonds of debt against one another, Admon says: [this one can say:] "If I had owed you money, how did you borrow from me?"[755] But the sages say: "This one collects his bond, and this one collects his bond."[756]

In addition to the clear grouping according to specific judges, Frankel noted a strong thematic connection among these laws, all of which seem to fit a certain characterization approximated by the German term *Politziarecht*, vaguely akin to the American legal notion of "small claims." Not completely based on a legal precedent, and of moderate import (certainly less so than larger civil or criminal cases), these laws saw to the smooth running of society, and were often based on the judges' *ad hoc* determination of justice in the case at hand.[757] Weiss, likewise, suggested that these two judges were involved in activities that increased peaceful coexistence in society at a time when the social fabric was fraying, during the fifty years leading up to the destruction of the Temple. Their decisions, Weiss agreed, were not based on legal precedent, but on pressing communal needs in a decaying political environment.[758] From a literary perspective, Albeck saw this grouping as an anomaly, stepping away from the usual thematic organization generally employed by M.[759]

The form of these *mishnayot* actually fits the two and seven pattern stated. In fact, this pattern of two and seven statements seems to consistently hold true throughout the later texts that evolve afterwards, in stark contrast with the development of the texts we saw above that followed the 18 decrees in the upstairs room of Hananya ben Hezekiah ben Gurion. That is not, however, to say that all is clear and consistent throughout the entirety of the divergent strands of this tradition, as we quickly learn first from PT Ket. 13:1, 35c, where the acceptance of the legal statements of Admon is called into question vis-à-vis the *halakhah*:

רבי זעירא, רב חננאל בשם רב, ר׳ זעירא בשם אבא בר ירמיה: שני דברים
אמר חנן, הלכה כיוצא בו. שבעה דברים אמר אדמון אין הלכה כיוצא בו.
רבי בא בר זבדא בשם רבי יצחק בר חקולא: בכל מקום ששנינו, אמר רבן
גמליאל רואה אני את דברי אדמון, הלכה כיוצא בו.

Rabbi Zeira, Rav Hananel in the name of Rav, Rabbi Zeira in the name of Abba bar Yermiyah [said]: Hanan said two things, and *halakhah* follows him. Admon said seven things, and *halakhah* does not follow him. Rabbi [Ab]ba bar Zabda said in the name of Rabbi Yitzhak bar Hakula: in any place where we learned, "Rabban Gamaliel said 'I recognize the words of Admon,'" [and this implies that] *halakhah* follows him.

Without any final word on the outcome of this *mahloket* in PT, we are simply left with two standing opinions, one that accepts the statements of both Hanan and Admon while the other rejects Admon's words despite their support by Rabban Gamaliel.

BT Ket. 105a, where we find a parallel *baraita* followed by interpretive material that informs us further about these judges and their activities:

ורמינהי, שלשה דייני גזילות היו בירושלים: אדמון בן גדאי, וחנן המצרי,
וחנן בן אבישלום; קשיא תלת אתרין! קשיא גזירות אגזילות! בשלמא
תלת אתרין לא קשיא, דחשיב ליה קתני, דלא חשיב ליה לא קתני, אלא
גזירות אגזילות קשיא! אמר רב נחמן בר יצחק: שהיו גוזרין גזירות על
גזילות; כדתניא: קיטמה נטיעה, ר׳ יוסי אומר: גוזרי גזירות שבירושלים
אומרים: נטיעה בת שנתה, שתי כסף; בת שתי שנים, ארבע כסף. ורמינהי,
שלשה דייני גזירות היו בירושלים: אדמון, וחנן, ונחום! א״ר פפא: מאן
תנא נחום? ר׳ נתן היא; דתניא, רבי נתן אומר: אף נחום המדי מגוזרי
גזירות שבירושלים היה, ולא הודו לו חכמים. ותו ליכא? והאמר ר׳ פנחס
אמר רבי אושעיא: שלש מאות ותשעים וארבעה בתי דינין היו בירושלים,
כנגדן בתי כנסיות, וכנגדן בתי מדרשות, וכנגדן בתי סופרים! דייני טובא
הוו, וכי קאמרינן, אגוזרי גזירות קאמרינן. אמר רב יהודה אמר רב אסי:
גוזרי גזירות שבירושלים, היו נוטלין שכרן תשעים ותשע מנה מתרומת

הלשכה, לא רצו, מוסיפין להם. לא רצו, אטו ברשיעי עסקינן? אלא לא
ספקו, אע"פ שלא רצו, מוסיפין עליהן.

A *baraita* conflicts [with the account of the mishnah]: There were three judges of theft in Jerusalem: Admon ben Gadai, Hanan the Egyptian and Hanan ben Avishalom. There is a contradiction between "two" and "three!" There is [another] contradiction between "*gezerot*" and "*gezelot*!" There is no problem between "two" and "three," [but this is] because the mishnah simply mentioned those judges it considered important [and did not mention those it did not consider important]. But between "*gezerot*" and "*gezelot*" there is still a problem. Rav Nahman bar Yitzhak said: they were decreeing decrees related to theft, as it was taught: [if one's animal] severed a plant, Rabbi Yossi says: the promulgators of decrees in Jerusalem say: for a plant in its first year, one must pay two silver coins, for a plant in its second year, one must pay four silver coins.

A[nother] *baraita* conflicts with this account: There were three judges of decrees in Jerusalem: Admon, Hanan and Nahum.[760] Rav Papa said: Who taught (in this *baraita*) this "Nahum?" It was Rabbi Natan, as it was taught: Rabbi Natan says: Even Nahum the Mede was among the promulgators of decrees in Jerusalem, but the sages did not accept [his decisions].

And no more judges? [Did not] Rabbi Pinhas say in the name of Rabbi Hoshaya: There were 394 courts in Jerusalem, and as many synagogues, and as many houses of study, and as many schools![761] There were many judges, and when we said [three], these were [only] the ones who promulgated decrees.

Rav Yehuda said in the name of Rav Assi: The enactors of decrees in Jerusalem took their compensation of 99 *minas* from the Temple *terumah* funds.[762] If they did not want [so little], they received more. Can you say that we are dealing with evil people [who looked to take more from Temple funds]? Rather, read instead "if it was not sufficient, even if they did not want it, then they received more." [Thus, an increase was granted them even if they refused it].

BT begins by harmonizing away the difference between judges who enacted *gezerot* and those who ruled on *gezelot*, and then solving the problem of two variant traditions of the number of these judges. Urbach, in particular, does not accept the idea that all these laws centered on the same topical focus. Instead, he believed that it was the prominent role of these judges that united these laws.[763] In BT's rehashing, no paucity of judges plagued Jerusalem during this period, but the two or three most prominent promulgators of *gezerot* were Admon, Hanan and either Nahum or Hanan the Egyptian. BT reflects, here, a certain outlook on formulating *gezerot* as a closely held and centralized activity. The task of making *gezerot* was not given to regular judges who existed in quantity, but was reserved for that special slice of the judiciary specifically housed in Jerusalem and charged with decreeing *gezerot*.

Urbach, in fact, relies on this text and others like it, to posit the existence of a centralized authority in Jerusalem that operated during the Second Temple period, and set the course of legal development by making and promulgating decrees:

> [We may trace] a phenomenon of disputed laws and varying customs in one locality—even within Jerusalem itself—which developed as a result of judges and sages specializing in defined areas of law with regard to which they possessed specific traditions. . . .

> On the basis of the theory we have proposed, it becomes possible to explain the difficult subject of the "Gezerah Judges." The Jerusalem Talmud (Shekalim 4:3, 48a) makes reference to "those who enact *gezerot*" thus: "Gidel b. Minyumi said in the name of R. Assi: The two *gezelot* judges took their fee from the *terumah* of the Shekel-Chamber," while the Babylonian Talmud (Ketubbot 105a) reports: "R. Judah said in the name of R. Assi: Those who enact *gezerot* [*gozrei gezerot*] in Jerusalem used to take their fee of ninety-nine *minas* from the *terumah* of the Shekel-Chamber." These sources constitute an ancient tradition concerning Temple officials whose function was to study and preserve the *takkanot* and *gezerot* and it is possible that this procedure originated from a Sadducean usage to keep a "book of *gezerot*. . . . " Even after the "book of *gezerot*" was abolished,[764] there was still a place for the *gozrei gezerot*; they had to preserve the *takkanot* and *gezerot* in their memories. [765]

While this strong statement is compelling in principle, it would seem to be hanging by a thread: there is simply not enough evidence in these texts (nor in the others cited by Urbach) to prove the existence of such an elaborate and organized system of judicial action and preservation. A total of nine decrees preserved in the name of these judges, all of which are later disputed by sages, priests or individual authorities, does not provide sufficient proof of the existence of such a highly developed and centralized system for legal oversight.

As opposed to the section from BT Shab. 13a-17a above, here BT does not attempt to pick up on a possible lacuna and fill it with *gezerot*, rather the choice was made by BT's editors to simply clarify any contradictions and move on to other topics. This is likely due to the individuals involved: while Beit Shammai and Beit Hillel retained authority long after their time, Hanan, Admon and the others mentioned in the Ketubbot passages appear only rarely, if at all, as tradents or authorities in later texts. Also, since the exact number of *gezerot* is exactly stated and fulfilled in M, there is less latitude for later imposition of ideas and rulings.

Here, then, we have a collection of *gezerot* that are centered on two (or potentially three, if we include Nahum/Hanan the Egyptian) specialist's legal decision-making. Since the laws stated certainly do not fit neatly into the category of theft, the resultant determination must be that these are grouped around Hanan and Admon. The use of the term *gezerot* indicates that these laws were more than simple court decisions, for they appear to have had a more binding and longer lasting effect. Nonetheless, this does not provide sufficient evidence for the conclusion that there was a larger, more complicated or permanent centralized judiciary acting in these areas. We can see, though, that the editors of later texts respected the authorities mentioned enough to include their opinions, noting they were *gezerot*, even if only some eventuated in halakhah.

Topically Grouped *Gezerot*

Our legal corpus contains three examples of texts that order their *gezerot* topically, addressing three vital concerns of the rabbinic mindset: idolatry,[766] Sabbath observance[767] and doubtfully tithed produce.[768] Each text gives ample opportunity to witness classic examples of rabbinic prohibitions that truly fit the accepted definition of "fences around the Torah." We will examine only one of these sections, the set of prohibitions centered on idolaters.

Fencing against Idolatry

In M AZ 2:6, we find an early example of the thread of prohibitions that limit interactions between Jews and idolaters. While M itself does not use the term *gezerah*, BT follows up on this pericope by using this term to describe these prohibitions, rendering them eligible for inclusion in our study. The initial mishnah (M AZ 2:6) reads:

אלו דברים של עכו"ם אסורין, ואין איסורן איסור הנאה: חלב שחלבו
עכו"ם ואין ישראל רואהו, והפת והשמן שלהן. רבי ובית דינו התירו בשמן.
ושלקות, וכבשין שדרכן לתת לתוכן יין וחומץ, וטרית טרופה, וציר שאין

בה דגה כלבית שוטטת בו, והחילק, וקורט של חלתית, ומלח סלקונטית.
הרי אלו אסורין ואין איסורן איסור הנאה :

These are the prohibited items related to an idolater, but they are not
prohibitions against benefit [from the item involved]:[769] milk [from an
animal] that an idolater milked without a Jew watching him, their
bread, and their oil. Rabbi [Yehuda Nesiah][770] and his court permitted
the oil.[771] And [also prohibited are] their cooked food, and their pickled
food where it is their custom to put wine and vinegar in,[772] and minced
fish, and brine made without fish floating in it, and *hilek* fish,[773] pieces
of asefetida[774] and seasoned salt.[775] These they are forbidden [to eat],
but it is not prohibited to derive benefit [from them].

No explicit sign of the word *gezerah* is present here at all; though the restrictions
imposed surely fit the general class of law we would name *gezerot* in that they
place a fence around activities that might lead to interaction with and practice of
idolatry. T, similarly, does not, at any point, refer to these laws as *gezerot*. In PT
AZ 2:8, 41d, though, there is a reference which does name the law prohibiting
use of heathen oil as a *gezerah*. It is then traced back to Daniel and his colleagues as its originators. The problem comes when PT tries to indicate that the
later court of Rabbi Yehuda Nesiah and his colleagues, of lesser prominence and
number than a prophet the likes of Daniel, attempted to uproot this *gezerah*:

ר' יוחנן בעי : ולא כן תנינן שאין בית דין יכול לבטל דברי בית דין חבירו עד
שיהא גדול ממנו בחכמה ובמניין! ורבי ובית דינו מתירין מה שאסר דניאל
וחביריו!?! רבי יוחנן כדעתיה : אמר ר' יוחנן מקובל אני מרבי לעזר בי רבי
צדוק שכל גזירה שבית דין גוזרין ואין רוב ציבור מקבלין עליהן אינה
גזירה. בדקו ומצאו בגזירתו של שמן ולא מצאו שקיבלו רוב הציבור
עליהן.

Rabbi Yohanan asked: Did we not learn (M Ed. 1:5) that a court is not
permitted to nullify the decisions of another court unless it is greater
than it in wisdom and in number? And [can it really be true that] Rabbi
[Yehuda Nesiah] and his court permitted what Daniel and his colleagues prohibited? Rabbi Yohanan [speaks] according to his opinion
[as it appears in other statements of his]: Rabbi Yohanan said "I have a
received tradition from Rabbi Eleazar son of Rabbi Tzadok that any <u>de-
cree</u> that a court <u>decrees</u> and the majority of the community does not
accept upon itself, it is no [longer considered an effective] <u>decree</u>. They
checked and found regarding the <u>decree</u> against [heathen] oil, and they

did not find that the majority of the community accepted it [thus nullifying it].

The editors of PT, as mentioned in the earlier part of this chapter, do recognize
the prohibition against heathen oil as a *gezerah*, both in name and in the way
they subject it to the principle that the community must accept a decree for it to
be efficacious. Its present, fence-like application is entirely consistent with the
definitions we have seen above.

BT AZ 36b, reading more broadly, declares all these restrictions *gezerot*:

וגניבא משמיה דרב אמר: כולן משום עבודת כוכבים גזרו בהן, דכי אתא
רב אחא בר אדא א"ר יצחק: גזרו על פיתן משום שמן; מאי אולמיה
דשמן מפת? אלא, על פיתן ושמן משום יינן, ועל יינן משום בנותיהן, ועל
בנותיהן משום דבר אחר, ועל דבר אחר משום ד"יא.

And Geneba said in the name of Rav: All [of these prohibitions], they
<u>decreed</u> against them because of [preventing] idolatry, for when Rav
Aha bar Ada came [from Palestine to Babylonia], he said in the name
of Rav Yitzhak: they <u>decreed</u> against their bread because of their oil.
Why be stricter about bread because of oil? Rather, read it this way:
[they decreed] against their bread and oil on account of their wine;[776]
against their wine on account of their daughters;[777] against their daughters on account of another matter;[778] and against another matter on account of still another matter.[779]

Here, we see a number of apodictically stated laws listed in M with no hint as to
their provenance, all related to the topic of idolatry, which are later recast as
gezerot in the discussion of their origin in BT. While the Gemaras differ on the
precise details and causes of the various prohibitions included in M, it seems
clear that the entirety of these narrowly focused individual prohibitions arise to
limit interaction with idolatry. The editors of M, PT and BT arranged them into
a topical unit. Yet, it is only in the Amoraic strata of PT and BT that they are
called *gezerot*. This represents a reclassification of prior laws as *gezerot*, and
shows that both BT and PT were not reticent to utilize such a rhetorical strategy
to enhance the observance and understanding of prior laws.

Throughout the preceding pages, we have seen that numerous *gezerot* are
presented in groupings that are based around individuals, historical events or
themes. Such collecting of decrees indicates a high degree of editorial work by
the editors of these texts, in creating and expanding the legal underpinnings of
various decisions. Utilizing tropes that existed in biblical texts, taking advantage
of the power of prior leadership and playing upon situations incompletely explained by earlier texts such as M and T were all strategies utilized by the edi-

tors of later texts, searching for ways to root conserving legal change into the prior traditions.

Most of these usages prove to be examples of the primary category of *gezerot*, that of fences around the Torah. As noted, the vast majority of *gezerot* were fences made to reduce the violation of pentateuchal laws. We will now turn our attention to other usages of the term *gezerah*. Though few, they do represent certain categories that should not be ignored.

Other Categories

The other uses of the root *gzr* follow along well-tread paths we have seen in prior chapters, and have little to add in the way of new rationales or modes of change in the rabbinic period. For the sake of completeness, we will briefly mention them in their categories, and list the involved citations

Initiation

In 13 cases,[780] we see the root *gzr* used to demarcate the presence of innova-tive activity, most similar to the predominate usage of the root *tkn*. The initia-tors, as we saw previously, range widely through the chronology of the ancient world, from Adam to the rabbis.

Changes in Authority Structures

In eight cases,[781] the root *gzr* reflects changes in authority structures, whether internal or external, that led to changes in rabbinic law.

An Incident Occurs

In eight cases,[782] the root *gzr* is utilized to reflect changes in rabbinic law after an incident occurred to show a problem with it, all in similar ways to what we saw in chapter one with the term *barishonah*.

Business and Agricultural Changes

In six cases,[783] *gzr* represents changes in business or agricultural practices that spur changes in rabbinic law.

Encouraging Proper Behavior

As we saw in chapter two, sometimes law is changed to encourage proper behavior among the populace. The root *gzr* is utilized to do this in six cases.[784]

For the Sake of Social Welfare

Three cases[785] of change in rabbinic law that concern social welfare (*tikkun haolam*) are registered with the root *gzr*.

Upholding the Words of Prior Sages

In a single case in our rabbinic texts, we find *gzr* used with a change in rabbinic law that upholds the words and actions of prior sages.[786]

Chapter Three—Conclusions

The most immediate and consistent result we found in our study of the use of the root *gzr* in rabbinic literature is that there is a significant difference in its meaning that divides roughly between the Tannaitic and Amoraic literature. In the Tannaitic texts (M, T and the Halakhic Midrashim), we found a wide range of meanings present, but only one (found in T[787]) case of the predominate usage so omnipresent in Amoraic texts: that of creating a fence around the law. Thus, our most important finding is that this meaning of "fence around the Torah" only came into wide written usage in Amoraic texts, thus no earlier than the Amoraic period itself. Aside from the lone citation in Tosefta, which could either have been a later addition or been written in the early part of the Amoraic period anyway, there is absolutely no foundation to show that this meaning was utilized before the Amoraic period at all.

Gezerot were disputed and rejected in far greater numbers than seen with the legal changes noted by the terms *barishonah* or *takkanot*. Disputed decrees fell into two categories: those where the standoff between two parties resulted in a draw, and those where a *gezerah* was instituted, but the authorities involved disagreed on the reason. Reasons for rejection include lack of communal acceptance of the *gezerah, gezerot* that focused on events that were too rare as to require legal change, knowledgeable parties who did not require the added protection of a *gezerah* and *gezerot* that were made upon other areas already protected by *gezerot* (only Torah law could be protected by a *gezerah*, not rabbinic law).

Those who violated *gezerot* were subject to lashes, but were also to receive punishment at the hands of heaven. The snakebite motif that recurs in rabbinic literature served as a caution against those who might contemplate violations of these fences, whether simply as Jews or as sect members of divergent religions such as early Christianity.

An oft-repeated statement suggested that decrees remained in effect until a court of greater number and wisdom voted to revoke them. There was also evidence that the rationales behind decrees were not shared until one year after their promulgation in Palestine. Another section suggested a forty-day waiting period before a *gezerah* went into effect, unless the *gezerah* is a correction of a prior mistake in law.

Table 8 on the opposite page, displays the distribution of rationales and the frequency of the various legal usages of this term. Unlike either of the two terms studied in prior chapters, *gzr* is only used in any legal sense quite sporadically in Tannaitic texts, a total of 23 times in all. It receives moderate usage in PT, a total of 42 times. It is in BT that it comes into its own, showing a whopping 270 distinct legal usages, even aside from the many rejected and disputed *gezerot* that appear. This means that BT contains over four times as many occurrences as we find in the entirety of the rest of rabbinic legal literature combined. Such a finding tells us that this term experienced a blossoming of use in the Babylonian editorial context, and supports the growing sense of Babylonian empowerment we found in the use of other terms that promoted halakhic change we studied in other chapters, though in this case in a conservative direction that protected the law as it was.

The Attributions of Fences Around the Torah

Keeping in mind the huge preponderance of the "fence" meaning present in Amoraic texts, we will now look at the distribution of authorities cited in relation to *gezerot* in both the Tannaitic and Amoraic periods. We note, first, exactly what is meant by the term "attribution" in this part of the study: these are attributed statements that indicate the presence of a *gezerah*. One short example from BT Git. 26b should make the point:

תניא : האומר כתבו גט לארוסתי לכשאכנסנה אגרשנה : אינו גט. ואמר
עולא : מה טעם? גזירה שמא יאמרו גיטה קודם לבנה.

It was taught: One who says "write a *get* for my fiancée, so that I may divorce her once I marry her," it is not a [legally valid] *get*; and Ulla said: What is the reason? It is a <u>decree</u> lest they say that her *get* came before her child [thus, once they were married, if she had a child, this could lead to suspicion of promiscuity, since the *get* could be seen as terminating the marriage immediately upon completion and before the conception].

Table 8
Rationales for Halakhic Change Utilizing
the Root *gzr* in Textual Sources

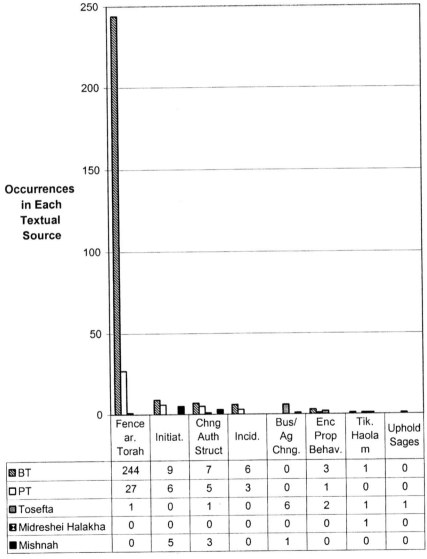

	Fence ar. Torah	Initiat.	Chng Auth Struct	Incid.	Bus/ Ag Chng.	Enc Prop Behav.	Tik. Haolam	Uphold Sages
BT	244	9	7	6	0	3	1	0
PT	27	6	5	3	0	1	0	0
Tosefta	1	0	1	0	6	2	1	1
Midreshei Halakha	0	0	0	0	0	0	1	0
Mishnah	0	5	3	0	1	0	0	0

Rationale Offered

The suggestion that the *get* at hand is not legally valid does not originate with Ulla. In fact, he is not responsible for it at all. However, the definition of this law as a *gezerah* and the indication of just what it protects against are both connected directly with Ulla's name. Note that these attributions are just that: attributions of statements that define legal decisions as *gezerot* and often supply their parameters and reasons. They may not represent a window into the originating parties of the laws that eventuate in *gezerot*, nor are they necessarily temporally proximate to those same parties. Viewed cumulatively over a number of sources, they do provide us with a rough understanding of when the terminology of *gezerah* took root, who utilized it and just how it was used throughout various time periods and locales.

Table 9
Occurrences of *Gezerot* Attributed to Tannaim in Textual Sources

	Pre-T / T1	T2	T3	T4	T5
▨ BT		1	4	3	1
☐ PT					
☐ Tosefta		1			
■ Mishnah					

Generations

Table 9 shows the distribution of statements attributed to Tannaim connected with *gezerot* that create a fence around the Torah. We note immediately that there are not many attributions to Tannaitic authorities of statements that have to do with *gezerot* as fences at all. A total of 10 occurrences link statements by Tannaim to *gezerot* that are fences. Remember, as well, that all of these statements attributed to Tannaim actually occur in the Amoraic strata of PT and BT.

Contrasting this with the Amoraic scene shown below in Table 10, we find a difference of an order of magnitude in the number of attributed statements that show *gezerot* connected with Amoraic authorities. This coheres with the upturn in Amoraic authorities connected with *takkanot* we saw in the prior chapter, but with *gezerot*, the difference is far more profound: .

Table 10
Occurrences of *Gezerot* Attributed to Amoraim in Textual Sources

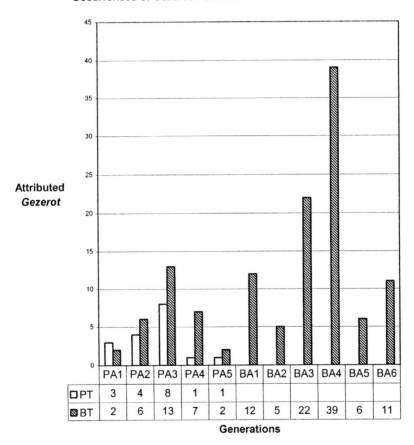

Attributed
Gezerot

	PA1	PA2	PA3	PA4	PA5	BA1	BA2	BA3	BA4	BA5	BA6
□ PT	3	4	8	1	1						
▨ BT	2	6	13	7	2	12	5	22	39	6	11

Generations

A few conclusions arise when we examine this chart in detail. First, there is significant peak of discussion about *gezerot* (meaning, again, the predominate meaning of "fences" only) during the third and fourth generations of Babylonian Amoraim. There is a smaller, but still noticeable rise in the *gezerot* connected with the third generation of Palestinian Amoraim. From these two facts, we can see that there was a trend upward during the third to fourth generations, significantly stronger in Babylonia, but still extant in Palestine. This result stands even when we compare it to the distribution of Amoraim and Amoraic *memrot* mentioned in BT and PT, as we noted before in the conclusion of chapters one and two.

Next, we notice the interesting fact that there is not one Babylonian authority cited as presenting a *gezerah* in PT. Every one of the attributed statements connected with a fence around the Torah in PT comes from a Palestinian Amora. Though the data are relatively scant (only a total of 17 occurrences), this is a reasonable basis upon which to conclude that PT's editors either did not know or were reluctant to recognize *gezerot* accepted by Babylonians. This may be based upon a general mistrust of Babylonian authority amongst the editors of PT, or it may represent a more moderate tendency when it came to imposing additional halakhic restrictions of the sort represented by *gezerot* that formed fences around the Torah. This result may either point to an exclusionary attitude on the part of PT's editors toward outsiders when it came to imposing conservative stringencies in legal matters, or an avoidance of overly conservative alterations to the law. It seems to reflect a Palestinian tendency toward more liberal, less conservative approaches to these sorts of legal limitations.

There is a vast number of statements that deal with *gezerot* in BT when compared with any other source, as we have now seen. The editors of BT were more open to the sort of radically conservative halakhic change represented by a fence around the Torah than the editors of any of our other rabbinic legal texts. This tendency is probably related to their willingness to analyze and explain law, and to search for underlying rationales. This points to a far greater Babylonian editorial willingness to discuss and consider the alteration of law in the service of conservative goals than that found in other sources.

Finally, the texts that mention *gezerot* utilize certain grouping patterns that have appeared before in some respects, but are somewhat novel. For instance, we find groupings of *takkanot* attributed to Ezra, Joshua and Rabban Yohanan ben Zakkai. With *gezerot*, however, the formal patterns tend to concentrate on incidents rather than individuals. While *takkanot* were generally grouped according to people who might have some relation to the subject matter, *gezerot* are more often grouped according to moments that changed communities: lost wars, the hostile incident between Beit Hillel and Beit Shammai and the judicial disputes of Admon and Hanan ben Avishalom. As we saw when these texts were addressed, each generation of editors tended to add their own embellishments to the core story, which reflected their own time and concerns.

With this evaluation of *gezerot* concluded, we will now turn to a summary of our overall conclusions.

Notes

585. See the active and passive forms of this verb as they appear in the Hebrew texts of Gen. 15:17 ("cut pieces," Lev. 16:22 ("cut off/inaccessible"), I Kgs. 3:25 and 26 (in the famous story of Solomon suggesting that two disputing prostitutes "cut" their baby in half), II Kgs. 6:4 ("cutting" timber for building), Is. 9:19 ("cutting") and 53:8 ("cut off, inaccessible"), Ez. 37:11 ("cut off, separated"), Hab. 3:17 ("cut off"), Psalms 88:6 ("cut off") and 136:13 (2 occurrences, "cutting" open the Sea of Reeds into "cut pieces"), Lam. 3:54 ("cut off, inaccessible") and II Chron. 26:21 ("cut off, inaccessible"). In the Aramaic of Dan., two passages reflect this early meaning: Dan. 2:34 and 2:45, where the term means "to hew stone."

586. See the Hebrew texts in Job 22:28 ("he will decree and God will make it so," one of the more famous prooftexts utilized in rabbinic literature to indicate that a magician or rabbi can invoke the power of God, cf. for example, BT Sot. 12a), Est. 2:1 (where Ahasheurus "decreed" a penalty upon Vashti) and the Aramaic texts of Dan. 2:27, 4:14 and 4:21 (where kings or kings' assistants "decree").

587. See Dan. 4:4, 5:7 and 5:11 (where a particular brand of magician is called a "decree-er," which the JPS version translates as "diviner.")

588. See "Job, Book of" *ABD* 3:858-868.

589. See "Esther, Book of," *ABD* 2:633-643.

590. See "Daniel, Book of" *ABD* 2:29-36.

591. For just three of the many examples, see Gen. 15:18 (subsequent to the earliest attestation of the root *gzr* in 15:17), where God makes a covenant with Abraham utilizing this term. Deut. 5:2-3 shows a double occurrence, again related to the "cutting of a covenant."

592. Delbert R. Hillers, *Covenant: The History of a Biblical Idea* (Baltimore: The Johns Hopkins Press, 1969), pp. 40-41.

593. See Liddell and Scott, *Lexicon*, p. 996 for examples and other definitions of this term. Josephus utilized this Greek verb in recounting decrees (both positive and negative) by the Roman government upon the Jewish community in *Antiquities*. Cf., for example, *Antiquities* 14:10:2-8 for a variety of decrees and the terminology used for them.

594. Cf. A. Dupont-Sommer, "Trios stèles araméennes provenant de Sfiré: un traité de vassalité de VIIIe siècle avant Jesus Christ," *Annales Archeologiques Arabes Syriennes* 10 (1960), pp. 21-54.

595. William F. Albright, "The Hebrew Expression for 'Making a Covenant' in Pre-Israelite Documents," *BASOR* 121 (1951), pp. 21-22.

596. Joseph A. Fitzmyer, *The Aramaic Inscriptions of Sefire* (Roma: Editrice Pontificio Istituto Biblico, 1995), pp. 44-47 for the text, where the term *gzr* appears in line 7 on p. 44. See also Fitzmyer's commentary on p. 69. Sincere thanks are due my colleague, S. David Sperling of the Hebrew Union College-Jewish Institute of Religion in New York, for sharing this reference.

597. Michael Sokoloff, *The Targum to Job from Qumran Cave XI* (Ramat Gan: Bar-Ilan University, 1974), pp. 36-7.

598. J.T. Milik, "'Prière de Nabonide' et autres écrits d'un cycle de Daniel," *RB* 63 (1956), pp. 407-415.

599. Frank Moore Cross, "The Prayer of Nabonidus," *IEJ* 34:4 (1984), pp. 260-264.

600. Cross, *op. cit.*, pp. 263-4.

601. See, for example, Honi the Circle Maker in M Ta. 3:8, BT Ta. 19a; see also T MS 5:24, where Hezekiah is reputed to have this power; and BT Ket. 103b, where all righteous people (*tzaddikim*) are able to invoke God's power by decree.

602. See, for example, Josephus' utilization of this term in describing the distribution requirements for the published decrees of Caesar in *Antiquities* 14:10:3. In 14:10:1, he uses the plural δόγματα in describing what is on the bronze tablet filled with decrees that Julius Caesar gave to the Jews of Alexandria.

603. Jastrow, *Dictionary*, pp. 231-2.

604. Sokoloff, *Dictionary of Palestinian Aramaic*, p. 126 and *idem, Dictionary of Babylonian Aramaic* (Ramat Gan: Bar Ilan University Press, 2002), p. 276.

605. See, e.g., *MRSBY* 14:15; BT Yoma 67B; BT Ket. 112a; BT BK 81b; BT BB 33b, 36a and 137b and BT Mak. 11a.

606. See *MRY Parashat Bo, Pasha Bo* 14.

607. See, among other examples: PT Suk. 2:5, 53a; BT Shab. 130b and PT Shab. 19:1, 16d.

608. See M Arakh. 3:5; M Neg. 12:5; BT Ket. 8b and PT Yev. 12:6, 13a among many others.

609. See *Sifra Aharei Mot* 2.

610. Many examples of this hermeneutic may be found throughout the rabbinic legal corpus. For an excellent and comprehensive study on the subject, see Michael Chernick, *Gezerah Shavah*.

611. Examples are scattered throughout M, T, BT and PT Ta. as well as (among others) *MRY Beshallah Masekhta DeAmalek Beshallah* 1 and *MRSBY* 17:9.

612. See, for example, M RH 2:9, BT Ta. 23a and BT Ber. 19a,

613. See *Mtan* 21:18 and BT Ned. 72b for just two of many examples. PT also has one odd phrase where the same idea is expressed differently in these words: אורייתא גזרת, in PT BM 2:5, 8c.

614. Examples may be found at M Oho. 8:2 and 14:1; BT Tam. 26b and PT Shevi. 3:5, 34c.

615. See M San. 9:6, M Men. 13:3 and T Kel. BK 1:6 for just three examples.

616. God is often portrayed as making decrees in rabbinic legal literature. See, for instance, M MS 5:13, M Ta. 3:8, T Sot. 12:1-3, T San.11:6, T Ker. 1:6, T Neg. 3:7, *MRY* 1:91 and elsewhere. One interesting instance occurs in BT Yoma 73b, where the *Urim* and *Thummim* (an oracular set of dice that the people in the desert utilized to divine God's will during their travels) make known a decree from God.

617. Kings' decrees include decrees of Pharaoh (see, e.g., BT Sot. 12a), the Roman Emperor Caligula (cf. BT Sot. 33a and PT Sot. 9:13, 24b) and others.

618. See BT Ber. 61b, BT Shab. 49a and 130a and BT Ta. 18a for a few examples.

619. A few of these exist, including one reportedly made by the Parsees (presumably the Parthians) at BT Yev. 63b; and one by the people of Kabul in BT Pes. 51a; as well as a decree made upon a demonic presence to limit her effectiveness in making trouble throughout the world in BT Pes. 112b.

620. This accounting is based on the results of a careful search of the Bar Ilan University Responsa Project database to find all occurrences of the root in rabbinic literature. Since some manuscripts utilize the root at certain points, and drop the root at other points, this exact total has some malleability based on manuscript selection. Nonetheless, on a statistical basis, the results of these comparisons are still quite valid and suggest certain tendencies on the part of the authors of the texts involved.

621. This number is based on the Bar Ilan University Responsa Project search indicated above, filtered through a personal reading of each and every result, and a determination of the meaning of the root involved. While we can be relatively confident that the selections made are accurate, still, there is always the possibility that one might read these sections differently, and results might well differ by a few occurrences in one direction or another depending on the reader. Nonetheless, as stated above, the results would remain statistically valid due to the large number of citations reviewed.

622. Note that the number of occurrences in both the BT and PT is based only on the respective Gemaras of these works, excluding the occurrences reproduced in the included mishnayot.

623. In total, in the two Gemaras, there are 134 examples of *gezerot* that are discussed, but ultimately rejected. The vast majority of these occur in BT (118) with only a few instances of rejected *gezerot* in PT (16). This indicates a significant difference in the editing and composition of BT and PT. PT is more reticent to delve into the hypothetical and rejected areas of changed law, whereas BT is more comfortable exploring the concept behind a decree it will ultimately discard, for the sake of understanding its ideology.

624. We find 51 examples of disputed *gezerot* in the two Gemaras. Here, the discrepancy between BT and PT is even more pronounced: BT shows 50 of these examples, and PT only one. Again, the tendency to discuss only resolved law is more pronounced in PT, while BT is more willing to go on fruitful excursions for the sake of understanding other viewpoints.

625. The "week of the son" is a euphemism for circumcision, since it took place one week after the birth of a son. The saving of the son has two possible meanings: Rashi suggests that it implies *pidyon haben*, the redemption of the first born that took place on the thirtieth day after his birth. Rabbenu Tam explains that it simply means the birth of the son itself. See Lieberman, *TK* 5:1186, where he discussed and defined the "week of the son," compiling a list of relevant citations that show that the meaning is related to the idea that it would take a few days to know (and let others know) that this was a son, and that the *brit milah* was to be celebrated on the appropriate day.

626. See, also, the parallel at T Sot. 15:10.

627. Circumcision was outlawed during the time of Hadrian's rule, *circa* 132 CE. The *Historia Augusta* suggests that outlawing circumcision was the *causus belli* that pro-

voked the Bar Kokhba revolt, though other sources disagree. See Smallwood, *Jews Under Roman Rule*, pp. 429-431, on the restrictions on circumcision.

628. See Gen. 1:22.

629. See T Sot. 15:10, BT BK 79b, BT Hor. 3b, BT AZ 36a-b, PT Shab. 1:4, 3d, PT Shevi. 4:2, 35b and PT AZ 2:8, 41d for other examples of this tendency. Frankel, *Darkhei HaMishnah*, p. 191, ties this to a tendency first enumerated by Rabban Shimeon ben Gamaliel, that all *halakhot* are promulgated *al tenai* (conditionally) until the community accepts them, when they become active law. I. H. Weiss, *Dor* 2:53, suggests that this is an overall category that encompasses three other smaller categories relating to *gezerot* and *takkanot*, including the principles that 1) one may not make a *takkanah* that causes losses or pain on the part of individuals or the community; 2) that one may not pass a law that might cause losses; and 3) that even an additional burden may be considered loss.

630. See also Rav Mesharshya as the initiator of a discussion on this topic in BT AZ 36a.

631. Cf. Lieberman, *TK* 8:771, where he cites Ms. Erfurt of T Sot. 15:10 to show an earlier version of the attribution of this passage, and Frankel's comments in *Darkhei HaMishnah*, p. 191.

632. Cf. Joseph M. Baumgarten, *Studies in Qumran Law* (Leiden: Brill, 1977), pp. 88-97.

633. Many scholars follow BT's version of this text and assign this lenient decision to Rabbi Yehuda Nesiah, grandson of Rabbi Yehuda HaNasi.

634. Cf. Hyman, *Toldot, s.v.* Rav Mesharshya and Rabbi Ada bar Abba.

635. See *MT Hilkhot Mamrin* 2:6-7 for Maimonides' version of this legal principle.

636. The act of pulling a piece of movable property indicates that the purchaser (who is doing the pulling) has taken ownership of it from the owner. See, for example, M Shevi. 10:9, one of a number of statements that bear witness to this legal position.

637. The situation is: a purchaser acquired some wheat with money but did not take physical possession of it, then went away for some period of time before picking it up from the seller. If a fire should break out, there would be two problems: first, the seller would have little impetus to protect the already-sold wheat, and would let it burn while he saved his other property. Second, if all the wheat were not segregated from the seller's other property and only some of the seller's wheat burned, the seller could craftily declare that the burnt part was the property of the purchaser, and reclaim the other parts for himself. In either case, the unclear ownership of the wheat would lead to trouble.

638. See other examples at PT Dem. 1:2, 21d; PT Yev. 6:6, 11a; BT Git. 5a and elsewhere.

639. Cf. BT BB 90a and BT Men. 90a.

640. See the parallels to this text in M Suk. 4:1 and 4:5, T 3:1 and PT 4:1, 54b, as well as Lieberman's discussion of these texts in *TK* 4:869.

641. Since this ceremony involved carrying a branch, it would not be permitted on Shabbat for a variety of precautionary reasons: one might accidentally prepare it after sunset on Friday, one might forget and tear or cut a branch from a tree or one might leave it at home and accidentally bring it to the Temple during Shabbat. Any of these would be

violations that could best be avoided by limiting the ceremony to non-Sabbath days of the festival.

642. The *lulav* of three elements (myrtle, willow and palm) is lifted up during the festival of Sukkot in accordance with Leviticus 23:40, but is not to be carried on Shabbat.

643. The idea, here, is that two large stones are set up next to one another, creating a sort of seat that allowed an individual to sit upon them and go about his/her business in the relative comfort of this primitive lavatory.

644. This would be making a stove on *yom tov*, and is forbidden, as it is considered building.

645. By placing a roof on the two-sided structure, a person is technically considered to have completed a structure that violates the prohibition on building.

646. According to Rav Nahman's logic, without some empty space enclosed, a solid chair made from a block of wood or other materials would not be considered a tent, and would therefore not be a violation of the prohibition against building on a festival. This is an untenable suggestion, and is immediately rejected.

647. See M Oho. for examples of the tent as prototypical dwelling.

648. Second degree incest regulations are prohibitions instituted by the rabbis against relationships with a man's maternal and paternal grandmothers, maternal and paternal great grandmothers, the wives of his grandfathers and a variety of other women who were not in his most immediate circle of family, but were still close enough to warrant prohibition.

649. Non-Jews were prohibited from marrying their mothers, see Rashi to BT San. 57b-58a. So, if in this state of sanctity (as non-Jews) they were prohibited from first degree incest, then it would be rather a poor reflection on Judaism if, after converting, they could then be permitted to marry their mothers.

650. See BT Shab. 11a, 21a; BT Eruv. 4b, 22a, 99a; BT Yoma 11a, 44b; BT Suk. 6b; BT Betz. 3a; BT Yev. 21b; BT Git. 21a; BT AZ 21a; BT Hul. 85b, 104a; BT Nid. 67b; PT Shevi. 2:4, 33d; PT Ter. 9:1, 46c and PT MS 1:1, 52c.

651. M Hul. 8:1.

652. Since this is permitted, it is clear that the rabbis did not create a fence around a fence, by limiting the eating of *hallah* at the table with a non-priest. Epstein, *Mavo Le-Nusah HaMishnah*, p. 786, notes that this represents a warping of the original meaning of M Hal. 4:8.

653. This is not prohibited according to the biblical verse, which only literally prohibits "seething a calf in its mother's milk." Cf. Ex. 23:19. Rav Sheshet contends that this implies that violation of the biblical prohibition requires actual cooking of milk and meat together, and would not count as a violation either proximate placement or consumption of unheated meat and milk together.

654. A כלי שני is a second vessel that is specifically not used for cooking or heating food, but one into which the food is poured after it is cooked. Thus, since cooking milk and meat together is the root violation, simply pouring them together into a second pot, where they are not heated thereafter, would then not violate the biblical injunction.

655. Rabbi Ba (PA2) is known in BT as Rabbi Abba bar Zabda. Rabbi La (PA3) is known as Rabbi Hela or Ela in BT. In PT MS 1:1, 52b, a parallel text has this interaction occurring between Rabbi Ba and Rabbi Ammi.

656. The printed edition has "מחרשין" here, as does Ms. Leiden, which could make some sense in the context (i.e., he may not plow his land on the basis of a *gezerah*), but ultimately fails to satisfy. The reading suggested by the *Penei Moshe* is preferable: "מחדשין." The repetition of this idea as the final clause of this paragraph seals its emendation to "מחדשין" as the correct reading. A further parallel in PT MS 1:1, 52c makes the evidence for this reading overwhelming.

657. There are a few occasions where undateable parties are included in the discussion: for example, *rabbanan* and the "men of Jericho" (BT Pes. 56b), the *stam* and "they said in the West" as the only respondents (BT Yoma 55b), *tanna kamma* and *rabbanan batraei* (BT Git. 4b) and Amoraic statements cited only as *mar savar* (BT Shab. 126b).

658. *Sekhakh* is the permitted natural covering material utilized for the roof of a *sukkah*.

659. Regular boards for the roofs of permanent homes were made of planed boards more than four handbreadths wide. This was set as the operative threshold between temporary roofing material and permanent roofing material. If a *sukkah* had planed boards that were at least this wide, Rabbi Meir declared it unsuitable, because of the use of regular, permanent housing materials in the place of the required, temporary *sekhakh*. Use of such boards might lead people to believe, incorrectly, that they could fulfill their Sukkot obligations by staying under the roof of their house.

660. Since most materials less than four handbreadths wide were not considered regular building materials for permanent dwellings, these were permitted for use in the roof of a *sukkah*.

661. Four handbreadths constitutes the minimum size for a place to be reckoned as its own domain, see Rashi, *ad loc*. Rabbi Yehuda believed that planed boards narrower than four handbreadths did not ever constitute a domain, and thus could not be considered similar to boards used in regular manufacturing, which would invalidate them for use in a *sukkah*. Thus, no *gezerah* was necessary.

662. לבוד (*lavud*, "joined") means that as long as the planed boards are no farther than three handbreadths apart, they are considered joined. Since boards over three handbreadths wide are larger than this threshold size, they are considered of a "significant size," because if they are missing, they cannot simply be ignored. Once they achieve this "significant size," they may end up being considered roofing material, thus leading to the aforementioned potential erroneous conclusion that one may fulfill his/her obligation while remaining at home. Thus, the rabbinic decree against their use.

663. Rav was concerned that if oil were permitted, onlookers might be wrongly convinced that wax, too, was allowed, which it was not.

664. Rashi explains that the problem addressed here is that the leaf must be detached before the *get* is written, and not afterwards. If the *get* were written on the leaf first, and the leaf were then detached, it would create an invalidating intermediate stage of action between the writing of the *get* and its delivery. This is based on the idea that a perforated pot resting on or in the earth is considered attached to the ground, since the perforations

do not create a complete boundary between earth and plant. Here, Rava is concerned that the husband will not detach the pot from the earth to give the *get*, but will instead pluck the leaf, thus invalidating the *get* with an intermediate action that severs it from the earth, explicitly forbidden by M Git. 2:4. To avoid this contingency, he decrees against the entire practice. Abaye believed it was permissible for the *get* to be written while the perforated pot was still attached to the earth, as long as the husband removed the pot in its entirety, and did not pluck the leaf alone. The presence of the perforated pot, to Abaye, appears to have provided enough separation to dismiss the problem of the intermediate step, if the husband removed the entire pot. Epstein, *Sifrut HaAmoraim*, p. 50, points to this *sugya* as an example of one with a number of historic layers that come before Rav Ashi's time, though the section we are observing only covers the time period of Abaye and Rava. Rambam rules that a perforated pot is the same as a plant planted directly in the ground, cf. *MT Hilkhot Kilayim* 5:16.

665. Since the same prohibitions on carrying are not in place for a festival, the Torah's prohibition against carrying on Shabbat cannot provide any justification for this practice on Yom Tov.

666. This Tannaitic statement supports the idea that immersion of vessels on a Festival is forbidden, which proves the point of Rav Bibi.

667. See, for example, Fish, *Is There a Text in this Class?*, and, for a concise treatment of Derrida's views on authorial intent as they apply to law, see the excellent article by J.M. Balkin, "Deconstructive Practice and Legal Theory" in Scott Brewer, ed., *Evolution and Revolution in Theories of Legal Reasoning*, pp. 743-786, with a focus on his section on "The Liberation of Text from Author," pp. 772-785.

668. The various disruptions that took place during the Tannaitic period may well have led to a serious disconnect between Tannaitic ideas and their reflection in Amoraic writings. This phenomenon is not entirely unknown in the modern world, as Haym Soloveitchik's, "Rupture and Reconstruction: The Transformation of Contemporary Orthodoxy," *Tradition* 28,4 (1994), pp. 64-130, suggests.

669. This is a vague formulation, interpretable in two distinct ways: Rashi, *ad loc.*, suggests that once an idolater has lent money to a Jew, he will rejoice that the Jew had need of him. The implication is that to add extra joy to an idolater's festival could be considered helping in its celebration, and is thus forbidden. Rabbenu Hananel, on the other hand, reads this statement more literally, explaining that when the idolater sees the Jew needing him, he will literally "give thanks" via extra sacrifices to his god(s). Thus, the prohibition against borrowing from a non-Jew in this three-day period is to avoid adding extra idolatrous offerings actually caused by the act of borrowing. See Roth, *Halakhic Process*, pp. 275-6 for his discussion of this issue.

670. Weiss, *Dor*, 3:175, remarks that Abaye makes an enormous contribution to the justification of *gezerot* that came before him, listing (in note 4) all 14 distinct occasions when Abaye does this.

671. David Weiss Halivni's theory of *shakla vetarya* suggests just this: see his introduction to *Mekorot UMesorot* to BT BK, especially pp. 7-13.

672. See the parallels to this Toseftan text in BT AZ 27b and PT AZ 2:2, 40d-41a and PT Shab. 14:4, 14d.

673. R. Travers Herford, *Christianity in Talmud and Midrash* (Clifton, NJ: Reference Book Publishers, 1966), pp. 103-108.

674. Urbach, *Sages*, p. 116.

675. Schiffman, *Who Was a Jew*, pp. 70-71.

676. A *tabala* was an instrument made of a series of bells that was often played at public processions, from the Greek ταβάλα. Cf. Liddell and Scott, *Lexicon*, p. 1752, which attributes its origin to Parthian.

677. Although T Ker. 1:6 stipulates that violating rabbinic enactments and decrees requires 40 lashes, as required with the violation of other negative commandments.

678. M MK 3:3.

679. T BM 1:9.

680. Cf. BT Betz. 3b.

681. For more on Roman taxation in Judaea, see Safrai, *Economy of Roman Palestine*, pp. 341-352.

682. Even if the rennet were proportionally so little as to be insignificant (less than 1/60th of the mixture), it was still enough to make the cheese unfit, because the rennet was the agent that changed the character of milk to cheese. It was thus identifiable because of its effect, and what was identifiable was forbidden.

683. Dov Zlotnick, *The Iron Pillar—Mishnah* (Jerusalem: Daf-Noy Press, 1988), pp. 165-6, explains that Rabbi Yishmael changed the subject to avoid teaching on this matter in a public setting. He sees this as one of a set of avoidances present in our texts when it was inappropriate for rabbis to make public comments on various issues.

684. The words of the Sages are sweeter than the written words of the Torah, for it is the unwritten law that supplements the written law and completes it.

685. Weiss, *Dor*, 2:55-6, asked: why publicize the reason behind a *gezerah* at all? After all, once any reason was made known, then those who opposed it had an opening to ignore the decree, and possibly work toward its elimination. Weiss suggested that the goal was to preserve the reason so as to allow future generations to recognize that if the reason ever became void, they could dismantle the prohibition. Lieberman, *Hellenism*, p. 139, goes so far as to suggest that "rabbis occasionally substituted some formal legalistic grounds for the real motive."

686. Shmuel Klein, ארץ יהודה (1939, תל אביב: דביר), p. 173 explains that this decision is reflective of the large number of foreigners living in Ashkelon in the time following the Bar Kokhba revolt.

687. These groupings are: M Shab. 1:4-9 (parallel to T Shab. 1:16-23, PT Shab. 1:4, 3c and BT Shab. 13b-17b); M Ket. 13:1 (parallel to BT Ket. 105a and BT BK 58b) and M Sot. 9:14 (parallel to T Sotah 8:10) around people and T Dem. 5:24; BT Betz. 36b-37a and BT AZ 36a-b around topics.

688. The massive list of 270 basic texts and their parallels that shows the term *gzr* used to signify a fence around the Torah includes: **in M**: Kil. 3:5, Shab. 1:4-9, Ket. 13:1 and Sot. 9:14; **in T**: Hag. 3:33 and Sot.13:10; **in PT**: Ter. 9:1, 46c; MS 1:2, 52d (two occurrences, one of them parallel to PT Betz. 3:6, 62b, BT Bekh. 15b, BT Tem.18a and 24a); Hal. 4:4, 60b; Shab. 1:4, 3c (parallel to PT Shab. 1:5, 27c, PT Ket. 8:1, 32b, BT Shab. 15b and BT AZ 8b) and another occurrence on Shab. 1:4, 3c (parallel to PT Ket.

8:1, 32c and BT Shab. 17a) and Shab. 1:4, 3d (parallel to PT Hag. 2:5, 78b, PT Ket. 8:1, 32c and BT Ber. 52a-b); Pes. 1:4, 27d and 3:8, 30b; Shek. 7:3, 50d and 8:2, 51a (2 occurrences); Yoma 1:1, 38b; MK 1:1, 80a (parallel to BT MK 4a); Ta. 2:11, 65d (2 occurrences, one parallel to PT MK 3:1, 81c); Yev. 8:1, 8d (parallel to BT Yev. 72a) and 10:6, 11a (parallel to BT Yev. 88b); Sot. 2:4, 18a and 5:2, 20b; San. 3:5, 21b and 4:9, 44b; **in BT**: Ber. 19b, 25a, 27b (parallel to BT Shab. 40b) and 53a; Shab. 8b, 9a, 9b (two occurrences), 11b, 14a-15a (group), 17a, 17b (four occurrences; one parallel to BT AZ 36b and BT AZ 59a, another parallel to BT Shab. 83a, BT AZ 36b and BT Nid. 34a), 18b, 21a (three occurrences), 22b, 23b (two occurrences), 25b (three occurrences), 29b, 34a, 34b, 38a, 39a, 46b, 48b, 49a (parallel to BT Shab. 58b), 53b, 62b (two occurrences), 85a-b, 113a, 117b, 122a, 122b, 124a, 125b, 128b, 129b, 146a, 146b and 149a; Eruv. 20a, 20b, 22a, 30b, 34a, 34b, 47a, 49a, 58b, 62a, 81b (parallel to BT Kid. 28b and BT Hul. 83a), 88b, 89a (two occurrences), 90b, 102b and 104a (two occurrences); Pes. 6b, 9b, 10b-11a, 12b, 29b, 30a, 33b (two occurrences), 46b, 51a, 56b, 69a, 73a, 78b, 84b and 110b; RH 21a, 22b and 29b; Yoma 10a-11b, 14a, 36a and 65b; Suk. 12b, 23a, 26a, 42b-43a and 50a; Betz. 2b, 8b, 15b, 17b, 18a, 21b, 32a, 32b, 36b (four occurrences), 37a (two occurrences), 38b and 39a; Ta. 17b, 26b and 27b; Meg. 4b and 21b; Hag. 21b, 24a and 24b; Yev. 12a, 19a, 20b (two occurrences), 21b (four occurrences), 29a (two occurrences), 31a, 31b, 35a, 40b, 41a, 42a (two occurrences), 50b (two occurrences), 51b, 61a (parallel to BT San. 19a), 66a, 94b, 102b, 108b, 113a (parallel to BT Git. 55a), 114a, 114b and 119b; Ket. 5a, 15a, 46a, 56a and 102a (parallel to BT Bekh. 51a); Ned. 39a, 42b, 43a and 60a-b; Sot. 6b; Git. 10b, 21b, 26b (parallel to BT Git. 79b), 54b, 55b, 71a-b, 73a, 81b and 84a; Kid. 5a, 17b (parallel to BT AZ 64a), 60a and 73a; BK 28a, 33b and 79b (parallel to BT Bekh. 28b); BM 6b (parallel to BT BM 47b-48a and 49b), 35a, 71a (parallel to BT AZ 6b), 72a-b and 93a; BB 145a; San. 25b and 25b; Mak. 20a (parallel to BT BM 53b and BT San. 113a); Shev. 12a; AZ 15a, 21a, 31b, 32a, 35a, 35b, 36b, 37b, 42a, 72b, 74b and 76a; Zev. 32a, 33a, 73b and 79a; Men. 14b, 18a, 46b, 52b, 67a, 79b and 90a; Hul. 6a-b, 8b (two occurrences), 15b, 72a (parallel to BT Nid. 42b), 85b, 88a, 94a, 104a-b, 116b, 122a and 123a; Bekh. 14a, 23b, 31b-32a, 33b, 38a (parallel to BT Nid. 7b), 45a and 53a (parallel to BT Tem. 24a); Tem. 11b; Ker. 26b and 27a; Nid. 7a, 32a, 34a, 66b, 67b, 68b, 69b, 72a and 72b.

689. Epstein, *Sifrut HaTannaim*, p. 423, shows that the term בו ביום appears in a number of texts and seems to indicate a specific time when important events happened all in one day.

690. A vetch is a plant with featherlike leaves that end in tendrils and small, variously colored flowers. Its colorful flowers were often used for dyes, after being cooked for some time.

691. Frankel, *Darkhei HaMishnah*, p. 51, suggests that this is one of the most frequent type of disagreements between Beit Hillel and Beit Shammai, where Beit Shammai took a more stringent approach to the limitation established through a *gezerah*, while Beit Hillel fought this tendency.

692. Until this point, the mishnah at hand may be explained by different understandings of the law of *shevitat kelim*, "the resting of vessels" owned by Jews on Shabbat. Beit Shammai holds that vessels owned by Jews (from pots and vats to traps for hunting) must

not be utilized for work on Shabbat, and thus this sort of work, if not completed by Friday at sunset, must not even be started. Beit Hillel does not believe in this concept, and thus work that may continue unaided by Jews, even if conducted in Jewish vessels, may be started until sunset and continue throughout the Sabbath.

693. Epstein, *Sifrut HaTannaim*, pp. 282-3, notes that this mishnah is probably not by the same editor as the prior ones, because of the change in permission granted by Beit Hillel, since here it is limited only to "as long as the sun is shining." Likewise, Epstein suggests that the difference in form in mishnah 1:9 indicates a different editor as well.

694. In mishnayot 7-9, the issue is that of the appearance of helping a non-Jew with an activity that will ultimately result in the violation of Shabbat by the Jew, because of the potential that the prohibited activity will not be completed before the onset of the Sabbath.

695. Since the majority of the squeezing takes place with the initial application of the heavy roller, the smaller, residual pressure applied over the Sabbath is negligible, and thus permissible to all.

696. The counting of the various groups of 18 is a significant problem for the later commentators. Our count is based on a straightforward reading of M, similar, but not exactly the same as the approach taken by the *Tiferet Yisrael*, beginning where the initial statement introduces the construct of the discussions in the attic, and ending where M moves on to a more apodictic statement that does not indicate dispute, in mishnah 1:10. This reading is at odds with the majority of commentators, who, it appears, attempt to harmonize the principle of 18 decrees with the decrees found in the texts at hand in a number of ways. Rabbi Obadiah of Bartenura explains that the 18 decrees are those listed in BT Shab. 13a-17a, thus entirely avoiding the question of resolving the enumeration in M's list. Maimonides, following PT, posits 18 decrees that were accepted (those listed in BT Shab. 13a-17a), 18 upon which they disagreed, and 18 upon which they ultimately agreed. The Meiri sees two sets of 18 matters: the first set are those laws taught in M Shab. 1-3, and the other set includes additional laws that were decreed that same day, as listed in BT Shab. 13a-17a. Such wide disagreement only points to the difficulty of understanding this tradition and the texts that comprise it. See the *hashlamot v'tosafot* of Albeck, *ad loc.*, and *TK* 3:13-23, for explanations of these and other views on the matter.

697. Pinhas Kehati, *Mishnayot Mevoarot, Moed* (Jerusalem: Heikhal Shlomo, 1991), p. 21.

698. M Mik. 4:1 explicitly states that Beit Hillel and Beit Shammai voted on this, making it a highly rational choice for inclusion in any list of the 18 decrees. The situation is this: one placed a vessel under a hollowed-out pipe that feeds rainwater into a *mikveh*. If rainwater descended the pipe and filled the vessels, Beit Shammai ruled that this constituted drawing water for the *mikveh*, which invalidated it, since *mikveh* water may not be drawn but must flow in of its own accord. Beit Hillel, on the other hand, assumed that the person who left the vessels simply forgot about them, and thus had no intention to draw water, therefore causing no invalidation of the *mikveh*.

699. It was a standoff—neither side would change its answer.

700. קילור, an eye medicine, comes from the Greek κολλύριον, a red eye medication.

701. In each event the secondary leader of the people (Aaron or Beit Shammai) temporarily dethrones the primary leader (Moses or Beit Hillel). Second, in the story of the golden calf there is also an element of group mentality run amok. The numerically superior and vastly nervous Israelites, stranded in the desert, give in to their latent desires and rule the day. So, too, do those students of Beit Shammai, who, in this one instance when they can, take over and give voice to their latent desires to rule and impose stringencies. Finally, as with the golden calf, this incident represents an overthrowing of the regular order of the community. Since Beit Hillel generally outnumbered Beit Shammai, they could usually make law as they saw fit.

702. Jastrow, *Dictionary*, equates this with the Greek πτῑσάνη, or "peeled barley." Cf. Liddell and Scott, *Lexicon*, p. 1548.

703. Cf., for example, *Korban HaEdah*, *s.v.* הלל בתלמידי הורגין והיו, which admits of their strong competition, but entirely dismisses the very idea that students might kill one another as impossible.

704. See Saul Lieberman, *HaYerushalmi Kifshuto* (Jerusalem: Darom Publishing, 1934), p. 38, where Lieberman cites both *MegTa* and *SZ* as prior sources that verify the violence between these two disagreeing groups of disciples.

705. See also two texts that have partial parallels to this section in BT Pes. 19b and BT AZ 36a.

706. Albeck, *Mavo LaMishnah*, p. 115 and p. 120, suggests that this is proof of the orality of the Mishnah. Had it been written, such clarification would not have been necessary.

707. Epstein, *Mavo LeSifrut HaTannaim*, p. 425, notes that this *baraita* only appears in BT, and never in any Palestinian texts.

708. This is the counting according to the *Penei Moshe.*

709. *Penei Moshe* equates this with BT's reading that every non-Jewish child is considered a *zav* from birth.

710. Rashi suggests that this was the practice when people were running in to take a vote.

711. As we have seen before, *gezerot* not accepted by the community were considered invalid. Here, probably due to the tension and threat of violence indicated, BT seems to suggest that the populace would have been loathe to follow this decree. Thus, we can read this as an indication that the decree did not gain immediate acceptance, until the students of the two schools re-decreed it, to ensure that it would take effect. Or, this may be an attempt to retroject these decrees back to Hillel and Shammai themselves, instead of simply to their schools.

712. Rashi understands רישבא as "fowl trapper," from the word רשבין, "trap." Cf. also Rashi to Hul. 116a, where some manuscripts have נשובין. Alternatively, this may be a last name, or a derivative of אבא בי ריש, meaning "head of the family."

713. BT AZ 36a and the Munich manuscript of BT both have נותאה, probably indicating that Abimi is a Nabatean, though many manuscripts leave the word out entirely in both AZ and Shab. Hyman, *Toldot Tannaim V'Amoraim* 1:89 suggests that Abimi is from a place called Notah, relying on BT Shab. 121b, and the suggestion originally offered in the medieval *Arukh* dictionary.

714. Rabbi Meir counts food and vessels as one *gezerah*, whereas Rabbi Yossi and Rabbi Tarfon count them as two.

715. Rabbi Meir and Rabbi Tarfon include forgotten vessels under a pipe as one of the *gezerot*, while Rabbi Yossi (BT Shab. 16b) believes that the discussion of this *gezerah* remains unresolved.

716. Rabbi Tarfon excludes the decree related to movable property larger than an ox-goad, which he sees as a mistaken interpretation, cf. BT Shab. 17a.

717. M (and all later sources) utilize the Greek word for war, πόλεμος. This is at least ironic, if not downright humorous, in the same mishnah where we find a ban on teaching children the Greek language.

718. The better manuscripts have קיטוס in place of טיטוס, which makes possible the understanding that this took place during the War of Quietus. Quietus was the general in charge of the army under Trajanus, who quelled the Diasporan uprising in 115-117 CE. This would suggest a later date, and, combined with the possible identification of the Bar-Kokhba revolt as the later war in the next part, gives this text a wider sweep of history.

719. Some say this means Greek language, while others argue that this implies Greek philosophy. Either way, this represents a turning away from friendly relations and social and intellectual intercourse with Judaea's captors. See BT Sot. 49b for the BT's opinion on exactly what learning Greek leads to—a derision of Jewish worship and its ultimate demise. The Gemara seems to indicate the context for the prohibition in this story. Cf. Tosafot to BT BK 82b, *s.v.* ואסור לאדם שילמד בנו חכמת יוונית, where it interprets the prohibition as against Greek wisdom, and suggests that this decree actually had its origins in the Maccabean period, but that the people did not accept it until it was re-decreed in the time suggested in M above. Also note that PT Peah 1:1, 15c preserves an alternate opinion that allows daughters to learn Greek as an ornament to their beauty.

720. Albeck, *Mishnah, Nashim*, p. 260, explains that this is Hadrian's war against the Jews, where the final taking of Betar represented a turning point in Jewish self-perception *vis-à-vis* the Romans. Other opinions, including Kehati, *Mishnah, Nashim, ad loc.*, suggest that this is the final part of the war against Titus, when his troops destroyed the Temple in 70 CE. This suggests a telescoping of the historical period covered in this mishnah, which seems rather unlikely.

721. See Albeck, *Mishnah, Nashim*, p. 394, in the *hashlamot v'tosafot, ad loc.*, where, relying on Rambam, he suggests that this indicates that Rabbi Yehuda HaNasi was the authority who permitted the bride to come out on a palanquin within the city, and that this final statement was a late addition to this mishnah. Albeck also admits of the possibility that it was Rabbi Yehuda Nesiah, based on a reading of M AZ 2:6 and BT AZ 37a, where permission is given to utilize Gentile oil by Rabbi Yehuda HaNasi and his court.

722. In BT Sot. 49b, the reason given for the rabbis allowing the use of a palanquin is that it encloses the bride, and allows a greater sense of modesty. Rashi reads this as a canopy that covers the bride as she walks through the city.

723. Again, Quietus is the better reading, preferred over Titus. Cf. Lieberman, *TK* 8:767.

724. There is an enormous divergence amongst the commentators on the meaning of this cap. Rashi to BT Sot. 49b, *s.v.* כיפה, suggests a cap of fine white wool, while Lieberman, *TK* 8:768, reads this as a cap decorated with salt. Lieberman cites Pliny the Elder's *Natural History*, book 31, chapter 41, where Pliny waxes eloquent about the many useful and lovely properties of salt, focusing on the fact that it comes in many colors. Ms. Erfurt leaves this phrase out entirely. Jacob Neusner translates it as "a cap of fine wool." The text is, at best, a difficult one.

725. Cf. Lieberman, *Hellenism*, pp. 102-127.

726. See Lieberman, Tosefta 3 (part 2), pp. 241-2 for additional variants. Here, we follow Ms. Erfurt.

727. Cf. especially, Josephus' *Bellum Judaica—The Jewish War*, Books IV-VI, for his detailed description of the battles and agony of those involved in the war. For a few of rabbinic literature's many accounts, see BT Git. 55b-57a, GR 10:7, LR 1:5, §32 and ARN chapters 4 and 6.

728. Lieberman, *Hellenism*, *loc. cit.*

729. For more proof of this idea, see BT BK 83a, where the explanation of why Greek is banned is: מפני המסורות, "because of the informers."

730. Cf. BT Men. 99b, where Josh. 1:8 is employed as a reminder that Jews are to "meditate upon the Torah day and night," thus leaving no time for any sanctioned study of Greek language and wisdom.

731. This is a very difficult text. Some manuscripts and parallels leave it out, including Ms. Erfurt and the *baraita* on BT Shab. 80b. The gist of this idea is that there was a certain kind of plaster utilized in Jerusalem before the destruction, and it was no longer permitted for use in the aftermath. It is impossible to determine any further specific characteristics from the limited texts we have before us. Mixing it with straw, however, takes away the concern, at least for the majority opinion, since it is no longer a purely forbidden substance.

732. Lieberman, TK 8:770, reads this not as the Bar Kokhba revolt, but instead as during the War of Quietus—the Diasporan Revolt. Cf. his basis in the *baraita* in BT Sot. 49b.

733. The Greek word for a kind of ointment, φουλιᾶτα, is transliterated thus in T. Based on a Latin cognate, *foliatum*, we can reconstruct the exact meaning: precious oil made from the fragrant leaves of a spikenard plant. According to Harold N. Moldenke and Alma L. Moldenke, *Plants of the Bible* (Waltham, MA: Chronica Botanica Co., 1952), pp. 148-9, spikenard was a native plant of high altitudes in Nepal, Bhutan and other areas of the Himalayan mountains, most likely imported to the Middle East from India, which explains its great expense and associated luxury status. Known as *Nardostachys jatamansi* to botanists, it was used for anointing kings and honored guests, and also had a role as one of the ingredients in the incense burned in the Temple.

734. דייני גזליות, "judges of robbery," is another possible reading. The Gemara resolves this problem by pointing out that they made *gezerot* related to *gezelot*—decrees relating to theft—harmonizing the two alternatives nicely into one solution. Cf. BT Ket. 105a.

735. Epstein, *Mavo LeNusah HaMishnah*, p. 67, points out that a similar statement is taught in PT Ket. 13:1, 35d, in the name of Rabbi Yehuda HaNasi.

736. In this case, a husband traveled abroad and left his wife alone, and she claims that she has no ability to sustain herself monetarily. Should the wife wish to claim support from the husband in court, asking the court to invade his property to support her, the question is when she may swear an oath that she is destitute. Hanan rules that the wife may not swear an oath that her husband abandoned her without money at the time of his initial departure. Instead, she must wait until either the time when he returns (and can tell his side of the story) or after he is declared dead, and only then may she swear an oath that he left her destitute.

737. Frankel, *Darkhei HaMishnah*, pp. 62-3 and Neusner, *A Life of Rabban Yohanan ben Zakkai* (Leiden: E.J. Brill, 1970) pp. 45-6, suggest that the "children of the high priests" was a euphemism for a priestly court that stood in competition with the municipal court. Urbach, *The Halakhah*, pp. 73-5, links this priestly court with another mentioned in T San. 4:7, who proofread the king's personal Torah scroll, mostly because they came with a traceable and unblemished genealogical record.

738. A parallel text that comments on the mishnah appears in T Ket. 13:4. Here, T probably knows the mishnah, as T shows a certain knowledge of the debate between Admon and the sages also present in M. This text also concludes with Rabban Gamaliel's statement accepting Admon's words.

739. Albeck, *Mishnah, Nashim*, p. 131, explains: a deer grows new horns each year, and runs quickly, thus the likelihood of him getting his money back if placed on the horns of a deer is slim to none. Therefore, by supporting the other's wife, this person has, to utilize an equivalent idiom in English, thrown his money to the wind.

740. This is a part of a condition imposed by the court in the *ketubbah*. See M Ket. 4:11 for the source related to this decision of the court. The daughters' support must be provided by the estate until they marry.

741. The sons must beg for food from house to house. They have no right to be sustained from the estate until there is enough to feed the daughters.

742. Neusner, *Pharisees*, 2:350-1, assigns this to Rabban Gamaliel HaZaken. Kanter, *Rabban Gamaliel II*, pp. 150-1, agrees with this assessment, and explains the logic of his inclusion: since he is the successor of Rabban Yohanan ben Zakkai, who validates the traditions of Hanan, it is quite logical to have Rabban Gamaliel I validate the words of Admon.

743. In other words, Rabban Gamaliel agrees with Admon's opinion. This entire mishnah is repeated verbatim at M BB 9:1.

744. Here, it is all a matter of definition: Admon sees the casks as part of the debt owed to the first party, while the sages do not consider the vessel to be a part of the debt at all, merely a container for the debt itself. One may only swear an oath to resolve a case of partial admission of a debt, not when there is denial of the entire claim by one party.

745. As a *nedunya*, a bridal gift. A parallel at the end of T Ket. 13:4 restates this law as applying to one who promised to give money to his daughter who is still a minor.

746. The bride must wait until the father-in-law can follow through on his promise, even if it takes so long that her hair turns white.

747. The bride is pointing out how unfair the situation is: her father is the one who agreed to this, not her, and so she should certainly not be the one to suffer for his mistake.

748. The situation is this: A signs a document as a witness when B sells a field to C. However, A now claims that B stole the field from him originally, and therefore, had no right to effect the sale to C. Thus, A is reclaiming the field after he served as a witness to its sale. The problem is that A should not have agreed to serve as a witness to the sale if he knew that B's ownership was in question and he claimed to be the owner.

749. Here, Admon's suggested statement works out to: C is easier to defeat, and A would have a fair chance of making a reasonable attempt at a claim against him. B, on the other hand, is a more formidable opponent (more politically powerful, or perhaps just downright intimidating). A's logic here, was to effect the sale to enable a fairer chance of his claim ultimately being handled appropriately.

750. In this case, if A sells a nearby field, and used the disputed field as a boundary in the sale contract, that, too, is enough to invalidate A's claim of ownership of the disputed field.

751. The neighboring owners took over the path to his field, assuming he was gone, and they now refuse to allow him right-of-way to pass to his property.

752. This implies he had lost his right to travel to the field.

753. The bill of sale must be dated later than the bond.

754. In this case, A claims that B owes him money. B, however, just sold a field to A. When A claims that B owes him a debt, B retorts that if he truly owed money to A, then A should have taken it back when he recently sold him the field, since that would have, of course, been an opportune moment to reclaim the debt. Admon views this as proof that the debt was falsified, and would thus allow its renunciation. The sages, however, see it as a shrewd maneuver, since now the loaner may reclaim the field itself as part of the debt, and he has the debtor's money used to purchase it already.

755. Since, technically, any transfer of funds from debtor to loaner would first constitute repayment, as this has priority over further loans, according to Admon.

756. The sages saw this differently: they rule that a court should honor the bonds as written, and the parties may collect, suggesting that prior debt repayment between parties is not automatically considered when making further loans.

757. Frankel, *Darkhei HaMishnah*, pp. 63-4.

758. Weiss, *Dor*, 1:181.

759. Albeck, *Mavo LaMishnah*, p. 88.

760. Nahum also appears in a parallel *baraita* in PT Ket. 13:1, 35c.

761. The count is 460 in PT Ket. 13:1, 35c.

762. A parallel text in BT BK 58b also recalls these judges receiving funding from public funds. The Gemara on BT Ket. 105a suggests that this monetary payment was not for the act of judging itself, but, instead, to compensate the judge for the loss of work that the hearing caused. Tosafot *ad loc.*, *s.v.* גוזרי גזרות שבירושלים, suggests that because they were full-time judges, they received payment from public funding, as they could not retain other positions that would provide them with appropriate compensation due to their busy judicial calendars.

763. Urbach, *The Halakhah*, p. 73.

764. This is mentioned in *MegTa*, see Lichtenstein, "Die Fastenrolle," p. 331.
765. Urbach, *The Halakhah*, pp. 71-2.
766. BT AZ 36a-b.
767. BT Betz. 36b-37a.
768. T Dem. 5:24.
769. In M AZ 2:4-5, we have just learned of a variety of prohibitions that are the strictest kind: those items where a Jew is not even allowed to benefit from the use, transport or sale of goods. Here, the prohibition is nonetheless serious, but not quite as strict. In this mishnah, the Jew may benefit from transactions related to these items (sale, transport, use, etc.) but may simply not eat the items mentioned.
770. Epstein, *Mavo LeSifrut HaTannaim*, p. 230 and Albeck, *Mavo LaMishnah*, p. 120, both agree that this is not Rabbi Yehuda HaNasi, but rather Rabbi Yehuda Nesiah ben Rabban Gamaliel, the grandson of Rabbi Yehuda HaNasi, though M itself simply says Rabbi, which usually indicates Rabbi Yehuda HaNasi himself. They base this on the reading in BT AZ 37a, which mentions Rabbi Yehuda Nesiah by name. Albeck, *Mishnah, Nezikin*, p. 331, further indicates that he sees the statement in M as a later addition, which it must be if it truly does represent the actions of Rabbi Yehuda Nesiah.
771. A parallel exists for this prohibition in *MegTa*, where oil touched by non-Jews was considered unclean. See Baumgarten, *Qumran Law*, p. 94, n. 29.
772. Wine creates the problem here, since the rabbis class all wine made or held by idolaters as inappropriate for Jewish use due to the high probability that it could have been used for idolatrous libations. Vinegar, since it was often made from soured wine, was likewise prohibited.
773. *Hilek* fish is a kind of fish that has no fins in its early stages of development, so there is a danger of it being confused with unclean species, thus M prohibits it.
774. Latin *assa foetida*, a coarse, umbelliferous plant indigenous to Afghanistan still eaten today in certain parts of Central and Eastern Asia, which grows large, cabbage-like heads. It is considered a remedy for heart and stomach ailments by some rabbis, and a poisonous substance by others. See Julius Preuss, *Biblical and Talmudic Medicine* (Northvale, NJ: Jason Aronson, 1993), p. 567, for a list of citations and short description. A useful description of the plant and its many uses was also available on-line at www.botanical.com/botanical/mgmh/a/asafe070.html#des. Kehati explains that this spicy plant was chopped up with a knife into tiny pieces. The rabbinic concern, here, was that non-Jews might chop it with a knife that had grease from a carcass on it, and the asafetida would absorb the grease and become more palatable. To prevent it from being eaten this way, the rabbis forbid its consumption if bought from a non-Jew.
775. Seasoned salt was a mixture of salt and various spices, into which non-Jews would mix lard and fat from unclean fish, rendering it forbidden for consumption, but not for benefit.
776. If one eats bread and oil with heathens, it is only logical to assume that the next thing shared at the table will be wine. To erect a fence around drinking wine used for idolatrous purposes, bread and oil must also be prohibited.

777. If a Jew and an idolater may drink wine together and share in this sort of close private contact, intermarriage also becomes possible. Limiting the drinking of wine prevented *yihud* and, ultimately, intermarriage with idolaters.

778. Another matter, here, implies idolatry in its most explicit sense. Once engaging in relations with heathen women, the next logical step is to engage in worshiping their gods. So, being involved with heathen women is fenced off, to prevent the ultimate violation: idolatry.

779. According to the reading of Rav Nahman bar Yitzhak, this further matter is the prohibition of having any contact with a heathen child from birth. The idea, here, is to erect a complete, airtight fence around idolatry, and in the service of this idea, any contact is considered off limits. One might argue that a child, as yet unschooled in the ways of idolatry, would be exempt from this prohibition. However, BT AZ 36b-37a refutes this position, and indicates (in highly derogatory terms with respect to heathen children, we might add) that they bring defilement from the time they are one day old.

780. The sources are: M MK 3:5 (two occurrences, one parallel to PT MK 3:5, 82a, PT MK 3:6, 83a and BT Nazir 16a-b); M Mid. 2:3 (parallel to PT Shek. 6:2, 50a); M Yad. 1:3 (two occurrences); PT Ber. 9:5, 14c; PT Yoma 2:2, 39d; PT Naz. 3:1, 52b; BT Ber. 31a (parallel to BT Sotah 46b); BT Shab. 30a; BT Yev. 78b-79a; BT Ket. 14a and BT Naz. 20a (parallel to BT Naz. 54b-55a and BT Git. 8b).

781. See M RH 2:9 (parallel to PT RH 2:9, 48b and BT RH 25a); M Ta. 3:8 (parallel to PT Ta. 3:8,67a and PT MK 3:1, 21d, BT Ber. 19a, BT Ta. 19a and 23a); M Ed. 8:3; T Par. 11b; PT Hag. 2:1, 77c; PT Kid. 2:7, 63a; BT Pes. 53a (parallel to BT Betz. 23a); and BT San. 5:2

782. The sources are all from Amoraic sources, interestingly enough: PT Shevi. 10:1, 36c (parallel to PT Git. 1:2, 43c); PT BK 4:3, 4b; BT Yev. 116b; BT Ket. 70b; BT Ned. 43b; BT San. 21b; and BT Hul. 6a (two occurrences).

783. The sources are all Tannaitic, in this case: M Kil. 3:5; T Dem. 5:25; T Shevi. 3:10, 3:11 and 3:13 and T MS 5:15-17.

784. The sources are: T Shab. 1:14; T YK 4:2; PT Ber. 3:1, 10a; BT Yoma 77b; BT Git. 8b and BT San. 82a.

785. See T BB 9:1, *Mtan Devarim* 24:11 and BT Ber. 16b.

786. See T Par. 3:6.

787. T. Sot. 13:10.

Conclusion

Engineers often utilize a "black box" model to understand complex systems. The experiment works this way: given a black (and thus opaque) box filled with connected components, an engineer attempts to determine, through applying certain inputs and observing the output, exactly what components are in the box, and how they are connected. The essence of this intellectual construct implies that a certain input applied to a given system will result in defined output. By thorough examination of how a given system responds to a wide range of input, the engineer can begin to predict how the system's input and output are related, and, eventually, with enough testing, can determine exactly what array of components are inside the "black box."

This study is an extension of that model, in certain ways. One can view the legal texts of the rabbinic period as the output of a black box. We know some (not all) of the input to the system in the form of earlier literary and legal traditions, because we have access to some of the texts and much of the history from the period preceding 70 CE. What often elude us are the complicated twists and turns of the components within: the values and ideals, the personalities and interactions, the historical triumphs and tragedies that shaped input into output. By analyzing both the input and output, we can begin to understand some of the components at work within that "black box" we call the rabbinic period.

Apart from the individual conclusions already reached in the three prior chapters, a number of general conclusions arise from the study of this particular black box that relate to legal evolution in the ideological system of the rabbis. We will mention each briefly.

The Anxiety of Innovation

One of the baseline repeating phenomena that tied this study together was the idea that changes in law required some sort of acceptable proof. This can best be observed in the fact that the vast majority of citations of legal change indicated by our semantic markers are accompanied by a rationale for that change. If legal change were easy and widely accepted, then such justifications would be completely expendable. In their inclusion, we learn that legal evolution was, for the rabbis, a matter of significant anxiety.

Retrojection of legal change, whether to an era in the past or onto the shoulders of a respected leader or group, further illustrates the point. As we noted in chapter two, many *takkanot* were tied to leaders to whom the Bible ascribed various attributes that made them perfect literary receptacles for legal evolution. With all three of the semantic markers, some legal evolution was said to arise from specific critical moments in the past that redefined the community's borders, practices or priorities. Different editors revised these tropes and ushered them from one focus to another for their own purposes. Had legal change been a welcome element in rabbinic law, none of this creative embellishment would have been necessary—the texts could simply have reported the prior and current states of the law, and that would have been sufficient.

Texts edited in or after the Amoraic period actually exhibit more anxiety about legal change than those created in the Tannaitic period. M, T and the Halakhic Midrashim often simply state earlier and later legal states directly, without wandering as far afield as PT or, to a greater extent, BT, in explaining, questioning and justifying legal change. PT and BT often rewrite prior legal decisions as *takkanot* or *gezerot*, indicating that the editors of PT and BT felt the need to distinguish legal change from straightforward statements of law, and to justify decisions made as authoritative by placing them into an acceptable evolutionary rubric. This was, no doubt, a side effect of BT's (and to a lesser extent, PT's) keen interest in greater explanation and justification.

The statements of the Amoraic tradents cited, and the apparent editorial acts of Stammaitic editors, especially, betray a tremendous angst about legal change. These authorities and editors go to great lengths to create plausible explanations for their actions, reflective of their great ideological anguish. Theirs was, in the end, a well-founded fear: after all, in any system with a core belief in a divinely-granted initial law, any change may well be perceived as betrayal of God's direct instruction. Nevertheless, the rabbis did not hesitate to change law, for they must have believed that their society's well-being, and their own proper observance of divine instruction, depended on it. While they utilized a rhetoric of disclosure, admitting that law was changing, they did not always admit that it was *their* decision to alter law. They often retrojected or demurred in other ways, bolstering and supplementing their own power with the weight of prior history and the authority of prior leadership. Their innovation was two-fold: to innovate by creating new law, but also to innovate in creating a new rhetoric that justified and explained that new law through utilization of the inherited tradition in novel ways.

Palestine and Babylonia

Major differences exist between Babylonian and Palestinian texts in their usage of the marker terms. Tannaitic (and thus Palestinian) strata tended to favor the terms *barishonah* and *takkanot*, and show little widespread interest in the use of *gezerot*. Palestinian texts never once include an initiation of new practice that is attributed directly to a rabbi or collective of rabbis through the term *takkanah*. Palestinian compilations also tended to favor various personalities whose influence with respect to legal change seems to have waned in later generations. Rabbi Akiba and Rabban Yohanan ben Zakkai, to choose but two prominent examples, were well represented in Tannaitic legal texts utilizing these marker terms, but these traditions did not continue in the same strong way into either the later Palestinian or Babylonian Amoraic strata.

The texts that collected around historical moments such as the battle between Beit Hillel and Beit Shammai in the attic of Hananya ben Hezekiah ben Gurion (in all four of its recensions) have a decidedly different flavor in their Palestinian and Babylonian versions. Where M, T and PT kept the passage's initial focus on Shabbat observance, BT warped the text into a set of laws related to purity concerns. Likewise, when confronting danger to life and limb, BT tended to embellish heartily, editing traditions to strengthen their message.

In an attempt to sum up the difference between Palestinian and Babylonian approaches, one might say that BT exhibits a far greater explicit flexibility and implicit self-confidence in its approach to legal change than what appears in PT or the other Palestinian texts. Flexibility is expressed in a few ways: first, in *takkanot*, BT's editors more frequently initiate new practices, and are more comfortable enhancing such practices' authority by assigning their origin to rabbis or retrojecting them onto pre-rabbinic figures. Second, BT includes discussion of numerous potential *gezerot*, even if they are ultimately rejected. PT, on the other hand, has only one example of a rejected *gezerah*, which indicates that these were either edited out of PT, or, conversely, the editors of BT constructed the discussions of rejected *gezerot* as a valuable intellectual exercise worth preserving. Third, BT incorporates *gezerot* with multiple possible reasons. Finally, the sheer number of *gezerot* accepted by BT is far greater (even when adjusted for relative size of the works) than the number found in PT.

All of these factors point to the conclusion that the editorial choices indicate a greater flexibility in ideology in BT and less interest in and self-confidence about legal evolution on the part of the Palestinian editors. When it came to the rhetoric of disclosure, BT ranged farther and was more explicit about disclosing its acceptance of legal change. PT followed suit, but with a less explicit commitment to disclosure. M, T and the Halakhic Midrashim exhibited some interest, but far less than PT. While some of this may be attributed to the general style of the works themselves, it surely points to a vital trend in intellectual history: the ideology of literary representations of Jewish legal change evolved from a closed, non-disclosing stance in the Bible, to more openness at the Tannaitic level in Palestine, then, eventually, to the greatest flexibility and self-confidence in Babylonia as expressed in BT.

When we say flexibility, though, it must be clear that flexibility goes in both directions. While BT includes an enormous number of *gezerot* that create more conservative laws, it is also responsible for the largest number of innovations, which must be considered more liberal. If there were a trend in BT, it would probably be on the conservative side, simply because there are four times as many *gezerot* in BT as there are *takkanot* of initiation.

Generations of Activity

All three marker terms showed their greatest attributed activity among the early generations of Amoraim. PA3 and BA3-BA4 showed particularly heavy concentrations of attributed statements, out of all proportion with the relative number of general occurrences of their authorities in PT and BT. When averaged over so many occurrences, these findings would tend to indicate a peak period for the attributed use of these terms in the late third to early fourth centuries CE, though they were certainly used both before and afterwards. Statements about *takkanot* had the smallest percentage of attributions, which may indicate that later editors' hands were at work, or that they wanted to maintain anonymity to imbue opinions with more power. *Barishonah* and *gezerah* exhibited fairly similar percentages of attributions.

Such a clear indication that authorities from this period discussed legal change regularly suggests that societal forces were mustering to propel such changes forward. Three forces could have propelled such evolution: the development of the new Babylonian rabbinic community in competition with the long established Palestinian rabbinic community; the creation and promulgation of M and T, which led to a new set of standards that required revision once promulgated; and the various political, economic, agricultural and military upheavals that occurred in both the Roman and Sassanian worlds in this historical moment. Any or all of these could have contributed to a blossoming in the ideology of legal change attributed to authorities of this period.

The Contribution of this Work

As noted in the introduction, prior scholarship tended to isolate various intriguing passages and mine them for their particular value. No study before this has looked comprehensively at the broader overall usage of these literary terms that admit of rabbinic legal change. Through this analysis, we have been able to discern concrete patterns that vary by locale, dating and specific literary work, all of which are useful in indicating the intellectual growth that took place in the rabbinic understanding of legal change.

Further, we have clearly demarcated the various rationales considered acceptable to rabbinic authorities and editors, thereby indicating the broad range of potential justifications for legal change considered, and then subsequently rejected or accepted. This has an added benefit: while no period in history is entirely beholden to the historical currents that came before them, a deeper understanding of both acceptable and unacceptable rationales for legal change in such a critical formative period of Jewish law is vastly useful for two groups in particular: scholars of later Jewish law and religious leaders. Scholars of later Jewish law can utilize this study's results to determine whether changes that arose in later periods either built upon or abandoned prior trends. Contemporary Jewish communal leadership can now attempt to evaluate their own choices and justifications in modern legal change against a more useful yardstick culled from the literary data of an important and formative prior age.

For scholars in literary and comparative legal studies, the results of this work should also be helpful. By noting the rhetorical patterns used for justifying legal change present in rabbinic literature, we have made possible future comparative legal study with Greek, Roman and Sassanian law. Literary scholars who analyze rhetorical patterns in ancient narrative will also benefit from this work's findings, as they may now comprehensively assess a facet of legal rhetoric heretofore unstudied.

Values and Ideals

Finally, in keeping with Alan Watson's theory mentioned in the introduction, this study has shown various values and ideals of the rabbis that were expressed through the rhetoric they utilized to justify alterations of law. Preventing danger, embarrassment and distress in social status fostered much change in rabbinic law. The teaching of a new philosophy by a great sage motivated subtle communal shifts that inspired legal evolution. Catastrophic historical moments (whether wars, the destruction of the Temple or persecutions) forced rabbis to rethink prior halakhic stands. Changes in leadership structures (both internal and external) and upheavals in business and agricultural practices all led to new legal opinions. The rabbis' perception of important communal needs, combined with the values they cherished, induced them to selectively alter law on hundreds of occasions. In each alteration is the kernel for understanding what the rabbis valued, individually and as a collective.

These and many similar reasons provided motivation for the rabbis to confront the daunting idea of legal change within their tightly constrained ideological system. In so doing, they made sure that Jewish law renewed itself, and stayed ever awake to the developing issues of the world around them. Ultimately, the rabbis firmly believed that new law, designed for a new moment, could rise to meet those challenges. The rhetoric of innovation they created helped it do so.

Bibliography

אלבעק, חנוך. "סמיכה ומינוי ובית דין." *ציון* 8 (1943) : 85-93.
——. *מבוא למשנה*. ירושלים : מוסד ביאליק, 1943.
——. *מבוא לתלמודים*. תל-אביב : דביר, 1969.
——. *שישה סדרי המשנה*. ירושלים : דביר, 1952-8.

Albright, William F. "The Hebrew Expression for 'Making a Covenant' in Pre-Israelite Documents." *BASOR* 121 (1951): 21-2.

Alon, Gedaliah. *The Jews in Their Land in the Talmudic Age.* Jerusalem: Magnes Press, 1984.

Amram, David Werner. *The Jewish Law of Divorce According to Bible and Talmud.* Philadelphia: Edward Stern & Company, 1896.

אנקר, אהרן ודויטש, סיני, עורכים. *עיונים במשפט עברי ובהלכה*. רמת-גן : אוניברסיטת בר-אילן, 1998.

Avi-Yonah, Michael. *The Jews of Palestine.* New York: Schocken, 1976.

Balkin, J.M. "Deconstructive Practice and Legal Theory," pp. 743-785 in Scott Brewer, ed., *Evolution and Revolution in Theories of Legal Reasoning.* Garland Publishing: New York, 1998.

Bar-Ilan, Meir. "Illiteracy in the Land of Israel in the First Centuries C.E.," pp. 46-61 in Simcha Fishbane and Jack Lightstone, eds. *Essays in the Social Scientific Study of Judaism and Jewish Society II.* Hoboken: Ktav, 1992.

Baumgarten, Albert I. "The Akiban Opposition." *HUCA* 50 (1979): 179-197.
——. "Rabbi Judah and His Opponents." *JSJ* 12:2 (1981): 135-172.

Bauer, Walter. *A Greek-English Lexicon of the New Testament.* Chicago: University of Chicago Press, 1979.

Baumgarten, Joseph M. *Studies in Qumran Law.* Leiden: Brill, 1977.

Berlin, Adele. *The JPS Bible Commentary: Esther.* Philadelphia: Jewish Publication Society, 2001.

Biale, Rachel. *Women & Jewish Law.* New York: Schocken Books, 1984.

ביכלר, אברהם. *הסנהדרין*. ירושלים : מוסד הרב קוק, 1974.

בלאך, משה אריה. *שערי תורת התקנות.* ירושלים: הוצאת מקור, 1971.

Birnbaum, Philip. *Daily Prayer Book.* New York: Hebrew Publishing Company, 1977.

Bokser, Baruch M. "Changing Views of Passover and the Meaning of Redemption According to the Palestinian Talmud." *AJS Review* 10:1 (1985): 1-18.

Bostock, John and Riley, H.T., translators. *The Natural History of Pliny.* London: Bohn, 1857.

Braude, Walter. *Pesikta Rabbati.* New Haven: Yale, 1968.

Brin, Gershon. *The Concept of Time in the Bible and the Dead Sea Scrolls.* Leiden: E.J. Brill, 2001.

Brunt, P.A. *Studies in Greek History and Thought.* Oxford: Oxford University Press, 1993.

Buckland, W.W. *A Text-Book of Roman Law.* Cambridge: University Press, 1966.

Büchler, Adolf. *Das Synedrion in Jerusalem.* Vienna: Verlag der Israel.-Theol. Lehranstalt, 1902.
———. *Der Galiläsche 'Am-Ha'rets Des Zeiten Jahrhunderts.* Vienna: N.P., 1906.

Bulsara, Sohrab Jamshedjee. *The Laws of the Ancient Persians As Found in the* "Mâtîkân Ê Hazâr Dâtastân." Bombay: Hoshang T. Anklesaria, 1937.

Cairns, Huntington. *Legal Philosophy from Plato to Hegel.* Baltimore: Johns Hopkins Press, 1949.

Cary, M. at al. *The Oxford Classical Dictionary.* Oxford: Clarendon Press, 1950.

Chajes, Tsvi Hirsch. *Mevo HaTalmud.* Lvov: Margulies, 1845.
———. *The Student's Guide Through the Talmud.* Translated by Jacob Shachter. London: East and West Library, 1952.

Charlesworth, James H. *The Old Testament Pseudepigrapha.* New York: Doubleday & Co., 1985.

———. *Graphic Concordance to the Dead Sea Scrolls.* Tübingen: J.C.B. Mohr, 1991.

צירניק, מיכאל. *לחקר המידות "כלל ופרט וכלל" ו"ריבוי ומיעוט" במדרשים ובתלמודים.* לוד : מכון הברמןלמחקרי ספרות, 1984
———. *מידת "גזרה שווה" צורותיה במדרשים ובתלמודים.* לוד : מכון הברמן למחקרי ספרות, 1994.

Clines, David J.A. *The Esther Scroll.* Trowbridge, England: Journal for the Study of the Old Testament Press, 1984.

R.J. Coggins. *Samaritans and Jews.* John Knox Press: Atlanta, 1975.

Cohen, Boaz. *Jewish Law and Roman Law: A Comparative Study.* New York: Jewish Theological Seminary, 1966. Repr. Holmes Beach, Florida: Gaunt, Inc., 2001.

Cohen, Matty. "La Maxime des Hommes de la Grande Assemblée: Une Reconsidération." Pages 281-296 in *Hellenica et Judaica.* Edited by A. Caquot, M. Hadas-Lebel and J. Riaud. Leuven-Paris: Éditions-Peeters, 1986.

Cohen, Shaye J.D., editor. *The Synoptic Problem in Rabbinic Literature.* Providence, RI: Brown Judaic Studies, 2000.

Cohen, Shaye J.D. and Greenstein, Edward L. editors. *The State of Jewish Studies.* New York: The Jewish Theological Seminary of America, 1990.

Cohn, Haim H. *Human Rights in Jewish Law.* New York: Ktav, 1984.

Crook, John. *Law and Life of Rome.* Ithaca: Cornell University Press, 1967.

Cross, Frank Moore. "Fragments of the Prayer of Nabonidus." *IEJ* 34:4 (1984): 260-264.

Crown, Alan D. *The Samaritans.* Tübingen: JCB Mohr, 1989.
———. "Redating the Schism between the Judaeans and the Samaritans," *JQR* 82 (July-October, 1991): 17-50.

De Zulueta, Francis, tr. *The Institutes of Gaius.* Oxford: Clarendon Press, 1946.

Di Lella, Alexander A. *The Wisdom of Ben Sira.* New York, Doubleday, 1970.

Duncan, David Ewing. *The Calendar*. New York: Avon Books, 1998.

Dupont-Sommer, A. "Trios stèles araméennes provenant de Sfiré: un traité de vassalité de VIIIe siècle avant Jesus Christ." *Annales Archeologiques Arabes Syriennes* 10 (1960): 21-54.

Dworkin, R. M., Editor. *The Philosophy of Law*. Oxford: Oxford University Press, 1977.

Eagleton, Terry. *Literary Theory*. 2nd Edition. Minneapolis: University of Minnesota Press, 1996.

Elbogen, Ismar. *Jewish Liturgy: A Comprehensive History*. Translated by Raymond P. Scheindlin. Philadelphia: Jewish Publication Society, 1993.

Elon, Menachem. *Jewish Law: History, Sources, Principles*. Translated by Bernard Auerbach and Melvin J. Sykes. Philadelphia: Jewish Publication Society, 1994.

Encyclopaedia Judaica. Jerusalem: Keter, 1972.

אנציקלופדיה תלמודית. ירושלים: הוצאת אנציקלופדיה תלמודית, 1951.

Enos, Richard Leo. *The Literate Mode of Cicero's Legal Rhetoric*. Carbondale: Southern Illinois University Press, 1988.

Epstein, Louis M. *The Jewish Marriage Contract*. New York: Jewish Theological Seminary of America, 1927.
———. *Marriage Laws in the Bible and Talmud*. Cambridge, MA: Harvard University Press, 1942.
———. *Sex Laws and Customs in Judaism*. New York: Bloch, 1948.

אפשטיין, י. נ. *מבואות לספרות התנאים*. ירושלים: מאגנס, 1957.
———. *מבואות לספרות האמוראים*. ירושלים: מאגנס, 1962.

Eshel, Esther and Kloner, Amos. "An Aramaic Ostracon of an Edomite Marriage Contract from Maresha, Dated 176 BCE." *IEJ* 46 (1996): 1-22.

Eusebius. *Ecclesiastical History*. Kirsopp Lake, tr. Cambridge: Harvard University Press, 1965.

Even-Shoshan, Abraham. קונקורדנציה חדשה. Jerusalem: Kiryat Sefer, 1987.
Feinberg, Joel and Coleman, James. *Philosophy of Law.* Belmont, CA: Wadsworth-Thomson Learning, 2000.

פלדבלום, מאיר ס. *דקדוקי סופרים מסכת גיטין*. ניו-יורק : חורב, 1966.

Feldman, Louis H. "Some Observations on Rabbinic Reaction to Roman Rule in Third Century Palestine." *HUCA* 63 (1992): 39-81.
———. *Jew & Gentile in the Ancient World.* Princeton: Princeton University Press, 1993.

פליקס, יהודה. *תלמוד ירושלמי מסכת שביעית*. הוצאת צור-אות : ירושלים, 1979.

Fenwick, Gruffydd Roger and Hanley, Anthony Bryan. "The Genus *Allium* – Part I." *CRC Critical Reviews in Food and Nutrition* 22:3 (1985): 199-271.

Steven Fine. *This Holy Place.* Notre Dame: University of Notre Dame Press, 1997.

Finkelstein, Louis. "The Birkat Ha-Mazon." *JQR N.S.* XIX (1928-9): 211-262.
———. *הפרושים ואנשי הכנסת הגדולה*. ניו יורק : בית המדרש לרבנים באמריקה, 1950.
———. *New Light From the Prophets.* London: Valentine, Mitchell & Co., 1969.
———. *Siphre ad Deuteronomium H.S. Horovitzii schedis usis cum variis lectionibus et ad notationibus.* New York, New York: Jewish Theological Seminary Press, 1969.
———. "The Men of the Great Synagogue (*circa* 400-170 B.C.E.)." Pages 229-244 in *The Cambridge History of Judaism II.* Cambridge: Cambridge University Press, 1989.

Fischel, Henry A. "Story and History: Observations on Greco-Roman Rhetoric and Pharisaism." Pages 443-472 in *idem*, ed., *Essays in Greco-Roman and Related Talmudic Literature.* New York: Ktav, 1977.

Fish, Stanley. *Is There a Text in the This Class?* Harvard University Press: Cambridge, 1983.
———. *Doing What Comes Naturally: Change, Rhetoric and the Practice of Theory in Literary and Legal Studies.* Durham: Duke University Press, 1989.

Fishbane, Michael. *Biblical Interpretation in Ancient Israel.* Oxford: Clarendon Paperbacks, 1985.

Fitzmyer, Joseph A. *The Aramaic Inscriptions of Sefire*. Revised Edition. Roma: Editrice Pontificio Istituto Biblico, 1995.

Fokkema, Douwe and Ibsch, Elrud. *Theories of Literature in the Twentieth Century*. New York: St. Martin's Press, 1978.

Fornara, Charles William. *The Nature of History in Ancient Greece and Rome*. Berkeley: University of California Press, 1983.

פראנקעל, זכריה. *דרכי המשנה*. סיני: תל-אביב, 1959.

Freedman, David Noel, ed. *Anchor Bible Dictionary*. Doubleday: New York, 1992.

Freyne, Sean. "Urban-Rural Relations in First-Century Galilee: Some Suggestions from the Literary Sources." Pages 75-91 in *The Galilee in Late Antiquity*. Edited by Lee I. Levine. New York: Jewish Theological Seminary, 1992.

Friedmann, W. *Legal Theory*. London: Stevens & Sons Limited, 1960.

Friedmann, Meir. *Pesikta Rabbati*. Vienna: Selbstverlag des Herausgebers, 1880. Reprinted Tel Aviv: Esther, 1963.

Gadamer, Hans-Georg. *Truth and Method*. Translation revised by Joel Weinsheimer and Donald G. Marshall. New York: Continuum, 2003.

Gafni, Isaiah. "Synagogues in Babylonia in the Talmudic Period," Pages 220-231 in *Ancient Synagogues*. Edited by Dan Urman and Paul V.M. Flesher. Leiden: E.J. Brill, 1995.

גאליפאפאח, אליהו. *ידי אליהו*. ברוקלין, ניו יורק: האחים ביגלאיזן, 1990/1989.

Garnsey, Peter. *Social Status and Legal Privilege in the Roman Empire*. Oxford: Clarendon Press, 1970.

Geiger, Abraham. *Judaism and Its History*. New York: Block Publishing Company. Reprinted New York: University Press of America, 1985.

Gerhardsson, Birger. *Memory and Manuscript*. Lund, Sweden: C.W.K. Gleerup, 1961. Reprinted Grand Rapids, MI: Eerdmans Publishing Company, 1998.

Gilat, Y.D. "בית דין מתנין לעקור דבר מן התורה" in *Annual of Bar-Ilan University* VII-VIII (1970): 117-132.

Gill, Christopher and Wiseman, T.P. *Lies and Fiction in the Ancient World.* Austin; University of Texas Press, 1993.

Ginzberg, Louis. *On Jewish Law and Lore.* Philadelphia: Jewish Publication Society, 1955.
――――. *Students, Scholars, and Saints.* Lanham, MD: University Press of America, 1985.

Goldberg, Avraham. *מסכת אוהלות.* Jerusalem: Magness Press, 1955.
――――. "התפתחות הסוגיא בתלמוד הבבלי" in *Memorial Volume for Rabbi Hanokh Albeck*, pp. 101-113. Jerusalem: Mossad HaRav Kook, 1963

Goldin, Judah. "The First Pair (Yose ben Yoezer and Yose ben Yohanan) or The Home of a Pharisee." *Association for Jewish Studies Review* 5 (1980): 41-61.

Goodblatt, David. *Rabbinic Instruction in Sassanian Babylonia.* Leiden: Brill, 1975.

Goodenough, Erwin R. *Jewish Symbols in the Greco-Roman Period.* Kingsport, TN; Kingsport Press, 1965.

Goodman, Martin. *The Ruling Class of Judaea.* Cambridge: Cambridge University Press, 1987.

Gordis, David. "Prozbul and Poseq" *S'vara* 2 (1991): 71-73.

Green, William Scott. *The Legal Traditions of Joshua ben Hananiah in Mishnah-Tosefta and Related Materials.* Ph.D. Dissertation, Brown University, 1974.
――――. "What's in a Name? – The Problematic of Rabbinic 'Biography," in *idem, Approaches to Ancient Judaism I.* Missoula: Scholars Press, 1978: 77-96.

Greenberg, Moshe. *Biblical Prose Prayer.* Berkeley: University of California Press, 1983.

גולאק, אשר. *החיוב ושעבודיו.* ירושלים: האוניברסיטה העברית, 1939.

Haas, Peter. "The Am Ha'rets as Literary Character." Pages 139-153 in *From Ancient Israel to Modern Judaism.* Edited by Jacob Neusner, Ernest Frerichs and Nahum Sarna. Atlanta: Scholars Press, 1989.

Hadas, Moses. *Aristeas to Philocrates*. (New York: Harper Brothers, 1951).

Halbertal, Moshe. *Interpretative Revolutions in the Making*. Jerusalem: Magnes Press, 1997.

Halivni, David Weiss. "Doubtful Attributions in the Talmud," *PAAJR* 46-7 (1979-80): 67-83
―――. *Midrash, Mishnah and Gemara*. Cambridge: Harvard University Press, 1986.
―――. *Mekorot U'mesorot Masekhet Baba Kamma*. Jerusalem: Magnes Press, 1993.
―――. *Revelation Restored*. Boulder, Colorado: Westview Press, 1997.

Harries, Jill. *Law and Empire in Late Antiquity*. Cambridge: Cambridge University
Press, 1999.

Harris, William V. *Ancient Literacy*. Cambridge: Harvard University Press, 1989.

Hauptman, Judith. *Development of the Talmudic Sugya*. Lanham: University Press of America, 1988.
―――. *Rereading the Rabbis*. Boulder, CO: Westview Press, 1998.

Hayes, Christine. "The Abrogation of Torah Law: Rabbinic *Taqqanah* and Praetorian Edict" in Peter Schäfer *The Talmud Yerushalmi and Graeco-Roman Culture*, pp. 643-674. Tübingen: Mohr Sieback, 1997.
―――. "Displaced Self-Perceptions: The Deployment of *Minim* and Romans in b. Sanhedrin 90b-91a" in Hayim Lapin *Religious and Ethnic Communities in Later Roman Palestine*, pp. 249-289. Bethesda: University Press of Maryland, 1998.

Hecht, N.S., et al., eds. *An Introduction to the History and Sources of Jewish Law*. Oxford: Clarendon Press, 1996.

Heinemann, Joseph. *Prayer in the Talmud*. Berlin: Walter de Gruyter, 1977.

Herford, R. Travers. *Christianity in Talmud and Midrash*. Clifton, NJ: Reference Book Publishers, 1966.

הר, משה דוד. "לבריית הלכות מלחמה בשבת בימי בית שני ובתקופת משנה
והתלמוד." *תרביץ* 30 (1961): 56-242 ו-561-341.

Hezser, Catherine. *The Social Structure of the Rabbinic Movement in Roman Palestine*. Tübingen: Mohr Siebeck, 1997.
———. *Jewish Literacy in Roman Palestine*. Tübingen: Mohr Siebeck, 2001.

Higger, Michael. *Treatise Semahot*. Jerusalem: Makor, Reprinted 1970.

הילדסהיימר, עזריאל. *ספר הלכות גדולות*. מקיצי נרדמים: ירושלים, 1971.

Hillers, Delbert R. *Covenant: The History of a Biblical Idea*. Baltimore: The Johns Hopkins Press, 1969.

הרשלר, משה. *תלמוד בבלי*. ירושלים: מכון התלמוד הישראלי השלם, 1972.

Hirsch, E.D., Jr. *Validity in Interpretation*. New Haven: Yale University Press, 1967.

האפפמאנן, דוד צבי. *המשנה הראשונה ופלוגתא דתנאי*. שמואל גרינברג, מתרגם.
ברלין: נארד-אסט, 1913.
———. *The First Mishnah and the Controversies of the Tannaim*. Translated by Paul Forchheimer. New York: Maurosho Publications, 1977.

Hoffman, Lawrence A. *The Canonization of the Synagogue Service*. Notre Dame: University of Notre Dame Press, 1979.
———. "The Origins of Ordination." *CCAR Yearbook* 90 (1982): 71-94.

Horovitz, H. S. *Mekhilta DeRabbi Yishmael*. Jerusalem: Bamberger and Wahrmann, 1931.
———. *Siphre D'be Rab*. Lipsiae: Gustav Fock, 1942. Reprinted Jerusalem:Wahrmann Books, 1966.

Howarth, William D. "'Droit du Seigneur:' Fact or Fantasy." *Journal of European Studies* 1 (1971): 291-312.

היימאן, אהרן. *תולדות תנאים ואמוראים*. ירושלים: מכון פרי הארץ, 1987.

Ilan, Tal. "Premarital Cohabitation in Ancient Judea: The Evidence of the Babatha Archive and the Mishnah (*Ketubbot* 1.4)." *HTR* 86:3 (1993): 247-64.

348   Bibliography

Jackson, Bernard. "Evolution and Foreign Influence in Ancient Law." *American Journal of Comparative Law* 16 (1968): 372-390.

Jacobs, Louis. "Are There Fictitious Baraitot in the Babylonian Talmud?" *HUCA* 42 (1971): 185-196.
———. *Teyku*. London: Cornwall Books, 1981.

Jaffee, Martin. *The Mishnah's Theology of Tithing*. Chico, CA: Scholars Press, 1981.
———. "The *Taqqanah* in Tannaitic Literature: Jurisprudence and the Construction of Rabbinic Memory," *Journal of Jewish Studies* 41.2 (1990): 204-225.

Jastrow, Marcus. *A Dictionary of the Targumim, the Talmud Babli and Yerushalmi, and the Midrashic Literature*. Repr., New York: The Judaica Press, 1996.

Jewish Encylcopedia. New York: Ktav Publishing, 1901.

Jewish Publication Society Hebrew-English Tanakh. Philadelphia: Jewish Publication Society, 1999.

Jolowicz, H.F. *Historical Introduction to the Study of Roman Law*. Cambridge: University Press, 1967.

Jones, John Walter. *The Law and Legal Theory of the Greeks*. Darmstadt: Scientia Verlag Aalen, 1977.

Kahana, Kalman. *Masekhet Sheviit*. Benei Brak: Lipa Freedman Press, 1972.

Kalmin, Richard. *The Sage in Jewish Society of Late Antiquity*. London: Routledge, 1999.

Kanter, Shamai. *Rabban Gamaliel II: The Legal Traditions*. Providence: Brown University Press, 1980

Katz, Jacob. *The Shabbes Goy: A Study in Halakhic Flexibility*. Translated by Joel Lerner. Philadelphia: Jewish Publication Society, 1989.
———. *Divine Law in Human Hands: Case Studies in Halakhic Flexibility*. Jerusalem: The Hebrew University Magnes Press, 1998.

קהתי, פינחס. *משניות מבוארות*. ירושלים : היכל שלמה, 1991.

Kellner, Menachem. *Maimonides on the "Decline of the Generations" and the Nature of Rabbinic Authority.* Albany: SUNY Press, 1996.

Kepnes, Steven. *Interpreting Judaism in a Postmodern Age.* New York: New York University Press, 1996.

Kimelman, Reuven Ronald. *Rabbi Yohanan of Tiberias: Aspects of the Social and Religious History of Third Century Palestine.* New Haven: Dissertation, Yale, 1978.
————. *"Birkat Ha-Minim* and the Lack of Evidence for an Anti-Christian Jewish Prayer in Late Antiquity," pp. 226-244 in *Jewish and Christian Self-Definition* 2 edited by E.P. Sanders *et al.* Philadelphia: Fortress Press, 1981.

Kirschner, Robert. *"Imitatio Rabbini."* *JJS* 17 (1986): 70-9.

קליין, שמואל. *ארץ יהודה.* תל-אביב: דביר, 1939.

Koch, K. "Ezra and the Origins of Judaism." *JSS* 19 (1974): 173-197.

Kraemer, David. *Stylistic Characteristics of Amoraic Literature.* Ph.D. Dissertation, Jewish Theological Seminary of America, 1984.
————. *The Mind of the Talmud.* Oxford: Oxford University Press, 1990.
————. "Prozbul and Rabbinic Power" *S'vara* 2.2 (1991): 66-70.
————. *The Meanings of Death in Rabbinic Judaism.* London: Routledge, 2000.

Kraft, Robert A. and Nickelsburg, G.W.E., eds. *Early Judaism and Its Modern Interpreters.* Philadelphia and Atlanta: Scholars Press, 1986.

Kuenen, Abraham. *Gesammelte Abhandlungen zur biblischen Wissenschaft.* Freiburg: Mohr Siebeck, 1894.

Kurtz, Donna C. and Boardman, John. *Greek Burial Customs.* London: Camelot Press, 1971.

Lapin, Hayim. *Economy, Geography, and Provincial History in Later Roman Palestine.* Tübingen: Mohr Siebeck, 2001.

לאו, ישראל מאיר. "בגדר שמיטת כספים ופרוזבול." *תורה שבעל-פה* 34 (1994): 33-38.

Lausberg, Heinrich. *Handbuch der literaschen Rhetorik*. Ismaning bei München, 1960. Translated by Matthew T. Bliss, Annemiek Jansen and David E. Orton. Edited by David E. Orton and R. Dean Anderson. Boston, Köln: Brill, 1998.

Lauterbach, Jacob Z. "The Ancient Jewish Allegorists in Talmud and Midrash." *JQR* (N.S.) 1 (1910-11): 291-333.

Levine, Baruch A. *Leviticus: The Traditional Hebrew Text with the New JPS Translation/Commentary*. Philadelphia: Jewish Publication Society, 1989.

Levine, Lee I. *Caesarea Under Roman Rule*. Leiden: E.J. Brill, 1975.
———. "Rabbi Abbahu of Caesarea," pp. 56-76 in *Christianity, Judaism and Other Greco-Roman Cults: Studies for Morton Smith at Sixty* 4 edited by Jacob Neusner. Leiden: E.J. Brill, 1975)
———. *Ancient Synagogues Revealed*. Detroit: Wayne State University Press, 1982.
———. *The Synagogue in Late Antiquity*. New York: Jewish Theological Seminary, 1987.
———. *The Rabbinic Class of Roman Palestine in Late Antiquity*. New York: Jewish Theological Seminary of America, 1989.
———. *The Galilee in Late Antiquity*. New York: Jewish Theological Seminary of America, 1992.
———. *The Ancient Synagogue*. New Haven: Yale University Press, 2000.

Levinson, Bernard M. "The Human Voice in Divine Revelation: The Problem of Authority in Biblical Law" in *Innovation in Religious Traditions* edited by Williams, Michael A.; Cox, Collett; and Jaffee, Martin S., 35-72. New York: Mouton de Gruyter, 1992.
———. *Deuteronomy and the Hermeneutics of Legal Innovation*. Oxford: Oxford University Press, 1997.

Lewin, Benjamin M. *Iggeret Rav Sherira Gaon*. Haifa: Golda Itzkofsky, 1921.

Lewis, Naphtali. *The Documents from the Bar Kokhba Period in the Cave of Letters: Greek Papyri*. Jerusalem: Israel Exploration Society, 1989.

Licht, Hans. *Sexual Life in Ancient Greece*. New York: Barnes & Nobles, 1963.

Lichtenstein, Hans. "Die Fastenrolle: Eine Untersuchung Zur Jüdisch-Hellenistischen Geschichte" *HUCA* 8-9 (1931-2): 257-351.

Liddell, Henry George and Scott, Robert. *A Greek-English Lexicon*. Oxford: Clarendon Press, 1968.

Lieberman, Saul. *HaYerushalmi Kifshuto*. Jerusalem: Darom Publishing, 1934.
————. *Greek in Jewish Palestine*. New York: Jewish Theological Seminary of America, 1950.
————. *Hellenism in Jewish Palestine*. New York: Jewish Theological Seminary of America, 1950.
————. ed. *The Palestinian Talmud, Leiden Ms. Codex Scaliger 3*. Jerusalem: Kedem Publishing, 1970.
————. *Tosefta*. New York: Jewish Theological Seminary of America, 1973.
————. *Tosefta Kifshuta*. New York: Jewish Theological Seminary of America, 1973.

Macrobius. *The Saturnalia*. Percival Vaughan Davies, translator. New York: Columbia University Press, 1969.

Mantel, Hugo. *Studies in the History of the Sanhedrin*. Cambridge: Harvard University Press, 1961.
————. ‏אנשי כנסת הגדולה. ישראל: דביר, 1983.‏

Martínez, Florentino García and Tigchelaar, Eibert J.C. *The Dead Sea Scrolls Study Edition* Leiden: Brill, 1997.

Marx, Alexander et al., eds. *Louis Ginzberg Jubilee Volume*. New York: American Academy for Jewish Research, 1945.

McCarthy, D. J. *"Berit* and Covenant in the Deuteronomistic History" in G.W. Anderson, *et al*, eds., *Studies in the Religion of Ancient Israel*. Leiden: E.J. Brill, 1972.

Mendenhall, George E. "Law and Covenant in Israel and the Ancient Near East." *The Biblical Archaeologist* 17:2 (1954):26-46 and 17:3 (1954):49-76.

Milik, J. T. "'Prière de Nabonide' et autres écrits d'un cycle de Daniel." *RB* 63 (1956): 407-415.

Mirsky, Shmuel Kalman, editor. *Sheiltot de Rav Ahai Gaon* (Jerusalem: Slomin, 1977).

Moldenke, Harold N. and Moldenke, Alma L. *Plants of the Bible*. Waltham, MA: Chronica Botanica Co., 1952.

Momigliano, Arnaldo. *Studies in Historiography*. New York: Harper, 1966.

Moore, Carey A. *Studies in the Book of Esther*. New York: Ktav, 1982.

Mulder, Martin Jan, ed. *Mikra*. Philadelphia: Fortress Press, 1990.

Murphy, Jeffrie G. and Coleman, Jules L. *The Philosophy of Law: An Introduction to Jurisprudence*. Totowa: Rowman and Allanheld, 1984.

Nahon, Gerard and Touati, Charles, editors. *Hommage à Georges Vajda: Études D'histoire et de Pensée Juives*. Louvain: Peeters, 1980.

Neusner, Jacob. *The History of the Jews of Babylonia*. Leiden: Brill, 1965-70.
———. *Development of a Legend: Studies on the Traditions Concerning Yohanan ben Zakkai* (Leiden: E.J. Brill, 1970).
———. *A Life of Rabban Yohanan ben Zakkai*. Leiden: E.J. Brill, 1970.
———, ed. *The Formation of the Babylonian Talmud*. Leiden: E.J. Brill, 1970.
———. *The Rabbinic Traditions About the Pharisees Before 70*. Leiden: Brill, 1971.
———. *Contemporary Judaic Fellowship in Theory and in Practice*. New York: Ktav, 1972.
———. *Talmudic Judaism in Sasanian Bablyonia*. Leiden: Brill, 1976.
———. "The History of Earlier Rabbinic Judaism," *History of Religions* 16 (1977): 216-36.
———. *Formative Judaism*. Chico, CA: Scholars Press, 1982.
———. "The Experience of the City in Antique Judaism." Pages 37-52 in *Approaches to Ancient Judaism Volume V: Studies in Judaism and its Greco-Roman Context*. Edited by William Scott Green. Chico, CA: Scholars Press, 1985.
———. *The Economics of the Mishnah*. Chicago: University of Chicago Press, 1990.
———. *Are There Really Tannaitic Parallels to the Gospels?* Atlanta: Scholars Press, 1993.

Oppenheimer, Aharon. *The 'Am Ha-aretz*. Leiden: E.J. Brill, 1977.
———. *הגליל בתקופת המשנה*. ירושלים: מרכז זלמן שזר, 1991.
———. *Babylonia Judaica in the Talmudic Period*. Wiesbaden: Dr. Ludwig Reichert, 1983.
———. "Those of the School of Rabbi Yannai." *Studies in the History of the Jewish People and the Land of Israel* 4 (1978): 137-145. Haifa.

Pastor, Jack. *Land and Economy in Roman Palestine.* London: Routledge, 1997.

Pelikan, Jaroslav. *The Vindication of Tradition.* New Haven: Yale University Press, 1984.

Perikhanian, Anahit, editor. *The Book of a Thousand Judgments: A Sasanian Law-Book.* Translated from Russian by Nina Garsoïan. Costa Mesa, CA: Mazda Publishers, 1997.

Phang, Sara Elise. *The Marriage of Roman Soldiers (13 B.C. – 235 A.D.).* Leiden: Brill, 2001.

Podro, Joshua. *The Last Pharisee.* London: Vallentine, Mitchell, 1959.

Porten, Betzalel and Yardeni, Ada, editors. *Textbook of Aramiac Documents from Ancient Egypt.* Jerusalem: Hebrew University, 1986.

Preuss, Julius. *Biblical And Talmudic Medicine.* Fred Rosner, tr. and ed. Reprinted, Northvale, NJ: Jason Aronson, 1993.

James D. Purvis. *The Samaritan Pentateuch and the Origin of the Samaritan Sect.* Cambridge: Harvard University Press, 1968.
———. "The Samaritans and Judaism." Pages 81-98 in *Early Judaism and its Modern Interpreters.* Edited by Robert Kraft and George W.E. Nickelsburg. Atlanta: Scholars Press, 1986.
———. "The Samaritans." Pages 591-613 in *Cambridge History of Judaism Volume II.* Edited by W.D. Davies and Louis Finkelstein. Cambridge: Cambridge University Press, 1989.

Rabbinovicz, Raphaelo. *Dikduke Soferim.* New York: M.P. Press, 1977.

רבינוביץ, מרדכי דב, עורך. *הקדמות לפירוש המשנה (של רבינו משה בן מימון).* ירושלים: הוצאת מוסד הרב קוק, 1961.

Rabinowich, Nosson Dovid. *The Iggeres of Rav Sherira Gaon.* Jerusalem: Moznaim Press, 1988.

רוזנטל, אליעזר שמשון. *ירושלמי נזיקין.* ירושלים: האקדמיה הלאומית הישראלית למדעים, 1983.

Rosner, Fred. *The Encylcopedia of Medicine in the Bible and the Talmud.* Northvale, New Jersey: Jason Aronson, 2000.

Roth, Joel. *The Halakhic Process.* New York: Jewish Theological Seminary, 1986.

Rubenstein, Jeffrey L. *Talmudic Stories: Narrative Art, Composition and Culture.* Baltimore: Johns Hopkins University Press, 1999.

Safrai, Shmuel, ed. *The Literature of the Sages.* Philadelphia: Fortress Press, 1987.

Sanders, E.P. *Jewish Law from Jesus to the Mishnah.* Philadelphia: Trinity Press International, 1990.

Satlow, Michael. *Jewish Marriage in Antiquity.* Princeton: Princeton University Press, 2001.

Schechter, Solomon. *Avoth De-Rabbi Nathan.* Vienna: Maurith Knöpflmacher, 1887. Repr., New York: JTSA, 1997.

שציפנסקי, ישראל. *התקנות בישראל.* ירושלים : מוסד הרב קוק, 1991.

Schiffer, Ira Jeffrey. "The Men of the Great Assembly." Pages 237-76 in *Persons and Institutions in Early Rabbinic Judaism.* Edited by William Scott Green. Missoula, MT: Scholars Press, 1977

Schiffman, Lawrence H. *The Halakhah at Qumran.* Leiden: E.J. Brill, 1975.
———. *Who Was a Jew?* Hoboken: Ktav, 1985.
———. "Samaritans in Tannaitic Halakhah," *JQR* 75 (April, 1985): 323-50.
———. "The Laws of War in XIQTemple," *Revue de Qumran* 13, 1-4 (1988): 299-311.
———. *From Text to Tradition.* Hoboken: Ktav Publishing House, Inc., 1991.
———. "Qumran and Rabbinic Halakhah." Pages 138-146 in *Jewish Civilization in the Hellenistic-Roman Period.* Edited by Shemaryahu Talmon. Philadelphia: Trinity Press, 1991.
———. "Was There a Galilean Halakhah?" Pages 143-156 in *The Galilee in Late Antiquity.* Edited by Lee I. Levine. New York: Jewish Theological Seminary Press, 1992.
———. *Reclaiming the Dead Sea Scrolls.* Philadelphia and Jerusalem: Jewish Publication Society, 1994.
———. "The Early History of Public Reading of the Torah." Pages 44-56 in *Jews, Christians, and Polytheists in the Ancient Synagogue.* Edited by Steven Fine. London: Routledge, 1999.

Scholem, Gershom. *Major Trends in Jewish Mysticism.* New York: Schocken Books, 1941.

Schürer, Emil. *The History of the Jewish People in the Age of Jesus Christ.* 4 volumes. Reprinted in Edinburgh: T & T Clark, 1973.

Schwartz, Joshua. "Tension Between Palestinian Scholars and Babylonian Olim in Amoraic Palestine." *JSJ* 11 (1980): 78-94.

Scott, S. P. *The Civil Law.* New York: AMS Press, 1973.

Segal, Moshe Tzvi. ‏ספר בן סירא השלם‎. Jerusalem: Mossad Bialik, 1958.

Shiffman, Pinchas. "Prozbul and Legal Fiction." *S'vara* 2.2 (1991): 63-65.
Smith, Morton. *Tannaitic Parallels to the Gospels.* Philadelphia: Society of Biblical Literature, 1951.

Silberg, Moshe. *Talmudic Law and the Modern State.* Translated by Ben Zion Bokser. New York: Burning Bush Press, 1973.

Smallwood, Mary. *The Jews Under Roman Rule.* Reprinted by Brill Academic Publishers: Boston, 2001.

Sokoloff, Michael. *The Targum to Job From Qumran Cave XI.* Ramat-Gan: Bar-Ilan University, 1974.
———. *A Dictionary of Jewish Palestinian Aramaic of the Byzantine Period.* Ramat-Gan, Israel: Bar Ilan University Press, 1992.
———. *A Dictionary of Jewish Babylonian Aramaic of the Talmudic and Geonic Periods.* Ramat Gan: Bar Ilan University Press, 2002.

Soloveitchik, Haym. "Rupture and Reconstruction: The Transformation of Contemporary Orthodoxy." *Tradition* 28,4 (1994): 64-130.

Sperber, Daniel. *Roman Palestine 200-400: The Land.* Ramat Gan: Bar-Ilan University Press, 1978.
———. *A Dictionary of Greek and Latin Legal Terms in Rabbinic Literature.* Jerusalem: Bar-Ilan University Press, 1984.
———. *The City in Roman Palestine.* Oxford: Oxford University Press, 1998.
———. "Social Legislation in Jerusalem During the Latter Part of the Second Temple Period." *JSJ* VI:1 (June, 1975): 86-95.

Stein, Peter. *Legal Evolution.* Cambridge; Cambridge University Press, 1980.

Stone, Michael, editor. *Jewish Writings of the Second Temple Period*. Philadelphia: Fortress Press, 1984.

Strack, H.L. and Stemberger, G. *Introduction to the Talmud and Midrash*. Philadelphia: Fortress Press, 1992.

Tcherikover, Victor. *Hellenistic Civilization and the Jews*.   New York: Atheneum Press, 1959.

Tigay, Jeffrey H. *Deuteronomy: The Traditional Hebrew Text with the New JPS Translation/Commentary*. Philadelphia: Jewish Publication Society, 1996.

Tov, Emanuel. *Textual Criticism of the Hebrew Bible*. Minneapolis: Augsberg Fortress, 1992.

Toynbee, J.M.C. *Death and Burial in the Roman World*. Ithaca: Cornell University Press, 1971.

Urbach, Ephraim E. "הדרשה כיסוד ההלכה ובעית הסופרים" *Tarbiz* 27 (1956-7): 166-182.
———. *The Sages*. Translated by Israel Abrahams. Jerusalem: Magnes Press, 1975.
———. *The Halakhah: Its Sources and Development*. Raphael Posner, tr. Israel: Yad LaTalmud, 1986.
———. *Collected Writings in Jewish Studies*. Robert Brody and Moshe Herr, eds. Jerusalem: Hebrew University Magnes Press, 1990.

Van De Sandt, Huub and Flusser, David. *The Didache: Its Jewish Sources and its Place in Early Judaism and Christianity*. Assen: Royal Van Gorcum, 2002.

Wald, Stephen G. *Perek Elu Ovrin: Bavli Pesahim, Perek Shlishi*. New York and Jerusalem: Beit Midrash La-Rabbanim Ba-Amerika, 2000.

Watson, Alan. *The Law of the Ancient Romans*.   Dallas: Southern Methodist University Press, 1970.
———. *The Evolution of Law*. Baltimore: Johns Hopkins University Press, 1985.
———. *Society and Legal Change*. Philadelphia: Temple University Press, 1977 and 2001.

Waxman, Mordecai. *Tradition and Change.* New York: The Burning Bush Press, 1958.

Wegner, Judith Romney. *Chattel or Person?* Oxford: Oxford University Press, 1988.
Weinfeld, Moshe. "Grace after Meals in Qumran." *JBL* 111 (1992): 427-440.

Weinstein, Sara Epstein. *Piety and Fanaticism.* Northvale, New Jersey: Jason Aronson, 1997.

Weiss, Abraham. לחקר התלמוד. (New York: Feldheim, 1954).

Weiss, Isaac Hirsch. *Sifra.* Vienna: 1852. Reprinted New York: Um Publishers, 1947.
——— . דור דור ודורשיו. ירודשלים : זיו, 1964.

Wettlaufer, Jörg. "The *jus primae noctis* as a Male Power Display." *Evolution and Human Behavior* 21:2 (2000): 111-123.

Widengren, Geo. *The Status of the Jews in the Sassanian Empire.* Jerusalem: Hebrew University Press, 1961.

Wiseman, T. P. *Clio's Cosmetics.* Totowa, NJ: Rowman and Littlefield, 1979.

Whiston, William, tr. *The Works of Josephus: New Updated Edition.* Peabody, MA: Hendrickson Publishers, Inc., 1987.

Williams, Michael A.; Cox, Collett; and Jaffee, Martin S., eds. *Innovation in Religious Traditions.* New York: Mouton de Gruyter, 1992.

Woodman, A.J. *Rhetoric in Classical Historiography.* Portland, OR: Areopagitica Press, 1988.

Yadin, Yigael. *The Scroll of the War of the Sons of Light Against the Sons of Darkness.* Oxford: Oxford University Press, 1962.
---------- *et al.*, editors. The *Documents from the Bar Kokhba Period in the Cave of Letters: Hebrew, Aramaic and Nabatean-Aramaic Papyri.* Jerusalem: Israel Exploration Society, 2002.

Yeivin, Israel. *Introduction to the Tiberian Masorah.* Atlanta: Scholars Press, 1980.

Zahavy, Tzvee. *Studies in Jewish Prayer*. Lanham, MD: University Press of America, 1990.

Zeitlin, Solomon. "The Am Haarez" *JQR* (N.S.) 23 (1932): 45-61.

Zlotnick, Dov. *The Iron Pillar – Mishnah*. Jerusalem: Daf-Noy Press, 1988.

Primary Source Index

Hebrew Bible

Exodus
15:26	274
18:13-26	33
16	275
20	275
20:8	286

Leviticus
5:21-26	57
18:29-30	128-9
30	273
23:44	148-9
25:29-31	22

Numbers
5:6-8	57
9:4	148
11:16-7	33
24-5	33
27:15-7	33
28:2	154-4

Deuteronomy
5:12	286
8:10	179
13:1	124
15:1-3	193, 197
9	192
17:8-13	125-7
22:1-3	57
24:1	135
25:5-10	43
5	47
6	46
26:5-10	62
31:1-8	33
32:7-9	125-7
34:9	33

I Kings
3:25-6	248

II Kings
17	37

Malachi
3:9	255

Job
22:27-8	248

Song of Songs
1:2	279

Ruth
4:7	4

Ecclesiastes
1:15	111
4:2	147
7:13	112
10:8	275-7
12:9	112

Esther
9:27	161-2
31	170

Daniel
1:8	258
4:33	112

I Chronicles
9:22	155
24:7-19	156

Babylonian Talmud

Index

Jacob Neusner

The Aggadic Role in Halakhic Discourses. Lanham. February 2001. University Press of America. Academic Studies in Ancient Judaism series. Volume I

The Aggadic Role in Halakhic Discourses. Lanham. February 2001. University Press of America. Academic Studies in Ancient Judaism series. Volume II

The Aggadic Role in Halakhic Discourses. Lanham. February 2001. University Press of America. Academic Studies in Ancient Judaism series. Volume III

A Theological Commentary to the Midrash. Lanham. April 2001. University Press of America. Academic Studies in Ancient Judaism series. Volume I. *Pesiqta deRab Kahana.*

A Theological Commentary to the Midrash. Lanham. March 2001. University Press of America. Academic Studies in Ancient Judaism series. - Volume II. *Genesis Raba.*

A Theological Commentary to the Midrash. Lanham. April 2001. University Press of America. Academic Studies in Ancient Judaism series. Volume III. *Song of Songs Rabbah*

A Theological Commentary to the Midrash. Lanham. April 2001. University Press of America. Academic Studies in Ancient Judaism series. Volume IV. *Leviticus Rabbah*

A Theological Commentary to the Midrash. Lanham. June 2001. University Press of America. Academic Studies in Ancient Judaism series. Volume V *Lamentations Rabbati*

A Theological Commentary to the Midrash. June 2001. University Press of America. Academic Studies in Ancient Judaism series. Volume VI. *Ruth Rabbah and Esther Rabbah I*

A Theological Commentary to the Midrash. June 2001. University Press of America. Academic Studies in Ancient Judaism series. Volume VII. *Sifra*

A Theological Commentary to the Midrash. July 2001. University Press of America. Academic Studies in Ancient Judaism series. Volume VIII. *Sifré to Numbers and Sifré to Deuteronomy*

A Theological Commentary to the Midrash. August 2001. University Press of America. Academic Studies in Ancient Judaism series. Volume IX. *Mekhilta Attributed to Rabbi Ishmael*

The Unity of Rabbinic Discourse. January 2001. University Press of America. Academic Studies in Ancient Judaism series. Volume I: *Aggadah in the Halakhah*

The Unity of Rabbinic Discourse. February 2001. University Press of America. Academic Studies in Ancient Judaism series. Volume II: *Halakhah in the Aggadah*

The Unity of Rabbinic Discourse. February 2001. University Press of America. Academic Studies in Ancient Judaism series. Volume III: *Halakhah and Aggadah in Concert*